Why QBASIC? Why the Revolu[...]

QBasic has stood the test of time. After being introduced to the MS-DOS community well over a decade ago, the language has now become much more than just another version of BASIC. As well as becoming the first language of choice for programmers new to computing, QBasic is also the language that professionals turn to when they want to knock up a quick simulation. Because of its long-time popularity across a wide section of computer users which has resulted in a wealth of experimentation, QBasic can now be pushed closer to its limits.

This Revolutionary Guide concentrates on the essentials of professional programming and development so, whether you are a novice programmer wanting to quickly attain the experience of other QBasic gurus, or a professional looking for a comprehensive reference guide to the best power tools in the QBasic world, you will appreciate the in-depth coverage of the essential QBasic features.

What is Wrox Press?

Wrox Press is a computer book publisher which promotes clear, jargon-free programming and database titles that fulfill your real demands. We publish for everyone, from the novice through to the experienced programmer. To ensure our books meet your needs, we carry out continuous research on all our titles. Through our dialog with you, we can craft the book you really need.

We welcome suggestions and take all of them to heart - your input is paramount in creating the next great Wrox title. Use the reply card inside this book or contact us at:

feedback@wrox.com

Compuserve 100063, 2152

http://www.wrox.com/

Wrox Press Ltd.
2710 W. Touhy
Chicago
IL 60645
USA

Tel: +1 (312) 465 3559

Fax:+1 (312) 465 4063

The Revolutionary Guide to QBASIC

Vladimir Dyakonov
Victor Munerman
Evgeny Yemelchenkov
Tatyana Samoylova

Wrox Press Ltd.®

The Revolutionary Guide to QBASIC

Published by Wrox Press Ltd. Site 16, 20 James Road, Birmingham, B11 2BA, UK
Printed in Canada
1 2 3 4 5 TRI 99 98 97 96

Library of Congress Catalog no. 94-78400
ISBN 1-874416-20-6

Trademark Acknowledgements

Credits

Authors
Vladimir Dyakonov
Victor Munerman
Evgeny Yemelchenkov
Tatyana Samoylova

Lead Editor
Adrian M Sill

Technical Editor
Graham J Butler

Contributing Editors
Tim Briggs
Paul Saville
Alex Stockton

Managing Editor
John Franklin

Beta Testers
Louis O'Brien
Peter Cooper
William Yu

Additional Material
Wouter Bergmann-Tiest
Dave Valentine

Translator
Vladimir Naidonov

Cover Design
Third Wave

Production Manager
Greg Powell

Design/Layout
Neil Gallagher
Graham J Butler
Damon Creed
Andrew Guillaume

Proof Readers
Pam Brand
Melanie Orgee
Emma Duncombe
Simon Gilks

Index
Simon Gilks

For more information on Third Wave, contact Ross Alderson on 44-121 236 6616
Cover photo supplied by Telegraph Colour Library

CONTENTS

Summary of Contents

WROX

Table of Contents

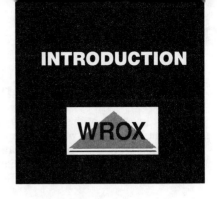

INTRODUCTION

Welcome to the latest Revolutionary Guide from the Wrox Press stable, The Revolutionary Guide to QBasic. This book has been designed as a guide to learning the essential and advanced techniques of one of the most popular and prevalent programming languages ever created. Introducing everything you need to know in order to become a capable and knowledgeable power programmer of the QBasic language, this book will enable you to understand the concepts and the best techniques involved. Because we at Wrox Press believe that our readers are intelligent creatures, we won't waste time by patronizing you with over-simplistic examples. We will be introducing new practical advice and a fresh approach to many exciting techniques from some of the industries finest developers.

What Can QBasic Do for Me?

The lifespan of a typical language often features a peak *after* the language has died a death. QBasic may not be at the forefront of the software revolution, but it has been distributed into millions of homes and offices during its stint as part of the MS-DOS and MS-Windows operating systems. It has even taken the next vital step in 1995, and been included on Microsofts latest operating system, Windows 95, which will ensure that it lives on into the next millenium.

It has survived for so long because it is so easy to understand. It is frequently the computer programming language of choice for beginners to computing, but this has also been a ball and chain around its neck too, forever labelling it with the 'beginners' tag. Unfortunately, this has also been the case with literature on the subject, which seems to fit into this one category. This book is revolutionary because it is the first to treat QBasic as more than a mere 'starter' language.

Who Should Use this Book?

The Revolutionary Guide to QBasic contains the information necessary to transform the reader with a limited knowledge of computers into an apprentice QBasic guru able to write efficient, well-structured, clear code. There are other types of people who are likely to benefit from this book too:

- The programmer who wants to know how to write powerful, creative, professional programs.
- The QBasic dabbler who needs a quick and comprehensive reference guide to state-of-the-art QBasic techniques.
- The amateur games programmer who wants to learn the tricks of the trade.
- Everybody who requires a concise and informative guide to all the important aspects of QBasic.
- Everybody who requires a one-stop QBasic resource package.

What You Should Know

To get the most out of this book, you should have some basic programming knowledge; you don't have to have spent five years of your life learning Assembler, but you should understand the basic concepts that are common to most programming languages. Since we are going to take this tour at quite a fast pace, we won't be dwelling on basic programming techniques that you already know. What you will be learning is how to program quality code in QBasic, and how to write programs that *you* want to write.

As all programming languages require a basic grasp of mathematics, we will assume that you understand some of the principles behind the major concepts. Don't worry, we won't be using calculus and umpteen different theorems, but you simply can't avoid brushing against the subject when you're dealing with programming.

Conventions Used

To help you find your way around this book easily, we have used various styles to highlight different references. Each style has been chosen to give you a clear understanding of the information that we have supplied.

All code and programs are highlighted with a gray background, so that you can locate them easily. For example:

```
REM This is a sample program

CLS
PRINT "Press the SPACE BAR to see a message.!"
LOCATE 10, 40: PRINT "I'm here!"
WHILE a$ <> "Q"
    a$ = UCASE$(INKEY$)
    LOCATE INT(RND * 21) + 3, INT(RND * 69) + 1
    COLOR INT(RND * 14) + 1
    IF a$ = " " THEN PRINT "No, I'm Here!"
WEND

END
```

Throughout this book we shall consistently use the following styles and fonts for a variety of textual distinctions:

When code or a command is mentioned in the middle of a sentence, we write it in **this style**, so as to emphasize its origin.

Filenames, such as **\GAMES\BATTLE.BAS** are always written in that style.

Important words and concepts are introduced in **this style**. These are significant words that we are meeting for the first time. They will appear subsequently as normal text.

Actual keys that you press will be displayed in *this style,* for example, when the *Esc* key needs to be pressed.

When we introduce the syntax of new code, we will use **this style**. We shall also be using the following bracket distinctions:

[ ]   Optional.

< >   Obligatory.

If a word needs to be emphasized, then we will *italicize* it.

We have attempted to break the text up, by using appropriate and consistent headings and with the judicious bulleting of lists.

> **When an important piece of information needs to be really emphasized, then we will place it in a stand-alone box like this.**

When we need to provide the reader with a useful, but not essential piece of background information we will use this style.

How to Use the Disk

To install the accompanying directories and programs place the disk in your A: drive and execute the file **SETUP.EXE**. The archive will create a new directory on your local drive named **REVQB** and extract all of the files to this directory. The disk includes the following items:

- ▲ Every major piece of source code listed in this book (each listing included on the disk features its path and filename in its first few lines).
- ▲ A host of programs referenced from the text as good examples of a particular concept or topic.
- ▲ A further array of quality QBasic programs for you to take a look at.

Every program or suite of programs included in the latter two entries of this table can be found listed and described in Appendix B. All the programs featured on the disk have been selected because they are the best examples of QBasic code ever written, and some require further payment for their use.

Further Information

If you require any more information about QBasic then look no further than Appendix A, which is *the* definitive one-stop guide for resources specific to QBasic. This is nothing more than a compilation of all the best sources of information, source code and contacts that have in some way contributed to the development of this book. If you require further information about ourselves, take a look at our web site, which can be found at the following URL:

http:\\\\www.wrox.com

For further information about what can be found on our site, check out the full-page advertisement at the back of this book.

Tell Us What You think

One last thing: we've tried to make this book as enjoyable and accurate as possible. We are here to serve the programming community, so if you have any queries, suggestions or comments about this book, let us know. We are always delighted to hear from you.

You can help us ensure that our future books are even better, by simply returning the reply card at the back of the book or by contacting us direct at Wrox. For a quick response, you can also use the following e-mail addresses:

      feedback@wrox.demon.co.uk   Compuserve: 100063, 2152

Please return the reply card at the back of the book and tell us what you think of the book, the style of presentation and the content. We are always ready to listen to comments and complaints (although we do prefer unadulterated adoration!).

Getting Started

Thank you for buying The Revolutionary Guide to QBasic. We hope you enjoy it and become a proficient programmer of QBasic. All our efforts have been aimed at bringing you maximum satisfaction, and if you want to learn QBasic properly, then we're convinced that this book will fulfill all your immediate requirements. Anyway, you've bought this book to learn QBasic, and we shall not hold you from it any longer. Dip in and enjoy!

The Essentials of QBasic Programming

CHAPTER 1

Before we jump in and start writing best-selling applications, we've got to take a look at the nuts and bolts of how to program in QBasic. This should prepare us for the following chapters where well take a more focused route through the language. The topics that we'll be covering here are:

- ▲ The concept of QBasic syntax.
- ▲ Program comments.
- ▲ The QBasic alphabet.
- ▲ Constants, variables and data types.
- ▲ String and numeric data control.
- ▲ QBasic's built-in math functions.

The Concept of QBasic Syntax

A BASIC program is in effect a list of instructions to the computer. These instructions are called **statements**. Statements must be written according to QBasic **syntax rules**. Why, for example, is the comment text in the **INPUT** statement enclosed in quotation marks, and the variable name placed after the comma? What's the difference between **X** and **X$**? All statements are governed by language syntax, which although simpler than the syntax of our own written and spoken languages still needs to be observed carefully.

Books on programming often begin with a description of a simple program which outputs a greeting on the screen. With QBasic, this type of program is surprisingly straightforward:

```
PRINT "Hello, my friend!"
```

You may ask whether this program can be represented in the following three ways:

```
PRINT "Hello"
PRINT ","
PRINT "my"
PRINT "friend"
PRINT "!"
```

```
PRINT "Hello, ";
PRINT "my friend!"
```

```
PRINT "Hello",","
PRINT "my friend!"
```

If you run each of these programs, you'll discover that only the middle one gives the same result as the initial program. Even something as seemingly insignificant as a comma or a semicolon following the **PRINT** statement can significantly change the appearance of the output, demonstrating the importance of accurate QBasic syntax.

The QBasic environment editor (in contrast to DOS Edit) is quite smart, checking the syntax of a program as it's typed in. It also has a number of features which make entering programs easier; for instance, you can type a question mark instead of the **PRINT** command. So, if you enter:

```
?"Hello my friend!"
```

QBasic will change it to:

```
PRINT "Hello my Friend!"
```

just as soon as you move the cursor off the line.

You can type keywords using upper-case letters, lower-case letters, or both: the editor automatically changes them to upper-case letters. For example, if you type **Input X**, the QBasic editor will replace this with **INPUT X**.

The syntax of QBasic isn't as academic as that of Pascal or C. These languages have a smaller number of syntactical constructions than QBasic and these can be strictly described; for example, by syntactical diagrams in Pascal. Unlike Pascal and C, where you have to use special libraries, QBasic offers most of the fundamental features like the input/output statements **INPUT** and **PRINT**, the clear screen statement **CLS**, and numerous graphic statements, as part of its keyword core.

Of course, this means that the syntax of QBasic is more verbose, but there's no denying that it has a human face - all the statements and functions are defined by everyday English words. As for getting to know how to use the program structures, QBasic readily forgives mistakes and prompts you as to where and what the error is. Syntax checking while a program is being developed will filter out any syntactical error no matter how small it is.

Program Comments

Even simple programs can be double-Dutch to an inexperienced programmer, but when programs consist of thousands of lines, the experienced programmer may have trouble understanding them. This is why **commenting** programs is useful. The first line of each program in this book is a comment, telling you the name and function of the program.

You can write a comment as follows:

REM Text

or

'Text

The text following the word **REM** (REMark) or the **'** sign (apostrophe) is a program comment and therefore it isn't executed. Its only function is to make the program clearer to read and understand. A comment line must only include comments - it's no good putting a statement to be executed after a comment.

For instance, the line:

```
'Calculate 2 + 2 =: PRINT (2 + 2)
```

isn't any good if you want it to calculate the **2+2**. Despite the fact that the **PRINT (2+2)** statement is separated from the comment by a colon, it won't be executed. The colon and all subsequent text is taken as part of the comment.

If a comment is placed at the end of a line, you don't need a colon before the apostrophe, for example:

```
PRINT (2 + 2) 'Calculate 2 + 2
```

The comment isn't executed, so when you run the above line, you'll get the result **4** on the screen.

It's good practice to use detailed comments in your programs to aid with debugging. Once again, we'll be returning to this subject later on.

The QBasic Alphabet

Every programming language has a set of rules which enable you to describe a problem or task in detail. Just like any oral language, it must have an **alphabet**, consisting of letters, numerals, and special characters. QBasic contains an alphabet in the form of ready-to-use characters which conform with the **ASCII** standard.

ASCII is the acronym for the American Standard Code for Information Interchange. Pronounced 'asskey', this 7-bit standard code was adopted to facilitate the interchange of data between different types of data processing equipment.

Typically, these characters include upper-case and lower-case letters, special symbols, and control characters. These form the basis for all QBasic data including commands, label identifiers, constants, variables, arrays, procedures, and functions.

The Standard ASCII Table

The **ASCII** character set corresponds to codes **0** through **127**, which can't be modified and are used to specify keywords and identifiers (names) of QBasic objects:

```
MS-DOS Prompt - QBASIC                                                    _ □ ✕
0          1  ☺     2  ☻     3  ♥     4  ♦     5  ♣     6  ♠     7
8  ◘       9         10        11        12        13        14        15
16         17        18        19        20        21        22        23
24         25        26        27        28        29        30        31
32         33  !      34  "     35  #     36  $     37  %     38  &     39  '
40  (      41  )      42  *     43  +     44  ,     45  -     46  .     47  /
48  0      49  1      50  2     51  3     52  4     53  5     54  6     55  7
56  8      57  9      58  :     59  ;     60  <     61  =     62  >     63  ?
64  @      65  A      66  B     67  C     68  D     69  E     70  F     71  G
72  H      73  I      74  J     75  K     76  L     77  M     78  N     79  O
80  P      81  Q      82  R     83  S     84  T     85  U     86  V     87  W
88  X      89  Y      90  Z     91  [     92  \     93  ]     94  ^     95  _
96  `      97  a      98  b     99  c     100 d     101 e     102 f     103 g
104 h      105 i      106 j     107 k     108 l     109 m     110 n     111 o
112 p      113 q      114 r     115 s     116 t     117 u     118 v     119 w
120 x      121 y      122 z     123 {     124 |     125 }     126 ~     127 ⌂
Press any key to display the characters with codes 128-255
```

Codes **0** through **31** are control characters used for popular key combinations, pseudo-graphic symbols and important characters. The QBasic alphabet uses the character codes **32** through **127** to depict the characters of the English alphabet, numerals and additional grammatical characters.

The Extended ASCII Table

The codes **128** through **255** correspond to the extended ASCII table, which extend the language features of your computer and are dependent upon the settings of your system. The tables include the characters of different languages; for example, the Cyrillic symbols (letters of the Russian alphabet) or graphical symbols. These ASCII charts are loaded using special programs called **display drivers**. The characters with codes from **128** to **175** and from **224** to **247** can be changed by loading different display drivers.

> *If you want to look through the complete character set of your PC, you can look at the*
> **REF\ASCII.BAS** *program on the accompanying disk.*

The character set and the type of characters available to you depend on the contents of the ROM, and on which character sets your PC or printer can load.

> **Characters with codes 128 through 255 should only be used in comments and dialogs; for example, when creating menus. You shouldn't use them in genuine code such as for the names of labels, constants, variables, procedures, or functions because they're unpredictable across different systems.**

Special Characters

The PC alphabet contains many **special characters**, used to specify detailed information. Here they are, in their specific groups:

Mathematical Operators

You use the following operators on numeric data, and you may be familiar with them as they form the basic functions of a simple calculator:

*	Multiplication symbol
–	Minus sign
/	Division symbol (forward slash)
+	Plus sign
.	Decimal point
\	Integer division symbol (back slash)
^	Exponentiation symbol (up arrow or caret)

Their syntax is straightforward and here are a few examples:

```
Pi = 22/7
PRINT 5*3
PRINT (Pi/2)*100
PRINT 2.705^8
```

As you would expect when you run this program, you'll see these results on the screen: 15, 157.0795 and 2866.408. You'll notice that we had to set the constant Pi before we could include it in an operation. We'll discuss setting constants a little later.

Relational Operators

Here's QBasic's logical or **relational** operators:

=	Equal to
>	Greater than
>=	Greater than or equal to
<	Smaller than
<=	Smaller than or equal to
<>	Not equal to

These are often used in decision making and are incorporated in statements in the following way:

```
IF Alcohol>Limit THEN PRINT "Walk Home"
```

General Symbols

Of course, there are always some symbols which defy categorization:

'	Comment line (apostrophe)
;	Controls **PRINT** and **INPUT** statement output
,	Controls **PRINT** and **INPUT** statement output
:	Separates multiple statements on a single line

?	**INPUT** statement prompt
=	Assignment symbol
_	Line continuation underscore (reserved for compatibility with other versions of Basic but not supported by QBasic)
$, #, !, %, &	Symbols to define data types

We'll discuss and use all these at the relevant stages throughout the book.

Keywords

The QBasic command set contains about 200 **keywords**, each of which is labelled by a sequence of characters. These are special QBasic words that mean something specific to the system, and are sometimes referred to as reserved words. A full list of all QBasic keywords can be found on the **Contents** page of the help system.

Some keywords, such as **TAB** and **USING**, are referred to as **modifiers** because they don't have a meaning of their own, but change the action of another statement, such as **PRINT**.

Identifiers

The main elements of the QBasic language - variables, constants, labels, procedures, and functions - have their own unique character names called **identifier**s. These labels must adhere to the following rules of thumb.

Naming Conventions

It's good practice to assign meaningful names for identifiers. For example, the identifier **lastname** might be used to store surnames in a database, **Xcoordinate** and **Ycoordinate** could specify the position of a particular point in a graphics program, and so on. If you use cryptic names like **atoz**, **ms13** or **xyzzy** then these can easily be misconstrued, forgotten or mispelled.

Of course, there are also illegal ways of naming specifiers. Here are examples of correct and incorrect definitions of identifiers:

Incorrect	Correct	Explanation
4Excel	Excel4	Identifier must not start with a numeral.
+DX	DX+	Identifier must start with an alphabetic character.
ASCII Code	ASCII_Code	Identifier must be a single character sequence.
%	X%	Identifier must not be a special character.

QBasic doesn't distinguish between upper- and lower-case letters in an identifier, so, as far as we're concerned, the names **Xcoordinate** and **xcoordinate** are identical. If you change the way you type an identifier whilst programming, Qbasic will automatically convert all occurrences of it to the latest version.

It's very unlikely that you should ever exceed the maximum limit on the number of characters in an identifier, but just for the record it's set at 40.

Nevertheless, using capital letters can make your programs clearer; for example, allowing you to distinguish between different words in a single identifier without the use of spaces. Keywords can also be entered in either upper or lower case. However, QBasic automatically converts all keywords to upper case (which tests the validity of the entry). It's because of this automatic capitalization that throughout this book we use lower case for all identifiers. This makes keywords and identifiers immediately distinguishable from each other.

> **Remember, keywords are special QBasic words that mean something specific to QBasic. You mustn't use them as identifiers because QBasic will get terribly confused and start misbehaving!**

Constants and Variables

Your PC works with a great diversity of data: numbers, characters, strings, arrays, etc. Imagine if every time we used one type or another we had to fully describe it. For example, if every time we wanted to use the value of Pi, we had to type in 3.14159 or 22/7 then it would quickly become very laborious. Fortunately, QBasic has special program objects which are capable of storing and operating various data using simple names. These program objects are known as **constants** and **variables**.

Specifying Named Constants

QBasic constants are program objects whose values are pre-assigned and unchangeable. Because they never change, they can be represented by either their names (identifiers) or by their values. For example, we could use the constant Pi with the expression value 3.141592654, but we could make it a lot easier for ourselves if we called this expression value a name, say **Pi_Value**. From this point on we could use this name instead of the actual value, every time we needed to specify Pi.

We prefix name constants with the **CONST** statement. When using this statement you can define several numeric and character constants in a single expression. Here are some examples:

```
CONST Pi_Value = 3.141592654
CONST Cents_In_Dollar = 100
CONST Year_Length = 365.25
```

It's nicer to work with named constants rather than common numeric or character constants: names are more descriptive of the value leading to less confusion in complex mathematical programs and they're often shorter than the number itself (take the example of **Pi_Value** instead of 3.141592654) This makes them convenient to use, *and* they can take up less RAM.

Specifying Named Variables

QBasic **variables** are program objects whose values are available and changeable throughout a module. Like constants, variables follow the same naming guidelines that apply to identifiers. Variables are the default program objects, and so don't require a statement to be applied before naming or declaration.

Pi could be a variable but, because it never changes, it should be implemented as a constant.

Assigning Data

When variables or named constants are first assigned data they're usually given names (or identifiers) to associate them with the expression value. You use the following construction to do this:

```
[LET] Name[S] = Data
```

In assignment operations QBasic always works out the righthand side of the = sign first and sends the result to the variable on the lefthand side. This action replaces the value that had been contained in the variable. For example, you can assign the value **6** to the variable **X** in any of the following ways (amongst others of course):

```
LET X = 6
X = 2 * 3
X = 6
LET X = 12/2
```

You can output the constant or variable value onto the screen using the **PRINT** statement. If you execute the statement **PRINT X** after any of these statements, the number 6 will be displayed on the screen. We'll look at the functions of the **PRINT** statement in more detail a little bit later on.

The optional suffix **S** in square brackets is used to indicate the data type of the variable:

Symbol	Data Type	Maximum Value	Minimum Value
%	Integer	32,767	-32,768
&	Long integer	2,147,483,648	-2,147,483,648
!	Single-precision (+ve)	3.402823E+38	2.802597E-45
	Single-precision (-ve)	-2.802597E-45	-3.402823E+38
#	Double-precision (+ve)	1.79769313486231D+308	4.940656458412465D-324
	Double-precision (-ve)	-4.940656458412465D-324	-1.79769313486231D+308
$	String		

In older versions of BASIC you had to use the **LET** statement to assign values to variables. In QBasic this isn't necessary, but this optional keyword has been retained to ensure compatability with these previous versions.

The following program shows how variables and constants are defined and how the **PRINT** statement is used to output their values:

```
REM Defining constants and variables
REM \CHAP1\CH1_1.BAS

char$ = "string"
c10% = 10
LI& = 123456789
CONST PI = 3.14159, HEX = 16
```

```
'Output of constants and variables

CLS
PRINT char$
PRINT c10%
PRINT LI&
PRINT PI, HEX
PRINT 2 * PI

END
```

If you run the program, the Output window will display the following results:

```
string
10
123456789
3.14159              16
6.28318
```

Notice also how the **CONST** prefix is used to define **Pi** and **Hex** as constants: you can't now change these values.

We shall be returning to the **CLS** statement later in the book, but for now it's sufficient to know that by itself it clears the screen.

Swapping the Contents of Two Variables

If you want to exchange the values of two variables, you can use the **SWAP** statement followed by the names of the two variables, separated by a comma:

SWAP Variable1, Variable2

The following program demonstrates how you use the **SWAP** statement:

```
REM The action of the SWAP statement
REM \CHAP1\CH1_2.BAS

CLS
A = 12
B = 34
SWAP A, B
PRINT "A="; A
PRINT "B="; B

END
```

This program, when run, outputs the following:

```
A= 34
B= 12
```

The **SWAP** statement replaces the inefficient construction:

```
C = A: A = B: B = C
```

by enabling you to avoid introducing the additional variable **C**.

Combining Data Types

Complex objects in diverse situations can be characterized by a number of different data types and not just a single variable. For example, each employee of a company could have the following information about them on computer:

Feature	Data Type
Name	String
Surname	String
Year of Birth	Integer
Place of Birth	String
Category	Numeric
Telephone number	String
Salary	Numeric

Of course, we could define a separate variable (numeric or character) for each of these characteristics, but it's more convenient to link all related data to one particular variable, such as the name of the object (in our case, the employee's name).

In QBasic we can define complex data types, (sometimes called data blocks or records), pertaining to several individual variables using the **TYPE** statement:

TYPE User type
Name of element AS Name of type
[Name of element AS Name of type]
[......................]
END TYPE

The individual variables in the block can be used in the same way as normal variables, but are accessed via a double name consisting of the name of the block followed by the name of the variable, separated by a period (**.**). Take these examples:

employee.surname$ or **employee.birthdate%**.

Using this statement:

DIM New name of block AS Old name of block

you can rename all the variables. Here's how we opted to show you the above features in action:

```
REM Specifying a data block - record
REM \CHAP1\CH1_3.BAS

CLS
TYPE vb
s AS STRING * 10
n AS INTEGER
dn AS LONG
xas SINGLE
dx AS DOUBLE
END TYPE

DIM VarBlock AS vb
VarBlock.s = "QWERTY"
vb.n = 3
vb.dn = 123456789
vb.x = vb.dn
vb.dx = 1 / vb.n
PRINT VarBlock.s, vb.n, vb.dn
PRINT vb.x, vb.dx

END
```

Here you can see how we identify individual variables in user-defined data types. Such combined data types are convenient for use in databases, the contents of which are modified and renewed as data is entered or corrected.

String Data Control

This is all well and good, but what we need is to print something meaningful on the screen. We can achieve meaning in our programs by making good use of textual characters. These, like program objects, can be split into variables and constants.

Character Constants

An unnamed character constant is a string of characters (including any spaces), enclosed in quotation marks; for example, **"2*3"**. Although this describes an arithmetic expression, it is in fact a character constant. So, the statement:

```
PRINT "2 * 3"
```

doesn't print 6 to your screen, just the straight character message:

    2 * 3

Character constants are widely used for organizing dialogs with computers, and creating control structures and databases.

Although you can't perform arithmetic operations with character expressions, the **+** sign can be used to combine character strings, for example:

```
PRINT "Hello, " + "my " + "friend"
```

will greet you once again with:

Hello, my friend

You'll see from the ground that we're about to cover that QBasic has a wide range of functions for dealing with character variables.

Character Variables

A string of characters enclosed in quotation marks is normally referred to as a **string constant**. Variables can also be defined as strings if their name is followed by the **$** sign, or if they're included in the variable list of the **DEFSTR** statement:

```
MyString$="QBasic"
DEFSTR variablelist
```

variablelist may consist of a simple comma-separated list of variable names; for example, **DEFSTR a,b,c,d,e**. It may also define a range of characters; for example, **DEFSTR a-d**.

> Note that by assigning the variable with one of the data type suffixes, such as $, %, or !, you can override the corresponding DEF statement.

Manipulating Strings: Character Operations and Functions

It's very important that a programming language offers a high degree of flexibility when dealing with text, and QBasic is certainly no exception. The following sections will show you just how to control your strings and characters.

Extracting Substrings

The ability to extract separate parts of a string expression is extremely important because it enables you to control strings and data easily. The following string manipulators are not statements, but functions, which modify data and are used in conjunction with statements like **PRINT**:

LEFT$ (s$,n)	returns the **n** leftmost characters in string **s$**.
RIGHT$ (s$,n)	returns the **n** rightmost characters in string **s$**.
MID$ (s$,m[,n])	returns a specified number, **n**, of characters in string **s$** beginning at a specified position, **m**.

We can illustrate these functions with this simple example:

```
REM Demonstration of character extracting functions
REM \CHAP1\CH1_4.BAS
```

```
CLS
$ = "OneTwoThree"
PRINT LEFT$(v$, 3)
PRINT MID$(v$, 4, 3)
PRINT RIGHT$(v$, 5)

END
```

And this is what's printed on the screen:

```
One
Two
Three
```

Note that there are two features of the **MID$** function which you should be aware of: if parameter **n** is omitted, or the number of characters in the string to the right of **m** is less than **n**, **MID$** returns all characters to the right of the start position; if parameter **n** is zero or **m** is more than the length of the string, **MID$** simply returns an empty string.

> *We shall return to the concept of functions in Chapter 2, but for now just try to understand how they're used.*

For an excellent example of just how useful **MID$** can be, take a look at **GAMES\ADVENTUR.BAS** on the accompanying disk. Take a close look at how we take the string input from the user, and convert it into several word strings, **W1$**, **W2$**, **W3$** etc.

Deleting and Inserting Characters

In character operations, a space is as meaningful as a letter or number. If you want to trim a string of its spaces, or insert a string of identical characters, QBasic provides a host of functions that will do this.

Removing Unwanted Spaces

If your string contains unwanted spaces at either the left or right end, you can remove them with one of these commands:

    LTRIM$ (s$)   removes leading spaces from a specified string.
    RTRIM$ (s$)   removes trailing spaces from a specified string.

Here's a demonstration of these two in action:

```
REM Demonstration of string trimming
REM \CHAP1\CH1_5.BAS

CLS
a$ = "   Qwerty   "
b$ = LTRIM$(a$)
PRINT a$
PRINT b$; "*"
b$ = RTRIM$(a$)
PRINT b$; "*"

END
```

Run this program and you'll see this:

```
Qwerty
Qwerty   *
Qwerty*
```

Filling a String with Specified Characters

If you want a string to contain a sequence of identical characters, there are two functions you can use:

SPACE$ (n) returns a string containing **n** spaces.

STRING$(n,s$) returns a string of length **n** made up of a repeated character. (Instead of the character itself, its ASCII code can be indicated.)

And here are **SPACE$** and **STRING$** in action:

```
REM A demonstration of string filling
REM \CHAP1\CH1_6.BAS

CLS
A$ = "Q"
B$ = STRING$(5, A$) + "*"
PRINT A$
PRINT B$
C$ = SPACE$(5) + "*"
PRINT C$

END
```

with this result:

```
Q
QQQQQ*
     *
```

Changing Letter Case

There are two functions in QBasic for changing the case of specified letters:

LCASE$ (s$) converts a specified string (**s$**) to all lower-case letters.

UCASE$ (s$) converts a specified string (**s$**) to all upper-case letters.

Here's how they work:

```
REM Demonstration of the 2 case functions
REM \CHAP1\CH1_7.BAS

CLS
a$ = "OneTwoThree"
b$ = LCASE$(a$)
c$ = UCASE$(a$)
PRINT b$; "*"
PRINT c$; "*"

END
```

and they produce this on the screen:

```
onetwothree*
ONETWOTHREE*
```

There isn't an actual function for converting letter case within a single line - in QBasic it's all or nothing. But because QBasic is so flexible we can achieve this with the following combination of functions:

```
REM Demonstration of mid-string case conversion
REM \CHAP1\CH1_8.BAS

CLS
a$ = "aaaaaaaaaaaaaa"
MID$(a$, 4, 3) = UCASE$(MID$(a$, 4, 3))
PRINT a$

END
```

which will output the following string:

```
aaaAAAaaaaaaaa
```

Character Statements

These statements are used for copying one variable into another whilst justifying left or right:

LSET a$ = b$	moves the string **b$** into the string **a$** and left justifies within the original length of **a$**.
RSET a$ = b$	moves the string **b$** into the string **a$** and right justifies within the original length of **a$**.

Here's some code showing you how **LSET** and **RSET** work:

```
REM Demonstration of LSET and RSET
REM \CHAP1\CH1_9.BAS

CLS
a$ = "OneTwoThree"
b$ = "Qwerty"
LSET a$ = b$
PRINT a$; "*"
PRINT b$

a$ = "OneTwoThree"
b$ = "Qwerty"
RSET a$ = b$
PRINT a$; "*"
PRINT b$

END
```

This is what you'll see on the screen:

```
Qwerty    *
Qwerty
     Qwerty*
Qwerty
```

You'll notice the asterisks placed at the end of each converted text field. We've included these to help you understand what's going on. The width of the field is predetermined by the length of the first string, in other words the one stored in **a$**. Therefore, the string is aligned either right or left depending on the function you use.

Searching a Character String

Occasionally you may need to determine whether a specified string, **a$**, forms a part of another string, **b$**, and if it does, you may need to know where it's located in that string. This function returns the position (as an integer) of the first occurrence of one string in another string:

```
INSTR ([n%] a$, b$)
```

The integer **n%** is the character position where the search begins (if **n%** is omitted, the search begins at the default position **1,** i.e. the start). Take this example:

```
REM Demonstrates substring searching
REM \CHAP1\CH1_10.BAS

CLS
b$ = "Two"
a$ = "OneTwoThreeOneTwoThree"
y1 = INSTR(1, a$, b$)
y2 = INSTR(7, a$, b$)
PRINT y1, y2

END
```

Here's what you get up on the screen:

```
4     15
```

The search for the substring **Two** starts at position **1** of string **a$**. The substring is found first at position **4**. The search is then resumed at position **7** and the substring is found again at position **15**. After a substring has been found, to continue searching through a string you need to program subsequent searches as we have just done with **y2**.

Numeric Data Control

Whilst characters and strings are important features of any programming language, so too are numbers. We'll now have a look at what means QBasic provides for dealing with them.

Preliminary Definition of Numeric Variables

It isn't good programming style to define variables solely by assignment. This can be confusing in large programs and can lead to the proliferation of bugs. This is a very real problem, and QBasic has a set of statements which enable you to predefine variables. You've already met **DEFSTR**, and the next four statements work on the same principal:

```
DEFINT  list_of_short_integers
DEFLNG  list_of_long_integers
DEFSNG  list_of_single-precision_reals
DEFDBL  list_of_double-precision_reals
```

These lists are sequences of one or more variable names separated by commas. This is the strictest way of defining variable types in the context of structured programming.

Here's our example defining variable type by this method:

```
REM Main variable types
REM \CHAP1\CH1_11.BAS

DEFSTR c
DEFINT i, 1
DEFLNG k
DEFSNG x
DEFDBL y

CLS
c = "String"
i = 123: 1 = 456
x = 1.2345E-06
y = .00000123456789#

'Output of variable values
PRINT c, i, 1
PRINT k, x, y

END
```

Run it and this'll hit the screen:

```
STRING    123      456
0      1.2345E-06  .00000123456789
```

You can define groups of variables as well, using either the **TO** modifier or the dash as in this expression:

```
DEFINT a TO k, p-v, z
```

All the variables whose names begin with the letters **a** through **k**, **p** through **v**, and those beginning with **z**, are declared as integers. These variables *don't* require a type suffix with their name.

Although the use of the **DEF** variable declaration statements makes programs shorter and stricter, it isn't essential that you use them. As we pointed out at the very start of the chapter, undeclared variables are real by default and other types of variables can be indicated explicitly by tagging their name with the appropriate suffix.

If you discover that your program makes calculation errors due to rounding, you can redefine single-precision real variables into double-precision ones. Note also that if your PC has a math co-processor, you'll have increased calculation performance. You can increase the speed of loop calculations by replacing the counter with a short integer. We'll return to the subject of program speed later on.

Numeric Decimal Constants

Numeric unnamed constants are just numbers in the program text. Look at this expression:

```
PRINT 2*3
```

2 and 3 are numeric unnamed constants and the execution of this instruction results in the number 6 being output.

Numeric constants can be either integer (short or long) or real (single- or double-precision). Since each constant type occupies a different number of memory cells, they should be specifically declared. The default numeric constant is a single precision real number. Using the corresponding suffix you can define the type of a constant explicitly; for example, `123456789&` is a long integer constant.

Real numeric constants can be represented both as common decimal fractions and in this form:

M*10p

where **M** is the mantissa and **p** the integer order. QBasic offers the letter **E** or **e** to separate the mantissa and the order; for example, `12.534E(3)` represents the number `123534`, and `-123.456E(-3)` is equivalent to `-0.123456`.

Arithmetic Functions

Using QBasic, it's possible to calculate arithmetic expressions. Arithmetic expressions consist of numeric constants, variables, math operations symbols, and functions. Functions return values. In other words, an arithmetic function converts arguments into numeric values which may, in turn, be the arguments of another function. You call functions in arithmetic expressions by expressing their names and arguments; for example, `2*SIN(1)` calculates the sine of 1 then multiplies it by 2.

QBasic comes equipped with a minimum set of elementary arithmetic functions:

ABS (x)	returns the absolute value of a number.
ATN (x)	returns the arctangent of the number **x**.
CINT (x)	rounds a numeric expression, **x**, to an integer.
COS (x)	returns the cosine of a specified angle.
EXP (x)	returns **e** raised to a specified power (**e** is the base of natural logarithms)
FIX (x)	truncates a floating-point expression, **x**, to its integer portion.
INT (x)	returns the largest integer less than or equal to a numeric expression.
LOG (x)	returns the natural logarithm of **x**.
SIN (x)	returns the sine of a specified angle.
SGN (x)	returns a value indicating the sign of a numeric expression.

SQR (x)	returns the square root of a numeric expression.
TAN (x)	returns the tangent of a specified angle.

Of course, to work with arithmetic functions requires a certain knowledge of mathematics. For instance, you should remember that the argument of a trigonometric function is expressed in radians. To convert from radians to degrees, just multiply the radians value by **(180/Pi)**. It's also worth remembering that you can't calculate the logarithm of a negative argument, that certain values of **x** for the function **TAN (x)** tend to infinity, and that the value **EXP (x)** increases very quickly when **x** is increased. This code gives you some examples of these functions:

```
REM Demonstration of Math Functions
REM \CHAP1\CH1_12.BAS

CLS
PRINT ABS(-234)
Pi = 3.141593
PRINT SIN(30 * Pi/ 180)
PRINT COS(30 * Pi / 180)
PRINT TAN(45 * Pi / 180)
PRINT ATN(1) * 180 / Pi
PRINT LOG(2)
PRINT EXP(1)
PRINT SQR(4)

END
```

You'll see these results when you run the program:

```
234
.5000001
.8660254
1
45
.6931472
2.718282
2
```

QBasic arithmetic functions are simple and limited, e.g. you won't be able to use functions like arcsine and arccosine, or any hyperbolic functions. Nevertheless, the available set is functionally complete and using the standard math relationships, you can easily calculate any elementary math functions, including special ones such as Bessell functions and the gamma function.

Integer Functions

The rest of the functions in our table (**INT**, **FIX** and **CINT** for rounding and truncating data) are demonstrated here:

```
REM INT, FIX and CINT functions illustration
REM \CHAP1\CH1_13.BAS

CLS
a = 9.123
b = 9.999
PRINT INT(a)
```

```
PRINT INT(-a)
PRINT INT(b)
PRINT INT(-b)
PRINT FIX(a)
PRINT FIX(-a)
PRINT FIX(b)
PRINT FIX(-b)
PRINT CINT(a)
PRINT CINT(-a)
PRINT CINT(b)
PRINT CINT(-b)

END
```

If you run this, this is what you'll see:

```
9
-10
9
-10
9
-9
9
-9
9
-9
10
-10
```

We recommend that you think carefully about rounding, and truncation operations using different functions, as any errors may not be readily apparent.

Retrieving the Sign of an Expression

The **SGN (x)** function is used to indicate the sign of an argument:

Value	Result
-4.5	-1
0	0
24.7	1

+1 if the argument is positive, **0** if it's zero, or **-1** if it's negative.

Understanding Arithmetic Operations

Arithmetic operations in QBasic are written as one-line expressions according to normal mathematical conventions. Often the function names differ from conventional math signs (for example, **SQR** instead of the square root sign) but you'll get used to these easily enough:

QBasic	Math representation
(a + b) / (c * d)	$\dfrac{(a+b)}{cd}$
2 * EXP(x)	$2e^x$
3^2 * SIN(q)	$3^2 \sin{(q)}$

We could carry on citing examples forever, but you're probably already familiar with this way of writing math expressions.

An incorrect math operation (division by zero, the logarithm of a negative number, etc.) results in calculations being suspended and the display of an error message. QBasic will also let you know where the error occurred. Later on, we'll cover the error processing mechanism which enables you to solve errors without suspending program execution.

Summary

We've decided to take the earliest opportunity to discuss how programming in QBasic works, and to show you what syntax rules you need to grasp, to get you thinking like a programmer from the outset. After swiftly running through the fundamentals, we took a look at commenting your code and how variables form the crux of your programs. We also examined important integral concepts such as string and numeric data control.

So, now that you've had a taste of things to come, and are sitting comfortably, let's not waste any more time, on with Chapter 2.

Controlling Program Flow

In this chapter we'll look at **control structures**; without these it's almost impossible to construct a serious piece of programming. If you want to refine your programming techniques then you won't be able to do so without conditional and unconditional jumps, conditional expressions, and a loop or two.

By the end of this chapter you'll understand exactly why well-designed programs rely on control structures. By building them properly into your routines, you can cut down on the amount of code you have to write, increase the speed of your program and drastically reduce the possibility of errors.

In this chapter, you'll learn about:

- The difference between linear and branching programs.
- The **IF** and **SELECT** constructs.
- Cyclic and looping constructs.
- Unconditional branching.
- Modular programming.
- Functions and procedures.
- Running external programs.
- Methods of exiting loops.

Controlling Program Flow

A QBasic program consists of text which contains a list of instructions, each of which must comply with certain syntax rules. Each instruction tells the computer to carry out a particular job, such as asking the user to enter data, accepting the data, processing it, and outputting the results to the screen or printer. There are basically three different ways in which we can structure a piece of code resulting in programs that may be linear, branching or cyclic.

Linear Programs

In a **linear** program, the instructions are executed strictly one after another, from left to right along a line, and from the first (uppermost) line to the last (lowermost) line in a program unit. Overleaf is an example of a linear program:

```
REM Example of a linear program
REM \CHAP2\CH2_1.BAS

CONST pi = 3.141
r=l=0
INPUT "Input radius r=";r: l = 2 * pi * r
PRINT "Circumference =";l

END
```

This program allows you to calculate the circumference, **l**, of a circle using the entered radius, **r**.

The program begins with the definition of the numeric constant **pi**. The **INPUT** command asks the user to enter the radius of the circle, then the circumference is calculated and the result is assigned to the variable **l**. The program finishes by displaying the comment Circumference = followed by the numeric value of **l**.

> Note that you can place multiple individual statements on a single line by separating them with a colon. Beware of using this feature too often though, because they can make your program look very cluttered and difficult to follow.

Unfortunately, this program has at least two defects: it can only be applied once without the user having to restart the program, and there's no restraint on the input values of **r**. In the case of the latter, if an incorrect input (for example, negative **r**) is given, then we'll obtain a negative and nonsensical value for the circumference. We'll discuss validating input later on in Chapter 7.

Structuring programs purely in a linear fashion is quite unusual unless they're very small, very simplistic or very well planned. All programs are linear in essence, but normally incorporate some branching and/or cyclic sections.

Branching Code

A program of any complexity will usually feature **branching**. Every so often the need arises to break the execution of a program into two or more branches, the path chosen depending, for example, on the input data or the results of the execution of another part of the program. Both of these possibilities are expressed as **conditional expressions**.

Conditional expressions play a large part in creating branching programs. Since the overwhelming majority of practical programs require some sort of branching mechanism, QBasic has advanced tools for defining conditional expressions. We'll illustrate these with the following example which calculates the function $\sin(x)/x$, a function of great mathematical significance.

The calculation of $\sin(x)/x$ causes no problems for most values of x, but one serious problem occurs when x is equal to the value zero. For those of us who have forgotten the significance of this, when x is zero, $\sin(x)$ should also be zero. Unfortunately, QBasic doesn't see it this way. Look at this program:

```
REM Demonstration of QBasic's problem with division by zero
REM \CHAP2\CH2_2.BAS

INPUT "INPUT x =";x
y = SIN(x) / x
PRINT "SIN(x)/x = ";y

END
```

It will quite happily calculate **SIN(x)/x** for all values of **x**, until **x = 0** is entered. At this point the program will stop working and tell us that, in its opinion, division by zero is impossible. It apparently doesn't know that **SIN(0)/0** is **1**. This is a problem with many versions of BASIC and something that we have to learn to live with.

> Note that QBasic also perceives the absence of any further code to execute as an indication of completion of the program. In other words, it automatically executes the **END** statement at the end of a program.

We'll have to help it understand by splitting the individual calculation of **SIN(x)/x** for **x = 0** into one branch, and the calculation for all other 'okay' values into another one. Now you should be able to see the need for carrying out conditional operations or expressions.

The IF...THEN Statement

The primary branching construct is the **IF. . .THEN** structure, whose syntax is as follows:

```
IF condition THEN statements
```

Here, when the **condition** is met, the **statements** will be executed. Now we can modify our program to the following form:

```
REM How we can solve QBasic's division by zero problem
REM PROGRAMS\CHAP_2\CH2_3.BAS

    INPUT "INPUT x =";x
IF x = 0 THEN y = 1
IF x <> 0 THEN y = SIN (x) / x
    PRINT "SIN(x)/x = ";y

    END
```

This program allows us to calculate our math function for any value of **x**, even when it's zero. The new line in the program allows us to do this by defining **y = 1** for **x = 0** (thus avoiding division by zero), and calculating **y = SIN(x)/x** for all the other values of **x**.

The ELSE Statement

There's another, more general, form of the conditional expression definition, where two expressions (one for when the condition is fulfilled and the other for when it's not) are defined as a single construction:

```
IF condition THEN [statements1] ELSE [statements2]
```

It's clear that if the condition is met, **statements1** is executed, otherwise **statements2** is executed. This construction is better in terms of structured programming as the structure of a program becomes clearer and more understandable.

This is illustrated by the next version of our math program:

```
REM How we can solve the problem more efficiently
REM \CHAP2\CH2_4.BAS

    INPUT "INPUT x =";x
IF x=0 THEN y=1 ELSE y = SIN(x) / x
```

```
PRINT "SIN(x)/x = ";y

END
```

The program has become shorter and clearer. Although we've been considering a very simple program, these advantages are of greater value in longer, more complicated programs.

Statement Blocks in IF Statements

This last method of writing conditional expressions is good in every respect, except for one - if the executable statement blocks are too large, they won't fit into one line. Fortunately, as a fully fledged representative of structural programming languages, QBasic has a conditional construction that enables multi-line executable blocks of code. This structure is as follows:

```
IF condition THEN
      [statements1]
ELSE
      [statements2]]
END IF
```

If the condition is fulfilled then the first statement block is executed, if it isn't then the second block is executed instead. If you require more than two blocks, you can include an additional expression, **ELSEIF**, which is our own version of the **SGN** function:

```
REM Application of the IF, ELSEIF and END IF statements
REM \CHAP2\CH2_5.BAS

CLS
INPUT "Enter a number x="; x
IF x < 0 THEN
    PRINT "The number x is smaller than 0"
    s = -1
ELSEIF x > 0 THEN
    PRINT "The number x is greater than 0"
    s = 1
ELSEIF x = 0 THEN
    PRINT "The number x is equal to 0"
    s = 0
END IF
PRINT "The sign of the number is "; s

END
```

If you run the program three times and enter the following values, you'll get this dialog:

```
Enter a number x=? 2
The number x is greater than 0
The sign of the number is 1

Enter a number x=? -6
The number x is smaller than 0
The sign of the number is -1

Enter a number x=? 0
```

The number x is equal to 0
The sign of the number is 0

Using Character Expressions

You can also use character expressions in conditional transfers; for example, you'll frequently come across the following query upon completing a program session:

```
REM Demonstration of Character Expressions
REM \CHAP2\CH2_6.BAS

INPUT "Do you want to restart this program (Y)es or (N)o ";answer$
IF UCASE$(answer$)="Y" THEN RUN
IF UCASE$(answer$)="N" THEN END

END
```

Here the **answer$** variable takes the value of the character entered, either **Y** (Yes) or **N** (No). If you type **Y**, then the program will restart. If you type **N**, the program will end. However, a small problem arises here - the user can enter either an upper or lower case letter Y or N and these are treated as distinct values of **F$**. We, therefore, explicitly define the condition of program termination to be fulfilled in either case. Of course, it isn't how the character looks, but its code that is perceived by QBasic. This is the key to understanding character data comparison operations. If strings of equal length are compared, then their equivalence means that the codes of all the corresponding characters, from the first character to the last, are identical. This is a technique that is often used when we need to sort strings - we can compare whether one is alphabetically before the other and then swap them. We shall return to sorting in Chapter 5.

> *Note the use of* **UCASE$** *to convert any lower-case letters in a text string into upper-case, thus replacing the statement* IF answer$="y" or answer$="Y".

The SELECT CASE Statements

Multi-directional branching is easy to do using another control structure, the **SELECT CASE** statement, which executes one of several statement blocks depending on the value of a single expression. When you require many different branches to select from, instead of using a long list of **IF** statements, use the **SELECT CASE** statement. The **SELECT CASE** statement is used as a part of the following construction:

```
SELECT CASE testexpression
    CASE expressionlist1
        [statements-1]
    [CASE expressionlist2
        [statements-2]]
    [CASE ELSE
        [statements-n]]
END SELECT
```

where

testexpression	is any numeric or string expression.
expressionlist	consists of one or more expressions tested as a possible match to **testexpression**.
statements-x	consists of one or more statements on one or more lines

This example demonstrates how you can use this efficient construct:

```
REM Demonstration of SELECT-CASE
REM \CHAP2\CH2_7.BAS

CLS
PRINT "Please enter a number 1 to 5 :"
INPUT choice

SELECT CASE choice
    CASE 1
        PRINT "One"
    CASE 2
        PRINT "Two"
    CASE 3
        PRINT "Three"
    CASE 4
        PRINT "Four"
    CASE 5
        PRINT "Five"
END SELECT

END
```

Start this program and you'll see a dialog similar to this:

```
Please enter a number 1 to 5 :
? 4
Four
```

The program asks for a number and, once it receives it, it outputs its equivalent in words.

The TO Modifier

However, we can extend the functionality of the **SELECT CASE** statement using the **TO** modifier, which allows you to switch according to the range of the argument:

```
REM Application of the TO statement for range testing
REM \CHAP2\CH2_8.BAS

CLS
INPUT "Enter the number of a month (1 to 12) : "; CHOICE
SELECT CASE CHOICE
    CASE 1 TO 3: PRINT "First quarter"
    CASE 4 TO 6: PRINT "Second quarter"
    CASE 7 TO 9: PRINT "Third quarter"
    CASE 10 TO 12: PRINT "Fourth quarter"
END SELECT

END
```

Running this program gives the following self-explanatory output:

```
Enter the number of a month (1 to 12) : ?10
Fourth quarter
```

Textual Expressions

The control variable can also be textual as well - a concept which can be illustrated by reversing the program we used earlier (**\CHAP2\CH2_7.BAS**) by having the user enter the name of a number and making our program respond with the number:

```
REM Demonstration of textual SELECT CASE expressions
REM \CHAP2\CH2_9.BAS

CLS
INPUT "Enter the name of an integer between 0 and 3 inclusive : "; n$
SELECT CASE n$
    CASE "Zero": PRINT "0"
    CASE "One": PRINT "1"
    CASE "Two": PRINT "2"
    CASE "Three": PRINT "3"
END SELECT

END
```

We get the following dialog when we run this program:

```
Enter the name of an integer between 0 and 3 inclusive : ?Two
2
```

The program performs an immediate conversion from the entered text into a number which is then displayed on the screen. You can also use the **TO** range statement with text-based expressions, because QBasic will first convert the text into ASCII codes and then perform the range evaluation.

The IS Modifier

There will be moments when the **TO** modifier won't allow enough flexibility, and you would like to make an expression using relational operators. To do this you must prefix your relational expression with **IS** modifier. For example, take the following program which decides whether to round a decimal fraction up or down:

```
REM Demonstration of the IS modifier
REM \CHAP2\CH2_10.BAS

CLS
INPUT "Enter your decimal fraction (between 0 and 1) : "; entry
SELECT CASE entry
    CASE IS < .5  : PRINT "Round number down"
    CASE IS >= .5 : PRINT "Round number up"
END SELECT

END
```

If the number entered is less than 0.5, we are to round the number down; but if it's greater than or equal to 0.5, we are to round it up. We listed the six relational operators back in Chapter 1.

Cyclic Code

We often need to execute many calculations in a **cycle**. You can see the importance of the code cycling technique by considering this example: create a table of the squares of all integers in the range of 1 to 999 inclusive. Imagine that you had to type the rest of this sequence of statements - it would result in rather a lot of lines of code:

```
REM Display the squares of all integers 1-999 #1

PRINT 1, 1 * 1
PRINT 2, 2 * 2
PRINT 3, 3 * 3
...
...
...
PRINT 999, 999 * 999

END
```

Instead of taking five weeks to finish this laborious program, we can write a simple cyclic program using special loop statements.

Loops with a Specified Number of Repetitions

You can write a more efficient program if you use loops, which are executed a definite number of times. In this example, we've used a **FOR...NEXT** loop:

```
REM Display the squares of all integers 1-999 #2
REM PROGRAMS\CHAP_2\CH2_11.BAS

FOR counter=1 TO 999
    PRINT counter, counter*counter
NEXT counter

END
```

Here we have an integer variable called **counter**, which starts with the value of one and with that value QBasic executes the code between the **FOR** and the **NEXT** statements. The construct then gives **counter** the next value in the series, here it's two, and executes the code again. This continues until the **FOR** runs out of values to assign to **counter**, in this case the loop finishes after executing the code when **counter** has the value 999.

You'll often find in your programs that you need to repeat a block of statements a specified number of times. The **FOR...NEXT** loop we've just used has the general format:

FOR n = start TO end [STEP increment]

> **[statements]**

NEXT [n]

Here **n** is a control variable used as a loop counter, the value of which changes as the loop is repeated from the **start** value to the **end** value. In the previous example it was called **counter**. If the expression **[STEP increment]** is omitted, **n** is increased by one if the **end** is greater than the **start** value. If the end is less than the start then the loop is skipped entirely - you must enter a negative **STEP** value if you want to reverse the loop. **STEP** can be either integer or fraction, positive or negative. You can't, however, specify **STEP** as zero or enter the loop other than at its beginning.

Start, **end** and **increment** can all be numbers, names of variables, or math expressions. If you use a math expression, then it's calculated before the loop is executed. You can't use the **IF. . .THEN. . .ELSE** construct to enter the loop body (as mentioned above, you can only enter the loop via its beginning). To exit the loop early, you can use the **EXIT FOR** statement. You could also use the **STOP** statement, which halts the program, or the **END** statement which ends a program, procedure, block, or user-defined data type. We shall look at the ways you can exit loops later.

The **NEXT** statement completes the **FOR. . .NEXT** construction. The control variable which follows **NEXT** doesn't need to be indicated, but it makes things much clearer if you include it, particularly if you're nesting loops within loops.

> If you're going to nest loops, be very careful that you control them in the proper manner. The control variable of each nested loop must be unique, although un-nested loops can have identical names. And always match each control variable to each **NEXT** statement, making sure that they're completed in the correct order (inner first, outer last)

FOR...NEXT Variations

So far we've assumed that **start** < **end**, and **increment** > **0**. However, you can create loops where the loop counter decreases. To do this, you should meet the conditions: **start** > **end** and **increment** < **0**. Values that don't meet these conditions, together with **increment** = **0**, aren't allowed and are classified as errors.

Here are some examples of valid loops:

Loop	Control variable values

`FOR n = 5 TO 1 STEP -1`
`...`
`NEXT n`
	$n = 5, 4, 3, 2$ and 1

`FOR n = 0 TO 1 STEP 0.25`
`...`
`NEXT n`
	$n = 0, .25, .5, .75$ and 1

`FOR n = 1 TO 0 STEP -0.25`
`...`
`NEXT n`
	$n = 1, .75, .5, .25$ and 0

The loop counter is fully available within the loop too; for example, its value can be used to output the current number in the sequence. The counter variable can also be changed within the loop; for example, assigning it the **end** value will force an exit from the loop. However, changing the control variable is a programming trick that's frowned upon in structured programming, because there are other types of loop better suited to such requirements.

> Loops with integer counters are executed noticeably faster than those with the default single precision variables. However, this is only becomes a factor when the number of loops is very large and speed is an issue.

Loops with Conditional Completion

Loops with a definite number of repetitions are useful programming constructs, but what happens if you want to execute a block of code until a specified condition is True. You can do this using the following construction:

```
WHILE condition

    statements

WEND
```

The statement block is executed while the condition is True and the following program demonstrates this:

```
REM Demonstration of WHILE...WEND
REM \CHAP2\CH2_12.BAS

CLS
n = 1
WHILE n < 5
    PRINT "n = "; n;
    n = n + 1
WEND

END
```

And the program prints the following output:

    n = 1 n = 2 n = 3 n = 4

The loop is terminated when the **WEND** can't return to the head of the loop, because the condition is invalid.

> You must always make sure that you allow the control variable the opportunity to actually get out of the loop, otherwise your program could be stuck in there for an eternity!

The DO...LOOP Construct

The **DO. . .LOOP** construction provides another way to execute statements in a program loop:

```
DO [{WHILE | UNTIL} condition]

    [statements]

LOOP [{WHILE | UNTIL} condition]
```

The **DO. . .LOOP** construction in its simplified form, without conditions, creates an infinite loop that you can get out of using the **EXIT** statement. Here, the **WHILE** statement is used to repeat the loop body as long as the condition is True, and **UNTIL** repeats until the condition is True. Only one of the **WHILE**'s or **UNTIL**'s can be used in any one loop. Here we'll show the differences between the different versions of the **DO. . .LOOP** construct:

```
REM The DO UNTIL...LOOP
REM \CHAP2\CH2_13.BAS

CLS
n = 0
DO UNTIL n > 5
    PRINT "n = "; n
    n = n + 1
LOOP
PRINT "End"

END
```

This produces the following results:

```
N = 0
N = 1
N = 2
N = 3
N = 4
N = 5
End
```

What's happening here is fairly straightforward: the loop increments the control variable *after* it has printed the first value, and the loop stops executing when **n** becomes six. The next loop construction, **DO WHILE...LOOP**, works the other way: it checks the value before it executes the code block. If the loop was entered with a False control variable, then the block of code wouldn't even be executed once:

```
REM The DO WHILE...LOOP
REM \CHAP2\CH2_14.BAS

CLS
n = 0
DO WHILE n <> 5
    PRINT "n = "; n
    n = n + 1
LOOP
PRINT "End"

END
```

And here's the results of this one:

```
N = 0
N = 1
N = 2
N = 3
N = 4
End
```

However, our next loop, the **DO...LOOP UNTIL**, executes at least once because the test appears after the block of code:

```
REM The DO...LOOP UNTIL loop
REM \CHAP2\CH2_15.BAS

CLS
n = 0
DO
    n = n + 1
    PRINT "n = "; n
LOOP UNTIL n = 5
PRINT "End"

END
```

This is what we get on running this program:

```
N = 1
N = 2
N = 3
N = 4
N = 5
End
```

Finally, the following program demonstrates the **DO...LOOP WHILE** cycle with the termination condition of the **WHILE** type:

```
REM The DO...LOOP WHILE loop
REM \CHAP2\CH2_16.BAS

CLS
n = 0
DO
    n = n + 1
    PRINT "n = "; n
LOOP WHILE n <> 5
PRINT "End"

END
```

This is what it gives us:

```
n = 1
n = 2
n = 3
n = 4
n = 5
End
```

You've realized by now that the **DO. . .LOOP** construction is the most flexible, because it allows you to define conditions of various types, both at the beginning and at the end of the cycle. However, be very careful that you know exactly what the values of the control variable are going to be at each stage of the loop - it can become very tricky when you include branching, nesting and the dynamic changing of the control variable.

Exiting Loops

Sometimes you need to exit a loop before it's finished. For instance, it may be necessary to end an infinite **DO. . .LOOP** cycle in order to terminate the execution of a program 'naturally', or to suspend a calculation if an error is encountered, for example in the case of an attempted division by zero.

Using a conditional jump to do this isn't possible in structured programming - this would be the equivalent of entering a **FOR...NEXT** loop without initializing the **FOR** statement. You can only exit a block through its natural end, a **WEND** or a **NEXT** or something similar. Violating this rule interferes with the operation of the stack which stores the addresses to the loop and sub-routines. This can result in the stack becoming over-filled and may cause program failure. You should use the **EXIT** statement to quit a loop since this ensures that the stack is correctly dealt with. We'll explain the operation of the stack in detail in a few pages time.

There's actually a whole group of early exit statements among the control structures. Apart from using **EXIT** on its own, you can also use the following statements in a loop: **EXIT DEF, EXIT FOR, EXIT DO, EXIT FUNCTION** and **EXIT SUB**. We will discuss exiting loops further at the end of this chapter.

Unconditional Branching

To create programs of even moderate complexity, you need tools to control the calculation processes. In QBasic, these software tools take the form of control structures. Using the various conditional and unconditional branches and expressions, loops, switch control statements, event handlers, etc., you can create sophisticated branching programs.

Using Numbering

As a legacy from earlier versions of BASIC, QBasic has retained line numbering as an option. You simply call a numbered line with the **Goto** statement to move the program flow:

```
GOTO Line_Number
```

For example, this line:

```
50 GOTO 1000
```

causes an unconditional jump to line 1000, and the program continues execution from there. In this example, the line number functions as a label.

Using Labels

QBasic allows you to define **character labels** in the following way:

```
Label_Name:
```

The colon has a special purpose here, indicating that the unique identifier preceding it is to be treated as a label rather than a common statement. Label names conform to the same rules as constant or variable names. The following short program demonstrates the definition and use of a label:

```
REM Using Labels to print 0 to 4
REM \CHAP2\CH2_17.BAS

CLS
i = 0
Label:
IF i = 5 THEN END
    PRINT i;
i = i + 1
GOTO Label

END
```

The **GOTO Label** statement causes a loop in which the value of variable **i** changes from 0 to 5. When **i** is assigned the value 5, the conditional expression:

```
IF i = 5 THEN END
```

executes the **END** statement, causing the program to end.

If you start the program, the following numeric string will be displayed on the screen:

```
0 1 2 3 4
```

The Dangers

You're restricted in what you can do with unconditional jumps in structured programming. For instance, you can't use them inside other control structures such as loops. You should also realise that if you use them recklessly, they can lead to confusing, badly structured 'spaghetti' code - this is very hard to debug. Quite often though, using the forbidden fruit of the **GOTO** statement carefully facilitates your work as a programmer. In fact, many good algorithms have been produced using both conditional and unconditional branches. As long as your program works, neither the user nor an external compiler (if one is used) will be aware of whether the program is written using structured programming or a multitude of unconditional jumps. All the same, avoid using the **GOTO** statement whenever you can apply other tools. Remember that in theory, programming can do without it.

Organizing a Multi-directional Branch

In theory, the **IF. . .THEN. . .ELSE** statements enable you to implement a multidirectional branch and serve as control switch statements. For example, you can switch subroutines while changing the variable **n** by using the construction:

```
IF n = 1 THEN GOTO Label1
IF n = 2 THEN GOTO Label2
IF n = 3 THEN GOTO Label3
 ...
 ...
 ...
```

However, instead of this cumbersome construction, QBasic offers several more up-to-date tools for multidirectional branching; for example, this statement:

ON expression GOTO label_list

This construction provides a branch to one of several locations, depending on the value of an expression. Here **label_list** is a set of labels or line numbers. If the value of **expression** is 1, the program branches to the first line in the list; if expression is 2, it branches to the second line, and so on. **expression** can range from 0 through 255. If **expression** isn't an integer it's rounded to the nearest integer value and if **expression** is beyond the specified range, no branching occurs. The **ON** construct can also be used with **GOSUB** and we'll deal with this later.

However, the best way of performing a multi-directional branch is to use **SELECT CASE**.

Modular Programming

A QBasic program is usually made up of a main module with one or more sub-programs and user-defined functions. A typical QBasic program has the following structure:

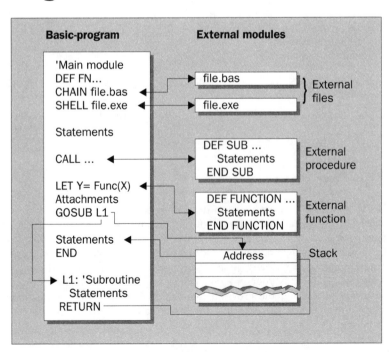

A **module** is a functionally complete section of code which performs a definite set of actions. Let us now look at some of the key concepts involved in modular programming.

Elements of Modular Programming

We can identify the following distinct elements in modular programming, and together they form a typical modular program.

Main Module

You should try to make the **main module** as illustrative and compact as possible. It contains the initial declarations of data types (arrays, constants, variable, user functions, etc.) and globally implements the algorithm for performing the specified task by calling sub-programs and external units which tackle simpler tasks within the module.

Functions

The role of a **function** is to return a value (numeric or character) in response to being addressed by name and its parameters passed to it. Functions may be mathematical; for instance, they can return the values of an exponent or the absolute value of a number; or they may consist of text operations and return a string.

Subroutines

Subroutines, or **procedures**, are more versatile than functions and allow you to perform all sorts of actions that can be separated from the main body of the program for example, you could write a procedure to handle keyboard input which could be called from anywhere in your program.

User-defined Functions and Subroutines

QBasic allows you to work with **user-defined** functions and subroutines, in addition to the built-in ones supplied with QBasic, and these may be internal or **external** to the module from which they are called.

External Modules

QBasic also allows you to create high level modular programs. For example, you could create three different programs to process data where the second processes the results of the first, and the third the results of the second, linking the programs together with the **CHAIN** statement. This modular approach allows you to attack a task with a range of programs with interchanges of data taking place between them.

Building a Subroutine

Modular programming is based on dividing a program into separate, functionally complete units. For a long time it was felt that BASIC was totally unsuitable for modular programming because earlier versions of BASIC, such as BasicA and GWBasic, had no tools for dividing programs into external units.

You'll often find that you'll need to repeat parts of your program several times throughout the duration of your application. If you Cut and Paste, or even worse, actually type in identical fragments of code over and over again, you'll not only waste a lot of time, but you'll also clutter your program up with unnecessary text, obscuring the main part of the program and causing problems in the debugging stage. To make life simpler, a block of code can be repeatedly executed by defining it as a subroutine. Subroutines are called from the main module using the construction **GOSUB Label** and they take the following form:

```
Label:

...

RETURN
```

where **Label** is the name that you give to your sub-routine and the ellipsis indicates the code that makes up your subroutine. Subroutines should be placed after the main program but in the main module. Take this example:

```
REM Organizing a subroutine using the GOSUB and RETURN statements
REM \CHAP2\CH2_18.BAS

x = 1: CLS
GOSUB HSN:
PRINT "HSN("; x; ")="; y:
PRINT "E ="; e

END

HSN:
e = EXP(x)
y = (e - 1 / e) / 2
RETURN
```

When running this program, you'll see the following result:

HSN (1) = 1.175201
E= 2.718282

Unfortunately, this method only gives the illusion of modular programming: the main program and the subroutine remain as a single unit, and the variables used (in this case **x, y** and **e**) are global, meaning that their values can be changed throughout the program (both in the main part and in the part allocated to the subroutine). This isn't always the ideal effect, since it makes it quite hard to keep track of changes made to variables throughout the program, and gives errors the opportunity to creep in. For this reason **GOSUB** isn't (or maybe *shouldn't be*) used very much any more. However, we'll be dealing with a suitable replacement in a few paragraph's time.

We mentioned earlier on in this chapter about the **ON** construct being used with **GOTO**'s. This method of branching can also be used in subroutines in the following form:

ON expression GOSUB label_list

As with **ON GOTO**, the value of **expression** decides the branch location; i.e. if the value of **expression** is 1 then the program branches to the first line and likewise, if the value of **expression** is 2, it branches to the second line. **expression** ranges from 0 to 255.

Introducing the Stack

A question may have crossed your mind: how does the sub-program know where to return the program control to after it has finished? This is the job of a **stack**, a chain of memory cells for storing numbers (**addresses**), organized on the principle of **last in, first out** (**LIFO**). It's like a stack of plates that can only be increased or decreased one plate at a time: the first plate we remove is always the one on the top and, therefore, the one that we added to the stack last. Only at the very end will we get to the plate that we put down first.

Each time a sub-program is called, the address in the program from which the call was made is added to the top of the stack. Each time the program reaches a **RETURN** statement, indicating the end of a sub-program, it reads the address from the top of the stack, removing the address in the process, and passes control back to the program at that address. Clearly, we can address many sub-programs, being limited only by the allowed size of the stack. If the number of calls is more than the number of the stack cells, then the stack overflows and an error occurs (too many plates stacked on top of one other has much the same effect). Note that the stack isn't only used for subroutines, but also for all similar modular operations covered in this chapter.

User-defined Functions

There are two different methods of defining a function, that the user can utilize, a simple one-line function or a more involved multi-line function. Here we will discuss both.

Defining a One-line User-defined Function

The simplest type of function that a user can define themselves is that of the one-liner, which has the following format:

DEF FNname (parameterlist) = expression

Here the **parameterlist** is a sequence of variables used in the **expression**, the numeric or character values that will be passed to the function when it's called. If this list contains several variables then they will be separated by commas.

For example, we can define the function to calculate the hyperbolic sine as follows:

```
DEF FNHSN (x) = (EXP (x) - 1/EXP (x))/2
```

The variable **x** used in the function definition is **local**, since its value is only specified when the function is called. Another variable **x** could also be used in the main program. When the function is called, it's not the current value of **x** that's used just the value given in brackets. In other words, the value of **x** used by the function is independent of any value that the other variable **x** may have in the main body of the program. For example,

```
REM Specifying a user function
REM PROGRAMS\CHAP_2\CH2_19.BAS

CLS
x = 5

DEF FNS (x) = (EXP(x) - EXP(-x)) / 2

y = FNS(1)
PRINT "HSN(1)="; y
PRINT "x="; x

END
```

When we run this program, we obtain the following results:

HSN (1)= 1.175201
X= 5

which prove the local nature of the variable used in the function.

Defining a Multi-line User-defined Function

Do you feel a little restricted by that single line? If so, you'll be glad to know that QBasic also allows you to define a function containing any number of lines:

```
DEF FNname (parameterlist)

    Statements

END DEF
```

The hyperbolic sine, for instance, can now be calculated like this:

```
REM Specifying a multi-line user function
REM PROGRAMS\CHAP_2\CH2_20.BAS

CLS
x = 5
e = 2
z = 3

DEF FNHSN (x)
    e = EXP(x)
    z = e - 1 / e
    FNHSN = z / 2
END DEF

y = FNHSN(1)
PRINT "HSN(1)="; y
PRINT "x ="; x
PRINT "e ="; e
PRINT "z ="; z

END
```

Running this program gives you:

```
HSN(1)= 1.175201
X = 5
E = 2.718282
Z = 2.350402
```

Note that, in this case, `e = EXP(x)` is calculated only once, greatly reducing the total calculation time. What's more revealing though, is that in the multi-line user function, the variables **e** and **z**, which appear both in the main module and in the body of the function, are subject to change when the function is called. In other words, the variables **e** and **z** (unlike the earlier variable-parameter **x**) behave like global variables. This means that the multi-line user function can't really be described as an effective modular programming tool, since not all the variables within it are local.

External Modules

QBasic is a strongly modular programming environment because it allows you to define external procedures and functions which are both complete and use local variables. Here we'll discuss both of these topics.

When a procedure or function is executed, the values of the variables are identical to those in the main module. The QBasic shell has the user define external procedures and functions and place them in its 'pockets', separate from the main module.

Defining an External Function

An external function is defined as a separate unit, like this:

```
FUNCTION Name (Variablelist) [STATIC]

    [Expressions]
    Name = Expression

 END FUNCTION
```

The **FUNCTION** and the **END FUNCTION** statements are created by the QBasic editor when you define your function. All you have to do is enter the name of the function and the block of statements which form the body of the function. The result of the executed function must be assigned to a variable of the same name as that of the function. This is necessary because the function's unique feature is that it returns a result when called by its name, making its behavior identical to that of any built-in QBasic function.

The **Variablelist** must include the variables which are passed as parameters from the main module of a program to the external function. The names of the variables are separated by commas. You can use standard variables of various types, index variables, or whole arrays. You can pass arrays by giving their name followed by empty parentheses, as in the following example:

```
MYFUN (n%,x,y,v(3),m())
```

In this case, the integer value **n%**, the single-precision real numbers **x** and **y**, the vector element **v(3)** and the matrix **m** will be passed to the function **MYFUN**. So that you recognize the type of an array and its index limits within a function, you should use the **LBOUND** and **UBOUND** functions. We cover these later on when we deal with arrays.

An external function must be declared in the program which uses it. The statement **DECLARE FUNCTION** is used to do this, followed by the name of the function and its variable list. You don't need to worry about this though, because as soon as the function is created, the editor automatically inserts the relevant declaration at the beginning of the program.

Global and Local Status of Variables

As you know, a program is made from different program modules: the main module, subroutines, functions, sub-programs, and, finally, external programs and procedures.

Variables are used within all of the sections: some locally within a single section, for example to control the flow within a sub-routine; others are used to pass information from one section of the program to another. Sometimes you may want information passed to internal modules only, at other times you may want to pass it to external modules, or some combination of the two.

You do this by using the following program statement: you place it at the top of all programs and external procedures you wish to share data:

```
COMMON [SHARED] variablelist
```

If you use **COMMON** by itself, then the variables specified in the list, are passed to external programs when you **CHAIN** to them. Adding the word **SHARED** allows you to share the specified variables with all the modules in the program, as well as making them available to the external ones.

One advantage of not using the **SHARED** option in your program, is that you can use variables of the same name in different program modules. Since they aren't shared, they don't affect each other's values.

For example, take the following program:

```
REM Use of STATIC keyword
REM \CHAP2\CH2_21.BAS

DECLARE FUNCTION ADDITION (X)

total = 0
CLS
x = 2
FOR n = 1 TO 10
    y = ADDITION(x)
    PRINT "ADDITION("; x; ")="; y; "   "; "TOTAL (Mainbody) = "; total
NEXT n

END

FUNCTION ADDITION (x) STATIC
    total = total + x
    ADDITION = total
END FUNCTION
```

As you can see, when the program is run with the **STATIC** keyword in place, the **ADDITION** function 'remembers' the value of the variable **TOTAL** each time the function is re-entered. The value of **total** in the main body isn't affected:

```
ADDITION( 2 )= 2    TOTAL (Mainbody) = 0
ADDITION( 2 )= 4    TOTAL (Mainbody) = 0
ADDITION( 2 )= 6    TOTAL (Mainbody) = 0
ADDITION( 2 )= 8    TOTAL (Mainbody) = 0
ADDITION( 2 )= 10   TOTAL (Mainbody) = 0
ADDITION( 2 )= 12   TOTAL (Mainbody) = 0
ADDITION( 2 )= 14   TOTAL (Mainbody) = 0
ADDITION( 2 )= 16   TOTAL (Mainbody) = 0
ADDITION( 2 )= 18   TOTAL (Mainbody) = 0
ADDITION( 2 )= 20   TOTAL (Mainbody) = 0
```

```
ADDITION( 2 )= 2    TOTAL (Mainbody) = 0
ADDITION( 2 )= 2    TOTAL (Mainbody) = 0
ADDITION( 2 )= 2    TOTAL (Mainbody) = 0
ADDITION( 2 )= 2    TOTAL (Mainbody) = 0
ADDITION( 2 )= 2    TOTAL (Mainbody) = 0
ADDITION( 2 )= 2    TOTAL (Mainbody) = 0
ADDITION( 2 )= 2    TOTAL (Mainbody) = 0
ADDITION( 2 )= 2    TOTAL (Mainbody) = 0
ADDITION( 2 )= 2    TOTAL (Mainbody) = 0
ADDITION( 2 )= 2    TOTAL (Mainbody) = 0
```

Remove **STATIC** from the function, and **total**'s value is forgotten when the program exits the function.

Defining an External Procedure

Despite the fact that functions offer powerful possibilities, their usefulness is quite limited. The ultimate aim of each external function is to return a result when it's called. External procedures are more flexible and are defined by the following QBasic construction:

```
SUB Name (variablelist) [STATIC]

    statements

END SUB
```

As with functions, procedures must be declared at the beginning of the main program and will be declared automatically by QBasic. The variables in the body of a procedure are local by default and may be defined as static using the **STATIC** keyword. As mentioned before, this keeps the last value of the variable inside this function.

The **variablelist** is just that - the list of variables separated by commas. In the variable list you can define the type of a variable using the following construction:

```
VariableName AS Type
```

The variables in the variable list are very important because they're the link between the external procedure and the main program. Certain variables may be used for passing data from an external program to the body of an external function. Others may be intended for transferring data from the external procedure to the calling program. The variable list can include numeric and character variables of any type, index variables, and even whole arrays. To pass a whole array you should give the array's name followed by empty parentheses. You can work out an array's dimensions and its index limits in the procedure (or function) using **LBOUND** and **UBOUND**.

Calling External Procedures

To call an external procedure, you can use the **CALL** statement:

```
CALL NameSUB (ParameterList)
```

or simply address it by name:

```
NameSUB ParameterList
```

In the second case, the variables included in the parameter list are used without parentheses. Both forms are interchangeable - it's up to you which one you use. **CALL** makes it obvious that you're calling an external procedure, while addressing by name is reminiscent of using statements.

Common and Shared Variables

Local variables have obvious advantages:you don't have to worry about using different names in the main module and in external functions or procedures; this decompartmentalization helps when it comes to debugging. However, every so often you may need to use global variables. You can declare the variables in the body of a function or a procedure global using the statements **COMMON** and **SHARED**:

```
REM Specifying and calling a procedure
REM \CHAP2\CH2_22.BAS

DECLARE SUB CalcSin (x)
COMMON SHARED x, y
x = 0: y = 0
CLS
INPUT "INPUT x ="; x
CALL CalcSin(X)
PRINT "y("; x; ")="; y

END

SUB CalcSin (x)
    y = SIN(x)
END SUB
```

When running this program, you'll obtain:

```
Input x=? 1
y( 1 ) =.841471
```

If we remove the **SHARED** option in the program, and we create a second external program with the same subroutine, we can demonstrate that the variables are indeed passed to the external procedure, but aren't available internally:

```
REM COMMON without SHARED
REM \CHAP2\CH2_23.BAS

DECLARE SUB CalcSin (x)

COMMON x, y
x = 0
y = 0
CLS
INPUT "Input x="; x
CALL CalcSin(x)
PRINT "Internal:"
PRINT "y("; x; ")="; y
CHAIN "C:\REVQB\CHAP2\CH2_23.BAS"

END

SUB CalcSin (x)
    y = SIN(x)
END SUB
```

Incidentally, we shall talk about the **CHAIN** command in a few pages time. For now, just note that it passes control to another QBasic program.

```
REM External program to demo passed variables
REM \CHAP2\CH2_24.BAS

COMMON SHARED x, y
DECLARE SUB CalcSin (x)

CALL CalcSin(x)
PRINT "External:"
PRINT "y("; x; ")="; y

END
```

```
SUB CalcSin (x)
    y = SIN(x)
END SUB
```

A procedure, unlike a function, doesn't return a value. Instead, it performs certain operations - logical, graphic, calculations, etc. For example, in the last program the procedure **CalcSin** assigns the value **SIN(x)** to the variable **y**. If **y** were local, it wouldn't be possible here to pass this value to the main program. This declaration:

```
COMMON SHARED x,y
```

assigns the variables **x** and **y** global status, allowing data to be passed between the procedure and the main module through these global variables. This method of attacking the problem (typically BASIC), is often very useful and convenient, but it doesn't conform to the requirements of structured programming. In fact, overuse of global variables is a much frowned upon exercise.

Meanwhile, as mentioned earlier, there's another way of interfacing external procedures with the calling program (or with another unit). It involves interchanging values through the variables of the external procedures parameters list only, as we demonstrate here:

```
REM Specifying and calling a procedure
REM \CHAP2\CH2_25.BAS

DECLARE SUB CalcSin (x, y AS DOUBLE)
CLS
INPUT "Enter x ="; x
CALL CalcSin(x, y#)
PRINT "y("; x; ")="; y#

END

SUB CalcSin (x, y AS DOUBLE)
    y = SIN(x)
END SUB
```

Running the program gives:

```
Enter x=?1
y (1 )= .8414709848078965
```

In this case, the parameter's list of the procedure **CalcSin** includes two variables: the function argument **x** as a single-precision real number (by default) and the variable **y** for passing data from the procedure, declared explicitly as a double-precision real number. The result of the calculations is given as a double-precision real number.

A Joint Use of External Procedures and Functions

It stands to reason that procedures and functions can be used in combination. You can see an example of this in the next program which calculates the **Gamma** function:

```
REM Combined Application of Functions and Procedures
REM \CHAP2\CH2_26.BAS

DECLARE SUB InpPrt ()
```

```
DECLARE FUNCTION GAMMA! (x!)
CLS
PRINT "CALCULATION OF GAMMA-FUNCTION"
CALL InpPrt

END

FUNCTION GAMMA (x)
    CONST Pi = 3.141592654#
    z = x
    FOR i = 1 TO 20
        z = z * (x + i)
    NEXT i
    b = x + 21: b1 = EXP(b * (LOG(b) - 1) + 1 / 12 / b)
    GAMMA = b1 * SQR(2 * pi / b) / z
END FUNCTION

SUB InpPrt
    DO
        INPUT "INPUT x ="; x
        PRINT "g(x)="; GAMMA(x)
        INPUT "REPEAT (y/n)"; m$
    LOOP UNTIL m$ = "n" OR m$ = "n"
END SUB
```

This program contains the **GAMMA(x)** function and the input/output procedure **InpPrt**. At this point two features are worth mentioning: the first is that the **GAMMA(x)** function aspires to be a library function on the quiet; and secondly, if you need to quit an external function or a procedure without disturbing stack operation, you should use the **EXIT FUNCTION** and **EXIT SUB** statements, respectively.

> Here it's significant to note that QBasic (unlike QuickBasic 4.0/4.5) has no means of creating external libraries of previously compiled procedures and functions. The only way of creating libraries is in the form of source code, which can be pasted into relevant programs as required.

When a program is printed, the main module listing is printed first and then the listings of all external procedures and functions follow on. However, when you display a program in the QBasic environment the functions and procedures can't be seen. As we mentioned earlier, these are stored in special windows or 'pockets' and edited separately from the main module.

Passing Control to Another QBasic Program

QBasic is able to work with external programs written in other programming languages and represented in machine code. Programs written in Assembly language are most frequently used since they're very efficient and have a high calculation rate.

The CHAIN Command

Before we move on to look at programs written in other programming languages, we should mention the **CHAIN** statement, that we used a couple of pages back, which transfers control from the current program to another BASIC program:

```
CHAIN filespec$
```

Suppose that you need to pass control to the program **TEST.BAS** which is currently in the **\BAS** directory on the **D:** drive. To pass control to this program you need to use the statement:

```
CHAIN "D:\BAS\TEST.BAS"
```

The RUN Statement

Alternatively, the **RUN** statement executes the current program or another specified one. It's used in the following format:

RUN [{linenumber | file$}]

If no line number is specified, execution begins with the first executable line. Before a program is executed, **RUN** closes all files and clears program memory. However, the **CHAIN** statement allows you to run a new program without closing the files of the old. For instance, to run the program **TEST.BAS** which is in the sub-directory **\BASPROG** on the **C:** drive, you would write:

```
RUN "C:\BASPROG\TEST.BAS"
```

which would run the following:

```
REM Calculating the Array of Values
REM \CHAP2\CH2_27.BAS

DECLARE SUB EvalProgram (f$, Maxx)
COMMON flag%, x(), y(), f$
Maxx = 20
IF flag% = 0 THEN
    CLS
    DIM x(0 TO Maxx): DIM y(0 TO Maxx)
    INPUT "Input function: y = ", f$
    INPUT "Input Xmin = ", x(0)
    INPUT "Input Xmax = ", x(Maxx)
    increment = (X(Maxx) - x(0)) / Maxx
    FOR i% = 1 TO Maxx
        x(i%) = x(i% - 1) + increment
    NEXT i%
    CALL EvalProgram(f$, Maxx)
    flag% = -1
    PRINT : PRINT "Loading EVALUATE.BAS. Please wait!"
    CHAIN "EVAL"
ELSE
    CLS : PRINT "Array X  and", " y="; f$
    FOR i% = 0 TO (Maxx)
        PRINT x(i%), y(i%)
    NEXT
    p$ = INPUT$(1)
END IF

END

SUB EvalProgram (f$, Maxx)
    OPEN "EVAL.BAS" FOR OUTPUT AS #1
    PRINT #1, "COMMON flag%, x(), y(), f$"
    PRINT #1, "FOR i% = 0 TO " + STR$(Maxx)
```

```
      PRINT #1, "   x = x(i%)"
      PRINT #1, "   y(i%) = " + f$
      PRINT #1, "NEXT i%"
      PRINT #1, "CHAIN " + CHR$(34) + "a:\PROGRAMS\EVAL.BAS " + CHR$(34)
      CLOSE #1
   END SUB
```

Note that the path of the final chain will need to be edited depending on where you've put your program file.

The program starts by asking for a function and the **Xmin** and **Xmax** limits of **x** as follows:

```
Input function: y = 10*(exp(-x)-1)
Input xmin = -10
Input xmax = 10
```

On entering the data, you'll notice that the program has addressed the disk and displayed the result immediately:

Array x	and	y=10*(exp(-x)-1)
-10		220254.7
-9		81020.84
-8		29799.58
-7		10956.33
-6		4024.288
-5		1474.132
-4		535.9815
-3		190.8554
-2		63.89056
-1		17.18282
0		0
1		-6.321206
2		-8.646647
3		-9.50213
4		-9.816844
5		-9.932621
6		-9.975212
7		-9.990881
8		-9.996645
9		-9.998766
10		-9.999546

Okay, now it's time to take a look at how this program works. When the program is started the variable **flag%** is defined as zero by default, so the first section of the main module, between the statements **IF** and **ELSE**, is executed. The program asks you to input a function, which it assigns to the character variable **f$**, and to input maximum and minimum values of **x**. It uses these values in the **FOR...NEXT** loop to form the array **x()** of the 21 possible **x** values for which the function will be calculated.

The key moment is when the procedure **EvalProgram** is called. This procedure creates a text file, **EVAL.BAS**, which calculates the **y()** array from the formula in the variable **f$** and the values of **x** in the **x()** array. In other words, the procedure produces a new program and writes it onto disk.

If you look for the program **EVAL.BAS** on your disk (it will be in the same directory as QBasic itself), it will appear like this:

```
COMMON flag%, x(), y(), f$
FOR i% = 0 TO 20
    x = x(i%)
    y(i%) = 10*(exp(-x)-1)
NEXT i%
CHAIN "a:\PROGRAMS\CHAP_02\CH2_28.BAS"
```

Remember that, at this point, control is still with the original program. Once **EVAL.BAS** has been created, the original program sets **flag%=-1** and then transfers control via the **CHAIN** statement to our newly created program. Now the initial program is erased from memory, and **EVAL.BAS** is stored in the RAM.

It's clear from its listing that **EVAL.BAS** calculates the elements of the arrays **x()** and **y()** (the elements of the **y()** array are worked out from the previously entered formula). Then, using **CHAIN**, the program erases itself from the memory and calls the original program. Since **flag%=-1**, the second section of the initial program, from the **ELSE** statement onwards, is executed and the results are printed to the screen.

It's important to note another fundamental feature of the interaction between the main program and **EVAL.BAS**: the use of the common variables **flag%, x(), y()** and **f$**. We declared these using the **COMMON** keyword at the start of both programs. If we hadn't done this, the values of these variables wouldn't have been maintained when control was passed from one program to the other, and the program wouldn't have worked.

We've conserved **EVAL.BAS**, but you can delete this program from the disk after having used it, using the **KILL** statement - you can always recreate it from the other program anyway.

The idea shown here is very useful, and we shall show you later some other examples of procreating programs. You can adapt such techniques to calculate any user-defined functions. You can also create text or graphic editors which not only develop and edit the screen images for you but create, in file form, programs in any programming language. Creating software to write programs for you is a great technique, and can drastically reduce the amount of work you have to do.

Terminating Modules and Programs

A program is automatically stopped when its final statement is executed, but there are also a number of statements in QBasic which allow you to force your program to stop. This can be of use if your program detects an error, and you don't want it to waste your time carrying on.

The STOP Statement

The **STOP** statement, which doesn't have any operands, is used to temporarily halt a program. When **STOP** is activated, any files that are already open remain open and variables retain their values. You can use **STOP** to help you debug your program, although it's more effective to set breakpoints using the QBasic system debugger. To continue program execution you can use the environment instruction Continue in the Run sub-menu.

The END Statement

The **END** statement is used to end a program and close all open files, but it doesn't necessarily have to be physically placed at the end of a program.

The SLEEP Statement

Every so often you may have to internally suspend program execution. You can do this with this statement:

```
SLEEP (P&)
```

The **P&** argument specifies the number of seconds that you want to suspend the program. If **P&** is **0** or is omitted completely, the program is suspended until a key is pressed. We've previously used the construction:

```
f$ = INPUT$(1)
```

to perform this function.

Exiting User-defined Functions

In certain instances, you'll need to perform a conditional exit from a user-defined function. To do this, you must use the **EXIT DEF** statement, as shown in the construction:

```
IF condition THEN EXIT DEF
```

This statement exits a procedure or function without interfering with the operation of the stack which controls the order of procedure and function execution. The next program calculates the factorial values, **n!**, for an integer, **n**, illustrating the use of the **EXIT DEF** statement. First though, the factorial of an integer number, **n**, is given by the formula:

```
n! = 1*2*3*...*n        when n > 0
n! = 1                  when n = 0
```

Our program calculates the factorial values for positive **n** up to a maximum of 50. If **n** is negative or exceeds 50, the program senses an error using the **IF...THEN** statement, assigns -**1** to the result and exits the function using **EXIT DEF**:

```
REM Factorial calculation
REM \CHAP2\CH2_28.BAS

DEF fnfactorial (x%)
IF x% < 0 OR x% > 50 THEN fnfactorial = -1: EXIT DEF
total = 1
FOR i% = x% TO 2 STEP -1
    total = total * i%
NEXT i%
fnfactorial = total
END DEF
```

```
'Main block of code
CLS
PRINT fnfactorial(10)
PRINT fnfactorial(80)

END
```

Running this program, we obtain:

```
3628800
-1
```

Here we can see that the core of the program works, when we enter the value 10. But when we give our user-defined function a value outside of its limits, e.g. 80, then the program responds to the error, defines the value of **fnfactorial** to be -1, and prematurely exits the function.

Summary

In this chapter, you've learned about typical QBasic control structures, though we haven't by any means covered them all. You've seen that QBasic has absorbed most of the common control structures that facilitate structured programming, and we've explored some of the uses which they can be put to. We've also introduced you to the modular programming tools, and described the operation of the stack. We've looked at various modular structures, such as external functions and procedures, which you can incorporate into your own programs. You've even seen how to use a QBasic program to create or modify another one.

Modular programming is a large subject so the programs we've used in this chapter serve only as an introduction to its concepts and practical applications. We'll come back to this topic and examine it in more detail in later chapters.

Input, Output and Printing

Introduction

As you're probably already aware, you are unlikely to meet a program that hasn't any input or output statements. So we'll now plunge head first into three of the most important programming topics by looking at the following:

- ▲ Inputting text.
- ▲ Outputting formatted text to the screen.
- ▲ Defining the cursor.
- ▲ The concept of video pages.
- ▲ Manipulating the screen.
- ▲ Making the most of colors.
- ▲ Drawing and painting graphics.
- ▲ Controlling windows.
- ▲ Printer management.
- ▲ Text and graphics printing.

Once you have grasped these principals you should be well on your way to becoming a QBasic guru, so lets move straight in and learn about input.

Understanding Input

Input can come from many different sources, of which the keyboard is only one. Peripheral devices, such as a joystick, a mouse or a disk system are obviously other frequently used input devices, but we shall concentrate at this early stage on the device that has made the computer its own - the keyboard.

The Simplest of All Input Statements

The **INPUT** statement is the most basic instruction used to accept input information from the keyboard. It effectively suspends PC operation, displays a specified comment and reads input data from the keyboard or a file (we shall discuss file management in Chapter 6 and concentrate on input from the keyboard here). The format of the **INPUT** statement is as follows:

```
INPUT [;] ["comment"{; | ,}] variablelist
```

where **comment** is an optional literal string to be displayed before the user enters data.

The semicolon after **INPUT** disables the line advance after data has been entered. You could also use it to suspend screen scrolling if, for example, you're using all 24 lines of the screen to enter data. The other semicolon, after the comment, adds a question mark to the comment string, but if you don't want to display a question mark, use a comma instead. Note that one of these two modifiers *must* be specified.

The **variablelist** consists of one or more variables, separated by commas, in which the data entered is stored. The variables can be any of the types covered in the first chapter. The type of data entered must correspond to the specified variable types, or QBasic will display the message Redo from start and wait for you to enter a valid input.

Here's the simplest demonstration of how you can use the **INPUT** statement:

```
INPUT x
```

This suspends calculations and outputs a question mark onto the screen. The variable **x** is assigned the value of the number that you enter. We know that the variable **x** is a number, because this is the type automatically assigned to it by default.

> When you use the **INPUT** statement and you're happy that the entry that you want to make has been entered correctly, for you are allowed to edit it, you must confirm entry by pressing the *Return* key.

But how would the user know that you need to enter a number? And how would they know what it was for? These questions are answered by the fact that the designers of QBasic included the opportunity to prompt the user with a comment:

```
INPUT "INPUT x = ";x
```

This is a lot better, because we're telling the user what type of data to input. We can see the benefit of this a little clearer if we form a sort of dialog with the program, like this:

```
INPUT "What is your name :";name$
```

Here we're prompting the user to enter a string, which we store in the variable **name$**. Another, last feature of the **INPUT** statement is that we can also ask the user to enter multiple entries all in the one line of code, like this:

```
INPUT x,y,z
```

Here you must type in three numbers separated by commas, values that will be assigned to **x**, **y**, and **z**.

Inputting Long Strings

Let's now take a look at a variant of the **INPUT** statement, **LINE INPUT**, which is used to let the user input long strings a bit more easily. It takes this form:

```
LINE INPUT [;] ["comment";] s$
```

The variable **s$** stores the character string entered from the keyboard.

In the **INPUT** statement, multiple variables are separated by commas. This means that commas can't be entered as part of the input string unless you enclose them in quotation marks. The **LINE INPUT** statement, on the other hand, reads all input characters (up to a maximum of 255) including commas and other awkward punctuation marks, until you press *Return*. Apart from this difference, these two statements work in identical ways.

In some cases it's more convenient to get data in your program from other sources, rather than directly from the keyboard, and we'll discuss such devices as the mouse, disk system and joystick later in the book.

Entering a Specified Number of Characters

Okay, so **INPUT** is a little open and clumsy, which is why the good designers of QBasic gave us a few more commands for inputting purposes. For example, when you want to enter a specified number of characters, **n**, you can use this statement:

INPUT$(n [, [#] filenumber%])

where **filenumber%** is the number of an open file (the subject of file manipulation is the topic we deal with in Chapter 6), but if **filenumber%** is omitted then the input will come from the keyboard instead. This is a very flexible statement, and clearly there are many uses for it. One line of code that you're likely to use is:

```
f$ = INPUT$(1)
```

This line will suspend calculations and wait for you to press a key. When you press a single key, that character is assigned to the variable **f$** and the program will continue on its way. You'll find that throughout this book we'll frequently use this method to pause the program.

Organizing a Dialog with Input and Print

The **INPUT** and **PRINT** statements are quite sufficient for organizing a simple exchange of questions and answers between you and your PC. A **simple dialog** of this nature runs as follows:

```
REM Program to illustrate dialog
REM \CHAP3\CH3_1.BAS

CLS
' GET user info
INPUT "What is your name"; name$
PRINT name$; ", what is your surname";
INPUT family$
INPUT "In what year were you born"; year%
LINE INPUT "Now tell me, where do you live? "; address$
INPUT "What is your home telephone number?"; tel$
' Output user info
PRINT
PRINT name$; " "; family$; " was born in"; year%
PRINT "and lives in "; address$
PRINT "His telephone number is "; tel$
a$ = INPUT$(1)

END
```

When you start this program it asks for your name. Then it asks you in a rather unceremonious manner to enter your surname, the year you were born, your address and finally your telephone number (I assure you that we won't sell your number to a direct mail company). The program finishes by displaying your details as a short summary. This is a typical dialog created with these statements:

```
What is your name? Chip
Chip, what is your surname? Andale
In what year were you born? 1970
Now tell me, where do you live? California, USA
What is your home telephone number? 465 7623

Chip Andale was born in 1970
and lives in California, USA
His telephone number is 465 7623
```

It is a *very* simple dialog, but as you progress through this book and master new QBasic features, you'll be able to write more sophisticated examples, involving color graphics, pull-down menus and a host of other professional features. Remember that the friendlier your program is, the better the response from the user.

Understanding Standard Screen Output

As we've already mentioned, **PRINT** is QBasic's main output statement. Formally, it has the following format:

```
PRINT [Using] [Expressionlist] [{; | ,}] [...]
```

where **Expressionlist** is a list of one or more numeric or string expressions, such as 2+2 or "Hello".

The following modifier characters define whether to send a carriage return after the string. To suppress a carriage return, you type a semicolon at the end of your statement: what you're saying is, in effect, that the next **PRINT** statement will appear immediately after this one, unless you've moved screen location in the meantime. If you include the comma as a modifier, the next **PRINT** statement will appear at the start of the next print zone (screen columns 14 characters wide).

We use the **USING** modifier to format output to the screen or onto a file. We'll talk about the **USING** modifier in a couple of pages time, but for now here's a quick overview of the **PRINT** statement:

```
PRINT  "Hello"                   Hello
PRINT  "my"                      my
PRINT  "friend!"                 friend!
PRINT  "Hello ";"my ";           Hello my
PRINT  "friend!"                 friend!
PRINT  "n =";123                 n = 123
PRINT  "n =";-123                n =-123
PRINT  1,2,3                     1         2          3
                                 --------------
                                 14 positions

PRINT  2 * (5 - 3)               4
PRINT  "x ="; 2 * (5 - 3)        x = 4
```

When you **PRINT** positive numbers, they're automatically preceded by a blank space and negative numbers are automatically preceded by a minus sign.

*This use of semicolons, commas, blank spaces and minus signs also applies identically to **LPRINT**, which sends output to the printer instead of the screen. We shall return to **LPRINT** and hard copy manipulation towards the end of this chapter.*

Formatting Output with the Using Modifier

By placing the **USING** modifier after the **PRINT** statement you can format your data output. The following modifiers can be used:

▲ The hash, comma and caret (^) symbols specify the actual format of your output. For example, **#.###** means that the output numbers have one digit before the decimal point and three digits after it. When dealing with numbers larger than the specified format allows, the % sign will appear in the output to indicate an error.

▲ Four ^ symbols in succession force the output into exponential form.

▲ The symbols **+** and **-** are used to output a number's sign.

▲ To output the dollar sign use **$$**.

▲ Empty output positions can be filled with the asterisk sign.

▲ The signs **\ !** and **&** in combination define text fields.

▲ Two back slashes **\ ** which enclose **n** spaces prints the first **n+2** characters from the text list.

▲ The **!** sign outputs only the first character of the string, and the **&** sign outputs the entire text.

▲ The **_** sign must be placed before you output control characters.

See how these modifiers work in the following piece of code. Here we're outputting numbers *and* characters. For the most part our examples are shown for the number **Pi = 3.141593**, and the formatting output of character data is shown for the string **"String"**:

```
REM Demonstration of the PRINT USING statement
REM \CHAP3\CH3_2.BAS

CLS
PRINT "Demonstration of the PRINT USING statement"
Pi = 3.141593
PRINT "Number Pi ="; Pi
PRINT "#.# -> "; : PRINT USING "#.#"; Pi
PRINT "#.### -> "; : PRINT USING "#.###"; Pi
PRINT "###.## -> "; : PRINT USING "###.##"; Pi
PRINT "+#.### -> "; : PRINT USING "+#.###"; Pi
PRINT "+#>### -> "; : PRINT USING "+#.###"; Pi; : PRINT " for Pi"
PRINT "-#.### -> "; : PRINT USING "-#.###"; Pi; : PRINT " for -Pi"
PRINT ".###^^^^ -> "; : PRINT USING ".###^^^^"; Pi
PRINT "#.###^^^^ -> "; : PRINT USING "#.###^^^^"; Pi
PRINT "###.###^^^^ -> "; : PRINT USING "###.###^^^^"; Pi
PRINT "$$#.## -> "; : PRINT USING "$$#.##"; Pi
PRINT "#- -> "; : PRINT USING "#-"; -Pi
PRINT "****#.### -> "; : PRINT USING "****#.###"; Pi
PRINT "#.### -> "; : PRINT USING "#.###"; Pi * 1000: PRINT "for 1000*Pi"
```

```
PRINT "Pi=#.### -> "; : PRINT USING "Pi=#.###"; Pi
PRINT "#.##_% -> "; : PRINT USING "#.##_%"; Pi
PRINT
s$ = "String"
PRINT s$
PRINT "! -> "; : PRINT USING "!"; s$
PRINT "& -> "; : PRINT USING "&"; s$
PRINT "\ \ -> "; : PRINT USING "\ \"; s$

END
```

If you run this program, you should see the following on your screen:

```
Demonstration of the PRINT USING statement
Number PI= 3.141593
#.#  -> 3.1
#.### -> 3.142
###.## ->    3.14
+#.### -> +3.142
+#.### -> +3.142 for PI
-#.### -> -3.142 for -PI
.###^^^^ -> .314E+01
#.###^^^^ -> 0.314E+01
###.###^^^^ ->   31.416E-01
$$#.## ->   $3.14
#- -> 3-
****#.### -> *3
#.### -> %3141.593
for 1000*PI
PI=#.### -> PI=3.142
#.##_% -> 3.14%

String
! -> S
& -> String
\ \ -> Str

Press any key to continue
```

The TAB Modifier

The **PRINT** statement can include the modifier function **TAB(n%)** which moves the cursor to a specified print location. The argument **n%** represents the column number of the new print position. Here's how the **TAB** function works:

```
REM Demonstration of the TAB modifier
REM \CHAP3\CH3_3.BAS

CLS
FOR y = 1 to 5
    PRINT TAB(2 * y); "HELLO"
NEXT y

END
```

Running the program gives us a result similar to the previous one:

```
Hello
 Hello
  Hello
   Hello
    Hello
```

The **TAB** modifier is only capable of shifting output in a horizontal direction. If the output data can't go in a single output line, part of it is transferred onto the next line.

Defining a Cursor's Position

You can pin down a cursor's location with the following functions, and you won't need any arguments:

CSRLIN   returns the current row position of the cursor.
POS   returns the current column position of the cursor.

This enables you to store the cursor's position so that you can return to this point after a number of applications of the **PRINT** statement. You'll find a use for this when you come to create menus or construct sophisticated tables.

The WRITE Statement

Instead of using the **PRINT** statement, you can use the **WRITE** statement:

WRITE d1, d2, d3, ...

WRITE inserts commas between items and quotation marks around strings. It also removes the space before positive numbers and after all numbers. See how the **WRITE** statement operates compared to the **PRINT** statement:

```
REM Demonstration of the WRITE statement
REM \CHAP3\CH3_4.BAS

CLS
a = 123
b = 4.56
c$ = "END"

WRITE a, b, c$
PRINT a; b; c$
PRINT a, b, c$

END
```

By running this program, you'll end up with this output:

```
123,4.56,"End"
123  4.56 End
123        4.56        End
```

Thus, you can see that the **WRITE** statement allows you to output information a lot more compactly than **PRINT**. However, the **WRITE** statement isn't used that often to output to the screen, but it's very useful when writing data to a file or peripherals, which we'll get to in Chapter 6.

Positioning the Cursor

The **PRINT** statement simply outputs the given information at the current cursor position. So how do you change this position? Well, you can use the **LOCATE** statement, for starters:

```
LOCATE row%, column%
```

If you just want to place the cursor at the start of a row, then there's no need to include the column parameter. However, if you want to move the cursor to a particular position along a row, then you'll need to use both **row%** and **column%**, like we demonstrate here:

```
REM Demonstration of the LOCATE statement
REM \CHAP3\CH3_5.BAS

CLS
FOR y = 1 to 5
    LOCATE y + 6, 2 * y
    PRINT "Hello"
NEXT y

END
```

Run this program and you'll be greeted with something along these lines:

```
Hello
 Hello
  Hello
   Hello
    Hello
```

Notice that we have used a **FOR...LOOP** here, forming a very popular statement combination, especially for repeated printing of certain areas of the screen.

The Form and Visibility of the Cursor

Not only can you move the cursor to a specified position with the **LOCATE** statement, but you can also control its visibility and appearance too. The cursor usually appears as a flashing underscore, but it's just a character which can move around the screen. If you want to control its visibility and appearance, you have to access the **LOCATE** statement in its full incarnation:

```
LOCATE    [row%][,[column%][,[cursor%][,start%[,stop%]]]]
```

where

row% and **column%**   specify the number of the row and column to which the cursor will move.

cursor%   specifies whether the cursor is visible. **0** for invisible, **1** for visible.

start% and stop%   are integer expressions between the range of **0** to **31** that specify the first and last cursor scan lines - you can change the cursor size by changing the cursor scan lines.

Take, for example, this statement:

```
LOCATE 10, 30, 0
```

It moves the cursor to the 30th position of the 10th line and renders the cursor invisible.

The following example, however, demonstrates the use of the last two parameters, which change the cursor form, making it thicker. They define the number of the first and final line of the cursor's character cell. So with this statement:

```
LOCATE 10, 30, 1, 1, 4
```

you transform the cursor into a visible rectangle formed by the upper four scan lines.

The Concept of Text and Graphics Pages

Information isn't actually output directly to the screen - it's first stored in the video adapter's memory, Video RAM (**VRAM**). In text mode a screen page occupies 2 Kb of VRAM, and since modern video adapters usually have between 512Kb and 2Mb of VRAM, video memory can hold a lot of text pages.

The image which is visible on the screen is called the **visible page**. However, data can be transferred into any page in VRAM; the page that's being written to is called the **active page**. If this page isn't visible at that moment, the output won't be visible on the screen. Any page can be chosen as the visible page. The concept of screen pages isn't unique to the text mode - it also applies to graphics mode. However, graphics mode pages require more memory, so the number of pages that can be stored in VRAM is considerably smaller than in text mode.

Let's take a closer look at how we can control the screen in both text and graphics modes. You'll notice that many statements of the QBasic language are used for manipulating both modes.

The Text Mode

Before you can output any information onto the display screen, you must first prepare the screen ready for use. The screen text mode (set by default) displays white characters on a black background. By using the **SCREEN** statement, however, you can control the display mode:

SCREEN   [mode][,[[c%][,ap][,vp]]

Here, **mode** represents the screen mode code (**0** for the text mode). **c%** can be either **0** or **1** to switch between a color and a monochrome display (for modes **0** and **1** only), **ap** is the active page and **vp** is the visible page.

If you don't specify a **SCREEN** statement in your program, text mode is set by default and the active and visual pages are one and the same, both assuming the number **1**. The maximum number of possible pages depends on the size of your video adapter's video memory. The **SCREEN 0** statement defines the standard text mode output: 25 lines deep, with 80 characters across. The last (25th) line is reserved for the system.

Here's an example of the **SCREEN** statement in action:

```
REM Demonstration of the SCREEN statement
REM \CHAP3\CH3_6.BAS

SCREEN 0, 1, 1, 0
CLS
PRINT "Hello!"
f$ = INPUT$(1)
SCREEN 0, 1, 0, 1
f$ = INPUT$(1)

END
```

It's worth taking a closer look at this program, short though it may be. If you run it you'll see that the **SCREEN** statement first specifies the active page number as **1** and the visual page as **0**, so the instruction **PRINT "Hello!"** puts the message Hello! on a currently invisible page, page **1**. If you press any key, the second **SCREEN** statement changes the pages and the message now appears in the upper left-hand corner of the screen.

Note that the appearance of characters on the screen depends on which screen mode you use, your video adapter and your PC's display, because each character on the screen is made up of pixels. The matrix of these pixels forms a character cell which is the same size for each of the video adapter standards. For example, the **CGA** mode has a matrix of 8x8 pixels for a character cell, so these pixels are quite large, chunky and clearly visible on the screen. **EGA**, and **VGA** video adapters have more pixels in the same sized character cell (14x8 for EGA and 16x9 for VGA), so characters appear clearer and smoother.

Clearing the Screen and Setting the Text Viewport

As you probably already know, the **CLS** statement clears the screen, and this is also true in text mode, which is normally invoked with the following command:

CLS [n%]

where **n%** is the type of clear that we wish to implement. Without a parameter, **CLS** is used to clear the entire screen. But there's a technique that we can use to clear only a certain area of the screen using the **CLS** command, which changes the area of the screen that can be affected by text. This area of the screen is commonly called a **viewport** and can be set with this statement:

VIEW PRINT [u% to d%]

where **u%** and **d%** define the number of the top and the bottom row of the text viewport. Typically, these values have minimum values of 1 and maximum values of 24. If you leave these arguments out, **VIEW PRINT** sets the entire screen as the text viewport by default.

Look at the following program which demonstrates a five-line text window and the peculiarities of the **CLS** statement at the availability of the window:

```
REM Statements CLS and VIEW PRINT demonstration
REM \CHAP3\CH3_7.BAS

CLS

'GET the CLS mode
INPUT "Which type of CLS 0 1 or 2"; Type.of.Clear
```

```
PRINT "Press any key to clear text"
VIEW PRINT 10 to 15
FOR i% = 101 to 180
    PRINT i%;
NEXT i%
f$ = INPUT$(1)

'Now clear as chosen
CLS Type.of.Clear

END
```

On execution, the first command, **CLS**, without an argument, completely clears the screen. Then, in the uppermost lines we're prompted with the mode that we wish to clear the screen with. After this, the **VIEW PRINT 10 to 15** statement sends all further output to go to a text window occupying the lines 10 through to 15. We fill this viewport with text so that we can see the effect of the **CLS** on the window. The string **f$ = INPUT$(1)** suspends the work of the program, allowing you to see two different types of text output - normal text and text in a window.

When you press any key, **CLS 2**, the last line of the program, is executed. Only the text window is cleared in the process, whilst the comments outside the window remain intact.

By re-running this program and replacing **CLS 2** by **CLS 0**, you can see that all the text on the screen is erased. If you try **CLS 1** you'll see that this form of the **CLS** command doesn't work in text mode - all the text beyond the scope of the window is left untouched. We'll discuss the peculiarities of the **CLS** statement when we meet the graphics mode in a few pages time.

Setting Text Color Attributes

When you output text information, you can specify the foreground, background and border colors. These are called text **color attributes**. To set these text attributes you'll need to use the **COLOR** statement:

COLOR [foreground%] [,[background%] [,border%]]

If you just use a single **COLOR** statement at the beginning of a program, it will set the colors for the entire program. However, you can use it repeatedly throughout the program and this means that you can output different letters, words or lines in different colors.

> *Of course, color is only available to you if your PC has a color display and a suitable video adapter, such as CGA, EGA or VGA! A lot of the programs in this book make use of color, but if you're stuck in two colors then check out Chapter 12 - Game Development - for tips on how to program for both color and monochrome in the same program.*

The following small program gives you an idea of which colors are available in text mode:

```
REM Demonstration of the COLOR statement for text mode
REM \CHAP3\CH3_8.BAS

SCREEN 0: CLS
FOR i% = 0 to 15
    COLOR i%
    PRINT i%;
NEXT i%

END
```

If you run that program, you'll see that the program displays a line containing the numbers **0** through to **15** which are the codes of the available colors. Each number should appear in its corresponding color. The zero is actually invisible since the code **0** corresponds to black which is the background color. If you change the background color, you'll see 0 where it should be.

Retrieving a Character from the Screen

Okay, so we can print text and characters onto the screen, but what if we want to retrieve what we originally put on the screen? Of course we can use the alternative version of the **SCREEN** statement which can determine which character is at a specified screen position and what its color attributes are. And this is how it works:

```
SCREEN (row%,column% [,f%])
```

If the color flag **f%** is specified as zero, **SCREEN** returns the ASCII code of the character at the screen location defined by **row%** and **column%**. If **f%** is **1**, then it returns the color of the character at that position instead.

That just about sums up the majority of the functionality that the text mode holds for us, so let's take a look at the graphics mode.

The Graphics Mode

One of the attractive features of a PC is that you can represent information graphically - in the form of simple geometric objects or the colorful animations common to modern computer games. QBasic has a small set of graphic tools which allow you to control the screen, draw simple geometric figures, paint closed figures, create windows, copy fragments of images and move them to a specific position on the screen. In this section we shall peek into the world of QBasic graphics, starting with a quick overview of the fundamental graphics concepts involved.

There are three important concepts associated with displaying graphics:

1   The general color of the working area of the screen is the **background** color.

2   The color used for drawing images is the **foreground** color.

3   The operation field, which is rectangular in shape, is surrounded by a non-working area, the **border**, which has its own color that's typically black.

It's no secret that complex images can be represented by a combination of points, particularly when plotting math functions. As you know, the geometric point is dimensionless (there's no point in increasing its size); however, to make it more visible, it's standard practice to depict it as a small filled-in circle, which is what we'll do.

It's usual for a point to be related to a system of coordinates, for example Cartesian (rectangular), polar or spherical. For the moment though, we'll consider the Cartesian system of coordinates, typically represented by two axes intersecting at right angles. Without wanting to delve deeper into the murky depths of mathematical theory, the vertical axis is the **y-axis**, and the horizontal axis is the **x-axis**. The point effectively has the coordinates (x,y):

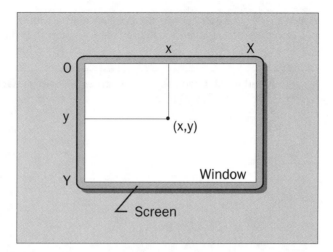

The graphic window contains **n** lines with each featuring **m** pixels, and the product **mxn** is referred to as the **resolution**. These pixels make up a two-dimensional array which is the matrix of the screen. The pixels are counted from zero, in other words, **0** through (**m-1**) on the horizontal axis, and **0** through (**n-1**) on the vertical axis.

The screen resolution and the number of colors available depend upon your current video adapter, monitor, and settings. Images are stored in VRAM in the video adapter, so the larger the VRAM, the greater the number of colors available, the higher the resolution and the greater the number of pages you can store. The older CGA adapters and displays provide a monochrome mode with a resolution of 640x200 pixels, and a 4-color mode with a resolution of 320x200 pixels. The more up-to-date VGA video adapters have 16 colors and a resolution of 640x480 pixels.

IBM-compatible PCs represent text and graphic information differently. There are a number of functions and statements which control graphics modes. All the examples we'll be using will need a graphics adapter and a CGA-, EGA- or VGA-compatible display.

Controlling Screen Modes

As we saw earlier, the **SCREEN** statement switches operation modes:

SCREEN [n%][,c%][,ap%][,vp%]]]

where **n%**, as we noted earlier, denotes the screen mode, **c%** switches between color and monochrome display, **ap%** is the active screen page and **vp%** is the number of the visible page. If graphics parameters are omitted, **SCREEN** sets both background and border colors to black (code **0**) and the foreground to white - the opposite of, for example, a newspaper.

If **n%** = 0, **SCREEN** sets the text mode. You can activate the graphics modes with **n%** values between **1** through **13**. A certain number of modes are reserved for future video adapters, but the rest are shown here in this table:

n%	Resolution	Number of attribute	Number of colors	Graphic Type
1	320x200	4	16	CGA
2	640x200	2	16	CGA
3	720x348	1	2	Hercules
7	320x200	16	16	EGA, VGA
8	640x200	16	16	EGA, VGA
9	640x350	16	64	EGA, VGA
10	640x350	4	9	EGA, VGA
11	640x480	2	256	VGA
12	640x480	2	256	VGA
13	320x200	256	256	VGA, MCGA

Clearing the Screen in Graphics Mode

As we mentioned earlier for the text mode, use the **CLS** statement in the following formats to clear the screen:

CLS   clears either the text or graphics viewport. If a graphics viewport has been set, **CLS** clears only the graphics viewport. Otherwise, it clears the text viewport or the entire screen.

CLS 0   clears the entire screen of both text and graphics.

CLS 1   clears the graphics viewport or the entire screen if no graphics have been set.

CLS 2   clears the text viewport.

You can see from these definitions that the **CLS** statement in a graphics mode doesn't behave in the same way as it does in a text mode. Its action depends on whether a window has been opened by the **VIEW** statement, and whether it's a text or a graphics window.

Setting and Changing Colors

The **COLOR** statement sets the screen display colors. Its three formats are:

```
COLOR [background%] [,palette%]       Screen mode 1
COLOR [foreground%]                   Screen modes 4, 12, 13
COLOR [foreground%] [,background&]    Screen modes 7-10
```

where

foreground%   is a number that sets the foreground screen color. In screen mode **0**, **foreground%** is a color attribute that sets the text color. In other screen modes, **foreground%** denotes the color attribute or 4-bit color value (screen mode **4** only) that sets the text and line-drawing color.

`background%`	is a number that sets the background screen color. In screen mode **0**, is a color		

`background&`   attribute. In screen mode **1**, **background%** is a 4-bit color value. In screen modes **7**
                  through **10**, **background&** is a color value.

`border%`   is a color attribute that sets the screen border color.

`palette%`   is a number (**0** or **1**) that specifies which of two sets of color attributes to use:

`palette%`	Attribute 1	Attribute 2	Attribute 3
0	Green	Red	Brown
1	Cyan	Magenta	Bright white

The color attributes and values available depend on your graphics adapter and the screen mode set by the last **SCREEN** statement.

As there are a great variety of different video adapters available, we won't waste page space or your valuable time discussing their color and attribute tables here - you can find this information in your graphic adapter's manual. However, the following code runs through the numbers **0 - 15** in the color which corresponds to your adapter:

```
REM USING operator COLOR for EGA mode
REM \CHAP3\CH3_9.BAS

SCREEN 9
FOR i% = 0 to 15
    COLOR i%
    PRINT i%;
NEXT i%

END
```

You'll see 15 numbers displayed in the colors corresponding to the codes **1** - **15** when you run the program. Don't worry, we haven't forgotten about **0** - this is displayed as well, but once again it's invisible since its code renders it the same color as the background.

Switching between Pages

If you have enough VRAM to store more than one page, then you can copy the pages to and from one another using the **PCOPY** statement:

PCOPY sourcepage%, destinationpage%

Here, **sourcepage%** denotes the number of the video page to be copied; **destinationpage%** denotes the number of the video page that you want to copy to. For example, **PCOPY 1,3** copies the contents of page 1 to page 3.

As you've already seen, only one page can be visible on the display screen at any one time. You can use other pages to construct images behind the scenes and then by making one of these pages visible, you can quickly output a complete picture straight to the screen. We'll come back to this exciting technique when we cover dynamic graphics and game development later on.

Drawing Geometric Figures

There would be little point in having a graphics mode if we couldn't access it very easily, and therefore we've kindly been given an extensive suite of drawing tools by the designers of QBasic. Using these commands we can set pixels, draw shapes and manipulate the graphics screen in a variety of very interesting and highly useful ways.

Drawing and Erasing a Point

You use the next set of statements - **PRESET** and **PSET** - to construct what are probably the simplest of geometric objects. These instructions draw single points (or set single pixels if you like) on the screen:

```
PRESET [STEP] (x!,y!) [,color%]
PSET [STEP] (x!,y!) [,color%]
```

where the **STEP** modifier indicates that the coordinates **x!** and **y!** are defined relative to the current graphic cursor position. If the **STEP** modifier is missing then the coordinates are relative to the point (0,0). If **color%** is omitted, **PRESET** will use the current background color, while **PSET** will use the current foreground color. In other words, **PSET** sets a point and **PRESET** resets it. Here's a quick example:

```
REM Demonstrates PSET and PRESET
REM \CHAP3\CH3_10.BAS

CLS : SCREEN 9
   PSET (0,0), 14              'Draws a yellow point in the upper
                       'left corner of the screen
f$=INPUT$(1)
   PRESET (0,0)                'Erases the previously constructed point

END
```

Setting and resetting points isn't a lot of fun though when you want to draw something larger than a rather small ant, unless you're very, very patient. So let's press on and have a look at some statements which enable you to construct images much easier.

Setting Color Palette

As memory is limited, so are the number of colors (this is especially true for some of the older video adapters). However, you can choose your limited color attributes from a wider color palette, with the following instructions:

```
PALETTE  [attribute%,color&]
PALETTE  USING arrayname#[(index%)]
```

where

attribute%	is the color attribute to change.
color&	is a color value to assign to an attribute.
Arrayname#	is an array of color values to assign to the current screen mode's set of attributes. The array must be large enough to assign colors to all the attributes.
index%	is the index of the first array element to assign to an attribute.

If we take the screen mode of 12, which has a resolution of 640x480, we can effectively assign any one of 64x64x64, or 262144, colors to any of its 16 color attributes. We shall demonstrate the **PALETTE** and **PALETTE USING** commands in a few pages time.

Drawing Lines and Boxes

The best and most popular command for constructing images is the **LINE** statement, which enables you to draw colorful lines and boxes. Its format is:

```
LINE  [[STEP](x1!,y1!)]-[STEP](x2!,y2!)  [,[color%][,[b|bf]  [,style%]]]
```

where the **STEP** modifier indicates that the coordinates are defined relative to the current cursor position, **(x1!,y1!)** and **(x2!,y2!)** indicate the screen coordinates of the start and the end of the line, respectively. The parameter **b** indicates that a rectangle (or box), as opposed to a line, will be drawn from corner to corner, whereas **bf** indicates a filled, solid box. The **style%** parameter is a 16-bit value which determines which pixels are drawn in a given line. It's used to draw dashed or dotted lines, for example:

_ _ _ _ _ _ _ _	Fragment of line
0101010101010101	16-bit number
5555	Hex number
__ _____	Fragment of line
1100111111111111	16-bit number
CFFF	Hex number

If the line is longer than the line section represented by the 16 style bits, then the subsequent line sections are simply copies or extensions of it. The **style%** parameter is the decimal or hexadecimal representation of the 16-bit binary number. Here's the **LINE** command in action:

```
CLS: SCREEN 9
LINE (319,0) - (319,349), 1
LINE (319,0) - (319,349), 12, &HCCCC
```

The first line clears the screen, sets the graphics mode and then draws a continuous line, breaking the screen into two parts. The second statement plots a dotted line over the top of it (so that the intervals will be blue). The hexadecimal value of the parameter style - **&HCCCC** - is chosen so that the length of the dash is two pixels, with four pixels between each one. The **style%** parameter is ignored if the **LINE** statement is used for drawing filled rectangles.

If the coordinates of a line or rectangle are beyond the scope of the screen, the protruding parts of the figure aren't displayed. Here's a closer look at the relative aspects of the **PSET** and **LINE** statements:

```
REM Demonstrates the LINE command
REM \CHAP3\CH3_11.BAS

SCREEN 1: CLS
PSET (50, 50)
LINE -(50, 150)
LINE -(150, 150)
LINE -(150, 50)
LINE -(50, 50)
LINE (60, 60)-(140, 140), 1, BF
```

As you'll see when you run the program, it starts by drawing a point with the screen coordinates (**50,50**) using **PSET**. Then, four **LINE** statements construct a rectangle from this point. The last **LINE** statement, which includes **bf** as its last parameter, draws a colored-in rectangle inside that box.

Using Different Palettes

Let's now take a look at how the **PALETTE** and **LINE** statements work together:

```
REM Demonstration of the PALETTE and LINE statements
REM \CHAP3\CH3_12.BAS

PALETTE 0, 1
SCREEN 1
FOR i% = 0 TO 3: a%(i%) = i%: NEXT i%
LINE (138, 35)-(288, 165), 3, bf
LINE (20, 10)-(160, 100), 2, bf
DO
    FOR i% = 0 TO 3
        a%(i%) = (a%(i%) + 1) MOD 16
    NEXT i%
    LOCATE 1, 16
    PRINT "PALETTE "; a%(0)
    s$ = INPUT$(1)
    PALETTE USING a%(0)
LOOP UNTIL a%(0) = 15
F$ = INPUT$(1)

END
```

Here, we draw two boxes in two different colors and proceed to run through the 15 different palettes to show just how simple it is to use the **PALETTE** statements and switch quickly between completely different sets of palettes.

One of the most popular uses of these statements is to provide fading effects - where you can scroll incrementally through the thousands of colors to create stunning effects. We shall demonstrate some of these effects later on in the graphics and games chapters.

Drawing Arcs, Circles and Ellipses

The **CIRCLE** statement enables you to draw arcs, circles and ellipses. Its format is:

```
CIRCLE [Step] (x!,y!),radius![,[color%] [,[start!] [,[end!]
[,aspect!]]]]
```

where

STEP	indicates that the coordinates of the figure are relative to the current graphics cursor position.
(x!,y!)	holds the coordinates of the center of the figure.
radius!	denotes the radius of the circle or ellipse in the units of the current coordinate system, determined by the last **SCREEN**, **VIEW** and **WINDOW** statements.
color%	denotes the color attribute of the circle or ellipse.

start!   indicates the starting angle of the arc in radians.

end!   indicates the final angle of the arc in radians.

aspect!   is the ratio of the length of the **y**-axis to the length of the **x**-axis, which is used to draw ellipses.

Although you may think that the **CIRCLE** statement is very simple, it actually allows you to draw some very complex and effective figures. Take this versatile and very concise example:

```
REM Operator CIRCLE - example 1
REM \CHAP3\CH3_13.BAS

SCREEN 2: CLS
FOR radius = 1 to 200 STEP 3
    CIRCLE (320, 100), radius
NEXT radius
m$ = INPUT$(1)

END
```

This draws a multitude of close concentric circles with gradually changing radii. The startling kaleidoscopic effect is caused by the superimposition of the pixels that actually make up the circles on the screen:

We'll come back to the features of the **CIRCLE** statement later. For now though, we'll take a look at painting closed objects, a technique which enables you to create more realistic and volumetric pictures.

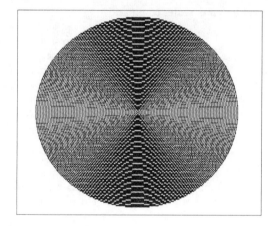

The Draw Statement

There are certain limits to what you can actually do with **PSET**, **PRESET**, **LINE** and **CIRCLE** - primarily they aren't very well suited to drawing complex figures. You'd have to use these statements many times to come up with something half-decent, increasing the size of your program and in our case, making it less illustrative.

The **DRAW** statement is a much more flexible alternative, a statement that has its own micro-language of graphics commands, consisting of a string of very short expressions - you can fit an almost unlimited number of these into a single line. Some of these commands are inherited from **LOGO** and effectively move the drawing point in a specific direction. This generally makes geometric objects easier to draw.

The format of the **DRAW** statement is:

DRAW commandstring$

Here, **commandstring$** is a string expression that contains one or more **DRAW** commands, illustrated in the following tables:

Line-drawing and cursor-movement commands

d[n%]	Moves cursor down **n%** units.
e[n%]	Moves cursor up and right **n%** units.
f[n%]	Moves cursor down and right **n%** units.
g[n%]	Moves cursor down and left **n%** units.
h[n%]	Moves cursor up and left **n%** units.
l[n%]	Moves cursor left **n%** units.
m[{+|-}]x%,y%	Moves cursor to point **x%,y%**.
	If **x%** is preceded by **+** or **-**, moves relative to the current point.
r[n%]	Moves cursor right **n%** units.
u[n%]	Moves cursor up **n%** units.
[b]	Optional prefix that moves cursor without drawing.
[n]	Optional prefix that draws and returns cursor to its original position.

Color, rotation and scale commands

an%	Rotates an object **n%**x90 degrees (**n%** can be **0, 1,2** or **3**).
cn%	Sets the drawing color (**n%** is a color attribute).
pn1%,n2%	Sets the paint fill and border colors of an object (**n1%** is the fill-color attribute, **n2%** is the border-color attribute).
sn%	Determines the drawing scale by setting the length of a unit of cursor movement. The default **n%** is 4,which is equivalent to 1 pixel.
Tan%	Turns an angle **n%** degrees (-360 through 360).

If you omit **n%** from the line-drawing and cursor-movement commands, the cursor will move 1 unit. For quick reference, the directions are as follows:

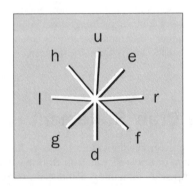

Let's consider for a minute specifying parameters of the **DRAW** statement using numeric variables. In the earlier versions of BASIC, this was straightforward since they were interpreting versions. However, with QBasic, you can't explicitly use numeric variables as parameters, instead you have to convert numeric variables into strings.

Look at how we draw a cube of a size defined by the **INPUT** statement:

```
REM Demonstration of the DRAW statement
REM \CHAP3\CH3_14.BAS

SCREEN 1, 0
```

```
PRINT "Draw various size cubes"
INPUT "Scale (1-255) "; scale
DRAW "S" + STR$(scale)
DRAW "bm +0,2 l3 u3 r3 d3 e1 u3 g1 e1 l3 g1"

END
```

And here's our cube:

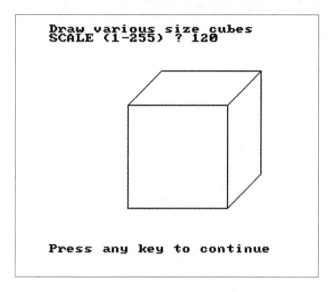

To execute a substring though, you must remember to include an **X** before appending it, like this example, which draws a 3D triangle in space:

```
REM Demonstration of the use of substrings with DRAW
REM \CHAP3\CH3_15.BAS

SCREEN 1
Triangle$ = "f90 l180 e100 f90 g10 h90"
DRAW "C2 X" + VARPTR$(Triangle$)
DRAW "bd30 p1,2"
f$ = INPUT$(1)

END
```

It's plain to see that the **DRAW** statement is a fantastically concise method of implementing fairly complex figures and 3D effects, and we'll be returning to it again and to show you some more advanced techniques.

Windows Control

Graphics drawings are performed in a graphics window which, by default, occupies the entire area of the operating screen. The graphics window, however, can be programmed to take up only a specific part of the screen - the **VIEW** statement allows you to do this:

```
VIEW [[SCREEN] (x1!,y1!)-(x2!,y2!)[,[color%] [,border%]]
```

SCREEN specifies that the coordinates are relative to the screen rather than the viewport defined by **(x1!,y1!)-(x2!,y2!)**, **color%** denotes the color attribute that sets the viewport fill color and **border%** denotes the color attribute that sets the viewport border color.

If there are no arguments, the viewport defaults back to the entire screen. Let's look at some code that draws a number of concentric circles in the upper-left quadrant of the screen, and then let's transfer these circles to the center of the screen using **VIEW**:

```
REM Application of the VIEW statement
REM \CHAP3\CH3_16.BAS

SCREEN 1: CLS : KEY OFF
GOSUB Figure
LOCATE 1, 1: PRINT "Drawing circles"
VIEW (140, 50)-(240, 150)
GOSUB Figure
LOCATE 7, 15: PRINT "Drawing after VIEW"
f$ = INPUT$(1)

END

Figure:
FOR r = 5 to 45 STEP 5
    CIRCLE (55, 50), r
NEXT r
RETURN
```

The **LOCATE** and **PRINT** statements work in graphics mode as well so you are still able to print text such as labels for your graphs. Here's the result on the screen:

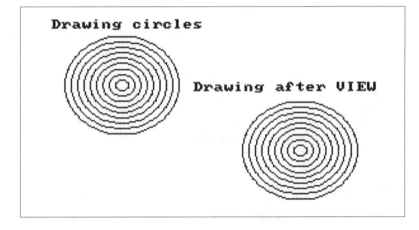

With **VIEW** you can also truncate the images that you create with **DRAW**, i.e. you can view a large object, say our cube, through a small window:

```
REM Clip a picture of a cube
REM \CHAP3\CH3_17.BAS

SCREEN 1, 0
VIEW SCREEN (120, 30)-(210, 110), , 3
DRAW "160 u60 r60 d60 e20 u60 g20 e20 160 g20"
f$ = INPUT$(1)

END
```

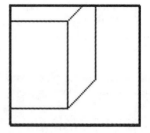

Here we're using the **VIEW** statement with the **SCREEN** modifier, and this is the section of the cube we see on the screen:

Changing the Origin of the Coordinate System

Up to now we've assumed that the points of the figures will be given in terms of screen coordinates, in other words, pixels. However, this isn't always convenient, especially if we want to plot math figures and functions. Fortunately, you can define the points of a figure as math coordinates using this statement:

WINDOW [[Screen] (x1!,y1!)-(x2!,y2!)]

Here, **SCREEN** inverts the normal Cartesian direction of the **y** coordinates so that the **y** values increase from the top of the screen to the bottom. **(x1!,y1!)** denotes the logical coordinates that map to the upper-left screen coordinates of the viewport; **(x2!,y2!)** denotes the logical coordinates that map to the lower-right screen coordinates of the viewport. If there are no arguments, **WINDOW** disables the logical coordinate system and switches to screen coordinates. To demonstrate this we're going to draw a set of ellipses using math coordinates:

```
REM Demonstration of the WINDOW statement
REM \CHAP3\CH3_18.BAS

SCREEN 1: CLS : KEY OFF
WINDOW SCREEN (0, 2)-(2, 0)
FOR r = .05 to .65 STEP .05
    CIRCLE (1, 1), r, , , , r
NEXT r
LOCATE 3, 9
PRINT "Drawing in mathematical"
LOCATE 4, 12
PRINT "coordinate system"
f$ = INPUT$(1)

END
```

Here's the screen you'll see:

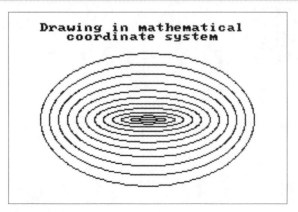

Note that the parameters of the **CIRCLE** statement are absurd in the context of raster graphics (**r** radius has a range of 0.05 through 0.65 with a 0.05 step) because you can't deal in fractions of a pixel. The conversion of math coordinates to raster is performed automatically. You'll find the **WINDOW** statement very convenient for drawing various figures in different sizes and positions. We can further illustrate this with:

```
REM Demonstration of the WINDOW statement #2
REM \CHAP3\CH3_19.BAS

Declare SUB DrawFigure ()
'DRAW 3 faces in different sizes and locations
SCREEN 1, 0
CALL DrawFigure
WINDOW SCREEN (0, 0)-(900, 600)
CALL DrawFigure
WINDOW SCREEN (-50, 50)-(190, 190)
CALL DrawFigure
f$ = INPUT$(1)

END

SUB DrawFigure
  CIRCLE (160, 80), 20
  PAINT (160, 80), 2, 3
  CIRCLE (150, 76), 2, 0
  CIRCLE (170, 76), 2, 0
  PSET (155, 90), 0
  LINE -(160, 92), 0
  LINE -(165, 90), 0
END SUB
```

Here we've created a subroutine which when called, draws a pumpkin-type head on the screen in a size and position dependent upon the current coordinate system. We draw the image three times in different positions and sizes to demonstrate this.

Combining VIEW and WINDOW

Used on their own, the **VIEW** and **WINDOW** statements are extremely versatile, but combined they have even more potential. Here's an example of how they can work together:

```
REM Demonstration of VIEW and WINDOW
REM \CHAP3\CH3_20.BAS

SCREEN 1: CLS : KEY OFF
LINE (9, 9)-(161, 161), , b 'Drawing a box
VIEW (10, 10)-(160, 160)
WINDOW (-15.7, -1)-(15.7, 1)
'Drawing function SIN(x)/x
PSET (-15.7, 0)
FOR x = -15.7 TO 15.7 Step .1
    LINE -(x, SIN(x)/x)
NEXT x
LOCATE 7, 23: PRINT "Plotting"
LOCATE 9, 23: PRINT "function"
LOCATE 11, 23: PRINT "SIN(x)/x "
f$ = INPUT$(1)

END
```

First of all we draw a box, to which **VIEW** then limits the viewport, and **WINDOW** converts the screen coordinates to mathematical coordinates, corresponding to the defined viewport. Finally, the graph of the function **SIN(x)/x** is plotted, which fits nicely into the selected viewport:

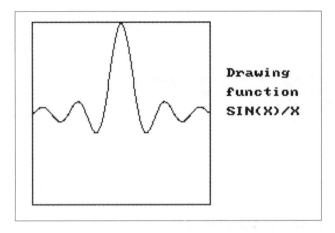

Note the way in which the function is plotted. First, the **PSET** statement specifies the initial point with the coordinates $(x0, y0)$, where **y0** is the value of the function when **x = x0**. Then, using **LINE - (x,y)**, a continuous curve is extended from one point to another.

This next example will give you a pictorial idea of how **VIEW** and **WINDOW** can work together. The program plots a linear diagram using the data in the **DATA** statement, and then, where these constructions are repeated, it opens a new window and a new system of coordinates. The new window with the new diagram is superimposed on the old one and partially covers it:

```
REM Demonstration of 2 linear diagrams in different windows
REM \CHAP3\CH3_21.BAS

Declare SUB LineChart ()
'DRAW a line chart and then the same line
'chart scaled by VIEW
SCREEN 2
WINDOW (-.5, -4)-(7.5, 16)
CALL LineChart    'LINE graph drawn first time
VIEW (130, 117)-(550, 180), , 1
CALL LineChart    'LINE graph drawn again in new viewport
DATA 0, 13, 9, 4, 6, 13
f$ = INPUT$(1)

SUB LineChart
  CLS
  RESTORE
  LINE (0, 0)-(7, 0)     'x-axis
  LINE (0, 14)-(0, 0)    'y-axis
  READ a
  PSET (1, a)
  FOR m = 2 TO 6
      READ a
      LINE -(m, a)
  NEXT m
END SUB
```

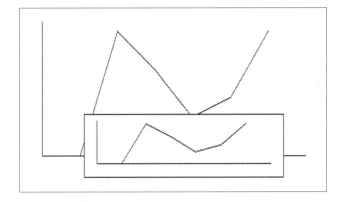

And here are our two linear diagrams drawn in different windows:

Converting Coordinates

The **PMAP** function converts screen coordinates to mathematical coordinates, or math coordinates to screen coordinates. It returns the window coordinate equivalent to a viewport coordinate, as defined by the **WINDOW** statement, and vice versa. Its format is:

```
PMAP (startcoordinate#, n%)
```

where **startcoordinate#** is a window or viewpoint coordinate, and **n%** is the value indicating which coordinate is returned, as shown in this table:

startcoordinate#	n%	Returns
Window x-coordinate	0	Viewport x-coordinate
Window y-coordinate	1	Viewport y-coordinate
Viewport x-coordinate	2	Window x-coordinate
Viewport y-coordinate	3	Window y-coordinate

By virtue of the fact that **WINDOW** automatically recalculates the screen coordinates to math ones, you'll seldom use the **PMAP** function by itself.

Controlling Color Attributes

There are a number of statements and functions that are used to paint closed figures. To start with you have to take control of the position of the graphics cursor and the pixel color attributes, and you can do this with the **POINT** function:

```
POINT {(n%) | (x%,y%)}
```

When used in the format **POINT (n%)**, the function returns one of the coordinates shown in the table opposite:

n%	Returns
0	The current viewport x-coordinate
1	The current viewport y-coordinate
2	The current window x-coordinate
3	The current window y-coordinate

In the other form, **POINT (x%,y%)**, it returns the color attribute of a specified pixel if the pixel is inside the current viewport, otherwise, it returns **-1**. You can see how **POINT** works here:

```
REM Using Point for CopyScreen
REM \CHAP3\CH3_22.BAS

DEFINT i-j
x = 71: y = 10: m = 2
SCREEN 1: KEY OFF: CLS
FOR r = 1 to 30 STEP 3
    CIRCLE (32, 35), r, 3, , , .65
NEXT r
LOCATE 3, 2: PRINT "Hello!"
FOR i = 0 to 70
    FOR j = 0 to 70
        sp = POINT(i, j)
        x1 = X + i * m: y1 = y + j * m
        LINE (x1, y1)-(x1 + (s - 1), y1 + (s - 1)), sp, bf
    NEXT j
NEXT i
LOCATE 17, 6
PRINT "This is new large figure!"
f$ = INPUT$(1)

END
```

A drawing is displayed in the upper part of the screen and then scanned line by line with **POINT**. The coordinates of each pixel of the image are used as the basis for a copy of this picture nearer to the center of the screen, each pixel being replaced by a 2x2 square of pixels, doubling the scale of the drawing:

This is a highly effective and very popular method of copying, especially if you want to increase the scale of a picture by an integer number of times. You can use it, for example, to

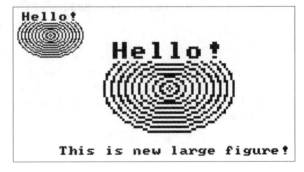

analyze the pixel structure of a letter in graphics mode. Unfortunately, copying is rather slow - the larger the picture, the longer the copying takes.

> *We can only increase the scale of an image by an integer amount of times, because fractional scales will cause distortion with part of the new image being in one scale, and the rest in another.*

We will show you some more uses of this technique in the graphics section later on.

Painting Closed Figures

Most images, such as geometric figures and pie charts, look a whole deal more attractive and much more effective in color. We can achieve this with the **PAINT** statement, which is used to color and pattern closed figures:

```
PAINT [STEP] (x!,y!)[,[{color% | tile$}] [,[bordercolor%]
[,background$]]]
```

The **PAINT** statement provides a quick way of painting any closed figure with a color defined by **color%,** or a pattern described by a string variable **tile$**. Painting begins at a definite point, **(x!,y!)**, and spreads outwards from this point to the figure's boundary. If you give the origin the coordinates **(0,0)**, the whole screen will be painted. Once again **STEP** specifies that the coordinates are relative to the current graphics cursor position, and **bordercolor%** is a color attribute that specifies the border color of the filled area.

PAINT stops filling in an area when it encounters a border of the specified color. **background$** is a 1-byte, 8-pixel background tile slice. By specifying a background tile slice you can paint over an area that's been painted already.

The **LINE** statement allows you to create a pattern using the same method you used when drawing lines with a given style. The surface you want to pattern is broken into rectangular pattern masks. Each mask is 8 bits along the x-axis and up to 64 bits along the y-axis. In other words, the mask is a set of parallel lines, each of which has its own style:

Line
8-bit number   **11001100**   **00110011**   **11100111**   **11111111**

Each 8-bit number can be represented by a decimal or a hexadecimal value. However, using a great many numbers is inconvenient so the mask is actually described using a character string, where each character is represented by **CHR$(arg)**, where **arg** is the decimal value of the 8-bit number. Take, for example, the following pattern defined by **tile$**:

    tile$ = CHR$(arg1) + CHR$(arg2) + ... + CHR$(argn%)

The arguments **arg1**, **arg2**, etc. are numbers 0 through 255. Each **CHR$(argn%)** defines a 1-byte, 8-pixel slice of the pattern based on the binary form of that number.

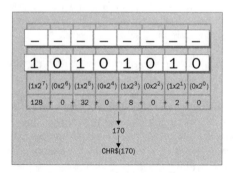

It's worth spending some time acquainting yourself with these rules so that when you use **PAINT** you can avoid making a serious mistake. Many programmers frequently make the frustrating mistake of painting the whole screen instead of a specified area if, for example, the area you want to fill isn't completely closed or if you choose the color of the boundary line incorrectly. A few examples showing how you can use **PAINT** will help you to understand its main characteristics.

First, a simple example: we'll draw two intersecting figures (a circle and a rectangle) and color in their intersection:

```
REM Demonstration of PAINT
REM \CHAP3\CH3_23.BAS

SCREEN 1
CIRCLE (106, 100), 75, 1
LINE (138, 35)-(288, 165), 1, B
PAINT (160, 100), 2, 1
f$ = INPUT$(1)

END
```

This is pretty self-explanatory - we're filling from the point (160, 100) with the color 2 and will not cross any boundaries of color 1. Here's how it looks:

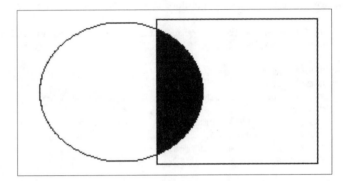

As our next example, we'll draw rings nested inside one another. The task seems simple enough - you just need to draw a series of concentric circles and color each one using **PAINT**. Of course, you can do it this way, but you have to be careful - every time the next circle is created, you should draw it with an available boundary color (it's better to choose the color which **PAINT** will use to fill it in). Our code does just this:

```
REM Create a dart board
REM \CHAP3\CH3_24.BAS

SCREEN 9, 0
COLOR 0, 1
FOR n = 1 to 15
    CIRCLE (320, 170), 15 * n, 3
NEXT n
FOR n = 1 to 15
    PAINT (310 + 15 * n, 170), n, 3
NEXT n
f$ = INPUT$(1)

END
```

Try it out and experiment by changing some of the variables - it's a very effective demonstration. But what if colors are beginning to bore you? Well, you could always use patterns instead; for example, you may want to fill in a closed area with an arbitrary pattern. We can easily draw any circle and fill it with N characters:

```
REM Demonstration of pattern filling
REM \CHAP3\CH3_25.BAS

SCREEN 2, 0
PRINT "Producing a circle filled with N's"
CIRCLE (140, 75), 130
t$ = CHR$(0) + CHR$(198) + CHR$(230) + CHR$(246)
t$ = t$ + CHR$(222) + CHR$(206) + CHR$(198)
t$ = t$ + CHR$(198) + CHR$(0)
PAINT (140, 75), t$
f$ = INPUT$(1)

END
```

Or we can employ several graphics statements together with the output of text information:

```
REM Demonstration of combinations of drawing statements
REM \CHAP3\CH3_26.BAS

SCREEN 1: CLS
LOCATE 1, 3
PRINT "Operators LINE, DRAW, CIRCLE and PAINT"
CIRCLE (160, 100), 60, 1, , , 5 / 6
PAINT (110, 100), CHR$(&HAA) + CHR$(&HAB), 1
LINE (140, 80)-(180, 120), 1, bf
DRAW "bm75,100 e85 f85 g85 h85"
f$ = INPUT$(1)

END
```

Unfortunately, the following screenshot doesn't show you the programs output in all its glory - instead, just imagine that the various shades of gray are bright, distinctive colors. To print a hard copy of a screen you have to use the key combination *Shift + Print Screen* (or *Print Screen* alone), provided that the **GRAPHICS.COM** driver is activated.

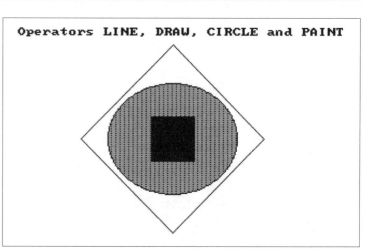

Programming for the Printer

There comes a time though, when looking at a screen all day begins to grate a little, and you need to sit down in a comfy chair and relax. And having a hard copy of your work to read through would be a great idea, and so you bought a printer. The following section will show you how to access your printer and get the most out of it from your QBasic programs.

Accessing the Printer

Interfaces are used to access peripheral devices which access the hardware through the input-output ports (I/O ports). These ports have their own numbers, and some of the most important ports are specifically named (for example, the printer parallel ports LPT1, LPT2 or the serial COM1, COM2 ports). QBasic provides both direct control of peripheral devices through specialized ports and access to any I/O port.

A PC transfers information to the printer either in parallel or serial transmission. Under the parallel transmission, the contents of every byte are transferred on 8 lines at once, i.e. each bit in parallel. This results in a high data transmission rate but requires a multi-strand ribbon cable, no more than a couple of meters long. Therefore, the PC and printer have to be quite close to each other. The interchange of information is proceeded through the parallel ports named as LPT1 and LPT2.

Serial transmission, however, is implemented via the infamous RS-232 interface, where every bit is transferred to the printer sequentially. The information transmission rate is obviously lower but you're able to use simpler cables, which have the added benefit of being much longer (normally up to 70 meters).

There are usually two serial ports on a PC, although there may be more, and these are referred to as COM1 and COM2 (COM3, COM4, etc.). It's quite common for the mouse to occupy one of these ports (normally COM1). A printer can use COM, COM2, LPT1 or LPT2 - it isn't particularly fussy. You just have the job of telling it which one you want it to use.

Text Mode Printing

If you look real close at a typical dot matrix printer, you'll notice that the print head is composed of a column of needles, and that the head moves along the page to produce the characters you see printed on the paper. In a text mode each character is formed from a number of such columns. This is reminiscent of how characters are represented in displays, with the only difference that a printer always prints characters by columns. In doing so, the data for several lines has to be stored concurrently (8 lines for a nine-needle printer). It is for this reason that the printer has its own memory - the buffer.

Dot matrix printers are rather slow devices - their printing rate ranges between 150 to 300 characters per second. So, the buffer is desirable because it enables you to transfer data to the printer quickly, leaving the printer to output it at its own speed. Once your PC has transmitted the data, and while it's waiting for the buffer to empty, your computer is free to do something else. The advantage this process gives you increases with the size of the buffer.

In text mode, the data passed represents common ASCII codes. Each printer has its own character generator to convert them into distinctive characters. Moreover, printers often contain several tables for character generation. These are used for national alphabets, pseudo-graphic sets and so on, and can be switched into play at will with the corresponding control commands.

Usually, in addition to standard data (as ASCII codes), special control codes can also be sent to the printer. For the moment though we shall highlight three of the most important codes which correspond to three commands: initialization of a printer, line feed and carriage return. The initialization of the printer prepares it for work and specifies the standard printing parameters; the line feed command prints the contents of a line contained in the buffer; and the carriage return command moves the carriage (print head) into the initial line position. The last two commands typically act concurrently so that the printing flow is maintained.

Simple Printing Commands

QBasic's **LPRINT** statement together with the **TAB** and **USING** modifiers, output formatted information to your printer. When the printer is connected to the I/O port LPT1, **LPRINT** is in fact analogous to the statement **PRINT #1**. The application of **LPRINT** has its own peculiarities, because it controls the printer by the transfer of special codes included in the statement itself. These may differ with various printer types, so from here on we will assume that we're dealing with the most popular type of printer - Epson compatibles.

First and foremost, note that **LPRINT** directs onto the printer any text enclosed in quotes, like this:

```
LPRINT "Hello my friend!"
```

The printer will most likely print this text in a draft mode. If the printer has its own tools for scripts and quality control (Near Letter Quality, for instance) it can manually be set to print with a specified script and quality.

> *There are lots of programs on the accompanying disk that make good use of the printer. For a good example of printer utilization take a look at **DSTORE.BAS**, a database which can output selected records to the printer.*

Setting the Width

Some printers have different operating sizes, whilst others can only use certain sizes of paper, which if you're not careful can make a real mess of your output. By using the **WIDTH** statement, you can define the width of a line when outputting to a printer or a file, or even change the number of columns and rows displayed on the screen. Its format is:

```
WIDTH [columns%] [,rows%]
WIDTH LPRINT columns%
```

where

columns%   indicates the desired width in columns. The screen display width must be 40 or 80 columns.
rows%   indicates the desired screen display height in rows. It can have a value of 25, 30, 43, 50 or 60, depending on your display adapter and screen mode.

Probably the most popular use of the **WIDTH** statement is to change the width of your printer's output. You can do this by accompanying **WIDTH** with a **#** sign, followed by the number of an open file or a device. For example, this statement sets up your program to take advantage of a wide-carriage (132 columns) printer:

```
OPEN "LPT1:" for Output as #1
   WIDTH #1, 132
```

Here we specify that data is to be output to the printer LPT1, with a print width of 132 characters. It allows you to overcome the limitation of 40 or 80 characters normally imposed on the **columns%** parameter.

Printer Control Codes

Nine times out of ten you'll find that you need a little extra program control over exactly what it is that you're printing. With QBasic, strictly speaking, **LPRINT** is all that we can work with. As we've just mentioned, the program control of a printer is performed by the transfer of special sequences of control codes which are included in the **LPRINT** statement.

You may know that ASCII codes from 0 to 31 are control codes, but what you may not know is which special codes we can use to squeeze that little extra functionality out of our printer. Here are some of the more popular ones:

ASCII	DEC	HEX	Operation
BELL	7	07	Sound the bell
BS	8	08	Backspace
HT	9	09	Horizontal tabulation jump
LF	10	0A	Line feed
VT	11	0B	Vertical tabulation jump
FF	12	0C	Form feed
CR	13	0D	Carriage return
SO	14	0E	Select double width
SI	15	0F	Select condensed mode
DC2	18	12	Cancel condensed mode
DC4	20	14	Cancel double width
CAN	24	18	Clear buffer
DEL	127	7F	Deleting last character from buffer

Although not all single control codes are listed here, even the full set would be insufficient to control some of the more advanced printer features; for example, landscape text printing. So, for enhanced program control, it's necessary to use **escape sequences**, whose telltale sign is the presence of code 27 (**ESC**) as the first character in the string. We pass or send such codes, characters and sequences with the **CHR$** function. Take the following examples:

```
LPRINT  CHR$(27);CHR$(69)
LPRINT  CHR$(27);"E"
LPRINT  CHR$(&H1B);CHR$(&H45)
```

These are three forms of the same command - selection of the bold text modifier. Here's a list of other widely-used **ESC** sequences:

ASCII	DEC	HEX	Operation
ESC + 0	48	30	Set 1/8 inch interval between lines
ESC + 1	49	31	Set 7/72 inch interval between lines
ESC + 2	50	32	Set 1/6 inch interval between lines
ESC + 3 + n	51 n	33 n	Set n/216 inch interval between lines
ESC + 4	52	34	Switch on italic mode
ESC + 5	53	35	Switch off italic mode
ESC + @	64	40	Initialize printer
ESC + C + n	67 n	43 n	Set the page length in lines n
ESC + C + 0	67 0 n	43 0 n	Set the page length in inches n
ESC + E	69	45	Select bold
ESC + F	70	46	Cancel bold
ESC + G	71	47	Select double strike
ESC + H	72	48	Cancel double strike
ESC + Q + n	81 n	51 n	Set right margin
ESC + R + n	82 n	52 n	Selection of an international character set
ESC + 1 + n	108 n	6C n	Set left margin
ESC + x + n	120 n	78 n	Toggles near letter quality on and off

As you can see from this selection of sequences (and there are many many more), **ESC** sequences allow you to initialize the printer, control its buffer, perform key operations on moving the printing head, switch print modes, change the font, etc.

Don't worry if these codes don't appear to work properly with your printer, you'll find that your particular printer will have a list of these escape sequences in the manual - all you need to do is find the ones that you want. Here's a typical program for the Epsom LX-800. Don't forget, it may need adapting if you're working with a different printer model:

```
REM Demonstration of Escape Sequences
REM \CHAP3\CH3_27.BAS

WIDTH "LPT1:", 80                              'Setting line width of 80 characters
LPRINT CHR$(27); "@";                          'Initializing the printer
LPRINT CHR$(27); "x0";                         'Printing in a draft mode
LPRINT "Hello my friend!"
LPRINT CHR$(27); "x1";                         'Printing in NLQ mode
LPRINT "Hello my friend!"
LPRINT CHR$(27); "!8";                         'Enhanced printing
LPRINT "Hello my friend!"
LPRINT CHR$(&H1B); "!B";                       'Printing in italic"
LPRINT "Hello my friend!"
LPRINT CHR$(&H1B); CHR$(&H21); CHR$(128);      'Printing with
LPRINT "Hello my friend!"                      'underlining

END
```

If everything goes according to plan your printer should have printed our favorite message in a variety of styles.

> **Many escape sequences require canceling sequences to cancel a particular style or effect, otherwise a combination of styles will occur. By experimenting with different combinations, you can produce some very effective printing routines.**

Redefining Characters

Since many printers also let you custom define your characters, you could for instance print in the Russian alphabet or even in Chinese pictograms. If you want to do this though, you need to compose the bit images of the characters yourself and enter them into a special storage area - the character generator memory. Most manuals that accompany printers feature programs to define your own characters, but for our purposes let's once again consider using the Epson LX-8OO as an example. In the usual draft mode, you can redefine only the following 6 characters:

Character:	:	;	<	=	>	?
Code:	58	59	60	61	62	63

Remember, you must form a character's bit image in order to redefine it. In draft mode, the bit image is built as a matrix of 11x9 points. Nine points are positioned vertically (the number of needles or pins of the print head), but the lower two points of each row aren't used and serve to create a vertical interval between the characters.

Let's assume that our goal is to replace the > character with the image of a small plane flying from left to right. The following drawing demonstrates the logical representation of the bit image using the rules we've described:

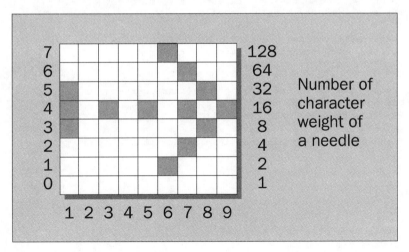

In order to define this image shown in the printer's memory, you'll need to calculate a code for each row by adding the weighting coefficients of the columns marked 1 to 9. Remember that a column may coincide with the separating line, so be careful. In our case, we can work these codes out like this:

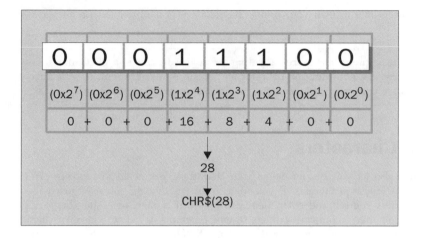

All the nine columns are represented by the following codes:

```
DATA 56,0,16,0,16,130,84,40,16
```

To make our printer actually print this little graphic we can use this program:

```
REM Define new printer symbol - airplane
REM \CHAP3\CH3_28.BAS

A = 60: 'The variable A defines the code of a character to be redefined
        '(in our case this is the character < with the code 60)

'This control sequence copies the new character into memory
LPRINT CHR$(27); ":"; CHR$(0); CHR$(0); CHR$(0);

'This control sequence specifies the choice of the set - the
'standard one or the user-defined set (latter - in our case)
LPRINT CHR$(27); "%"; CHR$(1); CHR$(0);

'This control sequence defines the codes of the characters to be
'redefined (code 60 in our case)
LPRINT CHR$(27); "&"; CHR$(0); CHR$(A); CHR$(A);

'Enter the definition of a new character into the printer's memory
LPRINT CHR$(128);
FOR I = 1 TO 9
    READ D
    LPRINT CHR$(D);
NEXT I

'Specifies the selection of a new character
LPRINT CHR$(0); CHR$(0);

'Contains the code set for defining a new character
DATA 56,0,16,0,16,130,84,40,16

'Specifies printing five new characters with spaces
FOR I = 1 TO 5
```

```
        LPRINT "< ";
    NEXT I
    LPRINT

    END
```

When preparing similar programs with the **LPRINT** statement you should keep an eye on the semi-colons following **LPRINT** statements. A casually omitted ";" will make the data being transferred to the printer append the line feed and carriage return codes after each character is printed, which corrupts the printing or the redefinition of the characters.

With most high quality printers, it's hard work redefining each character by hand, but many feature pre-installed fonts, or character sets that can easily be downloaded and used by your QBasic programs given the correct **ESC** sequences. Check out your printer's manual for further information on these features.

Graphics Mode Printing

All that we've said so far about the printer control is also relevant to the graphics mode. However, the data entering the buffer isn't ASCII code but full point-by-point (or pixel-by-pixel) graphics code. The volume of information transferred to the printer, therefore, is far greater and this explains in part why graphics printing is so slow.

Setting Up the Printer

You use the now familiar **ESC** sequences for switching between the printing density modes and for invoking special pixel-printing commands. These commands usually relate to the printing of a current line, but in case you need to use a command to print several lines, the various commands should precede the relevant line. For example, to define a single density mode, use the following command:

```
    ESC  K  n1  n2
```

where the numbers **n1** and **n2** specify the number of columns reserved for the graphics mode printing. This is how that command translates into QBasic:

```
        LPRINT  CHR$(27);"K";CHR$(n1);CHR$(n2)
```

If you need to obtain **n** columns in a full graphic line, the numbers **n1** and **n2** are calculated from these two expressions:

```
        n2  =  INT  (n/256)
        n1  =  n  -  n2*256
```

For example, if you want a width of 200, make **n = 200**, so you should find that **n2 = 0** and **n1 = 200**. For 400 columns, **n = 400**, **n2** should equal 1 and therefore **n1 = 144**.

The Graphical Printing Process

On receiving a graphic command that specifies the printing density, the printer prints the subsequent codes as graphic data. Because of this, their number must strictly correspond to the number of columns defined by **n1** and **n2**. If data is in short supply, the printer will pause and wait for additional data, which can make it look as if it has stopped working or even crashed. On completion of a graphics line, the printer returns to text mode and subsequent codes will be printed in ASCII. If you forget this, they will come out as meaningless characters.

Handling Line Feeds and Carriage Returns

Many program tools automatically insert the line feed and carriage return codes after each 80 or 132 characters, thinking that you need to start printing on the next line. In a graphic mode this can ruin your printing. There is, however, that special statement we mentioned, **WIDTH**, which specifies the line feed after the indicated value **n**:

```
WIDTH  "LPT1:",n
WIDTH  LPRINT  n
```

The value **n = 255** has a particular meaning though, in that it cancels the automatic line feed and carriage return codes. It's often necessary to do this when printing graphic images because there can sometimes be a large number of pixels in a line, e.g. in EGA or VGA mode the screen is 640 pixels wide so if you're intending to print such wide images, it's important to prevent any premature line feeds.

A Graphic Printing Example

A printer in graphics mode can print any image that can be represented by pixels on the screen. We'll illustrate this with a program that prints five graphic lines, each containing 5O pairs of exclamation marks. (In each pair one exclamation mark is normal and the other is upside down.) We accomplish this feat by forming a bit representation of each of these signs. Here's how we do it:

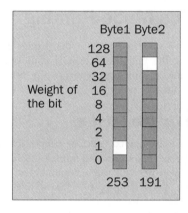

Each bit contributes to the byte value in relation to its weighting coefficient. So, in graphics mode, data is also transmitted to the printer byte by byte, but the difference here is that a byte defines only one column of 8 points rather than the whole character. This is demonstrated in the following program:

```
REM Demonstration of graphics printing
REM \CHAP3\CH3_29.BAS

'The automatic transfer of line feed and carriage
'return codes is cancelled
WIDTH LPRINT 255

'The line space of 8/72 inch, which provides dense
'vertical printing without intervals
LPRINT CHR$(27); "A"; CHR$(8);

'The loop for filling the buffer is specified
FOR I = 1 TO 5
    LPRINT CHR$(27); "K"; CHR$(100); CHR$(0);
    FOR X = 1 TO 50
        'Specifies printing two columns - of a normal and a turned
        'over exclamation mark
        LPRINT CHR$(170); CHR$(85);
    NEXT X
```

```
      'The empty LPRINT prints an empty graphic line
      LPRINT
NEXT I

'Initializes the printer, restoring its initial printing parameters
LPRINT CHR$(27); "@"

END
```

The most important general principles for controlling the printer in graphics mode are contained in this program. Notice the ";" character in the intermediate **LPRINT** statements. As we mentioned earlier, they prevent premature line feed. When writing graphics programs, missing out a ";" is one of the most common and frustrating errors and usually results in strangely printed characters and unforeseen line feeds.

> *For further examples of graphics printing check out the following programs on the accompanying disk:*
> *MUSIC.BAS, FRACTION.BAS and FONTS.BAS.*

We'll explore graphics printing in much more depth later when we discuss bitmapped graphics, but for the time being we'll round off this chapter with a reminder that each type of printer will have its own control codes and methods. Nevertheless, the methods we've covered here retain their usefulness for any kind of printer, be it the simple Epson LX-8OO, a Hewlett-Packard inkjet or even a laser printer.

Summary

Congratulations, you've graduated from the QBasic Guru College's apprentice course, and you should be ready to push on to cover much more interesting subjects. You've learnt all about how to get standard input, how to format text and graphics onto the highly flexible screen and how to make the most of your printer.

Understanding Memory, Data and Machine Code

Introduction

Up to now, we've examined a considerable number of ways to store and manipulate data. Because data is a very integral part of programming, we shall take a closer look. By extending our range of data types, and learning some new techniques, we shall be able to complete our data management apprenticeship with ease, and be able to move on to memory management.

In the world of professional programming, knowledge of the rules by which constants and variables are allocated in memory is of fundamental importance, so the remainder of this chapter will deal with the organization of the memory and the tools of direct memory access (the **POKE** statement and the **PEEK** function). By developing several practical examples, we'll then move on to machine code and assembly language integration in QBasic. The final example will demonstrate how to control the mouse using machine code in QBasic - a valuable addition to any programmers repertoire.

To summarize, in this chapter you'll learn about:

- Data conversion functions.
- RAM control.
- Arrays.
- Specialized data generation functions.
- Machine code integration.
- Events and manipulating the mouse.
- Shelling out.

Indexed Variables and Arrays

If you have a group of variables that contain the same type of data, and feature the same characteristics, you would previously have implemented them like this:

```
month1$="January"
month2$="February"
...
month12$="December"
```

Now obviously, this could get pretty hairy if you want to deal with a set of related data where the elements number considerably more than 12. What you need is some way to group all these together, whilst allowing easy access to any individual element. Well, this is where arrays enter the fray.

QBasic has tools for defining arrays as vectors (one-dimensional arrays), matrices (two-dimensional arrays) and even as multi-dimensional arrays. To get an idea of what these different arrays are, imagine shelves in a bookcase, filled with books. A one-dimensional array is simply a single shelf of books where each book has its own unique ordinal number - its index. A two-dimensional array could represent several shelves of books, whilst a multi-dimensional array could represent several book-filled bookcases.

Array Indexed Variables

Each array element is an indexed variable. This is a variable which, in addition to its name, is characterized by a set of indices which explicitly define its position in the array. The indices are placed in parentheses after the variable name, which is the same as the name of the array.

Setting the Index Base

Now before we show you an example, let's discuss the index base of arrays. Array indexes in the QBasic system are, by default, counted from zero, so the first element in our months of the year project would have the index of zero. If you wanted to change this, use:

`OPTION BASE n%`

This sets the initial integer index to the value of **n%** which can be 1 or 0. When considering such real life examples as the months of the year, the value **n% = 1** would appear to be the most natural choice since, in this case, the element index points directly to its ordinal number. However, some important math applications start counting from zero.

> One problem in particular that crops up is, if you have the OPTION BASE set to 0, and then you don't use the element zero, you *could* have problems when ascertaining which is the actual first element of the array.

Understanding Arrays

A one-dimensional array is a set of variables containing one index. For instance, **x(2)** is the second element of the array **x()** if the index base is 1, or the third element if the index base is 0. Indexed variables can be defined in the form **x(expression)**, where **expression** is a math expression calculating the index value. This value must be an integer. Non-integer numbers are rounded to integers.

One-dimensional Arrays

A one-dimensional array is defined simply by a set of **n** numbers:

```
x = x(1)  x(2)  x(3)  ...  x(i)  ...  x(n)
```

The structure of a one-dimensional array **x** is shown here (together with those of two- and three-dimensional arrays):

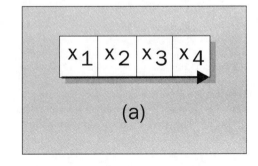

(a)

Two-dimensional Arrays

A two-dimensional array represents **m** one-dimensional arrays and can be written as a matrix of numbers like this:

```
X(1,1)   X(1,2)   X(1,3)   ...   X(1,n)
X(2,1)   X(2,2)   X(2,3)   ...   X(2,n)
...      ...      ...      ...   ...
X(m,1)   X(m,2)   X(m,3)   ...   X(m,n)
```

which can be diagrammatically represented with:

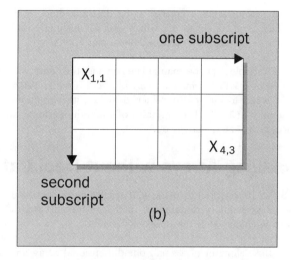

Three-dimensional Arrays

Going back to our 'book - shelf - bookcase' analogy, if there are several bookcases in a room, you would need a three-dimensional array to describe the books in them:

The number of pages in each book could be considered as the value of one element of the array.

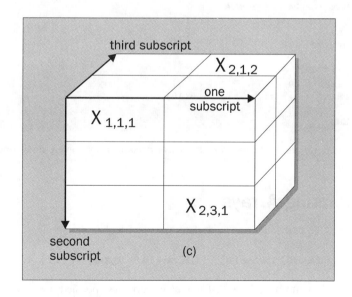

How to Use Arrays

In general, arrays can be both numeric and character. From our example, it's clear that the arrays have the following characteristics:

- ▲ A name (**x** in our case)
- ▲ A dimension (one-, two- or multi-dimensional)
- ▲ Lower and upper index limits

The name of an array is created along the same lines as that of the name of a variable. QBasic allows array dimensions of up to 60, which gets astonishingly difficult to imagine! For the most part, you'll only come across or use one- or two-dimensional arrays.

Indexed variables can be manipulated in just the same way. For example, **a(2) = r3** assigns the value contained in **r3** to the indexed variable **a(2)**, while **PRINT a(2)** outputs the value of the indexed variable **a(2)** to the screen. When dealing with two-dimensional arrays, you should indicate two indices, for example **a(2,3)**. The variables of multi-dimensional arrays are defined in the same manner, for instance **m(2,5,8)**, and so on.

Managing Arrays without Declarations

In QBasic, it's possible to work with small one-dimensional arrays with a top index of not more than 10, without a preliminary declaration. In this restricted case, the array is declared automatically as soon as you use any operation with the indexed variable.

Here is the definition of a small one-dimensional array and the use of indexed variables:

```
REM Defining a small one-dimensional numeric array
REM \CHAP4\CH4_1.BAS

CLS
OPTION BASE 1
a(1) = 1
a(2) = 2
a(10) = 10
PRINT a(1); a(2); "..."; a(10)

END
```

However, we would advise you to always declare arrays, even small ones, just to avoid confusion and mishaps.

Declaring Arrays

You use the **DIM** statement to declare arrays of higher dimensions:

DIM [SHARED] Name[s] [(Size)[AS Type] [...]

The word **SHARED** declares that the array variables specified are to be shared, and the remaining parameters have the following effects:

`DIM  v(100)`	defines a one-dimensional array of 100 real elements.
`DIM  m%(2,3)`	defines an integer matrix **m%** with a dimension of 2*3 if the **OPTION BASE** is set to 1, or with a dimension of 3*4 if the **OPTION BASE** is set to 0.
`DIM  text$(50)`	defines a string-array of 50 characters (**OPTION BASE 1**) or 51 characters (**OPTION BASE 0**).
`DIM  n% (10 TO 20, 3 TO 5)`	defines a two-dimensional integer array with indexes ranging from 10 to 20, and 3 to 5, respectively.
`DIM  m(100)  AS  Balance`	defines a one-dimensional array for data of the user-defined **Balance** type.

Therefore, using the **TO** modifier, indexing can start from any minimum index value to any maximum one. This method works well and is often very convenient. For instance, we can specify a one-dimensional array of our profits in the decade from 1980 to 1989 using an index that goes from 1980 to 1989, so relating each index directly to the year. This simplifies the program and makes it a lot more illustrative. The top index may be as high as 32,767, and you can even define the minimum index value as a negative number.

Controlling the Index Range

When applied to one-dimensional arrays, the functions **LBOUND (v)** and **UBOUND (v)** return the minimum and maximum values, respectively, of the index of the one-dimensional array **v**. For two-dimensional arrays you use them like this:

LBOUND(m,n%)

UBOUND(m,n%)

where **m** is the matrix name, and **n%** is the dimension of the array for which you wish to find the index limit. Here they are in action:

```
REM The illustration of the LBOUND and UBOUND functions
REM \CHAP4\CH4_2.BAS

CLS
DIM D%(80 TO 90, 1 TO 5)
D%(88, 2) = 2.34
D%(90, 3) = 5.67
PRINT D%(88, 2), D%(90, 3)
PRINT "LBOUND (D%,1)="; LBOUND(D%, 1)
PRINT "UBOUND (D%,1)="; UBOUND(D%, 1)
PRINT "LBOUND (D%,2)="; LBOUND(D%, 2)
PRINT "UBOUND (D%,2)="; UBOUND(D%, 2)

END
```

Several features of this piece of code are worth a mention. First, we demonstrate how non-integer values are rounded off when you try to assign them to integer type variables; and secondly, it shows how the functions **LBOUND** and **UBOUND** work. They are used extensively in creating universal library procedures for vector and matrix operations. These procedures allow arrays of any permissible dimension to be dealt with easily. You can see the results of the code on the following page:

```
 2       6
LBOUND (D%,1)= 80
UBOUND (D%,1)= 90
LBOUND (D%,2)= 1
UBOUND (D%,2)= 5
```

Static and Dynamic Arrays

Arrays can be static or dynamic. Static arrays take up a strictly specified place in RAM, which is defined when they are initially declared. Conversely, dynamic arrays have varying positions and size, which enables the PC's memory to be used more effectively. You can switch between these array types with these two compiler commands:

REM $STATIC   for static arrays
REM $DYNAMIC   for dynamic arrays

We've already noted that **REM**, or just the apostrophe **'**, are used for typing comments, but several keywords starting with the **$** sign take precedence over these. Among them are **$STATIC** and **$DYNAMIC**, which tell the compiler about the need for relevant memory distribution. Therefore, they're called **compiler directions** and are usually placed at the beginning of a program.

If you no longer need them, dynamic arrays can be redefined or removed during program execution, allowing you to free up memory.

Redefining an Array

It's often the case that, after performing a calculation, an array becomes redundant for the remainder of the program and just occupies valuable memory space. When this happens, a dynamic array can be redefined in order to change its dimension. The **REDIM** statement serves this purpose:

REDIM [Shared] Name [S] [(Size)] [As type] [...]

REDIM's syntax is very similar to that of **DIM**, but note that you can redefine an array without actually deleting it first.

Deleting an Array

ERASE is the statement you must use to delete or reinitialize arrays:

ERASE Arrayname [, arrayname2]...

You can clear one array with a single **ERASE** statement. However, static arrays can't be deleted, instead **ERASE** either sets each element of a numeric array to zero or each element of a string array to null. When **ERASE** deletes dynamic arrays, it frees the memory used by the array. Before you re-use an array, you must re-declare its dimensions using the **REDIM** or **DIM** statements.

Let's define and redefine a dynamic array:

```
REM Defining and rededining a dynamic array
REM \CHAP4\CH4_3.BAS
```

```
'$DYNAMIC
CLS
DIM A(80 TO 90, 10) AS INTEGER, B(20)
PRINT "Defining array A"
A(89, 5) = 123.456
PRINT B(12), A(89, 5)
ERASE A
REDIM A(80 TO 90, 10)
PRINT "Redefining array A"
A(85, 5) = 456.78
PRINT A(89, 5), A(85, 5)

END
```

Run it and you'll see these declarations:

```
Defining array A
0           123
Redefining array A
0           457
```

These powerful tools for defining and redefining arrays, together with the **LBOUND** and **UBOUND** functions, allow you to create independent functions and procedures which employ all the features of arrays.

Now that we have a fundamental understanding of arrays or indexed variables, it is important that we push on and learn how to convert data between different types.

Data Conversion Functions

When you're using arithmetic operations, it's very important to represent every operand correctly. This is often a very real problem though, because sometimes our variables are defined as a certain data type set. So, every now and again, you will need some way of converting certain values or variables from one type into another. Here we go.

Converting Real Numbers into Integers

One typical example is that an integer variable should never be assigned a fractional number, because it will be truncated. Therefore, QBasic includes a set of number-converting functions:

CINT(x)   rounds a numeric expression to a short integer.

CLNG(x)   rounds a numeric expression to a long integer.

CSNG(x)   converts a numeric expression to a single-precision float-point value.

CDBL(x)   converts a numeric expression to a double-precision float-point value.

We'll use these functions here:

```
REM Demonstration of conversion functions (example 2)
REM \CHAP4\CH4_4.BAS
```

105

```
CLS
n% = CINT(12 + 34)
PRINT n%
dn& = CLNG(25 * 400)
PRINT dn&
x! = CSNG(1 / 3)
PRINT x!
dx# = CDBL(2 / 3)
PRINT dx#

END
```

And we'll see this set of figures when we run that code:

```
46
10000
.3333333
.6666666666666666
```

These conversion functions are especially useful when you write data into files which must be accurate, byte-wise and of a pre-determined size.

Converting Character Data into Numeric Data

If the numbers are presented as characters or strings, the corresponding conversions are performed using the functions **CVI(x$)**, **CVL(x$)** and **CVD(x$)**. The numeric string used by the function **CVI** as its argument is a 2-byte one; for **CVL** it's 4-byte and for **CVD** it's 8-byte. The reverse conversion (numbers to numeric strings) is provided by the functions **MKI$**, **MKL$**, **MK$** and **MKD$**.

Here, all our new functions are dealt with in a simple example:

```
REM Conversion functions (example 1)
REM \CHAP4\CH4_5.BAS

CLS
n$ = MKI$(10000)
PRINT CVI(n$)
dn$ = MKL$(1000000)
PRINT CVL(dn$)
x$ = MKS$(123.456)
PRINT CVS(x$)
dx$ = MKD$(.123456789#)
PRINT CVD(dx$)

END
```

These are the figures we arrive at when we run this one:

```
10000
1000000
123.456
.123456789
```

These functions are also useful for dealing with files, since file data should be represented in character form. As a result, there's often the need to convert numeric data to strings to write them into a file and, vice versa, to convert strings to numbers to read information from files. We shall discuss file handling in Chapter 6 - File Management.

Converting between Number Bases

QBasic was designed to be backwardly compatible with BasicA and GWBasic, which predominantly used binary, octal and hexadecimal number systems. These representations are often used when setting patterns (masks) in graphics statements as well as whilst defining RAM addresses. Thus, the following functions are used to convert decimal numbers into octal and hexadecimal:

OCT$(n)	converts a decimal number **n** to octal.
HEX$(n)	converts a decimal number **n** to hexadecimal.

If **n** is a real number, it's either rounded to an integer or a long integer, as appropriate.

Other Conversion Functions

The full complement of conversion functions for numeric and character data is completed with these five functions:

ASC (s$)	returns the ASCII code for the first character in a string expression. (In the case of an empty string, **ASC** reports an error).
CHR$ (Code)	returns the character corresponding to a specified ASCII code.
STR$ (Expression)	returns a string representation of a number.
VAL (s$)	converts a string representation of a number to a number.
LEN (s$)	returns the number of characters in a string or the number of bytes required to store a variable.

We can see how they all work here:

```
REM Character functions (example 1)
REM \CHAP4\CH4_6.BAS

CLS
y$ = STR$(123)
PRINT y$
x = VAL(y$)
PRINT x
c$ = CHR$(65)
PRINT c$
PRINT ASC(c$)
PRINT LEN("Qwerty")

END
```

Our result is four figures and a letter:

```
123
123
A
65
6
```

Note that functions with the character **$** next to their name return character values, while the remaining functions return numeric values. The functions listed above are the ones that convert numeric values to characters and vice versa. Remember that character values, for example **"123"**, have nothing to do with numeric values, such as the number **123**. Characters and strings cannot be used in arithmetic expressions without first being converted to numeric values by the functions **ASC** or **VAL**.

Numeric Data Formats

QBasic operates with numbers represented in what is termed the **IEEE** format.

> *The acronym IEEE stands for the Institute of Electrical and Electronic Engineers, the organization that developed this standard.*

In an extended IEEE format for the double precision real numbers, an 8-byte number is stored in RAM in the following form:

63	62	....	52	51	....	0	Bits
s	ppppppppppp			mmm..................mmmmm			Contents

Here, **s** is a sign bit, the **p**'s are the bits representing the order, and the **m**'s represent the mantissa. This IEEE format is supported by math co-processors.

The **Microsoft Binary format** (**MBF**), as used by BasicA and GWBasic, is available in QBasic too. In this format, 4-byte single precision real numbers are stored in RAM in the following form:

Byte 4	Byte 3	Byte 2	Byte 1
spppppppp	pmmmmmmm	mmmmmmmm	mmmmmmmm

This form of storing single-precision real numbers is also used by the IEEE format. Both MBF and IEEE standards are methods of representing floating-point numbers internally. The IEEE format gives more accurate results than the Microsoft Binary format used in earlier versions of BASIC, and makes it easier to use a math co-processor. As we've just mentioned, QBasic has the functions **CVS**, **CVD**, **MKS$** and **MKD$** for reading and writing real numbers from and to random-access files. However, in QBasic, these functions deal with real numbers stored in IEEE format, not MBF. To work with numbers in Microsoft Binary format, QBasic has the following functions:

CVSMBF   converts a 4-byte string into a single precision value.
CVDMBF   converts an 8-byte string into a double precision value.
MKSMBF$ converts a single precision value into a 4-byte string.
MKDMBF$ converts a double precision value into an 8-byte string.

Generating Random Numbers

Why would you want a random number? Well, nearly all situations in life are at the mercy of random events - living would be a little dull if every thing was predetermined. This is a good enough reason why we need a way of generating random numbers.

Initializing the Random Number Generator

Many phenomena can be simulated using random numbers. For example, you can prove that when you flip a coin. The probability of it coming up heads and the probability of it coming up tails are both 0.5.

Random numbers may be governed by various distribution laws. You'll most frequently encounter the **uniform distribution law**, whereby the numbers are distributed evenly within an interval, and such numbers are said to be pseudo-random. In QBasic, you need a programmable random number generator to produce random numbers. This is normally initialized by the **RANDOMIZE** statement.

Obtaining Random Numbers

Pseudo-random numbers are produced using the **RND** function. We'll tell you what pseudo implies a few pages hence. Every time you invoke **RND**, a new random number, uniformly distributed between the range 0 to 1, is generated. Let's now create two sequences of five random numbers:

```
REM Demonstration of the RANDOMIZE(x) statement
REM \CHAP4\CH4_7.BAS

CLS
RANDOMIZE (1)
PRINT RND, RND, RND, RND, RND
PRINT RND, RND, RND, RND, RND

END
```

Ignoring the layout differences, here are our two sequences of five random numbers run together:

```
.7648737
.1054455
.6134542
.9377558
.1073679
.1084803
.7627969
.2643857
5.350369E-02
.7419969
```

The **RND** function can contain a parameter (a numeric expression in parentheses). The **RND** function, without an argument, is, in effect, equivalent to **RND(1)**. **RND(0)** returns the last number generated, and **RND(x)**, where **x** is less than 0, rounds **x** to an integer and uses it to initialize the random number generator again. If you don't want an interval of 0...1, you may use mathematical expressions to change it. Take this expression:

```
1 + INT (9 * RND)
```

It allows you to obtain integer random numbers within the 1 - 10 range.

One important point to remember, though, is that the random numbers are actually **pseudo-random**, which means that sooner or later there will be repeat sequences. By changing the parameter of the **RANDOMIZE** statement, you can make the sequence 'more random'.

There are many tricks you can use to obtain real random numbers. You can, for example, use the system time or the seconds between keypresses to initialize the random number generator. Check out random programs on our disk, such as **\GRAPHICS\LANDSCAP.BAS** and **\APPS\LOTTERY.BAS**, for examples of how such generators can be implemented. Anyway, that's enough data generation for now, how is your memory these days?

RAM Control

The Random Access Memory (RAM) of a PC stores the program and all the data it deals with, in particular, constants, variables and arrays. How the memory is distributed and in which cells particular program or data objects are stored is automatically dealt with by QBasic. Nevertheless, it's often necessary to know exactly where a particular object is and how many cells it occupies. You need memory control tools if you want to find out.

RAM Access

At some point, most professional programmers have to know something about the IBM PC addressing system. The full 20-digit address allows you to identify up to 1 Mbyte (1048560 bytes) of memory. Each address represents a cell or byte, which is a decimal number between 0 and 255. However, addressing the full 20-bit address is somewhat complicated.

The reasons for the address system are historical, dating back to Intel's early x86 chips which had a 16-bit bus, and whose numbers can be written in 16-bit binary, from 0 to 65535 (also written as 64 kilobytes). Thus, only 65536 bytes are directly addressable from the CPU. The designers decided to assign memory using *two* 16-bit numbers: a segment and an offset, written as:

```
segment : offset
```

where the addresses are in 4-digit hexadecimal (equivalent to 16-bit binary). Each can take values from 0 to 65,535. Now comes the problem; because the designers also reasoned that no-one would ever need more than 1 megabyte of memory for DOS, and set one segment equal to 16 bytes. This limits the amount of conventional memory accessible by a program to 640k, the rest being used by DOS. Most memory has a non-unique address under this scheme, for example the 31st byte may be addressed by 0000:001F or 0001:000F.

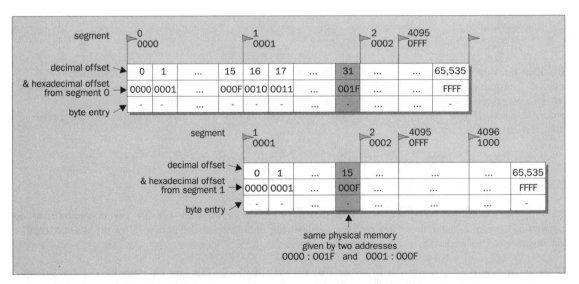

It's important to note that the segment does not start as the 5th hexadecimal digit and go to the 8th, it starts as another 2nd digit. The full address of any byte is, therefore, given by the following expression:

Address = 16 * b% + d%.

where b% is the **base** of a memory segment (with a value from 0 to 65535), and d% is the address **offset** (with the same range of values). The base of a segment is set with the **DEF SEG** statement:

DEF SEG [= b%]

If the operand isn't defined, the default base is set.

Writing Bytes to Memory

The **POKE** statement allows you to write a byte value (within the range 0 through 255) to a specified memory location. Its format is:

POKE address,byte%

Here's how **POKE** acts. This action relates to the segment defined by **DEF SEG**. If this statement isn't used, **POKE** acts by default within a zero segment.

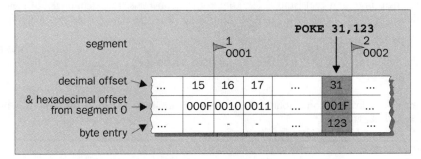

Here we have 'poked' the decimal value 123 into the memory address numbered 31 in the current segment (which is 0), equivalent to the QBasic commands **DEF SEG 0 : POKE 31,123**.

Retrieving Bytes from Memory

To retrieve a byte value stored in a specified memory location, you use **PEEK** as follows:

PEEK(address)

where address is the position of the byte relative to the current segment address set by **DEF SEG** − in other words a value in the range 0 through 65,535.

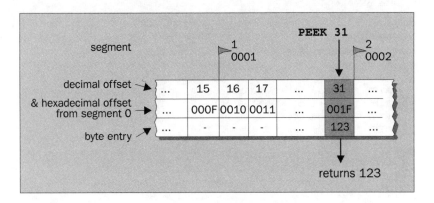

Look at this as an example of **PEEK** in action:

```
DEF SEG = 0
Status% = PEEK( &H417)                 'Reads the keyboard status
```

You must handle **POKE** statements with extreme care: if they aren't used carefully they can ruin your program, or worse, can cause data loss or system failure. This should come as no surprise since **POKE** modifies the machine code programs in RAM when writing new data into occupied memory cells. However, for those who know what they're doing, the **PEEK** and **POKE** instructions provide them with unlimited power over their PC.

In fact, we will now show you other memory related features of QBasic, learn how to actually write machine code programs that we can use in our QBasic programs.

Controlling RAM Variables

Constants and variables are actually collections of RAM cells, the addresses of which are indicated by their names. The number of cells (bytes) depends on the constant or variable type: 2 for short integers, 4 for long integers, 4 for single precision reals and 8 for double precision reals. Each character of a name takes up 1 byte. The value of a string constant or variable consisting of n characters, occupies n bytes of RAM.

The base of the segment where the value of the variable **v** is stored is given by the function **VARSEG (v)**, and the offset by the function **VARPTR (v)**. Use the function **SADD (v$)** to define the offset of a character variable, **v$**.

Remember, you can obtain information about the addresses of variables or arrays with the functions **VARSEG**, **VARPTR** and **VARPTR$**:

VARPTR (variablename)	returns the offset address of a variable.
VARSEG (variablename)	returns the segment address of a variable.
VARPTR$ (commandline)	returns the string representation of the variable address for use in the **DRAW** and **PLAY** statements.

Here are the three of them in action:

```
REM Demonstration of the VARx statements
REM \CHAP4\CH4_8.BAS

CLS
DEF SEG
c$ = "OneTwoThree"
x% = 123
Address = VARPTR(x%)
PRINT "Address x% ="; Address
PRINT "Address c$ ="; SADD(c$)
PRINT PEEK(Address)
PRINT PEEK(Address + 1)
PRINT "x% ="; PEEK(Address) + 256 * PEEK(Address + 1)
FOR i = SADD(c$) TO SADD(c$) + 10
    PRINT CHR$(PEEK(i));
NEXT i
F$ = INPUT$(1)

END
```

First, two variables are defined - one numeric, **x% = 123** and one string, **c$ = "OneTwoThree"**. Then we discover the initial addresses of these variables using the **VARPTR** and **SADD** functions. After this, using bytes located in these and the next addresses, we restore the variable values. This clearly demonstrates that the integer value of the **x** variable is located in 2 bytes and that the ASCII codes of the character variable **c$** take up 11 bytes.

Canceling Variable Definitions

On executing the Start command in the Run menu, all variable definitions are cleared from memory. You can also perform this function with the **CLEAR** statement:

```
CLEAR [,,m]
```

The optional parameter **m** stands for the number of bytes that you want reserved for the stack.

Controlling the Amount of Memory

The definition of variables calls for the use of memory reserves. Here's a function that will give you the size of all free memory blocks (or, as they say, 'bulk')and start the procedure of clearing 'dust' from the memory. When defining array storage space, use the **FRE** function in this format:

```
FRE(String Expression)
FRE(Numeric Expression)
```

If the argument of **FRE** is a string expression, the function returns the size (in bytes) of the free memory available for storing strings. If the argument is numeric, **FRE** returns different values depending on the numeric expression:

-1	the size of the largest non-string array you can create.
-2	the unused stack space.
Other	the unused free memory space for storing strings.

You can see just how important **FRE** can be when it comes to controlling free memory and the size of the stack. The amount of free memory will essentially define the maximum sizes of string arrays for you. Let's now move on from memory to address the scary world of assembly language (or machine code) programming.

Using Machine Code Programs

Although a full discussion of machine code and assembler programming isn't the task of this book, you can incorporate their capabilities by following some simple steps and using tools that you already have or are supplied with this book. Machine code programs offer the QBasic user:

- ▲ A huge increase in speed.
- ▲ Access to peripherals, ports and processors unavailable through the QBasic command set.

Unfortunately, machine code is also very difficult to learn and is such a vast topic that here we'll simply show you how to integrate them in QBasic. To use machine code subroutines in your QBasic programs, you need to go through these three steps:

▲   Acquire or build the subroutine.

▲   Build the code to load the subroutine in your QBasic program.

▲   Build the code to call and use the subroutine in your QBasic program.

Acquiring the Subroutine

There are many sources of subroutines. For example, there are libraries available for specific specialized topics such as math routines or graphics routines, and they can also be produced by hand with high level language compilers or assemblers. As a QBasic user, you will want your machine code in the shape of **COM** files.

There is a program that you can use to build your own machine code subroutines called **DEBUG.EXE**, which is distributed as a part of MS-DOS. Rather than describe the process, let's actually build a subroutine that we can use from QBasic. Our subroutine will give us the capability to do a print screen from within our QBasic program. We will be calling the BIOS interrupt 05H to perform this.

Type the following at a DOS prompt:

```
D:\>debug
-a100                    Tell DEBUG that we want to assemble at location 100.
10DB:0100 int 05         Type the instruction int 05.
10DB:0102 retf           Type the instruction retf.
10DB:0103                Type a carriage return to terminate the edit mode.
-npscreen.com            Tell DEBUG what to name our COM file.
-rcx                     Tell DEBUG to let us set how many bytes to write CX 0000.
:3                       Subtract 0100H from 0103H and tell DEBUG to write 3H bytes.
-w                       Tell DEBUG to write our file.
Writing 00003 bytes
-q                       Tell DEBUG to quit.
```

Although it's not necessary, we can look at our routine by doing the following:

```
D:\>debug pscreen.com
-u100,102                Tell DEBUG to unassemble locations 100H to 102H
10FF:0100 CD05           INT    05
10FF:0102 CB             RETF
-q
```

We now have a machine code subroutine called **PSCREEN.COM** which we need to load it into our QBasic program.

Loading the Subroutine into QBasic

There are several techniques that can be used to load the **COM** file into your QBasic program so that you can call it. Provided on the disk is a program, **COM2BAS.BAS**, to make the process a little easier - in fact, it will generate the QBasic code for you. Type the following:

```
D:\>qbasic /run com2bas
```

COM2BAS   Written by F.A. Gregory

COM file name? pscreen

COM file=pscreen.com   BAS file=pscreen.bas

OK (enter Y or N, Q to quit)? y

COM file length = 3

The **COM2BAS** program reads the **COM** file and generates the equivalent QBasic code into a new program called **PSCREEN.BAS**. To examine the results, load **PSCREEN.BAS** into QBasic and you should see the following:

```
DEFINT A-Z
GOSUB Loadpscreen
GOSUB Callpscreen

END

Loadpscreen:
  DIM pscreen( 2 )
  DEF SEG = VARSEG(pscreen(0))
  FOR i = 0 TO  2
      READ j
      POKE (VARPTR(pscreen(0)) + i), j
  NEXT i
  DEF SEG
  RETURN

Callpscreen:
  DEF SEG=VARSEG(pscreen(0))
  'CALL ABSOLUTE (,,VARPTR(pscreen(0)))
  DEF SEG
RETURN


DATA &HCD,&H05,&HCB
```

This is the QBasic code that **COM2BAS** has generated for you to load your machine code subroutine. We showed you earlier how one QBasic program can produce another, so we won't delve into the process again here. The final step that we have to do manually is to customize the **CALL ABSOLUTE** command and add the real processing to use the subroutine.

Using the Subroutine

This example does not pass any parameters, so the **CALL** is very simple. We'll look at passing parameters in another example later. Let's also add some **PRINT** statements so that we'll have something on our screen to print and then we can run our new creation. Our program now looks like this:

```
DEFINT A-Z

REM  Sample program to demonstrate a machine code subroutine that
REM  calls BIOS interrupt 05H to do a screen print.
```

```
PRINT
PRINT
PRINT
PRINT "This"
PRINT
PRINT "           is"
PRINT
PRINT "                    a"
PRINT
PRINT "                         TEST"

GOSUB Loadpscreen

GOSUB Callpscreen

END

Loadpscreen:
  DIM pscreen( 2 )
  DEF SEG = VARSEG(pscreen(0))
  FOR i = 0 TO 2
     READ j
     POKE (VARPTR(pscreen(0)) + i), j
  NEXT i
  RETURN

Callpscreen:
  DEF SEG = VARSEG(pscreen(0))
  CALL ABSOLUTE (VARPTR(pscreen(0)))
  RETURN
  DATA &HCD,&H05,&HCB
```

Now we have a completed machine code subroutine, built with **DEBUG**, loaded then called in our QBasic program. Let's do another one where we pass a parameter.

Passing Parameters

For this example, we will build a machine code subroutine that will return to us the name of the current directory. Here is what we are going to do. Run **DEBUG** just as in the previous example, starting with a100. Let's name it **CURRDIR.COM**. We will use interrupt **21h** function **47h** to return the name of the current directory to a string which we will pass to the subroutine. Run **DEBUG** as follows (you can also build a file using **EDIT** and redirect it into **DEBUG** - see **CURRDIR.DBG** included on the disk):

```
D:\>debug
-a100
10DD:0100 push bp
10DD:0101 mov bp,sp
10DD:0103 mov ah,47
10DD:0105 mov dl,00
10DD:0107 mov bx,[bp+06]
10DD:010A mov si,[bx]
10DD:010C int 21
10DD:010E pop bp
```

```
10DD:010F retf 2
10DD:0112
-ncurrdir.com
-rcx
CX 0000
:12
-w
Writing 00012 bytes
-q
```

Go ahead and inspect the subroutine by asking **DEBUG** to disassemble it:

```
D:\>debug currdir.com
-u100,111
10FF:0100 55          PUSH    BP
10FF:0101 89E5        MOV     BP,SP
10FF:0103 B447        MOV     AH,47
10FF:0105 B200        MOV     DL,00
10FF:0107 8B5E06      MOV     BX,[BP+06]
10FF:010A 8B37        MOV     SI,[BX]
10FF:010C CD21        INT     21
10FF:010E 5D          POP     BP
10FF:010F CA0200      RETF    0002
-q
```

Everything looks in order, so let's carry on and load it into our program.

Loading the Subroutine into QBasic

Now we need to run **COM2BAS** on our **COM** file and build our skeleton file:

d:\>qbasic /run com2bas

COM2BAS   Written by F.A. Gregory

COM file name? currdir

COM file=currdir.com   BAS file=currdir.bas

OK (enter Y or N, Q to quit)? y

COM file length =   18

Loading **CURRDIR.BAS** into QBasic we have:

```
DEFINT A-Z

GOSUB Loadcurrdir

GOSUB Callcurrdir

END
```

117

```
Loadcurrdir:
DIM currdir( 9 )
DEF SEG = VARSEG(currdir(0))
FOR i = 0 TO 17
    READ j
    POKE (VARPTR(currdir(0)) + i), j
NEXT i
DEF SEG
RETURN

Callcurrdir:
DEF SEG=VARSEG(currdir(0))
'CALL ABSOLUTE (,,VARPTR(currdir(0)))
DEF SEG
RETURN


DATA &H55,&H89,&HE5,&HB4,&H47,&HB2,&H00,&H8B
DATA &H5E,&H06,&H8B,&H37,&HCD,&H21,&H5D,&HCA
DATA &H02,&H00
```

Using the Subroutine

We will be getting the name of the current directory back in a buffer area and we need to allocate that string. We also need to pass its address which we get from the string address (**SADD**) function. Our program now looks like this:

```
DEFINT A-Z

GOSUB Loadcurrdir
CurrentDirectory$ = SPACE?(65)
GOSUB Callcurrdir
PRINT "Directory="; CurrentDirectory$
END

Loadcurrdir:
DIM currdir(9)
DEF SEG = VARSEG(currdir(0))
FOR i = 0 TO 17
    READ j
    POKE (VARPTR(currdir(0)) + i), j
NEXT i
DEF SEG
RETURN

Callcurrdir:
DEF SEG = VARSEG(currdir(0))
CALL ABSOLUTE(SADD(CurrentDirectory$), VARPTR(currdir(0)))
DEF SEG
RETURN


DATA &H55,&H89,&HE5,&HB4,&H47,&HB2,&H00,&H8B
DATA &H5E,&H06,&H8B,&H37,&HCD,&H21,&H5D,&HCA
DATA &H02,&H00
```

Sample COM Files

Included on the accompanying disk are lots of other great sample COM files, such as routines to find out how much free space is on a disk drive, how to read a CD-ROM and how to work with bits in a byte, and so on. There are also other great demonstration programs which show you exactly how to use them to your advantage. Take a look at Appendix B for a complete run down of all the files on the disk.

> **There are many good volumes that demonstrate the power of assembly language programming, but if you do want to learn more about this subject, take a look at the titles recommended in the QBasic Resource Guide in Appendix A.**

Using the techniques and tools we've just presented and the sample subroutines included on the disk, you can begin to add the power of machine code subroutines to your QBasic programs. Take your time, practice and be very careful where you poke!

But what do you do if something unexpected happens in your hybrid program? Or perhaps you would like your program to do something only when something in particular occurs. Well, what we need to understand in order to control these 'occurrences' are exactly how these events work.

Events and QBasic

Like real life, the operation of a computer, is accompanied by various **events**. An event may be thought of as something occurring suddenly and involving changes to the PC's schedule. Some events don't require a user's interference; for example, if it turned out that a maths coprocessor is required for a certain calculation, QBasic will automatically bring it into operation. Here's our definition of a QBasic event:

> **An event is a condition which, on being fulfilled, can or must involve a particular response by the program; for example, overflow when performing operations with integer numbers, division by zero, or reading information from one of the COM-ports. In other words, events interrupt program execution and require a response by the run-time system or the program. The response either clears up the trouble caused by the error or processes the information received.**

There is even a whole class of events that you may be unaware of which collectively handle the errors that suspend program execution and call for a user response. And sometimes, when programming in QBasic, you often find that you would like to control various internal (built-in) and external devices. Internal devices include the system timer, the keyboard and the display (although technically the last two are external, it is hard to imagine a PC without a keyboard or a monitor of some description). At the same time there are a lot of external devices without which the PC can still be considered able-bodied. These include a printer, light pen, mouse or joystick.

When you work with these devices, events often arise where you're required to take certain actions, and more often than not these are events associated with the keyboard and the processor. Events using the keyboard are typically defined by the programmer; for example, you often need to invoke particular actions by pressing a certain key (e.g. to move the cursor or another object on the screen). These types of events are intentional and so they can be planned for. Of course, it's never that easy because, in the real world, the most frequent type of events are unintentional occurrences associated with run-time errors.

QBasic, unlike the majority of PC programming languages, does not allow you to fully undertake the processing of nonstandard run-time events. This means that in some cases, for example, when an error or an interrupt occurs, the run-time system analyzes the cause on its own and decides what to do next without consulting you. The features inherent to Pascal or C which enable you to turn off the system error handler and analyze the cause of errors yourself are not present in QBasic. The complexity of interrupt processing in QBasic makes this impracticable.

Nevertheless, QBasic doesn't leave you completely out in the cold with these problems. You can always use the set of tools for event handling to allow you to organize error processing in each program, providing actions other than simply terminating the program. Aside from that, QBasic supports interrupt processing from the more popular external peripherals, allowing you to write complicated programs effectively under their control. It is these tools that we will look at now.

External Peripheral Interrupts

From here on, an **interrupt** will be considered to be an event associated with a signal from an active external device. Each interrupt is assigned a unique number. A PC's ROM contains a so-called **interrupt vector**, a cell of two bytes carrying the addresses of interrupt handler subroutines. For instance, if you send a message to the printer and the printer is turned off, the corresponding interrupt occurs and the subprogram response to that event is executed - the computer's operation is suspended with a message warning the user that the printer isn't ready. Knowing this, you could introduce an error handler into the program which, in this case, could cancel working with the printer and continue program execution.

'Interrupt' implies the completion of the current sequence of statements. The QBasic run-time system includes special interrupt handling procedures for the light pen, joystick, communication ports, keyboard and timer. You can, as the need arises, add a block to the system procedures which implements its own specific algorithms for interaction with these peripherals. We shall now discuss the tools which allow you to do this and cover the various methods of interrupt handling.

Event Trapping

The number of events of this type is enormous and it's almost impossible to have a specific response to each of them. Instead, QBasic has a uniform mechanism of event trapping which enables you to identify events and have the program execute one of the event trapping units. In this way, the decision of what to do when one of these events occurs is left to the user. This mechanism allows you to create event handlers based on the following unified QBasic constructions:

```
ON ERROR GOTO Label
ON Device GOSUB Label
```

where **Device** is the device (internal or external) that causes the event and **ERROR**, the internal error generator. Each device is assigned a unique name, for example:

COM	port for communication with peripherals
PEN	light pen
PLAY	music synthesizer
STRIG	joystick
TIMER	built-in system timer

Each device usually has a corresponding system variable or function. For instance, **ERR** returns the code of an error that has occurred, and the **TIMER** function returns the number of seconds that have elapsed since midnight. Calculations, depending on the value of one or another event, are not interrupted and the program branches to a specified program unit or subroutine. The following few sections will see us consider the identification and processing of some of those events which are typical of a personal computer, for example built-in event generators and first, the keyboard.

Keyboard Control

In addition to the **INPUT**, **INPUT$** and **INPUT LINE** statements, the function **INKEY$** (without arguments) is also used for input. It reads a character from the keyboard and, if there's no character waiting, it returns a null string. For standard keys, **INKEY$** returns a 1-byte string containing that character. For extended keys, **INKEY$** returns a 2-byte string made up of the null character (ASCII 0) and the keyboard scan code, for example, the second byte codes 3B through 44 (hexadecimal values) correspond to the function keys *F1* through *F10*, the codes 47 through 52 correspond to the numeric keys of the first group, and so on. Just like the **INPUT$** function, the input symbols are not displayed on the screen.

The value of the string returned by **INKEY$** is typically assigned to a particular character variable, for example:

```
REM Demonstration of INKEY$ harnessed within a WHILE loop
REM \CHAP4\CH4_9.BAS

WHILE Keypress$ = ""
    Keypress$ = INKEY$
    IF Keypress$<>"" THEN PRINT Keypress$
WEND

END
```

Here you can see the characters which are returned by pressing a key, or a key combination recognized by **INKEY$**.

Like **INPUT$**, the **INKEY$** function is most commonly used to create menus which offer the user a set of options activated by pressing a specified key. The fact that the selection isn't repeated has its advantages and disadvantages. The advantage is that a minimum set of keys are required to run a specified menu item, which also means, however, that it is impossible to change your choice. Therefore, menus are more often organized so as to allow the user to correct the input code or character before confirmation. This is usually done using the **INPUT** statement.

The KEY Statement

Sometimes you may also need to change the effect of one of the function keys, for example, we may want the *F1* key to bring up our own program's help screen rather than that of QBasic. To do this you use the **KEY** statement which assigns string values to function keys and lets you display the key values if you want to. It is used in the following format:

```
KEY key%, stringexpression$
KEY LIST
KEY ON
KEY OFF
```

Here, **key%** denotes the number of a key (1 through 10 for keys *F1* to *F1* plus 30 and 31 for *F11* and *F12* respectively). The variable **stringexpression$** is a string of up to 15 characters in length, returned when that key is pressed. **LIST** displays the assignments for each key, **ON** turns the function-key display line on, and **OFF** turns it off. The following is a simple example of using the **KEY** statement:

```
REM Demonstration of the KEY statements
REM \CHAP4\CH4_10.BAS

KEY 4, "MENU" + CHR$ (13)
KEY LIST
PRINT
KEY 4, ""
KEY LIST

END
```

There is another form of the **KEY** statement which enables, disables or suspends the event trapping of a key:

KEY(n%)	**ON**	enables event trapping for the specified key.
KEY(n%)	**OFF**	disables key event trapping.
KEY(n%)	**STOP**	suspends key event trapping. Events are processed once event trapping is enabled by **KEY ON**

where **n%** is one of these values:

0	all keys listed here
1-10	function keys *F1-F10*
11	up arrow key
12	left arrow key
13	right arrow key
14	down arrow key
15-25	user-defined keys
30,31	function keys *F11* and *F12*

Error Trapping

Loss of data caused by calculation errors is always a problem. The old interpreting versions of BASIC only allowed you to resume operation after you had eliminated the errors. This is impossible, however, with compiler-oriented versions, since the whole program has to be recompiled even when the slightest changes are made. Therefore, event handlers were introduced into QBasic. They process errors such as division by zero or an attempt to calculate the logarithm of a negative argument.

The system variable **ERR** is used to reveal errors. When an error occurs, **ERR** returns the run-time error code of the most recent error. This allows you to organize program operation properly after an error interrupt. A list of run-time error codes can be found from the QBasic Help contents page.

Working with the System Timer

IBM-compatible PCs contain a built-in timer in the form of a quartz clock. The ability of a program to retrieve the current time and date automatically from this clock is extremely useful, primarily to pamper the user with trivial but handy information. The following two commands effectively perform this function, and the third returns a relative time value:

DATE$	returns the current computer system date.
TIME$	returns the current computer system time, a string in the form **hh:mm:ss** where **hh** are hours, **mm** are minutes, and **ss** are seconds.
TIMER	returns the number of seconds elapsed since midnight up to the current moment.

Here is a simple program to test these functions:

```
REM Using the Functions of Time and Date
REM \CHAP4\CH4_11.BAS

CLS
PRINT DATE$
PRINT TIME$
PRINT TIMER

END
```

Run this short piece and you'll see output similar in style, if not exactly like this:

```
12-12-1995
09:53:38
80879.1
```

Look at this statement:

TIME$ = stringexpression$

It allows you to use the variable **stringexpression$** to set the current system time on your computer. The possible formats of **stringexpression$** are:

hh	sets the hour (0 through 23); minutes and seconds default to 00.
Hh:mm	sets the hour and minutes (0 through 59 for minutes); seconds default to 00.
Hh:mm:ss	sets the hour, minutes and seconds (0 through 59 for seconds).

The System Timer

Take the following form of the **ON TIMER** statement:

ON TIMER (n%) GOSUB line

Here the **TIMER** function returns the number of seconds in the range 1 through 86,400 (24 hours), and control is passed to the event-trapping subroutine started with a specified label.

The system timer can be used to test a PC's internal performance. You can, for instance, compare the speeds of two PCs by using the timer to provide a comparison of how long an algorithm takes to complete. Let's test for internal performance when calculating **SIN (1)**:

```
REM Demonstration of the TIMER function
REM \CHAP4\CH4_12.BAS

CLS
TIMER ON            'Timer initial
t = TIMER           'Start time
FOR i% = 1 TO 1000
```

```
     a = SIN(1)              'Testing function
   NEXT i%
   t = TIMER - t             'Calculate time
   PRINT t / 1000; " sec"    'Print time

   END
```

The calculation **a = SIN(1)** is carried out 1000 times in a loop to enable us to work out the calculation time for one algorithm more accurately. The calculated time turns out to be slightly longer than it should because it includes the time taken to execute the **FOR...NEXT** loop. You can probably guess how to avoid this - separately find out how long it takes to calculate 1000 empty loops and subtract it from the resulting time we obtain in our example, which is obtained as the difference between the initial variable **TIME** and its value after the execution of the loop.

The **ON TIMER** statement just assigns a subroutine. In order to actually pass control to it, the event trapping subroutine must be enabled by the **TIMER ON** statement. The **TIMER OFF** statement disables timer event trapping and **TIMER STOP** suspends event trapping until the reactivation of **TIMER ON**.

Input/Output Ports

As you know, the PC addresses peripherals through the **input/output ports** - each external device is assigned one or more ports with a distinct address. The information (contents of a byte) from a port reflects the current status of the external device. The CPU of IBM-compatible computers can address up to 65,535 such ports. In QBasic, there are specific tools to work with them. In particular, the function **INP (port%)** returns a byte read from a hardware I/O port identified by the number **port%** between the range of 0 through 65,535. For example:

```
   x% = INP(&H3FC)
```

assigns the value of the control modem register COM1 to the variable **x%**.

By contrast, the **OUT** statement sends the byte **data%** (a numeric expression in the range 0 through 255) to the hardware I/O port. For instance, the program line

```
   OUT &H3FC, (x% XOR 1)
```

changes the readiness bit of terminal data.

Finally, the **WAIT** statement suspends program execution until a specified bit pattern is input from an input port. It has the following syntax:

WAIT portnumber%, AND-expression% [,XOR-expression%]

Here, **portnumber%** is the number of the input port, and **expression%** is an integer expression that **WAIT** combines with the bit pattern value using an **AND** operator. When the result is non-zero, **WAIT** stops monitoring the port. **XOR-expression%** can be used to turn line bits on and off in the bit pattern before the **AND** operation is applied. For example,

```
   WAIT &H20, 1
```

reads the port **&H20** of the interrupt vector. The following procedure provides a practical illustration of controlling ports:

```
REM Creating and Using the Sounds Procedure with Ports
REM \CHAP4\CH4_13.BAS

DECLARE SUB Sounds (Freq!, Length!)

CONST WHOLE = 5000!, QRTR = WHOLE / 4!
CONST C = 523!, D = 587.33, E = 659.26, F = 698.46
CONST G = 783.99, A = 880!, B = 987.77, C1 = 1046.5
CALL Sounds(C, QRTR): CALL Sounds(D, QRTR)
CALL Sounds(E, QRTR): CALL Sounds(F, QRTR)
CALL Sounds(G, QRTR): CALL Sounds(A, QRTR)
CALL Sounds(B, QRTR): CALL Sounds(C1, WHOLE)

SUB Sounds (Freq!, Length!) STATIC
  Clicks% = CINT(1193280! / Freq!)
  LoByte% = Clicks% AND &HFF
  HiByte% = Clicks% \ 256
  OUT 67, 182
  OUT 66, LoByte%
  OUT 66, HiByte%
  SpkrOn% = INP(97) OR &H3
  OUT 97, SpkrOn%
  FOR I! = 1 TO Length!: NEXT I!
  SpkrOff% = INP(97) AND &HFC
  OUT 97, SpkrOff%
END SUB
```

This program generates a **Sound** procedure which works exactly like the QBasic **SOUND** statement, but it does this by using the system program tools which deal with port control. So you see, having access to the ports allows you to interfere with the operation of any external devices (not necessarily a good thing!).

Working with Communication Devices

With the fantastic growth of the Internet, computer communications have become a very important area. To communicate between computers over long distances, specialized modems are applied. These are supported by QBasic. The **OPEN COM** statement opens and initializes a communications channel for input and output through a serial RS232 interface, and must be executed before a device can be used for communication using an RS232 interface:

```
OPEN "COMn: optlist1 optlist2" [FOR mode] AS [#]filenum% [LEN=reclen%]
```

n	The communications port to open (1 = COM1, 2 = COM2).

optlist1	The most-often-used communications parameters:
	[baud] [,[parity] [,[data] [,[stop]]]]
	baud is the baud rate of the device to be opened:
	      75, 110, 150, 300, 600, 1200, 2400, 4800, 9600
	parity is the method of parity checking:
	      N (none) **E** (even) **O** (odd)
	      S (space) **M** (mark) **PE** (enable error checking)
	data is the number of data bits per byte: **5, 6, 7, 8**
	stop is the number of stop bits: **1, 1.5, 2**
	Defaults: 300 baud, even parity, 7 data bits, 1 stop bit.

optlist2	A list of less-often-used parameters, separated by commas:
	ASC Opens the device in ASCII mode.
	BIN Opens the device in binary mode.
	CD[m] Sets the timeout period (in milliseconds) on the Data Carrier Detect (**DCD**) line.
	CS[m] Sets the timeout period (in milliseconds) on the Clear to Send (**CTS**) line.
	DS[m] Sets the timeout period (in milliseconds) on the Data Set Ready (**DS**) line.
	LF Sends a line-feed character after a carriage return.
	OP[m] Specifies how long (in milliseconds) **OPEN COM** waits for all communications lines to become open.
	RB[n] Sets the size (in bytes) of the receive buffer.
	RS Suppresses detection of Request to Send (**RTS**).
	[n] Sets the size (in bytes) of the transmit buffer.
mode	**INPUT**, **OUTPUT**, or **RANDOM** (the default).
filenum%	A number in the range 1 through 255 that identifies the communications channel as long as it is open.
reclen%	Random-access-mode buffer size (default is 128 bytes).

Here is an example for trouble-shooting serial communications problems - notice the slow baud, that hardware handshaking is ignored and buffers are enlarged:

```
REM Demonstration of OPEN COM
REM \CHAP4\CH4_14.BAS

OPEN "COM1:2400,N,8,1,CD0,CS0,DS0,OP0,RS,TB2048,RB2048" FOR RANDOM AS #1

END
```

The COM Statement

The **COM** statement enables, disables or suspends event trapping on a communications port:

```
COM(n%)   ON
COM(n%)   OFF
COM(n%)   STOP
```

If event trapping is enabled, **ON COM** branches to a subroutine whenever characters are received at the port:

```
ON  COM(n%)  GOSUB  line
```

where **n%** is the number of a **COM** port (1 or 2).

Although QBasic supports work with telecommunication devices, we cannot seriously recommend their servicing using the QBasic programs. The point is that every modem is supplied with its own software, and terminal emulation packages are relatively inexpensive. However, if you are developing QBasic software that might automatically poll other users to interrogate their database or download information via a modem, then it's probably worth pursuing.

Managing the Mouse

A mouse works by moving mechanical or optical sensors incorporated into the mouse. The signals of these sensors allow the computer to judge the movement of the mouse. The QBasic editing shell supports mouse operations and most users appreciate the convenience of the mouse while switching the items of a menu, editing a text or running programs.

However, as a programming language, QBasic has no built-in mouse control tools. Hence, to use the mouse, we have to cheat a bit and use an external program - the standard mouse driver. This driver must be loaded into memory to work with the mouse. As a rule, it's run and loaded when you boot up your PC, and from here on we shall assume that this driver is already loaded.

The interrupt **33H** gives access to all the features of mouse control, and by using it you can get access to tens of functions operating various coordinate devices, including the mouse. For example, you can initiate the cursor on the screen, make it move about the screen and respond to the pressing of a key. You can determine the current coordinates of the cursor and define carrying out necessary actions if the mouse cursor falls into a specific screen area - e.g. is set on a chosen menu item. The **Int 33H**, however, is not a part of the BIOS and becomes available only while a mouse driver is loaded. To use the indicated interrupt, a small machine code program is required to ensure bit-by-bit control of the CPU's registers, allow access to the functions of **Int 33H** and determine the position and status of the mouse pointer.

Normally, we would want to perform some action in QBasic to compare the cursor's location with the positions of other objects on the screen and select the actions needed by the algorithm. Unfortunately, programs implementing both the keyboard and the mouse control are rather cumbersome and we're not able to present the full text of such a program. Luckily, all is not lost since what we can do is to look at a demonstration program which can easily be tailored to solve any mouse control problem.

This program activates the mouse, creates a simple menu of three items at the center of the screen and allows you to exert control over the menu. You can easily plagiarize this program to create a menu of any number of items and at any position on the screen.

The Functions of Interrupt 33H

To invoke the mouse driver from your program, you should load a number of the functions into the **AX** register and, if necessary, fill other registers too, following which you can activate the **Int 33H**. Let us consider the driver's functions:

Function 0000h   Driver reset
This function performs both hardware and software reset. Besides, it is intended to determine if the driver is stored in memory: if mouse support is set, the value **FFFFh** is returned to the register **AX**. It is good practice to reset the driver on finishing mouse use.

Function 0001h   Show the mouse
On resetting, the mouse pointer is invisible. To output it onto the screen, you must place the code **0001h** in **AX** and invoke the driver.

Function 0002H   Hide the mouse
To hide the mouse, you must enter the **0002H** code into the **AX** register.

Function 0003h   Asking for coordinates and status of the buttons

On invocation, the driver places the current coordinates **X** and **Y** into the **CX** and **DX** registers, respectively. The **BX** registers contain the status of the mouse buttons; if the lowest bit is set then the left button is pressed, and the second bit is set while the right button is pressed. Along with two previous functions, this one is most frequently used.

Function 000Ch   Setting external event handler

Parameters of this function are the address of the handler stored in **ES:DX** and the event mask in **CX**. This mask defines the events which cause the response of the handler - setting the mask to **FFh** makes the driver invoke the event handler whatever the interrupt. After setting up the handler, your program assumes the features of a multitask system because the event handler is called independently of the main module. The handler is usually a rather complicated program but, in our next example, its task is to sustain, in specially reserved memory cells, plausible values of the buttons status, so its size is minimal. When invoking the event handler, the registers of the CPU are loaded in the following manner:

AX	identifier of an event occurred
BX	status word of mouse buttons
CX	current **X** coordinate
DX	current **Y** coordinate
SI	last horizontal offset (in mouse coordinates)
DI	last vertical offset

It is significant that, to have access to memory, you should reload the **DS** register, because its value isn't restored by the mouse driver, or place the variables in a code segment in the manner it's done in our example.

Definition Block of the Program

Let's finally consider our program to utilize the mouse, the full text of which can be found on the accompanying disk, under the name **\CHAP4\CH4_15.BAS**. First of all, we reserve an array, **a%**, to store the assembler insertion of machine code:

```
DIM SHARED a%(34)
```

Next is the following minimum set of external procedures necessary to work with the mouse:

Procedure	Description
SUB MouseInit ()	Initialize the mouse.
SUB MouseReset ()	Deinitialize the mouse.
SUB MouseHide ()	Hide the mouse pointer.
SUB MouseShow ()	Show the mouse pointer.
FUNCTION MouseX% ()	Return **X%** coordinate of the mouse.
FUNCTION MouseY% ()	Return **Y%** coordinate of the mouse.
FUNCTION MouseButtons% ()	Return the sign of a pressed button.
FUNCTION MouseChoice% ()	Determine the number of a menu item pointed by the mouse.
SUB DrawMenu (current%, selected%)	Creating the menu.

Initializing the Mouse in the Main Module

The following listing contains the part of the main module which initializes the menu on the screen:

```
'Initializing menu and mouse
SCREEN 9: CLS
CALL DrawMenu(1, 1)
CALL MouseInit
CALL MouseShow
curChoice% = 1
curSel% = 1
doRedraw% = 0
LOCATE 1, 1: PRINT "Press Esc to exit ..."
```

The operation of this part of the program is rather evident - the graphics mode is set and the menu is displayed in the center of the screen. The **MouseInit** procedure provides the initialization of the mouse driver (**MouseInit** must be called *after* the graphic mode is set for the correct settings of the internal variables) and then **MouseShow** makes the mouse cursor visible (in the form of an arrow) on the screen.

Active Work with the Mouse

The next fragment of the main module serves to provide an active operation of the mouse. For active work with the mouse, the cycle of the **DO. . .LOOP UNTIL** is defined in this block - you can exit from the cycle pressing the *Esc* key. If the key isn't pressed, all the intermediate steps are repeated at regular intervals whilst inserting the actions corresponding to the pressed or released left button of the mouse:

```
'Mouse and menu active work
DO
  IF (MouseChoice% <> 0) THEN
    IF (curChoice% <> MouseChoice%) THEN
       curChoice% = MouseChoice%
       doRedraw% = 1
    END IF
    IF (MouseButtons% = 1) AND (MouseChoice% <> curSel%) THEN
      curSel% = MouseChoice%
      doRedraw% = 1
    END IF

    IF (doRedraw% = 1) THEN
      CALL MouseHide
      CALL DrawMenu(curChoice%, curSel%)
      CALL MouseShow
      doRedraw% = 0
    END IF
  END IF

  LOCATE 7, 35:  PRINT "Operation 1"
  LOCATE 9, 35:  PRINT "Operation 2"
  LOCATE 11, 35: PRINT "Operation 3"

  'Select menu operations
  IF MouseButtons% = 0 THEN
    LOCATE 14, 30
    SELECT CASE curSel%
      CASE 1: PRINT "This is Operation One"
      CASE 2: PRINT "This is Operation Two"
```

```
        CASE 3: PRINT "This is Operation Three"
    END SELECT
    END IF

LOOP UNTIL INKEY$ = CHR$(27)
CALL MouseReset   'Reset mouse
SCREEN 0
```

This program block is reasonably simple and easy to understand. Although pointing to the menu positions and changing the colors illustrates the technique of mouse control, by itself is of little use. In order to produce a practical application from the program, you should make it carry out these or other actions whilst pointing to a specified menu item. To accomplish this, the concluding block-switch can be appended to, so that actual functions or procedures can be executed. Depending on the parameter **curSel%**, one of the operations is performed while releasing the left mouse button (**MouseButton% = 0**) - displaying one inscription or another under the menu. This directly points to the possibility of carrying out operations whilst switching the active positions of the menu.

Building the Menu

This procedure, **DrawMenu**, which recreates the menu on the screen, like all the other procedures and functions in this program is implemented using just QBasic programming means, and not machine code or external programs. The parameters of the procedure are the variables:

selected%   indicates the selected menu item.
current%   indicates the menu item where the mouse pointer is currently set.

Depending on the values of these variables (ranging from 1 to 3), a rectangle is constructed in gray, with a tracing line if the mouse cursor is not over the menu item, and green line if it is over the item. Naturally, the painted rectangle changes from gray to green when the mouse button is pressed.

The Function of the Mouse Cursor Position Control

It is necessary to know exactly where the mouse cursor is while it moves. If the cursor is not over the menu, the movement of the mouse and pressing its buttons must not cause any actions. But if the cursor hovers over the menu area, we need to relay some sort of recognition of this. The **MouseChoice%** function serves to reveal that very indication:

```
FUNCTION MouseChoice%
  MX% = MouseX%: MY% = MouseY%
  IF (MX% < 220) OR (MY% < 76) OR (MX% >= 420) OR (MY% >= 166) THEN
    MouseChoice% = 0
  ELSEIF (MY% < 106) THEN
    MouseChoice% = 1
  ELSEIF (MY% > 136) THEN
    MouseChoice% = 3
  ELSE
    MouseChoice% = 2
  END IF
END FUNCTION
```

This function returns zero if the mouse cursor isn't over the menu, and 1, 2 or 3 if the cursor is over the first, second or third menu position, respectively.

Showing the Mouse Pointer

To retrieve the current coordinates of the mouse pointer, we use the following two commands:

```
FUNCTION MouseX%
   MouseX% = a%(0)
END FUNCTION

FUNCTION MouseY%
   MouseY% = a%(1)
END FUNCTION
```

The coordinates **MouseX%** and **MouseY%** have integer values within the limits defined by the selected operating mode (**SCREEN 9** in our case). These coordinates are used in the main program to define the mouse control logic. If you work in a text mode, you should divide the corresponding values by 8.

Illustration of Mouse Control

On starting the program, you will see a menu consisting of three menu items at the center of the screen. The position 2 (center) is active, and in the top left hand corner you can see an inscription which reports the action of the *Esc* key. At the bottom, the result of a performed operation is displayed. In this case, it is just a confirmation message:

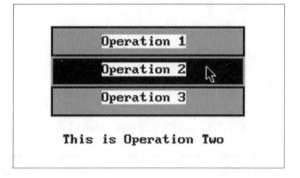

If you place the mouse pointer to the third position of the menu, the color of the tracing line will first be changed to green. This will happen as soon the pointer is placed over that menu item. After pressing and releasing the left mouse button, this menu position will be painted green and a new message will appear under the menu confirming our selection of the third operation.

Of course, instead of outputting those messages, you can define any other operations, including calling subroutines or external procedures. You can also change the size, the location, the colors and the whole structure of the menu, whilst maintaining control with the mouse. So, the presented example is not just a demo program, because by using it you can create mouse driven QBasic programs.

> *Check out the following program for a different use of the mouse in QBasic :*
> **\GAMES\MOLES\MOLE.BAS**

Shelling Out

Of course, if you want to program or access peripherals that aren't supported through standard QBasic means and you don't want to take time out to learn the intricacies of machine code, you can always shell out and run an executable file from there. This is, of course, a negative method of programming in QBasic and, if you intend to make progress in the language, then such methods shouldn't be relied upon. This said, there are many situations where the method of 'shelling out' is probably the best solution, and we shall examine these now.

CD-ROM Control

One common peripheral nowadays is the CD-ROM drive. If we had the time, we could develop a machine code program to read details from the CD drive, but let's say for now that we don't. The following program gives instructions for working with the Gold Star CD-player; by invoking the audio playing program **GSAUDIO.EXE**, turning the CD-player operation into background mode, provides 10 seconds of sound and, calling another program (**EJECT.EXE**), ejects the CD from the drive:

```
REM Demonstration of CD control
REM \CHAP\CH4_16.BAS

CLS
PRINT "Insert compact disk, press any key,"
PRINT "run CD-Player and press Power (off)"
F$ = INPUT$(1)
SHELL "C:\CDROM\gsaudio.exe"
PRINT "10 Seconds Play!"
SLEEP 10
SHELL "C:\CDROM\eject.exe"
CLS
PRINT "END"

END
```

Upon execution, you'll see the message:

> Insert compact disk, press any key,
> run CD-Player and press Power (off)

Having inserted the CD into the slot, it is sufficient to press any key and the CD-player interface created by the GSAudio program will appear on the screen. After turning off this program (using the Power key), it switches to a background playing mode, and the QBasic program resumes its operation forming a 10 seconds pause (of course, more useful functions can be specified).

This method of executing non-QBasic programs allows the QBasic programmer to quickly solve a difficult problem without having to resort to complex and considerable programming methods. You could, for example, run a speech program to produce speech from QBasic, or indeed create a menu system based in QBasic from where you can run several different executables - even a competitor to Windows perhaps!

Summary

On the basis of what we discussed at the start of this chapter, it's possible to say that, when we consider its inherent data types, QBasic hasn't progressed very far since older versions of BASIC. The only real addition is records as complex data types. The number of functions which operate with the data types is limited; for example, there are no matrix operations included in a number of BASIC versions. However, the tools that are available have been carefully chosen to make up a minimum 'gentleman's' set of tools which allow the implementation of crucially new data structures, such as stacks, queues, lists and trees, etc. without making the language excessively large. You can look forward to these because they form the bulk of the next chapter.

We have also opened up one of the most important features of the experienced programmers repertoire - access to assembly language programs. Once the forbidden domain of only the closet hacker and industry's finest programmers, machine code is now accessible to everyone. This vast topic, represented by many, many heavy volumes of stand-alone books and courses, allows you to delve into the inner workings of your computer and learn the oldest of computer languages.

Manipulating Data Structures

Introduction

In this chapter, we'll be taking the covers off some of the most popular data structures and taking a look at their interacting elements. We'll look at the typical set of operations associated with each of them and also show you how they're used. We'll discuss stacks, queues, and lists and explore the combinations of procedures that are relevant to each of these. We'll also demonstrate how you can apply these structures to solve a variety of problems.

Stacks

The stack is one of computing's most important and useful structures. A data structure is referred to as a stack if it accumulates elements and if the elements can only be retrieved in the reverse order to which they were added. This condition is often referred to as the 'Last In - First Out' (LIFO) principle. There are many real-life examples of practical stacks, such as 'The Towers of Hanoi', but here we'll take a look at a nice simple example:

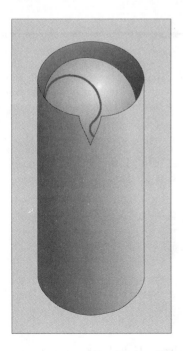

If you peep into the tube, you either see no balls at all or only the top one. You can't see whether there are any more balls underneath, and if there are then you have no way of telling how many there are or what color they are.

When you place a new element in the stack, you've **pushed** it on to the top. When you remove an element off the top, then you've **popped** it off. The only element that can be taken out, i.e. the uppermost one (the top ball), is the **top** of the stack. The stack is **bound** if the number of its elements can't exceed a certain value, e.g. 10, and this value is the stack's **depth**.

Implementing a Stack in QBasic

Before we write a program that involves a stack, we must first decide which of the QBasic tools will be used in the implementation. Because we can quite easily manipulate the elements with an array, this is perhaps the best choice for us to make. However, by using an array, we can only have a bound stack, since the dimensions of the array will limit the depth of the stack.

As an illustration of a stack, let's consider the problem of arranging parentheses. In all programs it's necessary to know whether the construction of an arbitrary math expression is correct. It's particularly important to know whether the parentheses of an expression are properly arranged.

For instance, in the expression,

$2 + (4 - x) * (3 * (y + x) - (2 + z) + 6)$

the sequence of parentheses for this expression is correct:

( ) (( ) ( ))

But take this expression:

$(2 + x) * (((x - y) * (z + 6) - 8) * 5$

Here, the sequence of parentheses is incorrect:

( ) ((( ) ( ))

In a more comprehensive mathematical context, an arithmetic expression may also contain square brackets [ ] and braces { }, making the sequence more complicated.

Suppose that we need an algorithm which determines the validity of a math expression according to the number of parentheses, square brackets and braces. To determine whether the brackets in an expression **Expression$** are correctly arranged, we can analyze the sequence of brackets by removing the rest of the characters.

You can set up a stack to keep track of whether the arrangement of brackets is correct - the length of the expression string will dictate the depth of the stack. Open the **\CHAP5\CH5_1.BAS** file to demonstrate this technique. As soon as an opening bracket is detected, its value (**x**) is pushed onto the stack using the procedure **InStack(x):**

```
SUB InStack (S() AS STRING, x$)
  IF Top = DeepStack THEN
    PRINT "Error: Stack is full!"
    STOP
  ELSE
    Top = Top + 1
    S(Top) = x$
  END IF
END SUB
```

When a closing bracket is detected, the contents of the stack are analyzed. If the stack is empty, determined by the value of the function **EmptyStack** (**True** or **False**), it follows that the opening bracket is absent and, therefore, the expression is incorrect. If the stack isn't empty, we pop an element from the stack, using the function **OutStack,** and check that it corresponds with the closing bracket. If there's a correspondence between the parentheses, the process continues.

It's clear, that where you require a bracket and it's absent, you can take the expression to be invalid. Therefore, for the expression to be valid, the stack must be empty when the program finishes.

You can see here how the stack changes when processing the a+([5-1]*{(4-a)*[(b+6)*c]-6}+d) expression:

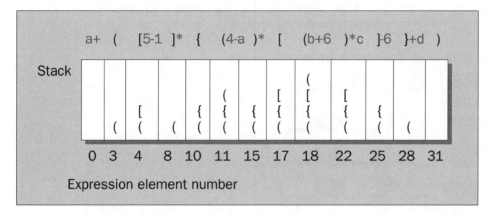

Okay, so we've covered some elementary uses for the stack. We'll consider several more examples of stacks in action later in this chapter, but right now it's time to look at another data structure: the queue.

Queues

Queues are among the simplest and most typical data structures and they're best applied when programming real processes and situations; for example, people queuing in a shop, cars at traffic lights, or a service machine that fills orders in sequence. If the system is free, i.e. there's no queue, then it can immediately start on any order as soon as it is given. If, however, it's already filling a particular order, the new one must join the end of the queue. Every time the service system finishes processing a current order, it moves to the order at the beginning of the queue. If orders arrive irregularly, the queue is sometimes longer or shorter and may occasionally disappear when all the available orders are filled and new ones haven't yet arrived.

In a queue, elements are retrieved from one end, the **front**, and added to the other, the **rear**. A linear array is normally used to simulate a queue; for example, **Queue(MaxLength)** and two integer variables **Front** and **Rear** which correspondingly point to the first and last elements of the queue.

Operating a Queue

Unlike real-life queues which shuffle forward as those at the front are dealt with, the elements in the computer queue occupy random access memory and have an address. The front and rear of the queue are pointers to the addresses of the first and last members of the queue, and these pointers move as items are dealt with. Changing addresses is much more efficient in the use of computer time, rather than shuffling all the queue contents along one element. In thinking about queues, instead of a line of customers at a cash-desk, it's better to think of a list, or queue of jobs to be done by a motorbike courier.

Take this example which shows how the queue operates:

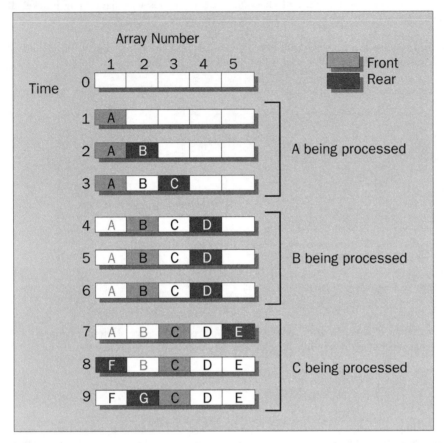

In this example, the maximum length of the queue (we shall call it **MaxLength**) equals 5, and the elements are labeled with the letters A through G. Let's suppose that a customer who is standing at the front of the queue is served in 3 units of time after which they leave the queue.

At the point when Time (we shall call it **T**) is equal to 0, the queue is empty, and hence the **front** and **rear** of the queue are 1 and 0 respectively. At the point when **T = 1** customer A arrives, waits for 3 units of time and leaves the queue when **T = 4**. Customers B, C, D, E, F and G arrive at times 2, 3, 4, 7, 8 and 9, respectively.

When customer F arrives at **T = 8**, the rear of the queue is at position 5 of the array - we have reached the end of the queue. However, because some earlier elements may have been removed, we will return to the start of the queue and look for the first free slot, which is position 1. We will, therefore, assign the **rear** to be 1. When customer G arrives at **T = 9**, the value 2 is assigned to **rear**, and at that instant the queue is entirely full. No more customers can join the queue until C leaves it.

Programming a Queue

The technique of returning to the front of a queue essentially forms an array rolled up in a loop, referred to as a **ring buffer**. The program **\CHAP5\CH5_2.BAS** demonstrates working with a queue consisting of a combined data type, **Record**, that defines and stores the names and dates of birth of contacts. This data is progressively added to the queue, simulating unpredictable (asynchronous) data arrival, and 'processed'. It's only removed from the array when new data arrives, and overwrites the previous entry. Let's take a look at how this program actually works.

The program creates a bound ring queue from the array **Queue(MaxLength)**, where we have defined the maximum size of the queue with the variable **Maxlength**. Basically, the main procedure runs through a sequence of reading data and making calls to the subroutines **InQueue(z)** and **OutQueue(z)**, in order to add and remove elements from the array.

The **InQueue(z)** subroutine first checks whether the queue is full. If it tried to add another element to the queue and the queue was full it would generate an error message but if everything is okay, it proceeds to add another element. It does this by assigning the next free array space to the variable **rear**, and then assigning the relevant data into the array. The length of the queue is also incremented:

```
SUB InQueue (Z AS Record)
'*** Adding an Element to the Queue ***
  IF LengthQueue = MaxLength THEN
    PRINT "Error: Queue is full!"
      STOP
  ELSE
    Rear = NextFR(Rear)
    Queue(Rear).X = Z.X
    Queue(Rear).Y = Z.Y
    LengthQueue = LengthQueue + 1
  END IF
END SUB
```

Removing an element from the queue is very similar, except that, afterwards, we also check whether the length of the queue is zero. If it isn't equal to zero, the front of the queue is equal to the front element of the **NextFR** array, and if it is empty, we make **front** equal to 1 and the **rear** to zero:

```
SUB OutQueue (Z AS Record)
'*** Removing an Element from the Queue ***
IF LengthQueue = 0 THEN
    PRINT : PRINT "Error: Queue is empty!"
  STOP
  ELSE
    Z.X = Queue(Front).X
    Z.Y = Queue(Front).Y
    LengthQueue = LengthQueue - 1
    IF LengthQueue <> 0 THEN
      Front = NextFR(Front)
    ELSE
      Front = 1: Rear = 0
    END IF
  END IF
END SUB
```

In the last two sections, we've defined the two major data structures - stacks and queues - and you've seen something of how they operate and how you can use them. They're also extremely useful when you want to 'find the solution' to a problem by eliminating all the other options. We will see how this works in the next section.

Exhaustive Searching

Stacks, queues and the problems associated with searching are a major feature of most artificial intelligence problems, irrespective of where it's applied, whether it be programming games, making decisions or recognizing images. In this section, we'll show you how to write several of the most useful search methods, some of which you may know by different names.

Having defined 'graphs', we start with the **backtrack method** (also known as the **depth first** search), which allows us to organize an exhaustive search for all the solutions of a problem without examining every possible version. The best way of illustrating this method is by example, so we'll use a couple of problems involving a labyrinth. We'll search for all the rooms of the labyrinth and then for a route between two rooms.

We'll introduce the **breadth first** search which is useful for finding the shortest route between two points and makes use of a queue instead of a stack.

These ideas are then put to use in some examples.

Graphs and Labyrinths

A graph is typically represented as a multitude of points connected by lines:

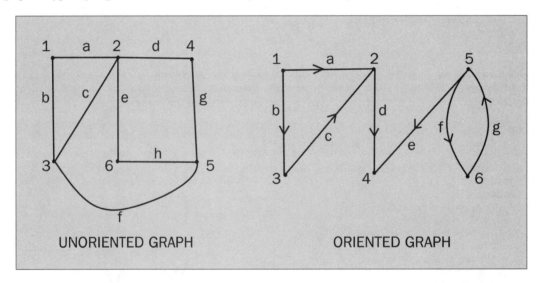

UNORIENTED GRAPH   ORIENTED GRAPH

The points are referred to as **nodes**, or **vertices**, and the lines which connect them are the **edges** of that graph. If the edges of a graph are labeled with arrows, those edges are denoted as **oriented**, or arcs. Passing between two connected points is only possible in the direction of the arrow. A graph with oriented edges is commonly referred to as an **oriented graph**.

If two nodes of a graph are linked by a line, those nodes are defined as **adjacent**, with the connecting line termed **incidental** to those nodes. The series of nodes including and between two separate nodes is known as a **path** (and who said math was difficult!). Finally, if the last node is connected to the first node, the graph is **cyclic**, i.e. you can travel between nodes in one direction for ever.

The best way to represent a graph is by the 'adjacency' matrix, defined as an array **b(n,n)** of dimension n x n. If there's an edge between nodes i and j, then **b(i,j) = 1**, and **b(i,j) = 0** if otherwise. Here, we can assume that the edge of an unoriented graph goes both from node i to node j, and from node j to node i, reflected in the adjacency matrices for those last two graphs:

	1	2	3	4	5	6			1	2	3	4	5	6
1	0	1	1	0	0	0		1	0	1	1	0	0	0
2	1	0	1	1	0	1		2	0	0	0	1	0	0
3	1	1	0	0	1	0		3	0	1	0	0	0	0
4	0	1	0	0	1	0		4	0	0	0	0	0	0
5	0	0	1	1	0	1		5	0	0	0	1	0	1
6	0	1	0	0	1	0		6	0	0	0	0	1	0

The adjacency matrix allows you to answer the question "Is there an edge from x to y?" in just one step.

There are two concepts which are commonly encountered with search algorithms, and which we need to review here: the **step** number and the **version** number. The step number of the current, or base node, gives its position in the searching order. The version number determines where the program checks for a new node.

Depth Searching

There are a lot of graph algorithms which are based on a systematic search for the graph's nodes, with the premise that each node is looked through only once. Using an unoriented graph, we'll cover a technique that's become one of the general methods in the development of graph algorithms. This method is called the **depth search**.

Going Round a Labyrinth

Theseus, a hero in ancient Greek mythology, set off to Crete to kill the Minotaur living in a labyrinth under the King's palace. The King's daughter, Ariadne, gave Theseus a ball of string to help him find his way around and out of the maze. With a leap of the imagination we can find a parallel with this myth in the computer world: the deeds of Theseus are repeated by computers, programs lead the computers in and out of the labyrinth of data to solve the problems which are the modern day equivalent of the Minotaur.

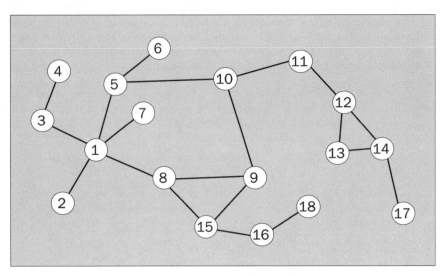

A less exotic example of a labyrinth is a logical graph (we won't go as far as to describe its nodes as ancient rooms and its edges as corridors) but it could represent any number of real-life situations - the layout of rooms in a building, the plan of a subway, relationships in a family, or a highway map, etc.

Essentially, the classic labyrinth problems are:

▲   Defining a path that links all the rooms of the labyrinth.

▲   Defining a path that links just two specified rooms.

Defining an All-linking Path

We'll set off on the first problem, using the backtracking algorithm to search for the desired path. The main role of backtracking is as follows:

▲   We go from a specified node V as far as possible along the edges of the graph, at each node choosing an edge which leads to a node that hasn't yet been passed. If we encounter a node from which there's no exit, we return to the last node with an edge that leads to a node we haven't yet met.

In this manner, we'll be able to visit all the nodes available from node V, and since the labyrinth is a connected graph, the first problem can be solved this way.

> *A connected graph is a graph where every node can travel a path to reach any other node, whilst a disconnected graph features some nodes that are unable to reach others.*

If you want to search for all the nodes of a disconnected graph, it's necessary to choose a new node that doesn't belong to the set of those already found and repeat the search on that connected component of the graph.

The program **\CHAP5\CH5_3.BAS** implements the **depth search** method for the aforementioned 18-node labyrinth, whose adjacency matrix is:

```
DataMatrix:
'V = 1  2  3  4  5  6  7  8  9 10 11 12 13 14 15 16 17 18
DATA 0, 1, 1, 0, 1, 0, 1, 1, 0, 0, 0, 0, 0, 0, 0, 0, 0, 0
DATA 1, 0, 0, 0, 0, 0, 0, 0, 0, 0, 0, 0, 0, 0, 0, 0, 0, 0
```

```
DATA 1, 0, 0, 1, 0, 0, 0, 0, 0, 0, 0, 0, 0, 0, 0, 0, 0, 0
DATA 0, 0, 1, 0, 0, 0, 0, 0, 0, 0, 0, 0, 0, 0, 0, 0, 0, 0
DATA 1, 0, 0, 0, 0, 1, 0, 0, 0, 1, 0, 0, 0, 0, 0, 0, 0, 0
DATA 0, 0, 0, 0, 1, 0, 0, 0, 0, 0, 0, 0, 0, 0, 0, 0, 0, 0
DATA 1, 0, 0, 0, 0, 0, 0, 0, 0, 0, 0, 0, 0, 0, 0, 0, 0, 0
DATA 1, 0, 0, 0, 0, 0, 0, 0, 1, 0, 0, 0, 0, 0, 1, 0, 0, 0
DATA 0, 0, 0, 0, 0, 0, 0, 1, 0, 1, 0, 0, 0, 0, 1, 0, 0, 0
DATA 0, 0, 0, 0, 1, 0, 0, 0, 1, 0, 1, 0, 0, 0, 0, 0, 0, 0
DATA 0, 0, 0, 0, 0, 0, 0, 0, 0, 1, 0, 1, 0, 0, 0, 0, 0, 0
DATA 0, 0, 0, 0, 0, 0, 0, 0, 0, 0, 1, 0, 1, 1, 0, 0, 0, 0
DATA 0, 0, 0, 0, 0, 0, 0, 0, 0, 0, 0, 1, 0, 1, 0, 0, 0, 0
DATA 0, 0, 0, 0, 0, 0, 0, 0, 0, 0, 0, 1, 1, 0, 0, 0, 1, 0
DATA 0, 0, 0, 0, 0, 0, 0, 1, 1, 0, 0, 0, 0, 0, 0, 1, 0, 0
DATA 0, 0, 0, 0, 0, 0, 0, 0, 0, 0, 0, 0, 0, 0, 1, 0, 0, 1
DATA 0, 0, 0, 0, 0, 0, 0, 0, 0, 0, 0, 0, 0, 1, 0, 0, 0, 0
DATA 0, 0, 0, 0, 0, 0, 0, 0, 0, 0, 0, 0, 0, 0, 1, 0, 0
```

Assuming that you are looking at the program, let's go through the salient points of the depth search as it's implemented.

At a current node, the subroutine **Version()** is called. This increments the current value of the version (stored as the **Y** coordinate in the data-type **Coord**), and checks whether there's an edge joining the current node and the **Y**th node, making use of the adjacency matrix. If there's a connecting edge, the value of **Flag** is set **True** and the program steps forward using the subroutine of that name. This pushes the value of the newly found node onto the stack, through a call to **InStack**. It's only removed from the stack after all the adjacent nodes have been looked through and the program has stepped back. As soon as a new node has been found, its number is displayed on the screen.

Also, in the initialization of the program, the eighteen nodes of the labyrinth are represented in an array **Vertex()**, each entry having the value **True**. Once the **J**th node has been visited, **Vertex(J)** is set **False** by **InStack()**, so that it won't be counted again if the search rolls back. It also stops over-counting when rooms of the labyrinth are connected in 'loops' (for example, 12, 13 and 14) and where there are multiple paths to a room.

The following diagram shows the graph with the nodes numbered according to the order of their depth search:

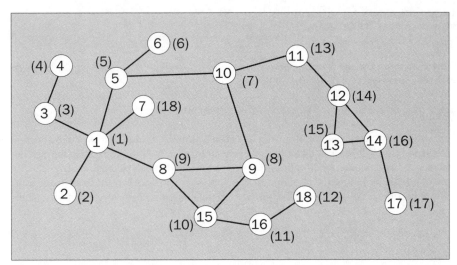

Here, the figures in brackets signify the order in which the nodes were found in the search. We started at node 1, but you can change the start of the path by changing the number 1 in the following line:

```
xy.x = 1 'Initialize the first step
```

Graph-related problems can often be solved with the depth search program. We'll now show you how you can use it to find the path through the labyrinth.

The Path in the Labyrinth

Suppose that we need to search for the path which connects two specified rooms in the labyrinth. To do this, we need to make a few alterations to our original depth search program.

First, we replace the first few lines of the depth search routine with the following lines, so that the user can define the start and end nodes:

```
CLS : PRINT "Search for a path in a labyrinth"
INPUT "Enter the number of the start node (1 - 18) = "; NumberBegin
INPUT "Enter the number of the end node (1 - 18) = "; NumberEnd

' *** Depth Search ***
xy.x = NumberEnd                         'initializing the first step
Vertex(xy.x) = False : xy.y = 0          'initializing the version
PRINT "List of the nodes detected:"
PRINT xy.x;
Finish = False
DO WHILE Finish = False AND NumberBegin <> xy.x
```

Notice how we assign the specified end node as the initial node in the first step of the algorithm; because of the way we accumulate the stack we have to do this. As the algorithm progresses, each key element of the path is added to the stack, so that when we've finished and found our path, we have to display the path to the screen. We do this by removing each element from the stack and printing them with the statement **PRINT xy.x**:

```
' *** Result ***
PRINT "Path from node"; NumberBegin; "to node"; NumberEnd; ":"
PRINT NumberBegin;
DO WHILE NOT EmptyStack
CALL OutStack(xy) : PRINT xy.x;
LOOP
```

If we started the first step with the **NumberBegin** variable, the path to be output would be in the form **NumberEnd** to **NumberBegin**, and not the other way round.

All these changes can be found in the **\CHAP5\CH5_4.BAS** program.

You'll notice that the paths calculated by the program aren't optimized, although a certain degree of path optimization is carried out. All the calculated paths are simple; that is, they don't pass through any room twice. Also, the result of searching for a path between two rooms depends a great deal on the room in which you start: the path from room 4 to room 16 consists of 5 corridors but the path from room 16 to room 4 contains 8 corridors. All the same, the program is still able to solve most of the problems it was designed for.

In order to optimize the path, we could use a variant of the depth first search: the **branch and bound** method. This is a simple version of the 'Traveling Salesman Problem'. In order to find the best path for minimum travel time between a connected set of nodes, one route (having depth, i.e. taking time x), is compared with another; the shorter route wins, and is used in the next comparison. By stopping the search whenever the depth of a branch exceeds the currently winning route, the search is made more efficient.

Breadth First Search in a Graph

Now let's consider a somewhat different searching method known as the **breadth first** search. It's important to note that in a **depth** search, the later a node is visited, the sooner it is used (the LIFO system). This is because the nodes previously visited but unused are accumulated in a stack. In the **breadth first** search, the stack is replaced with a queue, which means that the earlier a node is visited (placed in the queue), the earlier it is used (the FIFO system).

As in the previous section, we'll search for all the rooms in a labyrinth. This time, we'll use the breadth first search method. The program **\CHAP5\CH5_5.BAS** will print the order in which the eighteen rooms are found. Essentially, this program combines the ideas of node searching (that is the procedures **Version()**, **StepForward()** and **StepBack()**) seen in **CHAP_5\CH5_3.BAS** with the queue implementation (**InQueue()**, **OutQueue()** and **NextFR()**) of **CHAP_5\CH5_2.BAS.**

After initializing the labyrinth and setting the first room, **Version()** checks through the eighteen labyrinth nodes for a new node connected to the current node. It uses the adjacency matrix for this. If a corridor is found, and the room hasn't been previously visited, the program 'steps forward' and puts the new node at the rear of the queue. The next free position in the queue is calculated by **NextFR()**.

The program continues to check for connections from the node at the front of the queue, and doesn't necessarily consider the new node immediately. In our labyrinth example, starting with room 1 which is placed at the front of the queue, the program finds rooms 2, 3, 5, 7 and 8, and puts them on the end of the queue in that order. Once all possible connections from room 1 have been checked, it's removed from the queue, and the program checks room 2, and, finding no connections, moves on to room 3. Room 4 is found and put behind room 8 in the queue. And so the search progresses....

The breadth first search works rather like a wave rippling out from the first room, with increasing distance between the first and newly found nodes at each step. Therefore, the shortest route between two nodes will be the first ripple to reach the target node. Our path finding program **\CHAP5\CH5_4.BAS** can now be optimized by using queues instead of stacks.

The Search for the Shortest Path in the Labyrinth

The main difference between this program and the breadth first search is that the nodes form an entry to the array **Preceding()** as they are found:

```
DIM Preceding(MaxV) AS INTEGER     'Array of the preceding rooms
```

Finding the Jth node causes the program to enter the node from which connection was found as the Jth element in the array. So, in the following example, the third element of the array has the entry 4: room 4 *points* to room 3. Room 4, because it's where the search starts, has an entry -1:

```
xy.x = NumberBegin                    'Initializing the first step
Preceding(xy.x) = -1
```

When the search is complete, for every node examined the array **Preceding()** contains a pointer that points backwards one step in the search. The structure of the labyrinth can, therefore, be reconstructed.

Try it out with program **\CHAP5\CH5_6.BAS** on the disk. An example of the program execution for start node 4 and end node 16 is shown here:

i	1	2	3	4	5	6	7	8	9	10	11	12	13	14	15	16	17	18
Preceding (i)	3	1	4	-1	1	5	1	1	8	5	10	0	0	0	8	15	0	0

Notice how the nodes that aren't found in linking the specified start and end nodes have no preceding node, and still have their initial value zero. **OnScreen** outputs the results of the search.

The graph of the labyrinth may be marked with the direction of the pointers in the array, to make the results of the program easier to interpret. We have done this for you in the figure below:

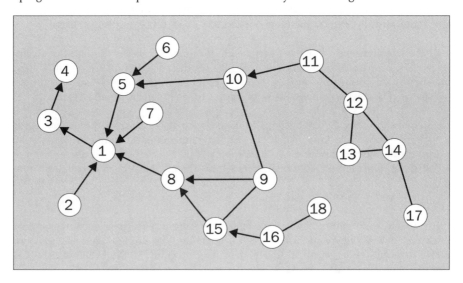

As we promised, we'll now illustrate the applications of these last few sections with some examples. Then we'll learn one more class of data structures: lists. We'll use these for the representation of graphs in memory.

Exciting Examples

We've seen how to move between nodes of a graph, or rooms of a labyrinth. In order to do this, a plan of the labyrinth corridors (stored in the adjacency matrix) is required. In the following examples, an ocean dotted with islands, and a chessboard overpopulated with aggressive queens, the moves allowed between squares (which are just the nodes of a larger graph) are predetermined by the 'version', i.e. the allowed moves from one square to another. On the island these are the compass points North, South, East and West, and on the chess board the accepted moves for a queen.

Here we're applying the same methods in more practical situations. By playing with these example programs you'll get a better feel for the theory of the previous sections.

Oceans and Islands

Our map is an expanse of ocean with several islands, and we want to find the island with the largest area. To begin with, we choose a data structure that can be processed by computer as a model to represent the map: a two-dimensional array seems more than suitable. Therefore, the map is divided into a matrix of small squares, **Map(16,18)**, where each location is numbered according to whether it belongs to the sea (**Map(x,y)**= 0), or to an island (**Map(x,y)**=-1):

	1	2	3	4	5	6	7	8	9	10	11	12	13	14	15	16	17	18
1	0	0	0	0	0	0	-1	0	0	0	0	0	0	0	0	0	0	0
2	0	0	0	-1	0	0	-1	-1	0	0	0	0	0	0	0	0	0	0
3	0	0	0	-1	-1	-1	-1	-1	0	0	0	0	0	0	0	0	0	0
4	0	0	0	0	0	-1	-1	-1	0	0	0	0	0	0	0	0	0	0
5	0	0	0	0	0	0	-1	-1	-1	0	0	-1	-1	-1	0	0	0	0
6	0	0	0	0	0	-1	-1	-1	-1	0	0	0	0	-1	-1	0	0	0
7	0	0	0	0	0	0	-1	-1	-1	0	0	0	0	-1	-1	-1	0	0
8	0	0	0	0	0	0	-1	-1	-1	0	0	0	0	-1	-1	-1	0	0
9	0	0	0	0	0	0	0	0	0	0	0	0	0	0	-1	-1	0	0
10	0	0	0	0	0	0	0	0	0	0	0	0	0	0	-1	-1	0	0
11	0	0	-1	-1	-1	-1	0	0	0	0	0	0	0	0	-1	-1	0	0
12	0	0	-1	-1	-1	-1	0	0	0	0	0	-1	-1	-1	-1	-1	0	0
13	0	0	0	0	-1	-1	0	0	0	0	0	-1	-1	-1	-1	0	0	0
14	0	0	0	0	0	0	0	0	0	0	-1	-1	-1	0	0	0	0	0
15	0	0	0	0	0	0	0	0	0	0	0	0	0	0	0	0	0	0
16	0	0	0	0	0	0	0	0	0	0	0	0	0	0	0	0	0	0

We could have chosen **+1** for an island, but in BASIC **-1** is a standard logic value for True, i.e. **PRINT 2*2=4** displays **-1**.

In the program that we'll be using, we'll define this map from **DATA** statements. However, if we wanted to, we could define the map from an image created on the screen. You would do this by looking through each line of the image, pixel by pixel, and, depending on the color of the current pixel, write **0** or **-1** into the appropriate element of the array.

Finding the Largest Island

You can answer a variety of questions using a geographic map like ours, including our search for the island with the largest area. In this case, we must define the concept of 'island' in our matrix model. We'll take an island to be the set of **m** squares which satisfies the following condition:

▲   For any two squares **a** and **b** from **m**, there's a sequence of squares **a => x1,x2,...xk => b**, where any two consecutive squares, **x1** and **x(i+1)** [i=1,2,...,k-1], in this sequence have at least one common side.

To put it another way, if we've agreed to consider *neighboring* squares as only those which have a common side (and not diagonals), then those squares which can be reached from a certain point by stepping no farther than to an adjacent square form an island. To make things simple, we'll set the area of the island to be equal to the number of constituent squares.

147

The problem of searching for the largest island is easy to solve if we have an algorithm which calculates the island's area using the coordinates **(x,y)** of an arbitrary square on the island. We can arrange this algorithm in the form of an external function **Area(x,y)**. We'll use a **Coord** type stack to store the coordinates of the squares:

```
TYPE Coord
    x AS INTEGER
    y AS INTEGER
END TYPE
```

The number of the current, or base square, **(x,y)** gives the step number if the squares of an island are numbered according to the order in which they are searched. The version number is the neighbor square being checked, defined by procedure **Version(x,y,k)**.

We'll conduct the search by considering squares which neighbor the current square **(x,y)** in turn, according to a searching order defined something like this:

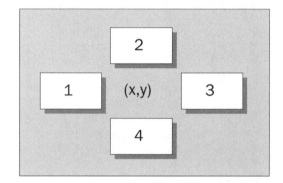

If the next square to be checked belongs to the island and hasn't previously been viewed (i.e. the entry to the array is still **Map(u,v)=-1**), then:

▲ We increment the number of the squares **s** which belong to the island.

▲ Set **Map(u,v)=1** so that the square isn't recounted in **s** if it's revisited.

▲ Push the coordinates **(u,v)** onto the stack.

Once we've examined all the neighbors of the current square, we'll pop the coordinates of the square at the top of the stack (the last to be found by the version). This is then the current square, and we take a look at its neighbors. If we hit a dead end, i.e. there are no adjoining squares with **Map(u,v)=-1**, the program returns (backtracks or rolls back) to the coordinate on the stack which it didn't have time to investigate earlier. These actions are repeated until the stack is empty. Thus, if all the neighboring squares of the current square are found to be part of the island, all four will be pushed onto the stack, and, one by one, *last first,* they'll be searched. Any new island squares from these are also pushed onto the stack. The value of the variable **s** will be the number of squares of the island that have been searched.

This to-ing and fro-ing between squares is a special feature of the backtracking search which doesn't fit in a ready loop structure common to most programming languages.

If, for example, the calculation of the area of the island on the map begins with processing the square **(7,1)**, **Stack** moves through a sequence of states, of which we show you the start:

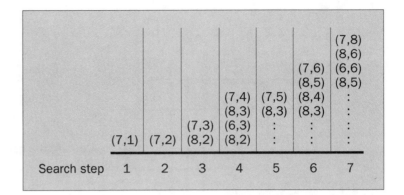

Search step	1	2	3	4	5	6	7
							(7,8)
							(8,6)
						(7,6)	(6,6)
						(8,5)	(8,5)
				(7,4)	(7,5)	(8,4)	:
				(8,3)	(8,3)	(8,3)	:
			(7,3)	(6,3)	:	:	:
	(7,1)	(7,2)	(8,2)	(8,2)	:	:	:

In the following figure, the squares of the island are numbered in the order that they were found with this algorithm; that is, the order in which they were put on to the stack:

	4	5	6	7	8	9
1				1		
2	24			2	3	
3	23	22	5	4	6	
4				7	8	
5				9	10	21
6			12	11	13	20
7				14	15	19
8				16	17	18

We can think of two sorts of squares: those whose coordinates were no sooner put on to the stack than they popped off (joined by a line, showing the path of the search), and those which are returned to, for further investigation (labeled **1**):

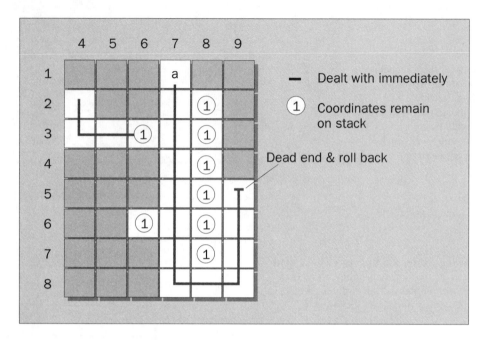

The algorithm that estimates the area of an island is illustrated in **\CHAP5\CH5_7.BAS**, and takes the form of the external function **Area(x,y)**. The program as a whole calculates the area of the largest island and identifies it by naming one of its coordinates. If you run the program you'll see the message:

The island which contains the point (12, 5)
is of the largest area S = 26.

Possible Improvements

If you've already tried this program, you may have realized that there are a few changes worth considering.

1 Searching by moving backwards is implemented by the external function **Area(x,y)**. When it's executed, the following program fragment checks at each step whether the next version is acceptable:

```
FOR i = 1 TO 4
   CALL Version(x1, y1, i)
   IF OnMap(NextX, NextY) AND Map(NextX, NextY) = -1 THEN
     s = s + 1
     CALL InStack(NextX, NextY) Map(NextX, NextY) = 1
   END IF
NEXT i
```

Here, there's a check on each square (**NextX, NextY**) of the next version to see if it falls on the map. You can abandon this checking if you increase the boundary of the **Map** array by **1** and 'frame' the map with squares of the value **-2**. If you want to do this, you should rewrite the section called **"Initializing the map"** as follows:

```
' *** Initializing the map ***
RESTORE DataMap READ MaxX, MaxY
DIM Shared Map(MaxX + 1, MaxY + 1) AS INTEGER
InitMap
FOR x = 0 TO MaxX + 1
    Map(x, 0) = -2
    Map(x, MaxY + 1) = -2
NEXT x
FOR y = 0 TO MaxY + 1
    Map(0, y) = -2
    Map(MaxX + 1, y) = -2
NEXT y
```

Now the condition

OnMap(NextX, NextY) AND

in the **IF** command can be replaced with:

Map(NextX, NextY) = -1

Once you've made these changes, the program will be slightly quicker in accomplishing its task and you can remove the external function **OnMap**.

2   While solving the problem of calculating the area of the largest island, only the squares with a common side were treated as neighboring. We'll change this definition: two squares of the island will be interpreted as neighboring if they have either a common side or a common node. Using this definition, we'll show only one island:

0	0	0	0	0	0	-1	0	0	0
0	0	0	-1	0	0	-1	-1	0	0
0	0	0	-1	-1	-1	-1	-1	0	0
0	0	0	0	0	-1	-1	-1	0	0
0	0	0	0	0	0	-1	-1	-1	0
0	0	0	0	0	-1	-1	-1	-1	0
0	0	0	0	0	0	-1	-1	-1	0
0	0	0	0	0	0	-1	-1	-1	0
0	0	-1	-1	-1	-1	0	0	0	0
0	0	-1	-1	-1	-1	0	0	0	0
0	0	0	0	-1	-1	0	0	0	0
0	0	0	0	0	0	0	0	0	0

It should be easy to modify the program version so that it will carry out its task using this new definition of an island.

3 If you call the **Area(x,y)** procedure and replace the line

```
Map(NextX,NextY) = 1
```

with

```
Map(NextX,NextY) = s
```

then during the execution of the new program, the squares of every island in the **Map** array will be assigned an ordinal number according to the sequence in which they're detected by the program.

4 We used a stack for storing the detected squares. If you use a queue instead of a stack, almost nothing will change except for the order in which the island's squares are used.

The Problem of Building a Sea Port

Let's suppose that port A is built at point (7,4) on one of the islands:

```
'                 10        20        30        40        50
'X =   12345678901234567890123456789012345678901234567890
DATA  "00000000000000000000000000000000000000000000000000"
DATA  "00010011000000000000000000000000000000000111110000"
DATA  "00011111000000000000000000000000001100000001110000"
DATA  "00000011100000000000000000001111111111111000000000"
DATA  "00000011100111000000000000001100000000000000000000'
DATA  "01110011100001100000000000110000000000000000000000"
DATA  "00110011100001110000000000110000000000000000000000"
DATA  "00100011100001100000000011111100000111110000000000"
DATA  "00001110000000110000000011111100011111000000000000"
DATA  "00000100000000110000000010001100001111100000000000"
DATA  "00111100000111110000000011000011100000000000000000"
DATA  "00111100000111100000000011000000111111111111110000"
DATA  "00001100001110000001100000000010000000001111000000"
DATA  "01101100000000000011111111100111000001111100000000"
DATA  "00100000000000000000000001110000000000000000000000"
DATA  "00000000000000000000000000000000000000000000000000"
```

We need to mark the place (point (12,5)) on another island so that we can construct the shortest possible route between ports A and B. We deal with this problem in the program **\CHAP5\CH5_8.BAS**, where we demonstrate the use of two stacks with a common memory whilst calculating the location of the second port using the **Wave** procedure:

```
SUB Wave (X, Y, L)
' ***             Wave Algorithm                 ***
' *** Plotting Isometric Lines on the Map         ***
' *** Beginning from the point (X, Y)             ***
' *** L is the distance from the point (X, Y)     ***
' *** to the island marked by the number (-3)     ***
TopStack = 0              'clearing the first stack
TopStack2 = DeepStack     'clearing the second stack
CALL InStack(X, Y)
St = 1
L = 1
Flag = False
```

```
WHILE Flag = False
  IF St = 1 THEN
    DO WHILE NOT EmptyStack
      CALL OutStack(XY)
      X1 = XY.X
      Y1 = XY.Y
      FOR I = 1 TO 4
        NextX = X1 + Delta(I).X
        NextY = Y1 + Delta(I).Y
        IF Map(NextX, NextY) = -3 THEN
          Flag = True
          Port2X = NextX
          Port2Y = NextY
          EXIT DO
        END IF
        IF Map(NextX, NextY) = 0 THEN
          Map(NextX, NextY) = L
          CALL InStack2(NextX, NextY)
        END IF
      NEXT I
    LOOP
    St = 2
  ELSE
    DO WHILE NOT EmptyStack2
      CALL OutStack2(XY)
      X1 = XY.X
      Y1 = XY.Y
      FOR I = 1 TO 4
        NextX = X1 + Delta(I).X
        NextY = Y1 + Delta(I).Y
        IF Map(NextX, NextY) = -3 THEN
          Flag = True
          Port2X = NextX
          Port2Y = NextY
          EXIT DO
        END IF
        IF Map(NextX, NextY) = 0 THEN
          Map(NextX, NextY) = L
          CALL InStack(NextX, NextY)
        END IF
      NEXT I
    LOOP
    St = 1
  END IF
  L = L + 1
WEND
END SUB
```

First, the squares of the second island are marked by a number (-3). This is performed by the **Mark** procedure using the search with return method. Next, isometric lines are plotted onto the map using the **Wave** iteration procedure.

At the first iteration, the squares which are one square away from port A are marked by the number **1** and pushed onto the second stack. At the second iteration, the squares are popped from the second stack. The sea squares lying near the retrieved ones are marked with the number **2** and stored in the first stack.

These are offset by a distance of two squares from port A. At the third iteration, the squares are retrieved from the first stack. The unmarked squares alongside them are marked with the number **3** and pushed onto the second stack, and so on.

This enumeration of the squares resembles a wave from port A, which is why the algorithm for plotting isometric lines is called a **wave** algorithm. The iteration process finishes as soon as the wave reaches the squares of the second island which are marked with a **-3**. The first square reached by the wave is the place where the new port B will be constructed.

To find the shortest route from A to B, we need to use a reverse move. The search for the shortest route begins at point B using the procedure **Path**:

```
SUB Path (X, Y, L)
'*** Searching for a Path of the L Length from the point (X, Y) ***
'***  to the First Port  ***
  TopStack = 0
  CALL InStack(X, Y)
  L = L - 1
  WHILE L > 0
    FOR I = 1 TO 4
      NextX = X + Delta(I).X
      NextY = Y + Delta(I).Y
      IF Map(NextX, NextY) = L THEN
        CALL InStack(NextX, NextY)
        X = NextX
        Y = NextY
        EXIT FOR
      END IF
    NEXT I
    L = L - 1
  WEND
  CALL InStack(Port1X, Port1Y)

' *** Displaying the Path from the First Port to the Second One ***
  PRINT
  PRINT "The path from the first port to the second:"
  WHILE NOT EmptyStack
    CALL OutStack(XY)
    X1 = XY.X: Y1 = XY.Y
    PRINT "("; X1; ","; Y1; ")",
  WEND
END SUB
```

First, it looks for a square which is marked by the number **(L-1)**, where **L** is the length of the path between A and B (which had previously been calculated by the **Wave** procedure). The coordinates of this square are pushed onto the stack, and the square itself is declared as the current square. Then it calculates the neighboring square, marked by a number one less than that of the current one. The process comes to an end when it reaches the square marked by a **1**.

By now, the coordinates of the squares which form the shortest path are stored in the stack. To print or find the path, all you need to do is pop these coordinates from the stack.

The program calculates the location of the second port and prints the shortest route between the two ports for the data defined in the block **Port1x**, **Port1y**, **Islandx** and **Islandy**. It's easy to improve the program by making only slight changes.

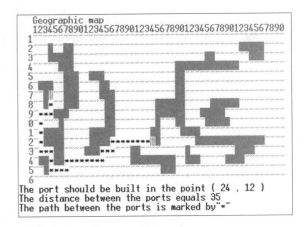

Our next version of this program will display a map with the port of departure on one of the islands and ask the user for the coordinates of a point on another island which is to be the location of the second port, or the destination port. When the user has responded, the program identifies the position of the destination port and plots the shortest route connecting the two ports, as shown here:

The program has found one of the possible locations for a port on our island (in reality, there can be several). It's fairly easy to change the program to make it calculate all possible locations for a port on the island, plot these on the map and, on request, draw the shortest sea route from the departure port to a chosen destination port.

You can also modify the program to ask for the island of departure and the island of destination and calculate the locations of the ports on these islands, so that the path from the first port to the second is the shortest possible.

The Problem of Eight Queens

The problem of eight queens is a well-known example using the trial-and-error method and the backtracking algorithms. In the 1850s, C.F. Hauss worked on this problem but didn't succeed in completely solving it. This isn't surprising: problems of this sort tend to lack an analytical solution. Instead, they require complicated, exhaustive calculations, patience and accuracy, so computers are ideally suited to solving such problems. For example:

> Arranging eight queens so that none of them threaten another.

We'll represent the chess board as a 2D array **Chess(8,8)**, with **Chess(x,y)=0** if the square **(x,y)** is empty, and **Chess(x,y)=-1** if the square contains a queen. We'll use the backtracking method to search for a successful possible arrangement of queens.

> *Incidentally, if you're unfamiliar with chess terminology, then let us explain what a queen is. Chess pieces move in different manners, and the queen is able to move horizontally, vertically and diagonally for any number of squares.*

We'll define the searching step as the choice of a vertical line to set the queen, and the version as the choice of a horizontal line. To store the order of queens at a recurrent step of the algorithm, we'll push the coordinates of the relevant square onto the stack. For each step we'll look for the appropriate version and, once we've found it, we'll move on to the next step, effectively finding the position of a queen in each column. If a version can't be detected, then the sequence of queens set thus far is incorrect, so we move a step back and continue searching for a new horizontal line from the last version checked. Therefore, for the duration of the program, it's likely that queens placed on the board will only later be found to be following an impossible solution. Eventually though, the program will find a correct way through and place eight 'safe' queens on the board.

155

Note that the first coordinate of a square coincides with the step number, and the second one with the version number at which this square is chosen.

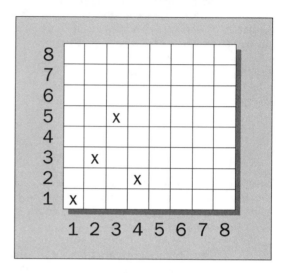

Now all we need to do is to think of a way of checking the validity of a version. The following diagram shows the arrangement at the fifth step of the algorithm. It must find the possible version (the horizontal number) for placing the queen on the fifth vertical line:

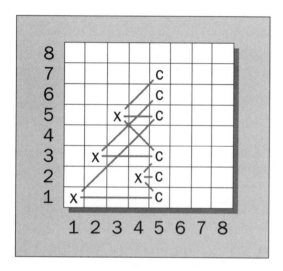

In order to check the validity of the **j**-th version of the fifth algorithmic step (i.e. the possibility of placing the queen on the square **(5,j)**), we must test to see if any of the four queens already placed threatens the square **(5,j)**. This could entail a lot of operations, so perhaps it would be better when setting a queen to mark the squares which it threatens, and then when we can test for this problem in one operation.

Here, we've marked each threatened version of the fifth step with a C. Unfortunately, it turns out that this wouldn't be very practical, not because marking the fields under threat would require a lot of operations, but because it would be difficult to unmark the freed squares when backtracking to the last step.

The solution to this lies in the following: we can define three arrays for storing the information on whether the horizontal or a diagonal (**1** and **2**) is threatened - **Horizontal**, **Diagonal1**, and **Diagonal2**. Then, when we set each next queen, we'll be able to mark the occupied horizontal and two diagonals in three operations.

Notice that we don't need an array to check vertically, because we already know from the searching step that there'll be only one queen in any one column.

While looking for the next version, we can check whether the square is safe, again in three operations. Note that while moving backwards from dead-ends, we can easily correct these arrays since only one queen can be located on any given horizontal or diagonal.

Implementing the Algorithms

We know that a characteristic feature of the top-left-bottom-right diagonal is that the sum of the coordinates of the squares is a constant. We'll declare this sum as the number of the corresponding diagonal - `Diagonal1(x+y)`. The bottom-left-top-right diagonal, however, has a constant difference of coordinates - `Diagonal2(x-y)`, as shown in the diagram:

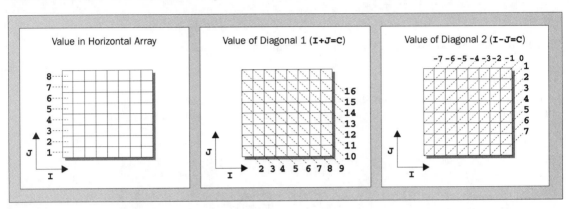

The array declarations will look like this:

```
DIM Shared Horizontal (1 TO 8) AS INTEGER
DIM Shared Diagonal1 (2 TO 16) AS INTEGER
DIM Shared Diagonal2 (-7 TO 7) AS INTEGER
```

When a queen is placed on a square, the horizontal and diagonals that it threatens are set **False**. The program fragment which implements the forward step (i.e. the setting of a queen on the square **(x,y)**) sets the three flags:

```
SUB StepForward (XY AS Coord)
'Steps forward a Square
   I = XY.X: J = XY.Y
   CALL InStack(I, J)
   Horizontal(J) = False
   Diagonal1(I + J) = False
   Diagonal2(I - J) = False
   XY.X = XY.X + 1   'Increments column for next queen
   XY.Y = 0
END SUB
```

For the new queen, the **Version** checks up the rows for a square which isn't threatened. It does this by looking for the first solution of the condition:

```
Horizontal(J) AND Diagonal1(I + J) AND Diagonal2(I - J)
```

If all these are true for the square **(I,J)**, then the queen can be placed here, by calling **StepForward()**. However, if no unthreatened square is found in the column, some reshuffling of the previously placed queens is necessary. The procedure **StepBack()** takes the coordinate of the last queen from the top of the stack and, from its current position, searches for the next place where the queen is unthreatened. If there is none, then the next column back is rechecked, by calling the next set of coordinates from the stack, and so on.

```
SUB StepBack (XY AS Coord)
'Steps Back a Square
  CALL OutStack(XY)
  I = XY.X: J = XY.Y
  Horizontal(J) = True
  Diagonal1(I + J) = True
  Diagonal2(I - J) = True
END SUB
```

Run the program **\CHAP5\CH5_9.BAS** to see this demonstration work.

The Results

In all, there are 92 different solutions to this problem. Among these, only 12 solutions are completely different, i.e. these can't be created by a simple rotation and reflection of another one:

Our program produces the first of these solutions.

The arrangement of queens can be determined by an eight-digit number, where the **i**-th digit equals the number of the row occupied by the queen which is in the **j**-th column of the chess board. For instance, the arrangement of queens deduced by our program can be identified by the number **15863724**.

The program could easily be modified to print the numbers of all 92 arrangements. Our program can be tailored to calculate all kinds of arrangements of n queens on a chess board of the size n x n, or Amazon queens (those that also have the knight's capabilities).

Lists

In this section, we'll introduce new data structures, lists, and illustrate working with them in the demo program **ListDemo**. Unfortunately, too many programmers still think that list processing methods are very complicated and that the only way to process lists is through a strictly defined procedure. You'll see, however, that there's nothing mysterious or too difficult in dealing with these structures; these methods are an important part of every programmer's repertoire, and you can easily use them while programming in QBasic.

A list is an ordered structure in which each element contains a reference which connects it to another element.

Each element of a list (denoted as a node) contains two fields: the information field (**Info**) and the pointer field (**Pntr**). The information field contains the information you want to process, and the pointer field contains the address of the next element on the list. This address used for access to the next element is referred to as the **pointer**.

The concept of a list generalizes everyday structures such as a list of telephone subscribers, a catalog of books in a library, the list of employees in an office, and so on. Lists are conveniently represented in the form of diagrams like this:

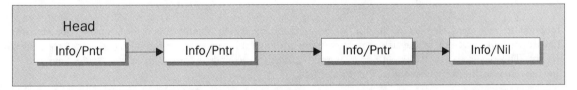

So that you know from which node the list begins, the external pointer **Head** points to the first element of the list. This external pointer isn't considered as an element of the list, and it doesn't include an information field **Info**.

Each list is related (apart from the external pointer) to one more pointer **PntrList** which contains a reference to one of the list's elements. The element pointed at by the **PntrList** pointer is referred to as the **current** element of the list.

The last element of the list contains the empty or null value **Nil** in the pointer field. This value isn't a significant address. **Nil** is used for pointing to the end of a list.

There are many types of lists, all differing from each other in the sets of operations that you can carry out with them.

Manipulating Elements of a List

In linear lists, we often need to add or delete data in the center of the list. For storing the elements of the list, we must choose methods of inserting and deleting which won't cause any movement of the elements, i.e. the position of the element, and the information must be independent of one another. The best way to understand this concept is to illustrate it with an example. Let's assume that we have the following small list, L1:

> Ivanov
>
> Sidorov
>
> Petrov

We'll limit the number of elements which the list can contain to 6. To store the list L1, we'll organize an array, **QList (-1 to 6)**, consisting of two-component records with the fields **Info** and **Pntr**, and arrange the elements of the list as here:

Index	Info	Pointer
-1		1 (Start Position of Head1)
0		
1	Ivanov	2
2	Sidorov	3
3	Petrov	Nil
4		
5		
6		

To point to each next element of the list, we've used indices which identify the records of the **QList** array. The record **QList(-1)** in the field **Pntr** contains an external pointer - a reference to the first element of the list. The records **QList(1)**, **QList(2)** and **QList(3)** contain information in the **Info** field and the reference to the next element in the **Pntr** field.

Adding Elements

Using this type of implementation, adding and deleting elements from the list doesn't call for large-scale movements. Assuming that we need to put the name **Romanov** into the center of the list, next to the current record containing the name **Sidorov**, we take the following steps:

1 Place the name **Romanov** in the free record of the **QList** array (e.g. into the element 4).

2 Put the **Pntr** field of this new record equal to the corresponding field of the current record **Sidorov**, 3.

3 Assign the **Pntr** field of the current record a new value equal to the index of the new record in the **QList** array.

As a result, the array takes this form:

Index	Info	Pointer
-1		1 (Start Position of Head1)
0		
1	Ivanov	2
2	Sidorov	4
3	Petrov	Nil
4	Romanov	3
5		
6		

So adding a new element to the center of the list appears to be a pretty simple operation. Adding an element to the beginning of the list is performed in a very similar manner:

Index	Info	Pointer
-1		5 (Start Position of Head1)
0		
1	Ivanov	2
2	Sidorov	4
3	Petrov	Nil
4	Romanov	3
5	Voronov	1
6		

Removing Elements

The removal of elements from the list is just as simple. For example, to delete an element which follows the current record **Sidorov**, i.e. **Romanov**, all you need to do is to change the value of the **Pntr** field in the current record to the value of the relevant field of the next record as follows:

Index	Info	Pointer
-1		5 (Start Position of Head1)
0		
1	Ivanov	4
2	Sidorov	4
3	Petrov	Nil
4	Romanov	3
5	Voronov	1
6		

Notice how Sidorov's record still appears to be present. This is because we haven't actually deleted the record, but merely changed the pointers so that it's never accessed and is not part of the actual list.

Controlling Free Elements

To include the elements just released into the number of free elements of the array, we use a different method known as 'gathering dust'. We perform this by placing the freed elements into a second list of free elements: list L2. After the removal of elements from the list, a place is free in the **OLIST** array which may be used for accumulating new elements. Therefore, we must somehow take into account the records that are freed. Have a look at how two lists can be supported within one array **OLIST**:

Index	Info	Pointer
-1		5 (Start Position of Head1)
0		2 (Start Position of Head2)
1	Ivanov	4
2	Sidorov	6
3	Petrov	Nil
4	Romanov	3
5	Voronov	1
6		Nil

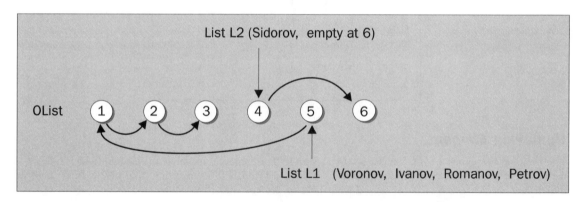

List L2 (Sidorov, empty at 6)

OList

List L1 (Voronov, Ivanov, Romanov, Petrov)

Now, to add a new element to the list L1, using the list L2, you simply calculate the index of a free record in the **OLIST** array (in this instance, where there was an entry for Sidorov) and place the new element at the address found. The following figure shows the state of the **OLIST** array after adding the element **Titov** to the end of list the L1:

Index	Info	Pointer
-1		5 (Start Position of Head1)
0		6 (Start Position of Head2)
1	Ivanov	4

Table Continued on Following Page

Index	Info	Pointer
2	Titov	Nil
3	Petrov	2
4	Romanov	3
5	Voronov	1
6		Nil

Implementation

The program **\CHAP5\CH5_10.BAS** demonstrates the different operations for manipulating lists. If you open it up you can take a look at how the source code works and perhaps modify it to thoroughly understand how we have implemented it. We've written it to sequentially display the current status of the **Olist** array which stores the list's elements, as we progress through some list operations, along with the current state of the list L1.

The program works through several list operations in a tutorial manner - by saying what we're doing to the list and then by showing the contents of the list after that operation. This is achieved by calling a standard list display routine, called **OListOnScreen**, which displays the first list to be shown.

We then proceed to add the first three elements into the list sequentially. In doing so, each of the elements to be added is placed at the end of the list. Anyway, run through the program and you'll understand what's going on, because everything is explained with this code.

Cycle Lists

Although the structure of a linear list is quite useful, it does have its share of drawbacks, such as its unidirectional access method. In this section, we'll discuss other methods of list organization and how to use them to remedy these problems. If we change the pointer **Nil** of the last element, Cycling Sally in our example, in a linear list so that it points to the first element, we'll obtain a new data structure similar to a ring buffer, called a **cycle** list:

Index	Information	Pntr
1	Jumping Jeremy	2
2	Ethel Frogkiller	3
3	Arthur Loosenoose	4
4	Admirable Adrian	5
5	Eddy Mophead	6
6	Gurgling Gither	7
7	Gregory Flapperback	8
8	Technical Tim	9
9	Gorgeous Graham	10
10	Cycling Sally	1

In a cycle list, we can access each element from any specified point. This causes full symmetry, so we don't need to distinguish between the 'last' and the 'first' nodes in the list. To point to a certain element of a cycle list, you just introduce an external pointer **Lst1**, which when blank contains **Nil** and represents an empty cycle list.

If we choose the array **CList** as a model of a cycle list then, to take account of the free elements of the array, we could also use a cycle list with the external pointer **Lst2**. Let's consider an example.

Assessing a Moving Target

For argument's sake, let's say that there are 10 children standing in a circle holding hands. Counting from the first child, every 3rd child is removed and the circle is closed again after they leave. You need to determine the order in which the children are removed from the circle. The program **\CHAP5\CH5_11.BAS** solves this problem.

The program takes **N=10** and an arbitrary **K>=2** defined from the keyboard by the user. The names of 10 children **Jumping Jeremy,...,Cycling Sally** are placed in the data block **Names**. The program reads these names and transfers them to the cycle list, simulated using the **CList** array, with sizes defined by the variable **Max Index**. So that it's easier to view (the contents of the **CList** array are displayed on the screen), we've limited the list's size to a smallish number - 14 elements.

The program is capable of supporting several lists defined by the value of the **NumberList** variable, the external pointers being stored in the array **Lst (NumberList)**. In this example, though, only one list is required to tackle the problem. Therefore, two external pointers are created, the first one (**Lst(1)**) points to the working list, and the second one (**Lst(0)**) to the list of free elements. These external pointers are records which consist of two fields, **L** and **Pntr**, with the field **Pntr** containing the pointer to the first record of the relevant cycle list, and the field **L** containing the length of this list.

The **L** field is the information part of the external pointer and is referred to as the list header. This may contain specific information about the list (no elements, a description of the list - the choice is yours). In our case, for instance, the heading allows you to find out the number of elements in the list without looking through the whole list.

The procedures are used in the following way:

InitList, **AddNode**, **DeleteNode**, and **NextNode**	Used to manipulate the list. Procedure **InitList** creates **NumberList** empty cycle lists on the basis of the array **CList**, where in our program **NumberList** equals **1**.
AddNode(ni,z,p)	Adds to the list number **ni** an element **z** after the pointer **p**. In case there are no free nodes in the list, the procedures output the corresponding message.
DeleteNode(ni,p)	Removes from list number **ni** an element, which follows after the pointer **p** and includes the freed element into the list of free elements.
NextNode(p)	Moves the pointer **p** of cycle list forward.
CListOnScreen	Outputs the nodes of list onto the screen.
Selection(k)	Recalculates the elements and removes every **k**th element from the cycle list. This procedure is easy to modify so as not to impose the restriction '**k>=2**' on the number **k**.

Try out the program with the value **K=7**. You should get the following:

Order in which the elements are removed:

> Gregory Flapperback
> Admirable Adrian
> Ethel Frogkiller
> Jumping Jeremy
> Arthur Loosenoose
> Gurgling Gither
> Cycling Sally
> Eddy Mophead
> Technical Tim

Element left: Gorgeous Graham

Methods of Sorting

Sorting is the process of ordering data, and its purpose is to make the data easier to find, retrieve, change, add and remove. If you've ever played cards, you'll understand the sorting process; depending on the game and the hand, you might sort the cards numerically, arbitrarily, by suit, or by a combination of these.

Let's take a simple example: the world's smallest English-Russian poultry dictionary. We have six English words with their Russian meanings and simply sort them into alphabetical order. That seems straightforward enough, doesn't it? But what you've actually done is only used the English words for the sorting - the Russian ones have no bearing on the sequence - a factor that all you Russians might want to change.

In computing terms we will store each English word and all the information associated with it as a record. This record is then divided up into fields, something like:

> English word
> noun / verb / adjective
> translation into Russian

Obviously, we've placed more importance on the English word, since this is what decides the order of our dictionary. The term for the field with this decisive ordering role is a **key** - and our English words will form our key field. Here's our fowl database:

English	Noun/Verb/Adj.		Russian
Chicken	n		Kuritsa
Egg	n		Yaitso
Feather	n		Pero
Fly	v		Lyetat'
Kiev	a		Kiev
Peck	v		Klevat'

If we shifted the emphasis, we could create the world's smallest Russian-English poultry dictionary, where the Russian words would become the key field. Alternatively, we could sort entries by number of characters, or by some other characteristic.

Computerized sorting can be done **internally** or **externally**. When sorting internally, the sorted data is stored in the RAM, while an external sort uses the disk. In this chapter, we'll stick to sorting our arrays internally. External sorting, the organization and programming involved will be covered in the next chapter, devoted to file management.

Sorting Terminology

There are a variety of sorting algorithms and to be able to choose the right one for carrying out a particular task, you'll need to be aware of a few things about each of them, namely:

▲ Programming time

▲ Machine time usage

▲ Data memory size

For regularly sorted data, sort methods that minimize machine time are your best option. On the other hand, if you only intend to sort a program once in a while, then programming time will govern your choice of method.

If you're going to make regular alterations to the ordered data (adding or removing records), then you'll find that re-ordering the data will take up a great deal of time. Hence, it's important that you choose the right one for the task you've set yourself.

Different Types of Sorting

Let's begin by taking a look at some popular algorithms and programs corresponding to six fundamental sort methods. The first three are very simple, although they can be a little bit slow:

▲ **select** sort

▲ **bubble** (and **shaker**) sort

▲ **insertion** sort

The other three sorting methods are improvements on the ones above:

▲ **shell** sort - an improved insertion method

▲ **pyramid** sort - an improved select method using a pyramid tree

▲ **quick** sort

The best way to determine the sort time is by running a sort program on a PC and determining its efficiency in absolute time units. To prevent you from choosing a method that's inefficient for your particular task, we've included timings for all the methods which will give you an idea of all their relative efficiencies. Furthermore, we'll also cover the best methods for minimizing the amount of memory you'll require when processing your data. Let's now take a closer look at how we can implement each of these in QBasic.

Select Sort

The select sort algorithm is based on a sequential search of an initial array which is looked through several times and, on the first run-through, the field key with the lowest value is selected and swaps position with the first element of the array. Selection continues using the remaining elements. Here's how the method works when sorting 8 key values:

```
Start:     30   9   11   2   35   5   16   19

1st Sort:   2   9   11   30  35   5   16   19

2nd Sort:   2   5   11   30  35   9   16   19

3rd Sort:   2   5    9   30  35  11   16   19

etc.
```

Using this algorithm, we have developed a subprogram **SelectSort** which uses two external variables **SortArray**, and **MaxRec**. The variable **SortArray** defines an array of records with the sorting key field **KeySort**. **MaxRec** stands for the number of records you're sorting:

```
SUB SelectSort
' ***         SelectSort        ***
' *** Inputs: SortArray,MaxRec
' *** Output: SortArray
' *** SortArray is sorted by the key field KeySort
' *** MaxRec -number of records in the array

FOR i = 1 TO MaxRec
  k = i                       'Initial value of the index of the minimum element
  FOR J = i + 1 TO MaxRec   'Minimum search cycle
    IF SortArray(J).KeySort < SortArray(k).KeySort THEN
      k = J                   'k-index of the smallest key
    END IF
    NEXT J
' *** k - index of the minimum element selected
' *** Swap elements, if the smallest one is found
    IF k > i THEN
      SWAP SortArray(i), SortArray(k)
    END IF
    NEXT i                    'Go to the next pass
END SUB
```

The Generic Program

The above procedure forms one of the sort subroutines in **\CHAP5\CH5_12.BAS**, which demonstrates the sorting of an array of records by a character key field. The definition of records of the **SortArray** array contains a key text field **KeySort** and the field for numeric information, the **Info** field:

```
TYPE SortType
   KeySort AS STRING * 20
   Info AS INTEGER
END TYPE
```

The **InArray** subroutine fills the records with the information from the **DATA** block. In doing so, the key fields are filled with the names of cities, and the information fields are filled with the dates that these cities were first mentioned in history. The **PrintArray** subroutine displays the list of records ordered according to the names of the cities.

The program includes commented-out calls to the subroutines of other select sort methods (bubble, shaker and insertion), which we will cover in the next few sections. Effectively, this program will demonstrate the differences between each of the methods. Here is the main procedure of the program from where we will call the various sorting subroutines:

```
'    **************************************************
'    *                Direct Sorting                  *
'    **************************************************
  DEFINT A-Z       'Default type: integer
  DECLARE SUB SelectSort ()
  DECLARE SUB BubbleSort ()
  DECLARE SUB InsertionSort ()
  DECLARE SUB ShakerSort ()
  DECLARE SUB InArray ()
  DECLARE SUB PrintArray ()

'Definition of a record
TYPE SortType
   KeySort AS STRING * 14
   Info AS INTEGER
'   KeySort AS INTEGER
'   Info AS STRING * 14
END TYPE

DIM SHARED SortArray(1 TO 1000) AS SortType
DIM SHARED MaxRec

CLS
InArray
PRINT "I N I T I A L      D A T A"
PRINT "record          key                information"
PrintArray
   SelectSort
'   BubbleSort
'   InsertionSort
'   ShakerSort
PRINT
PRINT "S O R T E D      D A T A"
PrintArray
RESTORE
END
'Number of records
  DATA  8
'Data for records being sorted, key - string
  DATA Smolensk,       863, Yaroslavl,  1010, Uglitch,   937
  DATA Moscow,        1147, Magadan,    1931, Novgorod,  859
  DATA Veliky Ustyug, 1207, Petersburg, 1703
```

```
'Data for records being sorted, key - integer
'  DATA 863, Smolensk,      1010, Yaroslavl,  937, Uglitch
'  DATA 1147,Moscow,        1931, Magadan,     859, Novgorod
'  DATA 1207,Veliky Ustyug, 1703, Petersburg

DEFSNG A-Z

SUB InArray
'Input of the array of records. MaxRec - number of records.
' A record consists of Info and KeyS fields
   READ MaxRec
   FOR i = 1 TO MaxRec
    READ SortArray(i).KeySort
    READ SortArray(i).Info
   NEXT i

END SUB

SUB PrintArray
    PRINT "-------------|-------------|--------------------"
    FOR i = 1 TO MaxRec
      PRINT i, SortArray(i).KeySort, SortArray(i).Info
      ' halt after each ten records
      IF (i \ 10) = (i / 10) THEN
        PRINT " Press Space to continue "
        WHILE INKEY$ <> " ": WEND
        PRINT "-------------|-------------|--------------------"
      END IF
    NEXT i

END SUB
```

You can also use this program to order records by the numeric key field. To do this, you first interchange the positions of the field types:

```
TYPE SortType
    Info AS STRING * 20
    KeySort AS INTEGER
END TYPE
```

You will then notice that, in the main procedure of the program, the order of the data should also be switched around:

```
DATA 863, Smolensk, 1010, Yaroslavl,  937, Uglitch
DATA 1147,Moscow, 1931, Magadan, 859, Novgorod
DATA 1207,Veliky Ustyug, 1703, Petersburg
```

The analysis of the number of comparisons through simple selection is quite evident. The first time through, **n-1** comparisons are carried out, the second time, **n-2** comparisons, and so on. Therefore, the total number of comparisons is:

$$C = (n-1)+(n-2)+(n-3)+ \ldots +1$$

which can be shown to equal **n*(n-1)/2** where **n** is the number of records. The select sort is, therefore, one of the best sorting methods for small tables.

Bubble Sort

The bubble sort algorithm is based on the repeated comparison and swapping of pairs of neighboring elements, until all the elements are in order. If we have an array of elements, the field of the sort key of the pairs of values `A(i)` and `A(i+1)` are compared and if `A(i) > A(i+1)`, then the values swap positions. Each time the array is passed through, the smallest elements of all the pairs are shifted towards the start (or the top) of the array, much like bubbles rising in a column of water. When the number of passes through the array equals `n-1`, the sort is over. Here we sort eight arbitrarily selected key values:

Start:

30	9	11	2	35	5	16	19

1st Sort:

9	30	11	2	35	5	16	19
9	11	30	2	35	5	16	19
9	11	2	30	35	5	16	19
9	11	2	30	35	5	16	19
9	11	2	30	5	35	16	19
9	11	2	30	5	16	35	19
9	11	2	30	5	16	19	35

Swapped Elements

No Change

2nd Sort:

9	11	2	30	5	16	19	35
9	2	11	30	5	16	19	35
9	2	11	30	5	16	19	35
9	2	11	5	30	16	19	35
9	2	11	5	16	30	19	35
9	2	11	5	16	19	30	35
9	2	11	5	16	19	30	35

3rd Sort:

2	9	11	5	16	19	30	35
2	9	11	5	16	19	30	35
2	9	5	11	16	19	30	35

etc.

You can see that the fourth pass through the data will give fully sorted data, yet there will be another three passes which have no effect on the order of the elements. One way to improve the algorithm is to check whether any rearrangements took place during a pass. If there were no rearrangements, the process has been completed. We can improve the algorithm further if we store not only the fact that an interchange occurred, but also the position (index `i`) of the last interchange in a pass. It's clear that all **pairs** of neighboring elements with indices higher than `i-1` are already in the required order. Hence, a further pass can be finished at that index.

Here is a bubble sort subroutine which demonstrates the improved algorithm:

```
SUB BubbleSort STATIC
' ***        BubbleSort        ***
' *** Inputs: SortArray,MaxRec
' *** Output: SortArray
' *** SortArray is sorted by the key field KeySort
' *** MaxRec -number of records in the array

Limit = MaxRec
DO                                   'For pass
  Switch = 0                         'There are, initially, no exchanges in a pass
  FOR i = 1 TO (Limit - 1)           'For each array element
                                     'Compare, swap, and store index
    IF SortArray(i).KeySort > SortArray(i + 1).KeySort THEN
       SWAP SortArray(i), SortArray(i + 1)
       Switch = i
    END IF
  NEXT i

Limit = Switch
LOOP WHILE Switch                    'Loop whilst no exchanges have occurred

END SUB
```

Its external loop controls the number of passes, while the internal one controls the interchanges in each pass. An interchange and its index are stored in the variable **Switch**. The value **Switch = 0** means that there are no interchanges in a pass, while the value **Switch = i** (**i** being any value other than zero) shows that there was an interchange and returns the index of the first element of the pair involved. The largest index of a switch provides the value of **Limit** for the next pass.

Next, we'll take our improvements on this algorithm a step further and take into consideration a slight asymmetry in the process. The 'light' element at the end of the array below will 'percolate' to the front of the array when bubble sorted (in size order from left to right) over the course of seven steps:

06 09 17 32 46 49 60 03

However, if you reversed the directions of the pass and the interchange, so that 'light' elements 'sink' to the (redefined) rear of the array, the array could be sorted in just one pass. This suggests that it would be better to alternate the sorting direction. The resulting algorithm is referred to as a **shaker** sort. Here's a shaker sort for the 8 elements of the moment. Note how the first left-to-right pass changes the value of **Switch** to (**i**) the index of the lower of the pair of values that are interchanged, every time a swap occurs. Since no more switches occur for array elements greater than (**i**), we may assume the array beyond here is sorted, and the return right-to-left pass can start at the array element **SortArray(Switch)**, rather like the variable **Limit** in the bubble sort procedure. Also, the second pass makes use of the same **SortArray(i)**. **KeySort** as the first, so its index for switching doesn't need to be changed. Here is the shaker sort subroutine:

```
SUB ShakerSort
' ***        ShakerSort        ***
' *** Inputs: SortArray,MaxRec
' *** Output: SortArray
' *** SortArray is sorted by the key field KeySort
' *** MaxRec -number of records in the array

L = 1                                'L-starting viewing from left to right
R = MaxRec - 1                       'R-starting viewing from right to left
```

```
DO                              'For pass
  Switch = 0                    'Existence of exchanges in a pass
  FOR i = L TO R                'For each element
                                'compare, swap, and store index
    IF SortArray(i).KeySort > SortArray(i + 1).KeySort THEN
        SWAP SortArray(i), SortArray(i + 1)
        Switch = i
    END IF
  NEXT i
R = Switch
  FOR i = R TO L STEP -1        'For each element
                                'compare, swap, and store index
    IF SortArray(i).KeySort > SortArray(i + 1).KeySort THEN
        SWAP SortArray(i), SortArray(i + 1)
        Switch = i
    END IF
  NEXT i
L = Switch
LOOP WHILE Switch               'Loop whilst no exchanges occur

END SUB
```

The number of comparisons, as with the select sort, won't exceed this value:

$$C = n*(n-1)/2$$

These improvements don't provide a considerable gain in efficiency, but the shaker sort is most successful when we have a set of elements that are almost ordered.

Insertion Sort

This method is widely used in card playing to arrange your hand. The elements (or cards) `A(1)`, `A(2),...,A(n)` are divided into two parts at step `i`: a 'ready', or ordered sequence `A(1),...,A(i-1)`, and the remains of the initial sequence `A(i), A(i+1),...,A(n)`.

As one list is always in an ordered state, we can copy the first element across and start at I=2. The following shows the process of inserting 8 arbitrarily selected numbers:

Start Step No.							
1	30	9	11	2	35	5	16	19
2	9	30	11	2	35	5	16	19
3	9	11	30	2	35	5	16	19
4	2	9	11	30	35	5	16	19
5	2	9	11	30	35	5	16	19
6	2	5	9	11	30	35	16	19
7	2	5	9	11	16	30	35	19
8	2	5	9	11	16	19	30	35

In our following subroutine, which mirrors this sorting technique, the initial and ready sequences are defined by the array of records **SortArray**. Its external loop controls the retrieval of each next element from the initial sequence for subsequent insertion, and the internal one controls the movement of the elements of the ready sequence.

```
SUB InsertionSort STATIC
' ***        InsertionSort        ***
' *** Inputs: SortArray,MaxRec
' *** Output: SortArray
' *** SortArray is sorted by the key field KeySort
' *** MaxRec -number of records in the array

DIM Xval AS SortType, x AS SortType
FOR i = 2 TO MaxRec                        'i-current index of the initial array
    x.KeySort = SortArray(i).KeySort       'taking i-th element for insertion
    Xval = SortArray(i)
    FOR J = i TO 2 STEP -1                  'j-current index of the ready array
                    'If J-1-th element is less than the element to insert,
                    'it is shifted to the right
    IF SortArray(J - 1).KeySort > x.KeySort THEN
        SortArray(J) = SortArray(J - 1)
                                           'Otherwise, exit the FOR...NEXT loop:
    ELSE                                   'as new element is largest in ready array
        EXIT FOR
    END IF
    NEXT J
    SortArray(J) = Xval                    'Inserting new element into the ready array
NEXT I
END SUB
```

The expression for the average number of passes is:

$$C = (n^2 + n - 2)/4$$

where n is the number of elements. Of course, when the initial sequence of elements is already ordered, we will require the minimum number of evaluations and, when the elements are arranged in no order at all, the program will take the maximum number of evaluations.

This method of sorting is convenient for adding new elements to an array that has already been sorted. In the program **\CHAP5\CH5_13.BAS,** a recurrent new element is immediately inserted into the array. The description of the array's record consists of the key field **KeySort** and the field **Info** for string information:

```
TYPE SortType
    KeySort AS INTEGER
    Info AS STRING * 40
END TYPE
```

The sub-program **InRecno** asks the user for the values of the new record fields (year of birth, name) and calls the **Appe** subroutine to add these values to the array. The subroutine **Appe** then inserts a new record at the location corresponding to its sorting key. The procedure **PrintArray** outputs all the data onto the screen.

At the outset of the process, there are no records and adding them means a new sorted array has to be created. You can also use this program (without changing the **Appe** procedure) for adding records to be sorted by the character key. You need only swap the field types in the head module of the program and the input messages in the **InArray** procedure. This would allow you to add records with their subsequent sorting by string key field.

Shell Sort

This is an improved sorting method that takes any of the search methods mentioned already and sorts them within groups. At the first iteration separate subsets of elements, spaced **h** apart, are sorted in the initial array **A(1), A(2),...,A(n)**. The value **h** is referred to as a step. For instance, if **h = 5**, the first elements to be sorted are the subset which consists of the elements **A(1), A(6), A(11), A(16)**, etc. Thus in total, five subsets, each containing 1/5 of the elements of the start array, are sorted in a similar manner:

```
1  ==>  A(1),  A(6),   A(11), A(16), ...
2  ==>  A(2),  A(7),   A(12), A(17), ...
3  ==>  A(3),  A(8),   A(13), A(18), ...
4  ==>  A(4),  A(9),   A(14), A(19), ...
5  ==>  A(5),  A(10),  A(15), A(20), ...
```

Once all five sequences have been sorted at the first iteration (using any direct method, often by simple insertions), a smaller **h** value is taken. With this smaller step, new subsets of the initial array are sorted once again. For example, with **h = 3** the following subsets are sorted at the second iteration:

```
1  ==>  A(1), A(4), A(7), A(10), ...
2  ==>  A(2), A(5), A(8), A(11), ...
3  ==>  A(3), A(6), A(9), A(12), ...
```

At the third iteration, the step is reduced further. Eventually, **h** takes the value **1** whereupon the whole array will soon be sorted. Here is a demonstration of the shell sort for 8 numbers with the set of steps **h = 5,3,1**:

h:								
5	71	32	98	17	56	79	13	44
	71					79		
		32					13	
			98					44
				17				
					56			
3	71	13	44	17	56	79	32	98
	71			17			32	
		13			56			98
			44			79		
1	17	13	44	32	56	79	71	98
	13	17	32	44	56	71	79	98

Because we focus on smaller sets of numbers, they become closer to being ordered than the initial array, with the consequence that insertion or bubble methods are more suitable for quick and efficient sorting. This applies to the nearly sorted array, when h=1. Obviously, it would be quicker and more efficient to sort the subsets using a method that is suitable for arrays which are almost ordered, such as, by insertion or bubble methods. The **ShellInsertSort** procedure in the program **\CHAP5\CH5_14.BAS** implements the shell method in combination with the insertion sort. This sub-program is only applicable for simple arrays of n elements.

The sequence of steps **h=5,3,1** in the shell method isn't fixed. It makes sense to use the following sequence (written in reverse order): **1,4,13,40,121,...** where **h(k-1) = 3*h(k) + 1** and this sequence: **1,3,7,15,31,...** where **h = 2*h+1**.

The set of steps **h=n/2, n/4, n/8,...1**, where **n** is the number of records in the array, works well for large arrays of data. The following code is a sub-program **ShellSort** from program **\CHAP5\CH5_15.BAS** which employs this set of steps and sorts sub-files with an improved 'bubble' method (speed increase of approximately n^2/n^1.2):

```
SUB ShellSort STATIC
'            ***        ShellSort      ***
'inputs: SortArray,MaxRec
'output: SortArray
'SortArray is sorted by the key field KeySort
'MaxRec -number of records in the array
' initial step of the method
 h = MaxRec \ 2

 DO WHILE h > 0            ' Loop until offset gets to zero.
 '                 **       BubbleSort     **
      L = MaxRec - h
   DO
         Switch = 0
      FOR i = 1 TO L
         IF SortArray(i).KeySort > SortArray(i + h).KeySort THEN
            SWAP SortArray(i), SortArray(i + h) '®¡¬¥-
            Switch = i
         END IF
      NEXT i

      ' Sort on next pass only to where the last switch was made:
      L = Switch - h
   LOOP WHILE Switch
 '             **    end  BubbleSort  **
      ' No switches at last offset, try one half as big:
      h = h \ 2      'Integer division
 LOOP
END SUB
```

Pyramid (Heap) Sort

If we have an array of elements with unordered keys, we may sort them efficiently and perform other operations such as adding or removing elements, or joining arrays, by using **priority queue operations**. These are a generalization of the queue and stack mechanisms we met earlier. The order in which the elements are processed is determined by some preset priorities: in a queue, the elements are processed oldest element first; in a stack, the newest elements have priority, and, typically, in a priority queue, the largest or most critical element is considered first.

The data structure we will use with the priority queue, is the **heap**. In a heap, keys of different elements of the array are related by some **heap condition** which is, basically, an inequality comparison of keys. In our particular example, the heap is a **binary**, or **pyramidal**, tree. They also have a complementary use in so-called binary searches which we will consider in a later section.

A binary tree, so-called because each node only has two branches, connects and labels the elements of the array as shown:

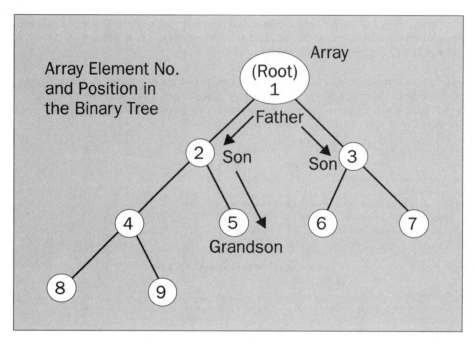

Its first or **root** node is at the top, and it's fairly easy to see that the two nodes branching from any arbitrary node, **A(i)**, the two 'sons' of the 'father', have labels, **A(2*i)** and **A(2*i+1)**. Thus, integer division (represented in QBasic by using '\' instead of '/') of either son's label gives that of the father. Therefore, we have a means of 'navigating' between elements of the array (between the second node and the fourth and fifth, for example). Also, there is only one path between any two nodes on the tree. The values of the elements in a heap are thus always 'related' as a 'family', and this *partially* orders the elements of a heap.

The pyramid (heap) sort consists of two stages: first you build the pyramid from an initially unsorted array, and then you sort its elements. The program can be found as a set of **SUBs** in **\CHAP5\CH5_15.BAS**.

We'll consider the stages involved using an example of a random array of 8 key elements:

```
A(1)  A(2)  A(3)  A(4)  A(5)  A(6)  A(7)  A(8)
 56    71    13    79    98    32    17    44
```

Building a Heap

We use, as a heap condition, the requirement that the magnitude of the entry to a parent node be larger than that to either of its children:

$$A(2*i) <= A(i); \quad \text{and} \quad A(2*i+1) <= A(i).$$

The entry to the root will thus be the largest at any time during the heap's construction.
HeapSort takes the unsorted array, and calls **PercolateUp(MaxLevel)** (MaxRec-1) times in order to construct the heap, as shown in the first part of the following listing. The program has two external variables, the **SortArray** variable is an array of records with the sorting key **KeySort**, and **MaxRec** is the number of records.

```
SUB HeapSort STATIC
' ***  HeapSort  ***
' inputs: SortArray,MaxRec
' output: SortArray
' SortArray is sorted by the key field KeySort
' MaxRec -number of records in the array

' Building a pyramid (heap)
   FOR i = 2 TO MaxRec
       PercolateUp i
   NEXT i
' Sorting the elements of the heap
   FOR i = MaxRec TO 2 STEP -1
       SWAP SortArray(1), SortArray(i)
       PercolateDown i - 1
   NEXT i
END SUB
```

In each call, the program starts at the highest numbered node **(MaxLevel)** and works up the tree to the root node, comparing values of parent and child and swapping where necessary to satisfy the heap condition. In doing this, the program is actually swapping entries in an array, and the binary tree is our visual aid.

```
SUB PercolateUp (MaxLevel) STATIC
'***  PercolateUp   ***
   i = MaxLevel
   DO UNTIL i = 1
       Parent = i \ 2        ' Get the subscript for the parent node.
       IF SortArray(i).KeySort > SortArray(Parent).KeySort THEN
          SWAP SortArray(Parent), SortArray(i)
          i = Parent
       ELSE
          EXIT DO
       END IF
   LOOP
END SUB
```

The start of this process is illustrated below, the shaded branches being those where swapping has occurred in building the heap:

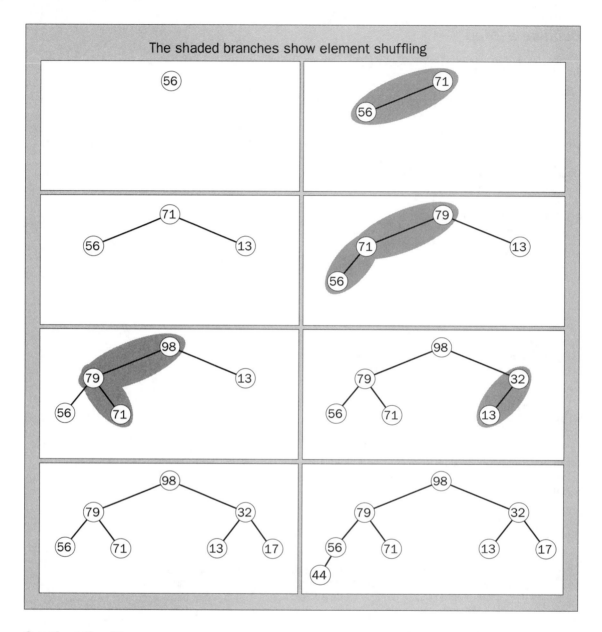

The shaded branches show element shuffling

Sorting the Heap

Having constructed a heap, where we know the local relation between entries to the nodes, the next task is to sort the array totally. Priority queue algorithms, such as our sorting program, work by making a simple structural modification and then rebuilding the heap so that the heap condition is again valid. For our example, sorting by magnitude, the program first swaps the current root entry **SortArray(1)** with **SortArray(i)** where **i** starts at **MaxRec** and gets incrementally smaller. Because of the heap condition, we know that the root value of the binary tree has the largest key of the array. If we put it at the end of the array (or the bottom of the tree), we are placing it in its final position in a sorted array, and we can subsequently ignore it.

However, the swap puts a low value key from the bottom of the tree at the root node, and violates the heap condition. The program then calls **PercolateDown(MaxLevel)** to rebuild the heap for the next swap. The procedure starts at the root node, then finds the node's children. It compares the two children, and whichever is larger is compared with its parent at the root node. Swapping occurs if the larger child is larger than the parent. The process carries on down the tree to the (Maxrec - 1)th node. This guarantees that the new root node of the smaller heap has the largest magnitude of the array.

```
SUB PercolateDown (MaxLevel) STATIC
'              ***    PercolateDown  ***
i = 1 'number of a layer of the heap
DO
   Child = 2 * i      ' Get the subscript for the child node.
   IF Child > MaxLevel THEN EXIT DO
   IF Child + 1 <= MaxLevel THEN
      IF SortArray(Child + 1).KeySort > SortArray(Child).KeySort THEN
           Child = Child + 1
      END IF
   END IF
   IF SortArray(i).KeySort < SortArray(Child).KeySort THEN
        SWAP SortArray(i), SortArray(Child)
        i = Child
      ' so exit:
   ELSE
        EXIT DO
   END IF
LOOP
END SUB
```

The following figure illustrates the process of heap sorting for the 8 elements in our array. The sorted elements, not involved in any further comparisons or exchanges, are shown in boxes.

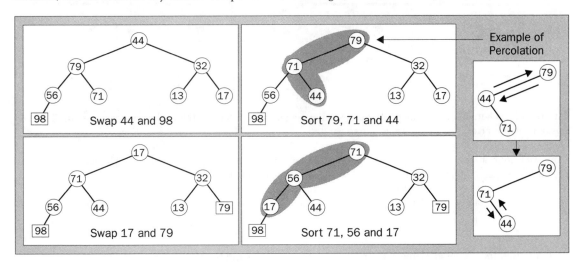

At first glance, it may appear that **HeapSort** doesn't work very well because the large elements, before reaching their positions, must first percolate upwards. Generally, the procedure isn't recommended for use with a small number of elements, **n**, as in our example. However, for large values of **n**, the **HeapSort** procedure is highly effective. For larger values of **n**, it is comparable with **ShellSort** and even outperforms it for randomly selected magnitudes of the array elements. Even in the worst case, **HeapSort** will require no more than **n*log (n)** steps.

QuickSort

Finally, we'll look at an improved sorting method based on exchanges. Its designer, C. Hoare, named the method **QuickSort**. It's aptly named since, compared to other methods, its performance is quite impressive.

The basis of the method consists of the following: among **n** values to be sorted, a value is chosen which is referred to as the partition element. The choice is random. The elements that are smaller than the partition element are then moved to the beginning of the array, and the rest are shifted to the end. The process is repeated with each of the resultant subsets until subsets of one or two elements are formed. At this point the array is sorted:

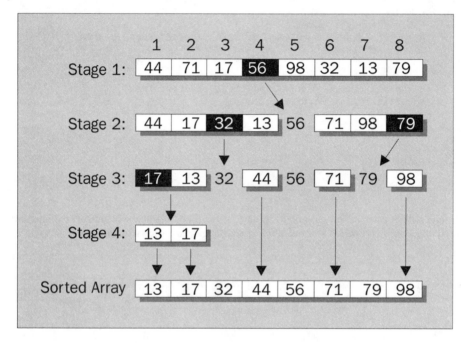

The partition elements are framed. At each sorting stage, the chosen partition element occupies its final position in the array, as the example demonstrates.

Now we'll look at the process of exchange at just one sorting stage in greater detail. We'll restrict ourselves to the first stage for our 8-element array. For the partition element **P=56**:

| 44 | 71 | 17 | 56 | 98 | 32 | 13 | 79 |

At the outset, the partition element temporarily swaps with the rightmost element **A(8)**:

| 44 | 71 | 17 | 79 | 98 | 32 | 13 | 56 |

The pointers **i=1** and **j=7** are set to the left and right boundaries of the array:

```
     *                                            *
    44        71        17        79        98        32        13      │ 56 │
    i=1                                                     j=7
```

Then the pointers begin moving towards each other under the following rules: the **i** pointer increments by **1** until the condition **A(i) > P** (**P** being the partition element) is fulfilled. The **j** pointer is decreased by **1** until **A(j) <= P**:

```
    ------->*                                   *<--
    44        71        17        79        98        32        13      │ 56 │
             i=2                                      j=7
```

If, as both inequalities are satisfied, **i < j**, the positions of the elements are interchanged:

```
             *                                            *
    44        13        17        79        98        32        71      │ 56 │
             i=2                                      j=7
```

The pointer continues moving up to the new exchange:

```
             -------------------->*          *<--------
    44        13        17        79        98        32        71      │ 56 │
                                 i=4        j=6
```

The elements **79** and **32** are swapped:

```
                                  *          *
    44        13        17        32        98        79        71      │ 56 │
                                 i=4        j=6
```

Now the pointers continue to move until they meet, that is when **i = j**:

```
             -------------------------->*<-------------
    44        13        17        32        98        79        71      │ 56 │
                                      i=j=5
```

Then the element at which they meet is swapped with the partition element, which takes its permanent place in the sorted sequence:

```
                                            *
    44        13        17        32      │ 56 │      79        71        98
```

At the next stage, this process is repeated with the sub-arrays **44, 13, 17, 32** and **79, 71, 98**, and so on until the sorting is complete.

The subroutine **QuickSort(Low,High)** presents the opportunity for its parameters to correspond to the indices of the rightmost and leftmost elements of the sub-arrays. When **QuickSort** is first addressed, **Low = 1**, and **High = MaxRec**. In subsequent calls the values of the parameters are defined by the pointer **i** at the instant it meets the **j** pointer. The subroutine uses two external variables **SortArray** and **MaxRec**. The **SortArray** variable denotes an array of records with the key field **KeySort**. **MaxRec** is the number of records being sorted:

```
SUB QuickSort (Low, High)
'                    *        QuickSort      *
'inputs: SortArray,MaxRec
'output: SortArray
'SortArray is sorted by the key field KeySort
'MaxRec -number of records in the array
' Low,High - bound indexes of the subarray sorted
   IF Low < High THEN
      IF High - Low = 1 THEN
         IF SortArray(Low).KeySort > SortArray(High).KeySort THEN
            SWAP SortArray(Low), SortArray(High)
         END IF
      ELSE
         RandIndex = RandInt%(Low, High)
         SWAP SortArray(High), SortArray(RandIndex)
         Partition = SortArray(High).KeySort
         i = Low: J = High
         DO

            DO WHILE (i < J) AND (SortArray(i).KeySort <= Partition)
               i = i + 1
            LOOP
            DO WHILE (J > i) AND (SortArray(J).KeySort >= Partition)
               J = J - 1
            LOOP
            IF i < J THEN
               SWAP SortArray(i), SortArray(J)
            END IF
         LOOP WHILE i < J
         SWAP SortArray(i), SortArray(High)
         ' Recursively call the QuickSort procedure
         IF (i - Low) < (High - i) THEN
            QuickSort Low, i - 1
            QuickSort i + 1, High
         ELSE
            QuickSort i + 1, High
            QuickSort Low, i - 1
         END IF
      END IF
   END IF
END SUB
```

The procedure is not recommended for use with already sorted arrays or those with a small number of elements. Although, in the worst case, the **QuickSort** procedure requires **n*log (n)** comparisons, its performance for random or inversely sorted elements is 2-3 times higher than that of **HeapSort**.

Assessment of Sort Programs

This is where we are going to summarize the preceding sections with the help of the program **\CHAP5\CH5_15.bas** which assesses the operation time of various sorting methods implemented in QBasic. The program sorts the array **SortArray** with a user-defined number of entries (**n<=1000**). **KeySort** is a key field, formed as a random integer value within the range 1-999, and **Str** is a string information field.

In addition to the sorting methods we've covered, another four subroutines can also be invoked from the main program:

- ▲ The subroutine **Initialize** specifies (using the **RandInt%** function), random values of the keys.
- ▲ The subroutine **SortMenu** asks the user for the sorting method and passes its code choice to the main program.
- ▲ The **PrintArray** subroutine outputs the key values onto the screen.
- ▲ The **Space** sub-program suspends calculation until *Space* or the *Esc* key is pressed and passes the code **Escape$** of the pressed key to the main program.

Try the program for yourself, preferably with a fairly large array size, so that the difference in computing time between methods can be compared.

This program can be used for more than simply estimating methods for random key values. The keys can also be sorted in increasing or decreasing order and to do either of these, you only have to replace one statement in the **Initialize** sub-program:

        Index = RandInt%(1, MaxIndex)

To sort in increasing order, replace it with:

        Index = 999 - MaxIndex

To sort in decreasing order, you'll need to replace it with:

        Index = MaxIndex

Try making these changes and testing the program. The following table presents the results of similar tests for arrays sized **n** = **50, 100, 500,** and **700** entries. These were the results on our computer, and they will not necessarily be true on yours, so prove them for yourself. Results, in seconds, for the three variations of sorting an array (elements ordered, random, or in reverse order) are shown in the tables on the next page:

Random:

No. Elements	50	100	500	700
Select	0.000	0.071	1.758	3.512
Bubble	0.059	0.168	4.941	10.051
Insert	0.000	0.109	2.469	5.270
Shell	0.051	0.051	0.391	0.651
Heap	0.059	0.059	0.332	0.488
Quick	0.051	0.063	0.219	0.383

Increasing order:

No. Elements	50	100	500	700
Select	0.000	0.051	1.758	3.461
Bubble	0.000	0.000	0.000	0.000
Insert	0.000	0.000	0.063	0.059
Shell	0.000	0.000	0.510	0.109
Heap	0.063	0.109	0.500	0.770
Quick	0.000	0.059	0.219	0.281

Reverse order:

No. Elements	50	100	500	700
Select	0.047	0.051	2.141	4.172
Bubble	0.113	0.277	6.809	13.230
Insert	0.051	0.160	4.121	8.020
Shell	0.000	0.000	0.223	0.332
Heap	0.000	0.051	0.328	0.488
Quick	0.000	0.047	0.219	0.281

Such experiments as these allow you to compare the practical implementation of the various sorting methods we've looked at, and therefore, to help you make the right choice of method when designing your programs.

Searching in Ordered Data

We've just covered ways of ordering data that you could use for database reports or to prepare data for processing in a program. Now we're going to look at data from the other direction - finding specific data within ordered sets.

Binary Search

We'll first consider searching in records ordered by key fields, where the **binary search** (or bisection) method is simple, fast and based on a 'divide-and-conquer' paradigm.

A binary search works on a large array organized according to the magnitude of a particular key field. The first element is taken, the array is then divided into two, and the element in the middle (or that given by integer division) is compared with the desired key. If the desired key's magnitude is less than that of the middle key, further searches will be restricted to the first half of the array, and if the key is greater than the middle key then further searching will be restricted to the other half, and so on until the position of the desired key is found. Each simple comparison reduces the amount left to be searched by half.

Let's take a look at a simple example using the following sorted sequence of keys:

A(1)	A(2)	A(3)	A(4)	A(5)	A(6)	A(7)	A(8)
13	17	32	44	56	71	79	98

We are going to try and search for the key element **A=32**. Here's the first step in our binary search for this value:

Iteration 1: Choose a value in the middle of the sequence:

13	17	32	**44**	56	71	79	98

Compare it to the desired key, and since **32** is less than **44** continue the search in the left half of the sequence:

A(1)	A(2)	A(3)
13	17	32

Iteration 2: Choose a value in the middle of this sequence:

13	**17**	32

Compare it to the desired key, and as **32** is more than **17** we restrict the search in the right half of sequence and, lo and behold, we find the single desired entry:

A(3)
32

To illustrate this, we'll present a binary search program **\CHAP5\CH5_16.BAS** which works on a sorted array **SortArray**. The records of the array consist of two fields:

Info	a string type key field.
Date	a field of data searched for.

The sub-program **InArray** fills the records with information from the **DATA** block. The key fields are filled with the names of the cities, and the search fields with the dates they were first mentioned. The subroutine **PrintArray** outputs an ordered list of the keys (cities) onto the screen. The subroutine **BiSearch** performs a binary search in a sorted array of length **MaxRec**. As you can see, the algorithm is fairly simple, taking the value midway between the first and last value, and then comparing the magnitude of the array's key at that point with the value of **KeySearch**. The comparison determines whether the search is completed, or needs to go to the left or right of the **i**.

```
SUB BiSearch
  PRINT
  INPUT "Name of the city"; KeySearch
  L = 1: R = MaxRec: p = 0' start value
      DO
        i = (R + L) \ 2
        IF KeySearch = SortArray(i).Info THEN
          PRINT
          PRINT "          Search is successful"
          PRINT i; SortArray(i).Info;
          PRINT " Year of foundation: "; SortArray(i).Date;
          p = 1
          EXIT DO
        END IF
        IF KeySearch < SortArray(i).Info THEN
              R = i - 1
        ELSE
              L = i + 1
        END IF
      LOOP WHILE R - L + 1
      IF p = 0 THEN
        PRINT " Record not found "
      END IF
END SUB
```

Binary Tree Search

Earlier, we used a binary tree in the pyramid sort to help order an array. The unordered keys of the array were partially sorted into a heap, using **HeapSort**. In this section, the order of the elements in the array is already fixed, although not necessarily in order of the magnitude of the key. What we have to do is assign these elements (for example, the characters of a word) to the nodes of a binary tree, so that they are searchable.

Representing data in the form of a binary tree is convenient when you're constantly adding new records or deleting records or parts of records from the array. However, there's very little point in using the binary tree search on a strictly ordered array because changing one record would cause many others to move, in order to retain the order.

The binary tree we use here differs subtly from that used in the pyramid sort. In the pyramid sort, the keys are ordered by magnitude, within each branch traced from the root node. In the **binary search tree** an arbitrary node **A(i)** has a 'left' and a 'right' son, as before, but they are related by the following conditions:

A(L) < A(i);   A(R >= A(i)

So a left son has a key of lesser magnitude than its father, while the right son has a key of greater magnitude. This gives us a tree consisting of partially ordered elements:

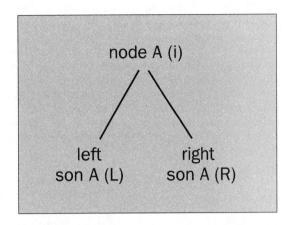

An example of a binary search tree for an array with the keys **14, 3, 27, 19, 5, 4, 1, 16** would be the following:

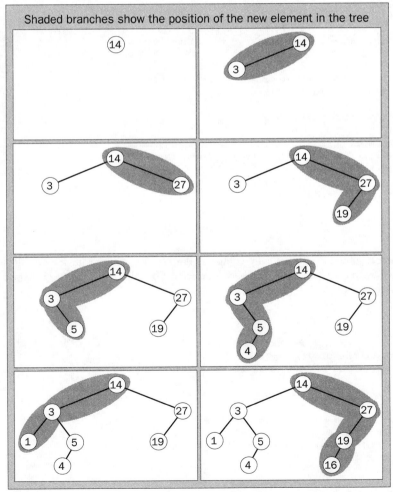

The algorithm for building a tree is as follows. The first key element, **14** in our case, is set as a root node. The next value, **3**, being less than **14**, is inserted in the tree as the left 'son'. Since **27** is greater than **14** it is inserted into the tree as the right 'son' of **14**. The number **19** is also greater than **14**, and so would normally be the right 'son' of **14**. But we already have **27** in its place, so we go down another level, and compare **19** to **27**, this means that **19** will be the left son of '**27**', and, therefore, one of **14**'s 'grandsons'.

If you look at our next program **\CHAP5\CH5_17.BAS,** you'll find a subroutine **Tree** which constructs a binary search tree for the array **TreeArray**. Each record is a node of the tree. The variable **i**, as the ordinal number, or index, of a record in the array, corresponds to the number of the node. A record must contain the three fields used by the sub-program:

> **Info** a key field of any type, e.g. String or Integer.
> **Left** & **Right** integer type fields where the numbers of the nodes corresponding to the left and right sons are formed while the tree is being created.

The subroutine fills the fields **Left** and **Right** according to the aforementioned algorithm. Here is the subroutine that performs this task:

```
SUB Tree

  FOR i = 2 TO MaxRec     'i-number of a pass
  q = 1 ' start value of the index of a mimimum key
    DO
      p = q
      IF TreeArray(i).Info < TreeArray(p).Info THEN
            q = TreeArray(p).Left
      ELSE
            q = TreeArray(p).Right
      END IF
    LOOP WHILE q
    IF TreeArray(i).Info < TreeArray(p).Info THEN
       TreeArray(p).Left = i
    ELSE
       TreeArray(p).Right = i
    END IF
  NEXT i
END SUB
```

The following **Search** subroutine sequentially compares the key **KeyTree** with the key fields of the records. The index of a record (the node number) is selected from the fields **Left** or **Right** depending on the result of the comparison.

```
SUB Search
  PRINT
  PRINT "          SEARCH ON THE TREE"
  INPUT "Name of the city"; KeyTree
  p = 1 ' start value of the index of the minimum key
      DO
          IF KeyTree = TreeArray(p).Info THEN
            PRINT
            PRINT "          Search is successful"
            PRINT p; TreeArray(p).Info;
            PRINT " Year of foundation: "; TreeArray(p).Date;
            EXIT DO
          END IF
```

```
        IF KeyTree < TreeArray(p).Info THEN
                p = TreeArray(p).Left
        ELSE
                p = TreeArray(p).Richt
        END IF
    LOOP WHILE p

    IF p = 0 THEN
      PRINT "Record not found"
    END IF
  END SUB
```

We'll demonstrate how useful these subroutines are with an example which searches for the first chronicled mention of a city. The demo program **\CHAP\CH5_17.BAS** uses the following sub-programs together with the ones we've already described:

▲ **InArray** inputs the unordered information about the cities from the **DATA** into an array.

▲ **PrintArray** displays the values of the nodes (names of the cities) in their tree order, and also the values of their left and right sons.

Here's a diagram showing the tree corresponding to the test run of the program:

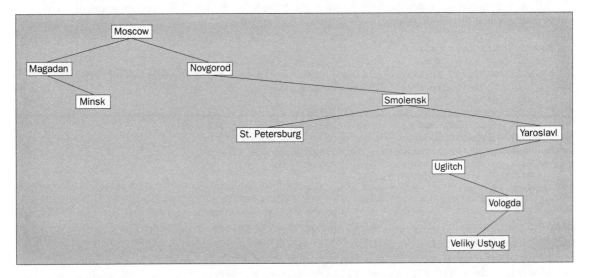

The tree search algorithm can be used to our advantage for developing sub-programs to add or remove records. We've seen in this section how, given an array which will regularly have records added to it, or whose initial order we want to keep, we can still order its keys by relative magnitude in order to perform a binary tree search, and locate them quickly.

Hashing

The search methods we've looked at so far have all been based on full (sort) or partial (tree) data ordering. However, the efficiency of the search can be increased if, instead of various ordered structures, you use unordered or mixed data structures, whose key directly addresses their index in the array. The **hashing** method deals with these structures.

Hashing is a compromise between the twin needs of saving time and space. Saving time in a search means that sequential searches aren't feasible, and saving space means that the minimum possible memory is to be used. These are its chief advantages.

With this method, the array index number of a record is calculated as some function of its key field. The simplest example is an ordered array with keys of 1 to 10, where the array index is just set to that of the key. The function that transforms the record key into its ordinal number is referred to as a **hash** function. A 'good' hash function has two properties:

 It's easily calculated and doesn't consume too much machine time.

 Its range of values must be relatively narrow, otherwise records will be wasted. However, it can't be too narrow, otherwise the same value will correspond to two different key fields: this is called **collision**. The number of collisions won't be high if the values being used are evenly distributed by the algorithm.

If there are collisions, a number of index records having the same array index, one collision-resolution technique is to order those records as a list, with the array index pointing to the beginning of the list.

We'll demonstrate the hash function for a string key field containing the name of a city.

The following program calculates the hash function **HashKey%** for the key field **x$** (the name of a city with length not less than 5 characters).

```
FUNCTION HashKey% (x$)
  IF LEN(x$) >= 5 THEN
    L1$ = MID$(x$, 1, 1)          'Takes first, third and fifth characters of city name
    L2$ = MID$(x$, 3, 1)          'for the Hash key
    L3$ = MID$(x$, 5, 1)
    Hundred% = ASC(L1$) MOD 2 'Calculates value of Hundreds, Tens and Units using
    Ten% = ASC(L2$) MOD 10       'the remainder from MOD division
    One% = ASC(L3$) MOD 10
    HashKey% = 100 * Hundred% + 10 * Ten% + One% + 1
  ELSE
    HashKey% = ConstHash * MaxRec
  END IF
END FUNCTION
```

Here, the built-in function **MID$** separates out the 1st, 3rd and 5th characters of the key field, and then the **ASC** functions calculates their numeric codes. The codes are divided by the integers 2 and 10 and the remainders of the division are used; for instance, for the string key '**Moscow**', the character codes '**M**', '**s**' and '**w**' will have the values **77**, **115** and **111**. The variables **Hundred%**, **Ten%**, and **One%** will be assigned the residual values: **77 MOD 2 = 1**, **115 MOD 10 = 5**, **111 MOD 10 = 1**. The hash function is calculated from these remainders:

$$HashKey\% = 100 * Hundred\% + 10 * Ten\% + One\% + 1$$

The value **HashKey%** for the "**Moscow**" key will be **100*1+10*5+1+1=152**. The range of the hash function (maximum number of records) is:

$$1 <= HashKey\% <= 200$$

In keeping with the known or estimated number of records, you can easily extend the set of values if you write, for instance:

```
Hundred% = ASC(L1$) MOD 10
```

In this case, there'll be 1000 values of the hash function. All applied hash functions use the functions **ASC** and **MOD**.

The Arrangement and Search for a Record Using the Hash Function

Suppose that we wish to place a new record into an array. The hash function, applied to the key field of a record, will define its number (index in the array). To find a record, you simply hash the key to give you the required number, and then check that the keys match. This is the quickest method of finding a record.

The program **\CHAP5\CH5_18.BAS** arranges and searches for records using the hash method. The array **HashArray** contains information about a city's first mention in the chronicles. This demo program also uses some other sub-programs:

- ▲ **HashInArray** 'clears' the array and inputs unordered information about the cities from the **DATA** block.

- ▲ The subroutine **PrintArray** displays the list of 'non-empty' keys together with their hash functions.

- ▲ **HashSearch** conducts the search for the information about the cities.

The collisions aren't analyzed in this program; the value **ConstHash** corresponds to the ratio of the hashed data area size to the initial data area, and the maximum size of the hash data area is 1000 entries. The results of this program are as follows:

Hashing:

City	Hash function
Petersburg	65
Novgorod	82
Vologda	84
Veliky Ustyug	88
Minsk	108
Smolensk	112
Magadan	131
Yaroslavl	146
Moscow	152
Uglitch	187

Summary

Data structures like stacks, queues and lists are the simplest and most abundant information structures. Using these as the basis, it's easy to create more complicated data structures, e.g. graphs.

Stacks and queues are used during programming when searching for variations and are an important method of processing finite data structures. This method forms the basis for solving a wide variety of problems - we've covered maps, chess problems and labyrinths but there are plenty more.

Lists allow the simulation of other data structures. In doing so, the memory for new data structures can be allocated dynamically; for example, when organizing several stacks or queues on the basis of one array. The ease with which lists can be changed makes them convenient for representing data that frequently changes shape.

We then took a look at some tried and tested methods of searching through data structures and we learnt the following points about the sort and search algorithms:

1 When evaluating their efficiency consider programming time, processing time and memory. Unless your data set is massive, you won't normally have a problem with memory.

2 The direct sort methods are simple, and they're most successful with small-size data.

3 The selection of an improved sort method depends on how ordered the initial data is. The shell method is well suited for sorting data that's already almost ordered, whereas the heap sort method doesn't work so well with ordered data. The quick sort method suits any kind of data, especially if it's in inverse order.

4 The binary method is only suitable for sorted data.

5 Use binary trees for partially ordering data when it will be subsequently added to, changed or searched.

6 Hashing is the fastest search method, though it's heavy on the memory.

By taking these conclusions into account, you'll be able to select the most appropriate sorting strategy for your application programs and make use of the advantages of working with ordered (sorted) data. We hope that the material we've looked at in this chapter has convinced you that there's nothing too mystical or difficult about working with complex data structures, and that when used properly they can greatly improve the efficiency of your programs.

File Management

Introduction

Data is stored in files and all applications which process large amounts of information, for example, databases and text editors, use a set of methods for organizing files to make searching for data as fast as possible. File organization, management and processing is something every good programmer needs to know.

In this chapter, we will first take a look at QBasic's built-in tools for file management - methods of accessing files, statements and functions to work with files and ways of storing files on disk. Then, continuing the work of Chapter 5's sorting and searching of data, we will discuss file processing.

In this chapter, you'll learn about:

- File classification
- DOS and QBasic file commands
- Sequential files
- Text files
- Random access files
- Binary files
- External sort and merging files
- File processing
- Indexation

The Main Concepts

A file isn't just a passive receptacle for data, as you will realize when we tackle a range of problems associated with file processing. Unfortunately, it's impossible to give a strict or full definition of what exactly a file is, since the concept of a file is one of the cornerstones of computer science. So we're limited to a descriptive definition which will be of use when designing file processing algorithms.

From the point of view of a PC user, a file is a named collection of data that gives a rather full description of some set of uniform objects, or objects of the same type, and is stored on external drives, typically a disk. Files are divided into **records**, each containing information about one of these objects. The records are then divided into smaller elements, referred to as **fields**, and each field carries a description of just one property of an object.

From this, we can provide the following definitions:

- A field is the smallest unit of named data. A field can be of any declared type, typically either numeric or string.

- A group is a named set of fields, considered as a single unit. A group can be defined using a user-defined type; for example, the group **Date** could consist of the fields **Month**, **Day**, **Year** of the type **Integer**.

- A record is a named set consisting of one or more fields or groups. Copies of this record template are used to store specific values associated with an object.

- A file is a named set of record copies of one type, located on a magnetic disk.

Such an information structure is perhaps best visualized by representing files as tables. As an example, consider a file called 'The Blue Ribbon' which contains information about record crossings of famous transatlantic liners:

Liner	Direction	Time of Crossing			Velocity
		Days	Hours	Minutes	
Normandy	West	3	23	2	30.58
Queen Mary	West	3	20	42	31.69
United States	East	3	10	40	35.6

From the table, you can see that the Days, Hours and Minutes fields are combined as the individual fields of the Time of Crossing group. Each row of the table contains a copy of a record from the file 'The Blue Ribbon'.

Classification of Files

There are two distinct ways that we can classify files which we will be looking at. Let's look first at classification via the organizational pattern of the data.

Classification by Way of Information Organization

In modern programming languages, there are three clearly defined types of files: text files, files with user-defined record types and binary files.

Text files

The organization of text files is determined by the requirements of the operating system and by compatibility problems in transferring information from one programming system to another. All software, though written in different programming languages on a PC, operates under the control of DOS.

How data is represented in these programs is defined by the programming languages (C, Pascal, Assembler, etc.) and by the programmer's choice. Yet, despite obvious differences in data representation, we can pass the resultant data from one program to another. For example, a file obtained as the result of a QBasic program can be easily transferred to a program written in the dBase environment for further processing. The majority of program systems, including QBasic, use two methods of organizing text files.

System Data Format

The first is referred to as the **System Data Format** (**SDF**). Here, the records of the text files represent continuous sequences of ASCII characters whose ends are marked by a record-end marker which is normally one or more special separation characters. In program systems that work under MS-DOS, the record-end marker is a pair of symbols **CR** (carriage return) and **LF** (line feed), with the codes **13(0Dh)** and **10(0Ah)**, respectively.

Text files prepared in this format are generally intended for preparing reports which are repeatedly output to the screen or to the printer or further used by word processors. Using data stored in text files for new calculations is difficult because you need complicated conversion procedures to separate the miscellaneous data within a line. This problem is further complicated by the fact that the lengths of the elements that make up a line may, in fact, differ.

Here is the general representation of a text file, containing n records:

Record 1   CR LF   Record 2   CR LF   ....   Record n   CR LF

Delimited Format

The second way of organizing a text file is referred to as the **Delimited Format**. In this format, elements of records are separated by commas. Characters, unlike numbers, are enclosed in quotation marks. As in the System Data Format, each record ends with two record-end markers. This format is used for the transfer of data from one program system to another. An example of the records of a textual file in this format is shown here:

"Reagan R.",1980,1988,"Republican" CR LF
"Carter J."1976,1980,"Democratic" CR LF

These records contain two character fields containing the names of USA presidents and the names of the parties they belonged to when they held office, as well as two numeric fields containing their first and final years of office.

Files with User-defined Record Types

As with all modern programming languages, in QBasic you can implement complex data structures which combine variables or fields under a single identifier called a **group**. Since each field is one of the language's built-in types, the length of a group is always the same and doesn't depend on the information it stores. Therefore, with user-defined record types we don't have to use record-end markers and field separators to separate variable entries.

However, distinctions in the representation of identical data types in various languages, and the differences in the syntax and the semantics of the user-defined type, do not, as a rule, allow the transfer of QBasic files of this type to programs written in other programming languages. For example, a field specified as a string of length up to 20 characters is defined in QBasic by type **STRING * 20**. In the record which contains this field, exactly 20 bytes will be allocated. In Turbo Pascal, the peculiarities of representing string variables means that 21 bytes of memory would be allocated for the equivalent field. So, although the records of files have an identical structure in programming terms, they'll actually have different physical lengths. Because of this, user-defined record types are only used for the internal storage of data amongst the same program systems.

In comparison to text files, files with user-defined record types provide simpler and faster data processing because, during reading or writing, conversion between numeric data and its string representation isn't required. For example, let's consider the output of the same data into a text file and to a file with user-defined record types. The source data is in the record **ExampleRec** of the following type:

```
TYPE ExampleRecType
    Field1 AS STRING * 15
    Field2 AS INTEGER
END TYPE
```

Assign the following values to the fields:

```
ExampleRec.Field1 = "Year of the Dog
ExampleRec.Field2 = 1994
```

If we enter the fields **Field1 Field2** into a text SDF-file, we'll get the record:

```
Year of the Dog 1994
```

In order to get this, the I/O system of QBasic actually carried out the following actions:

```
ExampleRec.Field1 + STR$(ExampleRec.Field2)
```

In other words, it converted the numeric field **Field2** into a string and added the result to the end of the string **Field1**.

If we output the whole record to a file, on disk we'll see this sequence of bytes:

```
Year of the DogCAh07h,
```

where the bytes **CAh** and **07h** present the physical standard representation of the integer 1994. These records reflect the way the data is stored in memory for use by the computer.

Binary Files

Binary files store numeric data as a sequence of bytes, the same format as that in the computer's RAM. It's the most efficient way to store numeric data. Each data entry is of a fixed size (integers occupy two bytes) with the result that, compared to ASCII's variable data lengths, the binary representation usually requires less memory.

Binary files have a structure that isn't recognized by QBasic's conventional I/O statements. The contents of a binary file are just a set of codes and contain no control characters to influence the data format, such as carriage returns, line feeds or tabs. The simplest way of reading or writing them is to use a byte-by-byte method. If you know the features of a particular binary file, you can sometimes read it partially or wholly into the variables of a complicated structure (a record or an array). We'll cover these methods in more detail in a later section devoted to binary file processing.

Binary files are used when the structure of the stored data goes beyond the scope of text files, or files with user-defined record types. Binary files are usually executable machine code files with the extensions **.COM** or **.EXE**, or graphics files with extensions like **.PCX**.

PCX files consist of a heading of fixed structure and a sequence of bytes which represent the graphics information in plain or coded form. This way of representing information is also used when transferring data through communication channels. An exchange of data with binary files is typically performed by the standard exchange statements of the QBasic language which we'll discuss later on. In practice, arrays are most frequently used to store blocks of binary files, although other types of data can also be used.

Classification by Length of Record and Access Method

In contrast, files can also be classified by these two features: the **length of the record** and the **access method**.

The record's length can be fixed or undefined, depending on the type of file. If a record type is user-defined, all records have the same length, so files that consist of records of this type are also called files with **fixed record length**. A text file is a typical example of a file with records of undefined length.

The access method is the way in which files are searched for a particular record. DOS doesn't implement access to separate records of files, so this is carried out by the run-time systems of programming languages. In QBasic, as in the majority of programming systems for PCs, there are two general access methods:

Sequential Access

In **sequentially accessed** files, the reading and writing of the data is performed in strict order (for example, the last element of data is available only *after* all the previous ones have been retrieved). The sequential access method is used for mass or group data processing when it's necessary to look through all the records of a file in order to get the necessary information to work on. This is very much like a cassette tape: it's impossible to play the last record without first going past all the others. Also, for an ASCII file, the variable data lengths for each entry mean that, in order to find an entry, all preceding entries must be read. A sequential file ends with a special character, the **EOF**, or **end of file** marker.

Random Access

With a **random** or **direct access** file, writing and retrieving an element of data can be performed without having to trawl through any irrelevant information. Rather like using a map where you locate places by their coordinates, the direct access method allows you to directly reference a particular record (byte) in a file. This access method is widely used when only a small part of the stored data is required. A classic example of its use is with help systems; for example, by entering the name of a person, you can find their telephone number and address.

File Channels

Files are inextricably entwined with the concept of **input/output** (I/O) channels, the paths along which information is transmitted. There are channels to the keyboard, display, printer and disk drives. The channel to a display is invariably unidirectional, as data from the source can only be transmitted to the display and not vice versa. The keyboard channel is also uni-directional - data can only be transferred *from* the keyboard. Disk drive channels, however, are bi-directional since the files can be transmitted both to and from the PC for reading and writing.

Files stored on magnetic disks have names which suit the requirements of the operating system, in our case DOS, whose names contain the file access path, the file name itself (up to 8 characters) and an extension (up to 3 characters) separated from the file name by a period.

Therefore, the file,

```
D:\QBASIC\PROGRAM\DEMO.BAS
```

has the name **DEMO** with the extension **.BAS** and is located on disk drive **D:** in the **\PROGRAM** subdirectory of the **\QBASIC** root directory. In this case, the extension **.BAS** tells us that the file is a BASIC program. Because such long names are inconvenient for use in input/output statements, files, once opened, are referred to by a hash mark followed by an integer, for example #1 or #2.

Managing Program Files

Before discussing the characteristics of data files, let's first consider operations with program files. Because of their importance, these files usually have special saving and loading instructions. In QBasic, there are the shell commands: **SAVE** (for writing programs) and **LOAD** (for reading programs). When program files are loaded, external procedures are sent to their 'pockets' and are put at the user's disposal separately from the main module (although included in the same file). DOS possesses a number of special commands for file operations which are included in QBasic as the following statements:

CHDIR path$	changes the current directory to a specified one.
FILES [file-spec$]	displays a specified file catalog.
MKDIR path$	creates a new subdirectory.
NAME old$ AS new$	renames files or catalogs.
RMDIR path$	removes a specified subdirectory.
KILL file-spec$	removes a specified file or group of files.

Here the dollar sign **$** indicates that the corresponding parameter must be a character string.

File Management in QBasic

File management consists of a number of operations: opening a file, sequentially or randomly writing to a file, reading data blocks, separating the records (in binary files) and closing a file. In QBasic, the following input/output statements are used for managing files and should be fairly familiar, having been introduced in Chapter 3:

OPEN	for opening a file.
PRINT [USING], WRITE, PUT	for outputting records to files.
INPUT, LINE INPUT, GET	for reading records from files.
SEEK	for positioning a record or a byte in a file with user-defined type of record or a binary file.
CLOSE	for closing a file.

The following functions also play an important role in file management:

EOF (n)	returns the value True, if the end of the file **n** is reached, and False if otherwise.
SEEK (n)	returns the number of the current record in a file **n** containing user-defined record types, or the current byte if **n** is a binary file.
LOF (n)	returns the size (or length) of a binary file in bytes.
INPUT$ (k, [[#]1])	returns the first **k** characters of the current record in file **n**.

We will explain more about these statements and functions in the next few sections as we further discuss sequential and random-access files.

Sequential Files

A sequential file can be likened to a record on a magnetic tape - the start of the file contains information about it and the rest is data. Apart from the beginning, every file contains an end marker, defined by the decimal code 26.

Information is written in the form of records. Each record consists of ASCII codes of the string to be recorded and the special characters - carriage return (CR), and line feed (LF). To recap, the decimal codes for CF and LF are 13 and 10, respectively. Thus, the structure of a sequential file may be represented as follows:

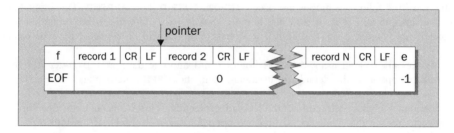

To read the file, the computer finds its beginning and puts a pointer on it which, in our cassette analogy, is like the playback magnetic head. It begins moving from the beginning of the file to the end, sequentially reading out all the records. From this, it's clear that within a sequential file it's impossible to read a particular record without reading all the records before it.

However, the magnetic head (pointer) must know where the records finish so as not to continue into the next file. The end of file marker is the cue here. QBasic's **EOF** function checks whether the end of a file has been reached. When reading files it returns a value of **0**, except at the end of the file when it returns a value of **-1**. Another function, **LOF** (standing for 'length of file') has a value equal to the length of a specified file.

Hold on, there's one more important feature. Because writing onto the disk is performed in blocks, there is another function, **LOC()**, the return value of which is the location of a previously opened file. For a sequential file, this location is the current position of the pointer with respect to the beginning of the file, measured in bytes divided by 128. For random access files, the return value is the number of the last file written to or read from the opened file. For binary files, the function has a value equal to the file pointer's current byte position.

Opening a File

In order to read or write to a file, be it sequential or random access, it must be **open**. To do this, you must use the **OPEN** statement:

```
OPEN file$ [FOR mode] [ACCESS access] [lock] AS [#]filenumber%
[LEN=reclen%]
```

where

`file$`	is the name of the file or device. The file name may include a drive and path.
`mode`	is one of the file modes: **APPEND**, **BINARY**, **INPUT**, **OUTPUT** or **RANDOM**.
`access`	indicates whether the file is open for **READ**, **WRITE** or **READ WRITE** access in network environments.
`lock`	specifies the file locking in network environments: **SHARED**, **LOCK READ**, **LOCK WRITE**, **LOCK READ WRITE**.
`filenumber%`	is a number in the range 1 and 255 that identifies the file while it's open.
`reclen%`	is the record length for random access files (the default is 128 bytes), or the number of characters buffered for sequential files (the default is 512 bytes). May be set to the length of a user-defined type.

For sequential files, the following modes are used: **INPUT**, **OUTPUT** and **APPEND**. The input file is only used for reading in data and, if it's a disk file, it must already exist. The file to be appended to must also exist. The output file is created on disk and, if it already exists, it will be replaced by a new one.

Random access files are created using **RANDOM** (for text and numeric data) and **BINARY** (for machine code). The **RANDOM** option is the default, so its inclusion in the **OPEN** statement is optional.

The **OPEN** statement includes instructions for file read protection. This is because the development of computer networks means that unprotected files are open for access by anybody. **SHARED** is used to indicate that the file is for common use, while **LOCK WRITE** prohibits the writing of information onto the file by other users and **LOCK READ** prevents other network users from reading the protected file.

Inputting Data in a Sequential File

So now you've opened the file, how do you put data into it? Sequential files have a simple structure and are thus widely used. To input data into a sequential file, you can use the **WRITE** or **PRINT** statements:

```
PRINT [[#]filenumber%,] variablelist
WRITE [[#]filenumber%,] expressionlist
```

where

`filenumber%`	is the number of an open sequential file. If `filenumber%` is omitted, **WRITE** writes to the screen.
`expressionlist`	is one or more variables or expressions, separated by commas, whose values are written to the screen or file.

WRITE inserts commas between items and quotation marks around strings as they're written and a new line for each **WRITE** statement. **WRITE** sends values to a file in a form that can be read by the **INPUT** statement.

The two simple programs contained in this program work with files which contain telephone number records:

```
REM Creating the sequential FTEL file and writing it onto a disk
REM \CHAP6\CH6_1.BAS

Num% = 3
Names$ = "Ivanov V.P."
Tel$ = "123-45-67"
MKDIR "C:\WROXDATA"
OPEN "C:\WROXDATA\FTEL.DAT" FOR OUTPUT AS #1
WRITE #1, Num%
WRITE #1, Name$, Tel$
CLOSE #1

END
```

In this case, the writing instruction includes three elements: an ordinal number, a name and a person's telephone number. The data in the file is presented in text format and, if you view the contents of the created file **FTEL.DAT**, you'll see this:

```
3
"Ivanov V.P.","123-45-67"
```

Each line in the **WRITE** statement creates its own line in the text file. If there are several pieces of data in a line, they're separated by commas.

Reading Input from a File

The statements **INPUT #**, **LINE INPUT #** and **INPUT$** are used to read input from files. Their syntax is the same as that of their analogous keyboard statements, without the **#** sign. We use the hash sign, followed by a number, to associate input with a specified channel.

The statements take this form:

```
INPUT #filenumber%, variablelist
LINE INPUT #filenumber%, variable$
```

where

variablelist   is one or more variables, separated by commas, in which data entered from the keyboard or read from a file is stored. Variable names can consist of up to 40 characters and must begin with a letter. Valid characters are **A-Z**, **0-9**, and period (**.**).

variable$ holds a line of characters entered from the keyboard or read from a file.

filenumber%   is the number of an open file.

INPUT uses a comma as a separator between entries, whilst **LINE INPUT** reads all the characters up to the next carriage return.

The following program reads the **FTEL.DAT** file created in the last program and displays the information contained in it:

```
REM Reading and using the sequential FTEL file from disk and
REM outputting onto the screen the information it contains
REM \CHAP6\CH6_2.BAS

CLS
CHDIR "C:\WROXDATA"
OPEN "FTEL.DAT" FOR INPUT AS #1
INPUT #1, Num%
INPUT #1, Name$, Tel$
PRINT "LOF ="; LOF(1)
PRINT "LOC ="; LOC(1)
PRINT "EOF ="; EOF(1)
CLOSE #1
PRINT "Data:"
PRINT Num%; " "; Name$; " "; Tel$

END
```

which appears on the screen as:

```
LOF = 30
LOC = 1
EOF =-1
Data:
3  Ivanov V. P. 123-45-67
```

As a file is read from disk, its data is treated as a continuous character string. When **INPUT #** and **LINE INPUT #** are executed, the characters are retrieved from the file in sequence and interpreted, depending on the variable type, either as a string or a numerical expression. Retrieval continues until a separator is met. For **LINE INPUT #**, the line-end marker is the carriage return character. The rest of the characters are referred to as data.

The function **INPUT$** is also often used when dealing with files. It returns a string of characters read from a specified file:

INPUT$(k[, [#]filenumber%])

where **k** is the number of characters (bytes) to be read and **filenumber%** is the number of the open file. If **filenumber%** is omitted, **INPUT$** reads data from the keyboard. See the on-line help for an example of its operation.

Appending a File

Let's return to **\CHAP6\CH6_1.BAS**, the program that created the file **FTEL.DAT** which so far contains just a single telephone number record. How can we add another person's data to the file? Easy - just use the **APPEND** modifier when opening the file. Then, while it's open, any new information is added to the end of the sequential file. If the file to be extended exists on a disk, you must open it using **APPEND** in order to add further information, otherwise it will be overwritten.

In this program, one more record is entered into the **FTEL.DAT** file:

```
REM Adding data to the file FTEL
REM \CHAP6\CH6_3.BAS

Num% = 4
Name$ = "Petrov I.L."
Tel$ = "654-32-10"
OPEN "C:\WROXDATA\FTEL.DAT" FOR APPEND AS #1
WRITE #1, Num%
WRITE #1, Name$, Tel$
CLOSE #1

END
```

If you run the program, you'll see that it opens and reads the file **FTEL.DAT** from the hard disk, makes additions to it and writes it back to disk again. If you look at the file **FTEL.DAT** now, its contents are:

```
3
"Ivanov V.P.","123-45-67"
4
"Petrov I.L.","654-32-10"
```

FTEL.DAT now consists of two records, each containing three components: a number, a name with initials and the telephone number of that person. If you're creating a database, you should make sure that you stick to the same file structure when dealing with various records. This isn't a hard and fast rule since you can add any data that you want to a sequential file, but making sense of it might be quite difficult if you haven't followed a strict pattern.

Closing a File

You'll have noticed that we've used the **CLOSE** statement in previous programs in this chapter. Basically, it closes the file after reading or writing and takes the following form:

CLOSE [[#]filenumber%[,[#]filenumber%]...]

CLOSE allows you to close the files numbered **filenumber1%**, **filenumber2%** and so on. The numbers that are released in the process can then be used to identify other files.

You can close selected files with this statement, but there are a number of commands that close all open files: **RESET**, **CLEAR**, **END**, **RUN** and **SYSTEM**.

Deleting, Renaming and Modifying Files

Unfortunately, a single item of data in a sequential file can't be arbitrarily selected and changed without a bit of thought. However, QBasic does include two statements which, if used correctly, will let you change any item in a sequential file:

KILL "Name"	deletes files of a specified name
NAME "Name1" AS "Name2"	renames file **Name1** as file **Name2**

We'll again use the previously created **FTEL.DAT** file containing just one record (if you haven't run **\CHAP6\CH6_1.BAS** yet, do so now).

Let's suppose that we need to change the ordinal number from 3 to 4 and the name of the person to that of his brother. The telephone number needs to be left the same. Although we can't do this directly, with a little bit of juggling it's possible. We have to open the file, output the information and send it to a new file (such as **NEWFTEL** for example), amending the information in the process. After that, **FTEL** should be deleted and **NEWFTEL** renamed as **FTEL**. This process is demonstrated here:

```
REM Correcting the file FTEL
REM \CHAP6\CH6_4.BAS

CLS
OPEN "C:\WROXDATA\FTEL.DAT" FOR INPUT AS #1
OPEN "C:\WROXDATA\NEWFTEL.DAT" FOR OUTPUT AS #2
INPUT #1, Num%
INPUT #1, Name$, Tel$
WRITE #2, 4
WRITE #2, "Ivanov S.P.", Tel$
CLOSE #1, #2
KILL "C:\WROXDATA\FTEL.DAT"
NAME "C:\WROXDATA\NEWFTEL.DAT" AS "C:\WROXDATA\FTEL.DAT"

END
```

If you view the file **FTEL** after executing this program, you'll see the following:

```
4
"Ivanov S.P.","654-32-10"
```

Mission accomplished! However, if you regularly want to do this sort of thing, it's probably better to use random access files.

Setting and Taking Off File Protection

Finally, files often contain important, confidential information; for example, your personal finances. Therefore, the need arises to *protect* files from unauthorized access, especially on networks. As well as allowing locking when using the **OPEN** statement, QBasic has instructions for setting (**LOCK**) and removing (**UNLOCK**) file protection within the program:

```
LOCK [#]FileNumber%, T
LOCK [#]FileNumber%, [T1] TO T2
LOCK [#]FileNumber%, [T1] TO END
UNLOCK [#]FileNumber%, T
UNLOCK [#]FileNumber%, [T1] TO T2
UNLOCK [#]FileNumber%, [T1] TO END
```

Here, the parameters containing the letter **T** refer to the record numbers or, in the case of binary files, to byte numbers. Locking a sequential file locks all the data. Locking a file stops other processes (programs which are running) accessing the data. It's important to **UNLOCK** the data before closing the program.

Text Files

Taking these file input/output functions, we'll now consider the management of text files using several examples. We begin with files in the System Data Format:

```
REM Example for Text File in System Data Format
REM \CHAP6\CH6_5.BAS

CLS
OPEN "CANDIES.TXT" FOR OUTPUT AS #1
DO
    'Read entries from the keyboard
    INPUT "   Candy   :            ", Candy$
    INPUT "   Weight  :            ", Weight
    INPUT "   Calories:            ", Cal%
    'Write entries to SDF-File
    PRINT #1, Candy$; Weight; Cal%
    INPUT "Add another entry"; r$
LOOP WHILE UCASE$(r$) = "y"
CLOSE #1

END
```

This simple program enters the name of a piece of candy, its weight and calorie content and then forms a corresponding record in the text SDF-file.

In such a file, the values of the character variable **Candy$** and the real and integer variable **Weight** and **Cal%** follow each other, occupying as many characters as is represented by their actual length. Because of this, the lengths of the line-records are different, which is clear here:

```
Snickers58.7425
Nuts50287
Twix58343
Picnic48.4265
```

Displaying information in this format is inconvenient when the variable values are of identical or similar types; for example, integer and real, but have different lengths. Looking at the first record, it's difficult to tell that the weight of the Snickers bar is 58.7g, and the calorie content is 425 cal.

To output information in a more convenient form, you can use **zone representation**. Here, each variable is allocated an integer number of **zones,** each of which is thirteen characters long. Each numeric variable occupies one zone, while text variables can take up several. The number of zones for a variable of random length, **v$**, is defined by the formula:

```
INT(LEN(v$/13))+1
```

If we replace this statement in our program,

```
        PRINT #1, Candy$; Weight; Cal%
```

with this line, using commas instead of semi colons,

```
        PRINT #1, Candy$, Weight, Cal%
```

we obtain this text file:

```
Snickers          58.7  425
Nuts                50  287
Twix                58  343
Picnic            48.4  265
```

This format, rather like the tabbing command, is more convenient for viewing on the screen and can even be used again for further processing. The variable values can be generated by the **INPUT$** function and the character-to-integer or character-to-real conversion functions. Notice that, in this case, the line-records can have different lengths as well, depending on the actual lengths of the character variables.

It's possible to structure the records of a text SDF-file by using the **PRINT USING** statement and declaring text variables with the statement:

```
DIM v$ AS STRING * k
```

In this case, the line-records are of the same length and the values of the numeric fields are more conveniently represented. The file can also be transferred to programs written in other programming systems. The only thing these programs need to know is how many characters are occupied by each field. As an example, we'll replace the variable **Candy$** in our program with the variable **Candy**, explicitly declared as:

```
DIM Candy AS STRING * 10
```

Now instead of the statement:

```
PRINT #1, Candy$, Weight, Cal%
```

we'll use this statement:

```
PRINT USING #1, Candy, Weight, Cal%
```

As a result, we get this structured text SDF-file:

```
Snickers          58.7  425.0
Nuts              50.0  287.0
Twix              58.0  343.0
Picnic            48.4  265.0
```

To create a text file in the **delimited** format (that is, with fields separated by commas), we replace the **PRINT [USING] #1** statement with:

```
WRITE #1, Candy$, Weight, Cal%
```

And as a result of this change, we obtain the file:

```
"Snickers",58.7,425
"Nuts",50,287
"Twix",58,343
"Picnic",48.4,265
```

Such a file can easily be understood by different program systems, irrespective of which programming languages they were developed in. In QBasic, reading the records of such a file is achieved by the **INPUT** statement which allows automatic division of the fields and their adjustment to the initial type. To accomplish this, you should observe a simple rule: read as you wrote - in other words, the lists of variables in the **WRITE** and **INPUT** statements must be the same.

Random Access Files

As we have seen, direct or random access files allow access to any record or set of records. In order to do this, the records must be of a predefined length so that the file position of any input may be known precisely. The structure of a random access file is as follows:

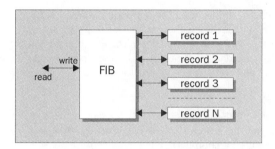

A random access file contains a special **file information block** (**FIB**). The file's name, its length and the locations of its records are stored in this block allowing you to address any record.

Creating and Reading a Random Access File

The output of records to the random access file is always carried out by the **PUT** statement, while their input from a file is carried out by the **GET** statement. Once the buffer is filled, it's saved onto disk using the **PUT** statement:

PUT [#]FileNumber% [,RecordNumber%] [,RecordVariable$]

where

#FileNumber%   denotes the file channel.

RecordNumber%   denotes the number of the record being formed, set by default to incrementally increase.

RecordVariable$ denotes the record variable to be put in the file. It can be any data type, including user-defined types with their grouped data.

The statements **PUT #** and **GET #** can also be used with binary files. In this case, the **RecordNumber%** parameter specifies the relative address of the byte in a file (counting from zero) rather than the number of the record.

In order to read data from a random access file, you have to open the file and specify the size of the buffer. Then the file is read from the disk with the **GET** statement:

GET [#]FileNumber% [RecordNumber%] [,RecordVariable$]

The variable, **RecordNumber%**, which is used to count the records of the file, plays an important role. If its value is less than or equal to zero, a system error code is generated. For example:

```
63 Bad record number
```

If it exceeds the number of records in the file, the **EOF(n)** function, after trying to read a record with this number, returns the value True.

Creating a Buffer for a Random Access File

When you open random access files (**RANDOM** mode), you have to allocate a buffer to temporarily store the file in the RAM. The same is true when preparing a current record before writing it to a file.

The most convenient way to allocate buffer area for temporary storage is by defining the structure of the record using a user-defined type and declaring the variable of this type using the **DIM** statement, as explained in Chapter 4. While the **TYPE** statement doesn't assign memory, it does define a collection of data and has a length but doesn't need all the entries to be character strings. It's extensively used in QBasic programs because of the ease with which it structures data, not just in program procedures but also in file handling.

Older versions of BASIC had no **TYPE** statement, so **FIELD** statements, with their string conversion functions, were necessary to define the random access file structure. You may need to use this statement if you're using older BASIC programs or compilers. For completeness, we will include an explanation of both.

User-defined Types

Traditionally, QBasic files with user-defined record types were called **random access files**. These files can be opened by the **OPEN** statement with the **FOR RANDOM** parameter. In doing so, it's assumed that direct access to a record with a random number is possible. However, this doesn't mean that the records of a random access file can't be written or read sequentially. To do this, you simply increment the record number variable after each reading to simulate the sequential file.

We'll look at an example of a program demonstrating various kinds of files with user-defined record type. You can find this program, **\CHAP6\CH6_5.BAS**, on the accompanying disk.

You can see that, from the very beginning, this next program is different from the previous text file example. The first differences are the explicit definition of the variables in the user-defined record type and, secondly, the reservation of an area for the records in the file **CANDIES.DAT**. Opening this file with the **FOR RANDOM** parameter, we set the size of the file's record in the **LEN** parameter, its value being equal to the total length of the constituent fields, in our case sixteen bytes:

```
TYPE Record
    Candy AS STRING * 10
    Weight AS SINGLE
    Cal AS INTEGER
  END TYPE
  'Reserving area for record
  DIM CandyRecord AS Record
  OPEN "c:Candy.dat" FOR RANDOM AS #1 LEN = LEN(CandyRecord)
```

The first section of the program, beginning with the comment,

```
' *** Creating Typed File on disk ***
```

is very similar to the program which created a text file. The difference lies in the need to initialize and make further changes to the **RecNum%** variable which determines the position of the next record in the file. Also, note that output is carried out using the **PUT** statement instead of **PRINT** or **WRITE**. This program section demonstrates the method of sequential output of the records to a random access file. Actions similar to those covered in this part of the program are necessary when creating a new file or preparing a file for subsequent or direct processing.

Note that the most widespread error when writing such programs is to forget to initialize the variable **RecNum%**, or to initialize it incorrectly.

```
'***          Creating Typed File on disk    ***
   RecNum% = 0
   DO
     'Read entries from the keyboard
     INPUT "   SWEET    :      ", CandyRecord.Candy
     INPUT "   Weight  :       ", CandyRecord.Weight
     INPUT "   Calories:       ", CandyRecord.Cal
     'Write entries to Typed File
     RecNum% = RecNum% + 1
     PUT #1, RecNum%, CandyRecord
     INPUT "Add another entry"; R$
   LOOP WHILE UCASE$(R$) = "Y"
   CLOSE #1
```

QBasic's run-time system reacts only when an attempt is made to output a record with the record number zero. The only other possible output error is when there isn't enough free disk space to accommodate the next record.

The second section of the program begins with the comment:

```
' *** Sequential Access to a Typed File ***
```

It demonstrates the sequential reading of the file prepared in the previous section. A typical error here is the incorrect organization of the loop for reading the next record. The features of the **DO... LOOP** construct mean that you can easily avoid this error. To make program debugging simpler, it's better to put the statement which changes the value of the record number variable as close as possible to the reading statement, hence:

```
'***          Sequential Access to Typed File   ***
   CLS
   LOCATE 1, 20
   PRINT "Record n     Candy  Weight  Calories"
   LOCATE 2, 20
   PRINT "_____"
   OPEN "c:Candy.dat" FOR RANDOM AS #1 LEN = LEN(CandyRecord)
   RecNum% = 1
   GET #1, RecNum%, CandyRecord
   DO UNTIL EOF(1)
     LOCATE RecNum% + 3, 25
     PRINT USING "###"; RecNum%
```

```
        LOCATE RecNum% + 3, 32
        PRINT CandyRecord.Candy
        LOCATE RecNum% + 3, 42
        PRINT USING "####.#"; CandyRecord.Weight
        LOCATE RecNum% + 3, 49
        PRINT USING "###"; CandyRecord.Cal
        RecNum% = RecNum% + 1
        GET #1, RecNum%, CandyRecord
    LOOP
    PRINT "Press any key to continue"
    WHILE INKEY$ = "": WEND
```

The third section of the program demonstrates working with a file in direct access mode. It begins with this comment:

```
'*** Random Access to Typed File  ***
```

We've already mentioned that implementing direct access isn't easy. We'll consider this in the section on 'hashing' later in this chapter.

In this section, we demonstrate how you could correctly read a particular record whose number is entered from the keyboard:

```
'***              Random Access to Typed File  ***
    CLS
    ErrCode% = 0
    LOCATE 1, 20
    PRINT "Record n      Candy  Weight  Calories"
    LOCATE 2, 20
    PRINT "_____"
    i = 4
    DO
       LOCATE 23, 31
       PRINT "          "
       LOCATE 23, 5
       INPUT "Do you want to continue? [y/n]"; r$
       IF UCASE$(R$) = "Y" THEN
          LOCATE 23, 55
          PRINT "          "
          LOCATE 23, 40
          INPUT "Press record number"; RecNum%
          ON ERROR GOTO ErrorHandler
          GET #1, RecNum%, CandyRecord
          ON ERROR GOTO 0
          IF ErrCode% = 63 THEN
             LOCATE i, 25
             PRINT USING "###"; RecNum%
             LOCATE i, 32
             PRINT "is bad record number"
             ErrCode% = 0
          ELSEIF EOF(1) THEN
             LOCATE i, 25
             PRINT USING "###"; RecNum%
             LOCATE i, 32
             LastRec% = LOF(1) / LEN(CandyRecord)
             PRINT "is after end of file, Max Record Num is "; LastRec%
```

```
      ELSE
        LOCATE i, 25
        PRINT USING "###"; RecNum%
        LOCATE i, 32
        PRINT CandyRecord.Candy
        LOCATE i, 42
        PRINT USING "####.#"; CandyRecord.Weight
        LOCATE i, 49
        PRINT USING "###"; CandyRecord.Cal
      END IF
      i = i + 1
    END IF
  LOOP WHILE UCASE$(r$) = "Y" AND i < 23
  CLS
  CLOSE #1
END

ErrorHandler:
  ErrCode% = ERR
  RESUME NEXT
```

A simple reading, using the **PUT** statement, can produce an error associated with the wrong record number. To handle the error, a special block with the label **ErrorHandler** is included in the program. The read statement is surrounded by the **ON ERROR GOTO ErrorHandler** and **ON ERROR GOTO 0** statements. The first statement cancels error processing, using the QBasic run-time system. If the input-output error occurs, its code is stored in the variable **ErrorCode%**. Only the error caused by an incorrect record number is of any importance to us. In this case, a corresponding message is displayed.

We check to see if the number of the requested record is bigger than the maximum number of records in a file using the **EOF(1)** function. If this function takes the value **True**, a message is displayed informing us of an attempt to read a record after the end of file is reached and telling us the number of the last record in the file.

The following table shows an example of the execution of this program. The first part, ending with the phrase Press any key to continue corresponds to the completion of the second section of the program:

Record N	Candy	Weight	Calories
1	Snickers	58.7	425
2	Nuts	50.0	287
3	Twix	58.0	343
4	Picnic	48.4	265
Press any key to continue.			

213

Record N	Candy	Weight	Calories
3	Twix	58.0	343
0	bad record number		
2	Nuts	50.0	287
6	after end of file, Max Record Num is 4		
1	Snickers	58.7	425
Do you want to continue? [y/n]		Press record number.	

The results log of the third section of the program then shows how the inclusion of error handling ensures the completion of the program irrespective of the errors caused by a user entering the number of a record.

The FIELD Statement

The buffer's structure is specified by the **FIELD** statement. This buffer is a continuous section of memory of a previously specified byte size, divided up into sub-sections allocated to the **character** variables used in the records. Here is the **FIELD** statement:

```
FIELD [#]N%, L1 AS A$, L2 AS B$, ... LEN = LC
```

The byte length of the sequential character fields is fixed by **L1**, **L2**, ... etc. for the named strings **A$**, **B$**, and so on. The total length, **LC**, of the fields assigned to the **LEN** parameter must coincide with the length of the record declared on opening the file or by default (to 128 bytes).

Here we show how a QBasic program creates a **FIELD** buffer and interacts with it and with the magnetic disk drive:

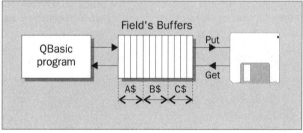

Each record of a random access file has its own number and contents. The contents, when using the **FIELD** function, are formed in two stages. First, the data is moved into a random access file buffer (declared by the **FIELD** statement) and the value of the string variable is left-justified (**LSET**) or right-justified (**RSET**).

The **LSET** and **RSET** statements can only assign values to the character variables whose names are indicated in previous **FIELD** statements. Therefore, to enter numeric data into a file it must first be converted to characters using the conversion functions we met in Chapter 4:

MKI\$(N%)	converts integers into 2-byte character strings.
MKL\$(N)	converts long integers into 4-byte character strings.
MKS\$(N!)	converts reals to 4-byte character strings.
MKD\$(N#)	converts double precision reals into 8-byte character strings.

When defining character variables in **FIELD**, you should take care to allow for their length in bytes, especially when variables are converted using the functions above. The length of common character data in bytes is simply the number of characters in the string. The length you define in the **FIELD** statement can be larger than the length of your string, if you so chose.

The character variables indicated in **FIELD** are assigned the values stored in the file. Then, each buffer field is processed. For example, to convert character data to numeric data you can use the following conversion functions:

CVI(V2\$)	converts a 2-byte character value into a short integer.
CVL(V4\$)	converts a 4-byte character value into a long integer.
CVS(V4\$)	converts a 4-byte character value into a single-precision real.
CVD(V8\$)	converts a 8-byte character value into a double-precision real.

These functions allow you to restore numeric data from their character representations which had been placed in a file. The **LTRIM\$** and **RTRIM\$** functions which delete start and end spaces of a character string, respectively, are also useful when converting expressions.

An Example of Working with Random Access Files

Have a look at this program which uses the **FIELD** statement. It first creates a random access file, saving it on disk and then reads this file and outputs the information it contains on the screen:

```
REM Creating a random access file FILEDAT.DAT
REM \CHAP6\CH6_6.BAS

OPEN "FILEDAT.DAT" FOR RANDOM AS #1 LEN = 32
FIELD #1, 2 AS Num$, 15 AS Name$, 15 AS Tel$
LSET Num$ = MKI$(3)
LSET Name$ = "Ivanov V.P."
RSET Tel$ = "123-45-67"
PUT #1, 1
CLOSE #1

'Reading the random access file FILEDAT.DAT
'and retrieving the information it contains
CLS
OPEN "FILEDAT.DAT" FOR RANDOM AS #1 LEN = 32
FIELD #1, 2 AS Num$, 15 AS Name$, 15 AS Tel$
GET #1, 1
Num% = CVI(Num$)
PRINT Num%; "|" + Name$ + "|" + Tel$ + "|"
CLOSE #1

END
```

When you run this program, you'll see the following information on the screen:

3 |Ivanov V.P. | 123-45-56|

Here, we've used the same information as in the sequential file examples. When the information is displayed, the symbol '|' is used to separate the output fields. This is to give you a clearer idea of how the **LSET** and **RSET** statements operate, essentially by justifying data to the left or to the right in the fields respectively.

Note that, once opened, a random access file may be both written to and read from. To modify a random access file, all you need to do is to define a buffer for the part of the file to be modified and change the corresponding variables. The number of the record being modified is indicated as the argument of the **PUT** statement.

Binary Files

As described earlier, binary files store the values of a set of bytes with specified addresses. These files can store Assembler subroutines or machine code programs. We've been using the term 'binary' up to now, but it isn't strictly accurate. In fact, these files store machine code strings (i.e. bytes), each byte containing 8 bits-worth of information. This section will draw on material covered in Chapter 4.

Saving and Loading Binary Files

BSAVE and **BLOAD** are the statements you use to read and write binary files. **BSAVE** allows you to write the contents of the RAM onto disk in the form of a string of **n%** bytes with a specified offset and a name (the file specification):

```
BSAVE file_spec$, offset%, n%
```

And **BLOAD** loads the file created by **BSAVE** into the PC's memory:

```
BLOAD file_spec$ [, offset%]
```

The value of the offset sets the start of the memory image. By default, this is considered to be in QBasic's data segment. If necessary, the **DEF SEG** statement can be used to set the address of the current memory segment:

```
DEF SEG [address]
```

where **address** is the address of the segment used by **BLOAD, BSAVE, CALL ABSOLUTE, PEEK** or **POKE**. The address of a current segment ranges between 0 and 65535. If the address is omitted, **DEF SEG** returns the address of the current segment.

The value of **offset%** gives the offset of the initial address of memory area in which the data will be loaded from the value given by **address**. It can also take values from 0 to 65,535. As we saw in Chapter 4, this means that the memory address is non-unique, each segment representing 16 bytes of memory.

Quickly storing and displaying a screen file using a CGA video adapter provides a good example of using the **BSAVE** and **BLOAD** statements. We know that in CGA mode, the video RAM starts with the address **HB800** and has a length of **H400** (in hexadecimal). Therefore, to write the current screen into a binary file, all you need to do is to include these three lines in your program:

```
DEF SEG=&HB800
BSAVE "Name_file",0,&H400
DEF SEG
```

In order to quickly retrieve the written image, read the file with these three:

```
DEF SEG=&HB800
BLOAD "Name_file",0
DEF SEG
```

Unfortunately, this simple method can't be used with the more up-to-date video adapters, such as EGA, VGA and SVGA, because their video-RAM is organized in a more sophisticated way, making it impossible to treat it as one block with fixed boundaries.

In older versions of BASIC (BasicA and GWBasic in particular), the **BSAVE** and **BLOAD** statements meant working with a tape recorder. Nowadays, tape recorders are seldom used with PCs, except for backup purposes.

File Processing

File processing is a major area of computer science. Methods of file processing form the base upon which software, such as database control systems, are built. The general problems associated with file processing revolve around choosing the best method of accessing a file for a particular task. There are two main file access methods: the sequential method, for mass or group file processing, and the direct, inquiry, or random method. The number of a file's record can't be used as the basic guideline for deciding whether a record should be involved in processing. Therefore, as in Chapter 5, we use the concept of a **key**.

A key is one or more fields in the record of a file, the values of which are used as the criteria while searching for records containing the necessary information. An example of such a structure is found in our program which demonstrates controlling random access files. The **Candy** field in that example assumes the role of a key. This field uniquely identifies the record and can be used when you want to obtain information about a particular candy. However, for those of you who combine your love for sweet stuff with the desire to preserve your figure, you may want to use the **Cal** field as a key, so you can find all the records that contain information about the candies whose calorie content is less than a certain number.

Choosing the most suitable file processing method isn't easy and requires a certain amount of programming skill. However, there's a way of assessing what you have to do that gives you a fairly accurate idea of which processing method you should use - we're talking about the **activity factor** of a file. The activity factor, k, of a file is defined as the number $k=m/n$, where n is the number of records in the file and m is the number of records to be processed by an inquiry. Clearly, k will, therefore, take a value between 0 and 1.

Let's calculate the activity factor for the tasks in the **Candy** example. If we use the random processing method for the first task, to obtain information about a particular candy, it's sufficient to read one record containing the information about the relevant candy. Since our example contained four records, k=0.25. If, however, we use sequential processing, on average we'll have to read half the records in the file, so here k may be close to 1. In this case, it's much better to use the random processing method. The second task (choosing all the candies whose calorie count is less than a certain number) on the other hand, requires viewing if not all, then the majority of the file's records, whichever method is used. Therefore, the activity factor k for this task will be near 1.

When choosing a method of file processing, it's good to follow this rule:

> **If the activity factor of a file is less than 0.5, apply random processing, otherwise use the sequential method.**

So, it's good practice to use direct access on the file's records (random processing) for the first task, and sequential access for solving the second problem. In general, the choice of file processing method is made after careful analysis of the features of the problem to be solved and by taking into account your own previous experience. We'll now consider in detail these different methods of file processing.

Sequential Processing

As you've already seen, the sequential accessing of records is used for sequential or mass processing. To access the **n**th record of a file, you have to make your way through **n-1** preceding records. Sometimes, the order in which these records are located in a file is of great importance.

Let's consider an example problem: the calculation of the average number of goals scored and goals conceded in the last ten years by several English soccer teams. The initial data for solving this problem is in the random access file, **FOOTBALL**, whose record structure is specified by the following user-defined types:

```
TYPE GoalsType
   Scored AS INTEGER
   Lost AS INTEGER
END TYPE
```

```
TYPE FootballType
   Team AS STRING * 20
   Season AS INTEGER
   Goals AS GoalsType
END TYPE
```

We hope that fans of the sport will forgive us for using random numbers as the values of the **Scored** and **Lost** fields. If you're a football fanatic, then you may want to modify the program to use the correct data.

It's highly likely that the data will be stored either in random order or in an order that doesn't help us with our task. Instead, we wish to arrange the data in order of increasing value of the key consisting of the pair of fields (**Team, Season**). This will result in the records in the file being split into groups of ten, each record in a group having the same value for the **Team** field (the name of one team) and the value of **Season** changing from the beginning to the end of the period under consideration.

It only remains for us to put the **FOOTBALL** file into order. We do this with a combination of algorithms and programs to sort the information. We'll, therefore, use external sorts.

External Sort

If we could completely accommodate a file in RAM, ordering it wouldn't worry us. For this you could use any of the algorithms suggested in Chapter 5. Unfortunately, this is but a dream because even the largest volumes of RAM aren't enough to hold all the data that you might want to search through - some databases hold millions of records. For this reason, external sort algorithms which were first developed when computers had little operative memory and information was stored on magnetic tapes are still important.

An external sort consists of two phases. We'll illustrate the algorithms which implement each phase in an example which sorts a small file **Players** containing information about popular soccer players using the **Name** key. Here are the values of the key in the records of the initial file:

Record Number	Name
1	Shearer Alan
2	Giggs Ryan
3	Beardsley Peter
4	Wright Ian
5	Le Tissier Matthew
6	Cantona Eric
7	Adams Tony
8	Walker Des
9	Bosnich Mark
10	Hoddle Glenn
11	McAllister Gary
12	Ferdinand Les
13	Platt David
14	Peacock Gavin
15	Jones Vinny
16	Gascoigne Paul
17	Sutton Chris
18	Waddle Chris

The first phase is frequently referred to as **partitioning**. During this phase, a file is read into RAM in pieces. The size of each piece, the **portion**, is limited by the size of the one-dimensional array allocated for sorting, with the elements of the array having the same user-defined type as the records in the file. Each portion is itself sorted and output into one of two target files: portions 1,3,5, etc. are sent to the first file, while portions 2,4,6, etc. are sent to the second. The partitioning process is finished after the output of the last portion, with the result that all the records of the initial file are transferred into two working files: **WORK1.TMP** and **WORK2.TMP**. The partition of the file **Players** for portions each consisting of four records is as follows:

WORK1.TMP Portion Number	Name	WORK2.TMP Portion Number	Name
1	Beardsley Peter	2	Adams Tony
1	Giggs Ryan	2	Cantona Eric
1	Shearer Alan	2	Le Tissier Matthew

Table Continued on Following Page

WORK1.TMP Portion Number	Name	WORK2.TMP Portion Number	Name
1	Wright Ian	2	Walker Des
3	Bosnich Mark	4	Gascoigne Paul
3	Ferdinand Les	4	Jones Vinny
3	Hoddle Glenn	4	Peacock Gavin
3	McAllister Gary	4	Platt David
5	Sutton Chris		
5	Waddle Chris		

The second phase of sorting a file is referred to as **merging**. There are various merging methods, but we'll just stick with one of them, called **balance** merging which uses four working files. This algorithm includes several stages. Each stage dealing with two source and two target files. The target files, obtained at the **k**th stage, become the source files at stage **(k+1)**, and the freed source files become the targets. At the first stage, the files obtained at the partition stage are used as the source files and the ordered portions scattered through these files are combined in pairs into portions of double length.

The sorting process is complete after the execution of **1 + INT (LOG2 (L/P))** iterations, where **L** stands for the number of records in the file being sorted, and **P** is the dimension of the array to which the ordered portions are read out during the partition phase. The last stage forms a single portion containing a completely ordered initial file in one of the output working files. These tables illustrate how the merging phase works:

WORK3.TMP Portion Number	Name	WORK4.TMP Portion Number	Name
1	Adams Tony	2	Bosnich Mark
1	Beardsley Peter	2	Ferdinand Les
1	Cantona Eric	2	Gascoigne Paul
1	Giggs Ryan	2	Hoddle Glenn
1	Le Tissier Matthew	2	Jones Vinny
1	Shearer Alan	2	McAllister Gary
1	Walker Des	2	Peacock Gavin
1	Wright Ian	2	Platt David
3	Sutton Chris		
3	Waddle Chris		

Work1.tmp Portion Number	Work2.tmp Name	Portion Number	Name
1	Adams Tony	2	Sutton Chris
1	Beardsley Peter	2	Waddle Chris
1	Bosnich Mark		
1	Cantona Eric		
1	Ferdinand Les		
1	Gascoigne Paul		
1	Giggs Ryan		
1	Hoddle Glenn		
1	Jones Vinny		
1	Le Tissier Matthew		
1	McAllister Gary		
1	Peacock Gavin		
1	Platt David		
1	Shearer Alan		
1	Walker Des		
1	Wright Ian		

Work3.tmp Portion Number	Name	Work4.tmp Portion Number	Name
1	Adams Tony	2	
1	Beardsley Peter		
1	Bosnich Mark		
1	Cantona Eric		
1	Ferdinand Les		
1	Gascoigne Paul		
1	Giggs Ryan		
1	Hoddle Glenn		
1	Jones Vinny		
1	Le Tissier Matthew		
1	McAllister Gary		
1	Peacock Gavin		
1	Platt David		

Table Continued on Following Page

| Work3.tmp | | Work4.tmp | |
Portion Number	Name	Portion Number	Name
1	Shearer Alan		
1	Sutton Chris		
1	Waddle Chris		
1	Walker Des		
1	Wright Ian		

Let's return to the problem of sorting the **FOOTBALL** file. This is implemented by the program **\CHAP6\CH6_7.BAS** which you can find on the accompanying disk.

This program consists of the main program, six **SUB**s, and one function. The head module sequentially calls the procedures **Initialize**, **PrintFile**, **Separate**, **ShellSort**, **Merge**, **StepMerge** and **PrintFile**. The **PrintFile** procedure, when first called, types the file obtained in the **Initialize** procedure and, at the second call, types the sorted file. In addition, the head module contains the error handling block which reacts to error 53 - File not Found. This may arise in this program if the file to be deleted (in the **KILL "C:FOOTBALL"** command) is absent.

The **KILL** statement deletes any old working files at the beginning of the program before the first merging stage recreates them for use in subsequent sorting. This isn't a fatal error in the sorting program. In order not to interrupt the program when this error occurs, control is passed to the next statement (here **CLS**) after the statement which caused the error interrupt. The occurrence of any other error stops or suspends the execution of the program.

The procedure **Separate** implements the first phase of sorting, dividing the initial file into two working files containing the ordered portions, whose length is specified by the **SortPortion** constant (set to 60 in the head module). The last portion can be of a smaller length if there aren't enough records. You can see a summary of the partitioning phase in the diagram shown here:

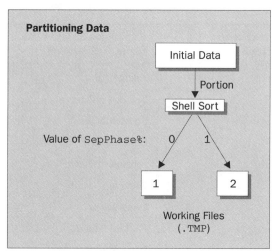

```
SUB Separate

'     ***    Separate Input File Phase    ***
  CLS
  LOCATE 8, 15
```

```
   PRINT "***    Separating Input File Phase    ***"
   KILL "C:*.TMP"
   OPEN "C:Work1.TMP" FOR RANDOM AS #1 LEN = LEN(WorkRec1)
   OPEN "C:Work2.TMP" FOR RANDOM AS #2 LEN = LEN(WorkRec1)
   OPEN "C:Football" FOR RANDOM AS #3 LEN = LEN(WorkRec1)
   RecNum1% = 0
   RecNum2% = 0
   AllRec = 1
   SepPhase% = 0
   MaxRec = 1
   GET #3, AllRec, SortArray(MaxRec)
   DO
     IF MaxRec = SortPortion THEN
       ShellSort
       FOR i = 1 TO MaxRec
 ' Selecting file for next portion to write to
       SELECT CASE SepPhase%
         CASE 0
           RecNum1% = RecNum1% + 1
           PUT #1, RecNum1%, SortArray(i)
         CASE 1
           RecNum2% = RecNum2% + 1
           PUT #2, RecNum2%, SortArray(i)
       END SELECT
       NEXT i
       MaxRec = 0
       SepPhase% = (SepPhase% + 1) MOD 2
     ELSE
       MaxRec = MaxRec + 1
       AllRec = AllRec + 1
       GET #3, AllRec, SortArray(MaxRec)
     END IF
   LOOP UNTIL EOF(3)
   ' Processing last portion
   MaxRec = MaxRec - 1
   ShellSort
   FOR i = 1 TO MaxRec
     SELECT CASE SepPhase%
       CASE 0
       RecNum1% = RecNum1% + 1
       PUT #1, RecNum1%, SortArray(i)
       CASE 1
       RecNum2% = RecNum2% + 1
       PUT #2, RecNum2%, SortArray(i)
     END SELECT
   NEXT i
   CLOSE #1, #2, #3
 END SUB
```

The ordered portions are recorded sequentially in one of the working files: **WORK1.TMP** or **WORK2.TMP**.

The **SepPhase%** variable acts like a railway point, defining the direction of the output. It takes the value 0 or 1, which defines the working file. The **AllRec** variable serves as a record counter in the initial file. Its final value is then used as a constant, corresponding to the actual number of records in the file. The **MaxRec** variable contains the actual number of records in the group being ordered and is used in the internal sorting procedure **ShellSort**. For all groups, except the last one, its value is equal to **SortPortion**.

The main part of the procedure is a loop which finishes with the end of the initial file **FOOTBALL**. At each iteration, **MaxRec** is checked to see if it has reached the value of **SortPortion**. If this condition isn't fulfilled, the next record is placed at the end of the **SortArray** array:

```
IF MaxRec = SortPortion THEN
     ShellSort
     FOR i = 1 TO MaxRec
  ' Selecting file for next portion to write to
     SELECT CASE SepPhase%
       CASE 0
         RecNum1% = RecNum1% + 1
         PUT #1, RecNum1%, SortArray(i)
       CASE 1
         RecNum2% = RecNum2% + 1
         PUT #2, RecNum2%, SortArray(i)
     END SELECT
     NEXT i
     MaxRec = 0
     SepPhase% = (SepPhase% + 1) MOD 2
  ELSE
     MaxRec = MaxRec + 1
     AllRec = AllRec + 1
     GET #3, AllRec, SortArray(MaxRec)
  END IF
```

If it is fulfilled, the following steps are performed: the array is sorted and all the records output to the selected working files, the direction of the output is switched and the next set of records from the initial file are read into the beginning of the array.

When the end of the file is reached, **SortArray** contains the last unordered portion of records from the initial file. It's sorted and output into the working file. At this point, the partitioning phase of the initial file is complete.

The next phase, the merging of the working files, is implemented by the **Merge** procedure, as shown in the figure.

```
SUB Merge
  '    ***    Merging Work Files Phase    ***

  Ready$ = ""      ' Sign of completing the last merging stage
  MergePhase% = 0
  MergePortion = 0 ' Size of portion at the recurrent merging stage
  RecNum% = 1
  CLS
  LOCATE 8, 15
  PRINT "***   Merging Work Files Phase    ****"
  DO
    StepMerge MergePhase%, Ready$
    MergePhase% = (MergePhase% + 1) MOD 2
  LOOP WHILE Ready$ = ""
  ' Copying the sorted file
  FileName$ = "C:Work" + Ready$ + ".TMP"
  OPEN FileName$ FOR RANDOM AS #1 LEN = LEN(WorkRec1)
  OPEN "C:Football" FOR RANDOM AS #2 LEN = LEN(WorkRec1)
  RecNum% = 1
```

```
    GET #1, RecNum%, WorkRec1
    DO
      PUT #2, RecNum%, WorkRec1
      RecNum% = RecNum% + 1
      GET #1, RecNum%, WorkRec1
    LOOP UNTIL EOF(1)
    CLOSE #1, #2
    KILL "C:*.TMP"
  END SUB
```

At the heart of this procedure is the loop which is performed until the **Ready$** variable takes on a value from the set {'1', '2', '3', '4'}. This value corresponds to the number of the working file which contains the sorted records of the initial file. The body of the loop includes the call to the **StepMerge** procedure which implements the recurrent stage of merging and changes the value of the **MergePhase%** variable:

```
    StepMerge MergePhase%, Ready$
    MergePhase% = (MergePhase% + 1) MOD 2
```

This variable takes on one of two values. If its value is **0**, the files **WORK1.TMP** and **WORK2.TMP** become the source files at the next merging stage and the files **WORK3.TMP** and **WORK4.TMP** become the targets. Otherwise, the working files are swapped. After the merging cycle is complete, the working file whose number is assigned to the **Ready$** variable is totally rewritten into the file **FOOTBALL**. The deletion of the working files completes the merging stage.

The procedure **StepMerge** implements the merging stage. It's quite an involved program with lots of switches to combine portions which we show in the figures shown here:

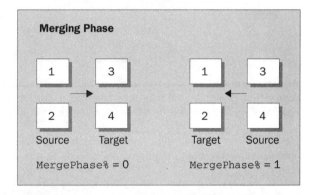

The input parameter **Phase%** takes the value of the **MergePhase%** variable and the procedure begins by setting up the source and target files according to the value taken:

```
'  Setting input and output files
  IF Phase% = 0 THEN
    FileName1$ = "C:Work1.TMP"
    FileName2$ = "C:Work2.TMP"
    FileName3$ = "C:Work3.TMP"
    FileName4$ = "C:Work4.TMP"
    KILL "C:Work3.TMP"
    KILL "C:Work4.TMP"
  ELSE
    FileName1$ = "C:Work3.TMP"
    FileName2$ = "C:Work4.TMP"
    FileName3$ = "C:Work1.TMP"
```

```
        FileName4$ = "C:Work2.TMP"
    KILL "C:Work1.TMP"
    KILL "C:Work2.TMP"
END IF
```

The general part of the procedure is a loop which is completed when both source files (we'll call them **1** and **2**) have been read to the end. After the current records of the source files **1** and **2** have been compared by the **KeyComparison%** function, the record with the larger value of the key is written into one of the target files. For example, if **WorkRec1%<WorkRec2%**, **WorkRec2%** will be written to the target file. The **OutPutSwitch%** variable performs a similar function to the **MergePhase%** variable earlier. Then the next record of the selected file (**2**) is read and compared to **WorkRec1%**. Let's recap with a diagram:

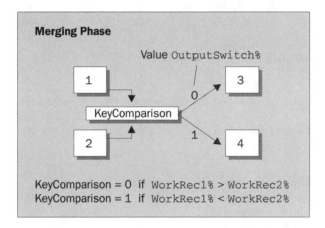

An important part is played by the two flags **EndGroup1%** and **EndGroup2%**. They're associated with the source files (**1** and **2**) and take the value 1 if a portion of the corresponding file is exhausted or if a file has been read to the end. In all other cases, the values of these flags are zero.

Having merged two portions, one from each of the two source files, the condition that determines the completion of merging, the absence of records in one of the target files, is checked:

```
IF Phase% = 0 THEN          ' Setting resulting file
    IF RecNum3% = 0 THEN
        Ready$ = "4"
    ELSEIF RecNum4% = 0 THEN
        Ready$ = "3"
    END IF
ELSE
    IF RecNum3% = 0 THEN
        Ready$ = "2"
    ELSEIF RecNum4% = 0 THEN
        Ready$ = "1"
    END IF
END IF
```

If the merging process is complete, the **Ready$** variable is assigned the number of the corresponding working file.

The function **KeyComparison%** compares keys in the current records of the source files at each merging stage:

```
FUNCTION KeyComparison (End1%, End2%)

' Returns
'      0 - if the record's key of the first working file isn't greater
'          than that of the second one,
'      1 - in the reversed case.

' Input parameters End1% and End2% take the value
'      0 - if the recurrent input ordered group or file
'          are not yet finished,
'      1 - otherwise

  IF End1% = 0 AND End2% = 0 THEN
    IF WorkRec1.Team < WorkRec2.Team THEN
      KeyComparison = 0
    ELSEIF WorkRec1.Team = WorkRec2.Team THEN
      IF WorkRec1.Season <= WorkRec2.Season THEN
        KeyComparison = 0
      ELSE
        KeyComparison = 1
      END IF
    ELSE
      KeyComparison = 1
    END IF
  ELSE
    IF End1% = 1 THEN
      KeyComparison = 1
    END IF
    IF End2% = 1 THEN
      KeyComparison = 0
    END IF
  END IF
END FUNCTION
```

It returns the value **0** if the value of the record's key of the first source file doesn't exceed the value of the record's key of the second source file. Otherwise the value returned is **1**. The input parameters **End1%** and **End2%** take the values of the flags **EndGroup1%** and **EndGroup2%** and are used for comparing records. Usually they are both equal to zero, meaning there are two records to be compared. At the end of a portion or a source file, if **End1%** or **End2% = 1** there is no need for a comparison. If both portions from the two source files have been merged, a new merging phase is called by **Merge**. If the end of one of the files has been reached, only those records from the unfinished file need be input, this forming the last section in the above code.

This, then, gives you a method for sorting files externally. Using our program as a basis, it's possible to write a similar one for any file that you need to sort. However, it should only be necessary to sort externally if the file is too large for all the records to be held in memory.

Processing Sorted Files

In the previous section, we considered a sorting program which not only demonstrated the algorithm for ordering a file but also showed you how two sorted files are merged. Basically, in any program which merges two or more files, each input file is considered to be one ordered group. Therefore, the rules of merging ordered groups can be carried over to merging ordered files.

We shall return to the merging algorithms, but for now we'll concentrate on how to sequentially process an ordered file, considering an example of the widespread convolution algorithm. By applying the convolution algorithm we'll be able to finish our calculation of the average number of goals scored and conceded.

As indicated earlier, further processing of the file reduces the search for one or more records whose fields' values define the further actions of the program. Selecting the records can be carried out using the keys. To recap, a key is unique if it identifies a single record. For example, in the **FOOTBALL** file, the keys **Team** and **Season** aren't themselves unique but, by combining them, we get the required unique key.

A file, ordered by a non-unique key, is split into several groups each containing the records with the same key value. There are as many such groups in a file as there are values of the key in the records of the file. In the **FOOTBALL** file there are 18 groups. In this file, each group contains ten records, defined in the creation of the file. In general, each group can contain an arbitrary number of records.

The file convolution operation consists of replacing each group with a record containing the value of the key and the results of the combined processing of several non-key fields.

In our example, all the records containing the same **Team** field value are replaced by a record of this type:

```
TYPE TotalType
  Team AS STRING * 20
  Goals AS GoalsType
END TYPE
```

which contains the key field **Team** and the group **Goals**, whose fields **Score** and **Lost** contain the final count for the scored and conceded goals over a ten year period. The field **Season** is absent in the record because its value isn't relevant to the task under discussion.

The program **\CHAP6\CH6_8.BAS** implements the convolution of the **FOOTBALL** file, so lets take a look at it in detail:

```
REM THE AVERAGING TYPED FILE PROGRAM
REM \CHAP6\CH6_8.BAS

  DEFINT A-Z        ' Default type integer
  DECLARE SUB SumGoals (TGoals AS ANY, CGoals AS ANY)
  DECLARE SUB PrintAV ()
  DECLARE SUB Total ()

' Define the data types
  TYPE GoalsType
    Scored AS INTEGER
    Lost AS INTEGER
  END TYPE
  TYPE FootballType        'Type of FOOTBALL file record
    Team AS STRING * 20
    Season AS INTEGER
    Goals AS GoalsType
  END TYPE
  TYPE TotalType           'Type of TOTAL record
    Team AS STRING * 20
    Goals AS GoalsType
  END TYPE
' Define the variables
```

```
   DIM SHARED TotalRec AS TotalType, CurrRec AS FootballType
   CLS
   LOCATE 8, 15
   PRINT "****    AVERAGING TYPED FILE    ****"
   LOCATE 10, 15
   PRINT "Press any key to continue"
   WHILE INKEY$ = "": WEND
   Total
   END


SUB PrintAV
' Calculating Mean Values and Outputting the Summarizing Line

   AverScored = TotalRec.Goals.Scored / 10
   AverLost = TotalRec.Goals.Lost / 10
   PRINT TotalRec.Team, AverScored, AverLost
END SUB


SUB SumGoals (TGoals AS GoalsType, CGoals AS GoalsType)
' Calculating Scored and Lost Goals

   TGoals.Scored = TGoals.Scored + CGoals.Scored
   TGoals.Lost = TGoals.Lost + CGoals.Lost
END SUB


SUB Total
' Controlling File Sequential Processing

   CONST SubLine$ = "_____", FileName$ = "Football"
   DIM Num AS STRING * 4
   CLS
   PRINT FileName$
   OPEN FileName$ FOR RANDOM AS #1 LEN = LEN(CurrRec)
   RecNum% = 1
   GET #1, RecNum%, CurrRec        ' Reading first record of file
   TotalRec.Team = CurrRec.Team    ' Setting up initial values
   TotalRec.Goals.Scored = 0       ' of summarizing variables
   TotalRec.Goals.Lost = 0         ' for first group
   PRINT "    Team", "", "Goals"
   PRINT "", "  " + SubLine$ + SubLine$
   PRINT "", "     Scored", "              Lost"
   PRINT SubLine$ + SubLine$ + SubLine$
   DO
     IF TotalRec.Team = CurrRec.Team THEN
       SumGoals TotalRec.Goals, CurrRec.Goals
       RecNum% = RecNum + 1
       GET #1, RecNum%, CurrRec
     ELSE
       PrintAV
       TotalRec.Team = CurrRec.Team  'Setting up initial values
       TotalRec.Goals.Scored = 0     'of summarizing variables
       TotalRec.Goals.Lost = 0       'for the next in turn group
     END IF
   LOOP UNTIL EOF(1)
   PrintAV
   CLOSE #1
END SUB
```

In the program **\CHAP6\CH6_8.BAS**, the type **Goals**, for the first time in our discussion, has an independent meaning. Here, the identifiers of the groups from different records are passed as parameters, to the **SumGoals** procedure:

```
SumGoals TotalRec.Goals, CurrRec.Goals
```

Such an approach shortens the source code and makes the program much more illustrative. The record of the **TotalType** type is used to accumulate the final values and output them onto the screen.

The **Total** procedure is the main controlling block of the program. It opens the input file **FOOTBALL**, outputs a page header onto the screen and, after reading the first record of the source file, establishes the initial values of the final record. Here, it's important to realize that, in the chosen convolution algorithm, the first record is processed in just the same way as all the subsequent ones. Therefore, the **Team** field of the final record accepts the value of the same record field of the **FOOTBALL** file and the **Goals.Score** and **Goals.Lost** fields are reset to zero.

The loop that follows the setting of the initial values implements the compression algorithm. The loop consists of a single conditional statement and its action is split into two parts:

```
      DO
        IF TotalRec.Team = CurrRec.Team THEN
           SumGoals TotalRec.Goals, CurrRec.Goals
           RecNum% = RecNum + 1
           GET #1, RecNum%, CurrRec
        ELSE
           PrintAV
           TotalRec.Team = CurrRec.Team 'Setting up initial values
           TotalRec.Goals.Scored = 0     'of summarizing variables
           TotalRec.Goals.Lost = 0       'for the next in turn group
        END IF
      LOOP UNTIL EOF(1)
```

The first part is carried out if the **Team** fields in the next record of the source file coincide with those in the final record, i.e. the records of one group containing identical key values are read from the **FOOTBALL** file. In this case, the values of the **Goals.Score** and **Goals.Lost** fields of the record of the source file are added to the final record.

The second part is executed when a record with a new value of **Team** field is found, in other words when the first record of the next group is read from the input file. The **PrintAV** procedure prints the final record which is then set to its initial state - as it was before it entered the loop.

The loop is complete at the end of the **FOOTBALL** file. However, the final record still contains the data from the last group of records in the source file. The **PrintAV** procedure is executed to output them. At this point, the **TOTAL** procedure has finished.

The **SumGoals** procedure summarizes the values of the **Goals.Score** and **Goals.Lost** fields and the **PrintAV** procedure prints the final records:

Football Team	Goals	
	Scored	Lost
Arsenal	22	21
Aston Villa	27	23
Blackburn Rovers	25	24
Chelsea	24	23
Coventry	24	24
Everton	24	24
Leeds United	24	24
Liverpool	25	26
Manchester City	22	23
Manchester United	25	24
Newcastle United	23	24
Norwich	24	22
Queens Park Rangers	24	21
Sheffield Wednesday	24	27
Southampton	27	26
Tottenham Hotspur	25	25
West Ham	23	29
Wimbledon	28	24

This section ends our look at sequential file processing algorithms. You can use the algorithms and the programs covered here for designing complicated data processing systems, including database control systems, of your own.

Random Processing

The random processing of a file, based on direct access to its records, plays an important part in data processing. Inquiries to reference databases, such as personal organizers, would be unthinkable without the quick searching of a small number of records, making random processing indispensable.

Randomization

Random processing is performed on files that are opened for random access. The file which we wish to search for data is opened with the **FOR RANDOM** parameter. Now it's possible to address any of its records by giving its number in the **GET** or **PUT** statement. Everything would be simple if the number of a record and the value of a key were the same. Unfortunately, this is seldom the case so, to search for a record with a specified key value, we must use special methods known as **randomization**.

By randomization we mean establishing a one-to-one correspondence between the value of a key and the number of the record containing this value.

The conversion that transforms the value of a key into the number of a record is referred to as the **randomization function**. Let's now look at two commonly used methods of randomization and their related functions.

The first is **hashing**, a method which makes use of the fact that a direct access file is like a one-dimensional array of records, where the role of the index belongs to the number of a record. The algorithms for creating a hash-array and searching for records in it, which are covered in Chapter 5, are easily transformed into algorithms for creating a hash-file and transforming the value of a key into the numbers of a record. The second method, **indexation**, is based on creating a special array or a file of indexes, which allows you to quickly find a required record using a specified key value.

Processing a File Using the Hashing Method

The way the hash-function is calculated depends on the features of the particular task and by the limitations on the amount of available disk space. Work with the hash-file is divided into two phases:

▲ The creation of a hash-file,

▲ The search for the record of a specified key value in it.

We'll consider these phases separately.

Creating a Hash File

When creating a hash-file, two main factors are taken into account: the number of the values of a hash-function and the possibility of collisions, as discussed in Chapter 5. For this reason, the hash-file is structured according to the following rules:

▲ The hash-file is a collection of zones, each of which is characterized by a single value of the hash-function. The zones are the possible integer values of the hash function.

▲ All the zones contain the same number of records, **R**, determined by the probable number of collisions.

▲ All the records located in one zone have keys, **k**, that give the same hash-function.

It may be thought of as shown in the figure, though in memory it's actually a linear array.

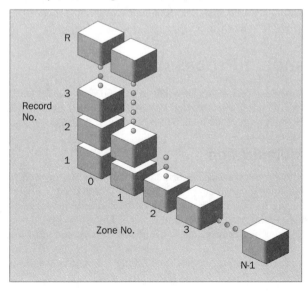

Therefore, if the hash-function can take values in the range **[0, N-1]** and we assume that each zone contains **R** records, the hash-file will contain **N*R** records.

The first step to creating a hash-file is to form an empty random access file on disk. This file contains the **forms** of all **N*R** records which can be located in it.

The second step is to fill the empty file. The data which we'll use later to answer inquiries to the file is entered any way you like: from the keyboard, using the **DATA** statement or from other files. After the data is entered in the buffer variable, the value of the hash-function is calculated from the value of the data's key. After that, an attempt to place a record in the file is undertaken. To do this, the number of the first record is calculated in a zone corresponding to the value of the hash-function using this formula:

```
FirstRec = h(k)*RpZ + 1
```

where **h(k)** stands for the value of the hash-function from the value of the key **k**, and **RpZ** is the number of records per zone. The records from these zones are then serially read until an empty record (form) is found or it's determined that all forms are already filled. In the first case, the information from the buffer variable is output onto disk and, in the second, the collisions are detected.

After the last source record is processed, the hash-file is considered complete. It's now possible to correct the file, add new records to it, exclude unnecessary or incorrect records and change, if necessary, the values of the non-key fields.

Searching in a Hash File

Once the file has been generated, we can turn to searching it for information. The search algorithm consists of calculating the number of first records in the zone, corresponding to the value of the hash-function with a specified key value, and reading all the records from this zone in sequence until either a record with the necessary value of the key is found, or all the records stored in the zone have been checked. In the former case, the search is considered to be successfully completed and, in the latter, it is unsuccessful.

Let's consider an example of creating a hash-file and searching for records in it. We'll use the program **\CHAP6\CH6_9.BAS** which you can find on the disk supplied with this book. This program carries on from the example of hashing given in Chapter 5, with the slight difference that the data which is searched is in the hash-file **Town.hsh**.

The head module contains the declarations of the type of the file record (**RecType**) and the constants **MaxHash** and **RpZ**. **MaxHash** sets the maximum value of the hash-function and **RpZ** sets the number of records in a zone:

```
'Definition of a record, its key is the Town field
  TYPE RecType
     Town AS STRING * 14
     Date AS STRING * 8
  END TYPE
  CONST MaxHash = 13 'Max value of hash-function
  CONST RpZ = 3        'Records per zone
```

After declaring the global variables and outputting the prompt on the screen, the head module serially calls the procedures for creating and outputting the hash-file on the screen followed by the procedure for searching for records. The head module contains an error-handling block which is activated when the **HashKey%** function isn't defined on a specified value of the key:

```
ErrorHandler:
  IF ERR = 5 AND ErrorCall = 0 THEN
    PRINT "Can't build hash-key for "; Info$
    ErrorCall = 1
  END IF
  RESUME NEXT
```

The head module ends with a block of data containing the descriptions of sixteen cities, each of them consisting of the name of a city and the year of its foundation. The number of cities is defined in the first **DATA** statement:

```
'Number of input data
DATA  16
'Data for records
DATA Moscow,      1147, Magadan,   1931, Novgorod,       859
DATA Smolensk,     863, Yaroslavl, 1010, Uglitch,        937
DATA Vologda,     1147, Minsk,     1067, New Orleans,   1718
DATA Novy Afon,   1875, New York,  1626, Magnitogorsk,  1931
DATA Newcastle,   1045, Newark,    1626, Veliky Ustyug, 1207
DATA Petersburg,  1703
```

The **CreateHashFile** procedure creates an empty hash-file and fills it with records. The loop that fills the file with records is executed as many times as there are cities defined in the data block:

```
SUB CreateHashFile
'    ***    Creating a hash-file and entering records in it   ***

  OPEN "town.hsh" FOR RANDOM AS #1 LEN = LEN(HashRec)
  ' Creating an empty file
  FOR i = 1 TO MaxHash * RpZ
    HashRec.Town = "            "
    HashRec.Date = "        "
    PUT #1, i, HashRec
  NEXT i
  ' Filling a file with records
  READ InData
  FOR i = 1 TO InData                   'Reading input data
    READ Info$
    READ Dat$
    Num = RpZ * HashKey%(Info$)
    ZoneTrashing = 1
    FOR j = 1 TO RpZ          ' Looking for a free place in a zone
        GET #1, Num + j, HashRec
        IF HashRec.Town = "            " THEN
          HashRec.Town = Info$
          HashRec.Date = Dat$
          PUT #1, Num + j, HashRec  'Outputting a record
          ZoneTrashing = 0          'on an free location
          EXIT FOR
        END IF
    NEXT j
    IF ZoneTrashing = 1 THEN '  Zone is overfilled,
                             '  no record output
        PRINT Info$, " - Number of collisions > ", RpZ
```

```
        END IF
      NEXT i
   END SUB
```

After the name of a city and the date of its foundation have been entered into the variables **Info$** and **Dat$** respectively, the value of the variable **Num** is calculated as **RpZ*HashKey%(Info$)**. The next loop, which is performed **RpZ** times, allows you to select all the records of a required zone. This loop is brought to an end if an empty record is found (the field **Town** contains only spaces) or if all **RpZ** records have been looked through and no empty record is found. In the former case, a record with a new key value is placed in the location of the empty record and the loop is interrupted.

A pseudo-logic variable **ZoneTrashing** is used as a flag signalling the occurrence of collisions. If, after the loop which accommodates a record in a zone is complete, its value equals **1**, a message is displayed which says that the number of collisions for the specified key has exceeded the permitted number of records in a zone:

```
     IF ZoneTrashing = 1 THEN '  Zone is overfilled,
                             '  no record output
        PRINT Info$, " - Number of collisions > ", RpZ
     END IF
```

The procedure **HashSearch** consists of a main loop which inputs the name of a city and searches for a record corresponding to this city. As you can see from the text of the procedure, the search is organized along the same lines as the search for an empty record with the difference that the field **Town** is compared with the name of the city entered.

```
   SUB HashSearch

   '   ***    Search in a hash-file    ***

     PRINT
     PRINT "    Search in a Hash-File "
     VIEW PRINT 21 TO 23
     R$ = "Y"
     DO
     CLS 2
     INPUT "Town: "; Info$    ' Enter the required key
     Num = RpZ * HashKey%(Info$)
     NoFound = 1
     FOR j = 1 TO RpZ
        GET #1, Num + j, HashRec
        IF RTRIM$(UCASE$(HashRec.Town)) = UCASE$(Info$) THEN
          PRINT "        Search is successful"
          PRINT HashRec.Town; " Year of foundation"; HashRec.Date
          NoFound = 0
          EXIT FOR
        END IF
     NEXT j
     IF NoFound = 1 THEN
        PRINT " Record not found   "
     END IF
     INPUT "Do you want to repeat the request [y/n]"; R$
     LOOP WHILE UCASE$(R$) = "y"
   END SUB
```

If the record is found, it's displayed on the screen. The pseudo-logic variable **NoFound** is used as a flag, signaling the failure of the search. This variable accepts the value **1** if the record with the specified key value isn't found. In this case, a corresponding message is displayed.

The integer function **HashKey%(x$)** accepts as its parameter a string variable containing the name of the city and returns the corresponding value of the hash-function. The choice of algorithm for this calculation will be covered in the subsequent discussion in more detail because it determines such important characteristics as the amount of disk space and the time necessary to search for a record by a specified key.

```
FUNCTION HashKey% (x$)

'   ***   Calculating a hash-function   ***

    ON ERROR GOTO ErrorHandler
    ErrorCall = 0
    L1$ = MID$(x$, 1, 1)
    L2$ = MID$(x$, 2, 1)
    L3$ = MID$(x$, 3, 1)
    Hundred% = ASC(L1$) MOD 2
    Ten% = ASC(L2$) MOD 10
    One% = ASC(L3$) MOD 10
    HashKey% = (100 * Hundred% + 10 * Ten% + One% + 1) MOD MaxHash
    ON ERROR GOTO 0
END FUNCTION
```

The results of the program **\CHAP6\CH6_9.BAS** are:

*** ORGANIZING A HASH-FILE AND SEARCHING RECORDS IN IT ***

Novy Afon	- Number of collisions >	3
Newark	- Number of collisions >	3
Veliky Ustyug	- Number of collisions >	3

Petersburg	4	13
Magadan	5	16
Magnitogorsk	5	17
Novgorod	6	19
Yaroslavl	6	20
Vologda	6	21
New Orlean	7	22
New York	7	23
Newcastle	7	24
Minsk	8	25
Uglitch	9	28
Smolensk	10	31
Moscow	12	37

Search in Hash-File
Town: New York
Search is successful.
New York   Year of foundation: 1626
Do you want to repeat the request [y/n] y
Town: Newcastle

236

```
          Search is successful.
Newcastle        Year of foundation: 1045
Do you want to repeat the request [y/n] y
          Town: Smolensk
          Search is successful.
Smolensk         Year of foundation: 863
Do you want to repeat the request [y/n] y
          Town: Novy Afon
          Record not found
Do you want to repeat the request [y/n] n
```

The output results of the program **\CHAP6\CH6_9.BAS** show that the choice of hash-function was far from ideal. Three of the sixteen records failed to be placed in the file because the zones corresponding to their keys appeared to be completely filled. Therefore, in a file designed for storing thirty nine records, we've located only thirteen, i.e. two thirds of the file remained empty.

A Good Hash Function

Hash-function selection is more or less arbitrary, depending on the skills of the programmer. To choose a good hash-function for any given file, it's necessary to work out a couple of things first:

- The approximate number of records in the file.
- How many records can be contained in one zone.

Using this information, we can determine the number of zones in the file and then the range of values of the hash-function.

If we allocate too few zones, some are overfilled and we lose part of the source records. By increasing the number of zones or the number of records in a zone, we can correct this but we then have to resign ourselves to a loss of disk space. Many think that the ideal is reached by filling approximately two thirds of each zone which gives the ideal ratio of record number to disk allocation.

As a bit of a recap, the following are three requirements for a good hash-function:

- Its value should be an integer from **0** to **n-1**, where **n** is the number of zones in a file.
- The calculation of the value of a hash-function should be performed quickly.
- For a set of possible values of the key, all the values of a hash-function should be equally likely.

If the hash-function satisfies the last condition, it's said to hash the value of the key well! If this condition isn't fulfilled, some of the blocks will be overfilled, while other blocks will contain only a small number of records.

In our previous example, the zones corresponding to values 6 and 7 of the hash-functions were overfilled; in the zone corresponding to the value 5, there were two records; in the zones corresponding to the values 4, 10, 12, there was only one record and the other zones were completely empty.

One way to ensure that the key values are uniformly distributed is to use a **prime** number of zones, **N**. Then, the last operation in calculating the hash-function's value is the modulus of the key, **k**:

```
HashKey(%)  =  k  MOD  N
```

So our program can be improved by using another hash-function. The defect in the function used for our data file is obvious: we should not take the first three letters of the names of the cities because they frequently coincide with each other. By replacing the computing part of the **Hashkey%** function with the following:

```
L1$ = MID$(x$, 1, 1)
L2$ = MID$(x$, 3, 1)
L3$ = MID$(x$, 5, 1)
Hundred% = ASC(L1$) MOD 2
Ten% = ASC(L2$) MOD 10
One% = ASC(L3$) MOD 10
HashKey%=(100 * Hundred% + 10 * Ten% + One% + 1) MOD MaxHash
```

and, given the values of constants **MaxHash=5** and **RpZ=4**, we obtain quite a different result:

*** ORGANIZING A HASH-FILE AND SEARCHING RECORDS IN IT ***

New Orlean	0	1
New York	0	2
Newark	0	3
Petersburg	0	4
Magadan	1	5
Yaroslavl	1	6
Magnitogorsk	1	7
Moscow	2	9
Novgorod	2	10
Smolensk	2	11
Uglitch	2	12
Minsk	3	13
Novy Afon	3	14
Newcastle	3	15
Veliky Ustyug	3	16
Vologda	4	17

In fact, the new function produced almost an ideal result on hashing. In addition, we have managed to fill 80% of the file which is a rare occurrence. The size of the zone has changed only slightly.

So, we've looked at the hashing method of randomization of a file. Now it's time to move on to the second method: indexation.

Indexed-sequential File Processing

Indexation as a means of accelerating the search for information has been successfully used for a long time. In front of me lies a copy of the *Dictionary of Programming (English-Russian-German-French)* - a perfect example of indexation. In this dictionary, terms are ordered according to their English spelling and presented in the following record format:

```
A189     e  array variable
         r  array m, variable f of the array type
         d  Feldvariable f
         f  variable f type tableau
```

This record is supplied with the index A189 which indicates that the record should be searched for among the terms beginning with the letter A, under the number 189. The letters e, r, d and f, preceding the terms, denote the language in which it's given. The letters f, m and n that appear among the words indicate the gender of the preceding word, feminine, masculine and neutral respectively.

The general text of the dictionary is followed by three index lists: RUSSIAN, GERMAN and FRENCH. These are alphabetically ordered and each term is assigned its corresponding record index from the general text. Therefore, if we look for the term *Schleifenrumpf* in the German index list, we shall find, from its corresponding index C427, the English term 'cycle body' and its Russian and French equivalents. You may be wondering why we're talking about a dictionary in this way. Well, the indexed sequential organization of a file is almost identical to the organization of a dictionary.

This is one of the earliest methods that offered the opportunity to organize direct access to a file. In some operating systems, it's even implemented as an independent Indexed Sequential Access Method.

There are various methods of indexed-sequential file organization and record access. As a rule, they are dependent on the capabilities of the computer, the operating system and the programming language. In this book, we'll cover a fairly simple but effective method of sequential file indexation which can be easily implemented in QBasic.

The essence of file indexing consists of creating additional information about it, allowing you to connect the value of the keys with the numbers of the records. If, as in the dictionary, each record is assigned an index, the indexation is referred to as unique. Unique indexation works very well in the search of records in files but calls for large volumes of RAM and, therefore, is badly implemented in QBasic.

Instead, we'll implement a classic version of the **indexed-sequential organization** of a file. The following are the various stages of the algorithm for indexing sequential files:

- ▲ The file to be indexed is sorted by the key to be subsequently used in any searches.

- ▲ The sorted file, consisting of **N*R** records, is conditionally broken into zones, each containing an identical number, **R**, of records.

- ▲ The records with the numbers **R*i+1, (i=0,1,2,...,N*R\k+1)** are serially read into the memory. The values of the keys from these records are stored as elements in a special array of indices. For each **i**, the record's keys and the number **R*i+1** is stored in the **i**th element of the array.

Instead of an **array** for storing the value of keys, it's possible to use any other data structure oriented to searching quickly, for example, the **binary tree**. If the file to be searched is rarely, if ever, changed, it makes sense to record the indices onto a disk and then read out the file of indices, speeding up the preparatory phase prior to the search itself.

The number of records in the zones shouldn't be too large. You have to get a balance when choosing the dimension of the array of indexes: for small **R** it's possible to overfill the operative memory, while large **R** may result in an infeasible search time.

It's difficult to give any recommendation on the choice of the value of **R**, but for large files you could, for example, choose a value of **R** equal to the number of records which are located in one cluster (the unit of exchange between the disk and the operative memory). The size of a cluster is typically defined by the operating system. In the majority of cases, your best advice is your own experience of searching for records in an indexed-sequential file.

A search in an indexed-sequential file is carried out by an algorithm which consists of the following sequence of actions:

▲ The value of the search key is entered.

▲ The largest index is found whose value isn't greater than the required value of the key. If the indices are organized in an array, the best results are offered by a binary search.

▲ **R** records are serially read from the file, beginning with the record with the number **R*i+1**, where **i** stands for the number of the found element in the array. If a record with the desired key value is found among these records, the search is successfully completed.

As an example of processing an indexed-sequential file, we'll take our example of searching for a record by a specified value of the **Team** and **Season** key in the file **FOOTBALL**, generated by the program **\CHAP6\CH6_7.BAS**. This file is already ordered by the **Team** and **Season** key.

You'll find the program **\CHAP6\CH6_10.BAS** on the disk. The head module contains the descriptions of the user-defined types necessary for the declaration of the variables. You already know two of these - **GoalsType** and **FootballType**. The third one, **IndexRecType**, is used for the definition of the **SearchRec** variable, where the search pattern is entered, and **IndexArray**, where the values of the keys for indexes are stored:

```
' Define the data type
TYPE GoalsType
   Scored AS INTEGER
   Lost AS INTEGER
END TYPE
TYPE FootballType
   Team AS STRING * 20
   Season AS INTEGER
   Goals AS GoalsType
END TYPE
TYPE IndexRecType
   Team AS STRING * 20
   Season AS INTEGER
END TYPE
```

The **ZoneSize** constant sets the size of a zone equal to six records:

```
CONST ZoneSize = 6  ' Size of index zone
```

After outputting a prompt onto the screen and completing the **Init** procedure which indexes the **Football** file, the head module starts the loop that forms its basis which you can interrupt if necessary:

```
DO
   BiSearch
   Search "C:Football"
   INPUT "Do you want to repeat the request [y/n]"; r$
LOOP WHILE UCASE$(R$) = "y"
```

The loop serially executes the **BiSearch** and **Search** procedures which implement the search for a key in an array and the search for records in a file.

The procedure **Init** opens the file **FOOTBALL** and, reading out the records with the numbers **ZoneSize*i+1** (i=0,1,2,...), fills the array **IndexArray** with the value of the keys:

```
SUB Init (FileName$)

  ' ***  Creating indexes for the Football file ***
  ' Input parameter contains the name of a file

  DIM Num AS STRING * 4
  CLS
  PRINT FileName$
  OPEN FileName$ FOR RANDOM AS #1 LEN = LEN(WorkRec)
  RecNum% = 1
  i = 1
  ' Reading the first record of a file
  GET #1, RecNum%, WorkRec
  PRINT " Array of indexes is being created"
  j = 0
  DO
    Num = RTRIM$(STR$(RecNum%))
    j = j + 1
    IF j > 20 THEN
      PRINT "Press any key to continue"
      WHILE INKEY$ = "": WEND
      j = 0
    END IF
    PRINT i; Num; " "; WorkRec.Team; WorkRec.Season
    IndexArray(i).Team = WorkRec.Team
    IndexArray(i).Season = WorkRec.Season
    RecNum% = RecNum% + ZoneSize
    i = i + 1
    ' Reading the first record of a next zone
    GET #1, RecNum%, WorkRec
  LOOP UNTIL EOF(1)
  MaxRec = i - 1
  CLOSE #1
  PRINT "Press any key to continue"
  WHILE INKEY$ = "": WEND

END SUB
```

The **BiSearch** procedure inputs the required value of the **Team** and **Season** keys and carries out a binary search in **IndexArray** for the element containing the largest key values not exceeding the required ones. The result of the search - the number of the array's element - is returned to the variable **Index**:

```
SUB BiSearch

  '*** Binary Search for the number of a zone by the key ***

  CLS
  PRINT
  INPUT "Team: ", SearchRec.Team       ' Input search pattern
  INPUT "Season: ", SearchRec.Season
  Index = 1  ' initial values of the variables
  R = MaxRec ' for binary search
  DO
    i = (Index + R) \ 2
    IF SearchRec.Team < IndexArray(i).Team THEN
R = i
```

```
      END IF
      IF SearchRec.Team > IndexArray(i).Team THEN
   Index = i
      END IF
      IF SearchRec.Team = IndexArray(i).Team THEN
        IF SearchRec.Season < IndexArray(i).Season THEN
   R = i
        ELSE
   Index = i
        END IF
      END IF
   LOOP WHILE R - Index - 1
   ' Variable Index contains the number of a zone
   ' with the record sought for
END SUB
```

The procedure **Search** reads the **ZoneSize** of the records of the file **Football** in sequence, starting from the one defined by the value of the **Index** variable, until either the necessary record is found or all records have been looked through. In the first case, the found record is displayed on the screen and, in the second, a message is displayed informing you of an unsuccessful search.

```
SUB Search (FileName$)
'  ***  Search in an indexed file  ***

   DIM Num AS STRING * 4
   NoFound = 1
   CLS
   PRINT FileName$
   OPEN FileName$ FOR RANDOM AS #1 LEN = LEN(WorkRec)
   ' Calculating the number of the first record in a zone
   RecNum% = ZoneSize * (Index - 1) + 1
   i = 1
                ' Searching for a record by the key
   DO
     GET #1, RecNum%, WorkRec
     IF SearchRec.Team = WorkRec.Team AND SearchRec.Season = WorkRec.Season THEN
       NoFound = 0
       LOCATE CSRLIN - 1, 35
       PRINT "       Search is successful"
       PRINT RecNum%; " "; WorkRec.Team; WorkRec.Season;
       PRINT WorkRec.Goals.Scored; WorkRec.Goals.Lost
       EXIT DO
     ELSE
       RecNum% = RecNum% + 1
       i = i + 1
     END IF
   LOOP WHILE 7 - i
   CLOSE #1
   IF NoFound = 1 THEN
     PRINT " Record not found "
   END IF
END SUB
```

The results of the program **INDFILE.BAS** are shown here:

```
***   INDEXING A TYPED FILE   ***
          C:Football
     Array of indexes is created
 1    1    Arsenal                  1985
 2    7    Arsenal                  1991
 3   13    Aston Villa              1987
 4   19    Aston Villa              1993
 5   25    Blackburn                1989
 6   31    Chelsea                  1985
 7   37    Chelsea                  1991
 8   43    Coventry                 1987
 9   49    Coventry                 1993
10   55    Everton                  1989
11   61    Leeds                    1985
12   67    Leeds                    1991
13   73    Liverpool                1987
14   79    Liverpool                1993
15   85    Manchester City          1989
16   91    Manchester United        1985
17   97    Manchester United        1991
18  103    Newcastle                1987
19  109    Newcastle                1993
20  115    Norwich                  1989
21  121    Queens Park Rangers      1985
22  127    Queens Park Rangers      1991
23  133    Sheffield Wednesday      1987
24  139    Sheffield Wednesday      1993
25  145    Southampton              1989
26  151    Tottenham                1985
27  157    Tottenham                1991
28  163    West Ham                 1987
29  169    West Ham                 1993
30  175    Wimbledon                1989
          Team: Aston Villa
          Season:  1989
     Search is successful.
15  Aston Villa        1989  22  31
          Team: Manchester United
          Season:  1991
     Search is successful.
97  Manchester United    1991  29  17
          Team: Tottenham
          Season:  1992
     Search is successful.
158  Tottenham          1992  28  16
          Team: Manchester City
          Season:  1980
     Record not found.
          Team: Iskra Smolensk
          Season:  1986
     Record not found.
```

This then, brings us to the end of our discussion on the methods of solving inquiry problems based on random access to a file. This section also concludes our look at the problems of processing files.

Summary

In this chapter, we've discussed the standard file management tools supported by QBasic. These are sufficient for developing simple databases and other programs that need to save data on disks.

We've presented you with different methods of file organization and processing. We've acquainted you with various ways of file classification by type and length of record, and by method of access. We've also discussed the basic methods of file organization, the algorithms of creating and processing files.

We've covered the following methods in detail:

- External sorting of sequential files.
- Searching for records using the hash method.
- Index-searching for records in an ordered sequential file.

The skills you develop in choosing the correct type of file and method of accessing its records will come in handy for tackling a wide range of problems.

CHAPTER 7

Program Design

Introduction

As any experienced programmer knows, the more complicated a program is, the more errors you're likely to create while designing it. However, reliability is a basic requirement for software, particularly in the commercial world where software failure can lead to disastrous results.

Because of the problems encountered when developing large programs, programmers now use stringent methods of writing and debugging while developing them to ensure reliability and maintainability. The methods they use have come to be commonly known as **programming technology** or **software engineering**. QBasic is one of a number of programming languages which allow you to use technological methods in your development of reliable programs.

In this chapter, you'll learn the main methods of programming technology: structural and modular programming. The section on style will then introduce you to an approach to programming that combines definite technique with artistic freedom. We demonstrate design methods using an example program which you can use later as part of more complicated programs.

The chapter concludes with sections on the art of program testing and debugging, often the most exasperating programming processes.

Program Design

One of the purposes of this book is to guide you through the development of serious program systems, allowing you to work with various types of menu, enter and analyze source data, create graphics and use complex algorithms to process data.

This can be more difficult to do in QBasic because of the limitations of its writing and debugging tools in comparison with more powerful programming languages like Turbo Pascal, C++ and the latest generation Visual OOP languages. However, the use of good technological programming methods allows us to avoid these difficulties.

Step-by-Step Programming

Without going into too much detail of program design theory, we're going to talk about a set of approaches which are part of one of the most popular technologies: **top-down programming**. When an entire program system consists of one very large program, we use top-down principles to divide the development process into several sequential stages. Each stage uses the results obtained in the previous stage and prepares the information necessary for the next one. The key advantages of this approach are simplicity and reliability. We explain the stages on the following pages.

The Specification

Drawing up the specification is the first stage and, although at first glance it has nothing to do with programming, ignore it at your peril. It's during this stage that you formulate all the problems that you're going to be faced with later.

The specification doesn't necessarily have to conform to any strict, formal rules, but it's important to include all the information necessary for further design. You should consider including the following sections:

▲ A comprehensive description of the purpose of the program you're designing.

▲ A comprehensive description of the input data with an indication of type, dimension and other restrictions.

▲ A comprehensive description of all the output data.

▲ Detailed descriptions of the data processing algorithms, taking into account the structures and types of intermediate data necessary for these algorithms.

If the specification is complete, you'll be able to debug and document the program with relative ease. You'll also be able to modify it more easily because you won't have to go through the frustration of trying to recollect what the program does and how it does it.

> It's important to permanently keep several backup copies of the specification across different mediums because the specification is integral to the project. It will also be very important a few years down the line when the program has been forgotten about and someone new comes along and wants to know what it does.

Splitting a Program up into Modules

If a program is large, it should be split up into interconnected sub-programs. Depending on the purpose of the subroutines and on the required results, these can be chained programs, external procedures or functions. Such subroutines are referred to as **modules**. When you split up a program, you must decide which variables will be common to all modules, and which will be local. At the same time, you should draw up a list of input and output parameters for each module.

You should draw up an individual specification for each separate module, defining the same sections as that of the head module.

Designing the Modules

At this stage, all the modules are designed to fit their specifications. In QBasic, this process begins with the head module and proceeds consecutively from one module to another. Here, structural programming is applied, which allows you to write programs which are read, tested, debugged and modified easily.

Program Testing

At the testing stage, data is prepared to check each module separately and the program as a whole. The purpose of testing is to detect errors in the program. This process of testing is directly associated with the debugging process. The results of testing become the source data for the debugging stage. Note that developing tests for checking the validity of program operation is as difficult and time-consuming as the design of the program itself. The art of testing is one of the major components of the art of programming.

Debugging

Debugging is essentially searching for, localizing and eliminating errors in a program. This stage is closely connected with the testing stage, the results of which serve as the source data for debugging . Debugging often leads to the modification of the source code of a program, so a return to the testing stage with changes to the tests is quite likely.

Optimization of a Program

This stage isn't always necessary. Usually, if the specifications were given sufficient thought in the first place, you'll end up with an adequate program. However, you may find that your program works slowly with real data or that you need to wring every last ounce of performance from your machine. In this case, you should return to your code and, wherever possible, remove all those excess actions which may have crept in, such as repeated checks of the same conditions. We will return to program optimization in Chapter 12 - Game Development.

If you're a conscientious programmer, be aware that any change to your code should result in a return to the testing and debugging stages.

A Program to Calculate an Arithmetic Expression

To illustrate the use of design technology, we'll use an example program which calculates the value of an arithmetic expression. The best way to demonstrate these techniques will be to run through each of the previous stages in turn, starting with the specification of the problem.

A Specification for the Whole

The source data of the program is an arithmetic expression in identifier form and the values of variables entered in the expression. The output data is the result of the calculation. So as not to burden you with difficult procedures for analyzing the initial expression, we'll restrict its definition.

We'll say that the arithmetic expression can consist only of variable identifiers and the signs of arithmetic operations: raising to a power, multiplication, division, addition and subtraction. To change the natural order of calculations, any number of brackets can be used, according to the standard algebraic rules.

We've deliberately turned away constants as their inclusion in the analysis and calculation of the expression doesn't require any great programming skill. It does, however, increase the size of the program, obscuring its more interesting features.

The identifiers consist of a pair: a letter from A to H and a number from 1 to 9, always starting with the letter. Lower-case and upper-case letters will be treated as indistinguishable.

This chessboard-like way of identification is accepted in electronic tables. A letter indicates the horizontal coordinate, and a number the vertical coordinate of the cell of a table. In general, the horizontal coordinate can contain up to two letters, and the vertical coordinate from one to four numbers. However, we'll restrict them to a letter-number pair so that we don't increase the size of the program unnecessarily. If you want to, you can quite easily redevelop the program to include numerical constants and identifiers of any length in the expression. The following are examples of valid and invalid identifiers,

al, B7, h3   valid identifiers
a0, Aa, 3, H, 5e, 34   invalid identifiers

and these are some examples of valid expressions:

    A1+B1
    (a1-b1)*(a1+b1)
    a5^(b3-a5)
    ((C2-A1*A2)/C2+B3)^A1

The program will ask you to enter an arithmetic expression, it will check its validity and then ask you to enter the values of the variables. To calculate the value of the expression, the program will transform it into a parentheses-free form, called **postfix** or **polish record**. The transformed expression is then calculated using the standard algorithm used for any valid expression.

The transformation and calculation algorithms used on the expressions are based on the use of the stack data structure that we discussed back in Chapter 5. Remember that data in a stack is like a pile of plates: it's subject to the LIFO (last in, first out) rule. In QBasic here, the stack is implemented by a pair: an array of variables whose type is defined by the type of data stored, and by an integer variable containing the index of the last value kept in the stack, called the **top** of the stack.

The output data of the program is a real number, the result of calculating the expression. We'll format it as the number with its sign and two digits after the decimal point, with the entire size of the output number being nine characters.

We'll call the program **\CHAP7\CH7_1.BAS** - you can find it on the disk.

This description of the program is actually our specification. From here onwards, it will be used at all stages of the program design, from dividing the program into modules right through to debugging.

Data and Algorithm Specification

The algorithm for converting an expression into postfix form is fairly simple and well-documented in literature on compiler design. During the conversion, all the brackets are excluded from the expression and the operation signs are moved from their natural positions between operands to the position after the second operand. Therefore, the expression A1 + A2, given in standard mathematical form, will become A1A2+, and the expression (A1+A2)/(A1-A2) becomes A1A2+A1A2-/.

There are different variations of the algorithm which transforms an expression from infix form to postfix, but all of them are based on scanning the initial expression from the first to the last character. In the algorithm that we'll use, the transformation is accomplished using special functions which determine the priorities of the operations. For each operation, two priorities are defined: the **in-coming priority** and the **in-stack priority**. To calculate these priorities, we use two functions **icp(Op)** and **isp(Op)** whose arguments are the operation signs. This table shows the operation priorities:

Operation	ICP	ISP
(	0	5
Unary minus	1	1
^	2	2
* /	3	3
+ -	4	4
#	-	5

The transformation of an expression is executed according to the following rules:

1 If the character being scanned is a letter or a number, it's added to the end of the resulting expression.

2 If the character being scanned is an operation sign or an opening parenthesis, (,then:

3 All operation signs whose ISP doesn't exceed the ICP of the character being scanned are popped and added to the end of the resulting expression.

4 The operation sign being scanned is stored in the stack.

5 If a closing parenthesis,) , is scanned, then all the operation signs up to the first occurrence of the, (, character are consecutively extracted and added to the end of the resulting expression.

6 If, when scanning is complete, the stack isn't empty, the characters that are left are put, in turn, at the end of the resulting expression.

Take, for example, the transformation of this expression,

$((A1-A2)/(A1+A2))*(A1 \wedge (-A3))$

from infix form into postfix form,

$A2A2-A1A2+/A1A3 \sim \wedge *$

using the described algorithm.

> **Incidentally, we shall be using the ~ character to designate the unary negation operator.**

Here is a step-by-step run through on how the algorithm will work:

Step	Scanning Character	Stack Contents	Postfix Expression
1	(	(	
2	(	((	

Table Continued on Following Page

Step	Scanning Character	Stack Contents	Postfix Expression
3	A	((	A
4	1	((	A1
5	-	((-	A1
6	A	((-	A1A
7	2	((-	A1A2
8	)	(	A1A2-
9	/	(/	A1A2-
10	(	(/(	A1A2-
11	A	(/(	A1A2-A
12	1	(/(	A1A2-A1
13	+	(/(+	A1A2-A1
14	A	(/(+	A1A2-A1A
15	2	(/(+	A2A2-A1A2
16	)	(/	A2A2-A1A2+
17	)		A2A2-A1A2+/
18	*	*	A2A2-A1A2+/
19	(	*(	A2A2-A1A2+/
20	A	*(	A2A2-A1A2+/A
21	1	*(	A2A2-A1A2+/A1
22	^	*(^	A2A2-A1A2+/A1
23	(	*(^	A2A2-A1A2+/A1
24	-	*(^(-	A2A2-A1A2+/A1
25	A	*(^(-	A2A2-A1A2+/A1A
26	3	*(^(-	A2A2-A1A2+/A1A3
27	)	*(^	A2A2-A1A2+/A1A3~
28	)	*	A2A2-A1A2+/A1A3~^
29			A2A2-A1A2+/A1A3~^*

After the expression has been converted into postfix form, its value is easily calculated. The transformed expression is scanned and the calculation is performed according to the following rules:

1 If two sequential characters form a variable identifier, the corresponding value is pushed onto the stack.

2 If a character being scanned is a binary operation sign, then:

the two upper elements are popped from the stack;

this operation is applied to the popped elements;

the result of the operation is stored in the stack.

3 If a character being scanned is a sign of unary operation, then

the stack's top element is retrieved;

this element is subjected to that operation;

the result of the operation is stored in the stack.

The following table illustrates the incremental calculation of the postfix expression A2A2-A1A2+/A1A3~^*, using the algorithm discussed. Every time a value is computed, it's stored in the temporary location **Ti**, where **i=(1,2,...6)**. **T6** contains the last calculated value, which is the result of the calculation of the whole expression:

Step	Scanning Identifier/Operation	Computing Value	Stack Containing
1	A1		A1
2	A2		A1 A2
3	-	T1=A1-A2	T1
4	A1		T1 A1
5	A2		T1 A1 A2
6	+	T2=A1+A2	T1 T2
7	/	T3=T1/T2	T3
8	A1		T3 A1
9	A3		T3 A1 A3
10	-	T4=~A3	T3 A1 T4
11	^	T5=A1^T4	T3 T5
12	*	T6=T3*T5	T6

Well, that concludes the definition of the problem, so now lets see how we're going to implement it.

Modular Programming

This is, in effect, the art of splitting a program into a number of different independent modules, allowing many programs to use standard units. In QBasic, standard, debugged modules can be stored on disk as independent source code and used in the main program with no change. This tried and tested code improves the reliability and reduces the development time of your programs, so most programmers have their own library of subroutines.

Principles of Modular Programming

The basic element of modular programming is the module - a separate, functionally complete program unit which is structurally identified and made in the standard manner. A program written using the principles of modularity has the following advantages:

▲ It has a tree-like structure, the head module of the program being the root. This means that intra-program communication and information flow isn't all that difficult to follow.

▲ It's easy to read and modify.

▲ There are a lot of natural breakpoints, which simplifies the debugging process and enables you to carry out more comprehensive testing.

When developing modules, you should bear in mind the following principles:

1 A module can only be accessed by calling it as a subroutine, using the identifier and the list of parameters.

2 A module should only pass control back to its calling module, and the head module only back to the operating system. The exceptions to this are the specialized modules that process run-time errors and which allow the use of termination statements when the further execution of a program is pointless or impossible.

3 Each module can call other modules.

4 A module is of limited size. The main limitation when defining the size of a module is that you have to be able to maintain an integral understanding of the algorithm and, preferably, see at a glance what the module does. Our experience suggests that, at least in QBasic, modules (including the head module) shouldn't exceed three screen pages. You can read and debug such modules quite easily.

5 A module should not preserve the history of its calls to control its functioning. Sometimes it's difficult to avoid the temptation of connecting the subsequent calls of a module with the previous ones. For example, the first call of a module differs from the subsequent ones in the initial values of some local variables. Such programming, though aspiring to good practice, usually ends with a long and fruitless search for errors. To avoid this sort of problem, you should make sure that all calls to a module have equality of rights.

6 A module carries out a quite definite transformation of the initial data during its operation. Ideally, each module accomplishes just one function which can be expressed by a single phrase and which can form the basis of the module's name. This principle will become especially evident when the program `\CHAP7\CH7_1.BAS`is broken into modules.

> **Fine examples of well-designed modular programs are the three sample programs you should have found with QBasic, `GORILLA.BAS`, `MONEY.BAS` and `NIBBLES.BAS`. Not that our programs are badly designed, but we are optimizing them slightly to fit into this book.**

When programming in QBasic, using these principles considerably simplifies and accelerates the process of developing sophisticated programs. Furthermore, QBasic's integrated environment, and the concepts of the language itself, are tailored and almost force you towards implementing programs in a modular and structured fashion.

Types of Modules

The definition of a module makes it clear that it's a sub-program called either by the head module or by another module. The connection between the calling modules and those being called is made either through the parameters or by using global variables accessible to both modules. The ideal way of doing it from a modular programming point of view is certainly the first one. However, in QBasic it may be appropriate to use global variables for the modules of a program. In this case, you should observe the following rules:

1 Global variables used by several modules should be declared in the head module.

2 In each module which uses global variables, there should be a comment indicating which variables are used and how. This should also be applied to local variables.

Traditionally, modules are divided into two types: procedures (or subroutines) and functions. There are certain distinctions between these two types of modules, which define their application fields:

1 A function can only be used as the operand of assignment and conditional statements, and as a parameter for other functions, procedures and statements.

2 A procedure always acts as an independent statement.

3 A function can accept any number of parameters but returns only one value which is directly substituted for the name of the function in the expression. Under no circumstances should the input parameters of a function be changed by calling it. In other words, after calling the function, they should have the same values as before.

4 As a rule, a procedure has changeable parameters.

5 The result of a function can't be structural (an array or a structure defined by the **TYPE** statement).

Failure situations which arise during the execution of a function are particularly complex. In a subroutine, the list of parameters can include a variable which returns an error code. However, this isn't allowed with a function.

In such cases, we recommend that you either trust the QBasic run-time system, or define a global variable in the head module which is available to all the modules where the function will return an error code. For example:

```
' ******** Main ******
    . . .
DIM SHARED ErrorCode%
    . . .
FUNCTION MY_FUNC% (p1%, p2%)
' Function to test for an error which may occur
' while raising zero in a negative power
FUNCTION MY_FUNC   (p1%, p2%)
    . . .
  IF p1% = 0 AND p2% < 0 THEN
    MY_FUNC% = 0
    ErrorCode% = 2
  ELSE
    MY_FUNC% = p1% ^ p2%
```

```
        ErrorCode% = 0
      END IF
         . . .
    END FUNCTION

    ' SUB-ROUTINE which calls the function and
    ' processes the error
    SUB MY_SUB
         . . .
      SumIntExp% = SumIntExp% + MY_FUNC (b%, e%)
      IF ErrorCode% = 2 THEN PRINT "Illegal operands in ^"      . . .
    END SUB
```

Each module should be preceded by a comment describing the purpose of the function, as well as the description of the parameters and local/global variables. To demonstrate what we mean, we're going to restructure the program **\CHAP7\CH7_1.BAS** according to the previously stated rules.

Partitioning into Modules

According to our specification, the program **\CHAP7\CH7_1.BAS** must execute the following actions for us to obtain a result:

1 Allow the input of an arithmetic expression and, at the same time, reduce it to standard format (remove spaces, replace lower-case letters with upper-case letters).

2 Check that the expression entered is correct (syntax control).

3 Transform the expression from a common record, containing brackets, into a postfix (parenthesis-free) record.

4 Accept the input of the values of the variables to be used in the expression.

5 Calculate the value of the expression.

6 Output the results.

The first five actions can easily be separated into modules. We shall now look at these individually and in more detail.

Program CALC: Head module

This module contains the declarations of all the procedures and functions which make up the program **\CHAP7\CH7_1.BAS**. Here are all the data types and global variables that are declared:

1 A record containing the variable identifier and its value:

```
TYPE  IdVal
    Ident  AS  STRING  *  2
    Value  AS  DOUBLE
END  TYPE
```

2 `IVArray(20) AS IdVal` is the array which accommodates up to 21 `IdVal` variables.

3 `NIdent%` is the number of variables in the expression to be calculated.

4 `ExpressVar$` is the source expression.

5 `PostExpress$` is the expression in postfix form.

6 `OpStack(20) AS STRING * 1` is a character array for the stack of arithmetic operators.

7 `ValStack(20) AS DOUBLE` is a numerical array for the stack of operands.

8 `HeadStack%` is a variable for storing the index of the top of the stack.

9 `Operand(2) AS DOUBLE` is an array for the value of the first and second operands.

The head module also consists of the following sequence of module calls:

1 `InExpression` is the input of the source expression and its transformation into standard form.

2 `TestExpression` is the syntax control of the source expression.

3 `InfToPostf` is the conversion of the initial expression to postfix form.

4 `InValues` is the input of the variable values.

5 `CalcExpression` is the calculation of the value of the expression.

Then come the statements which output the value of the expression that is stored in the top of the stack. The result has the form:

< initial expression > = < the value >

The value is output in the format "######.##".

And last, but not least, the head module contains the statement which processes arithmetic errors.

Here is a graphic illustration of the head module of
`\CHAP7\CH7_1.BAS`:

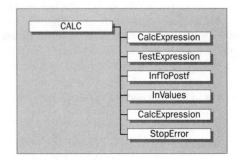

Drawing the plan or the route of the program logically is a vastly underrated and underused method of understanding what is required. We shall be showing you the schematic diagrams of all our modules here, hoping that you learn and practice this valuable technique.

Program CALC: InExpression Module

This module allows the input of the initial expression, replaces all lower-case letters with upper-case letters and removes the spaces between the identifiers and the operation signs. To make it easier to work with the expression, we recommend replacing the unary minus sign with another sign, so that you don't confuse it with the binary minus.

We'll use the ~ character to designate the unary minus. Since searching for and replacing the unary minus isn't particularly easy, it's implemented by a separate module - **ReplUnaryMinus**.

The **InExpression** module has no parameters. The source expression is entered into the global variable **ExpressionVar$** and stored there after the necessary conversions. Control is always passed back to the head module.

A graphic illustration of the **InExpression** unit is given here:

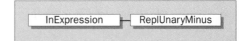

Program CALC: TestExpression Module

This module checks the syntax of the entered expression. The expression is considered correct if:

1 It contains an identical number of opening and closing brackets.

2 All the identifiers consist of a letter from A to H and a digit from 1 to 9.

3 It contains only the following operation signs: + - * / ^ ~

The initial expression is scanned, symbol by symbol, and the encountered letters and numbers are stored in the variable allocated for the current identifier. When an operation sign is met which is different from the unary minus, the **AddIdent** module is executed, the purpose of which is to store a new, correct identifier in **IVArray**.

If an error is detected during syntax analysis, control is passed to the **StopError** unit which signals the error and halts the program.

The **TestExpression** module has no parameters. The expression to be tested is taken from the global variable **ExpressionVar$**. Executing this module either stops the program if an error is detected, or generates the global array **IVArray** which contains all the variable identifiers, the number of which is stored in the global variable **NIdent%**. In the latter case, control is returned to the head module.

Here is a figure which shows the structure of the **TestExpression** unit:

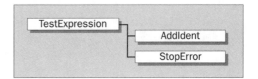

Program CALC: ReplUnaryMinus Module

This module is called from the **InExpression** module and replaces the unary minus with the symbol ~. To do this, it scans the source expression stored in the global variable **ExpressVar$**, assuming that the minus sign (-) corresponds to the unary minus if it's the first character in an expression, or if it's preceded by an opening bracket.

Program CALC: AddIdent Module

This module is called by the **InExpression** unit and accepts from it a string parameter which contains the next identifier. To check the validity of the identifier, the module-function **NoIdent** is invoked. If the identifier isn't valid, the **StopError** module is called with the error code **1** and the value of the invalid identifier as its parameters. A correct identifier is checked by the module-function **NewIdent** to see if it coincides with the identifiers previously stored in the global array **IVArray**. When it's found that this identifier doesn't coincide, it's stored in this array and the value of the global variable **NIdent** is increased by one. This module is shown schematically here:

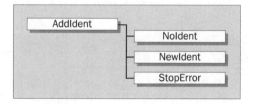

Program CALC: NoIdent$ Module

This module is a function called by the **AddIdent** module. It accepts the string variable containing the identifier being tested as its parameter. It returns the value **True**, if the string being tested isn't an identifier, in the previously defined sense, and **False** otherwise.

Program CALC: NewIdent$ Module

This module is a function called from **AddIdent**. It takes the same parameter as the **NoIdent$** function. The accepted value is compared with the value of the **Ident** field in all the elements of the **IVArray** array. If an element containing the value of the identifier is found, the function returns the value **False**, otherwise it returns the value **True**.

Program CALC: StopError Module

This module is invoked from the **BadOp** block of the head module and the **AddIdent** and **TestExpression** modules. The parameters of the module are the number of the message and a string containing the faulty character. The message text string is formed depending on the number of the message. When messages 1 and 2 are needed, either the first character of the incorrect identifier, or the character which can't be in the expression to be calculated, is inserted in the text. This table shows the corresponding error numbers and messages. As you can see, they all stop the program:

N	Message	Action
1	Invalid identifier <character>	Program Halted
2	Invalid character <character>	Program Halted
3	Unbalanced ( )	Program Halted
5	Illegal operands in ^	Program Halted
11	Divide by zero	Program Halted

In our example, the program calculates a single expression. Therefore, the **StopError** module causes an emergency stop. If your program is for calculating many expressions, this module can generate the value of a special variable for controlling the calculation of the expression. This value can terminate the processing of the current expression and invoke the input and calculation of the next one.

Making similar specifications for the rest of the modules, we'll obtain specifications for our program **\CHAP7\CH7_1.BAS**:

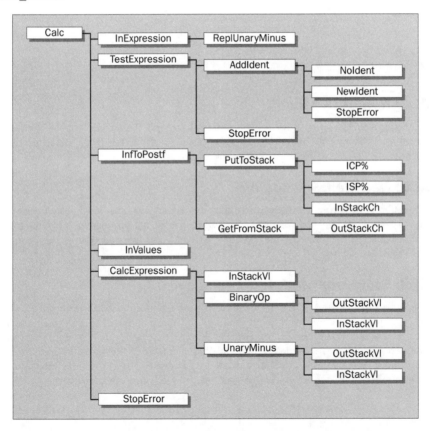

Once we've looked at the principles of structured programming, we'll show you how these specifications are transformed into real programs.

Structural Programming Technology

Structural programming came about from the need to write programs which would be easy to debug and correct after a lapse of time. The aim was to ensure that you could quickly make sense of a program written long ago if, for example, the program suddenly started throwing up errors or stopped working altogether.

It's not easy to give an exact definition of structural programming. The majority of definitions tend to be rather scientific-sounding and don't really give you a clear idea of exactly what it's all about. But structural programming is frequently defined as 'programming without the **GOTO** statement'.

The founder of structural programming, E. Dijkstra, wrote in 1968 that a programmer's skill is inversely proportional to the density of **GOTO**s in their programs. In his opinion, using this statement has fatal consequences and it should be forever excluded from programming languages. QBasic enables you to bypass the **GOTO** statement and use structural programming. It's still present in the language, but the use of the **GOTO** statement should be subjected to the severest restrictions.

Structural programming isn't just about designing programs without **GOTO**s. So, from here on we shall use the term 'structural programming' to mean the principles of writing programs according to a set of stringent technological rules and methods which allow you to design clear programs, whose debugging and subsequent modification will not pose serious problems.

If you've never programmed this way before, you may think that structural programming will take away the opportunities for creativity and make the programming boring. You'll find that this isn't the case - freed from having to devise various tricks while writing and debugging a program - you can spend the extra time looking for the best algorithms to do the job. Now isn't that the height of programming skill!

Developing Structured Programs

Structural programming is based on the sole use of three allowable structures: the **sequence**, **alternative**, and **cycle**. All these structures have one entrance and one exit.

The following figure shows a sequence, S, which consists of n elements S1, S2,..., Sn:

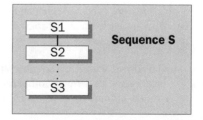

The elements of this sequence can be any statements of the programming language which perform some action and fulfill the one entrance (input) and one exit (output) condition. Typically, these are assignment and call statements and those implementing alternatives and cycles. Statements of the last two types are considered independent elements of a sequence, featuring one entrance and one exit.

To implement the alternative, one of three structures may be used. The next figure shows the constructions which select either of two possibilities. Structure (a) performs the actions defined by sequence S1, only when the conditional expression is **True**. Otherwise, no actions are executed. Structure (b) is used when one of two actions, depending on the value of the conditional expression, may be executed:

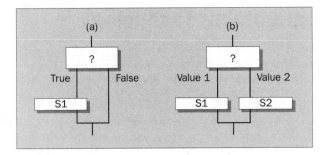

If the conditional expression takes the value **True**, the actions defined by sequence S1 are executed. If it takes the value **False**, those resulting from sequence S2 are executed. Both structures finish working by passing to the next element of the sequence, of which they are part.

This figure shows the structure which generalizes the alternative:

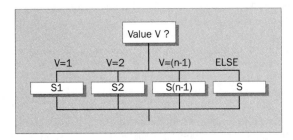

This structure provides a method of selecting from more than two options. We've used a control variable **i** (also called a selection variable) instead of the conditional expression. It's assumed that this variable can only accept one of n-1 values. In this case, one of the sequences Q1, Q2,..., Qn-1 is executed.

If the value of the variable doesn't correspond to any of these values, either sequence Qn is executed, or, if this isn't specified, no actions are performed. As with the previous structures, after completing the actions defined in the selection, control is passed to the next element of the sequence which employs this selection.

Alternative structures are used for calculations which are directly composed of sequentially numbered actions. The choice at each stage of program execution is defined either by a logic condition or by the value of the selection variable.

Those of you acquainted with programming at the level of the previous chapters will know that the given structures are inadequate for writing complicated programs. When an algorithm is implemented through a sequence of repeated actions, a cyclic structure is used.

A standard cycle consists of a condition and Q sequences, the latter being frequently referred to as the **body** of the cycle. A programming language usually has several statements with which this structure can be achieved. Their common feature is that they regularly check some condition which determines whether the cycle will be continued. Cycles are divided into two types: those with a pre-condition (a) and those with a post-condition (b):

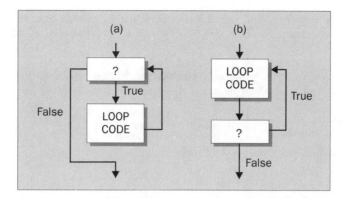

When a cycle with a pre-condition is implemented, the condition is checked every time before sequence Q is executed. If the condition is **True**, sequence Q is executed, otherwise control is passed to the next statement in the sequence. In a cycle with a post-condition, the condition is checked after the sequence Q is complete.

When programming cycles, you should remember that:

1 If the condition is **False** on the first check, a cycle with a pre-condition will never be executed.

2 The body of the cycle with a post-condition is executed at least once.

3 The constituent statements of the sequence Q should modify the value of the condition, otherwise the cycle can turn out to be an infinite one.

Developing a program using structural programming technology consists of superimposing these structures without using the **GOTO** statements. Structural programs, irrespective of their size and the complexity of the algorithms used, are simple in structure and easy to read and modify. In a structured program, there's no tangle of forward-backward transfers or the like.

Those of you who are accustomed to using **GOTO** with a free hand and a pure heart will probably need a little time to kick the habit. If you have decided to program in QBasic (which allows structured programming as easily as Pascal or C), it's worth trying to stick to structured programming. It will force you to think more about the design of a program. This means that you'll produce a better result first time round and, therefore, debugging time will be kept to a minimum. A quicker process altogether.

Implementing Structures in QBasic

Lets's take a look now at how we can utilize these structures within QBasic. You should already be quite familiar with some of the commands to achieve these flow controls because we discussed them fully back in Chapter 2 - Controlling Program Flow.

Sequence

This structure is implemented by placing any QBasic statements sequentially, one after the other. Among the statements that can be used in a sequence are the assignment, input, output, alternative, cycle and call statements. Unlike other programming languages, QBasic allows you to include statements such as **DATA**,

DIM, and **COMMON** in the sequence. Although this isn't particularly desirable from the point of view of good programming style, when defining dynamic arrays in QBasic, it's impossible to avoid including them in the sequence.

The following is a fragment from the program, **\CHAP6\CH6_7.BAS**, which we looked at in Chapter 5 - Manipulating Data Structures, and which illustrates the structure of a sequence:

```
RecNum1% = RecNum1% + 1
GET #1, RecNum1%, WorkRec1
IF EOF(1) THEN
   EndGroup1% = 1
END IF
```

Included in this sequence are an assignment statement which calculates the number of the next record in a file, a statement which reads a record with the calculated number and a conditional statement which processes the end of the file.

The following example from the same program demonstrates a fragment of the sequence which copies a file and contains a cycle statement:

```
RecNum% = 1
GET #1, RecNum%, WorkRec1
DO
   PUT #2, RecNum%, WorkRec1
   RecNum% = RecNum% + 1
   GET #1, RecNum%, WorkRec1
LOOP UNTIL EOF(1)
CLOSE #1, #2
```

Notice how everything is processed sequentially, including the **DO...LOOP** cycle statement.

Alternative

QBasic has two statements which are used to create this structure. One of them, a traditional **IF** statement, chooses one of two available options. It makes sense to use the modification:

```
IF condition1 THEN
    [statementblock-1]
[ELSEIF condition2 THEN
    [statementblock-2]]...
 [ELSE
    [statementblock-n]]
END IF
```

And, although in the simplest cases, BASIC's conventional modification,

```
IF condition THEN statement-1 [ELSE statement-2]
```

is quite allowable, it's worth using it with a great deal of caution. First, we can't predict precisely how many statements will follow the words **THEN** or **ELSE**, which provokes those not versed in structured programming to use **GOTO**s. Secondly, during step-by-step debugging, this statement is executed as one step, which doesn't allow you to see precisely where the program branches.

In contrast to similar statements in other programming languages, QBasic's **IF** is more expressive, thanks to the additional **ELSEIF** branch. Using this branch considerably reduces the amount of code you need to write. Take, for example, the following fragment of the **KeyComparision$** function also from the program**CHAP6\CH6_7.BAS**:

```
IF WorkRec1.Team < WorkRec2.Team THEN
  KeyComparision = 0
ELSEIF WorkRec1.Team = WorkRec2.Team THEN
  IF WorkRec1.Season <= WorkRec2.Season THEN
    KeyComparision = 0
  ELSE
    KeyComparision = 1
  END IF
ELSE
  KeyComparision = 1
END IF
```

Without using the **ELSEIF**, this fragment would be much clumsier:

```
IF WorkRec1.Team < WorkRec2.Team THEN
  KeyComparision = 0
ELSE
  IF WorkRec1.Team = WorkRec2.Team THEN
    IF WorkRec1.Season <= WorkRec2.Season THEN
      KeyComparision = 0
    ELSE
      KeyComparision = 1
    END IF
  ELSE
    KeyComparision = 1
  END IF
END IF
```

When you need to make a choice between more than two variable or expression values, you can use the following familiar construction:

```
SELECT CASE testexpression
CASE expressionlist1
  [statementblock-1]
[CASE expressionlist2
  [statementblock-2]]...
 [CASE ELSE
   [statementblock-n]]
END SELECT
```

Note that the values in all **expressionlist**'s should be of the same type.

The following example of the **SELECT CASE** statement enables the execution of various actions, depending on the different values of the character variable:

```
SELECT CASE CurrentChar$
  CASE "A" TO "H"
    CurrentIdent$ = CurrentChar$
  CASE "1" TO "9"
```

```
        CurrentIdent$ = CurrentIdent$ + CurrentChar$
        FOR j% = 1 TO NIdent%
           IF CurrentIdent$ = IVArray(j%).Ident THEN
              InStackV1 IVArray(j%).Value
           END IF
        NEXT j%
     CASE "+", "-", "*", "/", "^"
        BinaryOp CurrentChar$
     CASE "~"
        UnaryMinus
     END SELECT
```

Using the **IF** statement for tackling this task would considerably increase the size of the program and complicate its debugging.

Cycle

In the richness of its cycle structures, QBasic is unique. Two of these, the numbered cycle:

```
FOR counter = start TO end [STEP increment]
   [statementblock]
NEXT counter
```

and the conventional cycle with a pre-condition:

```
WHILE condition
   [statementblock]
WEND
```

are practically no different from the equivalent statements in other programming languages.

The **DO...LOOP** statement, the possibilities of which are practically limitless, is of special interest. In this modification,

```
DO [{WHILE | UNTIL} condition]
    [statementblock]
LOOP
```

it implements a pre-condition loop, while in this one,

```
DO
   [statementblock]
LOOP [{WHILE | UNTIL} condition]
```

it implements a post-condition loop. In both cases, the cycle can finish at both **True** and **False** values of the condition. The latter cycle version is very convenient in file processing, when processing ends while attempting to read the next record, because it's reached the end of the file.

The following fragment of the **Total** procedure from the program **\CHAP6\CH6_8.BAS** clearly demonstrates this method:

```
DO
   IF TotalRec.Team = CurrRec.Team THEN
      SumGoals TotalRec.Goals, CurrRec.Goals
      RecNum% = RecNum + 1
      GET #1, RecNum%, CurrRec
   ELSE
      PrintAV
      TotalRec.Team = CurrRec.Team            'Setting up initial values
      TotalRec.Goals.Scored = 0               'of summarizing variables
      TotalRec.Goals.Lost = 0                 'for the next in turn group
   END IF
   LOOP UNTIL EOF(1)
```

If you want to see a simultaneous use of both modifications of the **DO...LOOP**, the **ShellSort** procedure described in Chapter 5 - Manipulating Data Structures, provides a very good example.

Data Structurization

The structurization of data in a programming language begins with the introduction of the concept of **type**. This means that each variable, constant or expression is associated with one definite type, as discussed in Chapter 1 - The QBasic Essentials. Data type is a basic concept in programming theory and, therefore, it's impossible to apply a strict definition to it. However, we can give it the following description:

1 The type defines a set of values which can be accepted by a variable or an expression.

2 Each value belongs to one type, and to one type only.

3 For example, if we have the constant 25 in a program, it will be referred to as integer type only, the constant 2.5 as single and the constant 'a string' as string type.

4 The type of a constant, variable or expression can be determined either from the context of a program or from the appearance of the operand itself, without referring to the actual values being calculated in the program.

5 Regardless of the variable values, the expression **2*N%\3** has a value of integer type, the expression **2*N%/3** has a value of single type, and the expression **Name\$ + " " + Surname\$** has a value of string type.

6 For each operation, there's fixed types of operand and a fixed type (typically the same) of results. When the same character (for example, +, for adding values of different types) is applied to different operands types, it's assumed that this character designates several similar operations for different types of operands and results.

Therefore, the character,+, in expressions **N% + 2.5** and **Name\$ + " " + Surname\$** means, in the former case, the addition of numbers with a result of single type and, in the latter case, the concatenation of character strings with the result of the same type.

These properties allow the compilers and run-time systems of programming languages to implement correct data processing, including not only transforming types of operands, but also processing situations such as overflow which takes place when the absolute value of the result exceeds the maximum allowable value of the type of variable to which it's assigned.

Types are separated into **simple** and **structural**. All the types cited above are simple. They're also built-in types, which means that their definitions are part of the QBasic language. For example, if we want to define an integer constant or variable, we don't have to stipulate its length in bits, or the operations which are applicable to it. While preparing a program for execution, QBasic does all such necessary work on its own.

The first structural type we discuss is the fixed-length character string. The constants and variables defined in this type contain, apart from their own values, an additional value which defines the actual length of the string and which is invisible to the programmer.

Arrays are the first structural entity whose definition of the structure of its elements is completely carried out by the programmer. You've already met arrays, but still a reminder is in order here - an array is an indexed set of elements of the *same type*. Whatever dimension of array we set, each copy of the index values defines only one element, the type of which doesn't depend on the type and the values of the indexes.

The record type, as it's referred to in the majority of programming languages, is defined in QBasic rather confusingly by the **TYPE... END TYPE** statements. It gives the user maximum freedom to combine, under one name, a set of variables of different types. This type, which first appeared as a means of file typization in COBOL, very quickly found its way into all programming languages as a compulsory type. BASIC did not have this rather useful means for a long time, but they were specifically built into QBasic.

The main purpose of this type is to group polytypic data, describing the properties of a particular class of object, into structures of the same type . These structures, unlike arrays which are sets of elements of the same type, contain elements of various types. By way of an example, consider the structure **FootballType** from the program **\CHAP6\CH6_7.BAS**, which was used to define the structure of a record in the **FOOTBALL** file:

```
TYPE FootballType
    Team AS STRING * 20
    Season AS INTEGER
    Goals AS GoalsType
END TYPE
```

This structure contains not only two polytypic variables, **Team** and **Season**, but also a structure **Goals**:

```
TYPE GoalsType
    Scored AS INTEGER
    Lost AS INTEGER
END TYPE
```

The use of data structures of the record type allows for simplified programming and a reduction in the number of statements in the source code. For example, if we define two variables:

```
DIM Rec1, Rec2 AS FootballType
```

the assignment **Rec2 = Rec1** is equivalent to four assignments for each individual variable entered in the structure.

When transmitting parameters, it's also convenient to unite them in records to simplify the call statements. In the program, **\CHAP6\CH6_8.BAS**, the subroutine-procedure,

```
SUB SumGoals (TGoals AS GoalsType, CGoals AS GoalsType)
```

is declared and called as,

```
SumGoals TotalRec.Goals, CurrRec.Goals
```

with only two parameters. If we hadn't used a record of the **Goals** structure, we would have had to transmit twice as many parameters.

This brings us to the end of our discussion on data types and structures. Now you are familiar with the basic concepts which underlie good style and representation of data in a program.

Remarks About Style, or Let's Agree...

Few would disagree with the idea that a programmer should at least be able to read his own programs and that, for programmers working in groups, it's even more important that their code is clear and understandable. Hence, it follows that program writing style is very important.

Style is a collection of ways or methods of programming used by programmers to obtain correct, effective and readable programs. Rules of good style come about as a result of various programmers working together on large program systems, or when a programmer develops programs for his own use.

When a programmer has acquired a particular programming style, his or her programs are much simpler to understand. So here is our Programming Top Ten:

1   Remember that programs are read by people.

If you look at programs developed by various companies, although they may use different styles, they are clearly defined and their general aim is that any programmer can understand them at a glance.

2   If there's more than one way of doing something and the difference between one way and another is minimal, then choose one method and stick to it.

This is a very important rule in QBasic as the language allows you to solve the same problems in different ways. For example, calling sub-procedures can be performed directly by their identifiers, by previously declaring them using the **DECLARE** statements, or by using the **CALL** statement. You should stick with just one of these methods.

3   Write more comments than you think you need to.

The worst error that a programmer can make is to write a program without comments. It's evidence of an amateurish approach to his work. A good comment will remind the programmer of what he wanted to do in a given fragment of the program when, after half a year of normal operation, it suddenly bristles up and refuses to work when you expect it to.

It's best to write the comments as you write the program because that is the time when you have the clearest idea of what you are striving for. Generally, it's not a good idea to try commenting a program that you have already written - the results tend to be formal text that adds little to the code itself.

Sometimes, you may need to remove comments from a particularly critical program or from a section of a program, in order to make it achieve the desired speed. In these cases, always save this 'optimized' version under a different name and keep the master copy as the one with comments.

4   Comments should contain additional information; they shouldn't paraphrase the program.

In QBasic, it's good practice to use introductory comments at the beginning of each program or subroutine and explanatory comments accompanying separate statements or sequences of statements.

Introductory comments contain the main information about a program and should include at least the following items:

▲ The purpose of the program, taken from the specification.

▲ A list of parameters and global variables used (for subroutines).

▲ A list of files used by the program.

Information about the authors, the date and version number.

Look at this example from the **\CHAP6\CH6_9.BAS** program:

```
IF ZoneTrashing = 1 THEN ' Zone is overfilled,
                          ' no record output
   PRINT Info$, " - Number of collisions > ", RpZ
END IF
```

A comment like "Check of equality to 1" after the first line would serve no purpose, because even a basic knowledge of logic is enough for anyone to realize that this is just a check. The comment given in this example reflects the ideas incorporated in the algorithms for creating a hash-file.

5 Bad commenting is worse than no commenting at all.

6 The correct choice of variable and procedure names creates a program that is easy to read.

There's little point in being lazy or trying to save space when writing identifiers. Taken alone, a good identifier itself comments the program and makes it easy for us to understand what we want to achieve from a statement. The sequence of procedure calls from the head module of the program **CALC.BAS** tells us, practically without any additional comments, what this program does:

```
InExpression
TestExpression
InfToPostf                        'Infix to Postfix
InValues
CalcExpression
```

Obviously, the statement **CloseBracket% = CloseBracket% + 1** is infinitely more expressive than **C = C + 1**.

7 Try not to use defaults.

Note that an explicit instruction or definition of a variable type in the **DIM** statement is preferable to using defaults. The default mode isn't the best feature inherited from FORTRAN. Errors caused by using defaults are very difficult to locate.

8 Identifiers should be easy to understand.

It's good practice to begin the identifier with an upper-case letter. The exception are the identifiers of loop counters in cycles which usually consist of a single letter. If an identifier is made of several words, or abbreviations of the words, each of them should start with an upper-case letter; for example, **GetFromStack**, or **MergePortion**. This makes them much easier to read.

One stylistic error frequently made by beginners is the use of 'humorous' identifiers. For example, the expression:

```
Ketchup = Tomato + Salt + Sugar + Vinegar
```

Read for the first time, this may gladden the reader, but it may soon become a source of irritation.

9 One statement per line is enough.

QBasic allows you to write programs with lines containing more than one statement. As we've already pointed out, this considerably hinders debugging, and doesn't do much for readability either.

10 Use indentations to reveal the structure of a program.

Structured programs are different in that it's easy to understand when one or another sequence of statements should be executed. Indentations play an important role in this. For example:

```
FOR j = 1 TO RpZ
    GET 1.), Num + j, HashRec
    IF RTRIM$(UCASE$(HashRec.Town)) = UCASE$(Info$) THEN PRINT " Search is ⤶
successful "
        PRINT HashRec.Town; " Year of foundation"; HashRec.Date
        NoFound = 0
        EXIT FOR
    END IF
  NEXT j
```

In this program fragment, two sequences can clearly be distinguished: one sequence in the **FOR** statement, and the second one in **IF**.

These, then, are the golden rules of programming style. We aren't suggesting that following these rules will solve all your problems - the art of programming requires considerable knowledge, practice and skill - but, by using these rules and adding new ones, you can create your own style which will help you avoid many difficulties.

The Program

Now that we've learned the technology of programming, we can proceed to working over our expression program consisting of several modules.

This section contains the text of several modules of the program **\CHAP7\CH7_1.BAS**. We'll present the whole program but separate the procedures and functions by short comments. These listings will be used later to illustrate program debugging methods.

The head module begins with the declaration of procedures and functions:

```
DECLARE SUB AddIdent (IdentVar$)
DECLARE SUB BinaryOp (OpChar$)
DECLARE SUB CalcExpression ()
DECLARE SUB GetFromStack (Margin$)
DECLARE FUNCTION ICP% (OpChar$)
DECLARE SUB InExpression ()
DECLARE SUB InfToPostf ()
DECLARE SUB InStackVl (Value AS DOUBLE)
DECLARE SUB InStackCh (OpChar$)
DECLARE SUB InValues ()
DECLARE FUNCTION ISP% ()
DECLARE FUNCTION NewIdent$ (TestIdent$)
DECLARE FUNCTION NoIdent$ (TestIdent$)
DECLARE SUB OutStackVl (NOp%)
DECLARE SUB OutStackCh (DelCh$)
DECLARE SUB PutToStack (OpChar$)
DECLARE SUB ReplUnaryMinus ()
DECLARE SUB StopError (Message%, Symbol$)
DECLARE SUB TestExpression ()
DECLARE SUB UnaryMinus ()
    '************************************************************
    '*  Program of Calculating Arithmetic Expressions          *
    '************************************************************
' Declaration of variables
' A record containing variable identifier and value
TYPE IdVal
      Ident AS STRING * 2
      Value AS DOUBLE
END TYPE
' Common variables:
'     - array of records for 21 variables,
'     - number of variables in an expression,
'     - source expression,
'     - the exprerssion in a postfix form
DIM SHARED IVArray(20) AS IdVal, NIdent%, ExpressVar$, PostExpress$
'     - character array to organize a stack of operations,
'     - numeric array to organize a stack of operands,
'     - a variable for storing stack top's index
DIM SHARED OpStack(20) AS STRING * 1, ValStack(20) AS DOUBLE, HeadStack%
'     - array for the values of the first and of the second operand
DIM SHARED Operand(2) AS DOUBLE
ON ERROR GOTO BadOp
InExpression
TestExpression
InfToPostf
InValues
CalcExpression
PRINT
PRINT ExpressVar$; "=";
PRINT USING "######.##"; ValStack(1)
END
BadOp:
  StopError ERR, ""
  RESUME NEXT
```

This way of working with subroutines is used for two reasons: first, the program starts with a title which points to a good program-writing style; second, calling previously declared procedures doesn't require the use of the **CALL** statement and the absence of brackets enclosing the parameter lists brings the program text closer to real language.

The contents list is given in alphabetical order. This was done after the completion of program debugging. When working in the QBasic environment, this arrangement of identifiers facilitates the search for procedures and functions in a list. We also see the declarations of user-defined types and global variables, then the main procedures are called and the head module is completed by an error-handling block:

```
BadOp:
   StopError ERR, ""
   RESUME NEXT
END
```

The rest of the modules can be found in the program on your disk.

Summary

The aim of the advice in this chapter is to help you write error-free programs. However, there'll also be occasions when, despite all your efforts, you will not be able to make a program work. If, after going right back to the initial specification stage, you still have no joy, you will probably save time by starting all over again.

So, on that note we come to the end of our chapter on program development methods. In this chapter, we have looked at the most commonly used methods of program writing. If you are a relatively inexperienced programmer, you may well question the necessity of such a systematic application of methods. However, with more experience and as you develop more and more difficult programs, you will soon appreciate the importance of the areas we have covered here.

Bit-mapped Graphics and Animation

CHAPTER 8

Introduction

We've already seen how QBasic behaves with elementary geometrical figures, and it's now time to take a look at the more sophisticated bit-mapped graphics. We'll run through the basics to begin with and show you how to directly access RAM in both text and graphics video modes. We'll then look at developing drivers which enable the printer to copy the graphics screen pixel by pixel. We'll also demonstrate how an improved data math processing algorithm used within QBasic can improve copying performance, producing results comparable to those of some standard drivers.

We'll introduce a QBasic pattern editor for filling closed areas with solid color and specific patterns. And since we'll be just one step away from creating **sprites**, we'll touch on sprite-creating techniques and try out simple text and involved graphics examples. We'll explore the interaction between moving sprites and the background picture, and examine a sprite creator and drawing program which converts a picture or image you have drawn into data that you can include in any program.

Elements of Text and Graphics Representation

Your PC display is controlled by a special device known variously as a video adapter, a video card, or a graphics card. It contains circuitry to control display and carry out graphics operations, and to handle the memory (RAM, Video RAM) where your PC stores the images that you see on screen. There are also various screen modes split into two categories: the text mode and the graphics modes.

Text Mode

In text mode, it's easy to understand VRAM operation. The VRAM's address space is divided into fields called **pages**. Each page accommodates the text of one full screen. Each screen character is stored in 2 bytes of VRAM and the cells' contents describe the character and its attributes.

The first byte contains the character code in ASCII format which takes a value from 0 to 255. The second byte specifies the attributes of the character: its foreground and background colors and whether it flashes. You can find the rules for coding character color attributes in your video adapters manual.

The ratio between character positions and bytes per page is 1:2 because there will always be 2 bytes for every character position. Therefore, for a 25*40 page there'll be 2000 bytes. Let's look at a CGA color video adapter which has about 16 Kbytes of VRAM. At 4Kb or 2Kb per page, this works out at 4 or 8 pages of text.

> **Modern video adapters have higher resolutions and a greater choice of colors. They take up a lot more VRAM which limits the number of pages that you'll have available.**

Only one of these pages can be active at any one time. It's from this **active** page that you read information that appears on the screen. Although the other pages are passive, they are able to accumulate information in the background without being seen. QBasic allows you to switch between pages so that you can instantly change the page you're displaying.

If the code of a specified character stored in its code cell is on the active page, the character will immediately appear on the screen. The computer continually scans the VRAM and active information is automatically sent to the display. If the cell is of the low-address memory type, the character appears in the upper left of the screen. The next cell along stores the code of the second character of the line, and so on. So you can think of VRAM as a one-dimensional array.

When you directly access VRAM, the computer needs to know the starting point (initial address) of the VRAM in memory. Once you've given it this information, you can tell it which memory cells to use. This example illustrates the output of a line of characters using direct access to the VRAM of the EGA adapter:

```
REM Demonstration of simple direct access of VRAM
REM \CHAP8\CH8_1.BAS

CLS                     'Clear screen
DEF SEG = &HB800        'Set initial address of VRAM
POKE 0, 72              'Output of H character onto the screen
POKE 2, 69              'Output of E character onto the screen
POKE 4, 76              'Output of L character onto the screen
POKE 6, 76              'Output of L character onto the screen
POKE 8, 79              'Output of O character onto the screen
POKE 10, 33             'Output of the exclamation mark onto the screen
```

Run this program and the Hello! message appears in the upper left of the screen. The letter H is in the first position of the line, the letter E in the second, and so on. Notice that each step represents an increase of 2 because every memory cell containing character code information is followed by its counterpart containing code for that character's attributes. Enter different codes into this cell and you'll see a change of color in the corresponding character position.

It's quite obvious, though, that the following code fragment gives you exactly same result as the previous program:

```
CLS: LOCATE 1,1: PRINT "Hello!"
```

So, if you could avoid our time-consuming and pretty involved first approach to outputting a Hello! message, you would. QBasic provides an easier way out because it has convenient and simple commands to replace the code in our first attempt. We'll try a little experiment with this program:

```
REM Part one of 'direct VRAM access' v 'Built-in commands'
REM \CHAP8\CH8_2.BAS

CLS
t0 = TIMER
DEF SEG = &HB800
FOR a% = 0 TO 4000 STEP 2
    POKE a%, 72
NEXT a%
LOCATE 1, 1: PRINT TIMER - t0; "  ";
```

Here we've displayed 2000 H characters by directly filling the character VRAM with the code 72. And, using the system function **TIMER**, we've programmed for the time spent doing this routine to be printed in the upper left corner once it has finished. The time is calculated as the difference between the initial value of the **TIMER** function and its value on finishing the program. The time taken for the program to execute will depend on the type of PC you're using.

Here's the second half of this programming experiment:

```
REM Part two of 'direct VRAM access' v 'Built-in commands'
REM \CHAP8\CH8_3.BAS

CLS
t0 = TIMER
FOR A% = 0 TO 1999
    PRINT "H";
NEXT
LOCATE 1, 1: PRINT TIMER - t0; "   ";
```

It does exactly the same thing as the previous one, but this time we've used the **PRINT** statement to do it. If we compare the times that both programs take to fill the screen with H's, we'll see that by addressing the RAM directly, we've filled the screen in about a third of the time. We could have quite easily increased this speed difference further by using the **LOCATE** statement before **PRINT**.

However, now we've said this, we advise you not to use direct VRAM addressing in text mode too much. The QBasic statements **LOCATE** and **PRINT** offer a far more natural and illustrative way of outputting text information, and, generally, the speed with which the programs operate is quite sufficient. Use direct access to RAM in text mode only when the output rate of the **PRINT** and **LOCATE** statements really becomes a limiting factor; for instance, in dynamic graphics programs where speed is vital.

Graphics Mode

In graphics mode, each point of the screen is represented in binary format. Graphics images are kept in specialized RAM on your video adapter. Here are the resolutions of the most frequently used video adapters:

Graphic Type	Full Name	Resolution	No. of Colors	ScreenMode
CGA	Color Graphics Adapter	320*200 640*200	2 4	1 2
Hercules	Hercules Graphics Card	720*348	2	3
EGA, VGA	Enhanced Graphics Adapter	640*350	16	9-10
VGA	Video Graphics Array	640*480	256	11-12

This data isn't exhaustive because modern video adapters can have a number of operating modes, each with differing characteristics. However, this information shows how video adapters differ essentially in resolution and in the number of colors that can be displayed simultaneously (4 with the CGA adapter, 16 with EGA, etc.). Except for the Hercules video adapter, most of the later adapters support the graphics modes of the older ones - so VGA supports both CGA and EGA modes, etc.

> The number of available video adapters is growing as technology improves,
> resulting in partial, or sometimes complete incompatibility. This also means that,
> unfortunately, QBasic doesn't yet support such high resolution video adapters as
> SVGA.

EGA

For clarity, we'll refer to the EGA video adapter (and the compatible, improved VGA adapter). EGA video adapters allow you to create a 16-color image for every one of the 224000 (640*350) screen pixels. As we've mentioned before, there are several sets of colors, called **palettes**. The EGA video adapter has 16 special palette registers to facilitate changes from one color palette to another. These palette registers transfer information from each cell of the VRAM to the screen.

VGA and MCGA

The process is even more complex in the newer VGA and MCGA adapters. Besides the block of 16 color palette registers, they have a bank of 256 DAC (digit-to-analog converter) registers. This means that, with a limited VRAM size (up to 256 Kb), it's possible to obtain a picture of 640*480 (307200 pixels), 16 colors, 16 palettes and direct addressing of every pixel. You can still define a set of graphics pages but exactly how many will depend on the RAM available on the card.

Talking to the VRAM

QBasic supports dialog with the VRAM with the **PSET**, **PRESET**, **LINE**, **CIRCLE** and **DRAW** statements, which we covered back in Chapter 3. They send data, represented on the screen as one form of graphic display or another, to the RAM, using assembler or machine code drawing algorithms.

The **POINT** function calculates the address of the VRAM's cell, using specified coordinates, and tests the contents which define the pixel's attributes. The **PAINT**, **PUT** and **GET** statements are particularly important: they operate with whole areas of the VRAM rather than with separate points. The **POKE** statement stores a value in any memory cell; and the **PEEK** function checks and returns a cell's value. This is useful when working with the CGA and Hercules adapters, whose RAM is organized along fairly simple lines. However, there's little, if any, use for it if you're working with EGA, VGA and SVGA adapters, because they have a separate intricately configured VRAM.

However, you won't need to directly access video memory all that often. QBasic, like most languages, uses procedures written in assembler or machine code for most graphics operations. This means that you don't actually need to write specific programs for creating rectangles, circles, ellipses, lines, arcs or points, unless it's lightning speed you're after.

Even so, it's worth knowing how dialog with the VRAM can be organized in graphics mode. You can use the CPU ports for the necessary settings:

```
REM Accessing VRAM in graphics mode
REM \CHAP8\CH8_4.BAS

SCREEN 7                'Setting screen mode 7 of the EGA video adapter
DEF SEG = &HA000        'Setting the initial address of the video
RAM OUT &H3CE, 7        'Addressing the bit mask register
OUT &H3CF, 128          'Masking all bits except 7th one
OUT &H3C4, 2            'Addressing the map mask register
```

```
OUT &H3C5, 4          'Setting red color
POKE 0, 1             'Drawing a point
```

This program, at first glance, may not strike you as being very clear. It creates a red point in the upper left corner of the screen and, if you replace the last line with these lines

```
POKE 0, 170           'Drawing the first pair of points
POKE 80, 255          'Drawing the second pair of points
```

hopefully, you'll see that broken and unbroken lines are drawn in the same corner.

How to Poke

The first parameter of the **POKE** statement points to the address of the cell in the RAM which determines the screen position of the pixel. We need to do a spot of mathematics if we want to find out which address corresponds to which screen position. If we multiply the number of pixels along the X axis by the number of pixels along the Y axis, we get the total number of pixels on the screen. If we then divide this number by the number of bits in our address, which is 8, we get the total number of screen positions available to us. So, in screen mode 7 our calculation looks like this:

```
320 * 200 = 64000
```

Dividing this by the number of bits in our address gives us:

```
64000 / 8 = 8000
```

Therefore, in mode 7, we have a range of 0 to 7999 positions available to us, starting from the top left of the screen and finishing in the bottom right corner.

The second parameter is the value that we're writing to the address, defining the characteristics of the pixel. To work out this value, we simply take any binary number of up to 8 bits and convert it into decimal. For example, our broken line above looks like this in binary:

```
10101010
```

So, to convert it into decimal we have to add together the relevant bits, like we did earlier in Chapter 3 when defining a character bit image to send to the printer:

```
128 + 32 + 8 + 2 = 170
```

Our unbroken line looks like this:

```
11111111
```

```
128 + 64 + 32 + 16 + 8 + 4 + 2 + 1 = 255
```

Try experimenting with these parameters and you'll understand the organization of VRAM a lot better. You'll appreciate the convenience in defining a specified pixel using the following QBasic statement, as opposed to the program above:

```
PSET(X,Y), C
```

Although you may not want to directly change the memory contents with **PEEK** and **POKE**, if you understand the structure of the video memory, it will help later when we use video pages to move images smoothly round the screen.

Drivers for Copying a Plot to a File or a Printer

In every PC's life there comes a time when it has to print an entire screen image to a file or to the printer. In this instance, we need to call on the help of copy drivers which quite simply dump the entire screen, pixel by pixel, to the relevant buffer. Drivers of this type are normally executable **.EXE** or **.COM** files and, for the most part, use a special **.PCX** graphics format.

The Purpose of Copy Drivers

Before we describe plotting algorithms we'll ask a question: "Why do we need to create plots?" Perhaps it's because we like showing off to our less competent programming friends? Certainly, when you've mastered machine graphics you've really achieved something worth shouting about. So, up on our screen (as a tribute to one of our personality defects) we have our plot which we've shown to all our friends. What do we do with it? Sooner or later we'll need to know how to save it as a file and possibly how to print out a hard copy.

Even a simple plot consists of a lot of points. For example, in CGA mode with medium resolution, there are 320 x 200 = 64000 potential points, and in VGA mode with maximum resolution there are 640 x 480 = 307200! In addition, each point has its attributes - its chosen color and palette flags, and its coordinates. This means that saving or printing a plot as a file means moving large amounts of information someplace, so it's often difficult to get a high operating speed. The problems increase when you're writing copy drivers in BASIC. The best drivers are those written in a speedier high-level language like Assembler.

There are many ready-to-use drivers for copying a plot to a file, so there's no point in us trying to re-invent the wheel. They're usually included in integrated graphics systems, such as Harvard Graphics, PaintBrush and the like and you can also find them providing graphics import in text editors.

Some drivers (for example, **CAPTURE**) allow you to copy the screen image to a **.PCX** file *and* give you the option of changing the colors. Sometimes, this can be very useful.

As a rule, drivers are **terminate-and-stay-resident** (**TSR**) programs which means that they're loaded in the RAM and stored there until your PC is switched off. You typically use a key combination (such as *Alt+G* or *Shift+Print Screen*) to invoke them. The drivers either ask for the name of the file that they generate, or assign it their own name with an ordinal number. In the latter case, you should rename the files with appropriate names when you've finished working with them. Unfortunately, conflicts between resident drivers and other applications aren't uncommon, often resulting in a system crash unless you're using a TSR manager. Rest assured though, these crashes won't damage your hardware.

A commonly used driver, included in MS-DOS, is **GRAPHICS.COM** which is activated by pressing the *Print Screen* button. Unfortunately, **GRAPHICS.COM** isn't perfect:

- First releases didn't support EGA and VGA modes.
- The representation of colors using undertints isn't always particularly good (for example, on a multi-function plot some curves can appear faded or be completely invisible).

▲ High resolution plots (from CGA mode upwards) are printed along, rather than across the sheet of paper inserted in the printer.

▲ The plot dimensions are too large to be included into a review or an article.

▲ The printing time is quite considerable - 5-6 minutes when dealing with high resolution plots (this isn't particularly surprising given the large number of points there are).

Writing Your Own Copy Driver

Therefore, drivers in BASIC can be valuable, so we'll look at how you can create one for your own purposes.

The copy driver must scan each line of the screen and transfer data to the printer. In QBasic, you can use the function **POINT(x%,y%)**, which returns the point color code with the coordinates **(x%,y%)** to read point data. If you want to print color images in monochrome, all you have to do is replace the color generated by the **POINT(x%,y%)** with **1**. For instance, you can use the combined function **SIGN(POINT(x%,y%))** to speed up scanning.

The task of creating a driver in BASIC along these lines appears, at first, to be doomed to failure because of the low calculation performance ascribed to BASIC. However, clever use of QBasic features means that we can create drivers which are infinitely faster than **GRAPHICS.COM**. What's more, they even offer a more convenient print format and, of course, can be flexibly built into the main program. This driver is oriented at the printer Epson LX-800, but is relevant to all models of Epson printers.

QBasic Copy Drivers for the Hercules Video Adapter

Using QBasic drivers allows you to do away with TSR programs, such as **GRAPHICS.COM**. BASIC drivers may also turn out to be irreplaceable for special modes not supported by **GRAPHICS.COM**; for example, the monochrome mode **SCREEN 3** for Hercules video adapters with a resolution 720x348 pixels.

The procedure **CS3** contains two QBasic drivers for printing the graphics screen in **SCREEN 3** mode:

```
REM Demonstration of QBasic graphics drivers
REM \CHAP8\CH8_5.BAS

  SUB CS3

  DO
  M$ = INPUT$(1)
      IF M$ = "S" OR M$ = "s" THEN GOSUB CS3
      IF M$ = "C" OR M$ = "c" THEN GOSUB CS3N
      IF M$ = "Q" OR M$ = "q" THEN GOTO LEND
  LOOP

  CS3: 'Copy-screen for 720*348 pixels (turbo-mode)
      DEF SEG = &HB000 'Start address of video-RAM
      OPEN "LPT1:" FOR RANDOM AS #1: WIDTH #1, 255
      PRINT #1, CHR$(27); "3"; CHR$(24);
      FOR x% = 0 TO 89
          PRINT #1, CHR$(27); "*"; CHR$(0); CHR$(92); CHR$(1);
          FOR s% = 0 TO 7830 STEP 90: sx% = x% - s%
              FOR y% = 32316 TO 0 STEP -8192
                  a% = PEEK(y% + sx%)
                  PRINT #1, CHR$(a%);
```

```
            NEXT
        NEXT: PRINT #1, CHR$(10)
      NEXT: DEF SEG = 0: CLOSE #1
   RETURN


   CS3N: 'Copy-screen for 720*348 pixels (NLQ-mode)
   WIDTH "LPT1:", 255: LPRINT CHR$(27); "3"; CHR$(24);
   FOR y% = 0 TO 344 STEP 8
       LPRINT CHR$(27); "*"; CHR$(1); CHR$(207); CHR$(2);
       y1% = y% + 1: y2% = y% + 2: y3% = y% + 3: y4% = y% + 4
       y5% = y% + 5: y6% = y% + 6: y7% = y% + 7
       FOR X% = 0 TO 719
           a% = 16 * POINT(x%, y3%) + 32 * POINT(x%, y2%)
           a% = a% + 64 * POINT(x%, y1%) + 128 * POINT(x%, y%)
           IF y% < 344 THEN
           a% = a% + 8 * POINT(x%, y4%) + 4 * POINT(x%, y5%)
           a% = a% + 2 * POINT(x%, y6%) + POINT(x%, y7%)
           END IF
           IF a% = 13 OR a% = 9 THEN a% = 0
           LPRINT CHR$(a%);
       NEXT x%: LPRINT
   NEXT y%
   RETURN


   LEND:
   END SUB
```

This program module consists of three sections. The first section provides control by pressing key *S* for fast printing, *C* for medium speed printing with higher quality and *Q* to exit.

> You may have noticed that we were being very unfriendly to the user by not telling them what to press, but this is not the whole story. We couldn't print on the screen because it would corrupt the image we are storing, so, before running this program, the user must be familiar with what is expected of them.

The **DO LOOP** structure allows you to carry out more than one action; for example, if you need to make more than one hard copy of a plot.

Turbo Mode

The second block is the subroutine which fast prints the graphic copy of the screen. The printing speed, in this case, is increased by directly reading information about each pixel on the screen from the VRAM. To achieve this, scanning of the VRAM is organized to conform to the structure of the Hercules adapter.

A detailed description of memory distribution for this video adapter is beyond the scope of this book. However, we'll just point out here that RAM scanning starts from the hexadecimal address B000 and careful examination of how the loops are organized reveals the distribution of the information about the screen points in the VRAM. At the beginning of the program, the **DEF SEG** statement defines the starting address (segment) for the VRAM and, at the end of the program, the same statement sets the zero address used by default in the QBasic system.

The function **PEEK** (reading from memory) allows you to judge the presence or absence of points. Reading information is performed in the same way as organizing files but the values of the auxiliary variable **a%** are sent to the printer port rather than to a magnetic disk:

```
    a% = PEEK(y% + sx%)
    PRINT #1, CHR$(a%);
```

In this and other implementations of the printing operation, you'll meet the following, unusual line:

```
OPEN "LPT1:" FOR RANDOM AS #1: WIDTH #1, 255
```

This set of instructions is specifically associated with the **PRINT** command: it advances the line as soon as the number of data messages exceeds the values defined in **WIDTH** (typically 40 or 80). You can send information messages of unlimited length to the printer by opening the printer port as a channel for transmitting information to a file and setting the parameter 255 for **WIDTH**. Printing only takes place when outputting information from the buffer with line advance is indicated. When screen copy printing is complete, the open file is closed using the **CLOSE #1** statement at the end of the subroutine.

The subroutine **CS3** prints the screen image along the sheet of paper. The image fits loosely onto A4 and can produce the hard copy almost three times faster than with **GRAPHICS.COM**.

Near-Letter Quality

We use another method in the driver represented by the program **CS3N**. Here, to perform point-by-point scanning, we wheel in the function **POINT(x%,y%)**. The calculations are organized in such a way as to reduce any additional operations to a minimum. For example, the ordinates of a column are calculated before the loop, with **x%** as a loop counter, although, if these calculations were carried out within the loop, it would probably make the programs more illustrative. One more method is to directly use the **POINT** function in the expression which forms the column byte value. Printing using this subroutine is slightly slower than with **CS3**.

QBasic Copy Screen Driver for EGA and VGA Video Adapters

Here, we'll give you one more version of a screen dump driver, this time for EGA mode (and VGA, if used in EGA mode):

```
REM EGA/VGA Graphics driver
REM \CHAP8\CH8_6.BAS

CopyScr:
OPEN "LPT1:" FOR RANDOM AS #1: WIDTH #1, 255
PRINT #1, CHR$(27); "3"; CHR$(24);
FOR Y% = 0 TO 348 STEP 8: PRINT #1, CHR$(24)
    PRINT #1, CHR$(27); "*"; CHR$(4); CHR$(128); CHR$(2);
    y1% = y% + 1: y2% = y% + 2: y3% = y% + 3: y4% = y% + 4
    y5% = y% + 5: y6% = y% + 6: y7% = y% + 7
    FOR x% = 0 TO 639
        a% = SGN(POINT(x%, y7%)): IF y7% > 350 THEN a% = 0
        IF POINT(x%, y6%) <> 0 AND y6% < 349 THEN a% = a% + 2
        IF POINT(x%, y5%) <> 0 THEN a% = a% + 4
        IF POINT(x%, y4%) <> 0 THEN a% = a% + 8
        IF POINT(x%, y3%) <> 0 THEN a% = a% + 16
        IF POINT(x%, y2%) <> 0 THEN a% = a% + 32
        IF POINT(x%, y1%) <> 0 THEN a% = a% + 64
        IF POINT(x%, y%) <> 0 THEN a% = a% + 128
        PRINT #1, CHR$(a%);
    NEXT: PRINT #1, CHR$(10)
NEXT
```

```
CLOSE #1
RETURN
```

This driver uses another way of increasing performance. We have to multiply the values of the **POINT** **(x%,y%)** function by the weighting coefficients 0,2,4...128 to make up a column byte of 8 points. Meanwhile, especially when implementing math graphics, the majority of the screen points aren't active and the values of this function are **0**. A common QBasic program conscientiously multiplies the weighting coefficients by zero. In the given driver, the operations with zero values of the **POINT** function are completely eliminated using the conditional expressions **IF. . .THEN**, and multiplication is replaced with addition on the application of the previously calculated products of the function values by weighting coefficients.

Now that you know the basic principles, you can develop a VGA screen dump driver (640x480 resolution) by altering the above EGA driver. Similar drivers are worthy of inclusion in every serious BASIC program.

Graphics File Management

There isn't a programming language worthy of itself that doesn't manipulate graphics files in some form or other. As we've come to understand, QBasic isn't the most versatile of languages by any means, but it's quite capable of displaying various file formats.

GIF files were originally developed by CompuServe as a machine-independent image file format and are the most popular way of storing 8-bit, scanned or digitized images. It's time we showed you how to load and view a **.GIF** without a hitch. We won't go into too much detail here, as the code can simply be inserted into any program which requires a **.GIF**, but let's cover the main points just to give you a better idea of what's going on.

Our first job is to check the file header to ensure that we're using an 87a and not the almost unused 89a format:

```
INPUT "Type in Path and Filename..."; A$
IF A$ = "" THEN INPUT "GIF file"; A$: IF A$ = "" THEN END
IF INSTR(A$, ".") = 0 THEN A$ = A$ + ".gif"
OPEN A$ FOR BINARY AS #1
A$ = "      ": GET #1, , A$
IF A$ <> "GIF87a" THEN PRINT "Not a GIF87a file. ": END
```

Then the program checks the logical screen descriptor which contains the necessary parameters to display the image:

```
GOSUB GetByte: IF A% <> 0 THEN PRINT "Bad screen descriptor. ": END
```

Since our program only allows global color palettes, we must ensure that the local palette flag, in the data section of the **.GIF**, isn't set:

```
IF NoPalette = 0 THEN P$ = SPACE$(NumColors * 3): GET #1, , P$
DO
    GOSUB GetByte
    IF A% = 44 THEN
        EXIT DO
    ELSEIF A% <> 33 THEN
        PRINT "Unknown extension type. ": END
```

```
     END IF
     GOSUB GetByte
       DO: GetByte: A$ = SPACE$(A%): GET #1, , A$: LOOP UNTIL A% = 0
LOOP
Get #1, , Xstart: GET #1, , Ystart: GET #1, , Xlength: GET #1, , Ylength
Xend = Xstart + Xlength: Yend = Ystart + Ylength: GOSUB GetByte
If A% AND 128 THEN PRINT "Can't handle local colormaps. ": END
```

The rest of the program collects the image data in sub-blocks and, once the trailer block is found, displays the image from top left to bottom right:

```
SCREEN 13: DEF SEG = &HA0000
If NoPalette = 0 THEN
    OUT &H3C7, 0: OUT &H3C8, 0
    FOR A% = 1 TO NumColors * 3: OUT &H3C9, ASC(MID$(P$, A%, 1)) \ 4
    NEXT A%
END IF
LINE (0, 0)-(319, 199), Background, BF
DO
    GOSUB GetCode
    IF Code <> EOSCode THEN
        IF Code = ClearCode THEN
            NextCode = FirstCode
            CodeSize = StartCodeSize
            MaxCode = StartMaxCode
            GOSUB GetCode
            CurCode = Code: LastCode = Code: LastPixel = Code
            If X% < 320 THEN POKE X% + Ybase, LastPixel
            X% = X% + 1: IF X% = Xend THEN GOSUB NextScanLine
        ELSE
            CurCode = Code: StackPointer = 0
            IF Code > NextCode THEN EXIT DO '**Bad GIF if this happens**
            IF Code = NextCode THEN
                CurCode = LastCode
                OutStack(StackPointer) = LastPixel
                StackPointer = StackPointer + 1
            END IF

            DO WHILE CurCode >= FirstCode
                OutStack(StackPointer) = Suffix(CurCode)
                StackPointer = StackPointer + 1
                CurCode = Prefix(CurCode)
            LOOP

            LastPixel = CurCode
            IF X% < 320 THEN POKE X% + Ybase, LastPixel
            X% = X% + 1: IF X% = Xend THEN GOSUB NextScanLine

            FOR A% = StackPointer - 1 TO 0 STEP -1
                IF X% < 320 THEN POKE X% + Ybase, OutStack(A%)
                X% = X% + 1: IF X% = Xend THEN GOSUB NextScanLine
            NEXT A%

            IF NextCode < 4096 THEN
                Prefix(NextCode) = LastCode
                Suffix(NextCode) = LastPixel
                NextCode = NextCode + 1
                IF NextCode > MaxCode AND CodeSize < 12 THEN
```

```
                        CodeSize = CodeSize + 1
                        MaxCode = MaxCode * 2 + 1
                     END IF
               END IF
               LastCode = Code
            END IF
      END IF
LOOP UNTIL DoneFlag OR Code = EOSCode
BEEP
A$ = INPUT$(1)

END
```

The above program is quite complicated so don't worry too much if you're unsure about what's going on - you can find a full working copy on the disk under the name **\CHAP8\CH8_7.BAS**. However, if want to learn more about the internals of bit-mapped graphics, check out *The Revolutionary Guide to Bitmapped Graphics.* This book goes into much greater depth than we can hope to cover here, and comes with a CD-ROM packed with excellent code, info and images.

Manipulating Text

Bit-mapped graphics techniques offer many solutions to the old problem of how to create the large (or small), arbitrarily positioned text that is needed for things like superscript and subscripts, titles of drawings, and so on. Unlike the modern versions of Turbo Pascal and C, QBasic doesn't provide direct tools for solving this problem. Unfortunately, even in QBasic's graphics mode, the **PRINT** statement only outputs normal-looking text!

The available means for managing pixels in graphics mode, plus a little imagination, are all that's needed for a simple and original solution to this problem. The basic idea has already been discussed: you output a message somewhere on the screen (the less prominent the better), scan it using the **POINT (x,y)** function and reproduce it with a different scale in a new prominent position. A little mathematical transformation of the coordinates during transference can bring about miraculous changes in the text!

There are a number of ways of changing the style of the text:

- ▲ Reproducing each point in the form of a point with spacing produces soft and pale, dotted text.

- ▲ Reproducing each point in the form of a painted rectangle produces heavy and bright letters.

- ▲ Reproducing each point in the form of a little line gives a raised effect.

- ▲ Reproducing each point in the form of an arc or a circle of small radius gives unusual, rounded text.

- ▲ Adding the value **k*y** to the x coordinate, where **k** is a constant, outputs inclined letters (italics).

- ▲ Swapping the x and y coordinates outputs vertical text.

You can speed up the output of the message by carefully optimizing your code and removing any repeated arithmetic operations.

Here's a straightforward implementation of these ideas:

```
REM Demonstration of font manipulation
REM \CHAP8\CH8_8.BAS

SCREEN 9
DEFINT X-Y
LOCATE 25, 1
PRINT "Hello my friend!";
FOR Y = 0 TO 11
    Y2 = 2 * Y: Y3 = 3 * Y: Y4 = 4 * Y
    FOR X = 0 TO 319
        Z = POINT(X, 349 - Y)
        IF Z <> 0 THEN
        X2 = 2 * X: X3 = 3 * X
        ' Small font
        PSET (255 + .86 * X, 10 - .7 * Y), 15
        ' Italics
        PSET (250 + X + .3 * Y, 30 - Y), 11
        ' Double height and width
        PSET (200 + X2, 60 - Y2), 12
        ' Even larger font
        PSET (150 + X3, 110 - Y4), 13
        ' Bulky box font
        LINE (150 + X3, 165 - Y4)-(153 + X3, 169 - Y4), Z, BF
        XI = 150 + X3 + .6 * Y
        ' Large line-based font
        LINE (XI, 230 - Y4)-(XI + 2, 234 - Y4), 14
        ' Chubby rounded font
        CIRCLE (150 + X3, 300 - Y4), 3, 10
        ' Vertical italic font going upwards
        PSET (50 - Y2, 300 - X2), 15
        ' Vertical italic font going downwards
        PSET (530 + Y2 + .6 * X, 50 + X2), 15
        END IF
    NEXT
NEXT
F$ = INPUT$(1)
```

Like we said, the program draws the new text whilst it's scanning the original image, and speeds up what was a very slow routine into a manageable one. You'll no doubt have noticed that all the drawing is performed based on the current x and y scanning position which gives you total control over the result you want.

This program is both a demonstration program and a unit that can be inserted into your own program to obtain small or large text of various styles (with the precision of one pixel) and arbitrary positioning. In this case, you aren't likely to need many styles at once so you'll have to remove the redundant statements from the program.

It looks quite effective and, although the method retains the initial image of the text, the processing of its points mathematically changes it beyond recognition. This is particularly clear in the last of the large horizontal messages where each point of the initial image is replaced with a circle.

Here's one more program as a development of this method:

```
REM Modularized font manipulation program
REM \CHAP8\CH8_9.BAS

DECLARE SUB Title (T$, X0!, Y0!)
DECLARE SUB CharCir (C$, X0!, Y0!, R!, C!)
SCREEN 9
Title "The title is written!", 195, 200
CharCir "  Hello my friend!   ", 320, 180, 120, 15

SUB CharCir (C$, X0, Y0, R, C)
LOCATE 25, 1
PRINT C$;
FOR Y% = 0 TO 11
    YR = 3 * Y% + R
    FOR X% = 0 TO 319
        IF POINT(X%, 349 - Y%) <> 0 THEN
            W = .01964 * X%
            Xc = X0 - 1.5 * YR * COS(W)
            Yc = Y0 - YR * SIN(W)
            LINE (Xc, Yc)-(Xc + 2, Yc + 2), C, BF
        END IF
    NEXT X%
NEXT Y%
END SUB

SUB Title (T$, X0, Y0)
LOCATE 25, 1
PRINT T$;
FOR Y% = 0 TO 11
```

```
      DX = .6 * Y% + X0: DY = 2 * Y%
      FOR X% = 0 TO 319
          Z = POINT(X%, 349 - Y%)
          IF Z <> 0 THEN
          XI = DX + 2 * X%
          LINE (XI, Y0 - DY)-(XI - 1, Y0 + 2 - DY), 15
          END IF
      NEXT X%
   NEXT Y%
   END SUB
```

It contains two useful procedures: the first procedure **Title　(T$,X0,Y0)** outputs a short, enlarged message with the coordinates **(X0,　Y0)** of the lower left corner of the first character. You can use this procedure for creating short titles. The second, **CharCir　(C$,X0,Y0,R,C)** outputs a message (the contents of **C$**) along the outside of a circle of radius **R** with the center at the point at **(X0,Y0)**. You can use this procedure to create intricate and very effective messages which would leave anyone unfamiliar with these methods racking their brains.

This program gives us these messages:

These examples demonstrate two more unusual ways of creating arbitrarily positioned text of varying size and style. This method is ideally suited to anything requiring short lengths of unusual text, such as the introduction screen of a large program or the design of posters and drawings. We suggest that you don't try to use too many of these routines at once or too many large ones because, if you're not careful, they can take quite a long time to complete.

Editing Paint Patterns

We've already used the **PAINT** statement repeatedly to paint closed areas of a picture with both solid color and specific patterns. It's now time to look at a graphics program which enables you to edit these patterns with ease and find the parameters of the **PAINT** statement for creating them. This program also allows you to draw simple sprites which are used in fast, dynamic graphics.

The editing program **\CHAP8\EDPAT.BAS** is included in the system QuickBasic as a demo program. This program, slightly modified, is used as the basis of the following (you can find the full text of the program on the disk accompanying the book):

```
DECLARE SUB DrawPattern ()
DECLARE SUB EditPattern ()
DECLARE SUB Initialize ()
DECLARE SUB ShowPattern (OK$)
DIM Bit%(0 TO 7), Pattern$, Esc$, PatternSize%
DO
    Initialize
    EditPattern
    ShowPattern OK$
LOOP WHILE OK$ = "y"
END
```

The head module contains the definitions of the external procedures and the loop for executing the procedures **Initialize**, **EditPattern** and **ShowPattern**.

```
'Draws a patterned rectangle on the right side of screen
 SUB DrawPattern STATIC
 SHARED Pattern$
     VIEW (320, 24)-(622, 160), 0, 1  ' Set view to rectangle
     PAINT (1, 1), Pattern$            ' Use PAINT to fill it
     VIEW                              ' Set view to full screen
 END SUB
```

This procedure defines a window on the right of the screen. The window is filled with a multitude of patterns of the same kind (the pattern which is being edited).

Here's the main procedure of the pattern editor:

```
'Edits a tile-byte pattern
 SUB EditPattern STATIC
 SHARED Pattern$, Esc$, Bit%(), PatternSize%
 ByteNum% = 1          'Starting position.
 BitNum% = 7
 Null$ = CHR$(0)       'CHR$(0) is the first byte of the
                       'two-byte string returned when a
                       'direction key such as UP or DOWN is
                       'pressed.
 DO
     'Calculate starting location on screen of this bit:
     x% = ((7 - BitNum%) * 16) + 80
     y% = (ByteNum% + 2) * 8
     'Wait for a key press (and flash cursor each 3/10 second):
     State% = 0
     RefTime = 0
     DO
         'Check timer and switch cursor state if 3/10 second:
         IF ABS(TIMER - RefTime) > .3 THEN
         RefTime = TIMER
         State% = 1 - State%
         'Turn the  border of bit on and off:
         LINE (x% - 1, y% - 1)-STEP(15, 8), State%, B
         END IF
```

```
            Check$ = INKEY$          'Check for key press.
     LOOP WHILE Check$ = ""          'Loop until a key is pressed.
     'Erase cursor:
     LINE (x% - 1, y% - 1)-STEP(15, 8), 0, B
     SELECT CASE Check$              'Respond to key press.
     CASE CHR$(27)                   'ESC key pressed:
        EXIT SUB                     'exit this subprogram
     CASE CHR$(32)                   'SPACEBAR pressed:
                                     'reset state of bit
                                     'Invert bit in pattern string:
        CurrentByte% = ASC(MID$(Pattern$, ByteNum%, 1))
        CurrentByte% = CurrentByte% XOR Bit%(BitNum%)
        MID$(Pattern$, ByteNum%) = CHR$(CurrentByte%)
        'Redraw bit on screen:
        IF (CurrentByte% AND Bit%(BitNum%)) <> 0 THEN
        CurrentColor% = 1
        ELSE
        CurrentColor% = 0
        END IF
        LINE (X% + 1, Y% + 1)-STEP(11, 4), CurrentColor%, BF
     CASE CHR$(13)              'ENTER key pressed:
        DrawPattern                'draw pattern in box on right.
     CASE Null$ + CHR$(75)  'LEFT key: move cursor left
        BitNum% = BitNum% + 1
        IF BitNum% > 7 THEN BitNum% = 0
     CASE Null$ + CHR$(77)  'RIGHT key: move cursor right
        BitNum% = BitNum% - 1
        IF BitNum% < 0 THEN BitNum% = 7
     CASE Null$ + CHR$(72)  'UP key: move cursor up
        ByteNum% = ByteNum% - 1
        IF ByteNum% < 1 THEN ByteNum% = PatternSize%
     CASE Null$ + CHR$(80)  'DOWN key: move cursor down
        ByteNum% = ByteNum% + 1
        IF ByteNum% > PatternSize% THEN ByteNum% = 1
     CASE ELSE
        'User pressed a key other than ESC, SPACEBAR,
        'ENTER, UP, DOWN, LEFT, or RIGHT, so don't
        'do anything.
     END SELECT
  LOOP
END SUB
```

In the upper left of the screen, it displays a small ruled window in which the pattern is created. This procedure illustrates working with the bits and the editing keys.

The next procedure initializes the pattern editor:

```
'Sets up starting pattern and screen
SUB Initialize STATIC
SHARED Pattern$, Esc$, Bit%(), PatternSize%
Esc$ = CHR$(27)                    ' ESC character is ASCII 27.
'Set up an array holding bits in positions 0 to 7:
FOR i% = 0 TO 7:  Bit%(i%) = 2 ^ i%: NEXT i%
CLS
'Input the pattern size (in number of bytes):
LOCATE 5, 5: PRINT "Enter pattern size (1-16 rows):";
DO
```

```
        LOCATE 5, 38: PRINT "    ";
        LOCATE 5, 38: INPUT "", PatternSize%
LOOP WHILE PatternSize% < 1 OR PatternSize% > 16
'Set initial pattern to all bits set:
Pattern$ = STRING$(PatternSize%, 255)
SCREEN 2     ' 640 x 200 monochrome graphics mode.
'Draw dividing lines:
LINE (0, 10)-(635, 10), 1: LINE (300, 0)-(300, 199)
LINE (302, 0)-(302, 199)
'Print titles:
LOCATE 1, 13: PRINT "Pattern Bytes"
LOCATE 1, 53: PRINT "Pattern View"
'Draw editing screen for pattern:
FOR i% = 1 TO PatternSize%
    'Print label on left of each line:
    LOCATE i% + 3, 8: PRINT USING "##:"; i%
    'Draw "bit" boxes:
    x% = 80: y% = (i% + 2) * 8
    FOR j% = 1 TO 8
        LINE (x%, y%)-STEP(13, 6), 1, bf
        x% = x% + 16
    NEXT j%
NEXT i%
DrawPattern        'Draw  "Pattern View" box.
LOCATE 21, 1
PRINT "DIRECTION keys.......Move cursor"
PRINT "SPACEBAR...........Changes point"
PRINT "ENTER...........Displays pattern"
PRINT "ESC.....................Quits";
END SUB
```

The procedure asks for the size of a pattern, switches the display to graphics mode, creates the unfilled windows for editing and viewing patterns, and outputs a message containing the rules for working with the editor.

This subroutine completes the editing process:

```
'Prints the CHR$ values used by PAINT to make pattern
SUB ShowPattern (OK$) STATIC
SHARED Pattern$, PatternSize%
'Return screen to 80-column text mode:
SCREEN 0, 0: WIDTH 80
PRINT "The following characters make up your pattern:"
PRINT
'Print out the value for each pattern byte:
FOR i% = 1 TO PatternSize%
    PatternByte% = ASC(MID$(Pattern$, i%, 1))
    PRINT "CHR$("; LTRIM$(STR$(PatternByte%)); ")"
NEXT i%
PRINT : LOCATE , , 1: PRINT "New pattern? ";
OK$ = UCASE$(INPUT$(1))
END SUB
```

When you press *Esc*, the editing is completed and the procedure displays codes for the **PAINT** statement which you can use to specify the given pattern. Let's look at how the dialog with the pattern editor proceeds. On starting up, the editor asks the user for the dimensions of the pattern matrix:

Enter pattern size (1-16 rows):

A pattern always contains 8 pixels along the horizontal. The vertical can contain anything from 1 to 16 lines. Once you have indicated the size of the pattern, the editing screen appears:

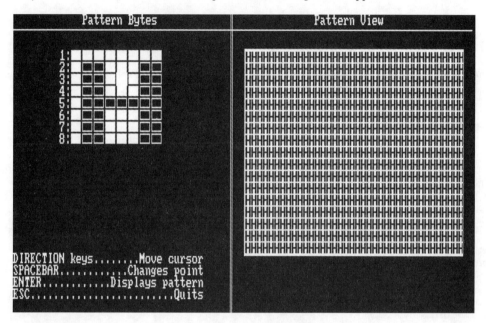

This demonstrates the construction of an upper case H and represents the window filled with this letter. On pressing *Esc*, the editor finishes working and outputs the message:

The following characters make up your pattern:

CHR$ (255)
CHR$ (156)
CHR$ (156)
CHR$ (156)
CHR$ (128)
CHR$ (156)
CHR$ (156)
CHR$ (156)

New pattern?

You can use this data to create the variable **P$** which carries information about the type of pattern for painting closed figures. This is illustrated by the following program:

```
SCREEN 2: CLS
LINE (0, 0)-(200, 96), 1, B
p$ = CHR$(255) + CHR$(156) + CHR$(156) + CHR$(156)
p$ = p$ + CHR$(128) + CHR$(156) + CHR$(156) + CHR$(156)
PAINT (10, 10), P$, 1
```

293

This program draws a rectangle and then fills it with H's.

Using this program, you can create whole sets of patterns (letters, symbols, small pictures, and so on) and then use them for special fonts or for generating simple sprites.

Simple Dynamic Graphics

One of the many things QBasic does particularly well is to manipulate sprites. Even in text mode we can produce some quite remarkable effects.

Operating Clock

Let's look at an example of a program where the low speed of the animated picture is integral to the image: a clock. The following program depicts a clock with minute and hour hands and also shows the time digitally (including seconds):

```
REM Program DCLOCK
REM \CHAP8\CH8_10.BAS

DECLARE SUB Cloc (Min$)
SCREEN 9: 'EGA mode
DO
    CLS
    Min$ = MID$(TIME$, 4, 2) 'Get the current minutes
    Cloc Min$
    DO
        LOCATE 10, 37
        PRINT TIME$
        Test$ = INKEY$
    LOOP WHILE Min$ = MID$(TIME$, 4, 2) AND Test$ = ""
LOOP WHILE Test$ = ""
END

SUB Cloc (Min$) STATIC
LOCATE 23, 30
PRINT "Press any key!"
LOCATE 6, 40: PRINT "12"
LOCATE 19, 41: PRINT "6"
LOCATE 13, 25: PRINT "9"
LOCATE 13, 57: PRINT "3"
CIRCLE (320, 170), 150
'Translate strings into number
Hr = VAL(TIME$)
Min = VAL(Min$)
'Translate numbers into angles
Little = 360 - (30 * Hr + Min / 2)
Big = 360 - (6 * Min)
'Drawing of hands
DRAW "TA=" + VARPTR$(Little) + "NU50"
DRAW "TA=" + VARPTR$(Big) + "NU75"
END SUB
```

The first loop uses **MID$** to get the current minutes and places them into the array **Cloc**. Next, the sub **Cloc (Min$)** is called, in which the hour and minute values are translated into angle coordinates and output to the screen in the form of hands.

The second loop simply displays the current time in the center of the screen and waits for a keypress to terminate the program. Before each new drawing, the previous one is erased. Since the hands move slowly, there are no problems as they change position.

Here's how the clock looks on the screen:

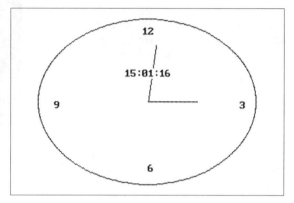

This program is interesting not only because it implements dynamic graphics (albeit tortoise-dynamic), but because it combines QBasic's system *and* graphics features. You can try adding a moving second hand and more detailed inscriptions on the clock face as an exercise if you like.

You may have already guessed that simply erasing and redrawing images is only one way of creating dynamic graphics. Other QBasic methods for creating them involve actual interaction with pixels on the screen.

Blanking Colored Pixels

Those of you familiar with Turbo Pascal and Turbo C systems may remember a colorful example - the drawing of a starry sky created by setting and resetting colored pixels. We can provide a similar example in QBasic. This program **\CHAP8\CHAP8_11.BAS** illustrates the capabilities of the **PSET** and **PRESET** statements:

```
SCREEN 9: CLS
n% = 4000 'Number of points
DIM x%(n%), y%(n%)
RANDOMIZE 1
FOR i% = 1 TO n%
    x%(i%) = INT(RND * 639)
    y%(i%) = INT(RND * 349)
    PSET (x%(i%), y%(i%)), RND * 14 + 1
NEXT i%

f$ = INPUT$(1)

FOR i% = 1 TO n%
    PRESET (x%(i%), y%(i%))
    a = SIN(1)
NEXT i%
```

The first section of the program forms two arrays, **x%** and **y%**, which store pixel coordinates generated by a random generator. These coordinates vary from **0** to **639** along the X axis, and from **0** to **349** along the Y axis (EGA mode). At the same time, **n%** pixels are created, their color also varying randomly (color codes from **1** to **15** - code **0** is omitted, because, in this case, the pixel's color is the same as the background). Overleaf there is a black and white view of the starry sky.

As soon as any key is pressed, the star-pixels begin to slowly disappear. The effect is caused by the second section of the program drawing exactly the same points once again, but this time back to black using the **PRESET** statement. It uses the current background color, so the pixels become invisible in the process.

The really observant among you may be perplexed by the expression **a = SIN(1)** which seems to be entirely meaningless. You're right - we've simply introduced it to increase the time taken to draw a pixel. Without it, the pixels disappear so quickly that you don't actually see the operation of the second part of the program. QBasic calculates trigonometric functions quite slowly, so the expression that we've used is one of a number of useful delaying techniques.

Imitating Sprites in Text Mode

Sprites are among the most important elements of dynamic graphics. A sprite is a set of graphic elements representing the various phases of movement of an object, such as a running man or a flying aircraft. Quickly changing the elements of the sprite and varying its current coordinates produces the effect of a complex movement, and it's this that forms the basis of computer animation.

An important aspect of working with sprites is their interaction with the background; for example, it's of little use, if a flying plane erases the background clouds. We must, then, deal with the problem of restoring those areas of the background image that are spoiled by a moving sprite. In the simplest case, when the background is an empty space, you just have to clear the position of the sprite before moving it to a new place.

Moving several sprites in different directions is also a problem, not because you have to create several objects and for each one define the changes of its coordinates - this is fairly easy - but because the movement of all the objects slows down the system considerably. This is because QBasic has no dedicated tools for simultaneously moving multiple objects. As a result, the movement of all objects is defined in one cycle by sequentially and alternately outputting and erasing them. As this takes place, the time taken to execute one cycle increases with the number of objects, and thus the motion of the objects becomes discontinuous.

We can demonstrate the general principles of sprite movement in either text or graphics mode: we'll choose text mode first as it's simpler to implement and, therefore, easier to understand.

Here's a simple sprite, a rotating line:

```
REM Sprite (rotation of a little line) demonstration
REM \CHAP8\CH8_12.BAS

 CLS : LOCATE 8, 32: PRINT "Press E for end! "
 DO
      LOCATE 10, 40: PRINT "-": GOSUB PAUSE   'Sprite element 1
      LOCATE 10, 40: PRINT "\": GOSUB PAUSE   'Sprite element 2
```

```
      LOCATE 10, 40: PRINT "|": GOSUB PAUSE    'Sprite elememt 3
      LOCATE 10, 40: PRINT "/": GOSUB PAUSE    'Sprite element 4
      F$ = INKEY$
      IF f$ = "e" OR f$ = "e" THEN END
  LOOP

  PAUSE:
  FOR i = 1 TO 1000: NEXT
  RETURN
```

Look at this program. You can see that the rotation effect is the result of the sequential output of several lines at various angles in the same screen position. Quickly switching between them produces the effect of rotation.

In the same way, you can rotate a more complicated figure, for example a torch which occupies a number of character positions. This is illustrated by the following program:

```
REM Sprite (rotating figure) demonstration
REM \CHAP8\CH8_13.BAS

 CLS : LOCATE 7, 31: PRINT "Press key E for end!"
 DO
     F$ = INKEY$
     IF F$ = "E" OR F$ = "e" THEN END

     LOCATE 9, 38:  PRINT "      "       'Sprite element 1
     LOCATE 10, 38: PRINT "*----"
     LOCATE 11, 38: PRINT "      "
     GOSUB PAUSE

     LOCATE 9, 38:  PRINT "*    "        'Sprite element 2
     LOCATE 10, 38: PRINT "  \  "
     LOCATE 11, 38: PRINT "     \"
     GOSUB PAUSE

     LOCATE 9, 38:  PRINT "  *  "        'Sprite element 3
     LOCATE 10, 38: PRINT "  |  "
     LOCATE 11, 38: PRINT "  |  "
     GOSUB PAUSE

     LOCATE 9, 38:  PRINT "    *"         'Sprite element 4
     LOCATE 10, 38: PRINT "  /  "
     LOCATE 11, 38: PRINT "/    "
     GOSUB PAUSE

     LOCATE 9, 38:  PRINT "     "         'Sprite element 5
     LOCATE 10, 38: PRINT "----*"
     LOCATE 11, 38: PRINT "     "
     GOSUB PAUSE

     LOCATE 9, 38:  PRINT "\    "         'Sprite element 6
     LOCATE 10, 38: PRINT "  \  "
     LOCATE 11, 38: PRINT "    *"

     GOSUB PAUSE
     LOCATE 9, 38:  PRINT "  |  "         'Sprite element 7
```

```
        LOCATE 10, 38: PRINT "  |  "
        LOCATE 11, 38: PRINT "  *  "
        GOSUB PAUSE

        LOCATE 9, 38:  PRINT "    /"         'Sprite element 8
        LOCATE 10, 38: PRINT "  /  "
        LOCATE 11, 38: PRINT "*    "
        GOSUB PAUSE

    LOOP

    PAUSE:
    FOR i = 1 TO 1000: NEXT
    RETURN
```

Note the use of a different delay method to the one used earlier. Being implemented as a subroutine, this can be conveniently called by the name **PAUSE** from anywhere in the program.

Here's our last text-based animation example: an asterisk (*) that rotates around a message:

```
REM Demonstration of an asterisk rotating around text
REM \CHAP8\CH8_14.BAS

CLS
  DO
      LOCATE 10, 30: PRINT "Press key E for end!"
      FOR W = .2 TO 6 STEP .24
          X = 40 + 15 * COS(W)
          Y = 10 + 6 * SIN(W)
          LOCATE Y, X: PRINT "*"
          GOSUB PAUSE
          LOCATE Y, X: PRINT " "
      NEXT W
      GOSUB PAUSE
  LOOP

  PAUSE:
  FOR i = 1 TO 1000: NEXT
  X$ = INKEY$
  IF X$ = "E" OR X$ = "e" THEN END
  RETURN
```

This program brings us closer to understanding the fundamentals of dynamic graphics. It illustrates the most important stages: creating an image, outputting it onto the screen for a period then erasing it, creating it in a new position and so on. In the first three examples, the erasing procedure was superfluous since every new image of the object erased its previous one. However, in this program, the object moves continuously so, before each of its shifts, it has to be erased. Otherwise, it would leave behind it an unsightly trail.

One more important feature here is the definition of a certain path for the object. In this case, the path, which is a circle, is defined by parametric equations. Using one or other mathematical means, it's easy to simulate more complex movements; for example, the path of a fired shell or a bouncing ball. We will be talking in more depth about sprite paths in Chapter 12 - Game Development.

Implementing Dynamic Graphics

In the early stages of computer development, simple game computers offered up to 200 pseudo-graphic symbols which was enough to design what were then considered fairly sophisticated games. However, you were usually fed up with them after a couple of months. Modern dynamic graphics use graphics modes with far more complicated sprites. You can create these using the pattern editor that we discussed earlier. Later, we'll look at two large programs which demonstrate the possibilities of applying pseudo-graphics.

Now is a good time for us to consider the implementation of dynamic graphics using the **GET** and **PUT** statements. Here we draw the outline of a truck and move it in a straight line from left to right across the screen:

```
REM Moving a truck across the screen
REM \CHAP8\CH8_15.BAS

 DECLARE SUB DrawTruck ()
 'Moving a truck across the screen
 SCREEN 1, 0
 CALL DrawTruck                       'Call subroutine and draw the truck
 DIM truck%(629)              'Define array
 GET (20, 21)-(119, 70), truck% 'Put Truck into array

 CLS                                 'Draw border and sun
 LINE (0, 0)-(319, 148), , B
 CIRCLE (0, 0), 20
 LINE (14, 14)-(50, 50)
 LINE (19, 3)-(70, 10)
 LINE (3, 17)-(12, 65)

 FOR n = 1 TO 210
     PUT (n, 100), truck%, PSET 'Draws truck, erasing the previous
     LINE (0, 148)-(319, 148)        'Re-draw the line under the truck
 NEXT n
 F$ = INPUT$(1)                       'Wait for a keypress
 END


 SUB DrawTruck
 CIRCLE (105, 60), 10                  'Draw front tire
 PAINT (105, 60), 3           'Paint front tire
 CIRCLE (35, 60), 10          'Draw rear tire
 PAINT (35, 60), 3            'Paint rear tire
 LINE (21, 21)-(101, 40), , BF    'Draw back of truck
 LINE (21, 40)-(119, 60), , BF    'Draw hood
 END SUB
```

The program consists of three blocks: the first block calls the **DrawTruck** subroutine to draw the initial truck then, using **GET** it stores it in the array **truck%**. The second block creates the rest of the picture - a frame and the image of the sun with the necessary three rays in the upper left corner of the screen. The third block performs the truck's movement along a horizontal road. The **PSET** parameter in the **PUT** statement is important here: it erases the image, moves it to a new place, and draws it again. However, as this takes place, part of the horizontal road is also deleted so, to reinstate this deletion, the line has to be redrawn each time the outline of the truck is created in the cycle.

Imitating a Bouncing Ball

One of the most popular sprites or moving images is that of a bouncing ball. There is something reassuring or therapeutic in watching a ball bouncing around the angles of the screen, so here's some code that bounces a ball (or your enemy's head) off some walls:

```
REM Bouncing a ball
REM \CHAP8\CH8_16.BAS

  SCREEN 2: CIRCLE (20, 20), 4, , , , .5
  PAINT (20, 20), 3: DIM ball%(10)
  GET (16, 16)-(24, 24), ball%
  'Set starting coordinates and their increments
  Xcor = 16: Ycor = 16
  dX = 1: dY = 1
  'Drawing frame and screen text
  LINE (0, 0)-(639, 199), , B
  LOCATE 8, 26: PRINT "Move a ball around the screen"
  LOCATE 12, 30: PRINT " Press any key to quit"
  'Move a ball around the screen
  DO WHILE INKEY$ = ""
      IF Ycor > 190 OR Ycor < 1 THEN dY = -dY 'Reflection of X
      IF Xcor > 630 OR Xcor < 1 THEN dX = -dX 'Reflection of Y
      oldXcor = Xcor: oldYcor = Ycor
      Ycor = Ycor + dY: Xcor = Xcor + dX
      PUT (oldXcor, oldYcor), ball%         'Put 1
      PUT (Xcor, Ycor), ball%               'Put 2
      FOR i = 1 TO 10: NEXT i               'Pause
  LOOP
  CLS : END
```

At the beginning of the program, the ball is defined as a painted circle and the **GET** statement copies the image of the ball into the **ball%** array. The subsequent part of the program moves the ball around the screen which has a border and contains messages. You can see that, while moving, the ball doesn't erase either the frame or the messages which it intersects in the center of the screen.

In this case, you can see that the background on which the ball is moving is restored naturally once the ball has passed across it. The parameter of interaction with the background is set by default to **XOR** in both **PUT** statements and it's this setting that restores the background as the ball-sprite moves.

The **IF** statements in the **DO WHILE** loop change the sign of the increments **dX** and **dY** along the X and Y axes, when the ball meets the horizontal or vertical barrier. This imitates the effect of the ball bouncing off the wall of the box. However, we haven't accounted for a decrease in the ball's energy and the movement is repeated indefinitely until it's interrupted by pressing a key.

Sizing up Arrays

When we grab images from the screen and put them into an array, it's always a good idea to make the array the exact size of the image being grabbed - mainly for efficiency and tidiness. In our next section, Inertia, we use an equation to calculate the exact size of an array. So, before we get ahead of ourselves, let's talk a little about the calculation involved.

The following table is the place to start:

Screen mode	Planes
1	1
2, 4, ,1	1
3	1
7	4
8, 9 (> 64K video memory), 12	4
9 (64K video memory), 10	2
13	1

Simply find out the planes value from the screen mode and insert the value into the following equation:

```
bytesize% = 4 + (INT(((x2 - x1 + 1) + 7) / 8) * planes% * (y2 - y1 + 1))
```

where

x2 is the bottom right x-coordinate

x1 is the top left x-coordinate

y1 is the bottom right y-coordinate

y2 is the top left y-coordinate

The resulting value, **bytesize%**, is the required size, in bytes, of the desired array.

Now, let's look at our equation in action, as we introduce inertia.

Implementing Inertia

The next program illustrates the motion of a ball bouncing back off the ground and the walls. This time though, as in real life, the ball loses momentum through energy loss. We use the function **ABS (COS(x))** as a model for the bouncing effect, and the **Decay** factor, which is constantly decreasing, models the ball's loss of energy. In this way, we can show a slightly more realistic motion for the ball:

```
REM Bouncing a ball (realistically)
REM \CHAP8\CH8_17.BAS

DECLARE FUNCTION GetArraySize (WLeft, WRight, WTop, WBottom)
'Define VIEW and WINDOW
SCREEN 2: : CLS : CONST Pi = 3.141592653589#
VIEW (20, 10)-(620, 190), , 1
WINDOW (-3.15, -.14)-(3.56, 1.01)
'$DYNAMIC

'Drawing and getting ball
WLeft = -.18: WRight = .18
WTop = .05: WBottom = -.05
ArraySize% = GetArraySize(WLeft, WRight, WTop, WBottom)
  DIM Ball%(1 TO ArraySize%) AS INTEGER
CIRCLE (0, 0), .18: PAINT (0, 0)
```

```
    GET (WLeft, WTop)-(WRight, WBottom), Ball%

    'Drawing arena
    CLS : LINE (-3, .8)-(3.4, .2), , B
    Pattern$ = CHR$(126) + CHR$(0) + CHR$(126) + CHR$(126)
    PAINT (0, .5), Pattern$
    LOCATE 21, 29: PRINT "Press any key to end"

    'Jumping ball
    StepSize = .02: StartLoop = -PI: Decay = 1
    DO
        EndLoop = -StartLoop
        FOR x = StartLoop TO EndLoop STEP StepSize
            y = ABS(COS(X)) * Decay - .14
            PUT (x, y), Ball%, PSET                        'Put 1
            FOR i = 1 TO 5: NEXT i
            IF y < -.13 THEN Decay = Decay * .9
            Esc$ = INKEY$
            IF Esc$ <> "" OR Decay < .01 THEN EXIT FOR
            PUT (x, y), Ball%, XOR                         'Put 2
        NEXT x
        StepSize = -StepSize: StartLoop = -StartLoop
    LOOP UNTIL Esc$ <> "" OR Decay < .01
    Pause$ = INPUT$(1)

    FUNCTION GetArraySize (WLeft, WRight, WTop, WBottom) STATIC
    VLeft = PMAP(WLeft, 0): VRight = PMAP(WRight, 0)
    VTop = PMAP(WTop, 1): VBottom = PMAP(WBottom, 1)
    RectHeight = ABS(VBottom - VTop) + 1
    RectWidth = ABS(VRight - VLeft) + 1
    ByteSize = 4 + RectHeight * INT((RectWidth + 7) / 8)
    GetArraySize = ByteSize \ 2 + 1
    END FUNCTION
```

If we use some additional code, we can illustrate the action of the **PUT** statement's affect on the track that the ball leaves, i.e. on its interaction with the background through its parameters. We'll replace the first of the **PUT** statements with this:

```
    PUT (x, y), Ball%, AND
```

The ball begins erasing the background as it moves. Because of the inaccurate definition of the initial array **ball%**, you see part of the ball's path giving you an idea of its trajectory. When it crosses the messages in the center of the screen, they are erased. Now try changing the parameter **AND** to **OR**: the path of the ball becomes totally visible and appears to be a wide band.

To move the image of the ball (a filled circle), change the program using **PUT** with the **PSET** parameter so that where the ball flies, the background is erased:

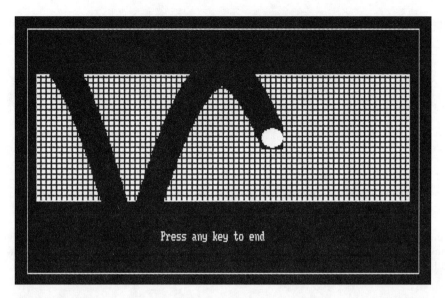

If we replace the **PSET** parameter with **XOR** in the statement denoted by the **Put 1** comment, the movement of the ball will not be accompanied by an erasure of the background. Try it and see.

By setting the **OR** parameter for both **PUT** statements, we can see the full track of the moving ball:

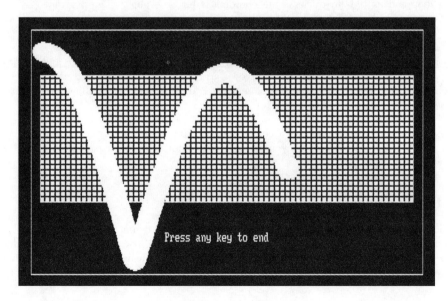

The four most important combinations of the parameters of the **PUT** statement, which give us different interactions of the sprite with the background, are shown below:

Put 1	Put 2	Effect on background
PSET	XOR	Sprite completely erases the background as it moves.
XOR	XOR	Sprite doesn't affect the background as it moves.
AND	XOR	Sprite leaves a track as it moves, spoiling background.
OR	OR	Sprite leaves a full track as it moves, spoiling background.

These combinations don't exhaust all the possible interactions between a sprite and the background picture, but they're the ones you're most likely to use in dynamic graphics programs.

These two programs, then, demonstrate creating a background, complicated motion of a ball (including 'real life' energy loss) and the interaction of the dynamic image with the background. They also show how to use **PMAP** to calculate the size of an array you'll use as a buffer for the **GET** statement.

A Parachute Jump

So far, we've considered the simple movements of one object. However, it isn't that difficult to make several objects move in different directions and along different paths at the same time. To do this, you need to organize a loop and use this to calculate the coordinates for each object. The program **\CHAP8\CHAP8_18.BAS** which you'll find on the disk shows you how you can represent a parachute jump.

Start the program and it draws the images of all the objects involved: a plane, a parachute and a small circle. Then, using **GET**, each of these is copied into its own array. After a key is pressed, the plane starts moving across the screen from left to right and the parachutist is dropped after it has flown a certain distance.

Of course, these examples don't really give you a comprehensive idea of the development of dynamic graphics programs but, hopefully, they've given you an insight into how they work and provide you with a starting point for your own experiments.

Video Memory Pages

Now we'll take a look at another form of animation involving the **PCOPY** command. Video memory pages can store an entire screen of both text and graphics. The number of pages that you have available depends on your screen mode and the amount of adapter memory you have. We touched on this at the beginning of the chapter. If you're interested in finding out more about this, there's information on QBasic's online help.

As we explained in Chapter 3, **SCREEN** is used to determine your mode, your active page and your visual page. **PCOPY** simply copies one video memory page to another, regardless of whether it's currently active or visible. When **PCOPY** is used alongside **SCREEN** to display pages other than those currently active, you have an exciting new technique at your disposal - the playground of animation opens up in a wholly different way. **PCOPY** itself looks like this:

PCOPY sourcepage%, destinationpage%

where **sourcepage%** is the number of the video memory page to be copied and **destinationpage%** is the number of the video memory page to be copied to. For example, **PCOPY 0,2** makes page 2 the same as page 0.

The following program illustrates a popular scenario where the **PCOPY** command is used to give the impression of animation. We start by displaying a message in the center of the screen, and then proceed to draw a set of blinds over the top, giving the appearance of having two planes, a foreground and background. Once fully closed, the blinds are then drawn open again, slowly revealing a message that is different from the first. It's an example that could be implemented in any number of ways; for instance as a 'between levels' effect in a game or a theater curtain for a presentation program:

```
REM Demonstration of PCOPY - Blinds
REM \CHAP8\CH8_19.BAS

SCREEN 7, 0, 1, 1

LOCATE 10, 10: PRINT "It's curtains for me"
WHILE INKEY$ = "": WEND

FOR T = 1 TO 84 STEP 4
SCREEN 7, 0, 2, 0: PCOPY 1, 2
LINE (0, 0)-(T, 200), 1, 2
LINE (80, 0)-(80 + T, 200), 1, BF
LINE (160, 0)-(160 + T, 200), 1, BF
LINE (240, 0)-(240 + T, 200), 1, BF
SCREEN 7, 0, 0, 0: PCOPY 2, 0: PCOPY 1, 2
NEXT

SCREEN 7, 0, 1, 0
CLS
LOCATE 10, 10: PRINT "But not for me....!"
FOR T = 84 TO 0 STEP -4
SCREEN 7, 0 2, 0: PCOPY 1, 2
LINE (0, 0)-(T, 200), 1 ,BF
LINE (80, 0)-(80 + T, 200), 1 BF
LINE (160, 0)-(160 + T, 200), 1, BF
LINE (240, 0)-(240 + T, 200), 1, BF
SCREEN 7, 0, 0, 0: PCOPY 2, 0: PCOPY 1, 2
NEXT

SCREEN 7, 0, 1, 1
WHILE INKEY$ = "": WEND
CLS
```

First of all, we display our message on a visible but inactive video page. The first loop then starts off by using a separate video page which is active but not visible:

```
SCREEN 7, 0, 2, 0: PCOPY 1, 2
```

Here the first section of the blinds are drawn. At the bottom of the loop this invisible page is then made visible and pushed into the foreground, on top of the message:

```
SCREEN 7, 0, 0, 0: PCOPY 2, 0: PCOPY 1, 2
```

Next, the second portion of the blinds are drawn on an invisible page and again suddenly made visible. The repetition of the process until the blinds are fully drawn gives the illusion of animation. The second loop simply repeats this process but gradually removes the number of rectangles so that the blinds appear to open.

Dynamic Graphics in Training and Physical Modeling

Dynamic graphics have a special role to play in training and modeling programs. For example, even a simple dynamic graphics imitation of the motion of the planets is superior to a still picture as an explanation of what's happening. The same goes for programs which imitate flying shells, bullets and other objects. You can use these to reveal new phenomena or features (either physical or mathematical), for instance, the effect of shooting pellets with a shotgun...

Shooting Pellets from a Shotgun

The program that we're about to show you models the shooting of five pellets from a shotgun and draws their subsequent paths. Air resistance is not taken into account, and the trajectories take the form of common parabolas. The x and y coordinates of each pellet are calculated from these expressions:

```
x = v0 * t * COS(a)              horizontal movement
y = v0 * t * SIN(a) - g * t^2 / 2    vertical movement
```

where **v0** stands for the initial speed of the pellets (m/sec) at the instant they are fired from the barrel of the gun, **t** denotes the current time (sec), **g** stands for the free fall acceleration and **a** denotes the angle of departure relative to the horizontal axis. The pellets are assumed to be dispersed at the gun angle. Here is the code:

```
REM Shooting pellets from a shotgun
REM \CHAP8\CH8_20.BAS

CLS : SCREEN 9
  v0 = 70
  g = 9.8
  ym = 0
  LINE (10, 10)-(10, 340)
  LINE (10, 340)-(630, 340)
  LOCATE 1, 1: PRINT "h"
  LOCATE 24, 79: PRINT "x";
  FOR t = 0 TO 13 STEP .04
      a = .78: GOSUB DrawTr
      a = .8:  GOSUB DrawTr
      a = .82: GOSUB DrawTr
      a = .84: GOSUB DrawTr
      a = .86: GOSUB DrawTr
  NEXT
  LOCATE 1, 20
  PRINT "xmax="; INT(x); "      Hmax="; INT(ym)
  LOCATE 20, 63: PRINT "<== Focus"
  f$ = INPUT$(1)
  END

  DrawTr:
  x = v0 * t * COS(A)
```

```
y = v0 * t * SIN(A) - g * t ^ 2 / 2
IF y > ym THEN ym = y
IF y > 0 THEN PSET (10 + x, 340 - 2 * y)
RETURN
```

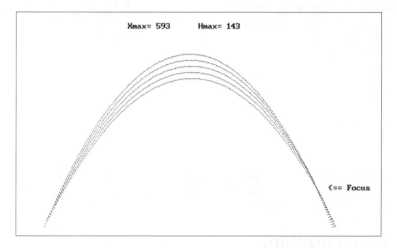

As you can see, the calculation of the flight path reveals an unexpected effect - towards the end of the flight, the pellets self-focus, i.e. converge together:

Our program uses simple dynamic graphics to draw the trajectories of the point-pellets as they move. Here we aren't using the animated cartoon style of erasing the objects drawn by the previous step because watching the full paths of the pellets tells us how they fly. The program calculates the average height (rounded to integers) of the flight and the distance from the starting point to the falling point. This data is displayed at the top of the drawing.

Imitation of Brownian Motion

Sometimes, very interesting drawings result from imitating random processes. The next program models the Brownian motion (random bouncing) of a particle and draws its trajectory within the boundaries of the screen:

```
REM Demonstration of Brownian motion
REM \CHAP8\CH8_21.BAS

CLS : SCREEN 9
 x = 320: y = 175
 PSET (x, y)
 DO
     RANDOMIZE (TIMER)
     dx = 30 * (RND - .5)
     dy = 20 * (RND - .5)
     x = x + dx
     y = y + dy
     IF x > 619 THEN x = x - dx
     IF x < 20 THEN x = x - dx
     IF y > 329 THEN y = y - dy
     IF y < 20 THEN y = y - dy
     LINE -(x, y)
 LOOP
```

In this program, the **x** and **y** coordinates of the point are incremented randomly. Experiment has shown that the point can very soon go off the screen, so a simple algorithm in the program returns the point to within the confines of the screen by changing the signs of the coordinate increments when **x** or **y** are outside of the defined limits. It isn't long before the random motion trajectory fills most of the screen:

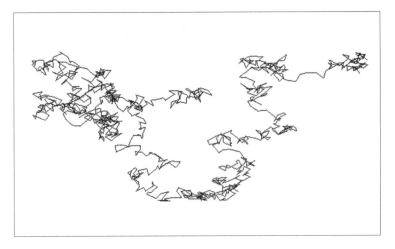

Like the program which drew a starry sky, the degree the screen is filled by the trajectory of the particle is a good test of the uniformity of the random number distribution law which we discussed in Chapter 3 - Input, Output and Printing.

A Celebration!

Let's return to the previously covered algorithm which output a set of multicolored points using the **PSET** statement and extinguished them with the **PRESET** statement. Remember that the algorithm is based on storing the coordinates of the pixels in an array. Instead of a starry sky, we'll use it to produce fireworks!

There are several useful dynamic graphics methods in this program. At the beginning, the program outputs a night landscape: the ground, the dark sky, a high building and groups of people. Then, on the left, a figure releases a rocket - you can see its gray smoke-trail. On reaching its maximum height, the rocket explodes into three colorful balls of sparks that gradually appear then slowly fade. On EGA or VGA monitors the imitation is quite realistic. Here's the picture at its culmination point:

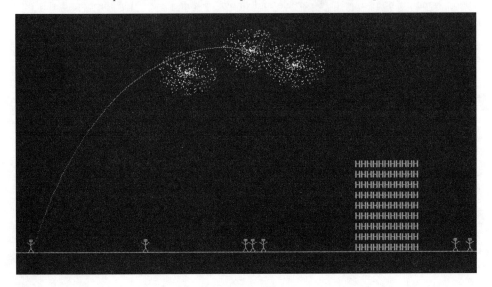

However, the rocket effect isn't over yet. If you've ever watched a rocket in the darkness, you know that the smoke trail slowly melts away. To imitate this, we erase the trail in two stages. First, we extinguish the pixels using the random number generator to give the impression that the trail is dissolving in the air.

```
'Draw fireworks
FIREWORKS X1, Y1, 30, 400
'Erase rocket's trajectory
FOR I = 0 TO 580
        I1 = INT(240 * RND)
        PRESET (X(I1), Y(I1))
        PAUSE
NEXT
FOR I = 0 TO 240
        PRESET (X(I), Y(I))
        PAUSE
NEXT
```

However, a number of non-extinguished pixels will be left. We erase these by extinguishing the whole array of pixels in the regular way. We carry out the whole exercise three times, so you get a triple salute.

We constructed the human figures by specifying their x coordinate. One of them walks up and down showing that two processes are taking place simultaneously (this and the flight of the rocket on a parabolic path).

Try modifying the program to make the figures sit on the roof of the house.

The house itself is just lines of H's one on the other. The three fiery balls use the same initial array of the points' coordinates, but with different palettes. The external procedure for drawing the flame-colored balls has the following parameters: the coordinates of the last point of the path, the radius of the balls and the number of small lights (the points in each ball).

If you have a 386DX or higher, the salute appears too fast, so it's deliberately slowed down using the **PAUSE** procedure which just executes 100 empty loops. However, you can change this number to achieve the effect you like. Have a look at the whole program **\CHAP8\CH8_22.BAS** on the disk.

Paint Basic

Imagine that you've just spent hours, days, weeks creating your pixel-perfect three-headed, fire-breathing dragon king. Now you're thinking, "If only I could get it into that game I'm writing." Well now you can, with *The Paint Basic Sprite Creator*.

In a nutshell Paint Basic, **\CHAP8\CH8_23.BAS**, is a drawing program written in QBasic. Using a pointer, it allows you to draw points, lines and rectangles. We can use this paint program, which introduces nothing that we haven't mentioned already, to create sprites in an easy-to-use environment.

Because we've already seen most of the paint program in one form or another, we will just look at the sprite creator here.

The Sprite Creator section **GET**s a section of the screen which contains an image, and stores those pixels into an array. Then the contents of the array are output to a brand new QBasic program file as hexadecimal **DATA** statements. These **DATA** statements can then be used to **PUT** the sprite anywhere on screen, maybe using motion and animation to give the sprite life.

Let's take a piece-by-piece look at the code:

```
'Define sprite array
 maxsizeofarray% = 8000
 DIM image%(maxsizeofarray%)
```

In the main program the array, **image%**, is set at 8,000 to allow for really large sprites (8,000 elements occupies more than enough memory). Since, some people like big, fire-breathing dragons as well as the little cute ones.

The actual sprite grabbing takes place in a subroutine where we perform various checks and calculations. Let's take a good look at it.

After removing the cursor and storing it safely away, our first move is to draw a box around the image using a 'rubber band' technique. This gives complete flexibility to the user when making the selection.

```
SUB Sprite (KXMin, KYMin, KXMax, KYMax)

BEEP: BEEP: BEEP
PUT (KX1, KY1), a%, XOR                    'Remove cursor
REDIM E%(10)                               'Array for storing picture
GET (KX1, KY1)-(KX1, KY1), E%              'A screen area is stored
KX2 = KX1: KY2 = KY1
KXMin = KX1
KYMin = KY1
DO
  DO
    KeyC$ = INKEY$
  LOOP WHILE KeyC$ = ""
' *** Detecting cursor offset ***
  CALL Displacement(KeyC$, flag)
' *** Responce on a key pressed ***
  IF flag = 1 THEN
    KX3 = KX2 + DX
    KY3 = KY2 + DY
    A1 = (KY3 >= 0) AND (KX3 >= 0)
    A2 = (KY3 <= MaxY) AND (KX3 <= MaxX)
    L1 = Bytes(KX1, KY1, KX3, KY3)
    A3 = L1 <= MaxInt
    IF A1 AND A2 AND A3 THEN
      PUT (KXMin, KYMin), E%, PSET
      REDIM E%(L1)
      KX2 = KX3: KY2 = KY3
      IF KX1 < KX2 THEN
        KXMin = KX1: KXMax = KX2
      ELSE
        KXMin = KX2: KXMax = KX1
      END IF
      IF KY1 < KY2 THEN
        KYMin = KY1: KYMax = KY2
      ELSE
        KYMin = KY2: KYMax = KY1
      END IF
      GET (KXMin, KYMin)-(KXMax, KYMax), E%
      LINE (KX1, KY1)-(KX2, KY2), CColor, B
    ELSE
```

```
      BEEP: BEEP
    END IF
  END IF
LOOP UNTIL KeyC$ = CHR$(13) OR KeyC$ = CHR$(27)

IF KeyC$ = CHR$(27) THEN 'No command execution
  PUT (KXMin, KYMin), E%, PSET
END IF

LINE (KX1, KY1)-(KX2, KY2), 0, B
```

The 'rubber band' can be manipulated until a key is pressed, so long as the key isn't *Esc*, which would cancel the whole operation.

Since QBasic has a limit of 64K on module size, we must ensure that this isn't exceeded when we create the **.BAS** file. To do this, we check that the size of the image doesn't exceed our **maxsizeofarray%** variable of 8,000. If it does, the program branches off to a sub called **BigSprite** where we inform the user that the image is too large to be written as a single module and needs to be smaller.

```
'Check for sprite > maxsizeofarray%
IF (KX2 - KX1) * (KY2 - KY1) > maxsizeofarray% THEN
  CALL BigSprite
ELSE
  GET (KX1, KY1)-(KX2, KY2), image%
  'Equation for calculating array size
  planes% = 4
  size% = 4 + (INT(((KX2 - KX1 + 1) + 7) / 8) * planes% * (KY2 - KY1 + 1))
  CALL SaveSprite
END IF

END SUB
```

Once we are happy that the image is below our limit, we store it in an array called **image%** which is used later on in the save routine. Before we save the sprite though, the program calculates the exact size of our sprite stored in the **image%** array. This is to ensure that we don't end up saving 8,000 **DATA** statements when we write to our new **.BAS** file when our sprite only uses say, 200.

Okay, so we've draw our sprite, we've checked that it's within QBasic's module limit, we've stored it in an array and calculated the number of DATA statements we are going to need. Now let's see how we create the new **.BAS** file.

Our first job is to ask the user to input the file name. We do this by using a routine which:

- ▲ stores an area in the centre of the screen.
- ▲ displays a window allowing the user to enter a string.
- ▲ and finally restores the stored area once the window closes.

The code which performs this operation is the **SaveSprite** procedure:

```
SUB SaveSprite
'    ***************************
'    * Saving Sprite to a file *
'    ***************************
SDY = INT(MaxY / 10)
SY = SDY
L% = Bytes(0, 0, MaxX - 1, SDY)
REDIM SC%(L%)
QX1 = 140: QY1 = 200
QX2 = 530: QY2 = 230
QL = Bytes(QX1, QY1, QX2, QY2)
REDIM QE%(QL)
GET (QX1, QY1)-(QX2, QY2), QE%
LINE (QX1, QY1)-(QX2, QY2), 0, BF
LINE (QX1, QY1)-(QX2, QY2), 15, B
LINE (QX1 + 2, QY1 + 2)-(QX2 - 2, QY2 - 2), 15, B
LOCATE 14, 20
PRINT "Enter filename: ";
PLAY "L24MNMBO1CDEFG"
CALL InputText(14, 36, 30, filename$, flag)
IF flag = 27 THEN
    PUT (QX1, QY1), QE%, PSET
    PUT (KX1, KY1), a%, XOR
    EXIT SUB
END IF
flag = 0
Flag1 = 0                    'Counting attempts of correcting error No71

IF flag = 0 THEN 'Save in file
PUT (QX1, QY1), QE%, PSET    'Restore screen section
```

Our next job is to create the **.BAS** file. Using the exact calculation of our sprite, we use a **FOR. . .NEXT** loop to output the data. First, the file is opened using the previously input file name, and the preliminary lines of code are printed:

```
'write file
datas% = 0
IF filename$ = "" THEN GOTO nosave
OPEN filename$ FOR OUTPUT AS #1
nextline:

PRINT #1, "REM Sprite Viewer : Automated from PaintBasic"
PRINT #1, "REM (c). Wrox Press Ltd."
PRINT #1, ""
PRINT #1, "SCREEN "; graphmode%
PRINT #1, ""
PRINT #1, "DATA ";
```

Next we start to print the contents of the array **image%** in the loop, converting each value to hexadecimal as we go:

```
linecheck = 0
FOR n = 0 TO size%                       'actual size of array
    datas% = datas% + 1
    linecheck = linecheck + 1
    temp = 4 - LEN(HEX$(image%(n)))
```

```
      PRINT #1, "&H"; STRING$(temp, "0"); HEX$(image%(n));        'print hex data
      IF linecheck > 7 THEN                              'only 8 statements to a line
          linecheck = 0
          PRINT #1, : PRINT #1, "DATA ";
      ELSE
          PRINT #1, ",";
      END IF
NEXT n

finish:
```

Finally, we print the last lines of code to the new file. This consists of a simple **READ** and **PUT** routine which, if you simply run the new file, will display your sprite on screen:

```
PRINT #1, "*** End of "; name$; " ("; (datas% - 1); ") statements ***"
PRINT #1, ""
PRINT #1, "DIM SHARED sprite%("; (datas% - 1); ")"
PRINT #1, ""
PRINT #1, "FOR loopcounter%= 0 TO "; (datas% - 1) - 1
PRINT #1, "    READ sprite%(loopcounter%)"
PRINT #1, "NEXT loopcounter%"
PRINT #1, ""
PRINT #1, "PUT (50,50), sprite%"
PRINT #1, ""
PRINT #1, "END"

CLOSE #1
nosave:
PLAY "L24MNMBO1GFEDC"
ELSE
PUT (QX1, QY1), QE%, PSET         'Restore screen section
END IF
ON ERROR GOTO 0                  'Disable error handling
PUT (KX1, KY1), a%, XOR          'Restore graphics pointer

END SUB
```

You can then go ahead and use this data in your own programs. Don't worry if you're unsure of how to go about this as we explain everything you need to know about Game Development in Chapter 12.

The combination of sprite creator and drawing software makes for an explosive development package which will help you to create fantastic, full-color sprites.

Summary

In this chapter, we've introduced you to the power of bit-mapped graphics and shown you the dynamic results that animation can achieve.

After examining the possibilities that Video RAM and graphics drivers hold for us, we took a look at some of the highly effective bit-mapped graphics commands:

- ▲ **POINT**
- ▲ **PAINT**
- ▲ **PCOPY**

In fact, if you're interested there are several other features that you can add to Paint Basic including:

- ▲ integrating the mouse with the ability to draw freehand.
- ▲ loading different file formats, such as **GIF**s and **PCX**s.
- ▲ providing the availability to switch between different modes.
- ▲ displaying a 'Please Wait' message when waiting for an image to load or save.
- ▲ integrating more drawing functions, such as an air brush or zoom function.
- ▲ allowing the user to copy areas of the screen.
- ▲ creating an undo option.

Advanced 2D Graphics

CHAPTER 9

Introduction

In Chapter 3 - Input, Output and Printing, we covered the essentials of machine graphics. In the last chapter, we introduced bitmaps and animation and, in this chapter, we'll consider some of the more advanced aspects of creating two-dimensional graphics. We'll show you how you can create usable graphics programs using various math coordinate systems, and we'll explain the differences between these pure math systems and their implementation as screen raster graphics.

This chapter won't provide exhaustive coverage of machine graphics - even a whole set of books this size couldn't do that - but we'll cover as much as we possibly can. From time to time, we'll refer to machine graphics algorithms and programs in combination with other PC features (math calculations, sound synthesis, etc.).

Here's the route that we'll be taking you on:

▲   LOGO graphics in QBasic

▲   Math and matrices

▲   No-fuss figure rotation and movement

The Math Essentials

Before we use LOGO graphics, we ought to recap and extend our knowledge of coordinate systems so that these concepts are understood. If you know your math, this will be an easy, even skippable section. If not, the next two chapters will be a taster of math making your job easier - not normally something with which it's associated!

As we saw in Chapter 3, graphics objects are described relative to a **coordinate system**. Generally speaking, a coordinate system relates a set of numbers, the coordinates, to a position in space. This space can have any number of dimensions, but in this and the next chapter we'll concentrate on 2- and 3-dimensional space, because this will be most useful for graphics applications.

A 2-dimensional space is referred to as a **plane.** All points in the plane can be uniquely described by two coordinates -any more is just overkill. Similarly, a point in three-dimensional space (usually just called **space**) can be described by just three coordinates.

For 2D planes, the choice of axes for those two numbers is up to you. However there are some particularly useful ones which we will cover next.

Cartesian and Raster Coordinate Systems

You're already familiar with the Cartesian coordinate system and its alternative, the raster coordinate system. They are both rectangular coordinate systems, which means that their axes are set at right angles to each other. They differ in the position of their basic point of reference, the **origin**, with coordinates (0,0) and in the direction of their y-axis.

Polar Coordinate System

In the polar coordinate system, the position of a point A is defined by its distance R from the origin (in other words, the length of the segment O-A) and by the angle the segment makes with the horizontal (x-axis). It's rather like drawing a circle from the origin with radius R and looking for the point on the circle's circumference:

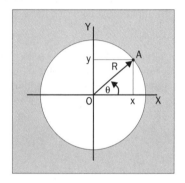 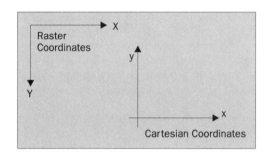

Segment O-A can be considered as a **vector** directed from point O to point A. It is sometimes referred to as the radius-vector of point A.

That's it for now; there's nothing to stop your enjoyment of LOGO!

LOGO graphics

LOGO graphics occupies a prominent position in the history of computer graphics. As well as being a stand-alone language for many years, it has also been introduced into a number of programming languages, for example Turbo Pascal and Prolog. QBasic's **DRAW** statement has its own micro-language which implements some LOGO graphics features, but these are limited and quite different from the proper LOGO graphics language. This means that direct translation of LOGO graphics programs into QBasic isn't possible.

The basis of LOGO graphics is very simple. The primary graphics object is the bird's eye view image of a turtle - actually, it's more like a small triangle. The user controls the movement of the turtle by giving it simple commands; for example, 50 steps forward, turn through 30 degrees, 10 steps backward and so on. The turtle is issued with a lightpen which can be raised or lowered. When it's lowered, all the turtle's movements make a mark on the screen. Don't worry if you don't have a lightpen, we don't either, so we'll use the keyboard instead.

Mutant Ninja Triangles

The aim of this section is to implement the LOGO graphics commands in QBasic by creating our own procedures. These will allow us to use the richest software created in LOGO from within QBasic. We won't provide a complete implementation of LOGO features, but we'll cover the most important LOGO graphics commands. In our version, though, we don't create the turtle - instead, we use a simple point for simplicity. We'll refer to our point as a turtle nonetheless.

Let's Go Turtle

In line with the concepts of LOGO graphics, you must initially locate the turtle in the center of the screen. This point coincides with the origin of the polar coordinate system, as you'll see when we draw a point, a triangle and a decagon later on.

The movement of the polar coordinate origin point is defined by two parameters - the angle `Q` and the distance `L` in steps. When the point is moved from position A to position B, its current coordinates `(Xc,Yc)` change to `(Xnew,Ynew)`, defined by these relationships:

```
Xnew = Xc + L * Mx * COS(HD)
Ynew = Yc + L * My * SIN(HD)
```

Here, `HD` stands for the angle the turtle's body is turned, and `Mx` and `My` are scale factors along their respective axes.

Let's look at the lightpen for a moment. If the status of the lightpen, `PS`, is equal to `0`, the pen is lowered and, while the turtle moves from position `(Xc,Yc)` to position `(Xnew,Ynew)`, it leaves a trail behind it. Logically, you could also join the points `(Xc,Yc)` and `(Xnew,Ynew)` with a line segment using the QBasic `LINE` statement. The simplest way of linking the beginning of each new line segment with the end of the previous one is to use this statement in the form `LINE (Xnew,Ynew)`.

Defining Procedures and System Variables

Here's the minimum set of procedures that you'll need to implement the main features of LOGO graphics in QBasic:

LOGO Procedure	QBasic Procedure	Action
DOT	DOT X,Y	Sets the point (X,Y)
PenDown	PD	Lightpen is down.
PenUp	PU	Lightpen is up.
ClearScreen	CS	Clears the screen.
SetPenColor	SETPC C	Sets lightpen color C.
SetScreen	SETSCR Mx,My	Sets scales along X and Y-axes.
SetPosition	SETPOS Xc,Yc	Sets the position of the point .

Table Continued on Following Page

LOGO Procedure	QBasic Procedure	Action
SetHeading	**SETH**	Sets the movement direction - the rotation angle **Q**.
Left	**LT Q**	Changes direction to angle **Q** left (counter-clockwise).
Right	**RT Q**	Changes direction to angle **Q** right (clockwise).
Forward	**FD L**	Moves the point **L** steps forward
Back	**BK L**	Moves the point **L** steps backward.
SetX	**SETX X**	Moves the point **L** steps in **X**-axis direction.
SetY	**SETY Y**	Moves the point **L** steps in **Y**-axis direction.

These 14 procedures in our QBasic version have a syntax similar to that in proper LOGO. The procedures which aren't found in this set are rarely used or have their direct analogs in QBasic; for example, the procedures defining the color of the background or border, setting window boundaries, etc.

The commonly-used LOGO graphics procedure,

```
REPEAT N [statements]
```

is easily substituted by this loop in QBasic:

```
FOR I=1 TO N
   statements
NEXT I
```

To implement LOGO graphics, we have to define the following global system variables available throughout the entire program:

Xcor   current coordinate of the point x
Ycor   current coordinate of the point y
PS   lightpen status (0 - down, 1 - up)
HD   current movement direction (angle or heading)
Col   color of the lightpen (codes 0 through 15)
Mx   scale factor along the **X** axis
My   scale factor along the **Y** axis
X0   raster (screen) coordinate x of the central point
Y0   raster (screen) coordinate y of the central point

On the basis of this, the main module of an empty LOGO graphics program is the following:

```
REM LOGO graphics for QBasic
REM \CHAP9\CH9_1.BAS

DECLARE SUB DOT (Xc!, Yc!)
DECLARE SUB LT (Q!)
DECLARE SUB RT (Q!)
```

```
DECLARE SUB SETPOS (Xc!, Yc!)
DECLARE SUB PD ()
DECLARE SUB SETPC (C!)
DECLARE SUB SETH (Head!)
DECLARE SUB CS ()
DECLARE SUB FD (L!)
DECLARE SUB BK (L!)
DECLARE SUB SETX (Xc!)
DECLARE SUB SETY (Yc!)
DECLARE SUB SETSCR (Msx!, Msy!)
COMMON SHARED Col, HD, PS, Mx, My, Xcor, Ycor, X0, Y0

'This is LOGO program:
'*********************************************************

'*********************************************************
```

The main module defines the procedures and system variables and marks the place for you to enter your own code. The system variables are listed as **COMMON SHARED**, which, as you already know, makes them available in any place throughout the main module and external procedures. Note that you have to initialize the values of **X0** and **Y0** in your own code, allowing you the flexibility of using different screen modes. In LOGO graphics, the central point of the screen is taken as the origin **(X0,Y0)**.

External Procedures

We thought it best not to implement the full range of LOGO tools, but to select only the most typical features which allow the construction of various figures in polar coordinates using a syntax close to that used in LOGO. The following code samples cover all the external procedures defining the LOGO graphics commands.

Initializing the Pen

Our first procedure **CS** clears the screen and initializes the system variables of LOGO graphics:

```
SUB CS
'Clearing screen and initializing
  CLS        'Clear screen
  HD = 0     'Set heading = 0
  Xcor = 0   'Set Xcor = 0
  Ycor = 0   'Set Ycor = 0
  PS = 0     'Set pen status 0 (pen down)
  Col = 15   'Color Col = 15
  Mx = 1     'Set scale Msx = 1
  My = 1     'Set scale Msy = 1
  PRESET (X0, Y0)  'Initial start point
END SUB
```

This procedure also places the invisible turtle at the origin of the LOGO coordinates **(X0,Y0)**, ensuring that the algorithm we use for extending lines from one point to another is valid. You use this procedure at the beginning of **grafc**   constructions.

So that the coordinates of the point correspond faithfully to the coordinates of LOGO graphics, you should leave **Mx=1** and **My=1** as they are, but you can change the screen scale if you wish, for example, using **SETSCR**.

Drawing a New Point

The second procedure **DOT** creates a point. It changes the current turtle screen coordinates **Xcor** and **Ycor** to the new values **Xc*Mx** and **Yc*My** and, if the status of the lightpen, **PS**, is zero, i.e. the pen is down, the procedure draws a point at this new position with color **Col**:

```
SUB DOT (Xc, Yc)
'Set point in position (Xc,Yc)
  Xcor = Xc * Mx
  Ycor = Yc * My
  IF PS = 0 THEN PSET (X0 + Xcor, Y0 - Ycor), Col
END SUB
```

Moving the Pen

The third procedure is the basic LOGO movement procedure, **FD**, and moves the point forward in the direction specified by the angle **HD** (in degrees) for a distance **L**:

```
SUB FD (L)
  'Forward in distance L
  PI = 3.141593
  HDR = HD * PI / 180
  Xnew = Xcor + L * Mx * COS(HDR)
  Ynew = Ycor + L * My * SIN(HDR)
  IF PS = 0 THEN LINE -(X0 + Xnew, Y0 - Ynew), Col
  Xcor = Xnew
  Ycor = Ynew
END SUB
```

This procedure does the following: defines the constant **PI**, converts the heading from degrees (**HD**) into radians (**HDR**) and calculates the new coordinates **Xnew** and **Ynew**. After that, if the lightpen status is **0**, i.e. the pen is down, it draws a line connecting the points **(Xcor,Ycor)** and **(Xnew,Ynew)**. If **PS=1**, i.e. the pen is up, no line is drawn. Finally, the variables **Xcor** and **Ycor** are assigned the new values **Xnew** and **Ynew**, respectively.

The **BK** procedure has no algorithm of its own to speak of - it simply calls the procedure **FD**:

```
SUB BK (L)
'Back in distance L
  FD -L
END SUB
```

To ensure that the movement is backwards rather than forwards, the **L** argument (number of steps) is specified with a negative sign.

Changing the Heading

To change the direction of the turtle, the following procedure **LT** is called:

```
SUB LT (Q)
'Left rotate in Q degrees
  HD = HD + Q
END SUB
```

The procedure increases the current value of the angle **HD** by **Q**, changing the direction of movement. This means that the imaginary turtle turns its head to the left from the initial direction. To turn in the opposite direction, simply supply the procedure with a negative value, or use the following procedure:

```
SUB RT (Q)
'Right rotate in Q degrees
  HD = HD - Q
END SUB
```

This procedure decreases the angle **HD** by **Q** degrees which means turning the turtle to the right, or clockwise, by **Q** degrees. Of course, if you want to be more precise, use **SETH**:

```
SUB SETH (Q)
'Set heading in Q
  HD = Q
END SUB
```

This procedure fixes the current direction angle **HD** and makes it equal to **Q**.

Lifting and Dropping the Pen

The procedure **PD** shown here lowers the lightpen:

```
SUB PD
'Set pen down
  PS = 0
END SUB
```

This procedure assigns the value zero to the lightpen status variable, **PS**. All movement of the turtle now leaves a trail on the screen until **PS** is changed to **1** with this procedure, to raise the lightpen:

```
SUB PU
'Set pen up
  PS = 1
END SUB
```

This procedure assigns the value **1** to the status variable **PS**. Although all math conversions are carried out as the turtle moves, it can make no mark on the screen while the pen is up.

Setting the Color

The procedure **SETPC** sets the current color of the lightpen by assigning the value **C** (color code) to the color variable **Col**:

```
SUB SETPC (C)
'Set pen color Col
  Col = C
END SUB
```

Remember that the procedure **CS** specifies the initial value **Col=15**, which corresponds to white.

Positioning the Turtle

The procedure presented here, **SETPOS**, places the turtle-point at a specified position in the current coordinate system:

```
SUB SETPOS (Xc, Yc)
'Drawing in position (Mx*Xc,My*Yc)
  Xcor = Mx * Xc
  Ycor = My * Yc
  IF PS = 0 THEN LINE -(X0 + Xcor, Y0 - Ycor)
END SUB
```

If the lightpen status is **0**, then the point leaves a trail whilst moving from the old position to the new one.

Setting the Scale

The **SETSCR** procedure sets the scales along the x- and y-axes by assigning specific values to the system variables **Mx** and **My**:

```
SUB SETSCR (Sx, Sy)
'Set scale coefficients Mx and My
  Mx = Sx
  My = Sy
END SUB
```

The procedure **CS** defines the initial values **Mx=1** and **My=1**, so the LOGO coordinate scale corresponds exactly to the screen coordinate scale. This may need to be changed to compensate for the different resolutions along the horizontal and vertical axes. For instance, to double stretch an image along the x-axis, you should specify:

```
    SETSCR 2,1
```

Note that the scale can also be changed by directly assigning the necessary values to the system variables **Mx** and **My**.

Perpendicular Movement

Perpendicular movement, in particular horizontal and vertical, movement of the pen can be extremely useful, especially when technical drawings are required. To move the pen in these directions we use the **SETX** and **SETY** procedures:

```
SUB SETX (Xc)
'Horizontal movement in distance Mx * Xc
  Xnew = Xcor + Mx * Xc
  IF PS = 0 THEN LINE -(X0 + Xnew, Y0 - Ycor), Col
  Xcor = Xnew
END SUB
```

This procedure moves the turtle along the x-direction for a specified distance, and is obviously used for drawing horizontal lines, whilst **SETY** is used for drawing vertical lines:

```
SUB SETY (Yc)
'Vertical movement in distance My * Yc
  Ynew = Ycor + My * Yc
```

```
        IF PS = 0 THEN LINE -(X0 + Xcor, Y0 - Ynew), Col
        Ycor = Ynew
    END SUB
```

Here, the procedure shifts our turtle along the y-axis for a distance **My*Yc**, in order to construct vertical lines.

A Demonstration of LOGO graphics

Let us consider an example which illustrates the use of the external LOGO graphics procedures that we have just discussed:

```
X0 = 320: Y0 = 175                'Set center point coordinate
SCREEN 9                          'Set EGA mode
CS                                'Clear screen, initial
PD                                'Pen down
SETSCR 1.5, 1                     'Set screen Mx=2, My=1
DOT 0, 0                          'Set point (0,0)
DOT -10, -10                      'Set point (-10,-10)
SETX 20:   SETY 20                'Drawing quadrat
SETX -20: SETY -20

DOT -50, 35                       'Set position (-50,35)
SETPC 14                          'Set pen color Col=14
FD 100                            'Forward in distance 100
SETH 60                           'Set head HD=60 deg.
BK 100                            'Back in distance 100
SETH -60                          'Set head HD=-60 deg.
BK 100                            'Back in 100 distance

DOT 95, -20                       'Set point (95,-20)
SETH 90                           'Set head HD=90 deg.
SETPC 12                          'Set pen color Col=13
    FOR I = 1 TO 10               '10 cicles
        FD 62                     'Forward in distance 62
        LT 36                     'Rotate left in 36 deg.
    NEXT                          'End cicles
f$ = INPUT$(1)                    'Stop programm
```

This fragment must be inserted between the comment lines containing asterisks in the main module that we showed you earlier. You will find it in **\CHAP9\CH9_1.BAS** on the enclosed disk. Here is the drawing constructed by this program:

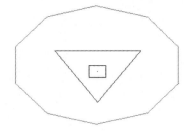

This LOGO program wasn't optimized, so its text includes all the LOGO graphics commands, even if they aren't used. Work through the commented lines one by one if you can't figure out how we have achieved the result - it's very straightforward, just take it one step at a time. In the next section, we'll consider a selection of the most typical examples of LOGO graphics applications.

Vector Graphics Using LOGO Tools

LOGO graphics allows you to implement the central idea of **vector graphics**, in other words the construction of complicated figures using points and line segments, which can be zoomed, rotated and output into any location on the screen. You can, for example, develop a set of procedures to construct vector symbols. The following program, **\CHAP9\CH9_2.BAS**, gives the main module and the non-LOGO subprocedure of a program that creates three versions of the lower-case letter q:

```
REM LOGO graφc for QBasic
REM \CHAP9\CH9_2.BAS

DECLARE SUB DOT (Xc!, Yc!)
DECLARE SUB letq (H!)
DECLARE SUB LT (Q!)
DECLARE SUB RT (Q!)
DECLARE SUB SETH (Head!)
DECLARE SUB CS ()
DECLARE SUB FD (L!)
DECLARE SUB BK (L!)
COMMON SHARED Col, HD, PS, Mx, My, Xcor, Ycor, X0, Y0

'This is LOGO programm:
'********************************************************
'Three letters "q"
X0 = 320: Y0 = 175
    SCREEN 9: CS
'1st
    DOT -150, 0
    SETH 40
    letq 20
'2nd
    DOT 0, 0
    SETH -10
    letq 30
'3rd
    DOT 100, 10
    SETH -130
    letq 10
F$ = INPUT$(1)
'********************************************************

SUB letq (H)
  LT 90
  FD 2 * H
  LT 45
  FD H
  LT 45
  FD H
  LT 45
  FD H
  LT 45
  FD 2 * H
  LT 45
  FD H
  LT 45
  FD H
```

```
        LT 45
        FD H
        LT 45
        BK 3 * H
        RT 30
        FD H
    END SUB
```

The procedure **letq** draws a letter q of any size. To do this, the movement of the turtle is defined by the parameter **H**. LOGO graphics also allows you to change the angle that the letter is inclined at, as well as its size. This screenshot shows the three letter q's created by the program:

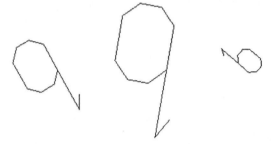

You've now (hopefully) seen a good illustration of locating, rotating and changing the dimensions of complicated figures, using LOGO graphics tools. Armed with patience, you can create a full range of screen characters, images and logos of any style. In the next section, we'll learn how to apply standard coordinate transformations to enable you to create these effects for any QBasic image.

Movement Math

Hoping that your appetite for vector graphics is now whetted, we've got to make use of some math to help.

If we want to move a vector object on screen, we really need to be able to relate the coordinates before and after, so we can make a quick and easy calculation. It's often best to consider the before and after as being described by two separate coordinate systems. Seems silly when you're just moving a line up and down the screen, but what about when you want to rotate a square? Then, it's much easier to let some pre-worked math take over and do the dirty work. Relax and read on!

Relating Two Coordinate Systems

In general, two rectangular coordinate systems are related by two things: the relative positions of their origins and the angle of rotation of their axes. Look at the diagram:

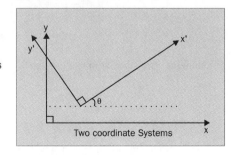

Two coordinate Systems

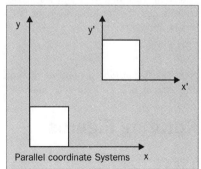

Parallel coordinate Systems

If the angle of rotation of their axes is zero, the systems are **parallel**, as you can see in the second figure. Think of each coordinate system as being two sides of a square, as shown. Move the square and the coordinate system moves with it.

Next question: point A can be described in both coordinate systems, by (x,y) and (x',y') respectively, so how can we relate their values?

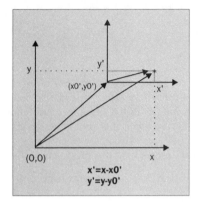

There is a constant difference between the origins (x0,y0), and (x0',y0'), like a vector. If (x0,y0)=(0,0), then this is just (x0',y0'). Subtracting this from any (x,y) coordinates will give (x'y') coordinates. This can be summarized as shown in the diagram.

These relationships are fairly obvious. A more general mechanism for converting objects from one system of coordinates to another is **matrix transformation**. It's more useful too, and remains a delight in school math. Basically, you represent the coordinates in brackets, as the components of a vector from the origin. Which origin? Whichever one you're working from at the time! So the above equation for object translation becomes:

$$\begin{bmatrix} x' \\ y' \end{bmatrix} = \begin{bmatrix} x \\ y \end{bmatrix} - \begin{bmatrix} x0' \\ y0' \end{bmatrix}$$

You can easily add and subtract these brackets - it's just like dealing with each of the two lines independently, but at the same time. Multiplication is a little tougher, and you'll have to look in a math textbook for details. For now, just note that, in order to deal with lots of coordinates, the multiplication of (ax + by) is written:

The equations
$$\begin{aligned} x' &= ax + by \\ y' &= cx + dy \end{aligned}$$
become
$$\begin{bmatrix} x' \\ y' \end{bmatrix} = \begin{bmatrix} a & b \\ c & d \end{bmatrix} \begin{bmatrix} x \\ y \end{bmatrix}$$

To multiply out a square matrix, multiply each element from the row of the square matrix with the corresponding element of the column. Here, the corresponding elements are shown by squares and circles.

$$\begin{bmatrix} x' \\ y' \end{bmatrix} = \begin{bmatrix} \boxed{a} & \textcircled{b} \\ c & d \end{bmatrix} \begin{bmatrix} \boxed{x} \\ \textcircled{y} \end{bmatrix}$$

Next, we'll consider a number of typical movements (transformations) that you'll use when moving from one system of coordinates to another.

Rotating Figures

Suppose we want to rotate a figure anti-clockwise about the origin by an angle, θ. Study the diagram on the following page:

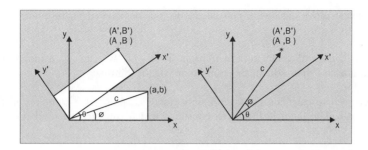

The new top-right corner of the shaded rectangle can be described by two sets of coordinates (A,B) and (A',B'). Note that the value of (A',B') is identical to (a,b), as we've just rotated the square. We don't really want to know (A',B') though. We want the new screen coordinates (that is, relative to the X and Y axes) (A,B), so that we can replot the object.

Concentrating on that one point (A,B), as in the second diagram, we describe it using polar coordinates, as (C,φ). Remember that ϕ is now measured from the X' axis. This makes use of the fact that the magnitude of C does not change with rotation. Polar and Cartesian coordinates are easily interchanged, so (A',B') can be written:

A' = C * Cos (φ)
B' = C * Sin (φ)

and (A,B) as:

A = C * Cos (φ + θ)
B = C * Sin (φ + θ)

We can now split the second pair of equations into cosines and sines that depend on φ or θ only - a standard math result which we just quote:

A = C * Cos(φ) * Cos(θ) - C * Sin(φ) * Sin(θ)
B = C * Sin(φ) * Cos(θ) + C * Cos(φ) * Sin(θ)

We already have expressions for C * Cos(φ) and C * Sin(φ), they are A' and B', so we write them in instead:

A = A' * Cos(θ) - B' * Sin(θ)
B = B' * Cos(θ) + A' * Sin(θ)

This may be represented in matrix form as:

Rotation Matrix

$$\begin{bmatrix} A \\ B \end{bmatrix} = \begin{bmatrix} \cos\theta & -\sin\theta \\ \sin\theta & \cos\theta \end{bmatrix} \begin{bmatrix} A' \\ B' \end{bmatrix}$$

or

$$\begin{bmatrix} A \\ B \end{bmatrix} = \begin{bmatrix} \cos\theta & -\sin\theta \\ \sin\theta & \cos\theta \end{bmatrix} \begin{bmatrix} a \\ b \end{bmatrix}$$

In order to make a shape move clockwise, you need only put negative θ in the matrix and the sine functions will reverse the sign.

If we wish to rotate a figure anti-clockwise and translate it as well, we can again make use of matrices. We just perform the rotation and then add in the translation vector. Simple!

Obviously, you don't need to calculate cos(θ) and sin(θ) for each point of a complicated figure. It's quicker to use a **FOR** loop to calculate them just once as constants which can then be used throughout the program:

```
FOR Q = 0 TO TWO.PI STEP TWO.PI / N
    C = COS(Q): S = SIN(Q)
NEXT Q
```

and define the coordinates of every next point from the expressions:

```
x' = x * C - y * S
y' = y * C + x * S
```

This method can significantly increase the calculation rate, because QBasic is rather slow when it comes to working out trigonometric functions.

Warping Transformations

We can also use matrices to zoom and stretch figures, which calls for another square matrix:

Square Matrix

No Change
$$\begin{bmatrix} x' \\ y' \end{bmatrix} = \begin{bmatrix} 1 & 0 \\ 0 & 1 \end{bmatrix} \begin{bmatrix} x \\ y \end{bmatrix} = \begin{bmatrix} x \\ y \end{bmatrix}$$

◄ *Identity Matrix*

Zoom
$$\begin{bmatrix} x' \\ y' \end{bmatrix} = \begin{bmatrix} 2 & 0 \\ 0 & 2 \end{bmatrix} \begin{bmatrix} x \\ y \end{bmatrix} = \begin{bmatrix} 2x \\ 2y \end{bmatrix}$$

You can see that multiplying the coordinates by the identity matrix doesn't change the coordinates at all. Slightly pointless! But, by using the second matrix, you can zoom towards (and thus enlarge) the figure, or, by using magnitudes less than one, recede away.

What about combining the zoom matrix with the rotation and translation matrices that we used earlier? Then we would have the ability to truly warp the figure! Have a look at these matrices and have a play with program **\CHAP9\CH9_3.BAS**. Don't worry about its code too much, we'll explain more in the rest of the chapter.

Warp Matrix

To rotate by angle θ and stretch in the y-axis:
$$\begin{bmatrix} x \\ y \end{bmatrix} = \begin{bmatrix} k\cos\theta & -\sin\theta \\ \sin\theta & k\cos\theta \end{bmatrix} \begin{bmatrix} x' \\ y' \end{bmatrix} + \begin{bmatrix} x2 \\ 0 \end{bmatrix}$$

To reflect in the y-axis:
$$\begin{bmatrix} x \\ y \end{bmatrix} = \begin{bmatrix} -1 & 0 \\ 0 & 1 \end{bmatrix} \begin{bmatrix} x' \\ y' \end{bmatrix}$$

To transform a geometric figure represented by a number of points, you simply carry out the same calculations for each point.

> *Remember to speed up the process by, wherever possible, calculating trigonometric functions only once, then assigning the results to a variable so that they can be re-used without taking valuable time to recalculate them.*

Figure Rotation

The rotation of various figures is often used in the design of national emblems and company logos. The eye-catching results of using rotation are not in doubt. There are few figure effects that are more effective and more frustrating than rotation techniques. Having introduced the math, we'll now try to clarify any misconceptions by examples that use rotation to its full potential.

Rotating a Square

Let's set ourselves the task of creating a program which outputs **N** squares to the screen by using an initial square:

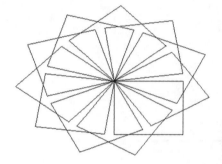

We'll rotate it about the origin (0,0). The length of the sides of the square can be arbitrary and are set as equal to **d**. Since the PC's coordinate system is different from the Cartesian system in which we showed our theory, you will see clockwise rotations reverse, and vice-versa, all because the y-axes are in opposite directions. Just change the sign of the sine functions to reverse the rotation. We must also provide zooming at least along the x-axis as, otherwise, the initial square may appear on the screen as a rectangle extended along the y-axis.

Each of the points given in the diagram must be processed by our formulae for rotating about the origin, but remember that we also use a scaling factor along the x-axis (because pixels aren't actually square) so that our squares look like what they're supposed to be - squares. Here's how we'd write this as a program:

```
REM Rotating N quadrates (var.1)
REM \CHAP9\CH9_3.BAS

  SCREEN 9: CLS
  x0 = 320            'Coordinate x0
  y0 = 150            'Coordinate y0
  d = 100             'Size of squares
  Mx = 1.35           'Scale x
  N = 11              'Number of squares
  TWO.PI = 6.282      'Constant 2*PI
```

```
FOR Q = 0 TO TWO.PI STEP TWO.PI / N
  C = COS(Q): S = SIN(Q)   'Calculating constants C and S
  'Drawing squares
  PSET (Mx * (0 * C + 0 * S) + x0, 0 * C + 0 * S + y0)
  LINE -(Mx * (0 * C - d * S) + x0, d * C + 0 * S + y0)
  LINE -(Mx * (d * C - d * S) + x0, d * C + d * S + y0)
  LINE -(Mx * (d * C - 0 * S) + x0, 0 * C + d * S + y0)
  LINE -(Mx * (0 * C - 0 * S) + x0, 0 * C + 0 * S + y0)
  'Pause loop
  FOR PAUSE.LOOP = 1 TO 1000
  NEXT PAUSE.LOOP
NEXT Q
F$ = INPUT$(1)

END
```

The figure created using this program for **N=11** is shown here:

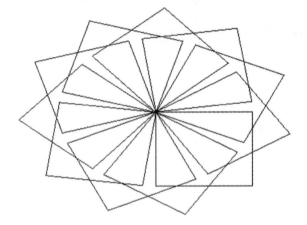

If you step through the program, you'll see that the starting square is in the bottom-right corner of the screen. You'll remember that this is because we're using raster coordinates, rather than the standard Cartesian variety, and the y-axis increases as it goes down the screen.

One more thing stands out - the code contains a number of meaningless multiplications by zero. We included these only to show you all the terms of the formulae for rotation. In general, of course, you must include all the terms but, in those cases where some of the terms are zero, it makes sense to remove them if you need to speed up your code.

Rotating an Arbitrary Figure with Four Nodes

Let's now look at the next progression from rotating a square - rotating an arbitrary figure, formed by four nodes and connected by line segments, 10 successive times about the origin:

```
REM Rotating N figures with 4 nodes
REM \CHAP9\CH9_4.BAS

SCREEN 9: CLS
x0 = 320                    'Coordinate x0
```

```
y0 = 150                        'Coordinate y0
Mx = 1.35                       'Scale x
N = 10                          'Number of squares
TWO.PI = 6.282                  'Constant 2*PI
'Nodes coordinates:
x1 = 0:     y1 = 50
x2 = -15:   y2 = 80
x3 = 0:     y3 = 110
x4 = 15:    y4 = 80
FOR Q = 0 TO TWO.PI STEP TWO.PI / N
    C = COS(Q): S = SIN(Q)    'Calculating constants C and S
    'Drawing figures
    PSET (Mx * (x1 * C - y1 * S) + x0, y1 * C + x1 * S + y0)
    LINE -(Mx * (x2 * C - y2 * S) + x0, y2 * C + x2 * S + y0)
    LINE -(Mx * (x3 * C - y3 * S) + x0, y3 * C + x3 * S + y0)
    LINE -(Mx * (x4 * C - y4 * S) + x0, y4 * C + x4 * S + y0)
    LINE -(Mx * (x1 * C - y1 * S) + x0, y1 * C + x1 * S + y0)
    FOR PAUSE.LOOP = 1 TO 1000 : NEXT PAUSE.LOOP
NEXT Q
F$ = INPUT$(1)

END
```

You can see that the second program block is very similar to the second block in the previous program. It calculates the coordinates in regard to rotating, shifting and zooming along the x-axis, and also draws the figure by sequentially connecting the nodes with line segments.

Here is our sample output, showing a figure made up of 10 parallelograms in a circle:

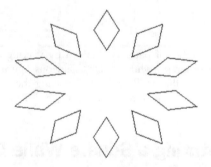

Our figures are indeed parallelograms but, by changing the node coordinates, you could create and rotate any four-cornered figure. You can also have any number of rotations by changing the value of **N**. Try **N=100, y1=90, y2=0, y3=300, y4=50**, for a completely different picture.

Rotating a Circle

You can get a variety of interesting geometric figures by arranging small-radius circles around a large-radius circle. You don't need to recalculate the coordinates of every point on the circle to do this - you just have to recalculate the center. The program shown here allows you to draw, by rotation, **N** circles of radius **R**, displaced from the origin by amount **d**:

```
REM Rotating N circles
REM \CHAP9\CH9_5.BAS
```

```
SCREEN 9: CLS
x0 = 320              'Coordinate x0
y0 = 150              'Coordinate y0
d = 50                'Displacement
Mx = 1.35             'Scale x
N = 16                'Number of circles
R = 80                'Radius of a circle
TWO.PI = 6.282        'Constant 2*PI
FOR Q = 0 TO TWO.PI STEP TWO.PI / N
   C = COS(Q): S = SIN(Q)    'Calculating constants C and S
   'Drawing circles
   CIRCLE (Mx * (d * C - d * S) + x0, d * C + d * S + y0), R
   FOR PAUSE.LOOP = 1 TO 1000: NEXT PAUSE.LOOP
NEXT Q
F$ = INPUT$(1)

END
```

The figure which results from running the
above program looks like this:

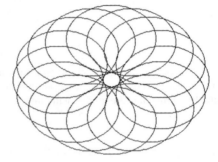

The number of patterns obtained by varying the parameters **N**, **d** and **R** is almost limitless. It's possible to
write programs which create analogous figures using a simpler method; for example, by calculating the
centers of the small circles and placing them on a large one divided into **N** parts. However, the program
we've used does have an advantage - it's based on a universal and flexible math instrument for coordinate
conversion.

Rotating a Square While Decreasing its Size

Another way to create interesting figures is to rotate them around their center at the same time as changing
their size. Here is a program which rotates a square about its center (coinciding with the origin of the
initial coordinate system), while making the square smaller:

```
REM Rotating N figures with 4 nodes
REM \CHAP9\CH9_6.BAS

SCREEN 9: CLS
x0 = 320              'Coordinate x0
y0 = 150              'Coordinate y0
Mx = 1.35             'Scale factor x
N = 40                'Number of figures
TWO.PI = 6.282        'Constant 2*PI
```

```
    d = 120

    FOR Q = 0 TO TWO.PI STEP TWO.PI / N
        'Nodes coordinates:
        x1 = d:    y1 = d
        x2 = -d:   y2 = d
        x3 = -d:   y3 = -d
        x4 = d:    y4 = -d
        C = COS(Q): S = SIN(Q)    'Calculating constants C and S
        'Drawing figures
        PSET (Mx * (x1 * C - y1 * S) + x0, y1 * C + x1 * S + y0)
        LINE -(Mx * (x2 * C - y2 * S) + x0, y2 * C + x2 * S + y0)
        LINE -(Mx * (x3 * C - y3 * S) + x0, y3 * C + x3 * S + y0)
        LINE -(Mx * (x4 * C - y4 * S) + x0, y4 * C + x4 * S + y0)
        LINE -(Mx * (x1 * C - y1 * S) + x0, y1 * C + x1 * S + y0)
        d = d / 1.1
        FOR PAUSE.LOOP = 1 TO 1000: NEXT PAUSE.LOOP
    NEXT Q
    F$ = INPUT$(1)

    END
```

The program recalculates the node coordinates **(x1,y1)...(x4,y4)** at every construction cycle, hence the calculations are included within the loop body. The square's dimensions are changed by dividing **d** by 1.1, so the square gradually shrinks. Here is an illustration of the result of running this program:

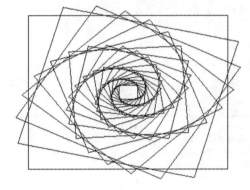

If you change this factor so that it's less than 1, you can make the square grow. However, it's best if you reduce the initial size of the square first. Try **d=3** and divide **d** by a factor of **.9** from within the loop.

Not a bad effect, is it? Using the above algorithms, you can create any number of programs to draw spectacular rotation patterns.

Drawing Polar Functions

You can construct similar figures using polar coordinates:

$$x = R * \cos(\theta) + x0$$
$$y = R * \sin(\theta) + y0$$

The plots of functions in polar coordinates are conveniently drawn using the **PSET(x,y)** and **LINE -(x,y)** statements. First, **PSET** draws the starting point, then **LINE-(x,y)** extends the line from one point to another.

There's little use in drawing circles to illustrate the use of polar coordinates because QBasic's built-in **CIRCLE** command is so very simple to use. Instead, we'll look at a few more complicated examples. These are all combined in **\CHAP9\CH9_5.BAS** which you'll find on the disk. Here, to make things more convenient, we'll split the program into a series of independent sections.

Drawing an Inclined Ellipse

Our first program allows you to plot ellipses whereby the main semi-axis is set at an angle to the horizontal:

```
REM Plotting Ellipses
REM\CHAP9\CHAP9_7.BAS

SCREEN 1: KEY OFF: CLS
Q = 45: R = 60: KR = 2 * R
C = COS(Q): S = SIN(Q): F = 1.745329E-02

FOR W = 0 TO 360
  A = W * F
  X = R * COS(A)
  Y = KR * SIN(A)
  X1 = X * C + Y * S
  Y1 = S * X - C * Y

  IF W = 0 THEN
    PSET (120 + X1, 100 + Y1)
  ELSE
    LINE -(120 + X1, 100 + Y1)
  END IF
NEXT W

LOCATE 1, 15
PRINT "Ellipse"
A$ = INPUT$(1)
```

This isn't possible using the **CIRCLE** statement alone. To draw an inclined ellipse, you have to use the ellipse parametric definition formulae and the formulae for conversion to a new system of coordinates. Here's what this program constructs:

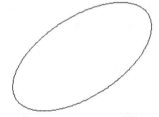

The formulae used are somewhat different from the initial ones. Why is this? It's not worth calculating the values **SIN (Q)** and **COS (Q)** within a loop, since the sine and cosine functions are processed rather slowly. Instead they're calculated beforehand and the relevant values are assigned to the variables **S** and **C**.

Parametric Examples

The next three programs draw spirals and illustrate quite well the features of parametric functions. The first version plots a spiral as a circle of varying radius, whilst the other two draw untwisting and twisting spirals:

```
REM Spirals
REM \CHAP9\CHAP9_8.BAS

SCREEN 1: CLS
LOCATE 1, 8
Kx = 1.2
X0 = 120: Y0 = 100
PSET (X0, Y0)
FOR W = .2 TO 40 STEP .2
  X = Kx * SIN(W)
  Y = COS(W)
  R = 2 * W
  LINE -(X0 + R * X, Y0 - R * Y)
NEXT W
PRINT "Spiral (normal)"
A$ = INPUT$(1)
```

The resulting spiral is:

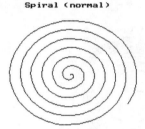

Here is a similar program which plots an exponentially untwisting spiral:

```
REM Untwisting Spiral
REM \CHAP9\CHAP9_9.BAS

'Spiral (exp)
SCREEN 1: CLS
Kx = 1.2
X0 = 120: Y0 = 100
FOR W = 1 TO 60 STEP .1
  R = 5 * EXP(W / 20)
  X = X0 + R * COS(W)
  Y = Y0 - R * SIN(W)
  IF W = 1 THEN PSET (X, Y) ELSE LINE -(X, Y)
NEXT W
LOCATE 1, 10
PRINT "Spiral (exp)"
A$ = INPUT$(1)
```

And this is what it looks like:

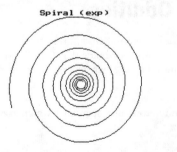

In comparison, here's the code for the third - a gradually twisting spiral:

```
REM Twisting Spiral
REM \CHAP9\CHAP9_10.BAS

'Spiral (log)
SCREEN 1: CLS
Kx = 1.2
X0 = 120: Y0 = 100
FOR W = 1 TO 80 STEP .2
  R = 20 * LOG(W)
  X = X0 + R * COS(W)
  Y = Y0 - R * SIN(W)
  IF W = 1 THEN PSET (X, Y) ELSE LINE -(X, Y)
NEXT W
LOCATE 1, 10
PRINT "Spiral (log)"
A$ = INPUT$(1)
```

The resulting figure is here:

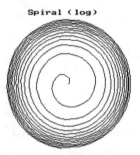

Spiral (log)

It's easy to see that, in spiral construction, the **W** parameter must range from small values to values over **2*PI**. If it doesn't, the spiral won't contain a sufficient number of turns.

For further examples of parametric effects, take a look at these programs included on the disk:

\CHAP9\CHAP9_11.BAS
\CHAP9\CHAP9_12.BAS
\CHAP9\CHAP9_13.BAS
\CHAP9\CHAP9_14.BAS
\CHAP9\CHAP9_15.BAS
\CHAP9\CHAP9_16.BAS
\CHAP9\CHAP9_17.BAS

QBasic Geometric Oddities

The pictures that you create with QBasic may not be entirely what you intend. Although you'll often be frustrated by the lack of resolution and color flexibility that QBasic offers, sometimes you may be pleasantly surprised by the results. The following two examples show the surprising effects that can result from **pixelation**.

The first program given here draws numerous line segments which rotate around the center of the screen (the point (160,100) in CGA mode):

```
REM Line segments
REM \CHAP9\CHAP9_18.BAS

PI = 3.141
SCREEN 1: CLS
FOR W = 0 TO 2 * PI STEP .025 * PI
  X = 150 * COS(W): Y = 90 * SIN(W)
  LINE (160, 100)-(160 + X, 100 - Y)
NEXT
F$ = INPUT$(1)
```

On the face of it, what's unusual about this piece of code? Well, nothing, but the drawing differs dramatically from the fan of common lines you might expect. You can see a rather intricate and almost spooky or gothic design in the center of the figure:

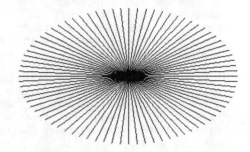

Let's also draw a pattern by rotating two lines around alternate angles of the window:

```
REM Rotating two lines
REM \CHAP9\CHAP9_19.BAS

SCREEN 2: CLS
FOR I = 0 TO 639 STEP 7
  LINE (0, 0)-(I, 199)
NEXT
FOR I = 0 TO 199 STEP 5
  LINE (0, 0)-(639, I)
NEXT
F$ = INPUT$(1)
```

Here's the surprising result:

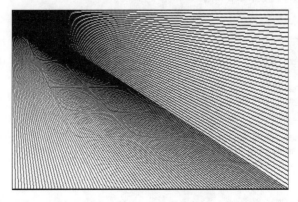

When straight lines cross each other, they share the same pixel and, if the angle between the lines is very small, you get a peculiarity similar to the above. The best way to explore these anomalies is to experiment with different angles and colors yourself, maybe even displaying more than one image on screen so they intersect. If you get anything really bizarre, don't forget to send them to us at Wrox!

Creating a Complex Multicolored Pattern

You can get spectacular visual effects by using the algorithms for drawing colored fractal images. The theory behind the construction of such objects goes far beyond the scope of this book, but here's a simplified version of the demo program **MANDEL.BAS**:

```
REM Mandel Fractals
REM \CHAP9\CHAP9_20.BAS


DEFINT A-Z
DECLARE SUB ShiftPalette ()
DECLARE SUB ScreenTest (EM%, CR%, VL%, VR%, VT%, VB%)
CONST FALSE = 0, TRUE = NOT FALSE
CONST MAXLOOP = 30, MAXSIZE = 1000000
DIM PaletteArray(15)
FOR I = 0 TO 15: PaletteArray(I) = I: NEXT I
'Set size of window and graphic mode control
WLeft = -1000: WRight = 250: WTop = 625: WBottom = -625
ScreenTest EgaMode, ColorRange, VLeft, VRight, VTop, VBottom
VIEW (VLeft, VTop)-(VRight, VBottom), 0, ColorRange
WINDOW (WLeft, WTop)-(WRight, WBottom)
'Drawing mandel
LOCATE 24, 10: PRINT "Press any key to quit.";
XLength = VRight - VLeft: YLength = VBottom - VTop
ColorWidth = MAXLOOP \ ColorRange
FOR Y = 0 TO YLength
  LogicY = PMAP(Y, 3): PSET (WLeft, LogicY): OldColor = 0
  FOR X = 0 TO XLength
    LogicX = PMAP(X, 2)
    MandelX& = LogicX: MandelY& = LogicY
    FOR I = 1 TO MAXLOOP
      RealNum& = MandelX& * MandelX&
      ImagNum& = MandelY& * MandelY&
      IF (RealNum& + ImagNum&) >= MAXSIZE THEN EXIT FOR
      MandelY& = (MandelX& * MandelY&) \ 250 + LogicY
      MandelX& = (RealNum& - ImagNum&) \ 500 + LogicX
    NEXT I
    PColor = I \ ColorWidth
    IF PColor <> OldColor THEN
      LINE -(LogicX, LogicY), (ColorRange - OldColor)
      OldColor = PColor
    END IF
    IF INKEY$ <> "" THEN END
  NEXT X
  LINE -(LogicX, LogicY), (ColorRange - OldColor)
  IF EgaMode THEN ShiftPalette
NEXT Y
DO
   IF EgaMode THEN ShiftPalette
LOOP WHILE INKEY$ = ""
SCREEN 0, 0: WIDTH 80: END

BadScreen:
   EgaMode = FALSE
RESUME NEXT

SUB ScreenTest (EM, CR, VL, VR, VT, VB) STATIC
```

```
      EM = TRUE
      ON ERROR GOTO BadScreen
      SCREEN 8, 1
      ON ERROR GOTO 0
      IF EM THEN              ' No error, so SCREEN 8 is OK
        VL = 110: VR = 529: VT = 5: VB = 179
        CR = 15               ' 16 colors (0 - 15)
      ELSE                    ' Error, so use SCREEN 1
        SCREEN 1, 1
        VL = 55: VR = 264: VT = 5: VB = 179
        CR = 3                ' 4 colors (0 - 3)
      END IF
   END SUB

   SUB ShiftPalette STATIC
      SHARED PaletteArray(), ColorRange
      FOR I = 1 TO ColorRange
        PaletteArray(I) = (PaletteArray(I) MOD ColorRange) + 1
      NEXT I
      PALETTE USING PaletteArray(0)
   END SUB
```

It displays probably the most well-known fractal, the Mandelbrot set. Start the program and it slowly draws a colorful image of the Mandelbrot set.

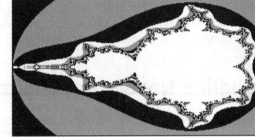

This intriguing effect is achieved not only by the technique applied to its construction, but also by switching the view and the active pages. Even the black and white image below gives you an idea of the beauty and mystery of the pattern:

Press any key to quit.

General Tips for Screen Graphics

When implementing 2-dimensional screen graphics in QBasic, it's worth bearing in mind the following:

1 It's recommended that you clear the screen before constructing graphics, otherwise previous outputs can obscure and confuse the current output.

2 When the graphics constructions are complete, the message Press any key appears on the lower line of the screen. If you don't want it to appear, you have to stop the program before it outputs the message.

3 Text will type over and delete plotted lines, but a plot drawn over text doesn't delete it. The starting position of the text in the graphics window is indicated by the invisible graphics cursor, positioned by the **LOCATE** statement.

4 The following method is the best one for creating plots: first the starting point **(x0,y0)** is drawn using **PSET** **(x0,y0)**, then the plot line is extended from one point to another using the **LINE (x,y)** statement.

5 If, during plotting, the coordinates (x,y) go out of bounds, you may get some unexpected results. You must resume constructing the initial point by the **PSET** statement. To do this, there are special variables or flags which take the values 0 and 1 (or -1), as the situation requires. However, a much simpler way is to artificially limit the coordinate values, for example, using the following expressions:

```
IF y> Ymax THEN y = Ymax
IF y< 0 THEN y = 0
```

Games frequently use this technique to keep characters within screen limits.

6 The coordinates of every point in screen graphics are integers. You can, however, define the parameters of graphics statements and functions as common fractional decimal numbers. Rounding is performed automatically, but not always in the way required by some complicated algorithms. Therefore, when implementing certain machine graphics algorithms, it makes sense to write code to round values yourself, when necessary. As you have defined the process, there should be less chance of unexpected results.

7 Different types of displays vary in their resolution capabilities. Because of this, geometric distortion takes place. For example, a figure specified as a circle may appear (or be represented on a sheet of paper) as an ellipse. This means that you need to change the image scale along the x- and y-axes (to do this you just multiply the x and y coordinates of every point by the corresponding factors, using the transformation discussed earlier).

You can save yourself a lot of time if you follow these recommendations when writing your graphics programs. As we saw earlier in Chapter 7 - Program Design, by sticking to a set of good rules or guidelines, you can keep to a routine and make the whole program development process that much easier.

Handling Resolution Limitations

As an example, we'll consider a program which creates a window containing a sine curve plot and a dotted horizontal axis. The curve is plotted using different resolutions (modes 1, 2, 9 and 10 which are inherent to the most widespread displays and video adapters of the CGA, EGA and VGA type):

```
REM SineCurve
REM \CHAP9\CHAP9_21.BAS

DO
   SCREEN 0: CLS : WIDTH 80: 'Text mode
   'Specifying the Number of Cycles and Screen Mode
   INPUT "Input Number of Cycles (0 for END)=", Cycles
   IF Cycles = 0 THEN END
   INPUT "Input Screen Mode (1,2,9,12)="; Mode

   'Selecting Screen Mode
   SELECT CASE Mode
     CASE 1: SCREEN 1: VIEW (20, 2)-(310, 172), , 1
     CASE 2: SCREEN 2: VIEW (20, 2)-(620, 172), , 1
     CASE 9: SCREEN 9: VIEW (20, 2)-(620, 300), , 1
     CASE 12: SCREEN 12: VIEW (20, 2)-(620, 420), , 1
   END SELECT
```

```
      CONST PI = 3.141592653589#
      ' Making window large enough to graph sine wave from
      ' 0 radians to ã radians:
      WINDOW (0, -1.1)-(2 * PI, 1.1)

      Style% = &HFF00                    ' Use to make dashed line.
      CLS
      LINE (2 * PI, 0)-(0, 0), , , Style%' Draw the x (horizontal) axis.

      'Plotting the sinusoidal function
        IF Cycles > 0 THEN
        'Start at (0,0) and plot the graph:
        FOR X = 0 TO 2 * PI STEP .02
          Y = SIN(Cycles * X)      ' Calculate the y coordinate.
          LINE -(X, Y)             ' Draw a line from the last
                                   ' point to the new point.
      NEXT X
      'Circle
        CIRCLE (.3, -.3), .25
      END IF

      'Print Mode comments
      IF Mode = 12 THEN LOCATE 28, 3 ELSE LOCATE 23, 3
      SELECT CASE Mode
        CASE 1: PRINT "CGA MODE 320*200 Graphic sin(x)"
        CASE 2: PRINT "CGA MODE 640*200 Graphic sin(x)"
        CASE 9: PRINT "EGA MODE 640*350 Graphic sin(x)"
        CASE 12: PRINT "VGA MODE 640*480 Graphic sin(x)"
      END SELECT
      A$ = INPUT$(1)  'Stop program
      CLS
   LOOP WHILE Cycles > 0
```

The program consists of five blocks separated by spaces. The main body is included within the general **DO...WHILE** loop, meaning that you can repeatedly execute the program as a whole. The five blocks are defined as follows:

▲ The first block, the input block, allows you to specify the number of **Cycles** and the graphics **Mode**.

▲ The second block specifies various graphics output modes and a variety of active window sizes, using the **SELECT** switching statement. In addition, it defines the constant **PI** and defines the coordinates in math form.

▲ The third block constructs the frame around the plot and the dashed horizontal axis.

▲ The fourth block plots the sine curve and a small circle under the first wave. The circle allows you to evaluate the extent of the geometric distortion of the figures in various graphics modes.

▲ The fifth block writes an explanatory message at the bottom of the plot. Note that, in VGA mode, the number of text lines is more than in CGA and EGA modes.

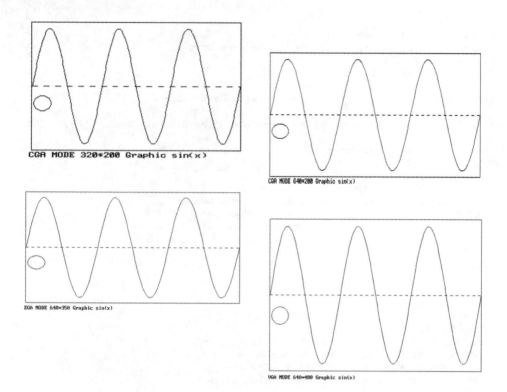

CGA MODE 320*200 Graphic sin(x)

CGA MODE 640*200 Graphic sin(x)

EGA MODE 640*350 Graphic sin(x)

VGA MODE 640*480 Graphic sin(x)

The following four figures show the results of the program for various graphics modes:

From comparing these figures, it's obvious how the image quality improves when you increase the display resolution. Note how, even in VGA mode, the graphic 'lumpiness' is still discernible, although I think you'll agree that it is far superior to the lower resolution modes. Low resolution modes are still useful, though, since they make it possible to obtain heavy lines which gives us a much more wholesome look.

Summary

In this chapter, we've covered a host of advanced 2D graphics concepts. We've looked at LOGO graphics and created a program which allows you to draw using LOGO commands. We then covered translation and rotation transformations which, although a little mathematical, enable you to manipulate graphics objects in a multitude of ways. Polar coordinates let you create objects that normally QBasic wouldn't allow, such as ellipses at an angle on screen. They're also the starting point for some of the most exciting developments in the last decade, as the Mandlebrot set program shows.

Finally, being structured, the procedures and functions in this chapter can also be used to supplement your program library, making it easier for you to write more complex and involved graphics programs. But lets leave flat graphics for now, and take a look at how we can add that extra dimension to our graphics.

3D Graphics Programming

Introduction

3D graphics are used to provide a realistic representation of the things that surround us. QBasic has no special means for building 3D objects - instead we have to construct figures based on a 2D representation of 3D objects.

We'll begin this chapter with intuitive examples of drawing 3D figures. We'll then cover the mathematical fundamentals of 3D graphics, including the general conversions of 3D figures, transferring to a new system of coordinates, rotation, erasing lines at the back of a figure, etc.

Later in the chapter, we'll look at a program which rotates a 3D figure defined by a combination of nodes. We'll also look at painting 3D figures and give a simple example of implementing dynamic graphics. We'll then be discussing the construction of contour graphs of 3D surfaces, known as level diagrams.

The grand finale of this chapter will see us take you on a grand tour of programming virtual environments in 3D, similar in effect to games like Wolfenstein and Doom. Hopefully, this will prove to all the doubters that, with just a little patience, QBasic can produce stunning effects.

Intuitive Drawing

3D graphics is one of the most impressive uses of personal computers, providing a source of fascination for computer users and non-users alike. Although PC-based stereoscopic representation of 3D figures has recently been made possible, it's still highly expensive in terms of software and hardware; all we can offer here is an imitation of 3D space on a flat screen. Most of us are able to draw simple 3D figures on a sheet of paper, but QBasic offers the opportunity of programming figures that would be very hard to draw accurately by hand, and even allows us to view them from different angles.

We'll start with a simple program that demonstrates the **DRAW** statement. It doesn't exactly break any new ground in terms of 3D graphics, but it serves as an apt introduction to the subject:

```
REM Cube in space
REM \CHAP10\CH10_1.BAS

SCREEN 1, 0
COLOR 1, 0
PRINT "  Draw a cube";
PSET (80, 90)
DRAW "L40 U40 R40 D40 E20 U40 G20 E20 L40 G20"

PRINT "   Draw a cube on an angle"
PSET (260, 75)
DRAW "TA45 L40 U40 R40 D40 E20 U40 G20 E20 L40 G20"

LOCATE 16, 40
PRINT "Paint a cube"
PSET (160, 150)
COLOR 2, 0
a$ = "TA0 L40 U40 R40 D40 E20 U40 G20 E20 L40 G20"
DRAW a$
DRAW "BF5 P 2,3"
DRAW "BR60 P 1,3"
DRAW "BH10 P 2,3"
LINE (160, 150)-(160, 110), 1

END
```

This program draws three images of a cube:

▲ Skeleton figure

▲ A cube turned in space

▲ A painted cube

You'll note that, in each case, the parameters of **DRAW** are very similar. We shall explain why this is in a few moments.

*The possibility of using **DRAW** to create volumetric figures with some parts painted is worth mentioning here. As it does a lot to enhance the appearance of figures, we'll discuss the problems of painting 3D figures later, in more detail.*

Fundamentals of 3D Graphics

Intuitively, perspective images are easily constructed, the basic definition being that lines directed into the distance intersect at a point. This is the idea behind perspective and it produces a realistic representation of 3D images on a 2D surface. It's quite likely that you did perspective drawing at school when you were younger. Typical examples involve railway tracks or a road that disappears into the distance.

Unfortunately, implementing perspective on a computer needs rather complicated algorithms which are really the domain of specialist 3D graphics programming books. All is not lost, however, because we can implement a special case of perspective which simplifies the calculations considerably - **parallel projection**.

In technical applications, it's often assumed that the convergence point tends to infinity and that the lines directed into the distance are parallel. This kind of representation, as well as being simple to achieve, has another important advantage: the same scale ratio is maintained for the foreground and the background.

Elements of Parallel Projection

In parallel projection, as well as the two axes x- and y-, another axis, z-, is introduced at an angle θ (most frequently 30 or 45 degrees) to the x-axis. A parallel projection picture is achieved by *projecting* an object into the plane formed by these axes.

This figure shows the most common positions of the coordinate axes for parallel projection images:

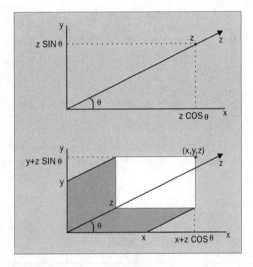

In general, each point of a 3D figure or surface is characterized by three coordinates X, Y, and Z. The x- and y-axes of our coordinate system coincide with those of the spatial coordinate system, and the z-axis of our coordinate system is imaginary. The Z value of a point's coordinate is placed on the screen by projecting its value onto the x-,y- (screen) axes using the formula:

$x = z * \cos(\theta)$

$y = z * \sin(\theta)$

where θ is the angle between the imaginary z-axis and the x-axis on a plane. For example, if θ =45degrees, sin(θ)=cos(θ)=0.707. Therefore, to specify a point (0,0,z), you just have to define:

x=0.707*z and y=0.707*z.

Normally, a point's 3D coordinates are linearly independent. So, to represent a point (x,y,z) in the parallel projection coordinate system, it is sufficient to add the above components of Z to the X and Y coordinates:

x'=x+cos(θ)*z   and y'=y+sin(θ)*z.

This principle provides the groundwork for constructing 3D figures and surfaces.

Simple Parallel Projection Drawings

The next program illustrates some methods of drawing simple 3D figures:

```
REM Elementary 3-D figures
REM \CHAP10\CH10_2.BAS

CONST PI = 3.141
SCREEN 2: CLS

'Cylinder
FOR W = 0 TO PI STEP .04 * PI
    X = 20 * SIN(W): Y = 35 * COS(W)
    LINE (X + 50, Y + 52)-(X + 200, Y + 52)
NEXT W
FOR W = 0 TO 2 * PI STEP .02 * PI
    X = 20 * SIN(W): Y = 35 * COS(W)
    PSET (X + 50, Y + 52)
    IF W < PI THEN PSET (X + 200, Y + 52)
NEXT W
```

This cylinder is created by constructing a set of line segments with their end points located on an elliptic curve. At the beginning, an ellipse is drawn and at the end, a semi-ellipse is drawn. Here is the second illustration:

```
'Paraboloid
FOR Z = -3 TO 3 STEP .1
    A = .5 * Z: Z2 = Z * Z
    FOR X = -3 TO 3.2 STEP .2
        Y = .5 * (Z2 + X * X)
        PSET (430 + 30 * (X + A), 90 - 8 * (Y - A))
    NEXT X
NEXT Z
```

This paraboloid is built point-by-point using the previous method for creating parallel projection pictures. The sub-program which draws the paraboloid illustrates the most typical algorithm for creating a 3D surface. It involves dividing the figure into a set of parallel planes; a line is drawn for each slice. This set of lines forms an image of the figure, or creates a surface.

In this case, each line is built by points. It doesn't matter whether a specified point is visible. The imposition of the points on each other enhances the 3D effect, giving the impression that the surface is made of a semi-transparent material. Unfortunately, this affects the quality of 3D images drawn with continuous lines. Later, we'll cover more complicated algorithms, based on deleting the lines at the back of the image which improve the perception of 3D figures.

The third illustration depicts a pyramid:

```
'Pyramid
N = 5
X = 130: Y = 97: D = 2 * PI / N
FOR W = 0 TO 2 * PI STEP D
    X1 = 130 + 80 * COS(W)
    Y1 = 72 + 15 * SIN(W)
    IF W = 0 THEN PSET (210, Y + 72) ELSE LINE -(X1, Y + Y1)
```

```
      PSET (X, Y): LINE -(X1, Y + Y1)
NEXT W
```

This pentahedral prism is constructed by connecting five points on an elliptic curve with line sections. These points are then connected by line segments to the peak of the pyramid.

Here is the last illustration:

```
'Sinusoid
LINE (380, 190)-(580, 190)
LINE (380, 190)-(380, 110)
LINE (380, 190)-(550, 135)
LOCATE 24, 45: PRINT "0";
LOCATE 24, 76: PRINT "X";
LOCATE 14, 45: PRINT "Y"
LOCATE 17, 71: PRINT "Z"
FOR W = 0 TO 4 * PI STEP PI / 5
    Z = 6 * W: X = 80 * SIN(W)
    IF W = 0 THEN
    PSET (380 + 2.2 * Z, 190 - .707 * Z)
    ELSE
    LINE -(380 + X + 2.2 * Z, 190 - .707 * Z)
    END IF
NEXT W

SLEEP
END
```

This program implements a number of simple algorithms for constructing elementary geometric figures (a cylinder, paraboloid, prism and sinusoid) in one of the planes. These figures are shown here:

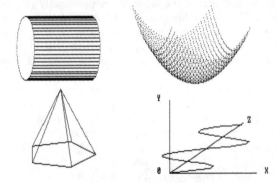

The algorithm of a point-by-point drawing calls for large volumes of calculations and is implemented by two nested cycles. This means that running them can be quite time-consuming. You need to be careful to avoid any repeating calculations in the internal cycle. For instance, in the paraboloid's subroutine, the calculations **A=.5*Z** and **Z2=Z*Z** are taken out of the internal cycle and placed in the external one, which greatly reduces the number of multiplications while processing the coordinates of each point of the surface. Even replacing **Z^2** with **Z*Z** can save time because the multiplication operation is carried out faster than raising to a power. These simple tips also work, sometimes critically, for more sophisticated 3D graphics algorithms.

The sinusoidal wave on the horizontal plane formed by the x- and z-axes (with z- being the time axis) is drawn in a similar way. The spatial representation of these geometric objects is very pronounced.

Constructing 3D Surfaces with Hidden Line Removal

Even from the simple constructions presented above, you can see that the spatial perception of 3D figures is notably improved when the lines that should be invisible are removed. For example, the picture of a cone would be nowhere near as effective if all of the lines that form it were completely visible. The technique for screening unwanted lines is called **hidden line removal**.

We'll now go on to algorithms for drawing 3D surfaces defined by the math function **Z(X,Y)**. Although there's a great variety of such algorithms, we'll consider just two of them. Let's look at the first.

The Z-Buffer Algorithm

The Z-buffer is an array of memory that stores the depth value of all the pixels in the figure. If part of the figure is about to be covered by something 'closer' to the viewer, the new pixel value must have a lower depth value. This algorithm is very costly in memory terms, so, in the following programs, the depth information is implicit - that is, the figures are drawn as lines, starting from the back and moving 'forward' (down the screen). The program structure may be summarized as follows. Note that the screen coordinates are **(y,z)** and **x** is the virtual axis in the program.

 A set of values **x=x1** is given, beginning with those referred to as the background lines.

 A set of values **y=yj** is given and, for each value, the points **(x1,yj,z)** are plotted. Then, the line of the background color (black) is plotted from the nearest point to the bottom edge of the window. Changing this color will enable you to see more of how the program works.

The second part of the algorithm is particularly important as it paints those background lines which lie below the current foreground. This method allows you to obtain fairly realistic 3D pictures quite simply. It doesn't require arrays to store the coordinates of the background points, which saves memory. However, this method does have a shortcoming - it cuts off the visible parts of complicated drawings which lie below the plane (y,z). However, it's possible to ensure that very few figures use negative coordinates.

The program **\CHAP10\CH10_3.BAS** draws any of the ten 3D figures and surfaces defined in it. The program is composed of several parts: the main module and ten subroutines. The full text of the program can be found on the disk. It allows you to print the drawn figures by inserting the procedure **CSEGA**, which copies the graphics screen. Here is a listing of the main module featuring an empty address to the procedure:

```
REM Program for drawing 3-D figures
REM \CHAP10\CH10_3.BAS

SCREEN 9: CLS
LOCATE 1, 12: PRINT "3-D-GRAPHICS"
LOCATE 3, 5: PRINT "Djakonov V.P. Smolensk 1994"
LOCATE 5, 3: PRINT "Program presents 10 algoritms"
LOCATE 7, 5: PRINT "FOR DISPLAYED 3-D-OBJECTS"
LOCATE 11, 3: PRINT "1 KNOLL          2 LETTER A"
LOCATE 12, 3: PRINT "3 WAVES          4 HOUSE"
LOCATE 13, 3: PRINT "5 LETTER O        6 CROS"
LOCATE 14, 3: PRINT "7 KONUS          8 PYRAMIDE"
LOCATE 15, 3: PRINT "9 OBJECT 1       10 OBJECT 2"
LOCATE 17, 7: PRINT "Press Q for quit"
LOCATE 18, 3: PRINT "Press C for CopyScreen"
```

```
LOCATE 19, 7: PRINT "Press M for menu"
LOCATE 21, 5: INPUT "Input menu position"; N$
IF N$ = "Q" OR N$ = "q" THEN END
IF N$ = "M" OR N$ = "m" THEN RUN
CLS : N = VAL(N$)
ON N GOSUB F1, F2, F3, F4, F5, F6, F7, F8, F9, F10
DO
    M$ = INPUT$(1)
    IF M$ = "C" OR M$ = "c" THEN GOSUB CSEGA
    IF M$ = "E" OR M$ = "e" THEN END
    RUN
LOOP
END


CSEGA:
'Include CSEGA if this necessary
RETURN
```

A 3D Knoll

The sub-program **F1** draws the image of a peak or a knoll. The math relationship for this figure is defined by the right part of the assignment expression for the variable **Z**. The text of this subroutine is given here:

```
F1:   LOCATE 1: PRINT " 1 Knoll"
      FOR X% = -44 TO 44 STEP 4
          X1 = X% - 150: X2 = X% + 60
          XT = X% * X% * .000025 + .001
          FOR Y% = -100 TO 100
              YT = Y% * Y% * .000025
              Z = 100 - 5 / SQR(XT + YT)
              NY = Y% - X1: NZ = Z + X2
              'Draws a black line from the new point down the screen
              'Change the 0 to change the background color
              LINE (NY, NZ)-(NY, 199), 0
              IF Y% = -100 THEN
               PSET (NY, NZ)
              ELSE
               'Draws a line segment from the old to the new point
               LINE (PY, PZ)-(NY, NZ)
              END IF
              PY = NY: PZ = NZ
          NEXT Y%
      NEXT X%
      RETURN
```

Here is a picture of the figure built by the **F1** subroutine:

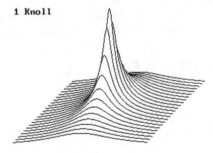

1 Knoll

The work of the algorithm in deleting the invisible lines is clearly demonstrated. The algorithm produces excellent results if the figure points in only one direction, upward, which is the case in our example.

3D Alphabetic Characters

The sub-program **F2** creates a 3D letter, A, positioned as if lying on a slanting plane. This sub-program addresses the subroutine **L2** which defines the math function **Z(X,Y)** for this figure:

```
F2:   LOCATE 1: PRINT " 2 Letter A"
      CC = 16.667
      FOR X% = -30 TO 130 STEP 5
          X1 = X% * .5 - 80: X2 = X% * .6 + 60
          FOR Y% = 0 TO 200
              GOSUB L2
              NY = INT(Y% - X1): NZ = INT(Z + X2)
              LINE (NY, NZ)-(NY, 199), 0
              IF Y% = 0 THEN
              PSET (NY, NZ)
              ELSE
              LINE (PY, PZ)-(NY, NZ)
              END IF
              PY = NY: PZ = NZ
          NEXT Y%
      NEXT X%
   RETURN

L2:   'Function Z(X,Y) for letter A
      Z = Y% * .1: XT = X% * .1
      Y0 = (.06 * (Y% + 120) - 10) * 3.333
      Y1 = Y0 - 10: Y2 = -Y0 + CC
      IF XT < 0 OR XT > 10 THEN GOTO L21
      IF XT < -Y0 + 10 OR XT < Y0 - 16.667 THEN GOTO L21
      IF XT < Y2 OR XT < Y1 OR (XT > 6 AND XT < 8) THEN Z = -20
L21:  RETURN
```

This geometric figure is remarkable because the description of a rather complicated 3D object is performed with the application of a mathematical instrument - not an intuitive approach. The letter A can be seen here:

2 Letter A

If you would like to improve this sub-program so that it draws a 3D letter from a character or string passed to it, make sure that you send us a copy - it will definitely take a lot of patience, time and effort.

A 3D Ripple Effect

The subroutine **F3** describes a ripple. The waves start in the center of the figure and gradually dampen out as they spread outwards. This dampening effect is obtained by using the function **Z=-300*SIN(D/5)/D**, where **D=SQR(X^2+Y^2)**. Unfortunately, this function gives an error at **D=0**. To prevent this, we use a conditional expression to directly define **Z=-60**, if **D=0**.

The text of the sub-program **F3**, together with the subroutine **L3** which gives the math description of the ripple surface, is as follows:

```
F3:   LOCATE 1: PRINT "   3 Waves";
      FOR X = -80 TO 70 STEP 4: X2 = X * X
           FOR Y = -100 TO 100
                   GOSUB L3
                   NY = Y - X * .5 + 150: NZ = Z + X * .7 + 120
                   LINE (NY, NZ)-(NY, 199), 0
                   IF Y = -100 THEN
                   PSET (NY, NZ)
                   ELSE
                   LINE (PY, PZ)-(NY, NZ)
                   END IF
                   PY = NY: PZ = NZ
           NEXT Y
      NEXT X
  RETURN

L3:  'Function Z(X,Y) for the figure WAVES
     D = SQR(X2 + Y * Y)
     IF D = 0 THEN Z = -60 ELSE Z = -300 * SIN(D / 5) / (D)
     RETURN
```

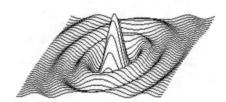

3 Waves

The following screenshot shows the wavy surface built by sub-program **F3**. You can see quite clearly the decreasing amplitude of the waves and how they spread out from the central point:

We won't guide you through the rest of the examples here, but suffice to say that this program, **\CHAP10\CH10_3.BAS**, defines and draws the 3D images of ten figures, providing a good demonstration of the algorithm which deletes invisible lines. All the subroutines that can be conducted in the external cycle are removed from the internal cycle.

If you take a look at the last two figures drawn by the program (not shown here), you can see that they demonstrate how mathematical surfaces in the form of bi-variable functions can have a complicated and unusual appearance. However, they don't always work properly when deleting the unwanted lines.

Now let's look at the second algorithm for **hidden line removal**.

The Floating Horizon Algorithm

This algorithm is based on storing the arrays of the previous and current lines of the drawing. Plotting the lines which imitate a 3D surface starts in the foreground with a control of the ordinates of the points. If a current ordinate is located higher than the previous one of the analogous number, the corresponding point is plotted. This algorithm lets you draw figures and surfaces with peaks and troughs.

The Cowboy Hat

The step along the z-axis is normally specified as greater than 1, otherwise the lines partially merge together, which impairs the perception of the figures. This does have disadvantages, namely that the definition of sharp edges can be a little bit flimsy, as demonstrated here:

```
REM Constructing a 3-D Surface applying the FH algorithm
REM \CHAP10\CH10_4.BAS

SCREEN 9: CLS
DIM U(424), L(424): XC = 320: YC = 50
XR = 175: ZR = 120: XA = 107
FOR I% = 1 TO 424
    U(I%) = 0: L(I%) = 1000
NEXT I%
FOR Z = -ZR + 1 TO ZR - 1 STEP 5
    Z2 = Z * Z
    XL% = INT(XR * SQR(1 - Z2 / (ZR * ZR)) + .5)
    X = -XL%
    GOSUB Func
    XZ = XC + Z: X1 = X + XZ
    Y1 = INT(199 - (YC + Y + Z / 2) + .5)
    YZ = 199.5 - YC - .5 * Z
    FOR X = -XL% + 1 TO XL% - 1
        GOSUB Func
        X2 = XZ + X: Y2 = INT(YZ - Y)
        N = X2 - XA
        DO UNTIL Y2 >= L(N)
        L(X2 - XA) = Y2
        IF U(N) = 0 THEN U(N) = Y2
        GOTO Lab
        LOOP
        DO UNTIL Y2 <= U(N)
        U(N) = Y2
Lab:    LINE (X1, Y1)-(X2, Y2)
        LOOP
        X1 = X2: Y1 = Y2
    NEXT X
NEXT Z
F$ = INPUT$(1)

END

Func: Y = 40 * SIN(.043 * SQR(X * X + Z2))
RETURN
```

The following screenshot shows the figure (a cowboy hat) constructed by this program. The figure isn't bad - only when viewed closely can you see weaknesses in the edges:

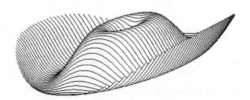

To view the peaks from the bottom, we'll replace the subroutine, **Func**, which calculates the function **Y(X,Y)** with the following subroutine:

```
Func:
a = SQR(X * X + Z2)
Y = -120 * COS(.05 * a) * EXP(-.01 * a)
RETURN
```

Now we get this picture:

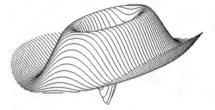

As you can see, the spike at the bottom is clearly distinguishable. If you remember, the first of the two algorithms didn't allow you to construct such a trough.

Using a Single Array

Here is a simplified version of this algorithm which requires the application of a single array but only draws bulging figures:

```
REM Drawing 3-D Figures using one array
REM \CHAP10\CH10_5.BAS

DECLARE FUNCTION z! (x!, y!)
SCREEN 9: CLS
DEFINT I
a = 155: k1 = 39
w = 75: k = .65
Xe0 = 320: Ye0 = 175
bm = 3.141 / 180
c = k * COS(w * bm)
s = k * SIN(w * bm)
dx = 2: dy = 7: af = a / 200
DIM H(640)
FOR I = 1 TO 640
    H(I) = -1E+30
NEXT I
FOR q = -160 TO 160 STEP dy
    y = q * af
    cq = Xe0 + c * q + .5
    sq = Ye0 + s * q + .5
    FOR m = -210 TO 210 STEP dx
        x = m * af
        Xe = INT(m + cq)
        Ye = INT(sq + z(m * af, y))
        IF m = -210 THEN
        f1 = 0: I = INT(Xe / dx)
        IF Ye >= H(I + 1) THEN F = 1: H(I + 1) = Ye
        x1 = Xe: y1 = Ye
```

```
        ELSE
        f2 = 0: I = INT(Xe / dx)
        IF Ye >= H(I + 1) THEN f2 = 1: H(I + 1) = Ye
        x2 = Xe: y2 = Ye
        IF f1 * f2 = 1 THEN LINE (x1, 350 - y1)-(x2, 350 - y2)
        x1 = x2: y1 = y2: f1 = f2
        END IF
    NEXT m
NEXT q

F$ = INPUT$(1)
END


FUNCTION z (x, y)
r = SQR(x ^ 2 + y ^ 2) * .017
z1 = (COS(r) - COS(3 * r) / 3 + COS(5 * r) / 5 - COS(7 * r) / 7)
z = 40 * z1 + 50
END FUNCTION
```

The figure that this produces is shown next. The corresponding math description is defined by **FUNCTION Z**:

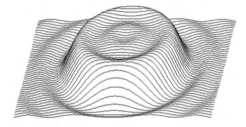

This gives a spatial interpretation of the waves resulting from the synthesis of odd harmonics - the sum of signals of the type **sin(k*x)/k**, where **k=1**, **3**, **5** and **7**.

Now we've familiarized ourselves with certain methods of constructing 3D surfaces and other geometric objects, using an algorithm which deletes invisible lines. But this topic isn't limited to the examples we've presented here: constructing 3D figures is one of today's most important and challenging problems. There'll always be a figure or mathematical surface which reveals the error of one or other of the algorithms for erasing invisible lines. So don't be surprised if, while you're experimenting, you expose their limitations.

Let's now take a look at adding dynamics to our 3D figures.

Moving and Rotating 3D Objects

Among the most complex aspects of 3D graphics is arbitrarily moving 3D figures in a space. This movement, however, can be broken down into a number of independent actions:

- ▲ A shift along the coordinate axes by incrementing the corresponding coordinates of every point.

- ▲ Changing the scale by multiplying the coordinates by the corresponding factors.

- ▲ Rotation around the coordinate axes by the relevant conversion of each point of the figure.

The first two operations are readily implemented and, in fact, have already been used in the previous examples. So, here we'll discuss the third and most complicated operation. It can be described with one 3x3 rotation matrix. If we consider rotation about just one coordinate axis at a time, we can write the rotation as the familiar 2D rotation matrix of the last chapter.

When rotating around the x-axis:

$$y = y' * \cos(\theta_x) - z' * \sin(\theta_x)$$
$$z = y' * \sin(\theta_x) + z' * \cos(\theta_x)$$

When rotating around the y-axis:

$$x = x' * \cos(\theta_y) - z' * \sin(\theta_y)$$
$$z = x' * \sin(\theta_y) + z' * \cos(\theta_y)$$

When rotating around the z-axis:

$$x = x' * \cos(\theta_z) - y' * \sin(\theta_z)$$
$$y = x' * \sin(\theta_z) + y' * \cos(\theta_z)$$

where θ_x, θ_y, and θ_z are the angles of rotation of the figure about the x-, y- and z-axes. Our next program lets you see the spatial rotation of a simple cube:

```
REM Rotating a 3D figure
REM \CHAP10\CH10_6.BAS

  DIM X(100), Y(100), Z(100)
  k = 1: sk = 15: pi = 3.141: alfa = .8
  kx = k * COS(alfa): ky = k * SIN(alfa): n = 0
  DEF FNX (a) = 320 + 1.5 * (sk * (X(a) + kx * Y(a)))
  DEF FNY (a) = 175 - sk * (Z(a) + ky * Y(a))

  DO
      READ Q
      IF Q = 1E+37 THEN EXIT DO
      n = n + 1
      X(n) = Q
      READ Y(n), Z(n)
  LOOP

  bx = 0: by = 0: bz = 0
  DO
      SCREEN 9: CLS
      RESTORE L1
      DO
          READ a
          IF a = 0 THEN EXIT DO
          READ b
          xe = FNX(a): ye = FNY(a)
```

```
        PSET (xe, ye)
        LINE -(FNX(b), FNY(b))
LOOP
M$ = INKEY$
' Quit program
IF M$ = "q" OR M$ = "Q" THEN END
' Move around x-axis
IF M$ = "x" OR M$ = "X" THEN
IF M$ = "x" THEN bx = bx - .001 ELSE bx = bx + .001
sx = SIN(bx): cx = COS(bx)
FOR i = 1 TO n
    y1 = Y(i): z1 = Z(i)
    Y(i) = y1 * cx + z1 * sx
    Z(i) = -y1 * sx + z1 * cx
NEXT
END IF
' Moves around y-axis
IF M$ = "y" OR M$ = "Y" THEN
IF M$ = "y" THEN by = by - .001 ELSE by = by + .001
sy = SIN(by): cy = COS(by)
FOR i = 1 TO n
    x1 = X(i): z1 = Z(i)
    X(i) = x1 * cy + z1 * sy
    Z(i) = -x1 * sy + z1 * cy
NEXT
END IF
' Moves around z-axis
IF M$ = "z" OR M$ = "Z" THEN
IF M$ = "z" THEN bz = bz - .001 ELSE bz = bz + .001
sz = SIN(bz): cz = COS(bz)
FOR i = 1 TO n
    x1 = X(i): y1 = Y(i)
    X(i) = x1 * cz + y1 * sz
    Y(i) = -x1 * sz + y1 * cz
NEXT
END IF
PRINT "x="; : PRINT USING "#.###"; bx;
PRINT "    y="; : PRINT USING "#.###"; by;
PRINT "    z="; : PRINT USING "#.###"; bz
PSET (20, 30): LINE -(20, 60): LINE -(70, 60)
LINE (20, 60)-(60, 35)
LOCATE 3, 2: PRINT "Z"
LOCATE 6, 9: PRINT "X"
LOCATE 3, 6: PRINT "Y"
SLEEP
LOOP

DATA -5,-5,-5,    -5,5,-5,    5,5,-5,    5,-5,-5
DATA -5,-5,5,    -5,5,5,    5,5,5,    5,-5,5
DATA 1e37

L1:
DATA 1,2,  2,3,  3,4,  4,1,  5,6,  6,7,  7,8,  8,5
DATA 1,5,  2,6,  3,7,  4,8,  1,6,  2,7,  2,5
DATA 0
```

The figure is specified by two data blocks in the list of **DATA** statements. The first data block defines the basic points of the figure (the coordinates X , Y and Z). The second block (after the label **L1**) contains the list of numbers of the double points which must be connected with line segments. The rotation angles θ_x, θ_y and θ_z are designated as **bx, by** and **bz** and can be changed by pressing the keys *x*, *y* and *z*, to decrease the angles, or by pressing these same keys while holding down *Shift* to increase the angles.

```
IF M$ = "x" OR M$ = "X" THEN                  'increase or decrease the angle
IF M$ = "x" THEN bx = bx - .001 ELSE bx = bx + .001
sx = SIN(bx): cx = COS(bx)                    'calculate angles
FOR i = 1 TO n
    y1 = Y(i): z1 = Z(i)                      'plot the Y points
    Y(i) = y1 * cx + z1 * sx
    Z(i) = -y1 * sx + z1 * cx
NEXT i
END IF
```

The following screenshot shows a view of the image created by this program:

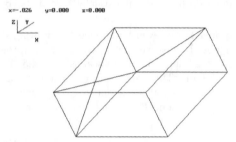

As you can see, the program constructs a cube. One of its sides is striped with two diagonal lines, and another with only one. This makes it easier to see the rotation.

Painting 3D Figures

Sometimes it's interesting to color-fill parts of a 3D image using the **PAINT** statement. This can be useful for creating depth-enhancing effects. Take a look at our following program which illustrates this method using a cone as an example:

```
REM Drawing a cone with painted rings
REM \CHAP10\CH10_7.BAS

SCREEN 9: R = 10: dH = 15: COLOR 0, 7
FOR I = 0 TO 15
    C = 15 - I
    LINE (320, 20)-(320 - 15 * R, 20 + 15 * dH), C
    LINE (320, 20)-(320 + 15 * R, 20 + 15 * dH), C
    CIRCLE (320, 20 + 15 * dH), R * 15, C, .27, 2.95, .2
    IF I <> 15 THEN CIRCLE (320, 20 + I * dH), R * I, C, .23, 2.9, .2
    PAINT (320, 24 + I * 13), C
NEXT I
```

```
CIRCLE (320, 20 + 15 * dH - 1), R * 15 - 2, 1, , , .2

END
```

The monochrome picture shown in a few seconds gives
you a rough idea of the picture constructed by the
program. To get the full effect, you need to see the picture
on a EGA or VGA display:

This example shows that painting even a simple 3D figure isn't easy, so drawing it in parts controls the
color of the tracing lines. The best way is to define the drawing color the same as the painting color. If
you don't do this, the paint usually spreads beyond the part you want colored.

This principle can even be applied for drawing dynamic
3D figures. This is exemplified by the demo program
TORUS.BAS supplied with QuickBasic 4.0/4.5. It works
well in QBasic. The program draws a multicolored
image of a torus rotating about its axis. A snapshot of
this image (in monochrome only) is shown here:

Unfortunately, we can't give you the program here as its listing, even without comments, is more than 20
pages, which gives you an idea of the complexity of a solution to a 3D graphics problem. If you can, have
a look at the program on your own - it contains a lot of useful external graphics procedures; for example,
for initializing the screen, checking the video adapter type, setting up the necessary screen resolution and
so on.

Color can be made one of the parameters of a 3D image. For example, a heated strip of metal can be
colored from dazzling blue to black - the color in this case telling us about the temperature of the strip.
Unfortunately, such programs, although based on QBasic features that we've already covered, are beyond
the scope of this book. The same goes for tinting and adding shadows to complicated 3D objects. There
are integrated graphic systems for doing this and you are better off using these for serious graphics tasks.

Drawing Contour Diagrams

The way the previous three-dimensional surfaces are represented isn't always the most convenient. If a
surface has a lot of peaks, they may obscure the background elements from view. Because of this, there's
another method of representing 3D surfaces: **contour diagrams** or equal-level curve diagrams. These are
extensively used in map drawing and for representing various math surfaces.

Imagine that a 3D surface **Z(X,Y)** is cut by a set of planes positioned at different heights (levels) and
parallel to the horizontal plane with the coordinates X and Y. The lines of intersection of the planes with
the 3D surface are referred to as equal level curves, and the projection of all this onto the horizontal plane
is the contour diagram. In order to distinguish the curves, you should draw them in different styles or
colors, or label them with their corresponding levels. The latter is impractical and difficult to implement
when there is a large number of curves.

It might seem that constructing a level diagram for the **Z(X,Y)** function isn't a great matter for concern - you draw a set of curves in a parametric form for different **Z = const** values. In general, however, finding the relationships in such a form isn't actually possible - the determination of **X** and **Y** under fixed **Z** often leads to transcendental expressions having no analytical solution. Because of this, you have to calculate a considerably large array of the points of the **Z(X,Y)** surface and build the level diagram by processing that array.

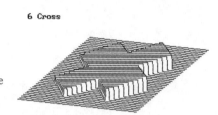

6 Cross

The program listed in a moment uses this approach, with every level curve drawn in a different color. The EGA graphics mode (screen number 9) supports up to 15 colors (without considering the background), which is usually more than enough for creating contour diagrams. Any more curves and the diagrams tend to lose their clarity because of the mass of complicated lines.

```
REM Drawing Contour 3-D diagrams
REM \CHAP10\CH10_8.BAS

DECLARE FUNCTION ZF! (X!, Y!)
SCREEN 9: CLS
DEFINT I
LOCATE 10, 34
PRINT "Please wait!"
'Calculate matrix Z for points 3-D surface Z(X,Y)
DIM H(15), X(60), XP(4), Y(60), YP(4), Z(60, 60)
NH = 15
NX = 0: Zmin = 1E+30: Zmax = -1E+30
FOR X0 = -5 TO 5 STEP .2
    NX = NX + 1: NY = 0: X(NX) = X0
    FOR Y0 = -5 TO 5 STEP .2
        NY = NY + 1: Y(NY) = Y0
        Z0 = ZF(X0, Y0): Z(NX, NY) = Z0
        IF Z0 < Zmin THEN Zmin = Z0
        IF Z0 > Zmax THEN Zmax = Z0
    NEXT Y0
NEXT X0
'Calculate values for heights H
M = Zmax - Zmin
FOR I = 1 TO NH
    H(I) = Zmin + .98 * (I - 1) * M / (NH - 1) + .01 * M
NEXT I
'Window define
CLS
LINE (0, 0)-(639, 328), 8, B
WINDOW SCREEN (X(1), Y(1))-(X(NX), 1.137 * Y(NY))
'Drawing contour lines
FOR IH = 1 TO NH
    HV = H(IH)
    FOR IX = 2 TO NX
        FOR IY = 2 TO NY
            IP = 0
            Z1 = HV - Z(IX - 1, IY - 1)    'Calculate
            Z2 = HV - Z(IX - 1, IY)        'height
            Z3 = HV - Z(IX, IY)            'differences
```

```
                    Z4 = HV - Z(IX, IY - 1)
                    IF SGN(Z1) <> SGN(Z2) THEN
                    IP = IP + 1: XP(IP) = X(IX - 1)
                    YP(IP) = Y(IY - 1) + (Y(IY) - Y(IY - 1)) * Z1 / (Z1 - Z2)
                    END IF
                    IF SGN(Z2) <> SGN(Z3) THEN
                    IP = IP + 1: YP(IP) = Y(IY)
                    XP(IP) = X(IX - 1) + (X(IX) - X(IX - 1)) * Z2 / (Z2 - Z3)
                    END IF
                    IF SGN(Z3) <> SGN(Z4) THEN
                    IP = IP + 1: XP(IP) = X(IX)
                    YP(IP) = Y(IY - 1) + (Y(IY) - Y(IY - 1)) * Z4 / (Z4 - Z3)
                    END IF
                    IF SGN(Z4) <> SGN(Z1) THEN
                    IP = IP + 1: YP(IP) = Y(IY - 1)
                    XP(IP) = X(IX - 1) + (X(IX) - X(IX - 1)) * Z1 / (Z1 - Z4)
                    END IF
                    IF IP = 2 THEN LINE (XP(1), YP(1))-(XP(2), YP(2)), IH
                NEXT IY
            NEXT IX
        NEXT IH
        LOCATE 25, 1
        FOR C = 1 TO NH
            COLOR C
            PRINT INT(100 * H(C)) / 100;
        NEXT C
        F$ = INPUT$(1)

        DEFSNG I
        FUNCTION ZF (X, Y)
        ZF = (X * Y) + (X * X)
        END FUNCTION
```

The first part of this program forms a surface matrix by calculating the values of the **Z(X,Y)** function for different **X = X0** and **Y = Y0**.

```
        'Calculate matrix Z for points 3-D surface Z(X,Y)
        DIM H(15), X(60), XP(4), Y(60), YP(4), Z(60, 60)
        NH = 15
        NX = 0: Zmin = 1E+30: Zmax = -1E+30
        FOR X0 = -5 TO 5 STEP .2
            NX = NX + 1: NY = 0: X(NX) = X0
            FOR Y0 = -5 TO 5 STEP .2
                NY = NY + 1: Y(NY) = Y0
                Z0 = ZF(X0, Y0): Z(NX, NY) = Z0
                IF Z0 < Zmin THEN Zmin = Z0
                IF Z0 > Zmax THEN Zmax = Z0
            NEXT Y0
        NEXT X0
```

To do this, we use a double nested loop. Because the calculation process takes a long time, the message "Please wait!" is displayed. During the course of the calculations, the minimum, **Zmin**, and the maximum, **Zmax**, values of the **Z(X,Y)** function are determined. After that, the number, **NH**, of level curves is defined in the range of heights from **Zmin** to **Zmax**, and the array **H(I)** is defined where **I** changes from **1** to **NH**. At this point, the preparation for plotting the graph is finished.

```
'Calculate values for heights H
M = Zmax - Zmin
FOR I = 1 TO NH
    H(I) = Zmin + .98 * (I - 1) * M / (NH - 1) + .01 * M
NEXT I
```

When the heights are calculated, there's a slight compression. For instance, if the **Z** values of a function range between **-1** to **+1**, the levels of the contour lines are defined in a more limited range, -0.98 to +0.98. A mental rounding off of the levels causes an error of about two percent, which is far less than the error resulting from the actual determination of the height of a point using a contour diagram.

The construction of a graph begins with the definition of a graphics window and the creation of a boundary. Further operations are performed in the main loop with loop counter **IH**. Using a double nested loop, the coordinates **(IX,IY)** of the points of the numeric matrix are defined, which specify the difference between the height, **HV**, of a given level curve and the values of the **Z(IX,IY)** function.

```
IF SGN(Z1) <> SGN(Z2) THEN
IP = IP + 1: XP(IP) = X(IX - 1)
YP(IP) = Y(IY - 1) + (Y(IY) - Y(IY - 1)) * Z1 / (Z1 - Z2)
END IF
```

These differences are the values of the variables **Z1**, **Z2**, **Z3** and **Z4** which characterize the position and dimensions of an elementary cell of the 3D surface. Processing them according to the algorithm above determines whether a specified level curve passes through the current cell of the 3D surface, and which **X** and **Y** coordinates characterize its projection onto the horizontal plane of the coordinate system.

If the signs of the variables **Z1**, **Z2**, **Z3** and **Z4** are identical (which is easily determined using the **SGN** function), the given curve doesn't pass through the current cell at all and isn't drawn. If the signs are different, the curve will be built with the current **X** and **Y** coordinates assigned to the variables **XP(IP)** and **Y(IP)**, after their calculation from the linear interpolation formulae. If a specified cell is too small, the level curve will either not pass though it at all, or will intersect it only once. Because of this, the constructed level curves may contain gaps. If a cell is intersected at two points, a line section connecting them is built.

In this way, the algorithm has a built-in error associated with the interpretation of a curve specified by an array of discrete points. So, it isn't surprising that some lines (typically near the extremes or far removed from the center of the figure) may appear to be dashed or dotted. This resolution problem may affect the images of small figures (closed contour lines) in the form of circles or ellipses by making them look like irregular rectangles. However, most of the level curves are constructed quite well.

Even the appearance of level curves can offer useful information. For example, they enable non-linearity, the steepness of slopes, etc. However, in general, it's necessary to know the values of the levels for each curve to be able to use the contour diagram for quantitative estimates. In this program, each line is drawn in its own color and the rounded-off level values are displayed in the form of a numeric string under the diagram. Each number is printed in the respective color of the level curve. As a result, we get a colorful contour diagram defined by the external function **Z(X,Y)** of the surface displayed on the EGA screen.

The following figure shows the level diagram for the surface **Z(X,Y) = COS (X)*COS(Y)**. Unfortunately, the drawing is in monochrome - all the colors appear as black and the background is white. By referring to the colors of the curves and to the level values, we can judge their locations fairly accurately:

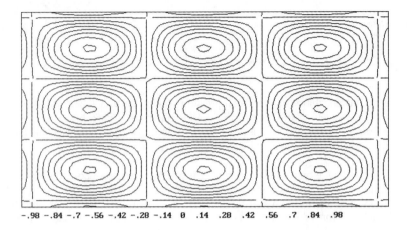

-.98 -.84 -.7 -.56 -.42 -.28 -.14 0 .14 .28 .42 .56 .7 .84 .98

This figure, however, shows the contour diagram for the function `Z(X,Y) = X*Y+X^2`:

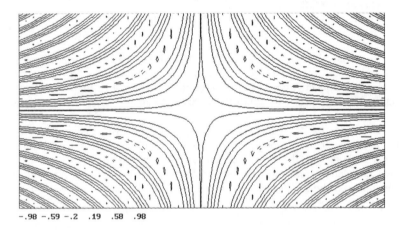

-.98 -.59 -.2 .19 .58 .98

This diagram gives you an idea of how much the appearance of a contour diagram depends on the defined function `Z(X,Y)`. You can modify the above program in different ways; for example, to specify a non-linear relationship for the level curves, or to enter the level values in dialog mode using the **INPUT** statement.

This really takes the topic of contour diagrams as far as we can go for our purposes, without adding dynamic aspects, such as real-time manipulation, to the data. This brings us neatly onto out next subject, ray casting, which creates a first-person perspective that can be manipulated in real-time.

Dynamic Ray Casting

We are hearing the obscure term **ray casting** more and more these days. We associate it with the technological wizardry and relatively new phenomena that we see in leading-edge games like Doom. Because of its recent effect on the games industry, you might think that it's incredibly complicated and difficult to do - something a green-skinned computer geek with a passion for twisted mathematics might invent. This simply isn't true, not that I have anything against Martian computer geeks. In its basic form, ray casting is very simple, and, really, you only need a good, firm grasp of basic trigonometry and the two dimensional coordinate system to get results. This doesn't mean that it's easy - just that it isn't impossible.

We are going to build a simple ray caster (**\CHAP10\CHAP10_9.BAS**) from the ground up. At this stage, it won't be all that fast as I have kept it simple just to make it easier to understand. You can re-work it to lightning speeds when you get to grips with what's going on.

If you haven't looked at the demo program yet, fire it up! Look at how the walls roll around, try to get a feel for the environment. Notice how the walls are all at ninety degree angles. Use the *Tab* key to bring up the information map which, although simple, contains valuable information. Here's a typical screen from the program:

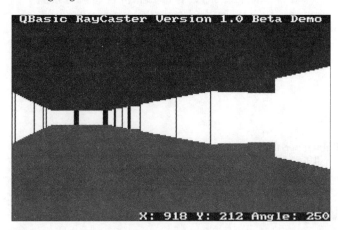

Once the craving for building the next Doom has begun, read on. Ray casting is very exciting and very innovative. You can do all sorts of different things with the basic engine, and truly make your ray casting engine scream. So let's get casting!

What Exactly Is a Ray Caster?

This is very hard to describe in words, since all explanations feature a host of visual-related adjectives. So, try to create a picture in your mind whilst you're reading.

A ray caster creates a three dimensional image from a map or grid. It does this by shooting out an arc of lines from your field of vision (which we'll describe later on). To see this, take this book and sit directly facing a wall. Place your arm directly forward and move it, say, thirty degrees to the left. Imagine a line coming straight out of your arm and continuing until it hits something (the wall right in front of you). This, we will call a **ray** or **beam cast**. The position that it hits is called an **intersection**. Imagine that all you can see of this ray cast is a vertical pixel width of the wall from the ceiling to the floor. All you can see, then, is a single strip of the wall. If you were to continue moving to the right, casting out beams as you go, you would cover your entire field of vision, which is an arc.

By reassembling the vertical strips on screen, according to size, we are able to create an image. This is what is seen on the screen of the computer. Be sure to have a good look at this diagram as all this is very visual and a picture really does, in this case, speak a thousand words:

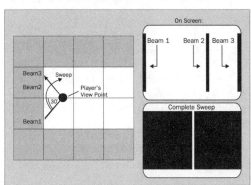

The diagram splits the two walls that you see, just like the included program that you've just run. That is the central line in the 'complete sweep' diagram.

Field of Vision

The Field of Vision, or FOV, is the length of the arc that we can see. The smaller the length, the narrower the field of vision.

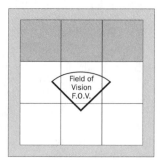

Remember that choosing large lengths allows you to see more than you would normally, and choosing small lengths reduces the view below normal level. I like a sixty degree field of vision as it gives a natural perspective on things.

Why Use a Grid?

A ray caster places the walls of your environment into a grid. The reason for this is simple: time and space. If we were to store a 1024 by 1024 world, with each point being a vertical strip of a wall, and, say, 64 pixels of 256 possible colors, we would require a machine with around 16384 megabytes of memory. I think you'll agree that this isn't practical. If we were to put our world into, say, a 16 by 16 grid, with a single 64 by 64 wall texture type, we would end up with the entire overhead of just 4 kilobytes.

Of course, we won't have just one wall type, but you can still see that it's just impossible to do without some kind of grid. For our ray caster, we will have a 16 by 16 world, with each wall being 64 pixels by 64 pixels. Also, when we place the world on a grid, tracing out the light rays, we only need to check a few squares to see if it's intersected, as opposed to checking a possible 1024 squares on a single cast. This also helps our slow QBasic interpreter to get through the horde of calculations that little bit quicker.

Implementing a General Ray Caster

The generic ray casting algorithm works as follows:

1 Start at the left of the computer screen and the left of the field of vision.

2 Cast out the a ray and its intersection with the closest wall.

3 Calculate the distance to the wall.

4 If the distance is great, draw a small strip for the wall, if it's close, draw a large strip.

5 Repeat steps 1-3, moving towards the right, until we have cast out our field of vision.

6 Display on screen (*fast!!!!*).

Let's now take a look at some of the issues that we come across whilst developing this engine.

Angles

Remember that we place all the vertical strips on the screen. The left part of the screen is 30 degrees to the left of our viewing path, and the right part of the screen is 30 degrees to the right, totaling 60 degrees across the screen. We then need to cast a total number of beams equal to the width of our screen. Most ray casters today are written for graphics mode 13h, therefore there are 320 beams for 320 columns on the video screen.

Because of this need, let's make a new unit. We'll call it a 'Beamie' whose plural is 'Beamies'.

Given that there are 360 degrees in a circle, 60 degrees splits this circle 6 times, and 60 degrees field of vision sweep out 320 pictures on pixel, there are at total of 6 * 320 possible beams to be cast in a complete circle. This number, 1920, is our Beamies unit, its angle equivalent being 360. Therefore, the current ray cast can be calculated from the following:

$$Beamies = Angle * (1920/360)$$

We can, of course, go the other way and calculate the angle from the Beamies unit with the following:

$$Angle = Beamies * (360/1920)$$

The general line equation we will use is $Y = MX$.

Remember that the slope of a line is defined by its rise over its run, or Y Delta / X Delta. When we deal with ray casting, we need to know the slope of a line. How can we get the slope? We use the tangent to obtain the quotient of the slope, and do a **CASE** statement in order to get the correct sign:

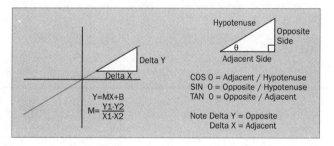

Once we have a line, we need to be able to use this line to scan for a wall hit on the map grid. We do this by manipulating the line equation. There are two types of hits: a hit on a vertical boundary of the grid called X intersection, and a hit on a horizontal boundary of a grid, the Y intersection. Because we don't know exactly where a wall is, we really need to test both if they exist. Once we've found an X intersection with a wall and a Y intersection with a wall, we decide which one to render by how close it is to the player. Take a look at the next figure.

Stepping (Rise & Run Tables)

Once we have found out our first intersection, we're able to compute the other intersections, step-by-step, either X Step or Y Step. We simply add them respectively to our old scanning position in order to calculate the new scanning position more quickly. For the X Step Distance, this is the Inverse Slope * Square Size while for the Y Step Distance this is Slope * Square Size:

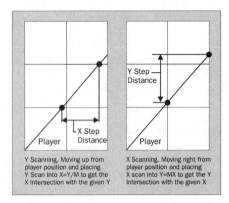

Y Scanning, Moving up from
player position and placing
Y Scan into X=Y/M to get the
X intersection with the given Y

X Scanning, Moving right from
player position and placing
X scan into Y=MX to get the Y
Intersection with the given X

This makes sense, especially in Y Step distance, because Slope = Rise / Run. Therefore, Slope * Run = Rise.

Computing Distance

Because we draw a larger or smaller vertical strip in relation to how far away our intersections are, we need to know how to calculate this distance. We could use the Pythagorean theorem, where Hypotenuse = Sqrt((X*X)+(Y*Y)), but calculating a square root isn't recommended as it takes up far too much computer time.

We can get around this processor-hog by finding out how to calculate the information by another means. We know that the cosine is the opposite/hypotenuse and that the inverse cosine is represented by the hypotenuse/opposite side. So, if we know the opposite side, we can multiply it by the cosine to get the angle. This is essentially just the calculation of the distance to an X intersection. The two formulas are as follows:

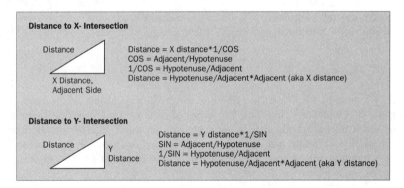

Distance to X- Intersection

Distance

X Distance,
Adjacent Side

Distance = X distance*1/COS
COS = Adjacent/Hypotenuse
1/COS = Hypotenuse/Adjacent
Distance = Hypotenuse/Adjacent*Adjacent (aka X distance)

Distance to Y- Intersection

Distance

Y
Distance

Distance = Y distance*1/SIN
SIN = Adjacent/Hypotenuse
1/SIN = Hypotenuse/Adjacent
Distance = Hypotenuse/Adjacent*Adjacent (aka Y distance)

Scaling

Once we have the distance, we need to calculate the actual distance according to the size scale. Since the further away the wall is, the smaller it is, the scale is 1/distance. 1/distance works but, to get more realistic drawings, I use 5000/distance. It's a matter of implementation and it only affects how much space is taken up on screen and its appearance.

Fudge Factors

The initial problem with a ray caster is slope. If we have a line straight up, it has infinite slope. To get around this, we fudge the values of the tan function, placing a very small error, by adding the small number, 1E-32.

The second problem is distance. When we look at something from the corner of our eye, the light travels further than if we looked at it straight on. The computer interprets this as being further way, but we don't. We need to multiply out the inverse cosine relative angle that we are casting (straight forward is zero in relative terms), to make all the distances equal to the center distance:

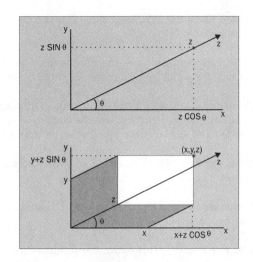

Simple Speed Issues

The program is slow. There are many things we can do to improve the speed, a few of which I have implemented in the program already. The video is rendered by an assembly language routine which makes the video updates very fast. We use previously built tables, such as trig tables, for anything we can.

We also have a factor called video quality. When video quality is 0, it renders the screen normally while, if it is 1, it skips every second ray. In the second case, when the screen is rendered, it doubles up on itself, so the light ray that wasn't cast is also shown. A video quality of 2 casts only every third ray and grabs the two missing ones from its closest neighbors. For this reason, as we skip more and more, the quality decreases and the resolution deteriorates proportionally. The positive side to this is a much improved frame rate!

Discussion of the Program Code

Let's take a look at the individual functions and procedures:

FUNCTION get.key% ()   When this is called, it gets a key from the user. It will accept forward, backward, left and right of both keypads, plus the *Escape* and *Tab* characters.

FUNCTION move.player% (X%,Y%,angle%,KeyPress%)   This function moves the player's position, passed to it as X, Y and the angle, following a certain key press.

SUB intro ()   This is a simple introduction routine. It describes the program and gives other start up information.

SUB load.asm.routine ()   To increase speed, we have made use of an assembly language routine. This routine is stored in binary format in the file **VIDEOASM.BIN**. This routine draws a vertical strip in pure assembly language. We will discuss the assembly language routine for this later in this chapter.

SUB display.map (X%,Y%,angle%) This procedure displays the map.

SUB build.tables ()   This procedure creates all the informational tables. These tables are used to cut down on critical calculation time. By storing a table of, say, the cosine values of 1920 Beamies, we never have to calculate the processor-hungry cosine again.

SUB display.hud (X%,Y%,angle%) This displays the "Head Up Display" located at the top and bottom of the screen.

SUB load.world () This procedure loads the ASCII world into its array. The wall character is X and you can edit the world by editing the file **WORLD.DAT**.

SUB cast.video (X AS INTEGER,Y AS INTEGER,Vang AS INTEGER) This is the meat and core of the engine. X, Y and Vang, are the respective current coordinates and viewing angle of the player. It casts the video and stores it into an array to be drawn later.

SUB update.screen () This calls the assembly language routine to draw everything to the screen in one huge, fast screen blast.

SUB get.parameters (X%,Y%,angle%) This subroutine gets the parameters that the user sets before he or she starts.

SUB end.message () This subroutine displays end of program information.

Constants

The constants used in the program are as follows:

ASMFILE is the name of the assembly language video routine file.

WORLDFILE is the name of the world data file.

MAX.ASM.ROUTINE.SIZE is the maximum size of the assembly routine.

PI is the defined value of pi.

NoZero is the tiny number added to fudge around the slope going to infinity.

SquareSize is the size in units of a square. This is 64.

EscapeChar,TabChar are the character sequences for the **get.key** routine.

MaxSlope is the maximum amount of slope allowed. A slope beyond 30 would exceed the map in one square, so we don't need it.

MaxScale is the maximum amount allowed on screen. In our case it's set at 100 units.

True,False are the QBasic constants. When a condition is evaluated, if it's true, it has a non-zero value and, if false, it becomes evaluated as 0. It's also possible to do an **IF True** then **BEEP** or an **IF -1** then **BEEP**.

WallChar is the character (**X**) used in the ASCII file to denote a wall.

WorldWide,WorldHeight are the dimensions of the grid world.

CordWide,CordHigh are the dimensions of the actual world.

MinWorld,WorldSize.MinCordTable,MaxCordTable are used for numbering in the world coordinate tables. Position one is 1***SquareSize**. Position 2, is 2***SquareSize** etc.

ViewArc,HalfViewArc are the degrees of our viewing arc, also known as FOV.

MinDeg,MaxDeg,MinBeam,MaxBeam are the maximum and minimum angles.

`MinX,MinY,MaxX,MaxY,HalfX` are the screen coordinates.

`ScanUp,ScanDown,ScanLeft,ScanRight.NoScan` are constants associated to the ray scanning direction.

`Forward,BackWard,Left,Right,TabHit` are constants associated with the pressing of a key.

`VideoConst` is the video constant.

`WallColor,EdgeColor,SkyColor,FloorColor` are the default colors.

`DefaultX = 95,DefaultY` are the default starting positions.

`MapViewmRendView` are the numbers associated to seeing the map or 3D picture.

`DefaultVQ` is the default video quality.

`DefaultAngle` is the starting angle.

`DefaultAngleShift,DefaultMove` are how far `move.player%` moves you in relation to one key press.

By playing around with all these aspects of our program, via this set of suitably named constants, you can, with very little knowledge of the inner workings, begin to build your own personalized environments.

Data Structures

The following data structures are used by our program:

`DrawBeam` is the array that contains the assembly language routine.

`AngleToBeams,BeamsToAngle` are the conversion arrays for Beamies and Angles.

`TanTable,CosTable,SinTable` are the trigonometric tables.

`InvCosTable,InvSinTable,InvTanTable` are the inverse trigonometric tables.

`WorldCordTable` is the table where the world coordinate table `WCT(1)` is 64, `WCT(2)` is 128, `WCT(3)` is 192, e.g. `WCT(n)*Square Size`.

`ViewFixTable` is the fix table coordinates.

`YStepTable,XStepTable` are the steps for next intersections.

`WorldData` is the array holding the world's data.

`Videoplot` is an array, 0-319, holding the size of each strip.

`VideoColor` is an array, 0-319, holding the color of each strip.

`VideoQuality` is the quality mode for rendering.

`ViewMode` is set to either Map or Rendering mode.

The Assembly Language Routine

The assembly language routine is what allows us to draw the screen very quickly. With this routine alone, I managed to get a total of about 30 frames per second on a non-local bus computer. Implementation is via the **CALL ABSOLUTE** function which we dealt with in Chapter 4; this function is one of the handiest things around when dealing with assembly language. Don't worry if you don't have much (or indeed any) idea of how this works - you would need to study assembler for an age to fully understand all the following material. You can still get the general drift of what is happening, so don't be put off - it's well worth reading.

Note that you're not obliged to use assembly language routines to build a ray caster - they just make it a lot faster.

Just as we learned back in Chapter 4 - Memory, Data and Machine Code, we have saved the **VIDEOASM.BIN** separately to keep the routine external to the program, although we could have used internal **DATA** statements just as easily.

When QBasic calls a routine, it pushes the return segment and address onto the stack, followed by each of the offsets of the parameters. To access these, we move the **sp** (stack pointer) into the **bp** (bit pointer) register so that, when we access what is on the stack, we don't corrupt it. **bp** is also important, so we save it. To prevent code trouble with 386s, we have manipulated the **ds** register and we save that as well. Note that, when we place something on the stack, after saving the top of stack pointer to **bp**, we don't need to worry about it because **bp** doesn't reflect the change.

The **ax**, and **bx** hold 'switch points'. When we draw the sliver from the top down, we will hit the wall (switch point a), then hit the floor (switch point b). These are held in **ax**, and **dx** respectively, and are calculated by 100-scale and 100+scale, where 100 is the center of the screen (64 hex).

Here's the assembly from the file, **VIDEOASM.BIN**, which draws the vertical strips quicker than you can say "eek!":

```
PUSH    BP              Save BP, by placing it on the stack
MOV     BP,SP           Get the stack pointer
PUSH    DS              Save the data segment
MOV     BX,[BP+0A]      Get the location of the first parameter,
                        skipping the return (4) skipping the saved bp(2)
                        and ds (2) and getting it's own (2) which is 10.
                        [Floor]
MOV     BX,[BX]         Get the value into bx from the location.
PUSH    BX              Push the value of the first parameter on the stack.
MOV     BX,[BP+0C]      Get the location of the second parameter. [Wall]
MOV     BX,[BX]         Get the value from the location.
PUSH    BX              Push the value of the parameter to stack.
MOV     BX,[BP+0E]      Get the location of the third parameter. [Sky]
MOV     BX,[BX]         Get the value from the location.
PUSH    BX              Push the value of the parameter to stack
MOV     BX,[BP+06]      Get the value of the fourth parameter [Column]
MOV     BX,[BX]         Get the value from the location.
MOV     DI,BX           Move into data index.  This is the screen
                        offset, since we want to draw starting our
                        column.
MOV     BX,[BP+08]      Get the location of the scale.
MOV     BX,[BX]         Get value of scale.
MOV     AX,0064         Move 100 into AX.
SUB     AX,BX           AX gets 100-scale (first switch point).
ADD     BX,+64          BX gets 100+scale.
MOV     DX,BX           DX,gets second switch point.
MOV     CX,A000         CX, gets the address of the video segment.
```

MOV	DS,CX	DS, gets the address of the video segment. Any data now goes there.
POP	BX	Pop the first color (Sky)
MOV	CX,0000	Move 0 into cx, total number of drawings.

Start:

CMP	CX,AX	Are we at the first switch point?
JZ	0151	If yes, jump to 0151 (Toggle A)
CMP	CX,DX	Are we at the second switch point?
JZ 0154		If yes, jump to 0154 (Toggle B)
CMP	CX,00C8	Are we at the bottom of the screen? (200 pixels drawn?)
JZ	014C	Jump to done.
INC	CX	Another pixel, add one.
MOV	[DI],BL	Draw pixel.
ADD	DI,0140	We are now 320 pixels left from original position. (1 down)
JMP	0135	Jump back up to start.

Done:

POP	DS	Restore Data Segment
POP	BP	Restore BP
RETF	000A	Return far, popping parameters off the stack before return address

Toggle A:

POP	BX	Get Wall color.
JMP	0139	Go back to start.

Toggle B:

POP	BX	Get floor color.
JMP	013DG	Go back to start.

Whenever you call this routine, you must *always* remember to change the default segment to the location of the array:

```
DEF  SEG=VARSEG(DrawBeam(1))
```

Otherwise, you might end up trying to run data, not code, and crashing all your hard work.

The Cast Video Routine

The first thing that the cast video routine does is to get the first angle we need to render, 30 (half FOV) to the left (-). It figures out which square we are in on the grid (PlayerY, and PlayerX) and sets the video column, rendered to the width of the screen:

```
        VangRend = Vang - AngleToBeams(HalfViewArc)
        PlayerY = Y \ SquareSize
        PlayerX = X \ SquareSize
        VideoCol = maxX
```

Then, we make a loop from the previously calculated angle to the angle + the FOV (view arc). When the video quality is set low, the rays themselves skip due to the step **VideoQuality**:

```
    FOR Ray = VangRend TO VangRend + AngleToBeams(ViewArc) - 1 ↵
        STEP VideoQuality
```

We render the angle **RayCast**, not **Ray**. If **RayCast** is negative, we flip it around (e.g. 360 and 0 are the same) so that it isn't negative any longer:

```
    RayCast = Ray
    IF RayCast < MinBeam THEN RayCast = RayCast + MaxBeam
    IF RayCast > MaxBeam THEN RayCast = RayCast - MaxBeam
```

Because we are commonly using slope, we will store them in inverse slope for our angle:

```
    Slope! = TanTable(RayCast)
    InvSlope! = InvTanTable(RayCast)
```

RayHitY and **RayHitX** tell us whether we've found an X intersection or Y intersection and set them to **false**. If they are **true** later, we know that an intersection was found:

```
    RayHitY = false: RayHitX = false
```

When slope increases in size, it's possible to exceed an integer too quickly, even when our coordinates should be 1024 in size. So, if our slope is too large, we clip it down a little:

```
    IF Slope! > MaxSlope THEN Slope! = MaxSlope
```

The following **CASE** statement is used to decide the scanning direction. If we are scanning right, we check the square just to the right of our first intersection and so forth:

```
    SELECT CASE RayCast

    REM *** Right ***
    CASE AngleToBeams(0), AngleToBeams(360)
    DirX = ScanRight
    DirY = NoScan

    REM *** Up and Right ***
    CASE AngleToBeams(1) TO AngleToBeams(89)
    DirX = ScanRight
    DirY = ScanUp

    REM *** Up ***
    CASE AngleToBeams(90)
    DirX = NoScan
    DirY = ScanUp
```

```
REM *** Up and Left ***
CASE AngleToBeams(91) TO AngleToBeams(179)
DirX = ScanLeft
DirY = ScanUp

REM **** Left ***
CASE AngleToBeams(180)
DirX = ScanLeft
DirY = NoScan

REM *** Down and Left ***
CASE AngleToBeams(181) TO AngleToBeams(269)
DirX = ScanLeft
DirY = ScanDown

REM *** Down ***
CASE AngleToBeams(270)
DirX = NoScan
DirY = ScanDown

REM *** Down and Right ***
CASE AngleToBeams(271) TO AngleToBeams(359)
DirX = ScanRight
DirY = ScanDown

END SELECT
```

This is our first render case. If we are scanning up, we want to start at our current position. If we are scanning downwards, we want to start at the position 1 down from us, so we boost our position by one:

```
REM *** Render Case ***
REM *** Scan for Y Intercect ***

IF DirY THEN
IF DirY = ScanDown THEN
ScanY = PlayerY + 1
ELSE
ScanY = PlayerY
END IF
```

This is the first intersection with the closest square:

```
XInterSectY = (Y - WorldCordTable(ScanY)) * InvSlope!
XInterSectY = XInterSectY + X
```

Next, is the main loop. It figures out where **Y** is, this is our scanner. We then figure out the square to look at, located in the grid. If we are out of the grid, we exit the **DO**, not finding a wall. If we find a wall, the **RayHitY** expression becomes evaluated to true, and the **DO** is exited.

```
RayHitY = WorldData(GridY, GridX) = WallChar IF RayHitY THEN EXIT DO
```

Given that we are not out of the world and haven't yet found a wall, we simply add the step, and loop:

```
      DO
          YInterSectY = WorldCordTable(ScanY)

          IF DirY = ScanDown THEN
              GridY = (YInterSectY \ SquareSize)
          ELSE
              GridY = (YInterSectY \ SquareSize) - 1
          END IF

          IF DirX = ScanLeft THEN
              GridX = (XInterSectY \ SquareSize)
          ELSE
              GridX = (XInterSectY \ SquareSize)
          END IF

          IF (GridX < 0 OR GridX > WorldWide) THEN EXIT DO
          IF (GridY < 0 OR GridY > WorldHeight) THEN EXIT DO
          RayHitY = WorldData(GridY, GridX) = WallChar

          IF RayHitY THEN EXIT DO
          ScanY = ScanY + DirY
          XInterSectY = INT(XInterSectY + YStepTable(RayCast))
      LOOP
END IF
```

The scan for X intersect is nearly identical to the scan for Y intersect:

```
REM *** Scan for X Intercect ***

IF DirX THEN
IF DirX = ScanRight THEN
ScanX = PlayerX + 1
ELSE
ScanX = PlayerX
END IF

YInterSectX = (X - WorldCordTable(ScanX)) * Slope!
YInterSectX = YInterSectX + Y
DO
XInterSectX = WorldCordTable(ScanX)

IF DirY = ScanDown THEN
    GridY = (YInterSectX \ SquareSize)
ELSE
    GridY = (YInterSectX \ SquareSize)
END IF

IF DirX = ScanLeft THEN
    GridX = (XInterSectX \ SquareSize) - 1
ELSE
    GridX = (XInterSectX \ SquareSize) '+ 1
END IF

IF (GridX < 0 OR GridX > WorldWide) THEN EXIT DO
IF (GridY < 0 OR GridY > WorldHeight) THEN EXIT DO
    RayHitX = WorldData(GridY, GridX) = WallChar
```

```
        IF RayHitX THEN EXIT DO
            ScanX = ScanX + DirX
            YInterSectX = INT(YInterSectX + XStepTable(RayCast))
        LOOP
    END IF
```

Now, we have three possible cases. We hit two walls, calculate the distance, decide which is closer and turn the other off:

```
REM *** If there are 2 walls then turn one off ***

IF RayHitX AND RayHitY THEN
DistanceX! = ABS((XInterSectX% - X) * (InvCosTable(RayCast)))
DistanceY! = ABS((YInterSectY% - Y) * (InvSinTable(RayCast)))

IF DistanceX! > DistanceY! THEN
    RayHitX = false
ELSE
    RayHitY = false
END IF
```

Here, we calculate the distance on the X intersection:

```
ELSEIF RayHitX THEN
    DistanceX! = ABS((XInterSectX% - X) * (InvCosTable(RayCast)))
```

And also on the Y intersection:

```
ELSEIF RayHitY THEN
    DistanceY! = ABS((YInterSectY% - Y) * (InvSinTable(RayCast)))
END IF
```

Now that we have the distance calculated, we place it into the video array. Note that, if it's close to an edge of the grid (i.e. +1 or -1 or actually on it) we change our default coloring in order to create dividers between the walls. If the intersection is on the grid, it will be divisible by 64 without remainder. Once again, we are using very handy Boolean expressions to do this. Note, also, that scale is the video constant / distance:

```
REM *** Plug into video buffer ***

IF RayHitX THEN
Scale! = VideoConst / DistanceX!
EdgeHit = (YInterSectX% MOD SquareSize = 0)
EdgeHit = EdgeHit OR ((YInterSectX% + DirX) MOD SquareSize = 0)
EdgeHit = EdgeHit OR ((YInterSectX% - DirX) MOD SquareSize = 0)

ELSEIF RayHitY THEN
Scale! = VideoConst / DistanceY!
EdgeHit = (XInterSectY% MOD SquareSize = 0)
EdgeHit = EdgeHit OR ((XInterSectY% + DirY) MOD SquareSize = 0)
EdgeHit = EdgeHit OR ((XInterSectY% - DirY) MOD SquareSize = 0)
ELSE
Scale! = 0
END IF
```

379

```
VideoPlot(VideoCol) = INT((Scale! * ViewFixTable(VideoCol)))
IF VideoPlot(VideoCol) > MaxScale THEN VideoPlot(VideoCol) = MaxScale

IF EdgeHit THEN
    VideoColor(VideoCol) = EdgeColor
ELSE
    VideoColor(VideoCol) = WallColor
END IF
```

Then we go to the next video column:

```
VideoCol = VideoCol - VideoQuality
```

And, finally, the ray loop ends:

```
NEXT Ray
END SUB
```

Above and Beyond, Improving the Ray Caster.

As you can see, there are a number of ways to improve our ray caster. It's very simple and has been written so that you can understand how it works. Now, we can talk about improvements.

Speed Improvements

To increase the speed:

1 Eliminate all the floating point math. You could do this by making the system 10* larger than normal (eliminating the last two decimal digits), then dividing at the end.

2 Make the routines in assembler. This is very hard and frustrating but, when you are looking for that extra zap, and you know you have made the QBasic code as best you can, put it into assembler. This is obviously not the answer for bad code, just for code that can't be made to run faster any other way.

3 Improve the scanning algorithm by making it more compact.

We will talk about optimizing your programs further in Chapter 12 - Game Development.

Textures

The most effective improvement would be to draw a texture instead of a simple line. To do this, we would use the grid to hold not just a wall, but a wall texture type. Then, depending on its offset to the intersection (i.e. where the ray hit the box in relation to the box), we would end up with a part of the bit map to draw. Drawing a scaled line is not difficult either. If we wanted to place a source of 64 pixels to 32 pixels, we would end up with a .5 ratio, i.e. 64/32. Now, we would simply scan the source image and place the pixel into the **int(new array*.5)**, then draw on top of approximately half the pixels. This is a very simple re-scaling system.

Lighting

This is what made Doom so much of an advancement over Wolfenstein 3D. The first lighting effects are palette-based and change the colors of the default so that our video looks red or green, adding a touch of realism.

The second, is the selection of the colors in the first place. When we get close to a wall, it gets brighter doesn't it? How could they do this when we only have 256 colors to work with? Look at this simple table:

1-16	Very Bright Colors
17-32	Fairly Bright Colors
33-48	Still Bright Colors
49-64	Bright Colors
64-80	Normal coloring
81-96	Shadowy
96-112	Very Shadowy
113-128	Fairly Dark
129-144	Very Dark
145-255	System

As you can see, we can create a palette with lighting inside so that, when approaching a wall, we would change the color rendered. If our bit map says 'light green', we might have a dark light green, a very dark light green, etc. As for the image, we would create a distance chart for the wall, so that, if we were within a specified distance, we would see bright colors. The further away we get, the darker the colours. When we take lighting into effect, the results can be staggering.

Doors

When we use doors, we are causing a wall to become transparent. What we need to do is to integrate into our scanner a special test for a transparent wall. This test, if true, would continue to the next wall, past our transparent one. Once it has dealt with the transparent wall, it would render the new wall (door) on top, drawing everything except for transparent pixels.

This type of thing is naturally recursive - door to door to door to door. If you implement this, be sure to do some reading up on recursive programming. It may seem impossible at first but, once you get the hang of a recursion routine, you'll see how simple it is.

Well, I have certainly left you with a lot to chew on. Although our program is simple, I think you'll agree that it has given you an excellent basis from which to delve further into 3D environments. You could even write your own killer Doom engine!

Unfortunately, the more advanced topics, such as adding ceilings and floors, are too much to cover here. (A hint is to look at everything sideways!) Take the demo and play around with everything that we've presented. The best discoveries are usually accidental. If you do build anything great, or notice something neat, be sure to let us know! May your quests be great, and best of all, fun!

Summary

In this chapter, we've discussed the main ideas for constructing realistic 3D images. We've tried to include both the simplest methods of drawing 3D figures and also the implementation of fairly complicated algorithms for creating mathematical surfaces using the algorithms that delete invisible lines.

As far as it's possible, given the confines of this book, we've tackled some of the complicated aspects of 3D graphics such as the painting of, the perspective representation of, and the spatial movement of complex objects.

We've also shown you how to create a unique virtual 3D world with the ray caster. We've given you the chance to break into this remarkable new technique with amazing ease and have shown how, with a little further thought, you could take graphics into seldom-charted regions.

The whole subject of 3D graphics is gigantic and we couldn't possibly cover every area here, but, hopefully, we've whetted your appetite for further study and development.

This Is Sound

Let's say it before we go any further - the PC was designed as a business machine and not as a tool for chart-toppers. This is why the PC speaker can't compete with your stereo. Now that we've said it, let's see exactly what it *can* do.

In this chapter, we'll start at the bottom - a beep. Then we'll alter the frequency and duration of the notes. We'll get to grips with changing octaves, producing half notes, sharps and flats, and sophisticated sounds with a touch of legato and staccato. You can't call a tune a tune if it hasn't got a melody, so we'll show you how to create one of those too.

And last, but by no means least, we'll show you how to program the Sound Blaster from within QBasic. Yes, we really will. Cool or what...!

Simple Sound Commands

Although there's a plethora of games for IBM-compatible PCs, nearly all of them use a Sound Blaster or compatible sound card. QBasic's sound synthesis tools are rather modest in comparison and can barely manage a beep, but they can do it in style - in a range of 7 octaves. So even programming a simple beep can be fun....

Generating a Brief Sound Signal

The simplest sound statement, **BEEP**, generates a beep from your computer's speaker. It's a beep of about 1/4 second in duration and it has a frequency of 400 Hz. Incidentally, you can get this signal if you try to output the control character with code **7**, i.e. if you execute the statement **PRINT CHR$ (7)**.

Here's a **BEEP** demonstration, just in case you haven't reached your annoyance threshold yet:

```
REM The action of the BEEP statement
REM \CHAP11\CH11_1.BAS

FOR I = 1 to 4
    BEEP
    FOR J = 1 to 1200
    NEXT J
NEXT I
BEEP: BEEP: BEEP
PRINT "END"

END
```

When you run this, you'll see that the End message isn't displayed on the screen until the sound has finished. This shows that **BEEP**, like most QBasic statements, suspends the operation of other statements whilst it runs. **BEEP**s are usually used to signify warning signals; for example, to indicate incorrect input, so suspending the program has a real benefit here.

Generating a Sound Signal of a Specified Frequency and Duration

When it comes to specifying the frequency and the duration of a sound, you need the (yes, it wasn't difficult to guess) **SOUND** statement. Its format is:

```
SOUND frequency, duration
```

The frequency of the sound ranges from 37 through 32,767Hz and the duration is expressed in system clock ticks, a value ranging from 0 through 65,535 - there are 18.2 clock ticks per second.

To create small delays in earlier chapters (remember the view of the starry sky in Chapter 8?), we've used a meaningless calculation, such as **SIN (1)**, or empty loops but, since we're dealing with sound, and since pauses are as integral to a musical composition as the notes, it is appropriate to introduce QBasic's own pause statement. Its format is

```
SLEEP t
```

which creates a delay of **t** seconds. However, you can also generate a pause with the **SOUND** statement by indicating 32,767 as the frequency parameter. This is a special frequency for this statement and suspends the operation of any program that it's part of by **18.2 * t** seconds. A sound of such a high frequency is beyond the range of the human ear, though it is audible to cats and dogs; so if you're feeling particularly vindictive, you can wake up your cat or dog at any time of the night or day without disturbing the rest of the house. So, back to the **SOUND** pause with this statement:

```
SOUND 32766, 18.2 * t
```

You'll delay program execution for **t** seconds.

If you like to write your own songs as a way of relaxing between more serious programming tasks, you'll need to know the frequencies that correspond to musical notes:

Note	Frequency	Note	Frequency
C	261.63	F#	369.99
C#	277.18	G	392.00
D	293.66	G#	415.30
D#	311.13	A	440.00
E	329.63	A#	466.16
F	349.23	B	493.88

The corresponding frequencies double if you move up an octave, and they halve if you move down one.

There are aspects of **SOUND** that you ought to be familiar with before you start writing your next hit. If **SOUND** is used once, it will generate the sound in the background without affecting the operation of the program. Run this and see (or hear) what happens:

```
REM Demonstration of playing sound in the background
REM \CHAP11\CH11_2.BAS

CLS
SOUND 1000, 18.2 * 5
PRINT "END", 2 * 2
f$ = INPUT$(1)

END
```

You'll hear a sound with a frequency of 1000 Hz lasting 5 seconds. However, at the very beginning of the sound, this message appears on the screen:

        End   4

This tells us that the program generated the sound signal, continued to operate, and immediately actioned the **PRINT** statement. When there are several **SOUND** statements in a program, the sound is again played in the background, but each sound continues only until the time allocated for it is up, or until a new **SOUND** statement occurs in the program.

> **The only exception to this is a new SOUND statement with zero duration which is useful for cutting a sound dead in any situation. This technique is widely used in games when, for instance, you've played through one level and moving up to the next one involves a change in background music.**

We can demonstrate how **SOUND** statements within a program affect each other with the musical notes of the first octave:

```
REM Demonstration of integration OF SOUNDs
REM \CHAP11\CH11_3.BAS

CLS
FOR i = 1 to 7
    READ f
    SOUND f, 18.2
NEXT i

DATA  261.63,293.66,329.63,349.23,392,440,493.88

PRINT "END"
f$ = INPUT$(1)

END
```

If you run the code, you'll hear how the **SOUND** statements work in succession, and you'll also see the word End appear on the screen the instant the last note begins its one-second salute to musical genius.

Generating Sound Effects

There are also various sound effects that you can create with the **SOUND** statement - the kind that you come across in lots of different game formats. Here are three popular samples:

```
REM Falling bomb, clock and siren sound effects
REM \CHAP11\CH11_4.BAS

t0 = TIMER
FOR i = 1 to 500: NEXT i
loopsPerSec = 500 / (TIMER - t0)
'loopsPerSec = # of passes through loop to delay about 1 second
CLS

'Bomb
PRINT "Falling Bomb"
FOR n = 1000 to 700 Step -5
    SOUND n, 1
NEXT n
FOR n = 1 to 500
    SOUND 50 * rnd + 37, .03
NEXT n
SLEEP 1

'Clock
PRINT "Clock"
FOR n = 1 to 5
    SOUND 500, .1
    FOR i = 1 to loopsPerSec * .4: NEXT i
    SOUND 2000, .1
    FOR i = 1 to loopsPerSec * .4: NEXT i
NEXT n
SLEEP 1

'Siren
PRINT "Siren"
FOR n = 1 to 10
    SOUND 1700, 5
    SOUND 1000, 5
NEXT n
SLEEP 1

END
```

A falling bomb and its explosion, the tick of a clock and an emergency vehicle siren. Each of these illustrations of the **SOUND** statement has an interesting aspect: the falling bomb is created by a gradual change in frequency and its explosion is a low-frequency signal generated using the random number generator; **TIMER** is a system function, used in this case to imitate the ticking of the clock; and the alternation of two distinctly different frequencies gives us our siren.

Creating Melodies

The **PLAY** statement provides even greater scope for synthesizing sound because, like the **DRAW** statement, it has its own micro-language. Its format is:

PLAY commandstring$

where **commandstring\$** denotes a string expression that contains one or more of the **PLAY** commands shown here in these tables:

Octave and tone commands	Action
O*n*	Sets the current octave to one of the seven available (0-6).
< or >	Moves up or down one octave.
A,B,C,D,E,F,G	Plays the specified note in the current octave.
N*n*	Plays a specified note (0 - 84) in the seven octave range. The value 0 is a rest.

Duration and tempo commands	Action
L*n*	Sets the length of each note (1 - 64). L1 is a whole note, L2 is a half note, L3 is a quarter note, etc.
ML	Sets music legato, where each note smoothly changes into the next.
MN	Sets music normal, where each note is played in its standard value.
MS	Sets music staccato, where each note is shorter and distinct from the rest.
P*n*	Specifies a pause (1 - 64). P1 is a whole-note pause, P2 is a half-note pause, etc.
T*n*	Sets the tempo in quarter notes per minute, the same way as a metronome. The range for **n** is 32 - 255, the default being 120.

Mode commands	Action
MF	Plays music in the foreground. No other QBasic statements are executed until **PLAY** has finished.
MB	Plays music in the background. QBasic continues to execute other statements while the music is **PLAY**ing.

Suffix commands	Action
# or +	Turns the preceding note into a sharp.
–	Turns the preceding note into a flat.
.	Plays the preceding note 3/2 times longer than specified, multiple periods will extend each note even further.

The parameters of these micro-language commands may be specified by numeric values. However, you can also define them through variables, using the variable conversion operations in the form of the **STR$** and **VARPTR$** functions:

```
REM Demonstration of PLAYs micro-language
REM \CHAP11\CH11_5.BAS

CLS
scale$ = "CDEFGAB"
PLAY "116"
FOR i% = 0 to 5
    PLAY "O" + STR$(i%)
    PLAY "x" + VARPTR$(scale$)
NEXT i%
PRINT "END"

END
```

By default, unlike **SOUND**, **PLAY** operates in the foreground. Run this program and the message End will appear on the screen only after the music has finished, showing that the music is playing in the foreground. You can use a special micro-language command, **MB**, to play music in the background, but it has to be the first command in the code. After this, the rest of the commands (up to 32 notes) are placed in **PLAY**'s buffer and executed without interrupting the program. We can see how this is done here:

```
REM Scale of D Minor
REM \CHAP11\CH11_6.BAS

CLS
PLAY "MB D E F G A B- O5 C D"
PRINT "END"

END
```

When you run this program, you'll hear the beginning of a musical scale. Notice that the message End appears at once, illustrating the background music mode. You use the micro-language command, **MF**, to switch within a program back to the default, foreground mode.

If you want a more complicated musical effect, you may find the following function useful:

PLAY (x)

x is a fictitious argument. This function returns the number of notes stored in **PLAY**'s buffer, in other words a number from 0 to 32. If a melody is played in the foreground, **PLAY (x)** returns **0**. Follow this code:

```
REM Demonstration of passing an argument to PLAY
REM \CHAP11\CH11_7.BAS

CLS
Music$ = "MBT128O2P2P8L8GGGL2E-P24P8L8FFFL2D"
PLAY Music$
WHILE PLAY(0) > 5: WEND
PRINT "Almost finished!"

END
```

Running it, you'll see that the message Almost finished! appears in the middle of the melody.

Here's how you can control the duration of the musical notes, using the **L** value. The larger the value, the shorter the note:

```
REM Varying the lengths of notes
REM \CHAP11\CH11_8.BAS

CLS : PRINT "This is a whole note."
PLAY "MF O3 C1"
FOR n = 2 to 64
    LOCATE 1, 10
    PRINT " 1 /"; n; "note."
    PLAY "L" + Str$(n) + "C"
NEXT n

END
```

On running this program, you'll hear notes of different lengths which are displayed on the screen. We can use the fragment of a popular song *Happy Birthday* to show how the playing style influences the sound of a tune:

```
REM Happy Birthday in three styles
REM \CHAP11\CH11_9.BAS

b$ = "CCDCFE"
PLAY "MS" + b$
PLAY "MN" + b$
PLAY "ML" + b$

END
```

And finally, before we look at a more complex musical program, we'll play another popular melody and display the text of this festive song along with it:

```
REM Jingle Bells
REM \CHAP11\CH11_10.BAS

CLS
PRINT "Jingle bells, Jingle bells"
PLAY "MF L8 N41 N41 L4 N41 L8 N41 N41 L4 N41"
PRINT "Jingle all the way"
PLAY "L8 N41 N44 N37. L16 N39 L4 N41 N0"
PRINT "Oh what fun it is to ride in a"
PLAY "L8 N42 N42 N42. L16 N42 L8 N42 N41 N41 L16 N41 N41"
PRINT "One horse open"
PLAY "L4 N44 N44 N42 N39"
PRINT "Sleigh"
PLAY "L1 N37"
f$ = INPUT$(1)

END
```

So we've just about covered QBasic's rather modest means for making music. You can't play polyphonic or multi-timbral compositions, or even control the volume with them, but then the IBM-compatible PC XT or AT, equipped with QBasic's music tools, wasn't meant to take the place of a synthesizer. We hope, though, that these examples inspire you to have a go at programming your own musical compositions. Do you think you might make it to the MTV awards?

A Musical Program

Next, we'll take a look at a QBasic remake of a popular program, **MUSIC.BAS**. This program was originally written in BasicA and has been on the scene in various guises for about ten years. It uses pseudo-graphics and the simplest methods of dynamic graphics with the best music you can get on a PC without a sound card!

Start the program and you'll hear Mozart's "Turkish March". The title of the program will gradually appear on the screen. What you're listening to is the **PLAY** statement used for music synthesis. Press *Space* and the program draws part of a piano keyboard using pseudo-graphic symbols and, at the bottom, displays a main menu bar which contains 11 melodies:

When you choose a particular melody, the program plays it and also indicates the keys that produce the notes. This is what we mean by a program combining sound *and* dynamic graphics! Even with its limited accomplishments, it's a pretty large program, so we'll split it into six sections which we'll examine in a moment.

Its programming style may well shock lovers of structured programming - because **MUSIC.BAS** wasn't designed for QBasic, there are numerous labels and unconditional jumps. As we've just pointed out, it was originally written in outdated BasicA. However, it's a fair demonstration of QBasic's downward compatibility with earlier versions of BASIC.

Now let's take a look at the individual sections of the program. The first section outputs the title in time with the "Turkish March", using the **PLAY** statement. Note the use of legato which smoothly changes each note into the next, and the change of octave using the characters < and >:

```
REM Program "Music for IBM PC"
REM QBasic version V.P. Djakonov
REM \CHAP11\CH11_11.BAS

L1: 'Print title and playing V.Mozart "Turkish March"
    SCREEN 1: CLS
    LOCATE 5, 19, 0: PRINT "IBM"
    PLAY "T120 ML L16 O2 B A G# A > C4 D C < B > C E4"
    LOCATE 7, 12: PRINT "Personal Computer": LOCATE 10, 9
    PLAY "    O3 F E D# E B A G# A B A G# A > C4"
    PRINT CHR$(213) + STRING$(21, 205) + CHR$(184)
    LOCATE 11, 9
    PRINT CHR$(179) + "         MUSIC         " + CHR$(179)
    LOCATE 12, 9: PRINT CHR$(179) + STRING$(21, 32) + CHR$(179)
    LOCATE 13, 9
    PRINT CHR$(179) + "     Version 1.10      " + CHR$(179)
    LOCATE 14, 9: PRINT CHR$(212) + STRING$(21, 205) + CHR$(190)
    PLAY "L8  O3 A B > C < B A G# A E F D C4 < B4 A4"
    LOCATE 17, 11: PRINT "QBasic version 1994"
    PLAY "    O3 A B > C#4 < A B > C# < B A G# F# G# A B G# E"
    PLAY "    O3 A B > C#4 < A B > C# < B A G# F# B G# E A. P16"
    PLAY "    O3 A B > C#4 < A B > C# < B A G# F# G# A B G# E "
    PLAY "    O3 A B > C#4 < A B > C# < B A G# F# B G# E A4"
    LOCATE 23, 7: PRINT "Press space bar to continue"
L2: IF INKEY$ <> "" THEN GOTO L2:
L3: CMD$ = INKEY$
    IF CMD$ = "" THEN GOTO L3:
    IF CMD$ = CHR$(27) THEN GOTO L16:
    IF CMD$ <> " " THEN GOTO L3:
    ON ERROR GOTO L4:
    PLAY "mf": GOTO L5
L4: RESUME L5
```

After drawing the main menu and the pseudo-graphic keyboard, you may notice that the structure of the program is a little offbeat. We have mentioned before that this program was originally written in BasicA and, since its conversion to QBasic was achieved mechanically, the melody section now appears below the playing section. This is what forces us to use conditional and unconditional jumps - it's the price you pay for recycling old code, but it does you a power of good to fall in with the rest of the world's recyclers since you'll quickly learn never to write code like this yourself.

The next section reads the data statements for a specified melody, i.e. the frequency and duration of each of the notes. We also output the musical symbol, ♫, to show which of the keys is played:

```
L7: 'Read datas for melodies
    READ J, K
    CMD$ = INKEY$: IF CMD$ = "" THEN GOTO L8:
    IF CMD$ = CHR$(27) THEN RETURN
L8: IF J = -1 THEN RETURN
```

```
      Q = O(J)
      IF J > 64 OR J < 39 THEN GOTO L9:
      IF SCREEN(5, Q) <> 32 THEN
            LOCATE 11, Q: PRINT CHR$(14): GOTO L9
      END IF
      LOCATE 7, Q: PRINT CHR$(14);
```

The specified melody is then played by the **SOUND** statement. Note the use of staccato here:

```
L9:   'Play selected melodies
      SOUND M(J), K
      IF J = 0 AND K = 1 THEN GOTO L10:
      'Skip next for staccato
      SOUND 32767, 1
L10:  IF J > 64 OR J < 39 THEN GOTO L7:
      IF SCREEN(5, Q) = 32 THEN LOCATE 7, Q: PRINT CHR$(32); : GOTO L7
      LOCATE 11, Q: PRINT CHR$(219); : GOTO L7
```

The actual notes for each song are stored as **DATA** statements at the end of the program and read in as pairs. The first value to be read in is the frequency, the second is the duration of each note.

```
L18:  DATA -2,"Blue Danube Waltz by J.S.Strauss"
      DATA 42,4,46,4,49,4,49,4,0,4,61,2,0,2,61,2,0
      DATA 6,58,2,0,2,58,2,0,6,42,4,42,4,46,4,49,4
      DATA 49,4,0,4,61,2,0,2,61,2,0,6,59,2,0,2
```

The **SOUND** statement is often pushed aside in favor of the more popular **PLAY** statement but, as we've seen here, if you apply a bit of thought to your programs, you can use the more primitive QBasic keywords very effectively.

As we said earlier, the structure of the program leaves a lot to be desired, but it's simple and effective.

The Piano

The following program is probably as close as we're going to get to emulating a piano keyboard through QBasic. It's not exactly a Steinway but, all the same, it's fun - even more fun than the **BEEP** statement. This example not only demonstrates a piano emulator but also how you can save a song to a text file and load it back in again. It also allows you to sit back, put your feet up, and watch as the computer plays the song back to you.

Let's dissect the program and look at, not only what it does, but how it does it.

Before we get to the introductory screen, we're going to draw and **GET** the keys needed for the piano keyboard. If you've ever looked closely at a piano keyboard, you'll have noticed that the white keys have four different shapes, like this:

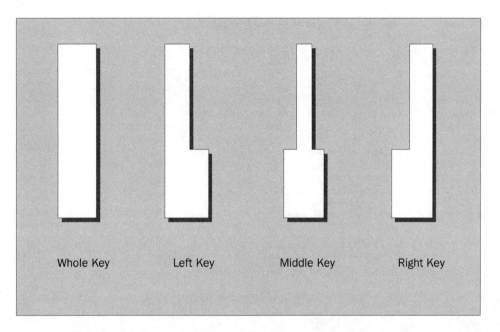

We need to draw these keys along with a single sharp key and **GET** them into an array. This is done for both the normal white and black keys, and also a set of green ones which are used in the program to highlight a key that has been pressed. Using the **SCREEN** statement, we're able to use an active but invisible video page to perform this task:

```
REM The Piano
REM \CHAP11\CH11_12.BAS

 SCREEN 7, 0, 1, 0

 dur% = 1000
 recordingflag% = 0
 songloadedflag% = 0

 'Arrays for the keys
 DIM song$(1000)
 DIM wholekey%(300)
 DIM leftkey%(300)
 DIM midkey%(300)
 DIM rightkey%(300)
 DIM sharpkey%(450)
 DIM midsharpkey%(450)

 'Drawing both Black & White and Green keys
 movekeys% = 0
 colorkeys% = 10
 FOR drawkeys% = 1 TO 2
     FOR x% = (20 + movekeys%) TO (70 + movekeys%) STEP 16
         LINE (10 + x%, 30)-((10 + x%) + 12, 100), colorkeys%, BF
     NEXT x%
```

In the figure above, the keys are labelled:

Whole Key   Left Key   Middle Key   Right Key

```
        FOR x% = (53 + movekeys%) TO (80 + movekeys%) STEP 17
            LINE (x%, 30)-((x%) + 13, 70), 0, BF
        NEXT x%
        movekeys% = 100
        colorkeys% = 15
    NEXT drawkeys%
    LINE (56, 30)-(64, 69), 10, BF
    LINE (156, 30)-(164, 69), 8, BF

    'GetKeys
    GET (130, 30)-(142, 100), wholekey%
    GET (146, 30)-(158, 100), leftkey%
    GET (162, 30)-(174, 100), midkey%
    GET (178, 30)-(190, 100), rightkey%
    GET (156, 30)-(164, 69), sharpkey%
    GET (156, 30)-(163, 69), midsharpkey%
```

Now that we've got our keys into their corresponding arrays, we can start the introduction. As the
introductory message is displayed, you'll hear a set of randomly generated notes. The duration of these
notes is as random as the note selection and this produces a rather spaced-out effect:

```
CLS 0

SCREEN 1, 0, 0, 0

'IntroScreen
LOCATE 8, 14: PRINT "The Piano"
LOCATE 19, 12: PRINT "by G.J.Butler"
FOR counter = 12 TO 24
    LOCATE 6, counter: PRINT CHR$(1)
    LOCATE 10, counter: PRINT CHR$(1)
NEXT counter
y = 12
FOR countertwo = 1 TO 2
    FOR counter = 7 TO 9
        LOCATE counter, y: PRINT CHR$(1)
    NEXT counter
    y = 24
NEXT countertwo
FOR counter% = 1 TO 10            'Random note/duration loop
    note = INT(RND * 2735) + 500
    duration = INT(RND * 3) + 1
    SOUND note, duration
NEXT counter%
PLAY "MS"
WHILE INKEY$ = "": WEND
```

The next step is to draw our main keyboard. As before, we use an active but invisible video page to draw
the keys, on which we earlier stored the arrays. We also show the corresponding computer keyboard keys
beneath the piano keys; it's handy to know which ones we have to press:

```
CLS 0
SCREEN 7, 0, 0, 2

'Drawing Whole Keyboard
PUT (30, 30), wholekey%
x% = 45
```

```
FOR counter% = 1 TO 2
    PUT (x%, 30), leftkey%
    PUT (x% + 15, 30), midkey%
    PUT (x% + 30, 30), midkey%
    PUT (x% + 45, 30), rightkey%
    PUT (x% + 60, 30), leftkey%
    PUT (x% + 75, 30), midkey%
    PUT (x% + 90, 30), rightkey%
    x% = 150
NEXT counter%
PUT (255, 30), wholekey%

x% = 0
FOR counter% = 1 TO 2
    PUT (54 + x%, 30), sharpkey%, OR
    PUT (70 + x%, 30), midsharpkey%, OR
    PUT (85 + x%, 30), sharpkey%, OR
    PUT (114 + x%, 30), sharpkey%, OR
    PUT (130 + x%, 30), sharpkey%, OR
    x% = 105
NEXT counter%

'Print Keyboard Keys
LOCATE 3, 8
PRINT "S D F  H J   3 4 5  7 8"
LOCATE 14, 4
PRINT "| Z X C V B N M W E R T Y U I O"
LOCATE 18, 14
PRINT "Note:"
LOCATE 24, 1: PRINT "F1 - Menu";
LOCATE 24, 31: PRINT "Q - Quit";
```

As soon as the screen is drawn, we make the page visible. This technique brings a professional touch to the program:

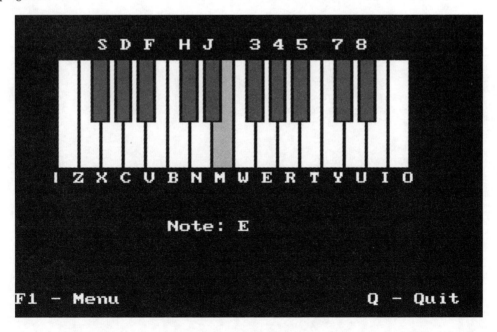

Now we're into the main body of the code. Since we're going to be processing a lot of single key presses, it's a good idea to use **SELECT CASE**, because it's ideally structured for this. We'll use the first couple of **CASE** statements for recording our songs later on, so don't worry about them for the moment. The third is executed when you press the *F1* key which brings up the menu in the section **menu**. The next choice in the statement is *Q* and, when we select this, we're sent off to the **quits** subroutine to confirm whether we want to exit the program. Then, we check for all the keys which correspond to the piano keyboard which are logically set on your keyboard as follows:

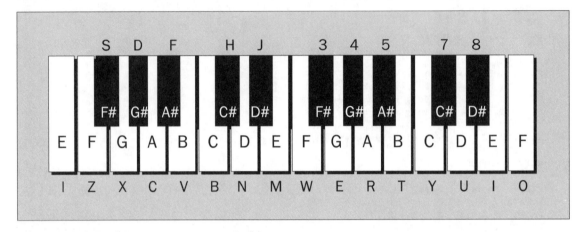

We use a separate loop because of the record and playback features which we'll discuss later:

```
SCREEN 7, 0, 0, 0

'GetNote
GetKey:
playingsonflag% = 0
a$ = UCASE$(INKEY$)
SELECT CASE a$
CASE CHR$(0) + CHR$(61)        'Cancel current recording
    IF recordingflag% = 0 THEN GOTO GetKey
    PCOPY 0, 1
    COLOR 3
    GOSUB drawbigmenu
    COLOR 10
    LOCATE 8, 13: PRINT "Are You Sure You"
    LOCATE 9, 13: PRINT "Want To Cancel.?"
    LOCATE 12, 15: PRINT "Yes or No"
    cancel:
    b$ = UCASE$(INKEY$)
    IF b$ = "" THEN GOTO cancel
    IF b$ = "N" THEN
        PCOPY 1, 0: SCREEN 7, 0, 0, 0
        COLOR 15
        GOTO GetKey
    END IF
    IF b$ = "Y" THEN
        recordingflag% = 0
        notecount% = 0
        PCOPY 1, 0: SCREEN 7, 0, 0, 0
        COLOR 15
```

```
            GOTO GetKey
        ELSE
            PCOPY 1, 0: SCREEN 7, 0, 0, 0
            GOTO GetKey
        END IF
    CASE CHR$(0) + CHR$(60)   'Save the current song
        IF recordingflag% = 0 THEN GOTO GetKey
        GOTO savesong
    CASE CHR$(0) + CHR$(59)   'Display main menu
        GOTO menu
    CASE "Q"
        GOTO quits                    'Do you want to quit?
    CASE " ", "\", "Z", "X", "C", "V", "B", "N", "M", "W", "E", "R", "T", "Y", "U"④
        "I", "O", "S", "D", "F", "H", "J", "3", "4", "5", "7", "8"
        GOTO notes                    'A Note has been pressed
    CASE ELSE
        GOTO GetKey
    END SELECT
```

This **CASE** statement, which takes all the key presses that produce a note, jumps to a separate loop where the individual notes are awaiting selection. In the next listing, we've only shown the first note since the process used in each **CASE** is the same.

Take the '\' key for example:

```
notes:
PLAY "MF"'Play all music in the foreground
 SELECT CASE a$
 CASE "\"
     note$ = "MFO1E"
     PAINT (30, 100), 10, 0
     LOCATE 18, 20: PRINT "E"
     PLAY note$
     FOR n = 1 TO dur%
     NEXT n
     LOCATE 18, 20: PRINT "  "
     PAINT (30, 100), 15, 0
```

▲ First, we assign the variable **note$** with the string **"MFO1E"**.

▲ Second, the piano key that corresponds to the note, in this case bottom E, is **PAINT**ed green. While the note is playing, we also output the name of the note to the screen and use a short

   delay to enable us to see the note.

▲ Third, the note's name is removed from the screen and the green piano key is returned to its original white color.

This is where things may get a little confusing, but don't worry…. At the end of our **SELECT CASE** we have a check on the **recordingflag%**. Since our record, playback and normal piano sections all use the same **SELECT CASE** structure, we need a flag to let us know which one of these processes is currently active. If we're recording, we start to store the played notes into an array called **song$**. It's from this array that we can save our song later:

```
END SELECT
IF playingsongflag% = 1 THEN
        GOTO playsongloop
END IF
length% = LEN(note$)
actualnote$ = RIGHT$(note$, length% - 4)
IF recordingflag% = 1 THEN
    notecount% = notecount% + 2
    IF note$ = "0000N0" THEN note$ = "N0"
    song$(position%) = a$
    position% = position% + 1
    song$(position%) = note$
    position% = position% + 1
END IF
GOTO GetKey
```

The menu section is simple in its design and uses nothing that we haven't covered so far. One point of interest is the use of **PCOPY** and **SCREEN** to save the piano keyboard's screen before drawing the menu on top of it:

```
'Draw Menu Box
menu:
PCOPY 0, 1
COLOR 3
GOSUB drawbigmenu
COLOR 10
LOCATE 7, 14: PRINT "R - Record Song"
LOCATE 8, 14: PRINT "L - Load Song"
LOCATE 9, 14: PRINT "P - Play Song"
LOCATE 14, 14: PRINT "X - Exit Menu"
GetMenuKey:
b$ = UCASE$(INKEY$)
SELECT CASE b$
CASE "R"
    GOTO record
CASE "L"
    GOTO load
CASE "X"
    GOTO exitmenu
CASE "P"
    GOTO playsong
CASE ELSE
    GOTO GetMenuKey
END SELECT
exitmenu:
PCOPY 1, 0: SCREEN 7, 0, 0, 0
COLOR 15
GOTO GetKey
```

The next section records a song by setting the flag **recordingflag%** to **1** (we saw this earlier), and then filling the array with each key that is pressed. We've also included a cancel button here because, from time to time, you're bound to misplay a note. World-class programmers aren't usually world-class pianists. Here is where we record a selection of notes:

```
record:
LOCATE 7, 13: PRINT "Type in the full"
```

```
    LOCATE 8, 14: PRINT "path & name of"
    LOCATE 9, 13: PRINT "your song below:"
    LOCATE 11, 12: PRINT "eg C:\SONGS\BOPPY"
    COLOR 3
    GOSUB drawsmallmenu
    tryagainrecord:
    COLOR 10
    LOCATE 18, 7: INPUT ; name$
    IF name$ = "" THEN GOTO tryagainrecord
    PCOPY 1, 0: SCREEN 7, 0, 0, 0
    PCOPY 0, 1
    COLOR 3
    GOSUB drawbigmenu
    COLOR 10
    LOCATE 7, 12: PRINT "Press F2 when you"
    LOCATE 8, 13: PRINT "are finished or"
    LOCATE 9, 13: PRINT "F3 to cancel at"
    LOCATE 10, 13: PRINT "any time......."
    LOCATE 13, 14: PRINT "Press Any Key"
    LOCATE 14, 16: PRINT "to Start"
    recordingflag% = 1
    notecount% = 0
    position% = 1
    WHILE INKEY$ = "": WEND
    GOTO exitmenu
```

Once a song is stored inside the array, we can save it out to a text file. The text file in which we save our song stores two values for each note: first, the key that you pressed on the keyboard, then the **PLAY** string.

```
    savesong:
    OPEN name$ FOR OUTPUT AS #1
    PRINT #1, notecount%
    FOR counter% = 1 TO notecount%
        PRINT #1, song$(counter%)
    NEXT counter%
    CLOSE #1
    PCOPY 0, 1
    COLOR 3
    GOSUB drawsmallmenu
    COLOR 10
    LOCATE 18, 7: PRINT "Song saved as "; name$;
    recordingflag% = 0
    position% = 0
    notecount% = 0
    WHILE INKEY$ = "": WEND
    GOTO exitmenu
```

You might want to take note of the three flags that we use here: **recordingflag%**, which we've just seen in action, **position%** and **notecount%**. They're all used in the recording and saving processes at the end of the notes section. The second flag, **position%**, stores the current position in the array, **song%**. And lastly, **notecount%** stores the number of notes in the array.

The load section quite simply loads a song into the array so that we can play it back:

```
    load:
    COLOR 3
```

```
GOSUB drawbigmenu
COLOR 10
LOCATE 7, 13: PRINT "Type in the full"
LOCATE 8, 14: PRINT "path & name of"
LOCATE 9, 13: PRINT "your song below:"
LOCATE 11, 12: PRINT "eg C:\SONGS\BOPPY"
COLOR 3
GOSUB drawsmallmenu
tryagainload:
COLOR 10
LOCATE 18, 7: INPUT ; name$
IF name$ = "" THEN GOTO tryagainload
OPEN name$ FOR INPUT AS #1
notecount% = 0
INPUT #1, notecount%
FOR counter% = 0 TO notecount% - 1
    INPUT #1, song$(counter%)
NEXT counter%
CLOSE #1
PCOPY 1, 0: SCREEN 7, 0, 0, 0
PCOPY 0, 1
COLOR 3
GOSUB drawbigmenu
COLOR 10
LOCATE 7, 15: PRINT "Song loaded"
LOCATE 9, 13: PRINT "To play the song"
LOCATE 10, 13: PRINT "select Play from"
LOCATE 11, 14: PRINT "the main menu."
LOCATE 14, 14: PRINT "Press Any Key"
songloadedflag% = 1
WHILE INKEY$ = "": WEND
PCOPY 1, 0: SCREEN 7, 0, 0, 0
COLOR 15
GOTO menu
```

Notice how we must make sure that the file saved earlier is read back in exactly the same way.

Finally, we play our song that is stored in the array. We do this by assigning the variable **a$** with the value of the corresponding keyboard key. This is then sent to our **SELECT CASE** routine near the top of the program. Using the **SELECT CASE** routine in this way, we've demonstrated how you can recycle parts of a program. Recycling like this saves time and space, and will probably speed up your program:

```
playsong:
IF songloadedflag% = 0 THEN
    COLOR 3
    GOSUB drawsmallmenu
    COLOR 10
    LOCATE 18, 7: PRINT "No Song Loaded...Press A Key"
    COLOR 15
    WHILE INKEY$ = "": WEND
    PCOPY 1, 0: SCREEN 7, 0, 0, 0
    COLOR 15
    GOTO menu
END IF
COLOR 3
GOSUB drawbigmenu
COLOR 10
```

```
      LOCATE 8, 14: PRINT "Press Any Key"
      LOCATE 9, 15: PRINT "to Play Song"
      COLOR 3
      GOSUB drawsmallmenu
      COLOR 10
      LOCATE 18, 7: PRINT ; name$
      WHILE INKEY$ = "": WEND
      PCOPY 1, 0: SCREEN 7, 0, 0, 0
      COLOR 15
      playingsongflag% = 1
      FOR counter% = 0 TO notecount% - 1 STEP 2
          a$ = song$(counter%)
          GOTO notes
      playsongloop:
      NEXT counter%
      playingsongflag% = 0
      GOTO GetKey

      END
```

You may already have a few ideas on how to improve the program, such as applying sustain to the notes or allowing the user to change octave. Feel free to alter the program in any way you choose and, as usual, if you come up with anything particularly interesting, do let us know.

Using a Sound Card in QBasic

Soon after the introduction of the personal computer, people began to realize its possibilities for playing games. The PC was equipped with a relatively adequate graphics system, but the sound capabilities were very limited. This changed with the introduction of special add-on sound cards, such as the AdLib card and the Sound Blaster card from Creative Labs. Nowadays, the majority of PCs have installed a sound card of some description, most of them compatible with the Sound Blaster card.

In this section, we will look at using a Sound Blaster compatible card with QBasic. Such a card actually combines different methods or systems for producing sound. These methods may include waveform sound, FM synthesizer music, sound from the Creative Music System (not used very much nowadays), MIDI compatibility and wave table sounds. Also, many sound cards are capable of digitizing sound. In this chapter, we will limit ourselves to discussing waveform and FM sound, because these two methods are the most prevalent and produce the best results from QBasic. With the experience gained from working with these methods and the specifications of the system, you will be able to work out how to control other sound systems.

Control

Controlling a sound card in QBasic is done by sending data to hardware ports by means of the **OUT** statement which we looked at back in Chapter 4 - Memory, Data and Machine Code. To recap a little, hardware ports are the connections between your computer and its peripheral devices, such as printers or modems. Data can also be sent the other way, from the device to the computer. In QBasic, this data is read in using the **INP** function.

The Sound Blaster card can be configured to use different sets of hardware ports, identified by their base address, which is the number of the first port in the set. For instance, if the card is set to use hardware port numbers 220h to 233h (and most are), its base address is 220h. To control the sound card, you have to find out this base address. Usually, the install program that comes with the sound card has set up an environment variable containing the base address. If you type the command, SET, at the DOS command line, a list will be printed with all the environment variables. There should be an item in the list that looks something like this:

BLASTER=A220 I5 D1 T3

The number just after the 'A' is the base address, in hexadecimal notation, in this case 220h. The other numbers specify the interrupt request number, the DMA channel number and the version number, but these don't concern us. The programs in this chapter will assume 220h to be the base address, so if your card is set to another address, you will have to change the value **BaseAddr** in each program.

Sampling sound

First, we will discuss sampling sound, or electronic sound recording. To do this, you need to connect a sound source, such as a microphone or a cassette player, to the MIC or the Line-In connector of the sound card. The Sound Blaster card is equipped with an analogue-to-digital converter, ADC for short. This is an electrical circuit that transforms the voltage on the connector to a numerical value which can be stored in a computer's memory. In this section, we will look at 8-bits mono sound sampling because this works on all cards. This means that one sample of sound is one byte long.

There are two ways of sampling sound: either through the processor or through DMA (Direct Memory Access). DMA means that the sound data goes directly into the computer's memory, without the intervention of the processor. DMA is faster, but fairly difficult, if not impossible, to accomplish in QBasic. Here, we will look at retrieving one byte of sound data at a time through the processor.

To let the sound card take a sample of the sound, we have to send the right command number to the command port. For DSP (Digital Signal Processing, what we are doing now), the number of the command port is **base + Ch**. Command numbers include **10h**, which means 'Output a value to the speakers' and **20h**, meaning 'Read a value from the microphone'. This subsequent value can then be read from the data port, which has number **base + Ah**. There are many other command numbers, but these can be found in more specific literature. To see how to use command **20h**, look at the following program **\CHAP11\CH11_13.BAS** which plots the sampled data on the screen:

```
CONST ScreenMode = 12, xMax = 640 'Change for other screen modes
CONST BaseAddr = &H220 'Change if your sound card uses another base address

CONST CommAddr = BaseAddr + &HC, DataAddr = BaseAddr + &HA

DEFINT A-Z
DIM Byte(xMax)
SCREEN ScreenMode
DO
    OUT CommAddr, &H20 'Give command to sample a byte
    PRESET (i, Byte(i))
    Byte(i) = INP(DataAddr) 'Read value from data port
    PSET (i, Byte(i))
    i = (i + 1) MOD xMax 'Wrap i when end is reached
LOOP
```

First, some useful constants are defined. If your hardware doesn't support screen mode 12, change it to another mode. **xMax** is the maximum x-coordinate which may have to change as well, depending on your screen resolution. An array is then defined, **Byte()**, to hold the value for each x-coordinate on the screen. In the loop that follows, the command **20h** is sent to the command port. Then, the sample value is read in from the data port and assigned to an element of the array **Byte()**. This value is then plotted on the screen. The **PRESET** statement clears the points of the previous plot. The variable **i** is incremented each time until it reaches **xMax**, and then it is set back to zero:

```
i = (i + 1) MOD xMax 'Wrap i when end is reached
```

This is the screen that you will see when you run **SAMPLE.BAS** and talk (or gibber!) into the microphone:

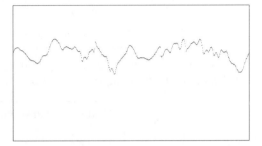

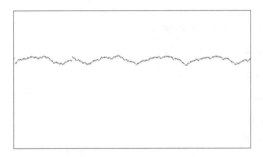

You can even play audio CD's from your CD-ROM drive for a visual image of a song. This is a sample we took of Bjork's 'It's Oh So Quiet' with a thick multicolor line.

This is a fascinating subject and it's possible that you could use your PC as an oscilloscope with this program. However, you can't measure voltages with it, because the Sound Blaster uses a technique called Automatic Gain Control (AGC), which automatically adjusts the recording level according to the level of the sound source. This means that (between certain boundaries) different levels of sound volume will produce the same level on the screen.

Try changing screen modes, thicker lines, adding color and using various types of sound. For something quite spectacular, how about a sprite that dances along to the music?

FM Synthesized Music

A very different form of sound output is FM synthesis. This section also applies to AdLib sound cards, but AdLib owners should change the base address in the next batch of programs to 380h. In this section, we will look at how to produce sound using the FM system. We will also experiment with some of the parameters used to define the sound.

FM stands for frequency modulation. The sound is formed by having a carrier sound being modulated by a modulator sound. We can define up to nine 'instruments', each consisting of a carrier and a modulator. We can let these nine instruments play different notes together, producing complicated tunes. The instruments are defined by a lot of parameters, of which we will discuss only a few.

The FM chip on the sound card is programmed by setting registers in the chip to certain values. There are 224 such registers, so you'll understand when we say that we won't be discussing every one of these. To set a register to a certain value, we send the number of the register to the Register Port, whose address is **base + 8**. Then we send the desired value to the Data Port, which has an address of **base + 9**.

The carrier and modulator of each instrument both have four registers in which parameters are placed. Since there are nine channels (instruments), that already gives us 72 (2 x 4 x 9) registers to program! Of course, we don't have to use all nine channels. The register numbers for the carrier of channel 1 are given here:

Number	Function
20h	Amplitude modulation/Vibrato/EG type/Key scaling/Octave shift
40h	Key scaling level/Output level
60h	Attack rate/Decay rate
80h	Sustain level/Release time

These functions will all be explained in a moment. To find the other 68 register numbers, add the offset numbers from the following table to the base numbers in the last table:

Channel	Offset for carrier	Offset for modulator
1	00h	03h
2	01h	04h
3	02h	05h
4	08h	0Bh
5	09h	0Ch
6	0Ah	0Dh
7	10h	13h
8	11h	14h
9	12h	15h

For example, to find the register number for the attack rate/sustain rate of the modulator of channel 6, add 0Dh to 60h which will find the value 6Dh.

To define an instrument, values should be assigned to parameters. As you can see in the function table, two or more parameters are combined into one register. Each register is eight bits wide, so the register values can range from 0 to 255. These eight bits are divided over two or more parameters, so each parameter has less than eight bits available. For instance, if a parameter has three bits available, its values will range from 0 to 7. The total register value is found by combining the values for the different parameters, using the appropriate coefficients.

We will now look at what the parameters mean. We will look at the registers for the carrier of channel 1, i.e. 20h, 40h, 60h and 80h, but the same goes, of course, for all the other channels.

Register 20h looks like this:

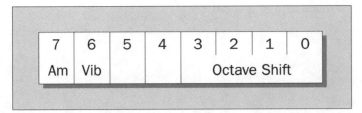

The value (ranging from 0 to 15) in bits 0-3 specifies whether the octave should be changed from the current value. If it's set to 0, the note is played one octave lower. If set to 1, there is no change and a value of 2 would raise the note one octave. There are other possible values, such as the functions of bits 4 and 5, but, due to the enormous scope of the topic we aren't able to discuss them here. Setting bit 6 applies vibrato to the sound and bit 7 causes amplitude modulation in the sound. The depth of the amplitude modulation and vibrato is specified for all channels through one register, BDh:

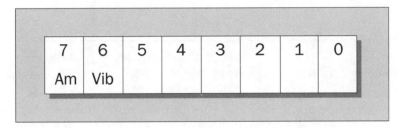

If bit 6 is set, the vibrato (if applied) is set to 14 percent. If clear, the vibrato is 7 percent. If bit 7 is set, the amplitude modulation depth (if applied) is 4.8 dB. If clear, it is 1 dB.

Register 40h looks like this:

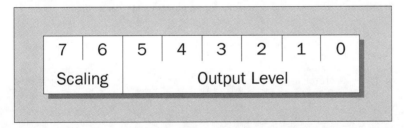

The output level value, bits 0-5, ranges from 0 to 63, where 63 corresponds to the lowest level, 0 dB, and 0 corresponds to the highest level, 47 dB. Bits 6-7 (ranging 0-3) specify how quickly the output level rises if the pitch of the sound goes up. 0 is no rise, 1 is 1.5 dB/octave, 2 is 3 dB/octave and 3 is 6 dB/octave.

Before we look at registers 60h and 80h, we first need to know a little bit more about how a note played on an instrument is built up. We distinguish four phases in the note:

▲ The 'attack' - this is the fast rise in level at the beginning of the note.

▲ The 'decay' - this is when, after reaching peak level, the sound volume drops to a certain level which is called...

▲ The 'sustain' volume - the sound stays at this level until the 'release' time is reached, at which point the sound stops.

Let's have a look at a graphical representation of this idea.

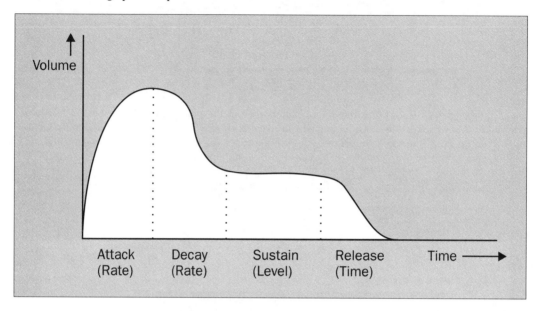

Now, the attack rate defines how quickly the sound level initially rises and the decay rate specifies how quickly it drops again to the sustain volume. The release time controls how long the sound stays at the sustain volume. These four parameters can be varied to produce different sound 'shapes'. A number of these shapes are shown here:

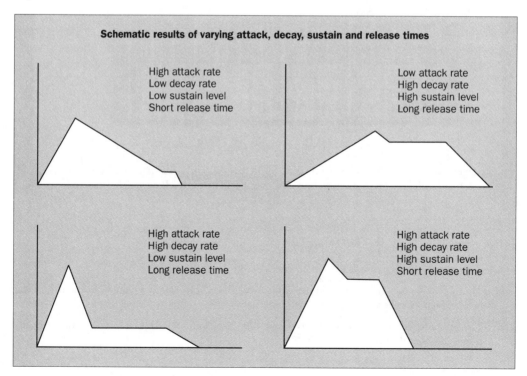

The attack rate and decay rate are specified by register 60h:

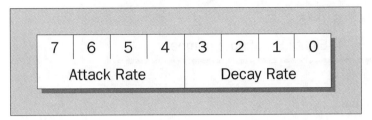

Bits 0-3 specify the decay rate, ranging from 0 (slowest) to 15 (fastest), while bits 4-7 specify the attack rate, a value between 0 (slowest) and 15 (fastest).

The sustain level and release time are controlled by register 80h, which looks like this:

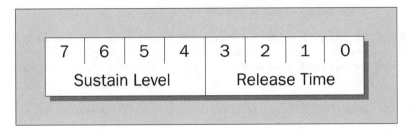

Bits 0-3 specify the release time, from 0 (longest) to 15 (slowest), while bits 4-7 specify the sustain level, from 0 (loudest) to 15 (softest).

As you can see, defining an instrument is not the simplest of tasks. There are still more registers, but I'm sure you've had enough by now.

Now we will have a look at how to actually use the instrument that we have just learnt to define. To hear a note play, we have to specify the note and the octave. We have eight octaves at our disposal, numbered 0-7. The notes, normally written down as letters, have numbers. These are as follows:

Note	Number
C#	16Bh
D	181h
D#	198h
E	1B0h
F	1CAh
F#	1E5h

Note	Number
G	202h
G#	220h
A	241h
A#	263h
B	287h
C	2AEh

As you can see, these numbers occupy ten bits, and because we only have eight-bit registers, the numbers have to be split into two parts. The eight least significant bits go into registers A0h (for channel 1) to A8h (for channel 9). The two most significant bits go as bits 0 and 1 into registers B0h (for channel 1) to B8h (for channel 9). Register A0h looks like this:

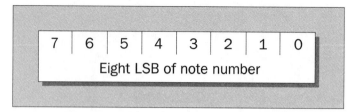

while register B0h looks like this:

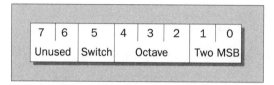

Bits 2-4 specify the octave that the note is played at. Bit 5 turns the channel on and off, and when it is set, the note starts playing. When it is cleared, the sound stops, and a new note can be played. Registers A0h and B0h are for channel 1, but the procedure is, of course, the same for the other channels (registers A1h-A8h and B1h-B8h).

Now we're ready to play some music. The following program shows how to play a simple tune, using channels 1, 2 and 3:

```
REM Play a sample tune using Sound Blaster
REM \CHAP11\CH11_14.BAS

DECLARE SUB SetReg (Reg%, Value%)
CONST BaseAddr = &H220 'Change if your sound card uses another base address

CONST RegAddr = BaseAddr + 8, DataAddr = BaseAddr + 9

DEFINT A-Z

FOR i = 0 TO 224
    SetReg i, 0 'Clear all registers
NEXT i
SetReg &H20, &H1                    'Plays carrier note at specified octave ch. 1
SetReg &H23, &H1                    'Plays modulator note at specified octave ch. 1
SetReg &H40, &H1F                   'Set carrier total level to softest ch. 1
SetReg &H43, &H0                    'Set modulator level to loudest ch. 1
SetReg &H60, &HE4                   'Set carrier attack and decay ch. 1
SetReg &H63, &HE4                   'Set modulator attack and decay ch. 1
SetReg &H80, &H9D                   'Set carrier sustain and release ch. 1
SetReg &H83, &H9D                   'Set modulator sustain and release ch. 1
SetReg &H21, &H1                    'Plays carrier note at specified octave ch. 2
SetReg &H24, &H1                    'Plays modulator note at specified octave ch. 2
SetReg &H41, &H1F                   'Set carrier total level to softest ch. 2
SetReg &H44, &H0                    'Set modulator level to loudest ch. 2
SetReg &H61, &HE4                   'Set carrier attack and decay ch. 2
SetReg &H64, &HE4                   'Set modulator attack and decay ch. 2
SetReg &H81, &H9D                   'Set carrier sustain and release ch. 2
SetReg &H84, &H9D                   'Set modulator sustain and release ch. 2
SetReg &H22, &H1                    'Plays carrier note at specified octave ch. 3
```

```
SetReg &H25, &H1                    'Plays modulator note at specified octave ch. 3
SetReg &H42, &H1F                   'Set carrier total level to softest ch. 3
SetReg &H45, &H0                    'Set modulator level to loudest ch. 3
SetReg &H62, &HE4                   'Set carrier attack and decay ch. 3
SetReg &H65, &HE4                   'Set modulator attack and decay ch. 3
SetReg &H82, &H9D                   'Set carrier sustain and release ch. 3
SetReg &H85, &H9D                   'Set modulator sustain and release ch. 3

READ NoOfNotes

FOR i = 1 TO NoOfNotes
    time! = TIMER
    FOR j = 0 TO 2 'Voices 0, 1 and 2
        READ octave
        READ note$
        SELECT CASE note$
        CASE "C#"
            SetReg &HA0 + j, &H6B 'Set note number
            SetReg &HB0 + j, &H21 + 4 * octave 'Set octave and turn on voice
        CASE "D"
            SetReg &HA0 + j, &H81
            SetReg &HB0 + j, &H21 + 4 * octave
        CASE "D#"
            SetReg &HA0 + j, &H98
            SetReg &HB0 + j, &H21 + 4 * octave
        CASE "E"
            SetReg &HA0 + j, &HB0
            SetReg &HB0 + j, &H21 + 4 * octave
        CASE "F"
            SetReg &HA0 + j, &HCA
            SetReg &HB0 + j, &H21 + 4 * octave
        CASE "F#"
            SetReg &HA0 + j, &HE5
            SetReg &HB0 + j, &H21 + 4 * octave
        CASE "G"
            SetReg &HA0 + j, &H2
            SetReg &HB0 + j, &H22 + 4 * octave
        CASE "G#"
            SetReg &HA0 + j, &H20
            SetReg &HB0 + j, &H22 + 4 * octave
        CASE "A"
            SetReg &HA0 + j, &H41
            SetReg &HB0 + j, &H22 + 4 * octave
        CASE "A#"
            SetReg &HA0 + j, &H63
            SetReg &HB0 + j, &H22 + 4 * octave
        CASE "B"
            SetReg &HA0 + j, &H87
            SetReg &HB0 + j, &H22 + 4 * octave
        CASE "C"
            SetReg &HA0 + j, &HAE
            SetReg &HB0 + j, &H22 + 4 * octave
        END SELECT
    NEXT j
        READ duration!
        DO
        LOOP WHILE time! + duration! > TIMER 'Wait as long as duration
```

```
      FOR j = 0 TO 2
          SetReg &HB0 + j, 0 'Switch voices off
      NEXT j
   NEXT i

   END
   DATA 15: REM Number of notes
   'Data below: octave1, note1, octave2, note2, octave3, note3, duration
   DATA 4,B,4,G,4,D,.5
   DATA 4,B,4,G,4,D,.5
   DATA 4,B,4,G,4,D,.5
   DATA 4,B,4,G,4,D,.5
   DATA 5,D,4,B,4,F#,.25
   DATA 4,C,4,A,4,E,.25
   DATA 4,C,4,A,4,E,.25
   DATA 4,B,4,G,4,D,.25
   DATA 4,A,4,E,3,C,1
   DATA 4,A,4,F#,4,D,.5
   DATA 4,A,4,F#,4,D,.5
   DATA 4,B,4,G,4,E,.5
   DATA 4,C,4,A,4,F#,.5
   DATA 5,D,4,A,4,F#,1
   DATA 5,G,5,D,4,B,.5

   SUB SetReg (Reg, Value)
      OUT RegAddr, Reg
      OUT DataAddr, Value
   END SUB
```

First, the procedure **SetReg** is declared, which puts the specified value into the specified register. Then, all registers are cleared:

```
FOR i = 0 TO 224
    SetReg i, 0 'Clear all registers
NEXT i
```

The registers for the first three channels are set to three identical instruments - some kind of electronic piano sound. The octaves and notes are read from the **DATA** statements and the **SELECT CASE** statement chooses the correct number for the note. The octave and note numbers are put in their respective registers and the note starts playing. We wait for a time specified by the duration variable using the **TIMER** system variable, and then registers B0h, B1h and B2h are set to zero, along with bit 5, to switch the channel off. The **DATA** statements at the end of the program describe the tune.

The first **DATA** statement specifies the number of notes and the statements that follow specify the octave and note for each channel and the duration of the note in seconds.

Working out the correct values for an instrument can be a long and tedious process. However, there are ways of making this easier. On the disk accompanying this book, the program **\CHAP11\CH11_15.BAS** can be found. This program lets you play with four of the parameters: the attack rate, the decay rate, the sustain level and the release time. When you run this program, a screen is printed as depicted here:

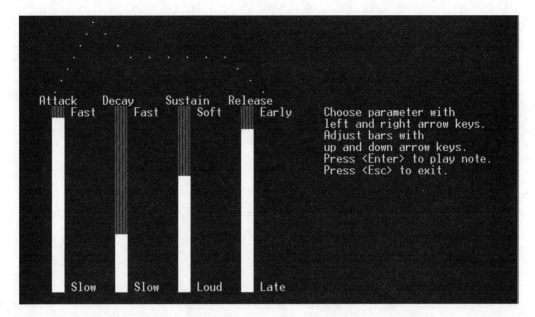

The parameter currently chosen is highlighted. You can adjust the value for this parameter using the up and down arrow keys. You can choose another parameter with the left and right arrow keys. Press *Enter* to hear the note that you have just defined. Pressing *Esc* ends the program.

This program demonstrates very well the effects that the different parameters have on the sound. You could expand this program to include the other parameters as well. When you are satisfied with the sound, you could use the values in a program similar to **\CHAP11\CH11_14.BAS**.

Summary

In this chapter, we have looked at the very basics of sound production and introduced a few programs which demonstrate how the **SOUND** and **PLAY** statements can be effectively used. We've also shown you how to talk to a Sound Blaster compatible sound card, using **OUT** and **INP** statements. We have also looked at a number of FM registers for specifying instruments, notes and octaves, using this knowledge to program a simple tune using three channels. Finally, we have experimented with four of the parameters: attack rate, decay rate, sustain level and release time. We hope that this chapter has given you some idea on Sound Blaster programming and has also encouraged you to perform some experiments of your own. Who knows? One day you could be walking into the local software store, only to hear your masterpiece blasting out as the latest No.1!

Game Development

Introduction

So you have the bricks, you have the mortar, and you want to build a house. How are you going to do it? Unless you already have some experience of writing applications and programs, you're probably wanting a gentle push in the right direction. If you're not already itching to write your own masterpiece, you will be after this chapter! And what better way to pull everything together than to write the type of programs that entertain - that's right, games.

If you aren't particularly interested in writing games (yes, some people aren't), don't discard this chapter as being trivial - it isn't. Computer entertainment is as valid a use of a computer's resources as any other program. We will show you that, because entertainment drives the computer industry, the most powerful techniques, skills and lessons are best learnt by examining game development. This is true not just for QBasic but for all languages and systems - we can all learn a great deal from writing a game or two, as well as generating a bit of fun and entertainment for everyone.

Amongst the whole enchilada of topics discussed in this chapter, the most significant ones are:

- Storing dynamic data
- Traditional game design
- Game control techniques
- Manipulating sprites
- Advanced graphic tips
- Program optimization
- Smoothing out the wrinkles in your programs

Have fun!

Games and QBasic

You've probably already played **GORILLA.BAS** and **NIBBLES.BAS**, the two games that accompany QBasic everywhere it travels. These two fine exponents of structured QBasic programming demonstrate, at the lowest - just by existing, that excellent games can, in fact, be written in QBasic. This first section has thus been devoted to the how, why and where of this well-known fact.

What QBasic Can Offer the Games Programmer

Well okay, QBasic isn't as fast as C++, and maybe it isn't even as sophisticated as Visual Basic or Delphi, but what it lacks in modern programming facets, it more than makes up for in programming ease. The fact that QBasic is one of the easiest languages to pick up serves us well not only for writing games, but for composing any program. If you know what you are doing and you have planned your program, it shouldn't take very long at all to implement the majority of the functionality of the program. Of course, many would-be programmers write programs without planning and without following sensible guidelines, such as those we outlined in the chapter on program design. This type of 'programming', is often called 'hacking', and adds considerable amounts of time and effort to the development of a program, especially in the debugging stage.

As well as the ease of programming that is inherent in most BASIC languages, QBasic also offers the games programmer a host of useful features:

▲ A highly flexible language, such as QBasic, enables programmers to choose between a variety of methods to solve a particular problem. This allows the programmer to examine each method and weigh up the advantages and disadvantages of each approach in order to find the most suitable solution.

▲ QBasic features a horde of flexible and built-in graphics functions that allow the user to draw and manipulate color images of their own choosing.

▲ Sound and music can easily be incorporated into games and other programs to enhance the effect and atmosphere.

▲ The modular aspect to QBasic programming offers the experienced programmer the chance to create re-usable libraries of frequently used functions and subroutines.

▲ There are a large number of different types of resolutions and color schemes that can be accessed by the **SCREEN** command. This also allows the programmer to pick and choose which type of screen particularly suits the type of program that he or she wants to write.

▲ The ability to incorporate external programs, for example assembly language routines or shelling out to DOS programs, allows your program to access features that are beyond the capabilities of mere internal QBasic commands.

But, alas, there are also a few disadvantages that you've got to be aware of when writing entertainment-intensive programs in QBasic.

The Limitations of Games Writing in QBasic

Okay, so QBasic isn't very fast when it comes to writing programs featuring lots of screen updates in a short time. However, this isn't the end of the world because we outline plenty of optimization tips and tricks later on in this chapter. In the meantime, let's look at some of the other hassles that QBasic games programmers have to endure and work around:

▲ File and code limits can be a crippling menace to the ambitious programmer who wants to write large applications; and large applications can sometimes be unavoidable when you need to use libraries of commonly used routines.

▲ QBasic is very slow when drawing large and not particularly complex images or drawings.

▲ There are no built-in 'just-for-games/graphics' routines in QBasic. Instead, we have to make do with **GET**, **PUT**, **DRAW**, **LINE**, **PAINT**, etc.

▲ QBasic slows down terribly when you try to interleave sound or music into your programs.

So, now that we know what problems can occur, and what QBasic's advantages are, we can start examining what types of games we can try to write.

What Types of Games Can We Write?

Well, we can write simple action games like **GORILLA.BAS** and **NIBBLES.BAS**, but *that* you already know. We can, in fact, write any type of game, but not necessarily up to the high quality that commercial games offer - but you can't have everything can you? In fact, this chapter will give you a thorough grounding for writing any type of game - the techniques that we will show you here will endow you with twenty years of games programming knowledge. Whether you want to continue writing games in QBasic indefinitely, or whether you intend to move on after mastering QBasic, this chapter will hold you in good stead for writing games, period.

If you want to put the disk that accompanies this book in your machine, you could try out some of the example programs that we've written for your amusement:

▲ Strategy Games - such as Super Soccer Manager (**SSM.BAS**), are ideally suited to QBasic's modular features and are CPU non-intensive. This type of game, such as The Book Publishing Game (**BOOK.BAS**), can be easily completed in pure text.

▲ Puzzle Games - such as Animal Vegetable Mineral (**AVM.BAS**), are also easily programmable in text alone. Our Quiz Game is a perfect multiple-player exponent of this hugely popular genre.

▲ Adventure Games - such as The Adventure (**ADVENTUR.BAS**), is predominantly text-based too, although static graphics of each location render a better atmosphere.

▲ Action Games - such as Battle (**BATTLE.BAS**), is a very broad area but, fortunately, they are also the most popular so the most research has gone into developing this type of game. Try out Dodge Pro (**DODGEPRO.BAS**) and Hour of the Beasties (trust me, try **BEASTIES.BAS**) for two vastly different action games.

Have these whetted your appetite to write some better games? If so, read on, because we'll be telling you how to get the most out of QBasic and your entertaining ideas.

There are literally thousands of QBasic games knocking around and, if you check out Appendix A, you will find a comprehensive resource for finding the best in QBasic development.

Writing Text-only Games

Most people think that games can only be written using graphics. This is simply not true - a lot of the best games are in fact text-only. QBasic is particularly adept at text-based games because it has a fantastic array of text-handling functions and commands that make a mockery of other languages. Text is also very quick compared to hordes of graphics and can be stored a lot more efficiently, making it ideal for many types of game that we discussed a few paragraphs ago.

The perfect example of how text can be used to create other worlds of entertainment and vision is the ageless classic, the text adventure game.

Writing Adventure Games

The origin of textual adventure games goes back a very long way. Before computers, we had books, music, movies and television to take us to far off places, but what they couldn't do was to let you do *incredible* things. One of the first types of game, the text adventure game, could take you anywhere and let you do anything. This new media could let you (yes, *you*) fight dragons, fly to Mars, command an army or be ruler of a kingdom. The power of words had been taken to new lengths and was exploding the imagination of millions of computer users around the world.

But what is more important is that, today, with all our SVGA monitors, sound cards and multimedia capabilities, the structure and concepts behind these ancient founders of video games still exist in modern games. It's now time for us to rediscover these golden rules that have stood the test of time.

What Is a Text Adventure Game?

The game drops you, the lead character, into a new land, where you must fulfill tasks or aim for goals. Basically, you do this by picking up and using objects, and talking to, persuading and fighting with other characters. You are able to move about in this land by typing GO EAST, RUN NORTH, CLIMB UP, etc. Everything you want to do must be typed in in plain English, which made these games highly accessible to a lot of people. Here is a screenshot from our QBasic adventure game that we'll be looking at in a few moments:

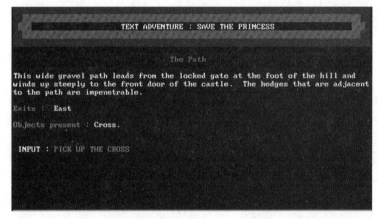

If you want to try this game out before we start discussing it, you can find it in the **GAMES** directory on the accompanying disk. It's called **ADVENTUR.BAS**. The first thing that we must discuss once you have played around with it is what data we have to store, and why. So here we go.

Storing our Data

All programs need to store data, and games, in general, are no exception. Whilst different games require different data storage techniques, our adventure game is probably the best example with which to examine the issues involved in storing our data. By following our thinking, you can perhaps begin to practice the techniques behind visualizing a whole program, before you've started to write code. So, as a kind of exercise from Chapter 7 - Program Design, let's look at what data we need to store. This will act as our specification document.

Locations

First of all, we need some way of storing information about all our locations in the game. For example, we will need the following data readily at hand for *every* location:

Name	`"On top of Big Bob's Mountain."`
Description	`"The air is very thin up here at the top of the world, but, in between breaths, you can make out that the world is indeed round, and a lot bigger than you'd ever thought as a child. You are surrounded by craggy rocks and very little vegetation."`
List of Exits	`"23120300000002000400"`

Here, we have specified all three items of data as strings, which is no surprise for the first two, but the last one could easily be represented numerically. This field is used to determine which location to go to (if any) when the user enters North, Southeast or Up for example, and works like this:

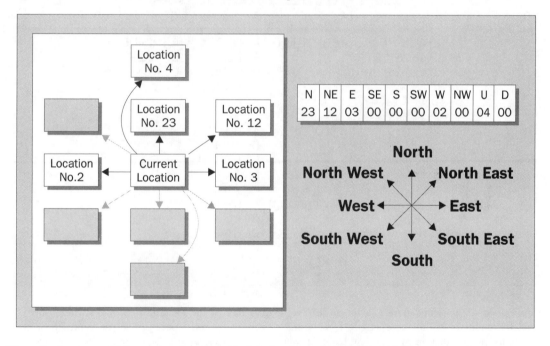

N	NE	E	SE	S	SW	W	NW	U	D
23	12	03	00	00	00	02	00	04	00

Alternatively, we could have stored each exit's location in an individual variable, or even in an array. There's a lot information detailed here, but the reason we have opted for the string option is purely the fact that the representation is easy to access, concise and readily understandable.

> Notice how the description of the example entry is devoid of 'variable' factors, such as light, objects, state of the surrounding area etc. The description we use for each location should always be as general as possible, so that we never get static, conflicting problems. A good example could be a cave. If we described it as dark, what would happen if the user lit a torch in the cave? The description field would lose its authenticity, appeal and effect.

Objects

We need very similar data for all our sticks, gems and rocks. But we do actually need a complex information field too, to store details like weight, location, condition, etc. We require all these for each object that we define in the game:

Name	`"A big stick"`
Description	`"This is one huge meaty twig, ideal for clogging someone with."`
Information	`"0010002030405055064"`

Here, the same applies to the description field, as it did for the location information. But, once again we have also included an initially indecipherable string of numbers to depict all the information required to control the object. Luckily, we've provided a diagram to explain it:

LOCATION	WEIGHT	USE	TYPE OF USE	POSITION	INSIDE WHAT?
01	02	A	A	C	00

	0 - FLYWEIGHT	A - CLOTHING	A - FEET	A - INSIDE
	3 - BRICKWEIGHT		B - LEGS	B - FIXED
	5 - BAG OF BRICKS		C - TORSO	C - NONE
	10 - HEAVY		D - HANDS	
	15 - TON		E - HEAD	

B - FOOD	A - HUNGER
	B - THIRST
	C - HEALTH
	D - BAD

C - WEAPON	A - SHOOT
	B - CLUB
	C - STAB

D - KEY

The information represented here is a lot more diverse than that of the location's exit field which only featured ten numbers of the same length. Here, using a string is essential because we can represent a great deal of different information in very few bytes of memory. This technique of squeezing a lot of related data into one very small, but accessible, unit is invaluable as lack of memory space can be crippling in large applications.

You may have been wondering earlier why we didn't include a field in the locations section for those objects that are present at that location. Well, as you can see from the diagram, we have included that function here, within the object information field. Because we have a sub-field detailing the location of the object, we can assign the following values:

00	The user is holding it
01-49	The actual location 1-99
50	Doesn't exist or has been destroyed
51-99	It is inside the object numbered n+100

Some programs feature a separate array to fulfill this role, often called **inventory()**, but this is just a good example of inefficiency.

Getting our Line of Input

"What is wrong with the **INPUT** command then?", I here you ask. Well, without wanting to hurt it's feelings, it is a little bit simple, I'm afraid. You see there's very little flexibility in there - it's designed to be multi-purpose, and in doing so it has had to compromise a fair bit. For example, if we wanted the user to enter a name, we might want to stop them using the number keys and, whilst they're typing away, convert the first letter of each name into upper case. The **INPUT** command doesn't allow us to do any of this. If we had a little man on the screen, who we wanted to move about, how could we do that with the **INPUT** command? This is where **INKEY$** steps into the ring.

Harnessing the Power of INKEY$

As we discovered back in Chapter 3 - Input, Output and Printing, the **INKEY$** statement is of little use without a suitable control structure to harness its basic control features. So, if we use a simple **WHILE...WEND** loop to encapsulate our input command, we find that we can poll very easily for exactly what we want:

```
REM Demonstration of controlling input via WHILE...INKEY$...WEND
REM \CHAP12\CH12_1.BAS

LOCATE 1,1:PRINT "Press a key to test this routine"
a$=""
WHILE a$=""
a$=UCASE$(INKEY$)
WEND
LOCATE 5,5:PRINT "You pressed the ";a$;" key"

END
```

Now what you do with the key code that is returned, here by **a$**, is central to successful control of your dynamic input routines. We have simply output the code in this example, but we could have played a tune instead, dropped a coconut, quit the program, or made our lead character jump in the air. We shall come back to the important topic of control in action games but, for now, let's concentrate on entering a text string. To enter a whole string, though, we will need to go that little bit further and turn this single-character routine into a module that can enter a full string, whilst maintaining the same control over the keyboard.

> Notice that we use the UCASE$ function to return just the upper-case version of every alphabetic character entered. This doesn't restrict entry to just alphabetic characters, but merely converts them if they are entered. Obviously, if you want to use lower-case letters, this routine will need slight modification.

If we want to use the last routine as the basis for inputting a whole string, we need to control the following variables:

The whole string	**st$**
The last character	**a$**
The current X screen coordinate	**x**
The current Y screen coordinate	**y**
The maximum number of characters	**maxchar%**

The problem with the previous routine is that it will only input a single character. This poses some awkward questions for us: how do we construct a string?, how do we control the input?, and what editing features can we incorporate? This last question is extremely important, especially since the **INPUT** statement that we are replacing offered us some excellent editing features, such as the ability to amend keypresses that were incorrect.

Basically, what happens is that we use the **st$** variable to store the whole string, and each valid character entered is added onto the end of the string (assuming that we haven't already filled up the whole string). We also manage to include a fully working *BackSpace* key to delete the last character entered. The whole input process is confirmed when you press the *Return* key.

```
COLOR 7: LOCATE 18, 2: PRINT "INPUT :": COLOR 2
X = 10: Y = 18: MAX% = 50: EntryString$ = "": a$ = ""


StartTextEntry:
a$ = "": WHILE a$ = "": a$ = UCASE$(INKEY$): WEND
SOUND 137, .1
IF a$ = CHR$(13) AND EntryString$ <> "" THEN GOTO StartAnalysis
IF a$ = CHR$(8) AND EntryString$ <> "" THEN
    EntryString$ = LEFT$(EntryString$, LEN(EntryString$) - 1): LOCATE Y, X:
    PRINT EntryString$; "      ": GOTO StartTextEntry
IF (ASC(a$) < 64 OR ASC(a$) > 91) AND (a$ <> " " AND a$ <> "-"
    AND a$ <> "." AND a$ <> ",") THEN GOTO StartTextEntry
IF LEN(EntryString$) > MAX% - 1 THEN GOTO StartTextEntry
EntryString$ = EntryString$ + a$
LOCATE Y, X: PRINT EntryString$ + " "
GOTO StartTextEntry
```

Notice that, after waiting for a key, we operate a filter system to weed out keypresses that won't be put into the string, such as *Return*, *BackSpace*, numbers or non-alphabetic characters. For the most part, if we receive an illegal character, we choose to ignore it and pass control back to the start of the loop so that we can get a proper input. If the key that the user pressed is okay, though, we add it on to the end of the string **st$** and print the whole string out again.

> *The reason we have used the audio command,* **SOUND 137, .1** *is so that the user can get that extra bit of tactile feedback from the keyboard. By making this noise every time the user presses a key, we can emulate the clicking sound made by a noisy typewriter.*

We may indeed be using this as our basis for string input for our adventure game, but this doesn't restrict its use at all. In fact, by using variables such as **x**, **y** and **maxchar%** , this routine can, with very few changes, be re-used in almost any string-entry scenario. The number of string-entry scenarios you come across in the average program can be phenomenal.

We shall return to the subject of refining our data input routines when we discuss the subject of keyboard input in the Chapter 13 - Programming a User Interface.

All that we have to do in our program now is work out how we can analyze this string so that we can act on the commands given by the user.

Acting on Input

We have our user input string, **EntryString$**, and what we have got to do is to examine its contents and act on them. Nothing hard about that you may be thinking, but let's assure you that you'd be wrong. Okay, so we could simply do something like this:

```
IF EntryString$="GO NORTH" THEN CALL MoveNorth
IF EntryString$="EAT FOOD" THEN CALL EatFood
IF EntryString$="HOP ON 1 FOOT WHILST CARVING A WOODEN PIG" THEN CALL WhichFoot?
```

which would work admirably; but definitely in the face of sensibility, because this is so inflexible that we would have to write hundreds of lines of code if we were to make our interpreter understand a potentially infinite number of commands.

Many programmers of text adventure games have fallen into the trap of only offering the user a very limited array of commands with which to 'live' in their virtual world. For example, to move your characters north, you should be able to use any of the following:

NORTH, MOVE NORTH, GO NORTH, WALK NORTH and RUN NORTH

amongst many others. But some programmers only incorporated one or two of these methods for each command, and left the user to get really frustrated by the interpreter's fundamental lack of knowledge, which leads it to frequently tell the user, 'I don't understand!'.

String Analysis

What we need to do, then, is write a routine that will translate our string into a format akin to the way we understand our own verbal languages - by splitting it up into separate chunks, or words. To do this, we need the following variables:

NumberOfWords%	Number of words separated by a space.
NumberOfSentences%	Number of sentences.
WordLength%	Length of the current word.
B$	Current character being analyzed.
WORD$(A)	Storage of separate words after analysis.

Before we start analyzing our string, one of the first things we must do is to check that the user has typed in a full stop at the end of the string, and if not, add one ourselves:

```
IF RIGHT$(EntryString$, 1) <> "." THEN EntryString$ = EntryString$ + "."
```

This is so that our program can recognize when a sentence has been terminated.

Once everything has been initialized and is ready, we can start to analyze our string at last. We shall do this by once again scanning our string character by character:

```
   FOR a = 1 TO LEN(EntryString$)
      B$ = MID$(EntryString$, a, 1)
      IF B$ = "." THEN NumberOfSentences% = NumberOfSentences% + 1
      IF B$ = " " AND WordLength% = 0 THEN GOTO EndLoop
      IF (B$ = " " OR B$ = "(" OR B$ = ")" OR B$ = "?" OR B$ = "!" OR B$ = CHR$(34) OR
   B$ = "." OR B$ = "," OR B$ = "" OR a = LEN(EntryString$)) AND WordLength% > 0 THEN
   GOSUB GetWord: GOTO EndLoop
      WordLength% = WordLength% + 1

   EndLoop:
    NEXT a
```

Here, the program runs through the string one character at a time, waiting for the chance to store a whole word in the **WORD$()** array. The main line here checks for all the 'end-of-word' characters, such as a new space, a comma, full stop or the end of the string. When it finds one, it jumps out to a subroutine which extracts the word and stores it in the aforementioned array:

```
   REM ########### SUBROUTINE ##########
   NumberOfWords% = NumberOfWords% + 1
   flag% = 0
   Word$(NumberOfWords%) = MID$(EntryString$, a - WordLength%, WordLength% + 1)
   WordLength% = 0
   RETURN
```

Notice that we increment the number of words variable here and, after we have extracted the word, we reset the word length variable to zero, ready for the next word to be analyzed.

We siphon the word off to the **WORD$()** array, by extracting it with the **MID$** function passing the parameters of **a**, the pointer to the current character in the routine, less the length of the string, and the length of the string plus one. This works as long as the pointer minus word length is positive.

Incorporating a Debugging Function

If you haven't managed to bend your head around the logic that flows through this system, and rest assured all programmers get that feeling, take it one step at a time and work out exactly what is happening every step of the way. If you had written such a logic intensive program as this, or beyond this, you will probably hit some problems or conundrums along the way. One of the best ways to overcome your lack of understanding is, like we showed you in Chapter 4 - Understanding Memory, Data and Machine Code, to write some short subroutine that shows you, whilst your program is running, what the contents of all your pertinent variables are. Such a subroutine can be run when you press a certain key, can be programmed to execute at a certain stage, or it can simply be included in the program listing but not normally called, except when you're having a debugging fest.

Take a look at our variable printing stub here:

```
   InputStats:
   REM ########### INPUT STATS ##########
   LOCATE 11, 1: COLOR 7: PRINT "Number of words : "; NumberOfWords%
   PRINT "Number of Sentences : "; NumberOfSentences%
   PRINT "Average sentence length was : "; (NumberOfWords% / NumberOfSentences%); "words
   long"
   LOCATE 17, 1: FOR a = 1 TO 8: PRINT Word$(a); "   "; : NEXT a
   WHILE INKEY$ = "": WEND
   RETURN
```

Here, we present a variety of variables and other statistical information that should tell us that our routine, and those who feed it, are running smoothly.

Acting on our Analysis

The method that we outlined earlier for acting on input was dismissed as being extremely verbose and very inflexible, so how does our new string analysis routine help us? Well, it enables us to make much more efficient use of logic, and also to keep everything concisely segmented into reasonably short modules. Take our action section:

```
Reply$ = UnknownResponse$((RND * 14) + 1)
WHILE a$ <> "": a$ = INKEY$: WEND
W1$ = LEFT$(Word$(1), LEN(Word$(1)) - 1)
IF Word$(2) <> "" THEN W2$ = LEFT$(Word$(2), LEN(Word$(2)) - 1)
IF Word$(3) <> "" THEN W3$ = LEFT$(Word$(3), LEN(Word$(3)) - 1)
IF Word$(4) <> "" THEN W4$ = LEFT$(Word$(4), LEN(Word$(4)) - 1)
IF Word$(5) <> "" THEN W5$ = LEFT$(Word$(5), LEN(Word$(5)) - 1)
IF W1$ = "DROP" AND W2$ <> "" THEN GOSUB DropObject
IF W1$ = "DROP" AND W2$ = "" THEN Reply$ = "Drop what?"
IF (W1$ = "GET" OR W1$ = "GRAB" OR W1$ = "TAKE") AND W2$ <> "" THEN W4$ = W2$: GOSUB
GetObject
IF (W1$ = "GET" OR W1$ = "GRAB" OR W1$ = "TAKE") AND W2$ = "" THEN Reply$ = "Try again
- what do you want?"
IF (W1$ = "GO" OR W1$ = "RUN" OR W1$ = "WALK" OR W1$ = "CRAWL" OR W1$ = "HOP") AND
(W2$ = "NORTH" OR W2$ = "SOUTH" OR W2$ = "EAST" OR W2$ = "WEST") THEN GOSUB
MoveRoutine
```

First of all, we select a random response just in case the user has typed something that our interpreter doesn't understand. We use a random response instead of a fixed 'I don't understand!' because it surprises the user and increases the length of time before he or she gets frustrated and quits our game.

To keep this section of code as short as possible, and keep the length of possibly very long lines to a minimum, we transfer the contents of the **WORD$()** array into the shorter, and more manageable strings, **W1$**, **W2$**, **W3$** etc. We decrement the length of the word in the **WORD$()** array because the originals are stored with an extra character on the end.

We are now able to fit all like verbs together on one line - a vast improvement on what would have occupied at least five separate lines.

Implementing Other Features

There are so many interesting and valuable features of a well-written adventure game that we can't possibly mention them all here. But what we will do is to outline some of the more advanced features of typical adventure games so that you can have a go at implementing them yourselves. None of the concepts introduced here are particularly difficult, and neither are they particularly involved. All we are manipulating is arrays, and all we are writing is text.

Objects

Objects are the lifeblood of the text adventure game - without them you can't achieve anything more substantial than mere traveling around the virtual world. Objects should be programmed to be used in the following ways:

To be picked up	TAKE EGG, PICK UP EGG, GET EGG etc.
To be dropped	DROP ROCK
Use object	USE BRUSH (or the specific verb such as PAINT WALL WITH BRUSH)
Eat/drink object	EAT CARROT, CONSUME BEER, SWALLOW FOUL YOGHURT
Wear object	WEAR RED SCARF, PUT ILL-FITTING JEANS ON

It would be inadvisable for us to explain how each of these could work, and indeed these are only ideas that could easily be incorporated into your adventure - we haven't necessarily included them in **ADVENTUR.BAS**.

We showed you earlier how we are going to store the object data in memory, and a quick revision of that, will show you how easily it is to implement these features. For example, if the user had typed in TAKE EGG, the module for the 'Pick Up' action would be processed with these operations:

▲ Check that the object is present in the locality. If not, display 'Cannot see EGG' message.

▲ If the object is currently held by the user, display 'EGG is already held' message.

▲ Check that the user has enough space to carry the object. If not, display 'Your pockets are full' message.

▲ Check the objects weight and its ability to be carried. If it can't be carried, display 'You cannot carry the EGG' message.

To perform all these checks you must first find which object in memory, the user has referred to. You can do this by simply searching through the object names until you reach one called 'EGG', then you assign a variable to the number of that record. The code should look something like this:

```
flag% = 0
FOR a% = 1 TO Objects%
   IF UCASE$(ObjectKey$(a%)) = W4$ THEN flag% = a%
NEXT a%
```

Now you can use the **flag%** variable to manipulate the relevant data in the object information string. Assuming that the situation when the user typed 'TAKE EGG' passed all the checks, we must change the location attribute of the 'EGG' object to signify that we are holding it:

```
ObjectInfo$(flag%) = "00" + RIGHT$(ObjectInfo$(flag%), 7)
```

Here, we have used the value 7 to represent the rest of the string which is 9 characters long, less the first 2 characters designating the location. By using string modifiers such as **MID$** we can perform almost any function on our objects that we care to imagine.

Characters

It's infeasible that any world you place the user in will be uninhabited. It would, therefore, be useful to learn how to control other characters (**npcs** or non-player characters). Although we didn't define any data structures for characters in our earlier section, we are sure that by following the structure of the objects database, you can define your own system.

> *It's important not to think of our method of data storage as being the 'best way' - every adventure game will require different attributes, features and data. If you don't design any of your applications before you start writing them, you'll spend far too much time trying to convert old code which was originally designed for a different purpose.*

There are many ways that you can design your characters to interact with your world; they can be developed so that they can talk with you, help you, give you objects, threaten you, laugh at you or even ignore you. Characters can also be given tasks to perform in the game, like guard a bridge, find a pot of gold, mug people, follow you, etc.

The Concept of Time

But when do you check whether a character has hit you? Or whether they have taken your wallet and left the scene? Well, this is where you have to decide how you wish to implement the concept of time in your text adventure game. For instance, most games take the easy route and simply check a character-handling routine after each command has been entered. This has the effect that the whole virtual world waits for the user to finish their cup of coffee and type in a command before making any changes - hardly realistic. The alternative is a lot more difficult to implement, that of incorporating a timer so that, whilst you're still typing instructions, a message will pop up saying 'Big Bad Bob has come into the room' or something else just as scary.

The reason that this method is so difficult to implement is two-fold: first you have to try to give the user the perception that time passes at a constant rate - quite difficult when the user is typing, or the program is doing something else, and second you must give the effect that character processing is transparent, i.e. allow the user to perform actions during the character processing. This is a quite complex subject and obviously requires a great deal of precision and control.

Pictures

Text adventures, by definition, are purely textual systems, but when video displays evolved, programmers soon learnt to incorporate graphics into their games. Instead of, or perhaps as well as, the textual description of each location and object, we can depict 'The Hairy Cave' that little bit better. Of course, the improvement over text depends purely on the quality of the artistry. You could draw each picture using QBasic's drawing functions, or you could store them as bitmaps on a non-visible background video page, or even draw them in your favorite paint package and load them in when you visit each new location.

There are, in fact, too many things with which you could improve any application, not just text adventure games. All it takes is a little application and thought when you are designing your project. Hopefully, this text adventure has proved to be a great help to understanding how flexible QBasic really is, and how important text can really be to a game.

Traditional Game Design

Thousands and thousands of computer games have been written over the past twenty years, with the number growing exponentially every day. And just like any other medium, most titles feature popular concepts that have gradually matured into regular beasts that developers think players like. This next section will pinpoint exactly what these 'traditions' are, show you how you can implement them and demonstrate some good examples on the accompanying disk.

Different Formats

The way that you intend to use your program when it is finished will impact strongly on the different formats that you want it to take. For example, you may just want to produce one version of the game and continually update it - the most popular format. Or, you may want to produce a couple of formats aimed at different people; for example, one version of a calculator program for students, and another version for engineers. For a good example of different versions of software, take a look at the three versions of the game Dodge that appear on the accompanying disk.

Another scenario is that of shareware, whereby you produce and freely distribute one limited version of your software which has some important features missing. This has the advantage of letting people look at your software and if they like it, they can send away for the **registered version** which they have to pay for.

Security and Piracy Issues

There are a multitude of reasons for wanting to prevent users from giving illegal copies of your programs to their friends, colleagues or even selling it themselves. Whilst you may not be concerned with such matters at the moment, you may develop a program at some point in the future that you wish to be used by only those people who have paid for your hard work. The main principle involved in solving this problem is based around a variation on the theme of password management.

The easiest method is to give the user a list of passwords that correspond to certain codes. When the program starts, the user is given a code and then he or she has to look up that code in their list of passwords. They type in the appropriate password and if they are correct, the program continues. If they enter the wrong password, the application is closed.

Because QBasic programs don't readily change hands for large sums of money, security can seem rather pointless. But, nevertheless, this is an important topic and one that should be practiced or at least considered at this early stage in your programming career.

Take, for example, the following subroutine which utilizes an array of statistics, **STATS%(100,5)**, for characters in a role-playing adventure game:

```
CLS
XVal% = INT(RND*100)+1
YVal% = INT(RND*5)+1
LOCATE 5,5:PRINT "Enter security code for entry : ";XVal%;", ";YVal%
LOCATE 30,5:INPUT ":";code$
IF VAL(code$)<>STATS%(XVal%, YVal%) THEN PRINT "Incorrect!": SYSTEM
LOCATE 30,6:PRINT "Correct!"
```

Here, we have selected a random entry from our characters data table and ask the user to enter the correct code from the manual.

There are several other issues to be considered here, though:

▲   The legal user must have a printed copy of all the codes.

▲   The codes must not be accessible to an illegal user.

▲   A listing of the program must never be made accessible to any user.

▲   The codes must never change.

Extravagance and Showing Off

Whilst other types of 'serious' applications have to fulfill a certain role, such as display business information, write letters or calculate equations, every game *must* fulfill one goal - to entertain. Of course, most games perform this function satisfactorily with just the actual game itself, but because games programmers want to entertain the user, they are prone to showing off. This gratuitous creativity overflow enables the developer to scare their competitors at the same time as causing users to drool over luscious graphics and incredible sound - and they haven't even started the game yet! In fact, many 'amateur' programmers allow their games to be overshadowed by their flashy introductions and sideshows, and some just create stand-alone 'demos' which you are supposed to just watch goggle-eyed, whispering "How do they do that?".

Introductory Sequences

The main concentration of 'flashy sequences' can be found at the start of games, in the introduction before the game or menu starts up. Normally, introductions are used to serve as a gentle preamble to the game, where credits, instructions or the story-line are given. Many modern commercial games spend millions of dollars developing long, introductory video sequences that consume amazing chunks of your hard disk. Think hard before you embark on creating an involved introduction in QBasic, and don't forget that players want to play the game, not watch the intro every time they load your game.

Pre/Post-Game Interfacing

So, how long does it take from selecting Start on the QBasic Run menu, before you can actually start firing at aliens, or playing the game? Well, most programs, not just games, have an initial interface that is situated after the introduction and before the game. We discussed them earlier and you've all seen them, the most common one for games being the menu list.

A typical menu could consist of the following menu items:

> Play Game
> See Introduction Again
> See Instructions
> Examine/Change Game Controls
> See Hi-score Table
> Examine/Change Game Options
> See Credits
> Fill in Order Form
> Exit Game

This menu would normally be shown after the introduction has finished, after a game has been finished, and if during the game the player wants to change the controls or options, or just wants a breather from the action. We have already seen that QBasic is more than capable of coping with such a menu system, so implementing it around a game is an excellent method of controlling the program flow.

Of course, you don't have to follow this interfacing method. It would be just as valid to use any one of the other systems, a combination of these or even one of your own. Many programmers forget that all the best programs offer a very stable and informative environment and solely concentrate upon the actual game, to the detriment of the final system.

Originality and Concept Integration

Many users, myself included, complain that programs written by the same programmer always look the same. I suppose that this is similar to suggesting that a rock band always sound the same. This isn't necessarily a good or a bad thing - merely a point of view. But it's possible for people to get into a certain habit that stagnates a program and becomes old hat. This is why many programmers fuse their introductions into their interfaces and vice versa, in order to produce an astonishingly flashy interface.

What we are trying to say is that there are no hard and fast rules to game design - QBasic is *so* flexible that you're able, with practice, to achieve virtually anything. Incorporating an original (and awe-inspiring) idea into the introduction or interface-system of a program is a difficult thing to achieve and can only be done through experience, patience and effort. In the meantime, check out some of these programs on the accompanying disk, for example, the information screen in Extreme Velocity, `\GAMES\EV.BAS`.

Establishing the Level of Difficulty

This is crucial to the average length of time that a player of your game will spend playing it. Perhaps they will play it twice, finish the game, put it back in the box and never let it see the light of day again. Or maybe the user will give up after a couple of tries because it's "obviously impossible". It's evident that the writer of the game has to come to some compromise with the level of difficulty.

This kind of mastery of game design is a black art where many a hopeful programmer has come a cropper. But there are certain corrections that you can follow to ensure that your game doesn't make the fatal mistakes like this:

▲ Increase the minimum length of time *you* need to complete the game. You can do this by making your playing area bigger, adding more puzzles, including new levels, or making your opponents nastier!

▲ Make sure that you have a gradual grading of the actual difficulty of the game. In Tetris, the blocks fall faster, in Doom the monsters get bigger and in Chess the players get even better. Always start with a few easy stages and then up the tempo once the player has begun to acclimatize.

▲ Add the ability for the user to play against another human being. This increases the interest and shelf life of your game.

▲ If at all possible, allow the user to define the level of difficulty before they start. This enables them to play the whole game once on the easy level, and then on the next level, and so on. Effectively, this can create multiple instances of one game - increasing the size of your game by the number of difficulty levels.

▲ Give the user the chance to customize the game before (and/or during) the game. Offering them the chance to change racing cars or use a different weapon will also increase the chances of them keeping the game on their hard disk.

Let's now look at some of the concepts involved with difficulty-level programming.

Splitting the Game into Different Levels

There are many ways of splitting a game into logical chunks and they all depend purely on the type of game that you want to write. For example, a platform game can be split into different 'buildings', 'worlds' or 'levels', where the programmer can give each area a distinct personality or style of its own. Many programmers try to make each area into a sub-game, where the difficulty rises steadily from the start of each level to the end, where a huge end-of-level beasty appears.

This encapsulatory effect allows programmers to split the whole game conveniently into sub-games that, frankly, provide the project manager with some flexibility, such as the ability to scrap later levels if work falls behind schedule. Individual levels can also be distributed between a team, to get the job done a lot quicker.

Using the Concept of Lives

Many games, especially action games, implement the concept of multiple lives. Where your character can actually die, the user feels comfortable with having some reserve 'life' to rely on for continuing the game. Normally, games give the user three lives with which to complete the game and maybe even win a bonus life later in the game.

Storing Snapshots

When games get too big to finish in one go, such as a thinking game like our text adventure, you have to think about implementing a snapshot routine to save all the variables in your game to disk. Basically, you need two routines, one to save the snapshot and another to recover a saved snapshot.

We've already discussed how to store files on disk, so there are only a few pieces of advice left that we can give on the subject:

▲ You should allow the user to specify the name and path of the snapshot. This primarily enables different users to store separate snapshots, dependent upon the amount of free disk space, not restricting them to just a small set of snapshots.

▲ Because QBasic can sometimes be a little sluggish, try to implement some sort of progress bar, giving the user some sort of indication as to how long is left before they can resume their game.

▲ Try to make the process as quick as possible - some adventure games are so large that it can take minutes for a snapshot to be saved.

▲ Hi-score tables are often by gamers as a method of easing the difficulty level. This is achieved by saving the game just before a possibly fatal section. Programmers can get around this by limiting the places or times when the user can save or load a game.

Hi-score Tables

Most games implement some sort of scoring system with which the user can be graded and rewarded. A close acquaintance of most scoring systems is the fabled **hi-score table**. Hi-score tables use the tried and tested league tabling technique to add that extra competitive edge to games - the incentive to beat not only the game, but also the previous best scores. Basically, these hi-score tables contain the following information:

▲ Position in table

▲ Name of achiever

▲ Total score

for each entry in the table, which normally holds between ten and twenty of the best-ever scores. It could look something like this taken from Hour of the Beasties:

```
          HOUR OF THE BEASTIES HI-SCORE TABLE
        1 ___ Big Bob the Wild Axe-man_____ 70
        2 ___ Fat Jack the Rabid Veterinarian_____ 63
        3 ___ Loose Jim the Mad Milkman_____ 58
        4 ___ Thick Phil the Daft Goose-Chaser_____ 52
        5 ___ Bouncy Bertha the Bobbing Duck_____ 50
        6 ___ Sick Sam the Great Goonybird Hunter_____ 47
        7 ___ Bad Boris the Fractal Freak_____ 43
        8 ___ Flat Phyllis the Fool_____ 38
        9 ___ Edible Egbert the 'Orrid Egg_____ 34
       10 ___ Tricky Tom the Green Grass Lover_____ 29
       11 ___ Horseman Harry the Bee-Tamer_____ 25
       12 ___ Radioactive Ronny the Rooster_____ 22
       13 ___ Slick Simon the Slippery Stone_____ 18
       14 ___ Juicy Jill the Jar of Gel_____ 15
       15 ___ Hold-The-Horses Henry the Bowl_____ 12
```

The implementation of a hi-score table is not very complex. It is but a simple sorted array of data - the key of the sort being the score achieved. When a player's session has terminated, the program will check the hi-score table to see if the score that has just been accumulated warrants a place in the table:

```
REM ###### UPDATE HI-SCORE TABLE ######

VAR% = 0                               ' Check whether score is good
FOR A = 15 TO 1 STEP -1                ' enough to make the hi-score table
   IF SCORE% > HI%(A) THEN VAR% = A
NEXT A
IF VAR% = 0 THEN GOTO 2780

CLS
LOCATE 1, 1: COLOR 9: PRINT STRING$(80, "Û");
LOCATE 25, 1: PRINT STRING$(80, "Û");
FOR A = 2 TO 24
   LOCATE A, 1: PRINT "Û";
   LOCATE A, 80: PRINT "Û";
NEXT A

COLOR 14: LOCATE 3, 15: PRINT "CONGRATULATIONS YOUR EFFORTS HAVE BEEN REWARDED"
COLOR 7: LOCATE 6, 5: PRINT "Your name must now be engraved upon the high score 
trophy for 'The Hour"
LOCATE 7, 5: PRINT "Of The Beasties'.   Please enter how you wish it to be 
represented : "
FOR A = 14 TO VAR% STEP -1
   HI$(A + 1) = HI$(A)
   HI%(A + 1) = HI%(A)
NEXT A
HI%(VAR%) = SCORE%
COLOR 15: LOCATE 10, 15: INPUT "Enter your name : "; HISIG$
IF LEN(HISIG$) > 25 THEN HISIG$ = LEFT$(HISIG$, 25)
HI$(VAR%) = HISIG$

OPEN "BEAST_HS" FOR OUTPUT AS #1
FOR A = 1 TO 15
   WRITE #1, HI$(A)
   WRITE #1, HI%(A)
NEXT A
CLOSE #1
RETURN
```

If the last game is good enough to warrant recognition, it must be inserted in the sorted array at the correct place and the existing entries from that position, down the table, must be lowered down a place:

```
FOR A = 14 TO VAR% STEP -1
   HI$(A + 1) = HI$(A)
   HI%(A + 1) = HI%(A)
NEXT A
HI%(VAR%) = SCORE%
```

Don't forget that your hi-score table must always be saved to disk after each update of the table, or at the end of a session, so that the new entries can be seen when the user returns to the game a week later.

Multiple Human Players

There's a time in the career of most games where the user will become bored with or be able to predict the actions of the computer opponent. If, however, your game allows you to play against other people, the challenge is sustained a little longer. There are two ways of allowing for more than one player to compete in a single game:

- Take turns to make a move (the Chess method)
- Simultaneous actions (the Tron method)

Each has its merits, depending on the type of game you wish to implement. For example, the game of **\GAMES\DODGE3.BAS** on the disk, is a three-player game where each person has a set of four keys on the keyboard with which to control their character - a crowded scene! The game of Battle **\GAMES\BATTLE.BAS** features a style of game where the two players take tension-building turns to fire a cannon at the other player.

Game Control Techniques

Different games, like different programs, need different controls. All programs (except totally non-interactive rolling demos) require you to control the flow of the program and without it the user would only be able to watch the program. So, in order to sustain even the minimum of interest, you will need to write routines which will let the user think that they are in control of the program.

We have already looked at programming a user interface, which covered all the standard methods of allowing the user to have a say in your program. What we are going to do in this section is to take a look at how we can write intuitive input routines that can not only be used in games, but in any program you care to write. We will start off by taking a peek at how we can control the keyboard a little better.

Using the Keyboard

Earlier on in this chapter, we looked at how we can create a routine to harness the power of the **INKEY$** command to accept exactly what we want from the keyboard, in respect to a string. You have probably already thought of how we can modify that routine to adapt it into other scenarios - this is what we are going to discuss now.

Polling for Standard Keypresses

In action games, you need to process the pressing of a small set of keys as quickly as possible, a technique which can be achieved in a variety of creative ways. Take the following method which acts upon the four control keys, *Q, A, O* and *P*:

```
WHILE pressakey$<>"X"
pressakey$=""
WHILE pressakey$="": pressakey$=UCASE$(INKEY$): WEND
IF pressakey$="Q" THEN moveup
IF pressakey$="A" THEN movedown
IF pressakey$="O" THEN moveleft
IF pressakey$="P" THEN moveright
WEND
```

Like earlier on, we have eliminated the possibility of wasted loop checking slowing our system down, and thus we only act upon those keys that are strictly necessary.

Polling for Extended Keypresses

We can improve the user-friendliness of this technique by utilizing the extended keyboard, and most importantly, the convenient arrow keys. The following keys are of particular use:

59	F1	71	Home
60	F2	72	Cursor Up
61	F3	73	Page Up
62	F4	75	Cursor Left
63	F5	77	Cursor Right
64	F6	79	End
65	F7	80	Cursor End
66	F8	81	Page Down
67	F9	82	Insert
68	F10	83	Delete

Now we can use these the arrow or cursor keys in the code sample to give the games player a better set of keys with which to control their character:

```
Move$ = UCASE$(INKEY$)
SELECT CASE Move$
CASE CHR$(0) + CHR$(77)
   X = X + 1
CASE CHR$(0) + CHR$(75)
   X = X - 1
CASE CHR$(0) + CHR$(72)
   Y = Y - 1
CASE CHR$(0) + CHR$(80)
   Y = Y + 1
```

In this manner, we can access and make use of some of the most popular keys on the keyboard.

Managing the Joystick

Computer games aren't that much fun using the keyboard, they're not much fun for the keyboard either. At times children and even adults (not that we bought our computer to play games on, you understand), in the heat of the moment, strike the keys so hard that sooner or later they're bound to fail. And after a month or two of Doom deathmatch mode, your keyboard will have really taken some punishment. Using a joystick makes much more sense.

There's a special statement in QBasic for controlling the joystick - **STRIG**, which enables, disables, or suspends joystick event trapping. If event trapping is enabled, **ON STRIG** branches to a subroutine whenever a specified joystick trigger is pressed. The format of the **STRIG** statement is as follows:

STRIG(n%) **ON**		Enables joystick event trapping.
STRIG(n%) **OFF**		Disables joystick event trapping.
STRIG(n%) **STOP**		Suspends joystick event trapping. Events are processed once event trapping is enabled by **STRIG ON**.
ON STRIG(n%) GOSUB line		Branches to an event trapping subroutine.

Here, **n%** is a value that specifies a joystick trigger - a binary switch that controls the joystick. Here are the acceptable values of **n%**:

n%	Trigger
0	Lower trigger, joystick A
2	Lower trigger, joystick B
4	Upper trigger, joystick A
6	Upper trigger, joystick B

If the joystick is connected to your computer, the next example will show you the action of the above:

```
REM Joystick button detection
REM \CHAP12\CH12_2.BAS

CLS
ON STRIG(0) GOSUB Handler
STRIG(0) ON
PRINT "Press Esc to exit"
DO UNTIL INKEY$ = CHR$(27): LOOP
END


Handler:
   PRINT "Joystick Trigger is Pressed "
RETURN
```

To exert a full control over the joystick, QBasic includes the function **STICK(n%)**, which returns the coordinates of a joystick according to the following:

n%	Returns
0	x coordinate of joystick A
1	y coordinate of joystick A
2	x coordinate of joystick B
3	y coordinate of joystick B

You must call **STICK(0)** before **STICK(1)**, **STICK(2)**, or **STICK(3)**, because **STICK(0)** records the current coordinates into memory. The following example illustrates the operation of this function:

```
Temp% = STICK(0)
PRINT STICK(2), STICK(3)
```

Here's another joystick function, **STRIG(n%)**, which returns the status of a joystick trigger with the value of its **n%** parameter:

n%	Condition
0	Lower joystick A trigger was pressed since last STRIG(0)
1	Lower joystick A trigger is currently pressed
2	Lower joystick B trigger was pressed since last STRIG(2)
3	Lower joystick B trigger is currently pressed
4	Upper joystick A trigger was pressed since last STRIG(4)
5	Upper joystick A trigger is currently pressed
6	Upper joystick B trigger was pressed since last STRIG(6)
7	Upper joystick B trigger is currently pressed

This next example illustrates the function **STRIG**:

```
REM Joystick button beep
REM \CHAP12\CH12_3.BAS

CLS
PRINT "Press Esc or joystick button to exit"
DO
    IF STRIG(0) OR INKEY$ = CHR$(27) THEN EXIT DO
LOOP
DO
    BEEP 'Generates a sound signal (BEEP) when trigger A is  pressed
LOOP WHILE STRIG(1)
```

We can demonstrate the use of the joystick with the following program which responds to presses of the joystick by showing you a cursor in text mode:

```
REM Joystick tester in text mode
REM \CHAP12\CH_4.BAS

CLS
X=40:Y=12
WHILE INKEY$<>"X"
    DX=X:DY=Y
    COLOR 11:LOCATE 1,1:PRINT "HORIZONTAL : ";STICK(0)
    LOCATE 2,1:PRINT "VERTICAL : ";STICK(1)
    LOCATE 3,1:PRINT "Button One : ";
    IF STRIG(0)=-1 THEN PRINT "Down" ELSE PRINT "Up"
    COLOR 10:LOCATE 1,74:PRINT "e(X)it";
    IF STICK(0)<120 AND X>1 THEN X=X-1
    IF STICK(0)>170 AND X<79 THEN X=X+1
    IF STICK(1)<70 AND Y>1 THEN Y=Y-1
    IF STICK(1)>130 AND Y<24 THEN Y=Y+1
    LOCATE DY,DX:PRINT " ";
    COLOR 14:LOCATE Y,X:PRINT "Û";
WEND
```

Likewise, we can provide a more accurate joystick program by applying graphics coordinates and commands to it:

```
REM Joystick tester in graphics mode
REM \CHAP12\CH12_5.BAS

CLS
X=320:Y=175
WHILE INKEY$<>"X"
    DX=X:DY=Y
    COLOR 11:LOCATE 1,1:PRINT "HORIZONTAL : ";STICK(0)
    LOCATE 2,1:PRINT "VERTICAL : ";STICK(1)
    LOCATE 3,1:PRINT "Button One : ";
    IF STRIG(0)=-1 THEN PRINT "Down" ELSE PRINT "Up"
    COLOR 10:LOCATE 1,74:PRINT "e(X)it";
    IF STICK(0)<120 AND X>1 THEN X=X-1
    IF STICK(0)>170 AND X<639 THEN X=X+1
    IF STICK(1)<70 AND Y>1 THEN Y=Y-1
    IF STICK(1)>130 AND Y<349 THEN Y=Y+1
    PSET (DX,DY),0
    PSET (X,Y),14
WEND
```

Beware that analog joysticks may require re-calibration. If you're thinking about including a joystick option in your games, then you should always ask the user to re-calibrate.

Manipulating Sprites

Although we covered animation back in Chapter 8 - Bit-mapped Graphics, the combination of graphics and games is much more involved than simply scrolling images across the screen, and so natural that we are going to discuss it in further detail here.

What Are They?

Right, hands up anyone who's never heard of a sprite. Aaaaargh...there's always one isn't there? Okay, so maybe not everyone really knows what a sprite is and I bet there are quite a few.

A **sprite** is quite simply a bit map. It's very common for bit maps to move across the screen, animated via a series of transitional bit maps, or both, to give the sequence life. However, not everything that flies around the screen blasting away at poor defenseless aliens, are sprites. An opening door, rippling water and flashing lights are also good examples of stationary sprites and are handled by the computer in much the same way as any psychotic spaceship traversing the galaxy. Controlling a sprite can be achieved in a number of ways, the most obvious one being player control. Computer control comes a close second. But what if we were to create a sprite that reacted to another sprite's actions (remember those cute little spiders in Arachnaphobia?).

Sprites are the essence of the vast majority of games that we play, and in this section we will show you how to make your characters walk, run, hop, fly, swim, skate...

Designing Sprites

Okay, so how do you design it? Well, to create your data, you could use our sprite creator that we introduced in Chapter 9. But before we go ahead and draw our 3 mile high megasaurus and convert it into hex, we need to cover a few points.

- First, we need to decide on size, bearing in mind that the bigger it is doesn't necessarily mean that it is better. Large sprites are much more difficult to manipulate than smaller ones and require much more RAM, especially if animation is involved. Our megasaurus would look lovely with 8 frames of animation, but 4 or even 2 frames would conserve vast amounts of much needed memory. In 256 color modes, a bit map takes up 1 byte of RAM per-pixel, so a sprite of say 80 x 80 pixels would need 64,000 bytes of RAM. Get a few sprites of this size in your game and you can kiss your RAM goodbye!

- Color is also limited depending on the screen mode you're in, so bear this in mind also when designing sprites.

If you do find yourself struggling with the arty side of things (exactly how many programmers are artists too?) you can always take a look at other games and applications for ideas. Icons are also an excellent example of how to create small but effective images using the simplest of designs.

> We'll talk much more about optimization a little later on but, for now, remember a golden rule which has always worked for me - generally, the simpler it is, the faster it is.

So how DO you do it? Okay, okay let's get down to the meaty stuff. Because the sprite creator is the easiest way for us to design our sprites, we shall be using this QBasic program to create all our sprites. Let me recap how the sprite creation process works:

- The best method of handling sprites is to use an old favorite - the array.

- After deciding on your screen mode, draw your sprite.

- We then **GET** it and put all the values into an array in hexadecimal form, the values of which can then be listed as a series of **DATA** statements which are output to a new **.BAS** file.

- Then, at the start of the program, each sprite's **DATA** can be **READ** into their respective arrays, ready for use in the game.

Following this process will leave you with an array (a bit map or sprite) that can be **PUT** anywhere on the screen any number of times.

So, you've drawn your sprite and it's looking all cute and cuddly. Now - how exactly do we move it?

Moving Sprites

This is where we can breath life into a stationary sprite's dull existence. Movement gives a whole new dimension to play with and I'm sure you're all gagging to see your creation take great leaps and bounds across the screen.

Moving sprites across the screen is relatively easy and, with a little care, can be made to look very professional. Smoothness is our first goal as this makes games look polished and often easier to play.

> It's worth mentioning here that the higher your screen mode's resolution, the smoother the scrolling will be, due simply to the greater amount of pixels. Unfortunately, the downfall to this is the considerable drop in available video memory pages and a much higher consumption of RAM. Most QBasic games use screen mode 7 since this is a fairly good compromise between the two.

Since we now have our sprite in an array, the process of displaying and moving it across the screen is very easy. All we need to do is **PUT** our sprite on screen at a certain position using the **XOR** keyword. Then, we change the values of the X and/or Y coordinates accordingly and **PUT** the sprite on the screen, with **XOR** again, using the new coordinates.

There are a number of keywords available which will create different results when moving sprites. As we have already covered these in Chapter 8, we won't go over them again, but do experiment as clever manipulation of these keywords can create some remarkable effects.

Over Backgrounds

Moving a single color sprite over a background of the same color is very easy and, as we've seen, **XOR** comes in very handy when moving objects about the screen with the minimum of fuss. But when we need to move sprites over a background of a different color, we run into a small problem. If you run the program **\CHAP12\CH12_6.BAS** you will see what we mean. The background actually shows through the sprite and produces a very unsightly effect. This is a problem that even **XOR** can't get around, and requires us to call on a clever 'masking' technique.

What we need to do is to create a single colored mask or template which is exactly the same height and width as the sprite. We then **PUT** the mask on to the screen using the **AND** keyword just before we **PUT** the sprite, using **XOR**, and at the same position. A mask of our spaceship, which we saw in the previous example would look like this:

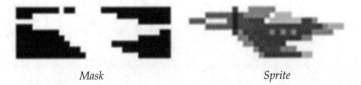

Mask   *Sprite*

When we use this technique in conjunction with **SCREEN** and **PCOPY** to draw on invisible video pages and then make them suddenly visible, the 'ghosting' problem can be overcome. Take a look at the program **\CHAP12\CH12_7.BAS** and you'll see the difference. The way the video pages are used is slightly confusing, so let's cover this technique in detail.

Using Video Pages

If you imagine how a cartoon works:

First we display the background,

then we draw the characters,

and, finally, the characters are put on the background.

The advantages of doing this are:

- It gets rid of spooky ghosting.
- It's smooth.
- It's cool.
- Best of all, it's really fast. While the background and character are being viewed, the computer is processing the new coordinates of the character and pasting them onto a copy of the background, ready to be made visible.

We do this in QBasic by first creating our background screen and storing it in a video page, say 1:

```
SCREEN 7, 0, 1, 1
```

We then copy this page into another, non-visible page (effectively the drawing board) onto which we put our sprites and characters:

```
SCREEN 7, 0, 2, 0: PCOPY 1, 2
```

Now we copy this 'merged' screen onto our visible page, replacing the previous screen. And so the loop continues.

```
SCREEN 7, 0, 0, 0: PCOPY 2, 0: PCOPY 1, 2
```

> **This is a very important, powerful and prevalent concept for action game programming, especially when smooth and quick graphics movement is required.**

Let's illustrate the process with our spaceship and star-field:

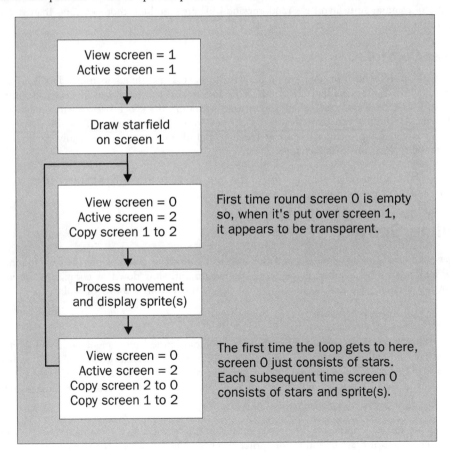

It may look a little confusing but we haven't used anything that we haven't already explained, so try following it through, statement by statement, and all will become clear.

Following Paths

One of the most memorable examples of sprites which follow paths or pre-determined routes must be Pac-Man. Although it's very out-dated now, the process used was very interesting and involved a very primitive version of artificial intelligence.

The method used was to allow the main sprite only to move in one of two ways: either left and right or up and down. When the sprite came to preset 'junctions' along these paths, it was given the option to turn the corner. This created a superb maze effect and the more complex the maze, the harder the game got. The ghosts which ran after the main sprite were simply programmed to take the shortest route possible to get our little hero, which gave the illusion of intelligence. Throw in a few bonus points at certain places in the maze and you had an excellent example of simple, but effective programming.

But sprites following paths aren't limited to maze games. An awful lot of today's shoot-em-ups use pre-determined paths and formations to give their aliens life.

When it comes to creating your own games, make your sprites swirl, bounce, rotate, hover and dive, and don't forget the old games-guru favorite - randomization. There's nothing more exciting than not knowing when or where the baddy will pop up from next.

Under User Control

When it comes to sprite control in your game, it's wise to bear a few things in mind. Firstly, if your choice of input is the keyboard, use keys that are comfortable to use and it's not a bad idea to use some sort of standard layout. It can be a real pain when you're used to hitting the space bar for your mega-weapon, only to find in this game that you have to use the *Alt* key instead. Even better, allow the player to select their own keys - which has the added bonus of creating that all important 'user-friendly' feeling. We shall discuss configurability later on in this chapter.

When it comes to the actual programming, one of the best methods to use is **SELECT CASE**, as it's simple in construction and flexible when things get more complicated.

Controlling Sprites

Right, so now we know how to move around the screen, we need to create some lifelike motion. Our sprites would look a lot more realistic if they could speed up and slow down or comply to the laws of gravity. So, in this section we'll look at how to make things move with a touch of reality.

Speed

It can be very difficult trying to get just the right speed for our sprites' movements and you could tweak it for ever and a day and still not be happy. It's a good idea to use a variable to control the number of pixels distance a particular sprite is moved in one iteration of the loop, and try out different values until you're happy. As the speed increases and the number of pixels per move increases, the image may begin to jump, so try to find that happy medium between the two.

Including a variable for each sprite on the screen may slow the game down too much, and so you may need to group the speed of a set of similar of sprites (such as alien invaders) together.

Inertia

One thing that makes sprites act realistically is inertia (speeding up or slowing down). This technique can make your game look very impressive if it's handled in the right way. Let's have a look at how we can do this.

Take our spaceship, traveling across the screen. If we use the polling method, the sprite moves because the player has the key held down continuously. So, if our spaceship is traveling at, say, 3 pixels per move, and a key is released or a change in direction is requested, we could follow this procedure to give the impression of deceleration:

▲ Keep moving the sprite at 3 pixels and at the same time, start a counter going, adding one to itself each time the sprite is moved.

▲ When the counter equals 30, decrease the pixels to 2 which will start to slow the sprite down.

▲ Then, once the counter reaches 50, decrease the pixels moved to 1 and, finally, when the counter reaches 60, stop moving completely and the craft comes to rest.

▲ For acceleration, you simply reverse this, and, as the counter reaches the certain values, the number of pixels moved increases.

▲ If you play around with the counter values you can change the rate of inertia; for example, if you were to set the values at 20, 40 and 70, you would create the impression of slow deceleration.

Gravity

The force of gravity and inertia act very similarly to each other and are, therefore, programmed in much the same way. Very simply, if you created a constant acceleration on a sprite in a downwards direction, you would have the effect of gravity. But if the poor old sprite is to have any chance of surviving a crash landing, you must allow an opposite inertia effect in an upwards direction.

If the directions were reversed, you'd have an underwater effect, ideal for that man-eating shark game.

Range Checking

The last thing you'd want to see in any game is your budding hero gallantly trotting across the screen only to disappear off the edge, never to be seen again. This is where we need a routine which will constantly check the position of our sprite every time a movement is processed. If, for example, we were using mode 7, and our sprite was 10 pixels wide, the following line of code would suffice:

```
IF sprite_x_pos > 310 THEN sprite_x_pos = 310
IF sprite_x_pos < 10 THEN sprite_x_pos = 10
IF sprite_y_pos > 190 THEN sprite_y_pos = 190
IF sprite_y_pos < 10 THEN sprite_y_pos = 10
```

When this is used in conjunction with an inertia routine, you get a very nice 'bouncy wall' effect. Note how we allow a border of ten pixels all around the screen to safeguard against sprites that jump more than one pixel in a single go.

If you wanted your sprite to wrap-around, i.e. disappear off one side only to reappear on the other, the following line of code would suit:

```
IF sprite_x_pos > 310 THEN sprite_x_pos = 1
IF sprite_x_pos < 1 THEN sprite_x_pos = 310
IF sprite_y_pos > 190 THEN sprite_y_pos = 1
IF sprite_y_pos < 10 THEN sprite_y_pos = 190
```

Don't worry about angles or speeds either - because both of the above examples will handle sprites moving off the playing area at any angle or speed (less than the border width of course).

Of course, should your playing area be confined to a certain sized window or to a different screen mode, you will have to alter the values of the boundaries.

Collision Detection

We could convert the previous example to check for our sprite crashing into the furniture, but it would be slow and tedious if the room were full of armchairs. So we must use another method for detecting collisions between sprites. One way is to check certain pixels around our sprite for a change in color, using **PSET**, and react according to the color found. If, for example our spaceship encountered an asteroid field which consisted of brown asteroids, we could check all the points around the spaceship every time it is moved and, if a brown pixel was detected, an explosion would occur. But checking every point around our sprite is very time consuming. A much better technique is to check the most prominent points - 5 points at the nose, 5 at the tail and perhaps 10 points above and 10 points below. This would enable us to keep detecting while maintaining an adequate speed. Let's take a look at this next piece of code which you can find at work in **\CHAP12\CH12_8.BAS** on the disk:

```
starcolor% = 2                                    'Select green stars
FOR top% = Ship.X% TO Ship.X% + 10                '10 pixels above sprite
pixelcolortop% = POINT(top%, Ship.Y% - 1)         'Get pixels color
IF pixelcolortop% = starcolor% THEN               'Is it green?
LOCATE 1, 1                                        'If it is...
PRINT "Top hit!"                                   '...then print this...
GOTO Finishdetect                                  '...and exit loop
END IF                                             'Or else...
NEXT top%                                           '...try next pixel
FOR bottom% = Ship.X% + 5 TO Ship.X% + 15         '10 pixels below sprite
pixelcolorbottom% = POINT(bottom%, Ship.Y% + 10)
IF pixelcolorbottom% = starcolor% THEN
LOCATE 1, 1
PRINT "Bottom hit!"
GOTO Finishdetect
END IF
NEXT bottom%
FOR left% = Ship.Y% TO Ship.Y% + 5                '5 pixels left of sprite
pixelcolorleft% = POINT(Ship.X% - 3, left%)
IF pixelcolorleft% = starcolor% THEN
LOCATE 1, 1
PRINT "Left hit!"
GOTO Finishdetect
END IF
NEXT left%
FOR right% = Ship.Y% + 2 TO Ship.Y% + 7           '5 pixels right of sprite
pixelcolorright% = POINT(Ship.X% + 25, right%)
IF pixelcolorright% = starcolor% THEN
LOCATE 1, 1
PRINT "Right hit!"
GOTO Finishdetect
```

```
END IF
NEXT right%
Finishdetect:                        'End detection
```

The listing is fairly straightforward and has the added bonus of ending detection immediately when a collision has been detected.

Good collision detection is essential and the lack of it is one the main reasons for games receiving poor comments from reviewers. Test, test and test it again.

Animating Sprites

I know I've said it a thousand times, but don't expect too much here from QBasic . Although, if you do keep your animation simple you can achieve some quite impressive results. As we said earlier, since frames are memory, try to keep your frames down to as few as possible - ideally 2, 4 or 6 at the most.

The method we're going to use involves the masking technique that we encountered earlier with a little counter just to keep things ticking along nicely. We'll call upon the use of the spaceship again to illustrate our frames and corresponding masks:

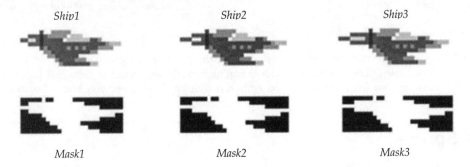

Ship1   *Ship2*   *Ship3*

Mask1   *Mask2*   *Mask3*

What we want is our spaceship to be animated with a burst of flame appearing from the exhaust. We only have three sets of sprites and masks but we're going to be using the second one again as our fourth frame, to complete the effect. The process is very simple and is as follows:

- We **PUT** our mask of sprite1 using **AND** as the keyword, closely followed by sprite1 itself, using **XOR**.

- Then we start off a counter which adds a value of one to itself each time we run through our main 'polling for a keypress' loop.

- When the counter reaches a certain value, let's say 10, the next mask and sprite (#2) are **PUT** to the screen, using the usual combination of keywords.

- We run through the main loop again and, when the counter reaches 20, the 3rd set of mask and sprite is **PUT** to the screen.

- Then, when the counter reaches 30 we use our 2nd set to complete the cycle. Each frame is, therefore, visible for a total of 10 loops, which produces the effect that we're after. If the counters steps are increased, animation is slower, and vice versa.

- We must remember to reset our counter to zero once all the frames have been used and our cycle is complete. Then the whole process can begin again.

Take a look at this bit of code from **\CHAP12\CH12_8.BAS**:

```
IF counter% = 20 THEN counter% = 0              'reset counter to zero
IF counter% < 20 THEN counter% = counter% + 1   'adds one to itself
IF counter% > 0 AND counter% < 11 THEN          'first 10 loops
PUT (ship.X%, ship.Y%), ship1mask%, AND         'display mask
PUT (ship.X%, ship.Y%), ship1%, XOR             'display sprite
GOTO sprite1done                                'frame displayed-exitloop
END IF
IF counter% > 10 AND counter% < 21 THEN         'second 10 loops
PUT ((ship.X% - 2), ship.Y%), ship2mask%, AND   'display mask
PUT ((ship.X% - 2), ship.Y%), ship2%, XOR       'display sprite
GOTO sprite1done                                'frame displayed-exitloop
END IF
IF counter% > 20 AND counter% < 31 THEN         'third 10 loops
PUT ((ship.X% - 4), ship.Y%), ship3mask%, AND   'display mask
PUT ((ship.X% - 4), ship.Y%), ship3%, XOR       'display sprite
GOTO sprite1done                                'frame displayed-exitloop
END IF
IF counter% > 30 AND counter% < 41 THEN         'fourth 10 loops
PUT ((ship.X% - 2), ship.Y%), ship2mask%, AND   'display mask
PUT ((ship.X% - 2), ship.Y%), ship2%, XOR       'display sprite
GOTO sprite1done                                'frame displayed- exitloop
END IF
sprite1done:
```

This is an excellent example of masking and, once you've run the program, I think you'll see just how easy it is to write hot animated games in QBasic with the minimum of fuss. Take the code and bolt on some of your own ideas or start from scratch. If you come up with anything good, you know the score - don't forget to send us a copy.

Multiple Sprites

What fun would it be with just one sprite in a game? Not, much. Multiple sprites are what's needed and the way we do this is relatively easy. Let's look at how…

We've got the code which animates our main sprite every 10 loops. What we need to do is to **PUT** another sprite at a different position on screen, at the same time that we are **PUT**ting our main one. We can do this as many times as we like, but remember QBasic's speed limits, because to create hordes of good guys and bad guys will slow the program down.

All you need to do is to process the motion and draw your second sprite at the same place in the program that you drew the first. If you want a different frame rate to the first, say twice as fast, just halve the number of counter loops to 5.

Let's take a Space Invaders scenario. Each time the program polled for a keypress, an alien counter, let's be obvious and use **Counter,** would start ascending from 1 to 5. When **Counter** reaches 5, the aliens movement and animation would be processed. Then **Counter** is reset and the whole process starts over again.

The way the aliens speed up as time goes on is to keep a variable, perhaps called **Restarts**, which stores the number of restarts to the animation loop. When **Restarts** reached 20, for instance, the initial alien movement variable of 5 would drop to 4 and when **Restarts** reached 25, the animation counter would drop to 3, and so on until the aliens were whizzing down the screen at a heart-stopping pace.

The player's sprite would be able to move each time the main loop polled for a keypress and, therefore, wouldn't interfere with the alien's movement.

"What about the bonus ship?" I hear you say. Well, using either a random number or a preset counter to choose when it appears you could animate and move the bonus ship once every two polls for a keypress. This would enable the main sprite to travel twice as fast as the bonus ship, thus giving the player a fairly good chance of destroying it.

Advanced Graphical Techniques

A competent game is fine, but to make a game stand out from the crowd, it has got to entertain the user. We can do this by incorporating spectacular graphics, good sound and hundreds of other tried and tested techniques. Here, we shall introduce you to some add-ins that you can use to spruce up your games.

Explosions

Most action games follow the Hollywood technique of using huge explosions to signify the end of a life. There are many different techniques for achieving explosions which we will now demonstrate.

The Simple Circles Method

To create possibly the easiest explosion, we can draw a series of yellow and red circles that emanate out from the center of the explosion, and recede when the fire dies down. Our **\GAMES\BATTLE.BAS** game shows you just how this effect works.

The Sprite Method

The sprite method of drawing explosions is, strangely enough, based around a series of sprites that represent a roaring fire. Despite taking up a lot more memory and being dependent on your artistic skills, this method is probably the most realistic way of creating explosions.

The Fireworks Method

The fireworks method is a stylish variation of the circles explosion effect, whereby particles, not circles, of the explosion emanate out from the center of the explosion. This can create a smooth and impressive effect, but probably wouldn't be suitable for very large explosions.

The code for this is as follows:

```
REM Fireworks
REM \CHAP12\CH12_9.BAS

CLS
PRINT "PLEASE WAIT WHILE WE CALCULATE THE SINES AND COSINES. CHEERS."
DIM S(360),C(360)
FOR T=0 TO 360
    S(T)=SIN(T):C(T)=COS(T)
NEXT T

CLS
LOCATE 24,1:PRINT "Press a key and wait to end"
```

```
WHILE INKEY$=""
    X=RND*500+100:Y=RND*300+20
    COL=RND*14+1
    FOR T=1 TO 53
        FOR W=0 TO 324 STEP 36
            PSET (S(W)*T+X,C(W)*T+Y),COL
            IF T>10 THEN PSET(S(W)*(T-12)+X,C(W)*(T-12)+Y),0
        NEXT W
        IF T>40 THEN COL=0
    NEXT T
WEND
```

Notice that, as suggested in Chapter 10 - 3D Graphics, we calculate all the sine and cosine values before we actually run the critical code. This enables us to draw our firework explosion effect a lot quicker.

Audio

Let's face it, there's nothing worse than playing a game that has no sound effects or music. Audio adds a whole new dimension to the environment and can help create suspense, mystery or even violence. As we know from Chapter 11, QBasic can whip up some remarkable effects when it wants to and can even create funky tunes and melodies. Since we have already covered sound, there's no need to go into great detail here, but there are a few points I'd like to mention.

Have you ever booted up a program only to be greeted by an annoying piece of 'music' that makes your dog howl like a wolf or persuades your cat to pack his bags and leave home? And what if you can't switch it off and are forced to listen to every single 'note'. Not a good start in the world of user-friendliness is it?

This is a golden rule in audio programming - only force the player to listen to music when it's necessary. For example, when the player dies, you could have a short burst of music while simultaneously displaying a death screen, emphasizing the fact that all of his/her lives have gone. You wouldn't necessarily have to play a tune after every single life has gone, restricting this to when they've all gone would suffice. An alternative to this would be to play the tune in the background so that the program can carry on as the music ends. This is a great technique to use when a player starts the level, as an introduction to the action.

Don't forget sound effects either. QBasic may not be the hottest synth around, but it can bleep and bloop as good as any other basic language. An example of this would be if the player has achieved something of significance, you could have a short run of ascending notes, played in the background, of course, which would the notify the player of the event.

The list of possible sound effects that you could create is extensive and the best way of creating them by experimenting. If you're a little stuck for ideas, refer back to Chapter 11, and you'll find some examples which can be easily incorporated into any program. Just try to keep things friendly and you won't go far wrong, but above all - have fun! And remember - rock hard, rock heavy, rock animal.......meow!

Humor

Commercial comedy is probably one of the most difficult tasks to achieve, especially in our media, computer programming. But that doesn't mean that you shouldn't try to make the user of your games laugh.

There are many different ways in which you can add humor to your games, or indeed base your games around humor:

Include a funny plot or story-line. This naturally involves a good dose of comedy writing skills which also much be evident at other stages of the game, such as between levels or at the end of the game.

Use funny sprites, characters or backgrounds. Adding humorous touches to graphics requires a great deal of time, skill and patience, but is well worth it. A character who winks, smiles, or displays other 'character-forming expressions', such as tapping a foot in impatience, is a lot more fun than a static one-dimensional sprite. Adding humorous characters into text-based games is a lot easier than using graphics because you have a lot more memory and flexibility with which to add character forming expressions.

Use relevant captions. Adding an unexpected one-line quip here and there brightens up a dull scenario no end. For example, if the user's character dies, you could add such dodgy quips as "You can do better, can't you?", "Let's face it - that was BAD!", or "Try harder next time, punk.". Make sure that they are relevant and that they vary, depending on different situations.

Wipes

Wipes are the intermediate routines between levels where the last screen is removed in a certain way and the new one is brought in using a certain method. Such transitional routines are part of the entertainment and can effectively simulate actions such as cinema curtains or shutters. There are lots of wipes that you can implement, and here's one of the best ones:

```
REM Blinds
REM \CHAP12\CHAP12_10.BAS

SCREEN 7, 0, 1, 1

LOCATE 10, 10: PRINT "It's curtains for me"
WHILE INKEY$ = "": WEND

FOR T = 1 TO 84 STEP 4
    SCREEN 7, 0, 2, 0:  PCOPY 1, 2
    LINE (0, 0)-(T, 200), 1, BF
    LINE (80, 0)-(80 + T, 200), 1, BF
    LINE (160, 0)-(160 + T, 200), 1, BF
    LINE (240, 0)-(240 + T, 200), 1, BF
    SCREEN 7, 0, 0, 0: PCOPY 2, 0: PCOPY 1, 2
NEXT

SCREEN 7, 0, 1, 0
CLS
LOCATE 10, 10: PRINT "But not for me...!"
FOR T = 84 TO 0 STEP -4
    SCREEN 7, 0, 2, 0: PCOPY 1, 2
    LINE (0, 0)-(T, 200), 1, BF
    LINE (80, 0)-(80 + T, 200), 1, BF
    LINE (160, 0)-(160 + T, 200), 1, BF
    LINE (240, 0)-(240 + T, 200), 1, BF
    SCREEN 7, 0, 0, 0: PCOPY 2, 0: PCOPY 1, 2
NEXT
SCREEN 7, 0, 1, 1
WHILE INKEY$ = "": WEND
CLS
```

Here we have used the concept of video pages to imitate the action of a set of four blinds or curtains which scroll across our stage, removing the old screen, and then scroll back, revealing the new screen. The technique for performing this is nothing new: we simply write over the front screen, write the new screen to a back page and then take slithers from this background page and put them back onto the visible page, one slice at a time.

Take a look at **\GRAPHICS\WIPES.BAS** and **\GRAPHICS\FADE.BAS** for further examples of how you can implement your own special versions of these techniques.

Scrolling

The scrolling of the screen, or areas of the screen, is a very popular video gaming technique, and one which is not properly supported by QBasic commands. But that hasn't stopped us before has it? The problem with scrolling in QBasic is that to move large areas of the screen *very quickly* takes a lot of work. We can achieve a variety of scrolling techniques in QBasic, but we'll struggle to do it fast enough to make it of any use. What we'll do in this section is outline some of the ways that we can scroll parts of our programs, and demonstrate some good examples.

Scrolling is basically just another style of animation programming where a section of the section, albeit larger than sprites, is removed and replaced by the next frame in the sequence. There are two distinct scrolling types.

Scrolling a Text String

This simple ticker-tape style special effect is very eye-catching and very easy to implement. If you take a long string, say this paragraph, we could scroll it through a box on the screen, using this simple method:

```
REM Simple demonstration of text scrolling
REM \CHAP12\CH12_11.BAS

CLS
ts$ = "This simple ticker-tape style special effect is very eye-catching and very ↵
easy to implement. If you take a long string, say this paragraph, then we could ↵
scroll it through a box on the screen, using this simple method:         "
looppos% = 1
sizeofbox% = 70
finalstring$ = ""

WHILE keyinput$ = ""
    IF looppos% > (LEN(ts$) - sizeofbox%) THEN finalstring$ = MID$(ts$, looppos%, ↵
    LEN(ts$) - looppos%) + LEFT$(ts$, (sizeofbox% - (LEN(ts$) - looppos%))) ELSE ↵
 finalstring$ = MID$(ts$, looppos%, sizeofbox%)
    LOCATE 5, 5: PRINT finalstring$
    looppos% = looppos% + 1' increment position
    IF looppos% = LEN(ts$) THEN looppos% = 1 ' check for wraparound
    FOR B = 1 TO 500: NEXT B                              ' delay loop
    keyinput$ = INKEY$
WEND

END
```

Despite this horrendous long line, the general routine is very straightforward, in that we just increment a counter corresponding to the position in the string. After each increment we print the next 70 characters onto the screen, at the same place as the last one. If done at the correct speed, and smooth enough, we can produce quite effective ticker-tape simulators.

Scrolling Areas of the Screen

This arcade-style effect is most often used in video games, such as the classic game Defender. This is a method where you can scroll a huge landscape across the screen giving the smooth effect that you're moving through more than just a single screen of a virtual world. Here is a similar implementation:

```
REM Scrolling Landscape Example
REM \CHAP12\CH12_12.BAS

'Define Land array and Land variables
DIM height%(232)    'size of landscape
chunk% = 10         'width of land gradients
landwidth% = 100
```

After defining the arrays and the size of each 'block' of land we move on to the actual generation of the landscape. The following piece of code uses the random number generator to choose whether the land will rise, fall or remain horizontal. It does this by returning a random value which is either greater than or less than .5:

```
RANDOMIZE INT(VAL(RIGHT$(TIME$, 2)))

height%(0) = 120
FOR land% = 1 TO landwidth%
    height%(land%) = height%(land% - 1)
    randomnumber = RND
    IF randomnumber > .5 THEN GOSUB down
    IF randomnumber < .5 THEN GOSUB up
NEXT land%
```

This value determines whether the program draws an ascending slope or a descending one. This is with the aid of a couple of subroutines, called **down** and **up**. These routines add or take away a value of **chunk%** which is currently set at 10 from the previous value and then stored in the array **height%**. This is essentially the height of the landscape in 10-pixel-width 'chunks'. Any smaller and the landscape would be too flat, any larger, too craggy. An upper and lower limit is adhered to within the two subroutines, these being - maximum **x**= 190 and minimum **x** = 70. The whole process is repeated until there are 100 height values stored in **height%**. Then we take these values, reverse them and add them on to the end of **height%**, thus giving us a mirrored landscape.

```
'Generate \ Land In Array
down:
IF height%(land%) > 180 THEN      'Maximum depth of valleys
height%(land%) = 190
ELSE
height%(land%) = height%(land%) + chunk%     'Create new height
END IF
RETURN

'Generate / Land In Array
up:
IF height%(land%) < 120 THEN      'Maximum height of hills
height%(land%) = 120
ELSE
height%(land%) = height%(land%) - chunk%     'Create new height
END IF
RETURN
```

Since we are in screen mode 7, there are 320 pixels on the x-axis. So, if we are going to draw our landscape in 10-pixel 'chunks' we need to get the first 32 (320/10) values from our array **height%**. These 32 values are placed on screen 10 pixels apart and joined up with the **LINE** statement. We do this again directly below, just to give us a nice, thicker line:

```
'Draw Landscape
FOR pixel% = 0 TO 320 STEP chunk%
   LINE (pixel%, height%(currentbun%))-(pixel% + chunk%, height%(currentbun% + 1)) ,6
                                      'draw first line
      LINE (pixel%, height%(currentbun%) + 1)-(pixel% + chunk%, height%(currentbun%
+ 1) + 1), 6                                      'draw second line
      currentbun% = currentbun% + 1              'next array value
NEXT pixel%
PAINT (319, 199), 6
currentbun% = (currentbun% - (320 / chunk%)) + 1     'move 1 array value along
IF currentbun% > 200 THEN currentbun% = 1            'redraw from start
```

The program pauses for a moment to allow the player to see the landscape before it is erased and to eliminate flicker. Then we move along one value in our **height%** array and plot another 32 points on screen before joining them up with **LINE**, and so the loop goes on.

We add some collision detection just to spice things up a bit, though we've left a few things for you to think about, namely, some sort of laser which would blast across the screen at a horde of oncoming aliens. All of which would be placed within the usual **SCREEN/PCOPY** loop that we discussed earlier.

Fading

The ability to fade parts of the screen in and out is a trick and special effect often used in commercial TV, movies and video games. The problem with achieving it in QBasic is that we don't have as many colors available to us to implement it smoothly enough. We can, though, use some tricks to get similar effects.

We can, for example, use the limited colors that we have to give the impression of a gradual fade, by selecting the palette command to scroll through the available colors in both directions (to black, and to white). Take the following program, a modified version of the text scrolling program:

```
REM Simple demonstration of text scrolling with fading
REM \CHAP12\CH12_13.BAS

CLS
COLOR 15
ts$ = "This simple ticker-tape style special effect is very eye-catching Ã and
very easy to implement. If you take a long string, say this paragraph, Ã then we
could scroll it through a box on the screen, using this simple Ã method:         "

looppos% = 1
sizeofbox% = 70
finalstring$ = ""

WHILE keyinput$ = ""
IF looppos% > (LEN(ts$) - sizeofbox%) THEN finalstring$ = MID$(ts$, Ã looppos%,
LEN(ts$) - looppos%) + LEFT$(ts$, (sizeofbox% - (LEN(ts$) - Ã looppos%)))
ELSE  finalstring$ = MID$(ts$, looppos%, sizeofbox%)
```

```
COLOR 8: LOCATE 5, 5: PRINT LEFT$(finalstring$, 1);
LOCATE 5, 70: PRINT MID$(finalstring$, 66, 1);
COLOR 7: LOCATE 5, 6: PRINT MID$(finalstring$, 2, 1);
LOCATE 5, 69: PRINT MID$(finalstring$, 65, 1);
COLOR 7: LOCATE 5, 7: PRINT MID$(finalstring$, 3, 1);
LOCATE 5, 68: PRINT MID$(finalstring$, 64, 1);
COLOR 15: LOCATE 5, 8: PRINT MID$(finalstring$, 4, sizeofbox% - 10);

looppos% = looppos% + 1                    ' increment position
IF looppos% = LEN(ts$) THEN looppos% = 1   ' check for wraparound
FOR B = 1 TO 5000: NEXT B                  ' delay loop
keyinput$ = INKEY$
WEND

END
```

By printing the start and end of the string in gradually darkening colors, we can create the effect of fading:

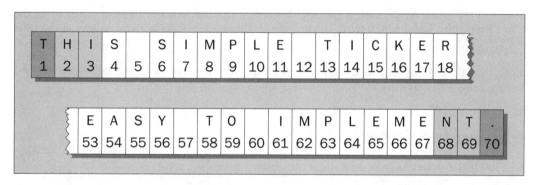

We can also produce effective fading effects using graphics too. Try the following program, which accesses the video RAM directly:

```
REM Demonstration of Graphical Fading
REM \CHAP12\CH12_14.BAS

SCREEN 9

FOR boxes = 1 TO 30
  LINE (RND * 640, RND * 350)-(RND * 640, RND * 350), RND * 15, BF
NEXT boxes

WHILE INKEY$ = "": WEND

 FOR colors% = 0 TO 63
   FOR fade% = 0 TO 30
     OUT 967, fade%
     Red = INP(969)
     Green = INP(969)
     Blue = INP(969)
     Red = Red - 1
     Green = Green - 1
     Blue = Blue - 1

     IF Red < 0 THEN Red = 0
```

```
        IF Green < 0 THEN Green = 0
        IF Blue < 0 THEN Blue = 0

        OUT 968, fade%

        OUT 969, Red
        OUT 969, Green
        OUT 969, Blue

        FOR delay = 1 TO 15: NEXT delay

     NEXT fade%
  NEXT colors%

  WHILE INKEY$ = "": WEND

  END
```

Here, we read and write the decreasing values of the red, green and blue components of colors on the screen using the video address 969. By decreasing the brightness, via address 968, we fade all the colors between 0 and 30 to black.

Obviously, this effect can be used as a kind of screen wipe, to bring screens in and fade them out. We shall look at some other effective methods of screen wiping later in this chapter.

The Need for Speed

Let's face it, QBasic is very slow when it comes to shifting graphics around the screen. But there are ways in which we can minimize the effect of this lethargy - we've already mentioned several subtle techniques, such as using video pages. But if you don't understand fully what is slowing your program down, it can be a very frustrating (and sometimes fatal) period in your program's life cycle. What you can do is to follow a few golden rules of code optimization and examine some tricks to smooth out the wrinkles in your program.

Golden Optimization Rules

We're about to list a few tried and tested techniques for making your programs as lean as can be, but please don't assume that these will eliminate all your personal ailments (see a doctor for them). No, the ones listed shortly will improve the efficiency of your program, but it's up to you to make sure that you implement them fully.

Most of these are also best implemented in the design stage of program development, and not as immediate solutions to existing sluggish programs. It's suggested that you think about these issues and then plan your program bearing them in mind.

Use fewer statements in the main loop. We demonstrated in Chapter 8 - Bit-mapped Graphics and Animation, that a 4000 cycle loop with just a **PRINT** statement inside operated a great deal faster than with a **LOCATE** statement as well. Be stringent in what you allow to stay inside your critical loop.

Include the % modifier on all integer variables and constants. If you use integers in your programs (and who doesn't?), make sure that you allocate the smallest amount of memory space available by forcing

QBasic to store it as an integer. By replacing all occurrences in your existing programs with % equivalents, you can gain a surprising increase in speed.

Use video pages. By writing to a non-visible background page, you can cut out a lot of time-consuming work. As we've already discussed, this neat method can produce very smooth and very quick graphics routines.

Minimize the amount of active data. By keeping the sheer amount of data being displayed on the screen or being processed to a minimum, you can concentrate on those elements that matter and reduce the amount of work the processor has to do.

Keep chunks of data small. Large sprites and large sets of data slow your programs down - try to minimize them as far as possible.

Crunch processor-hungry calculations beforehand. By moving slow calculations out of a critical loop, you can speed up your programs a great deal. Examples of slow calculations include trigonometric functions, such as **SIN** and **COS**.

Use a lower resolution. If your program doesn't necessarily need a high resolution, try using a lower one. This can considerably increase the speed of your programs.

Keep two versions of each program. The first with long variable names, extensive comments, pieces of code to help you to understand or test the program but which aren't part of the final program, and the second without all these. The latter will be quicker than the former.

Compile your program. If you can afford the QuickBasic 4.5 version of QBasic which features a compiler to turn your programs into executables, you can speed up your programs a great deal.

Hiding Sluggishness

Sometimes, though, you can never get away from the fact that some processor intensive programs are just too slow in QBasic. This is obviously a huge problem, and one which causes many less patient and less devoted programmers to turn elsewhere for there lust for speed. But, for the most part, this is unnecessary, and there are also a few well-known techniques for hiding the fact that your routines are lagging behind the mind of the user.

If you use Windows, you will no doubt be aware that icons inform you of what the computer is currently doing. If there's no problem with the system, the cursor will be normal, but if the system is busy doing something, the cursor will change to something visually descriptive, like an hourglass.

You have probably also come across status bars that can often be seen when installing a program or saving or loading a large file. Typically, they inform you of how long you will have to wait for the processor to complete the task.

If you haven't already guessed, the reason we *need* to implement these features is so that user feels in control. If the program just seems to stop working for no apparent reason, and it doesn't immediately respond to their keypresses, it's possible that they will exit the program, assuming that it has crashed. This isn't the fault of the user, but the result of bad programming.

We can implement both of these methods in QBasic because neither are particularly involved nor do they require you to learn different or new techniques. The best way is for a routine which is busy to implement one of these methods to call a suitable procedure whilst it is operating.

> This may seem rather odd to some people, adding more code into the critical loop,
> following on from a section where we outlined that we need to remove code from
> the critical loop in order to speed your programs up. The truth of the matter is that
> the user needs to be in control of the program at all times, and it's worth a slight
> extra delay to achieve this.

Take a look at this procedure:

```
SUB DelayManager (percentage)

pc = percentage
LOCATE 1, 1
PRINT "##################################"
IF pc <> 100 THEN PRINT "### Percentage Completed = "; pc; "% ";
IF pc <> 100 THEN PRINT STRING$(4 + (LEN(STR$(pc)) <> 2), "#")
IF pc = 100 THEN PRINT "###        ALL DONE !         ###"
PRINT "##################################"

END SUB
```

By displaying the message in a box we can keep up with the Jones' and demonstrate our programming
dexterity. How do we do this when the problem is so easy? Well, you haven't seen the problem yet have
you with aligning the right of hand side of the center line?

Yes, the top border of the box and the bottom border are just a set string of hashes, but the center line
changes in length throughout the process, because we will have 5%, 10% and 100% if we implemented it
fully. To get around this, we print the start of the line, and then we calculate the length of the number *as a
string* and feed that correctly into the **STRING$** function to output the correct number of hashes at the end.

Of course, to catch the third number size, three digits, we have cheated and just used the **IF** statement to
separate the three-digit numbers and the one- and two-digit. This simply serves to demonstrate that there's
always more than one solution to every problem. All you have to do is think about what you want and
how you're going to get it. Simple.

To call this function, look at this program:

```
REM Demonstrating the Status Bar
REM \CHAP12\CH12_15.BAS

DECLARE SUB DelayManager (percentage!)
SCREEN 9
CLS

FOR i% = 1 TO 1000
    DelayManager (i% \ 10)
NEXT i%

DelayManager (100)

END
```

We aren't just restricted to icons or status bars either, because we can keep the user informed of the
progress of the current task by all manner of different methods. You could just as easily implement any of
the following:

Color cycling. This is a popular (if sometimes garish) method whereby the program quickly changes the color of a certain area of the screen, usually the background, border or a particular text string. This quick switching of colors is very striking and gives the user a sense of activity.

Using audio. Another good example of a system illustrating activity is the use of audio. Often accompanied with one of the other methods too, this one is particularly adept at annoying the user, so don't over use it.

Using movement. Here's another effective 'activity-informing' technique that usually is a little more involved than the previous two. Back in Chapter 8 we showed you a very popular program used for exactly this purpose - the rotating line.

Metaphorical Inbetweening

When one part of a program is completed, how do you normally go into the next section? Do you keep both sections totally separate by any chance? Most programmers do. But what if you could offload the processing of one particularly sluggish section onto another, less intensive part of your program? Well, it might be cheating, but I tell you it works!

This style of creative flow management is used a lot by professional programmers and can effectively mask the obnoxious long pauses between sections. Sometimes, it can be as simple as just stringing the user along, i.e. give them a screen of text to read, or controls to calibrate, and whilst they are doing this, you load your data or prepare your sprites or whatever. A lot of commercial games, in fact, lead you through a very long-winded introductory sequence, not just to set the scene, but to load a massive amount of data into memory too.

For example, if we had to store all the sine values of degrees between 0 and 90, to two decimal places, i.e. 9000 different floating point values, we would use something like this:

```
CLS
DIM sinvalues(9000)
FOR A = 0 TO 90 STEP .01
sinvalues(A * 100) = SIN(A)
LOCATE 1, 1: PRINT INT(A)
NEXT A
```

But this is painfully slow, and we couldn't possibly let the user wait until our code completes this. We could optimize it a bit more, but the user would still be sat around waiting for a while.

What we could do is to try to mask it by partitioning it between intermediate sections of code. For instance, we could separate this awkward task into nine segments which we execute at different moments before we need them to be completed. We could partition them into these nine procedures:

```
DECLARE SUB getvalues1 ()
DECLARE SUB getvalues2 ()
DECLARE SUB getvalues2 ()
DECLARE SUB getvalues3 ()
DECLARE SUB getvalues4 ()
DECLARE SUB getvalues5 ()
DECLARE SUB getvalues6 ()
DECLARE SUB getvalues7 ()
DECLARE SUB getvalues8 ()
DECLARE SUB getvalues9 ()
```

Now we can process each of these individually any place, any time, because they only take a fraction of the time to complete, and are independent of one another.

What most programmers familiar with this technique would do is the following, bearing in mind that we have split the processing into nine sections:

- Complete two procedures at the start of the program, or the end of the current section.

- Draw a screen full of information, whilst processing the third procedure.

- Process as many as possible whilst waiting for the user to press a key, or instruct the program what to do next. Hopefully, the user will not respond immediately, and as many procedures are completed as possible.

- Another procedure (if there are any left) is completed before the next screen is shown.

- Another procedure (if there are still any left) is completed whilst drawing the second information screen.

- Process as many of those left as possible while waiting for the user to press a key, or instruct the program what to do next. Hopefully, the user will not respond immediately, and as many procedures are completed as possible.

- All the remaining procedures are completed before the start of the game.

The number of procedures and number of intermediate screens will, of course, determine how well you can hide the slow processing speed of QBasic. But don't worry about inserting any extra screens than you had planned, they don't have to take up a lot of space, and they make your program look:

- More professional

- More instructive

- More friendly

- Better value for money

The wipes we saw earlier can also be implemented with such intermediary screens, and masking routines, although should they run too slowly, then this may look rather unsightly.

If you think about your programs, there are probably hundreds of different screens that you could insert in between their sections, of which these are only a few:

A hi-score table
A credits page
A reminder to register
An instructions page
A list of the controls
A detail of the story
An image to act as the header

A system information page
A summary of your last performance
A gratuitous advert
A summary of selected options
A screen shot from the game
A small introductory sequence
An epilepsy warning

Incidentally, this last example, an epilepsy warning, is required in several countries to be included in all new commercial games. Details of this can be found in the documentation of all latest games releases.

Controlling your Speed

Speed isn't all about the faster the better, though, because if you're not careful, you can lose control of your sprites, an effect than can mean unsightly flicker and/or disproportionate speed of sprites. The key to mastering this problem, is the ultimate test of games programming control - the use of timers.

Let's consider the example of the classic game, Tetris, which everyone is undoubtedly familiar with. If you aren't, let me recap a lost childhood. You are given a dropping block to control by moving it either left or right, or rotating it, until it hits the bottom of the screen when it stops. This continues until the blocks fill the screen, which is what you are trying to stop. Your weapon to stop this happening is the fact that if you fill a horizontal line without gaps then it disappears. Simple. But it isn't, the blocks drop faster, have awkward shapes and fill up the screen rather quickly. On the accompanying disk, we feature two similar versions, which you are free to try out; **\GAMES\BLOCKM.BAS** and **\NOCTURNAL\MATRIX.BAS**.

In a game like this, we would want to introduce a delay in the program, since it would probably run far too fast for us to follow. Such a delay is usually implemented by means of an empty **FOR...NEXT** loop. However, this construction has some drawbacks. First, it isn't machine-independent; what on one computer may be much too slow may be far too fast on another. Second, nothing can be done while the computer is in the loop - it just isn't possible to react to keypresses, or update the screen. A much better construction would be the use of the **TIMER** system variable.

In Tetris, the blocks drop one row every half second or so, but in that half second, the player can move and rotate it several times. In this case, the following construction is ideal:

```
DO
   Time! = TIMER + 0.5
   DO
      ' Place code for moving and rotating block here
      ...
   LOOP UNTIL Timer > Time!
   LowerBlock
   ' Place code for checking if the block has landed here
   ...
LOOP UNTIL BlockLanded=True
```

Here, the innermost **DO...LOOP** is executed as many times as will fit into 0.5 seconds. This is done by checking if the system variable **TIMER** has caught up with the single precision variable **Time!**, which got a 'head start' of 0.5 seconds. In this loop, the player can rotate and move the block as often as they wish within those 0.5 seconds. After the loop exits, the **LowerBlock** procedure is called, which displays the block one row down.

In general, the construction looks like this:

```
Time! = TIMER + DelayTime
DO
   ...
LOOP UNTIL TIMER > Time!
```

This will ensure loops of equal time length, with the possibility of executing code while in the loop.

Check out the two Tetris variants, listed at the start of this section, for further details of how this program can be practically implemented.

Putting It All Together

There's a very large gulf between having written a program and having written a proper application. What this means is that anyone can write the basis of a good working game, but it takes a really competent programmer to turn that 'core' code into a full-blown application. Of course, this doesn't matter if you only want to play your game amongst friends, and it doesn't matter when you want to teach a particular concept, but it *will* make all the difference if you send it to total strangers who'll judge it on substance alone.

So what is this substance that we're talking about? Well, imagine this book without all its complementary features; an index, a contents page, any headings, appendices, cover information etc. Pretty dull, eh? Well, now picture your favorite word processor without any of its menus, functions or help. It might be a very good word processor, but it's not a great application.

Let's now take a look at how we can avoid such problems with our programs and especially our games.

User Customization

One of the best ways to prolong the lifetime of a game is to offer the user the ability to customize as many facets of the game as they wish. This has the effect that the user will be able to use the software, or play the game, in a different manner if they choose. If you don't offer customizable features, and many commercial applications don't, then the software will have to be that much better than one than that offers a little variety so that it can occupy the user for as long as possible.

If we turn back to the word processor analogy once again, we can look at the various user customizable options that seem to offer most the user. For example, many give you the chance to select the size and orientation of your page. Without this option, the user would have to use the standard page layout for every document they created - a remarkably infeasible option.

In games, the most popular customizable options are normally these:

- Keyboard preferences
- Other control preferences and configuration
- Sound configuration
- Video and screen configuration
- Difficulty level

Extra Enhancements

If you've finished your game and tested it thoroughly, you might want to start thinking about enhancing its functionality. By adding extra features you can make your game really stand out from the crowd. We shall use this section to simply give your creative side a little nudge in the right direction.

We've already discussed obligatory inclusions such as hi-score tables, introductory sequences and special effects, but have you ever considered any of the following enhancements:

A level editor. Most games should be able to allow the user to define their own scenarios for playing the game in. For example, the Quiz game, **\GAMES\QUIZ.BAS**, features a complimentary program, **\GAMES\QUIZMAKE.BAS** which allows you to create your own question files. The same could quite easily be achieved for *any* other type of game.

A small bonus game between levels. A completely different, and very, very simple game that pops up in between levels, if you do particularly well, is a great reward for a job well done. It also helps keep the user's interest in the game alive.

Include a boss key. No-one likes to admit to playing games whilst they should be doing something more constructive, and so a lot of games now feature a boss key. This is so called because, if the boss walks in, you can press this key, and a 'serious' screen will be instantly displayed, giving the impression that you're doing some work.

Allow the user to change certain options during the game. Sometimes, if your sound is from the PC speaker, it can, trust me, get quite annoying. If people can't switch things like the music on and off at will, they will either stop playing or remove the offending statements from the program.

Create a form screen for registration. Everyone likes to do less work, and have everything automated for them. This is why including an on-screen form will make it a lot easier (and pressure the user) to register your work of art.

Include a positive way to exit your game. Some games don't allow you to exit from them very easily - an arrogant and unfriendly way of sustaining interest (or annoyance). Every program you write should include a logical way of quitting, and don't forget, this is also a golden opportunity for you to sell the full version, or other wares.

Depending on the type of game you want to write, the type of possible enhancements will vary a great deal and, without a doubt, new ones will present themselves. It's up to you to take full advantage of these 'breaks' and make your program the best in its field.

Programming for Multiple Systems

Not every computer user who has a copy of your program will have the exact same system specification that you have - in fact, this is very, very rare! Fortunately, these days most users can enjoy facilities such as a color screen and a reasonably fast processor, but we can't rely upon every user of our programs actually having these facilities. So what can *you* do? Well, you could design your programs with these aspects of your game or program as being customizable.

We've already talked about controlling the speed that the program runs at, so here we shall discuss how you can offer the monochrome user some welcome support.

Well, for a start you could write all your programs in black and white, but that wouldn't ingratiate color screen users very much would it? So what we have to do is have a feature at the start of your program which asks the user (in black and white if you like) whether they wish to be in monochrome or color for the duration of the program. It's as easy as that!

I'm sorry but I lied, it's not as easy as that because throughout your program you've got to select the correct color each time you change it, depending on the mode you've just chosen. You can do this in a number of different ways, the simplest being this:

```
LOCATE 1,1
IF chosen_screen_type$="color" THEN COLOR 3          ' Select Green
IF chosen_screen_type$="monochrome" THEN COLOR 15    ' Bright White
PRINT "Colored text on a black background"
```

But if you have a lot of different colors in your program, this method would undoubtedly become very tiresome after a while. So, a better method would be to write the program as if it were for color screen users and then, when we have to change a color, we send a copy of that color to a subroutine which changes the color if the user is driving monochrome. We would implement such a routine in exactly the same way, like this:

```
SUB ColorChange (Colortochange)

IF chosen_screen_type$="monochrome" AND Colortochange > 0 AND Colortochange < 10
THEN Colortochange = 15 ELSE Colortochange = 0

END SUB
```

Notice here that if the user isn't running in monochrome mode, this subroutine won't change anything. But if the user has selected monochrome, the colors 1 through 9 will become bright white (15), and all others will be black (0).

Of course, you'll have to change which values to change to black or white depending on the colors that you want to use in your program, because you may wish to use a color between 10 through 14 to signify white too.

> If you offer the user the chance to switch between these two modes at will, you will be able to test how your color schemes look in monochrome a lot more easily.

If you want to see a fully working program that caters for this, then check out the first part of the Super Soccer Manager, `\GAMES\SOCCER\SSM1.BAS`.

Summary

Games aren't to be treated trivially. More than any other computer-related topic, they are constantly at the cutting edge of technology. This, as we have seen, is just as evident in the world of QBasic. We have seen, on the accompanying disk, a collection of astonishing games. But they aren't astonishing because they have decent graphics, sound or effects. They are astonishing because they are *fun*. You have seen a lot of different versions of classic games, and many of these QBasic implementations stand up rather well against versions written in more modern languages.

We have also used this chapter to ingrain a sense of adventure, invention and creative license, which, hopefully, will give you the confidence with which to tackle almost any problem that you wish to solve in computer programming. This 'attitude' is very important, and should hold you in good stead for when the time comes to write your own applications, if you haven't done so already.

Programming a User Interface

Introduction

The user interface is a set of tools for creating a dialog interaction between the user and a program. A good interface effectively controls information, representation and processing and reduces the likelihood that you'll make mistakes while you're working with a program.

The user interface in the QBasic environment is designed according to the IBM standard (Systems Application Architecture: Common User Access, Panel Design and User Interaction, SC26-4351-0, IBM Corporation (1987)). Every company involved in software development has its own user interface standards. You can even develop your own if you don't want to use somebody else's.

In this chapter, we'll look at QBasic's user interface components and how you can implement them. You can spend an awful lot of time developing an interface and yet it can quite easily turn out to be inefficient in practice. We hope that the examples given here will help you to choose an optimal balance between the effort you put into the design of the interface and its efficiency as a dialog between the user and the program.

The Components of a User Interface

Designing a user interface involves constructing screen panels, developing the user's interaction with the panels and creating dialog windows. A panel (or window or form) is a part of the screen where grouped information is located. The elements of this information may be:

- Menus.
- Fields for data entry and editing.
- Illustrations, text, messages and references.
- The results of data processing.
- Selection fields - lists of objects, from which the user chooses one (one selection) or several (multi-choice selection) objects.
- Pause fields which output messages and wait for a key to be pressed.
- Program titles and stages of execution, labels or headings of data groups and entry fields.
- Explanation of control and function keys.

In real panels, these types of information are often combined so, typically, we classify a panel by the main type of information that it contains.

User-program Dialogs

The **dialog** is a sequence of requests directed at the program by the user, and vice versa: a user requests an action in response to a request by the program, and so on. The rules of conducting such a dialog are an important consideration when programming the user interface. These include the rules for moving the selection cursor, data input, exiting a program, or going back to the previous dialog, canceling actions, and finally, working with windows.

These rules should not only be implemented in the program, but also be brought to the user's attention by on-panel prompts, explanations of the entry fields, information about the features of a specified program and the functions of the control keys. It's because of these rules that the user interacts with the panel during the dialog.

The Selection Cursor

The information that the user is going to work with is usually marked on the panel by the selection cursor. The rules of moving the selection cursor should be the most effective way of choosing the necessary information for each dialog situation.

Windows

A window is a bound rectangular area of the screen which we use to display a set of related information. The dialog typically begins in the primary window which occupies the whole screen. Secondary windows are invoked from within the primary window. They can either be **dialog** windows or **help** windows.

The dialog between the user and the computer is conducted in a dialog window. This dialog is either simultaneous with that in the primary window, or it is a continuation of it. In a help window, there will be references or messages relating to the dialog in the primary window. The user should also be able to switch from the primary window to its secondary ones, and vice versa.

As an example, take a look at a standard entry and edit panel from the QBasic programming environment:

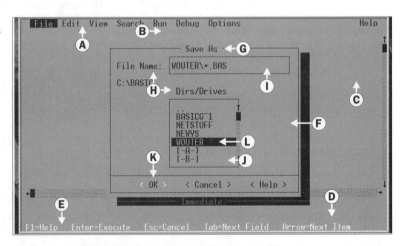

Here, the contents of the primary window is a QBasic program and, in a secondary pop-up window, the user indicates the name of a file for the chosen Save As menu item. The component elements of the panel are as follows:

A - main action bar
B - panel title
C - program entry and edit field
D - 'immediate' field
E - function and control keys
F - pop-up dialog window
G - pop-up window title corresponding to chosen menu item
H - field titles
I - entry field
J - selection field
K - pop-up window menu
L - selection cursor

Let's now take a look at the different ways of interfacing the user-computer dialog through the use of menus.

Organizing a Dialog Using Menus

Menus are one of the more common types of PC-user dialog and they've become essential in the competitive world of applied program packages for personal computers. Menus qualified software for the *user-friendly* label when they were less prevalent than they are today, and it won't come as a surprise when we tell you that the Windows 3.1 graphical user interface is largely responsible for their current popularity.

The term *menu* refers to the similarity between what you see on screen and a restaurant menu - in both cases you're given a list of options to choose from. There are various ways in which you can represent a menu on screen. Here's a menu from program **CH13_1.BAS** which occupies the whole screen:

Here, the numbers serve to identify the options: by pressing one of the identifier keys *1 - 5*, you choose the relevant option. The choice of method for identifying options is arbitrary - you could have used letters. Using letters as identifiers would be convenient when the program contains a small number of menus and we can mnemonically assign connected letters to the options, for example R for Rectangle.

The letters which identify an option are marked in different ways (more often than not by size or color). It's logical to expect that an identifier and its corresponding option are somehow connected. If there's no connection, it's probably better to designate numbers to the options.

Function keys can also act as option identifiers, as the following shot illustrates. It shows a menu from the QBasic environment where choosing options is carried out through the function keys:

```
<F1=Help> <F2=Save> <F3=Load> <F4=Edit> <F5=Calculate>
```

We'll illustrate ways of representing menus using a program which calculates the areas of the four classes of geometric figure : Rectangles, Trapezoids, Triangles and Circles. In this program, the user has to choose a type of figure and enter the required data items, for which the area will then be calculated. Once an option has been chosen, the program calculates the area of a figure using the numeric data that the user entered.

467

The first kind of menu that we'll look at in more detail is the full-screen menu.

Numeric Menu Selection

Program **CH13_1.BAS** demonstrates a menu which occupies the whole screen and in which your choice is made by selecting a numeric value. The user interaction rules are very simple. In the primary dialog window shown earlier, the choice of option is made using one of the keys *1 - 5*. Pressing other keys produces no effect other than a warning sound.

Choosing options 1, 2, and 4 results in closing the menu panel and executing the program fragment appropriate to the chosen menu item. When the Triangle item is chosen, a secondary window opens, in which the user is requested to fill in the details of the chosen option:

```
          D A T A :

1    Three sides
2    Base and height
3    Two sides and angle
4    Main menu
```

In this way, program **CH13_1.BAS** implements a full screen two-level menu. Typically, the second level menu provides an option enabling the user to return to the main menu. This is accomplished in our menu by the Main menu option.

After choosing options 1, 2, or 3 in the secondary menu, the corresponding program fragment is executed and the program returns to the second-level menu.

Run the program and the menu shown earlier appears in the center of the screen. The **Menu** procedure outputs the menu onto the screen and waits for the user's response, which is defined by subtracting the value 48 from the ASCII value of the character entered. If the value entered doesn't have an ASCII value of between 49 and 48+**N%** (the number of menu items), you'll hear a beep:

```
'*** Selection of item ***
DO
    DO
        A$ = INKEY$
    LOOP WHILE A$ = ""
    NT% = ASC(A$) - 48
    IF NT% < 1 OR NT% > N% THEN
        PLAY "C+"
    ELSE
        EXIT DO
    END IF
LOOP
END SUB
```

The key value chosen is returned in the variable **NT%**, and when you select the menu items 1, 2, or 4, procedures **Rectangle**, **Trapezium**, and **Circle1** are called. Each of these displays a corresponding drawing, asks the user for the source data and calculates the area of the geometric object for the values entered.

When you choose item 3, the second-level menu appears on the screen and the user is asked to specify the type of parameters from which to calculate the area of the triangle.

When you choose items 1, 2, or 3 in the secondary menu, the control is passed to procedures **Triangle1**, **Triangle2**, or **Triangle3**, respectively. These procedures output diagrams onto the screen, explaining the parameters you need to provide, and then ask the user for the necessary parameters and calculate the area of the triangle.

To return to the main menu from the secondary one, choose option 4, and to exit the program from the main menu, select item 5.

Using a Pointer to Choose Options

Program **CH13_2.BAS** demonstrates the use of a full-screen menu in which an option is chosen using a pointer:

Only three keys are involved in menu control - the *Up* and *Down* cursor arrows and *Enter*. The first two serve to move the pointer, while the third one serves to activate the currently highlighted item. The small number of control keys is one advantage of a menu of this kind.

Program **CH13_2.BAS** differs from program **CH13_1.BAS** only by changes made to the **Menu** procedure:

```
SUB Menu (X0, Y0, IM$, NT%)
'    *****************************************
'    *                  Menu                 *
'    *    Items are selected using a pointer  *
'    *****************************************
' X0, Y0 - coordinates of upper left corner of menu
' IM$ - selection of data block for menu
' NT% - number of selected option

SCREEN 0
CLS
WIDTH 40
Wide% = 40                        'screen width
SELECT CASE IM$
CASE "Main"
    RESTORE DataMenuMain
CASE "Triangles"
    RESTORE DataMenuTriangles
END SELECT
READ N%, Title$                   'number of menu items and a title

' *** Centering and outputting title ***
T = (Wide% - LEN(Title$)) / 2
LOCATE X0 - 2, T
PRINT Title$

' *** Output of menu onto screen ***
FOR I = 1 TO N%
```

```
      READ B$
      LOCATE X0 + I - 1, Y0
      PRINT B$
   NEXT I

   ' *** Selection of item ***
   X = X0: Y = Y0 - 2                    'current position of pointer
   NT% = 1
   DO
      LOCATE X, Y
      PRINT "->"
      DO
         Key$ = INKEY$
      LOOP WHILE Key$ = ""
      SELECT CASE Key$
         CASE CHR$(0) + CHR$(72)        'Up
            NT% = NT% - 1
            IF NT% < 1 THEN NT% = N%
         CASE CHR$(0) + CHR$(80)        'Down
            NT% = NT% + 1
            IF NT% > N% THEN NT% = 1
         CASE CHR$(13)                  'Enter
            EXIT DO
      END SELECT
      LOCATE X, Y: PRINT "  "
      X = X0 + NT% - 1
   LOOP
   END SUB
```

Let's look at how an option is selected. In the section marked *****Selection of Item*****, first the current coordinates (**x**, **y**) of the pointer are determined, then the number, **NT%**, of the chosen option is initialized and the pointer (in the form of an arrow (**->**)) is placed in the given position. When a key is pressed, the **SELECT** command analyzes it.

When you press either of the *Up* or *Down* keys, you correspondingly change the value of the variable **NT%**, erase the old pointer by outputting two blank spaces over the top of it, and create a new pointer in the correct position. You'll notice that the pointer moves around as if on a loop: if the pointer is on the last menu option, pressing the *Down* key will move it onto the first option, and vice versa.

These circular menus are convenient because you can quickly move the pointer up or down to the option you require. The amount of key presses it takes to move the pointer from its present position to a desired one is never more than half the number of items in the list. For example, in a ringed menu with five options, no more than two key presses are needed to get to any option. This compares with a possible four key presses in a simple, linear menu with five options.

Using a Graphics Pointer to Select Options

In programs which work with menus on a graphics screen, the pointer is typically represented by some kind of icon. Let's look at how a menu of this sort can be organized, using program **CH13_3.BAS** which calculates areas:

The main module of program **CH13_3.BAS** is different from that of **CH13_1.BAS** only in the first four lines:

```
COMMON SHARED A%()
SCREEN 9, 1, 0
CALL Pointer (1,1)
SCREEN 0, , 0, 1
```

The **Pointer** procedure, which is called in the third line, creates the graphics pointer:

```
SUB Pointer (X, Y AS INTEGER)
'    ***********************************
'    *  Definition of graphic pointer  *
'    ***********************************

' *** Defining form of graphic pointer ***
RESTORE Cursor
FOR I = 1 TO 16
   FOR J = 1 TO 18
      READ C
      IF C = 1 THEN PSET (J, I)
   NEXT J
NEXT I

' *** Determining number of bytes to store pointer ***
L = 4 + INT(((18 + 1) + 7) / 8) * 4 * (16 + 1)

' *** Storing pointer in array A%() ***
DIM A%(L)
GET (X, Y)-(X + 18, Y + 16), A%
END SUB
```

The data defining the appearance of the pointer is taken from the block of data labeled **Cursor** at the end of the main module. If you look at this **DATA** block from a distance, or if you squint, you should be able to see the outline of the pointing finger even before printing it to the screen:

```
DATA 0,0,0,0,1,1,1,1,1,1,1,1,1,1,1,1,1,0
DATA 0,0,0,1,0,0,0,0,1,0,0,0,0,0,0,0,0,1
DATA 0,0,1,0,0,0,0,0,0,1,0,0,0,0,0,0,0,1
DATA 0,1,0,0,0,0,1,0,0,0,1,0,0,0,0,0,0,1
DATA 1,0,0,0,0,0,1,0,0,0,0,1,1,1,1,1,1,0
DATA 1,0,0,0,0,1,0,1,0,0,0,1,0,0,0,0,0,0
DATA 1,0,0,0,0,0,0,1,1,1,1,0,1,0,0,0,0,0
DATA 1,0,0,0,0,0,0,1,0,0,0,0,1,0,0,0,0,0
DATA 1,0,0,0,0,0,0,1,1,1,1,1,1,0,0,0,0,0
DATA 1,0,0,1,1,1,1,0,0,0,0,1,0,0,0,0,0,0
DATA 1,0,0,0,0,0,1,0,0,0,0,1,0,0,0,0,0,0
DATA 1,0,0,0,0,0,1,1,1,1,1,1,0,0,0,0,0,0
DATA 1,0,0,0,0,1,0,0,0,0,1,0,0,0,0,0,0,0
DATA 0,1,0,0,0,1,0,0,0,0,1,0,0,0,0,0,0,0
DATA 0,0,1,1,1,1,1,1,1,1,0,0,0,0,0,0,0,0
DATA 0,0,0,0,0,0,0,0,0,0,0,0,0,0,0,0,0,0
```

Moving the pointer is carried out in two stages. First the pointer is placed onto its old image using the **PUT** statement with the **XOR** parameter as we discussed in the Chapter 8 - Bit-mapped Graphics and Animation.

This results in the extraction of the pointer from the screen. Then, the pointer is displayed in its new position. An option is then selected in just the same way as in program **CH13_2.BAS**.

As well as the menus that we have discussed, there are many other ways of organizing menus which include varying the representation of the menu text and the marking of a current option. **Highlighting** is a popular method for marking a current option - you can see its extensive use in the QBasic environment menus.

Using a Cursor to Select an Option

Here's a full-screen menu, from program **\CHAP13\CH13_4.BAS**, in which highlighting marks the current option:

A menu option is highlighted by placing a colored rectangle over the text of the chosen option, using the **PUT** command again with the **XOR** parameter. Placing the rectangle a second time returns the text to its initial state.

The advantages of such a method are freedom of movement and control, and can best be seen in action in most graphical operating systems such as the many versions of Windows.

So far, we have looked at menus from which the user chooses just one option. Now, we'll move on to consider a menu from which you can select a host of options.

Optional Selection Buttons

You may wish your users to choose more than one item at a time from a menu. This may, for example, be necessary when specifying the screen mode, the name of a friend, or the parameters of a font before outputting text to the screen or to the printer. This kind of selection is known as **multi-alternative**.

To mark the selected options we've chosen buttons - so an unpressed button marked with the text Off represents an unchosen option, while a pressed button marked with the text On represents a chosen one.

When you start the program (**CH13_5.BAS**), it outputs the text of the menu and draws a button to the left of each item: all the buttons are unpressed and marked Off. The text of the current option is yellow; movement is again provided by the *Up* and *Down* keys; and you can toggle the current menu option on and off by pressing the *Space* bar.

Here's the screen after options 1, 2 and 4 have been chosen (the options are stored in the **Buttons** array):

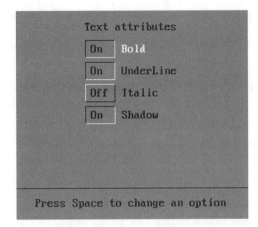

Pressing *Enter* finishes the menu option selection and displays a list of the chosen options on the screen.

Menu Design Tips

The most important design tip for any sort of user interface is consistency. If there are several menus in one program or one system, you should always try to use the same method. From the user's point of view, consistency speeds up the understanding of the program.

However, you'll often find that a lot of programs let you choose menu items in two different ways: either from the keyboard or by moving the cursor. Experienced users, and particularly proficient typists, who like to skip through menus, take advantage of the **shortcut keys** (keys which mirror the selection of particular popular items from the menus).

Finally, the most commonly used options should be nearest the default cursor position in the menu. This speeds up choice selection - remember, users don't want to navigate menus, they want to use the program!

Integral Screen Menus

Menus which occupy just part of the screen are more typical of most programs. These are usually displayed at the same time as other information located in the rest of the screen. They are often used for manipulating the display, controlling data input or performing other actions, relevant to information on the same input screen. In this way, they're different from the full-screen menus that we've seen so far.

The typical menu bar has the following characteristics:

- It takes up one line at the top of the screen.
- It's differentiated from the rest of the screen by the panel color.
- The current menu option is highlighted.
- The menu is not titled.
- There's a status bar or prompt line located at the bottom of the screen, in a color similar to that of the menu bar.

▲ The menu and the prompt line are constantly available on the screen.

Menus which occupy just part of the screen like this can be used in any screen location and appear in many different guises.

Notice how, when one of the menu items here is selected, a secondary menu drops down. This menu has slightly different characteristics:

▲ The menu options are located vertically, not horizontally.

▲ The menu is differentiated from the rest of the screen by the color of its panel and the border.

▲ The menu title is the name of an item from the menu bar e.g. File.

▲ The current menu option is identified by a cursor.

▲ The help line is located in the bottom part of the screen and is highlighted only by color.

▲ Unlike the previous menu, it isn't constantly on screen; also when an item is selected from this kind of menu, it normally disappears. The shadow cast by the menu panel emphasizes that it's above the screen and, when it disappears, the screen area which was underneath is completely restored.

You can select the top-level items on the menu bar by highlighting your option with *Left* and *Right* arrow keys and pressing *Enter* (or the *Up* and *Down* arrow keys) to activate it. Pressing *Esc* returns you to the main menu without having to chose a new item in the sub-menu.

The *Enter* key is used to select an option and exit from the **Menu** procedure, passing three variables, **Esc**, **Vers** and **SubVers** to the calling procedure. If the value of **Esc** is True, the **Menu** procedure has been exited by pressing *Esc*, in other words, canceling selection from the new menu. The variables **Vers** and **SubVers** store the values of the chosen items in the main menu bar and in the corresponding pull-down menu.

The values of the variables **Esc**, **Vers** and **SubVers** are processed by the procedure **Result**. So as not to complicate the program, to show the results of option selection in the menu, we either output the corresponding text onto the screen (items Laws, Principles, Axioms), or change the screen colors (option Colors). Interesting color effects are obtained by choosing items from the Colors sub-menu. The **PALETTE USING** statement changes the color palette.

Let's now look at the program itself. The head module of the program begins, as usual, with the declaration of procedures, constants and global variables.

Among the global variables, five arrays are declared: **C**, **P1%**, **P2%**, **P3%**, and **P4%**, which are all used in the statements **COLOR** and **PALETTE USING** for changing the color palette. Colors on the screen are defined in accordance to those depicted in this diagram:

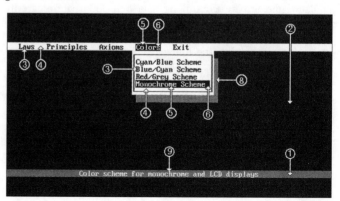

The array **C** is used to store the ten color attributes:

C(1), C(9)	color of the background and the information messages
C(2), C(10)	color of the background and the text of the main screen
C(3), C(4)	color of the text and background in the menu
C(5), C(6)	color of the text and background of the cursor
C(7)	color of warning message (not shown)
C(8)	color of the shadow

The procedure **InitMenu** initializes the variables and defines a current palette. Then, control is passed back to the main module, the main loop is started and will continue until the Exit option is chosen from the menu bar. At the beginning of the loop, the **Menu** procedure is called.

The first parameter of the **Menu** procedure is a variable, **NP**, equal to the number of options in the main menu. The results of the procedure are stored in the variables: **Vers** (the number of the highlighted item in the main menu bar), **SubVers** (the number of the highlighted option in the subsequent pull-down menu) and **Esc** (the attribute for canceling in the main menu).

In the **Menu** procedure, a text view area is set and the internal variables, **Version** (the number of options in the main menu bar) and **SV** (the number of options in the pull-down menu), are initialized:

```
VIEW PRINT
Version = 0
SV = 0
```

The **InitTextMainMenu** sub-program then initializes the texts of the menu options and the Help information of the status bar at the bottom of the screen. The subroutine **MainMenuOnScreen** outputs the main menu onto the screen.

Since the parameter **Version** equals 0, the highlight is missing in the main menu. The information line contains the value of the variable **Help$(0)** (in our case, this is an empty line).

The internal variable **Version** is then assigned the number **Vers** of the current main menu option. The subroutine **MainMenuOnScreen** is called again, which outputs the highlight onto the current position in the main menu and the corresponding message in the prompt line.

The last sub-program called in the **Menu** procedure is **SelectVersion**, which processes the keys *Esc*, *Left*, *Right*, *Up*, *Down* and *Enter* when they are pressed. Pressing *Left*, *Right*, *Up* or *Down* changes the value of one of the internal variables **Version** or **SV**, and moves the cursor in the relevant direction.

Cursor movement is executed as follows:

▲ The screen memorized on the first screen page at the beginning of the **Menu** procedure (**PCOPY 1,0**) is restored.

▲ The item **Version** in the main menu is marked by the cursor (subroutine **MenuOnScreen**).

▲ If **SV <> 0**, a second level menu with the cursor in position **SV** (subroutine **SubMenuOnScreen**) is displayed.

When the *Enter* key is pressed, it's processed according to the values of the variables **SV** and **NV**, the latter being the number of options in the **Version** menu of the main menu bar. If **NV(Version)<>0** and **SV<>0**, the corresponding assignments to the variables **Vers** and **SubVers** are made and the execution of the subroutine **SelectVersion** is complete.

If **NV(Version)<>0** and **SV=0**, the corresponding pull-down menu becomes active (the subroutine **SelectVersion** is not exited). Therefore, pressing *Enter* results in exiting the subroutine **SelectVersion** when the current option has no pull-down menu, otherwise the menu of the current option is called.

Pressing *Esc* results in returning to the main menu bar if a pull-down menu is currently active, or exiting the subroutine **SelectVersion** if the main menu bar is active. In the latter case, the values of **Vers** and **SubVers** don't change - the selected new menu option is canceled.

The procedure **Menu** finishes with the call to the subroutine **SelectVersion**, and control is passed to the **Result** procedure.

The arguments for the procedure **Result** are the variables **Vers, SubVers** and **Esc**. The **Esc** variable tells the **Result** procedure how the procedure **Menu** will be exited. If **Esc** = True, the message Selection not made is output and the procedure **Result** is exited.

If the value of the variable **Esc** is False, the **Result** procedure executes the actions associated with the chosen menu option. These actions are defined by the value of the variable **Vers** (the number of the current main menu item) and **SubVers** (the number of the current option in the pull-down menu). If the value of **Vers** equals 1, 2 or 3, some text is displayed on the screen while, if **Vers** = 4, the screen color palette is changed.

Changing the Palette

The change of palette in the **Result** procedure is carried out using the **PALETTE USING** statement, according to the numbers of colors defined in one of the arrays **P1%()**, **P2%()**, **P3%()** or **P4%()**. The number of an array depends on the number of the selected option in the Colors sub-menu, for example, if you select Red/Gray Scheme:

```
PALETTE USING P3%(0)
```

This statement establishes the conformity between the color attributes and the numbers of colors. Remember that, in the **SCREEN 0** video mode, you can choose a color number from the range [0, 63], and the attribute number from [0, 15].

The **PALETTE USING** statement changes the color palette in this program because we want to be able to quickly change the colors on the screen. If you don't need to change the color palette in a program, it can be significantly simplified by changing the procedures **InitMenu**. Every so often, you may need to output the menu text together with an information line on the screen, but without choosing an option.

For this purpose, it makes sense to introduce a global logic variable **ActiveMenu** into the program, depending on the value of which activation of the menu does (**ActiveMenu=False**) or doesn't (**ActiveMenu=True**) take place. For convenience, we've made the alterations in **CH13_5.BAS** on your disk.

The disk also contains **CH13_6.BAS** which demonstrates the use of menus in a graphics screen mode. **CH13_6.BAS** is intended for the calculation of areas of different geometric objects and differs from **CH13_1.BAS** - **CH13_4.BAS** only in its interface.

Data Input

Remember that, when organizing a dialog between the user and the PC, the user will make mistakes of one sort or another - it's human to err. Your program may have to cope with input that you hadn't envisaged during its development. The user may press *Enter* without having typed anything in, type in upper-case letters where your program is expecting lower-case ones (or vice versa), or use a different format for entering dates and telephone numbers from the one you've catered for. All of these things can destroy your program's view of the world!

You should do as much as you can to insure against user errors. For example, when you are requesting numeric data, you can analyze the input to make sure that it really is numeric and is written in a recognized format. If a discrepancy is detected, the program should tell the user, in as much detail as is necessary, what the problem is and then allow for the error to be corrected. If possible, this should be done without forcing the user to input all the data again if some of it was correct first time round. This is particularly relevant when you're entering large amounts of data.

You will remember from the previous chapter that we can build our own routines to eliminate or control these mistakes. Unlike the simple method implemented in the text adventure game, the following routines can be manipulated to capture the keys you desire:

CH13_7.BAS includes a procedure which only allows the input of numeric data by switching off the keys that could interfere with the syntax during data entry. The program also prevents the user from entering more than one decimal point, or a minus sign in a position other than at the front of the data, and sounds a warning beep when the user makes any of the anticipated mistakes.

CH13_8.BAS demonstrates how to enter numeric and text data to satisfy some of the requirements listed above. You can use this procedure as an example from which to develop your own input procedures.

Another condition frequently imposed on data input is the restriction of the length of an entered string. The input procedures from **CH13_7.BAS** and **CH13_8.BAS** contain parameters which limit the maximum number of characters for the entry.

We'll begin our look at data input with a comparison of the elementary data input statements. QBasic has the following statements for data input during a dialog with the PC: **INPUT**, **LINE INPUT**, **INPUT$**, and the system variable **INKEY$**. Which of these will be most suited to your needs depends entirely on the features of your particular program.

To enter a character value corresponding to the code of a pressed key, without displaying the character on the screen, you can use the system variable **INKEY$**. Bear in mind though, that the reference to the variable **INKEY$** doesn't wait for a key to be pressed. The length of a string line transmitted through **INKEY$** can equal **0**, **1**, or **2**. If, when this system variable is invoked, no key is pressed, the assignment:

```
A$ = INKEY$
```

transmits a character line of zero length (empty line). If the length of the line transmitted using the variable **INKEY$** is equal to one, the value of the character variable is the character which has just been typed on the keyboard.

Extended ASCII codes are transmitted using two characters. The first character of the two-character code is equal to zero. The code of the second character is defined by the extended code of the pressed key.

system variable **INKEY$** transmits most two-byte codes which are the result of pressing a control key or their combinations. The exceptions are the *Print Screen* key and the combinations *Ctrl + Break*, *Ctrl + NumLock*, *Ctrl + Alt + Del*, *Ctrl + Print Screen*, whose codes can be used.

In many cases, these statements are sufficient to create a simple dialog with the user. However, in more complicated programs you have to turn to other specially developed input procedures. We'll start with numeric data input.

Keyboard Numeric Data Input

Numeric data often needs to be input during user-computer dialogs. In this section, we look at a procedure for entering numerical data which doesn't allow the user to make an error when entering a real number. We'll proceed from the following assumptions:

1 The first character of a number can be either a digit, a minus sign or a decimal point. All the other keys are disabled at this stage.

2 The second character in the number can be either a digit or a decimal point. At this stage, the minus key is added to the list of disabled keys.

3 The decimal point can't occur twice in the number, so, once it has been entered, this key is also switched off.

4 Entries consisting only of a minus sign, a decimal point, a minus sign and a decimal point, or no characters at all, aren't numbers so aren't allowed.

Therefore, the sequences 0.12, -.5, 3, 4, and -123456 are valid numbers, whereas the sequences -.1., -123-4, 4.-5, and + 23 aren't considered numbers and so can't appear in the input field.

Our procedure for entering numbers uses the ten numeric keys, and the *BackSpace* key for deleting a character to the left of the cursor.

The text of **CH13_7.BAS** illustrates numeric data entry. The main load of the program is born by the procedure **NumberAnswer (X0,Y0,LAns,Number)**, the first three parameters of which are arguments. They define the location and the length of the entry field into which a number will be entered. The length of the entry field sets the maximum allowable number of characters that the number to be entered can have.

The **NumberAnswer** procedure is fairly simple: using the system variable **INKEY$**, the variable **L$** is assigned a string value corresponding to the key pressed by the user, which is then analyzed. If **L$** is a figure, the subroutine **AddSymbol** is used to join the value **L$** to the string **Nmbr$**, in which the input result is stored. At the beginning of the procedure, this string is empty:

```
    AddSymbol:
            IF LEN(Nmbr$) < LAns THEN
        Nmbr$ = Nmbr$ + L$
        GOSUB OnScreen
    ELSE
        BEEP
    END IF
RETURN
```

If **L$ = "."**, the subroutine **FullStop** analyzes the presence of a decimal point in the string **Nmbr$**. If a decimal point hasn't yet been entered, it's added to the right of **Number$**:

```
FullStop:
  IF INSTR(Nmbr$, ".") = 0 THEN
    GOSUB AddSymbol
  ELSE
    BEEP
  END IF
RETURN
```

The **Minus** subroutine is organized in a similar way and only enables you to enter the '-' character if it's the first character of the string variable **Nmbr$**.

When the *BackSpace* key is pressed, the subroutine of the same name deletes the last character in the string **Nmbr$** :

```
BackSpace:
  LN = LEN(Nmbr$)
  IF LN > 0 THEN
    Nmbr$ = LEFT$(Nmbr$, LN - 1)
    GOSUB OnScreen
  ELSE
    BEEP
  END IF
RETURN
```

The input or removal of any character is accompanied by the corresponding alterations in the entry fields. The output of data onto the screen is provided by the subroutine **OnScreen**:

```
OnScreen:
  Nmbr1$ = Nmbr$ + SPACE$(LAns - LEN(Nmbr$))
  LOCATE X0, Y0
  PRINT Nmbr1$;
  GOSUB Cursor
RETURN
```

This subroutine supplements the string **Nmbr$** with blanks up to the length **LAns** and outputs it on the screen in an entry field.

A blinking cursor is used to highlight the location in which the next character in the entry field will appear:

```
Cursor:
  LN = LEN(Nmbr$)
  IF LN < LAns THEN
    COLOR CC
    LOCATE X0, Y0 + LN
    PRINT "Û"
    COLOR CI
  END IF
RETURN
```

When the entry field is filled, the cursor is removed, which warns the user that no more characters can be entered. In this case, only the *BackSpace* and *Enter* keys are operational. Pressing any other key produces a warning beep.

479

Once a number has been typed in it is confirmed by pressing *Enter*. The subroutine **Enter** transforms the **Nmbr$** string into a number using the **Val** function, assigns this number to the output parameter **Number** and removes the cursor in the entry field:

```
Enter:
   Number = VAL(Nmbr$)
   LN = LEN(Nmbr$)
   IF LN < LAns THEN
      COLOR CI
      LOCATE X0, Y0 + LN
      PRINT " "
   END IF
RETURN
```

After the **NumberAnswer** procedure has been completed, this is the result on the screen:

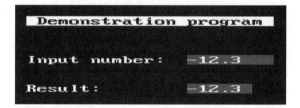

In the next section, we'll consider the input of text and numeric data.

Text and Numeric Data Input with Extended Editing Features

For correct programming of data input, it's not enough to write the **INPUT** statement to cope with the just the following:

Henry Simpson

In this section, we'll consider a procedure (**Answer**) which enables us to enter a long text message in an entry field of limited size. The need to do this may arise, for example, when defining the whole access path of a file.

In **CH13_7.BAS** we looked at a procedure for entering numeric data. This procedure provided just one way of editing the data being entered - by deleting a character to the left of the cursor. This is reasonably acceptable as far as entering numeric data is concerned. However, it would sorely try the patience of the user who has entered a 40-character text message only to discover that the third character is wrong.

In this case, expanding the editing features becomes a necessity and it's not unreasonable to expect the following editing features as a minimum:

- ▲ Moving the cursor one position left.
- ▲ Moving the cursor one position right.
- ▲ Replacing a character at the cursor.
- ▲ Inserting a character before the cursor.
- ▲ Deleting the cursor.
- ▲ Deleting a character at the cursor.

▲ Moving the cursor to the beginning of the text string being entered.

▲ Moving the cursor to the end of the text string being entered.

Of course, we could probably cope without the last three, but it only means a couple of extra lines of code, so why not?

To make the procedure **Answer** suitable for entering numeric data as well, we'll add a function **Number(Txt$)** which checks whether the string **Txt$** is a number record.

In the procedure under discussion, seven control keys are used: *Left*, *Right*, *Home*, *End*, *BackSpace*, *Del*, *Ins*, *Enter*. They provide easy editing of the entered data and are widely implemented in most commercial applications.

CH13_8.BAS implements the **Answer** procedure:

```
REM Data Input Demonstration Program
REM \CHAP13\CH13_8.BAS

DECLARE SUB Answer (X0!, Y0!, LX!, MaxLText!, Text$, NumberText$)
DECLARE FUNCTION Number! (Txt$)
DECLARE SUB Box (X1!, Y1!, X2!, Y2!, Version!, Clr1!, Clr2!)
DECLARE SUB NumberOrText (L$)

CONST False = 0
CONST True = NOT False

SCREEN 0
CALL NumberOrText(L$)
WIDTH 40
COLOR 15, 7: CLS
CALL Box(1, 1, 25, 40, 4, 8, 7)
CALL Box(4, 9, 6, 31, 2, 8, 7)
CALL Box(9, 3, 11, 38, 3, 8, 7)
CALL Box(19, 3, 21, 38, 1, 8, 7)
COLOR 15, 7: LOCATE 5, 10
PRINT "Demonstration program"
COLOR 4, 7: LOCATE 17, 14
PRINT "R e s u l t :"
COLOR 15, 7: LOCATE 10, 4
IF L$ = "N" THEN
    PRINT "Your number:"
    CALL Answer(10, 29, 8, 34, T$, "Number")
    Nmbr = VAL(T$)
    COLOR 15, 4: LOCATE 20, 4
    PRINT Nmbr
ELSE
    PRINT "Your text:"
    CALL Answer(10, 18, 20, 34, T$, "Text")
    COLOR 15, 4: LOCATE 20, 4
    PRINT T$
END IF
L$ = INPUT$(1)
END
```

First, the program sets a screen text mode and, using the procedure **NumberOrText**, asks whether the user wishes to input a number or text. Frameworks of various kinds are then drawn by the **Box** procedure and the explanation messages are displayed:

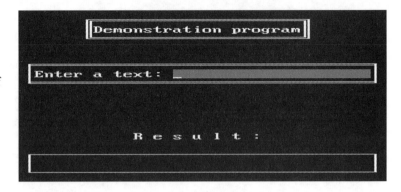

Then, the control is passed to the **Answer** procedure:

```
SUB Answer (X0, Y0, LX, MaxLText, Text$, NumberText$)
' ************************************************
' * Input of a number or of a character string *
' ************************************************
' NumberText$ = "Number" - input of a number
' NumberText$ = "Text" - input of character string
' X0, Y0 - coordinates of the beginning of the input zone
' LX - length of input zone   ( LX <= MaxLText )
' MaxLText - maximal length of a string to enter
' Text$ - result of input

CI = 14                                'foreground color
CB = 1                                 'background color
GOSUB Init
GOSUB OnScreen
DO
   DO
      L$ = INKEY$
   LOOP WHILE L$ = ""
   SELECT CASE L$
   CASE CHR$(0) + CHR$(82)             'Ins
      GOSUB Insert
   CASE CHR$(0) + CHR$(83)             'Del
      GOSUB Delete
   CASE CHR$(0) + CHR$(75)             'Cursor-left
      GOSUB CursorLeft
   CASE CHR$(0) + CHR$(77)             'Cursor-right
      GOSUB CursorRight
   CASE CHR$(0) + CHR$(71)             'Home
      GOSUB Home
   CASE CHR$(0) + CHR$(79)             'End
      GOSUB End1
   CASE CHR$(8)                        'BackSpace
      GOSUB BackSpace
   CASE CHR$(13)                       'Enter
      IF NumberText$ = "Text" THEN
         Text$ = RTRIM$(Text$)
         LOCATE , , , 7
         EXIT DO
      ELSE
```

```
        GOSUB EnterNumber
        IF Number(Text$) = True THEN
   LOCATE , , , 7
   EXIT DO
        END IF
     END IF
   CASE CHR$(32) TO CHR$(255)            'Characters
     GOSUB AddSymbol
   CASE ELSE
     BEEP
   END SELECT
LOOP
EXIT SUB

...                                      'Sub-procedures removed from this listing

END SUB
```

The **Answer** procedure is the most important procedure of the program. It enters a character string **Text$** of length **MaxLText** in an entry field of **LX** characters in length, beginning from the position **(X0,Y0)**. Here are the variables dealt with in the **Answer** procedure:

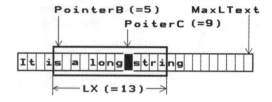

The **Answer** procedure begins by initializing the variables **CI** and **CB** which define the colors of the display and the color of the background in the entry field:

```
CI = 14               'foreground color
CB = 1                'background color
```

If we remove these variables from the procedure and declare them global, then initialize them in the calling module, we could use the **Answer** procedure with various display and entry field backgrounds in one program. Other variables are initialized using the **Init** procedure:

```
Init:
' *** Initialization of procedure ***
   COLOR CI, CB
   LOCATE X0, Y0
   Text$ = SPACE$(MaxLText)
   PointerB = 1
   PointerC = 1
   Ins = False
RETURN
```

Then, the **Answer** procedure calls the **OnScreen** subroutine which outputs an entry field in the form of a rectangular band on the screen:

```
OnScreen:
' *** Output a text fragment onto screen ***
   COLOR CI, CB
   LOCATE X0, Y0
   PRINT MID$(Text$, PointerB, LX);
```

```
      IF PointerC <= LX THEN
         NL = PointerB + PointerC - 1
         LOCATE X0, Y0 + PointerC - 1, 1
      ELSE
         LOCATE , , 0          'hide cursor
      END IF
   RETURN
```

First, the **OnScreen** subroutine cuts out a substring of length **LX** from the **Text$** variable and outputs it on the screen in the entry field. Then it outputs the cursor as a blinking line or rectangle at the current position. The shape of the cursor is defined in the subroutine **Insert** and depends on the status of the insertion/replacement mode.

Then, a loop in the **Answer** procedure waits for a key press. A pressed key is analyzed using the **SELECT** statement. First, the keys which, when pressed, pass a two-byte string to the system variable **INKEY$** are analyzed. These include *Ins*, *Del*, *Left*, *Right*, *Home* and *End*.

To process the *Ins* key, the subroutine **Insert** is called which toggles the value of the logic variable **Ins** and the form of the cursor, using the **LOCATE** statement:

```
Insert:
' *** Change value of  Ins and form of cursor ***
   IF Ins = True THEN
      Ins = False
      LOCATE X0, Y0, , 7
   ELSE
      Ins = True
      LOCATE X0, Y0, , 0, 7
   END IF
   GOSUB OnScreen
RETURN
```

To process the *Del* key, we use the **Delete** subroutine:

```
Delete:
' *** Delete a character at cursor ***
   NL = PointerB + PointerC - 1
   IF PointerC <= LX THEN
      TL$ = LEFT$(Text$, NL - 1)
      TR$ = RIGHT$(Text$, MaxLText - NL)
      Text$ = TL$ + TR$ + " "
      GOSUB OnScreen
   ELSE
      BEEP
   END IF
RETURN
```

This subroutine deletes the character at the cursor position by cutting the **TL$** substring from the **Text$** variable to the left of the cursor and the **TR$** substring from the right of the cursor. The strings **TL$** and **TR$** are pasted together and a space is added to the end. The resulting string becomes the new value of the variable **Text$**.

To move the cursor one position left or right in the entry field, we use the subroutines **CursorLeft** and **CursorRight**:

```
CursorLeft:
' *** Move cursor left ***
    Crsr$ = "left"
    GOSUB Cursor
    GOSUB OnScreen
RETURN
'===========================================================
CursorRight:
' *** Move cursor right ***
    Crsr$ = "right"
    GOSUB Cursor
    GOSUB OnScreen
    RETURN
```

These simply assign the appropriate value - **"left"** or **"right"** - to the variable **Crsr$** and call the subroutines **Cursor** and **OnScreen** for further processing:

```
Cursor:
' *** Change position of cursor ***
SELECT CASE Crsr$
    CASE "right"          'move cursor right
        IF PointerC < LX THEN
            PointerC = PointerC + 1
        ELSE
            IF PointerB + PointerC - 1 < MaxLText THEN
    PointerB = PointerB + 1
        ELSE
    IF PointerC = LX THEN
        '*** cursor at the end of word Text$ ***
        PointerC = PointerC + 1
    ELSE
        BEEP
    END IF
            END IF
        END IF
    CASE "left"        'move cursor left
        IF PointerC > 1 THEN
            PointerC = PointerC - 1
        ELSE
            IF PointerB > 1 THEN
    PointerB = PointerB - 1
            ELSE          'cursor at the beginning of word Text$
    BEEP
            END IF
        END IF
END SELECT
RETURN
```

The **Cursor** subroutine is central to the **Answer** procedure. It calculates the new position of the cursor in the entry field, as well as the value of the variable **PointerB**, indicating the number of the first character of the substring of the **Text$** variable which is output on the screen in the entry field. The keys *Home* and *End* are processed by subroutines of the same name and shift the cursor to the beginning or the end of an entered line:

```
Home:
' *** Move cursor to the beginning of string ***
```

```
        PointerB = 1
        PointerC = 1
        GOSUB OnScreen
RETURN
'============================================================
End1:
' *** Move cursor to end of string ***
    LTxt = LEN(RTRIM$(Text$))
    SELECT CASE LTxt
    CASE IS < LX
        PointerB = 1
        PointerC = LTxt + 1
    CASE IS = MaxLText
        PointerB = MaxLText - LX + 1
        PointerC = LX
    CASE IS >= LX
        PointerB = LTxt - LX + 2
        PointerC = LX
    END SELECT
    GOSUB OnScreen
RETURN
```

The subroutine **BackSpace** processes the *BackSpace* key which deletes a character to the left of the cursor:

```
BackSpace:
' *** Delete a character to the left from cursor ***
    NL = PointerB + PointerC - 1
    IF NL > 1 THEN
        TL$ = LEFT$(Text$, NL - 2)
        TR$ = RIGHT$(Text$, MaxLText - NL + 1)
        Text$ = TL$ + TR$ + " "
        GOSUB CursorLeft
        GOSUB OnScreen
    ELSE
        BEEP
    END IF
RETURN
```

To enter any character with an ASCII code greater than 32, we use the subroutine **AddSymbol**:

```
AddSymbol:
' *** Add a character to string Text$ ***
    NL = PointerB + PointerC - 1
    SELECT CASE Ins
        CASE True              'insertion mode
            IF RIGHT$(Text$, 1) <> " " THEN
    BEEP
    PointerC = PointerC - 1
        ELSE
    IF NL = MaxLText THEN
        MID$(Text$, NL) = L$
    ELSE
        TL$ = LEFT$(Text$, NL - 1)
        TR$ = MID$(Text$, NL, MaxLText - NL)
        Text$ = LEFT$(TL$ + L$ + TR$, MaxLText)
    END IF
```

```
          END IF
      CASE False                  'replacement mode
          IF PointerC <= LX THEN
   MID$(Text$, NL) = L$
          ELSE
   BEEP
          END IF
    END SELECT
    GOSUB CursorRight
    GOSUB OnScreen
 RETURN
```

Depending on the value of the logic variable **Ins**, the subroutine **AddSymbol** adds a character entered from the keyboard to the string **Text$**. If **Ins = True**, the character is inserted into the string before the cursor. However, if the length of the entered string is equal to **MaxLText** (in this case, the last character **RIGHT$ (Text$, 1)** of the variable **Text$** isn't blank), the character isn't inserted. When **Ins = False**, the character entered from the keyboard replaces the character in the variable **Text$** at the cursor location.

After a character has been added to the variable **Text$**, the cursor is moved one position right (subroutine **Cursor**), and the corresponding fragment of the **Text$** string is displayed on the screen in the entry field (subroutine **OnScreen**).

The string is finally entered or confirmed by pressing the *Enter* key. The way that this key is processed depends on what the user has entered - text or a number. If text is entered, all the right blanks are excluded from the **Text$** variable and the procedure **Answer** is executed. If a number is entered, the subroutine **EnterNumber** is called:

```
EnterNumber:
' *** Complete input of number ***
   IF Number(Text$) = False THEN
      PCOPY 0, 1
      X3 = 12: Y3 = 11
      CALL Box(X3 + 1, Y3 + 1, X3 + 4, Y3 + 19, 4, 0, 4)
      CALL Box(X3, Y3, X3 + 3, Y3 + 18, 2, 15, 5)
      CALL Box(X3 + 1, Y3 + 1, X3 + 2, Y3 + 17, 4, 5, 15)
      COLOR 31, 5
      LOCATE 13, 18
      PRINT "Error!"
      COLOR 15, 5
      LOCATE 14, 12
      PRINT " Enter a number! "
      L$ = INPUT$(1)
      PCOPY 1, 0
      GOSUB OnScreen
   ELSE
      Text$ = RTRIM$(Text$)
   END IF
RETURN
```

Here we call the function **Number**, which checks that the variable **Text$** is a number. If **Text$** isn't a number, a warning message is displayed and control remains with the **Answer** procedure. The user is then given the opportunity to correct the errors.

In contrast to **CH13_7.BAS**, in which any character prohibited by syntax isn't allowed in the entry field, in the present program, any characters can be entered. A sequence of characters is analyzed only after *Enter* is pressed. The permissible ways of writing a number (the syntax of an object of the 'number' type) are defined by the **Number** function:

```
FUNCTION Number (Txt$)
' *************************
' * Txt$ - number or not? *
' *************************
T$ = Txt$
T$ = RTRIM$(T$)
T$ = LTRIM$(T$)
SELECT CASE LEN(T$)
CASE 0
   Flag = True
CASE 1
   IF T$ < "0" OR T$ > "9" THEN Flag = False ELSE Flag = True
CASE IS > 1
   Flag = False
   SELECT CASE LEFT$(T$, 1)
   CASE "+", "-", "0" TO "9"
      Flag = True
   CASE "."
      IF INSTR(2, T$, ".") = 0 THEN Flag = True
   END SELECT
END SELECT
IF Flag = True THEN
   FOR I = 2 TO LEN(RTRIM$(T$))
      SELECT CASE MID$(T$, I, 1)
      CASE "."
         IF INSTR(I + 1, T$, ".") <> 0 THEN Flag = False
      CASE IS < "0", IS > "9"
         Flag = False
      END SELECT
      IF Flag = False THEN EXIT FOR
   NEXT I
END IF
IF T$ = "+." OR T$ = "-." THEN Flag = False
Number = Flag
END FUNCTION
```

When checking the syntax of the variable **T$**, the function **Number** ignores the leading left and concluding right blanks. They're discarded using the **LTRIM$** and **RTRIM$** functions. Analysis is then carried out, depending on the length of this converted **T$** variable. If the length of **T$** is equal to **0** (i.e. **T$ = ""**), the value of the **Number** function is set as **True**.

If the length of **T$** is equal to **1**, the value of **Number** is set as **True** if, and only if, **T$** is a figure. If the length of **T$** is more than **1**, additional analysis of the characters in **T$** is carried out:

```
CASE IS > 1
   Flag = False
   SELECT CASE LEFT$(T$, 1)
   CASE "+", "-", "0" TO "9"
      Flag = True
   CASE "."
```

```
        IF INSTR(2, T$, ".") = 0 THEN Flag = True
    END SELECT
```

This analysis is the same as for **CH13_7.BAS**, except that we also allow the initial character to be a plus sign.

Once the **Answer** procedure is complete, control is transferred to the main module of the program. The result entered by the user is displayed on the screen and remains there until you press any key.

We'll show how this program works by entering a familiar example phrase "English-Russian Dictionary". After you've entered "English-Russian Dic", the cursor is in the right most position on the screen:

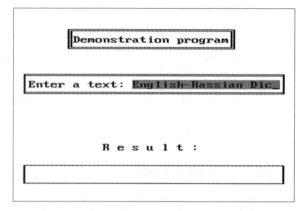

If we continue the input, as new characters are entered, the text displaces to the left and disappears from the entry field. To see the entered string, use the *Home* key to move the cursor to the beginning of the line, and then the *Right* arrow key to scroll the string horizontally in the entry field.

To edit the entered text, you can use the *Ins*, *Del*, *Left*, *Right*, *Home* and *End* keys. When you use the *Ins* key, the cursor changes form: in insertion mode it's displayed in the form of a rectangle and, in the replacement mode, in the form of a short line. Here's the entry field at the insertion point before the word 'Dictionary':

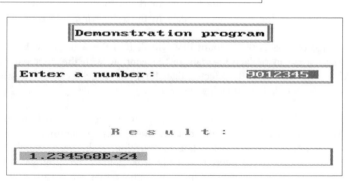

This is the result of entering a number with a lot of digits:

Although this data input procedure is fairly powerful, it can't, of course, satisfy all possible user requirements. Nevertheless, there's no harm in improving it. Try to modify the **Answer** procedure so that the concluding blanks aren't discarded when you enter text data.

Improvements

CH13_8.BAS can serve as a basis for you to create your own input procedures. It's often possible to modify data input with minimum changes to a program. Two possible modifications are:

If we exclude the line,

```
Text$ = SPACE$ ( MaxLText )
```

from the **Init** sub-program and declare the variable **Text$** as a global variable, we get a new procedure enabling us to edit previously entered data.

If you want to end data input by pressing a key other than just the *Enter* key, all we have to do to modify the program is change one line in the **Answer** procedure. Another method for letting your users enter long text is discussed in the following section.

Sample Data Input

During certain tasks the user needs to be able to give the computer information about a fixed subject area. These include, for example, the following:

- Choosing the font for printing.
- Entering the name of a file for copying.
- Indicating the exact name of a company producing certain goods.

It isn't as simple as it may seem at first sight to answer these sorts of requests. For one thing, the names of objects can be rather long and, for another, it's difficult to remember the names of all the objects in a particular subject area. **Sample data input** is frequently used to get round these problems.

CH13_9.BAS shows how you can organize viewing a large amount of data in an entry panel of limited size. To view data in the entry panel use the *Up*, *Down*, *PageUp* and *PageDown* keys. If you press *Up* or *Down* the cursor moves one line up or down in the data view window. When the cursor is at the top or the bottom of the window, the data in the view window scrolls down or up to reveal the next data item.

A **page** of data is the amount that will fit into the window without scrolling. If you press *PageUp* or *PageDown*, you replace the data in the window with the next page of data in the relevant direction. Choosing the currently selected data for input is achieved by pressing *Enter*. Data selection in the entry panel is canceled by pressing the *Esc* key.

The sample input is implemented using the procedure **ChoiceExample (X0,Y0,LH,LW,Variant)**. The **ChoiceExample** procedure contains the necessary parameters, enabling you to use it in various situations. The arguments **X0** and **Y0** define the position of the entry panel and the arguments **LH** and **LW** define the size of the panel. An internal variable **Num** defines the number of selectable data. At **Num = LH**, all possible input data can be seen in the entry panel, so, in this case, vertical scrolling in the entry panel isn't necessary. At **LH = 1**, only one string can be seen in the entry panel. Here, the *PageUp* and *PageDown* keys will perform exactly the same function as the *Up* and *Down* arrow keys.

Remember then, that, when developing dialog programs, you must have the user in mind. You should take into account that there's nothing to prevent the user from pressing any key at any instant, so you must develop your programs to react to any keyboard eventuality.

Programming Data Entry Panels

Now we'll have a look at designing a user interface for a program containing data entry panels which have several numeric or string fields. Our basic assumption here is that only those who do nothing make no mistakes. This also applies to the process of data input, as it's not difficult to make mistakes while entering even a small number of elements. This being the case, you want to think carefully at the design stage about making editing convenient. Here are three situations where entered data needs editing:

- There are errors in the entered data that are detected before the data is displayed in the entry panel. However, you've gone past the field containing the inaccurate data. In this case, it's necessary to provide transfer back and forth from field to field, with the opportunity to edit the fields.

- There are errors detected when there's no panel with the entered data, but the data is stored in the operative memory as the values of variables. In this event, the user must be given the chance to return to the corresponding screen form and edit these values.

- There are errors detected once the program's work is complete; for example, while viewing the listing of entered data. In this situation, the user needs a means by which he can edit the data stored as a file on an external information carrier.

We'll consider **CH13_10.BAS** which provides data editing for these three situations. The data we'll process is information about the winners of the 'Blue Ribbon'; it's stored in the file **LINERS.DBF** as records with the following structure:

```
TYPE RecordType
    Liner         AS STRING * 20
    YearofLaunch  AS STRING * 4
    Dockyard      AS STRING * 20
    Country       AS STRING * 16
    Town          AS STRING * 15
    ShipOwningCo  AS STRING * 20
END TYPE
```

The program enters and edits the data to fit the screen forms given here:

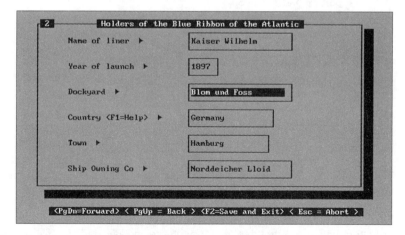

CH13_12.BAS has three possible operating modes: view, edit, and input mode. The view mode is executed by default. By pressing control keys, we can 'turn the pages' of the data records forwards and backwards.

The entry fields are edited according to rules similar to those considered in the previous section. The editing field is chosen by moving the selection cursor with the *Up* and *Down* keys. With editing complete, the changes are stored in an array of records. Editing is completed, with or without storing the changes in the file **LINERS.DBF**.

In input mode, with the absence of the data file **LINERS.DBF** on disk, the file is created automatically and consists of empty records into which the user can enter new data, using the edit mode.

At the bottom of the main window, there's a help bar containing a list of command keys and their effects. In addition to the main window there's also a secondary window which can be activated by pressing *F1* when the cursor is in the Country entry field.

The main rules of user interaction with the secondary dialog Help window are as follows:

- ▲ The dialog with the pull-down window should be finished before the dialog in the main window resumes.

- ▲ When an object is chosen from the list of prompt fields, the pop-up window disappears and the object appears in the field of the primary window. Dialog with the primary window is resumed.

- ▲ When an inadmissible key is pressed, a signal sounds.

The declared subroutines **Box**, **Center**, **PrintHelpLine**, **TextHelp**, **MaxLen** draw, in text mode, the frames of windows, and write the window titles and prompt text, as well as calculating the sizes of output fields and carrying out other service functions. The subroutines **Answer** and **Number** edit the entry fields. Subroutines **LoadBase** and **SaveBase** read a file from the disk with the data to be edited and write it back to disk after the editing. **EditRecords** is a basic editing module. **PosChoice** is a function to determine the number of position in the entry field.

Along with the declarations of the subroutines, functions, variables, constants and arrays, the above module also includes the routine for processing the pressing of the *F1* function key:

```
'F1- pop-up help window
ON KEY(1) GOSUB F1help
KEY(1) ON
```

This interrupt passes control to the label **F1Help**:

```
'Pop-up menu for the fourth field, "Country"
F1help:
IF NumField = 4 THEN
    PopUpWindow 13, 41, 22, 68
END IF
RETURN
```

This checks whether the cursor is in the Country field of the entry panel and if it is, calls the procedure **PopUpWindow** which activates a secondary dialog window containing the names of countries.

The control part of the main module consists of a sequence of calls to the external procedures **LoadBase**, **EditRecords** and **SaveBase**. The **LoadBase** module reads the file **LINERS.DBF** into an array of records called **Record**, whilst the **SaveBase** module saves the data to **Record**. The editing of the **Record** array by organizing a user's entry panel is accomplished by the **EditRecords** module.

This module begins with the description of operation arrays and with calls to the subroutines **InitVar** and **DrawScreen**. **InitVar** initializes the variables while the **DrawScreen** subroutine draws the dialog window in text mode. This is followed by the two main cycles of the **EditRecords** module:

```
DO

    'Transfer record to one-dimensional array edit()
    GOSUB EditRecordsLoadData
    GOSUB PrintEdit

    'Editing fields of record
    'edit$(NumField) - field to edit
    'NumField - number of field
    NumField = 1
    FinishDo = FALSE
    DO
        'RN,Col -location of field on screen
        VN = Vis(NumField)                          'length of field
        RN = Row(NumField)
        'editing field edit$()
        Answer RN, Col, VN, VN, edit$(NumField), "Text"
        'analyze control key pressing
        GOSUB Control
    LOOP UNTIL FinishDo OR Finished

    'record m is followed by record 1
    IF NumRec > m THEN NumRec = 1
    IF NumRec < 1 THEN NumRec = m

    IF Finished THEN
        EXIT SUB
    END IF
LOOP
```

The first cycle's varying parameter **NumRec** equals the number of records in the entry panel. The visual effect of 'turning the pages' of information about the liners, by pressing *PgUp* and *PgDn*, is implemented in the next cycle of this loop. The subroutine **EditRecordsLoadData** forwards the fields of a record under editing to an n-element array **edit()** (the record **LINERS.DBF** has six fields, therefore n=6). The subroutine **PrintEdit** outputs all the values of **edit()** in the panel. You can exit the cycle upon termination of the editing process by pressing the keys *Esc* or *F2*.

The second cycle, nested inside the first, executes the actual editing of the panel data:

```
DO
    'RN,Col -location of field on screen
    VN = Vis(NumField)                          'length of field
    RN = Row(NumField)
    'editing field edit$()
    Answer RN, Col, VN, VN, edit$(NumField), "Text"
    'analyze control key pressing
    GOSUB Control
LOOP UNTIL FinishDo OR Finished
```

At each cycle, the next element of the array **edit()**, corresponding to the record field, is edited. Editing is performed by the **Answer** module which has been changed slightly from our earlier versions to combine input and edit functions. After editing, the **Answer** module passes the code of the pressed control key to **EditRecords**. The analysis of this code is executed by the **Control** subroutine.

Control moves the selection cursor from the current field to another field. The parameter **NumField** in the nested cycle corresponds to the number of the field being edited. The cycle is exited when the last field of the current record is filled or either *PgDn* or *PgUp* are pressed.

The majority of the subroutines in, or called from, the module **EditRecords** are similar, if not precisely the same, to those covered earlier in the chapter. These subroutines include those which process and control separate fields, analyze the control key codes, and control the selection cursor.

The subroutine **EditRecordsLoadData** fills the array **Edit$()** with the values of the fields of the record being edited. You can familiarize yourself with its text, as well as with the texts of the subroutine included in the module. The subroutine **PrintEdit** outputs a group of the field values into the corresponding positions of the panel. The subroutine **Answer** puts the selection cursor in to the field with the number **NumField**.

A help window appears if the user asks for help while filling the fourth field of the Country panel by pressing *F1*. The displayed list allows you to choose the name of a country where a liner was built:

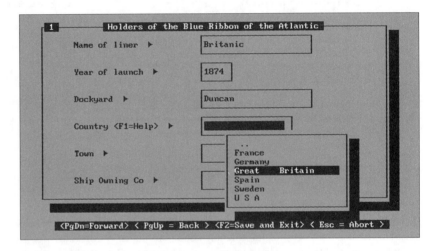

For example, you can choose 'USA' or, in the absence of the necessary country, you can choose the element '..'. The pop-up window effect is achieved in the module **PopUpWindow** by storing an area of video memory corresponding to the window being displayed and subsequently restoring it.

Entering Data in Tables

In this section, we'll consider **CH13_11.BAS** for editing data in a table. Our table holds information about the Atlantic crossing records of the liners and is stored in the file **RECORDS.DBF** like this:

```
TYPE RecordType
      Year              AS STRING * 4
      Liner             AS STRING * 20
      Direct            AS STRING * 4
      Days              AS INTEGER
      Hours             AS INTEGER
      Minutes           AS INTEGER
      Velocity          AS SINGLE
END TYPE
```

The program provides view, edit and data input modes within a unified dialog panel. Input is regarded as editing 'empty' records.

Despite the difference in the representation of the information between **CH13_10.BAS** and **CH13_11.BAS**, the two programs are identical in structure and their modules are analogous. Unlike **CH13_10.BAS**, all the records forming a table in **CH13_11.BAS** are located in one entry panel, which prevents you having to turn the pages of data during dialog. As well as the primary dialog entry window, the program also provides a secondary window, containing brief information about the purposes of the control keys for interacting with the main window. The Help window is activated by pressing *F1* and disappears when you press any further key.

Unlike **CH13_10.BAS**, the file which is to be edited in **CH13_11.BAS** contains both string and numeric fields. They are edited by a unified module **Answer**, which is covered in the section *Data Input*.

The control part of the head module calls in sequence the external procedures **LoadBase**, **EditTabRecords**, and **SaveBase**. The modules **LoadBase** and **SaveBase** which read and write the file during editing we considered earlier, so we'll only expand on the features of data editing present in the **EditTabRecords** module:

```
SUB EditTabRecords
'Full screen editing array of records. Number of records m <= 16,
'corresponds to the number of screen lines to edit.
'Source data:
'Record() - source array of records,
'm - number of records in Record().
'n - number of fields of one record equals to number of screen columns.
'Target data:
'Record() - edited array of records.

    REDIM Help$(n), col(n), Vis(n), edit$(m, n)
    'TextHelp variables
    GOSUB InitVar

    'Send records to two-dimensional array edit$()
    GOSUB EditTabRecordsLoadData

    'Draw the screen
    GOSUB DrawScreen

    'Start of full-screen editing a two-dimensional array
    'of string elements edit$(CurrRow,CurrCol).
    'CurrRow, CurrCol - parameters of main cycle
    CurrRow = 1 'initial number of string to edit
    CurrCol = 1 'initial number of field to edit
    PrintHelpLine Help$(CurrCol)
    Finished = FALSE

    'Loop until F2 or <ESC> is pressed
    DO
        GOSUB EditTabRecordsShowCursor                          'Show Cursor
        Ro1 = CurrRow + 4
        Co1 = col(CurrCol)
        Vi = Vis(CurrCol)

        'Editing one field on screen (text or number)
```

```
        IF CurrCol = 1 OR CurrCol = 2 OR CurrCol = 3 THEN
            answer Ro1, Co1, Vi, Vi, edit$(CurrRow, CurrCol), "Text"
        ELSE
            answer Ro1, Co1, Vi, Vi, edit$(CurrRow, CurrCol), "Number"
        END IF

            'Analyze of  control key pressing, which completed
            'field editing
    GOSUB Control
    LOOP UNTIL Finished

    IF Save THEN
        GOSUB EditTabRecordsSaveData
    END IF
    EXIT SUB
```

The **EditTabRecords** module begins by addressing the three subroutines: **InitVar**, **EditRecordLoadData** and **DrawScreen**. **InitVar** assigns the coordinates of the panel's fields to the working variables. The **EditTabRecordsLoadData** subroutine transfers the fields of a record during editing to a two-dimensional array **Edit()** of size m*n, where m is the number of screen lines, and n is the number of data columns, equal to the numbers of fields in the records of the file **RECORD.DBF**. The **DrawScreen** subroutine draws, in text mode, a screen for inputting and editing tables. The preparation for the main cycle of the module concludes with a specification of the initial coordinates of the selection cursor. These coordinates - **CurrRow** and **CurrCol** - correspond to the number of the line and the column where the cursor highlight is located.

The main cycle **DO...LOOP UNTIL Finished** executes the actual editing of the m*n fields given in the table. At each cycle, the module **Answer** edits the next field. Depending on the type of field, the call to **Answer** contains the parameters **"Text"** or **"Number"**:

```
'Editing one field on screen (text or number)
IF CurrCol = 1 OR CurrCol = 2 OR CurrCol = 3 THEN
    answer Ro1, Co1, Vi, Vi, edit$(CurrRow, CurrCol), "Text"
ELSE
    answer Ro1, Co1, Vi, Vi, edit$(CurrRow, CurrCol), "Number"
END IF
```

Once editing is complete, the **Answer** module passes the code of the pressed control key to **EditTabRecords**. Analysis of this code is executed by the **Control** subroutine. This subroutine moves the selection cursor from the current field to another one. The new position of the selection cursor is set according to the user interaction rules with the main dialog window. The cycle is exited when the editing process is completed by pressing the function keys *Esc* or *F2*.

The pop-up help window is implemented by the module **PopUpWindow**, which differs only slightly from the same module in **CH13_10.BAS**.

Programming Combined Panels

In this section, we'll discuss programming a composite panel which combines information areas of different types. The modules of **CH13_12.BAS** are also part of the structure of the database control program, which can be found on the accompanying disk, under the name **\APPS\BLUE.BAS**. Here, we'll just look at the preparation of data for operations with the database: the selection of the database file names, the selection

selection of the file record field names, and the definition of the requests for the database. For the sake of simplicity, we'll look at just two demonstration positions: Select and Project. The choice of either of these invokes an appropriate dialog window:

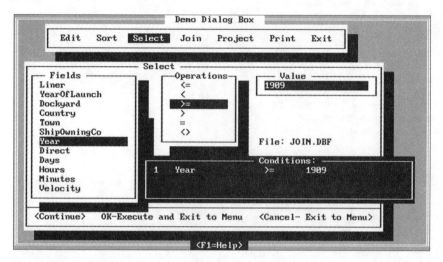

The following are the groups of information given in the dialog windows:

▲   File name selection field

▲   Single-alternative selection field of the file record name field

▲   Multi-alternative selection field of the file record name field

▲   Input and value editing field

▲   Results of selection and input

▲   Dialog window menu

▲   Help information

▲   Window and field headings

The rules of user interaction with the panel dialog window are presented in the secondary help window which is activated by the *F1* key.

The main purpose of the subroutines and functions declared in the main module is to display the elements of the panels and implement the above rules for conducting a dialog.

The full text of **CH13_12.BAS** is contained on the disk accompanying the book. Here, we'll consider some of the declared modules, the ones most characteristic of dialogs with combined panels.

The controlling part of the head module consists of calls to the external procedures **Initialize** and **ControlPanel**. The module **Initialize** sets the colors of the screens, specifies the positions of the menu names, their explanations and the headings of the selection fields.

The **ControlPanel** module operates the sequence of activations in the main menu, dialog windows and its component elements:

```
SUB ControlPanel
'Managing main menu and dialog window.

    'Set  Select for demonstration.
    PosM% = 3
    FinishMenu = FALSE

    'Cycle of activization of main menu and of corresponding dialog window
    DO
      DemoText
      PosM% = PosMenuMain(Menu$(), 7, 2, 7, PosM%)
      IF FinishMenu = TRUE THEN EXIT DO
      FinishWindow = FALSE
      SELECT CASE PosM%
        CASE 3
          InitSelect

    'Cycle of activization of selection fields and of window menu Select
        DO
            'Selection of file name
            FileToSelect 3, 11, 6, 7, 4
            IF FinishWindow = TRUE THEN EXIT DO
            'specifying several conditions for this file
            DO
              FieldOpToSelect 7, 4
              PosW% = PosMenuWin(MenuW$(), 3, 21, 3, PosW%)
              IF FinishWindow = TRUE THEN EXIT DO
              SELECT CASE PosW%
                CASE 1
                  PosW% = 1
                CASE 2
                  '"Plug" for the command Select.
                  ResultSelect
                  FinishWindow = TRUE: EXIT DO
                CASE 3
                  FinishWindow = TRUE: EXIT DO
                CASE 4
                  PosW% = 1: EXIT DO
              END SELECT
            LOOP
            IF FinishWindow = TRUE THEN EXIT DO
        LOOP
      CASE 5
        InitProject
        DO
          FileToProject 3, 8, 10, 7, 28
          IF FinishWindow = TRUE THEN EXIT DO
          SELECT CASE PosW%
            CASE 1
              '"Plug" for the command •roject.
              ResultProject
              EXIT DO
            CASE 2
              EXIT DO
            CASE 3
              PosW% = 1
          END SELECT
```

```
            LOOP
        CASE 7
            EXIT DO
        CASE ELSE
            '"Plug" for Edit, Sort, Print.
            SortAndOther
        END SELECT
    LOOP

  END SUB
```

The external cycle of this module activates the main menu and opens one of the dialog windows corresponding to the chosen operation in the database. The cycle 'menu - window' is repeated until the main menu is exited. Each of the internal cycles activates the selection fields corresponding to the dialog window. The internal cycle 'field - ... - field - menu of window' is repeated until the window is exited to the main menu of database operations.

The body of the external cycle begins with the procedure **DemoText**, which creates a frame and outputs brief information about the features of the demonstration program on the screen. Then, the **PosMenuMain** function activates the main menu.

After the user chooses a position in the main menu, the parameter **PosM%** in the external cycle of the **ControlPanel** module is assigned the value of the ordinal number of the chosen position. The **SELECT CASE PosM%** statement of this module then passes control to a block corresponding to the database operation.

Select is executed when **PosM% = 3**. At the beginning of the block, the **InitSelect** module outputs (opens) a dialog window with a window menu at the bottom of the screen and sets the parameters of the selection fields.

The screen panel after the completion of the **InitSelect** procedure contains just the heading of the opened window and its non-activated menu:

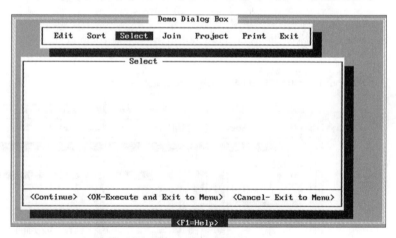

Addressing **InitSelect** is followed by the first internal cycle of the **ControlPanel** module, corresponding to Select. This cycle controls the dialog inside the opened window of the panel. The Select dialog window has three selection fields and one entry field, enabling us to set a condition of the kind File RECORDS.DBF: Liner = Germanic for the file.

499

The first selection field defines the name of the database file (**RECORDS.DBF**), the second one defines the file record field (**Liner**), and the third one, its processing operation (**=**). The right part of the condition (**German**) is entered in the entry field. The field priorities are established so that, when the dialog window is opened, the first field (file name selection field) is always active. It's activated by the module **FileToSelect**, which also displays the other window fields:

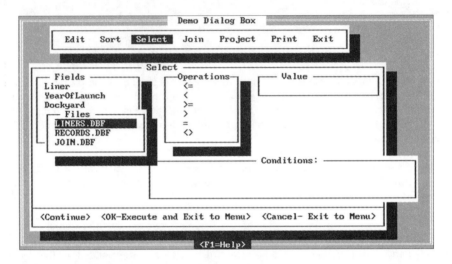

Using the Select dialog window for one file, it's possible to choose several conditions, for example:

File RECORDS.DBF:
  1) Liner = Germanic
  2) Direct = West
  3) Days < = 7

To define several conditions, a subroutine activating its component fields - **FieldOpToSelect** - is enclosed by one more nested loop in the module **ControlPanel**.

The result of executing **FieldOpToSelect** is this:

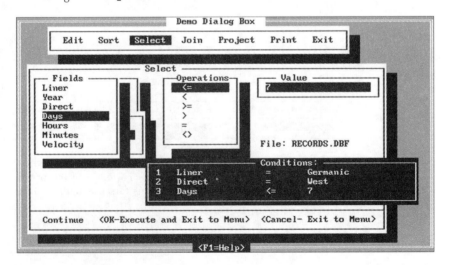

The initialization of the entry area is simple: a rectangle is created which defines the length of the entry line on the screen. Entering the value of the string variable with full control is executed by the **Answer** procedure covered above in the corresponding section.

After condition 1 has been chosen, and the full text of the condition output to a separate area of the panel, control of the dialog is passed to the area of the window menu. Its options Continue, OK and Cancel allow you to continue the window dialog or close the window. The function **PosMenuWin** activates the window menu. The call of this function and the analysis of its value is carried out in the **ControlPanel** module. The number of the position, equal to the value of the function, is assigned to the variable **PosW%**. On choosing the first position (Continue), the next field activation cycle is performed and the dialog continues.

When the OK position is chosen in the window menu, control is passed to a module-plug **ResultSelect**. Then, the field activation cycle is exited and the Select dialog window is closed.

We'll now consider the implementation of a dialog window for the Project operation, in which it's necessary for a database file to choose a subset of fields from the full list of its record fields.

Let's return to the **ControlPanel** module and consider its block corresponding to Project. After opening a dialog window using the procedure **InitProject**, a cycle is executed activating its selection fields. Included in the body of the cycle, the **FileToProject** module activates two selection fields: the first one contains the list of file names, and the second contains the list of field names in this file.

After the file name has been chosen, activation of the second field of the multi-alternative selection takes place:

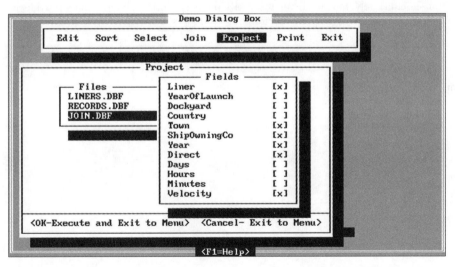

You can choose one of these options by placing the cursor over it and pressing *Enter*. To cancel the choice, you press *Enter* or *Space* again. Once an object has been chosen, a small cross appears in the brackets after it.

The help mode which provides information on controlling the fields of the dialog window, can be activated by pressing *F1*. The Help sub-system in the form of a pop-up window is provided by the module **PopUpWindow** and is common for all the primary dialog windows.

Closing the Project window is performed, as in the case of Select, via the window menu by the **PosMenuWin** module called from the **ControlPanel** module. When the OK item is chosen, control is passed to the module **ResultProject** which closes the window.

For now, this concludes our discussion of various elements of a user interface. For further details of user interface programming, examine the following programs on the accompanying disk:

The spreadsheet program: **\CHAP14\CH14_1.BAS**.
The database program: **\CHAP14\BLUE.BAS**.

Summary

To summarize, we'll remind you of some of the important concepts that you should bear in mind when designing user interfaces:

▲ During the dialog, the user's attention must be centered on the data and they must have easy access to it.

▲ Indicating or selecting an alternative is simpler than recalling data and typing it in from the keyboard.

▲ Using windows provides parallel output onto the screen and inter-dependent information.

▲ The user's actions should be convertible - within a dialog the cancellation of an action (Cancel item) returns the user to the previous condition.

▲ You shouldn't rely too much on the user's memory. Instead, you should provide him or her with various kinds of help in the form of reminders, references, and prompts.

Using BASIC for Business

Introduction

Whilst most programs, with the possible exception of games, can be used in a business context, several genre of programs have emerged as essential over the last twenty years. The most prominent are spreadsheets and presentation programs, both of which we will be looking at in this chapter.

In this first section, we shall acquaint ourselves with our simple spreadsheet, EasyCalc, written in QBasic. The program **\CHAP14\CH14_1.BAS** demonstrates the use of the following techniques:

- Drop-down menus
- Controllable data input with extended editing possibilities
- Context-sensitive help
- Recursive implementation of a formula interpreter

In the business world, graphs are frequently used to present financial information in a more meaningful manner than it appears in a table format. Examples of such information might include a manufacturing company's monthly output, changes in prices or payments over time or a company's market share.

Clearly, there is a connection between spreadsheets and graphs, so after the discussion of our spreadsheet, we will show you how to create the various types of graph to properly illustrate your data. We'll also look at programs for normalizing the dimensions of the charts, highlighting parts of them with color and writing text or legends at the necessary places in the diagrams.

> *You should note that spreadsheets and graphs are firmly situated in the world of mathematics. However, as this book is about the use of QBasic and not about why the algorithms work, we shall not be discussing them in detail. Fortunately, the algorithms are not too complex, and if you are interested, the sample programs should provide you with enough explanation to understand them.*

What is a Spreadsheet?

A spreadsheet is a computer program intended for processing information given in a tabular form. The spreadsheet is the technical amalgamation of three common office tools: a calculator, a pencil and a sheet of paper. The spreadsheet transforms your monitor into the paper, the keyboard into the pencil and the computer itself into the calculator.

However, this is not the end of the story. The spreadsheet also brings several other advantages to the business user:

▲ The ability to store the results of several calculations in a more permanent manner than a piece of paper.

▲ The ability to retrieve those calculations at anytime for review or modification.

▲ The ability to alter several core entries and have the entire set of calculations update based on these new values.

Let's take a closer look at the subject of this chapter, first by getting some of the terminology clear in our minds, before looking at what our spreadsheet has got to offer and how it works.

Describing the Spreadsheet

The rows of the table are designated by numbers, the columns by letters. At the intersection of a row and a column a square (or cell) is formed. In a similar manner to the squares on a chessboard, each cell has its own name (or address) consisting of a letter and a number, and it is with this name that you can refer to the contents of a given cell. Examples of cell names include A5, D12 or even W284 if it's a really big table.

	A	B	C	D
1				
2				
3				
4				
5				
6				
7				

The size of an electronic table basically depends upon the size of your computer's RAM and can normally be measured by the tens of thousands of cells. For simplicity's sake, we have limited the EasyCalc's maximum table size to 26 columns (A-Z) and 100 rows (1-100).

Displaying the Data

Even by limiting the size of an EasyCalc table, we can't manage to fit all the rows and columns on the screen at the same time. In order to get around this problem, we are going to use a 'window'. By scrolling out of the window, you can change the focus of the window to another part of the spreadsheet.

The idea of a windowed spreadsheet is illustrated here:

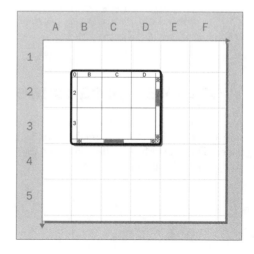

Cell Functionality

Each cell can be used for one of three main purposes:

▲   The storage of numerical data

▲   The storage of text - headings, labels, comments etc.

▲   The storage of mathematical formula. This formula is usually composed using references to other cells and the usual mathematical operators.

It is the last of these purposes that is the most interesting to understand. If, after entering a formula into a particular cell, the values in previous cells change, the output displayed in the cell can be automatically recalculated. Thus, by placing a formula in a cell, we are not just setting that cell to a single value, we are making that cell dependent upon others.

This technique comes into its own when you have a key value that is used a lot, but may change. One example of such a value is that of the tax rate. If you create a spreadsheet to track the pay of your employees and hard code the current tax rate into the calculations, when the rate changes you will have to visit every cell that refers to it and manually change it - don't forget any or your employees will start complaining. However, it you assign the tax rate to a cell and refer to this cell in the pay calculations, you will only need to update the contents of this key cell to get the required results.

Using a Spreadsheet

At any one time, just one single cell can be in use, and this is commonly considered to be the current, or **active** cell. When we are looking at the spreadsheet, the current cell is defined by a pointer (or table cursor) which can be moved by pressing the arrows keys. This mode of operation is also used for all the editing purposes of the spreadsheet.

As an example we shall consider a fragment of the table "AVAILABILITY", containing information about the availability of goods in a warehouse:

	A	B	C	D
1	WARES	PRICE	QUANTITY	SUM
2	butter	1.5	36	
3	rice	1.8	23	
4	flour	.9	0	
5	cheese	2.14	15.4	
6	milk	.21	73	
7			Total	

As you can see, the cells from A1 to D1 (written as A1:D1), A1:A6 and C7 are being used to store text, while B2:C6 are storing numbers. Clearly, from the layout of these key values, the cells D2:D7 will be used to display the results of several calculations.

> *Note the new terminology - A1:D1 represents successive four cells, starting at A1 and ending at D1, thus describing part of column 1. You should also note that this terminology is not restricted to lines of cells. You can also describe rectangular areas of cells by giving the top left cell and the bottom right cell as reference points, i.e. B2:C6 describes a two by five cell rectangle.*

To complete this spreadsheet, we need to understand how to create the formulae that we require for the appropriate calculations. Clearly, the cell D2 should show the product of cells B2 and C2, with the cells D3:D6 following a similar pattern. To create the total for the whole spreadsheet, D7 must display the sum of D2:D6. So how do we enter these formulae so that the spreadsheet understands what we are trying to do?

To enter a formula, you simply type it into the active cell where you want it to be held. In other words, cell D2 should contain the formula 'B2*C2'. If you wish to place text in a cell, you must inform the spreadsheet of this requirement so that it doesn't attempt to evaluate the text as a formula. In EasyCalc, this task is performed by placing a double quote before the text you wish to appear in the cell. Check out the spreadsheet that appears on the disk to see these techniques in action.

One point that you must understand is that the actual formulae are not displayed in the cells; the results of the calculations appear instead. If you wish to view the formula associated with a cell, move the table cursor to the cell and look at the data entry panel at the bottom of the screen. In this region of the screen, you will see the current value associated with the cell, whether it is text, a value or a formula, together with the name of the currently active cell.

This concept is described by the following sentence: the spreadsheet displays the **logical** contents of each cell, while the data entry panel describes the **physical** contents of the currently active cell.

The Calculation of Formulae

If we change any of the data in the QUANTITY and PRICE columns, the spreadsheet will instantaneously recalculate the formulae for the new data. The ability to quickly query data is one of the spreadsheet's most important features and enables users to quickly and easily obtain new information based on a set of given criteria (the formulae given in the spreadsheet).

For example, you may want to know 'What will happen to the final cost of goods, if the price of milk drops from 0.78 to 0.72, flour increases from 0.90 for 0.98 and we ask for 44 packs of butter instead of 36?'. With the spreadsheet, you simply change the three numbers and wait for the spreadsheet to perform the calculations. Strenuous, huh?

When the formulae in tables depend on the cells associated with other formulae, the result of recalculation of this table will depend considerably upon the order in which the formulae are calculated.

In EasyCalc the recalculation of formulae is made in strict order. When recalculating, the formulae are advanced by rows: first the formulae of the first row are calculated from left to right, and then those of the second row and so on down to the last row of your table. The formulae should be designed bearing this calculation order in mind, otherwise the results of calculations may not correspond to those expected.

The Main Concepts Behind EasyCalc

Okay, now we understand the major ideas behind why we would want a spreadsheet, what a spreadsheet can do and why an accountant might want to use one instead of pencil and paper. Now let's move on to examine how EasyCalc is coded to provide these features.

The EasyCalc Environment

The screen of a typical spreadsheet consists of several distinct sections, Easycalc's looks like this:

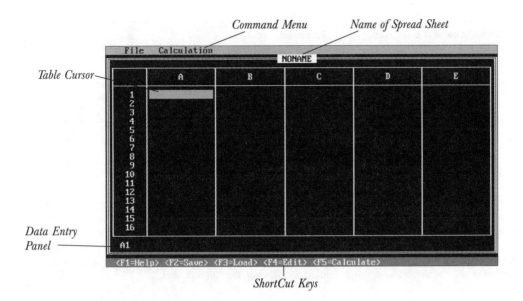

The Main Window

Beginning from the second line, the spreadsheet's scrollable window appears containing a 5 column (13 characters each) by 16 row section of the underlying table. If you wish to move this window around the table, simply try to move the table cursor out of the window - hit the right arrow key when the table cursor is in the far right column - and the table cursor will appear to drag the window in that direction, revealing the next row or column.

This window is labelled with the name of the current spreadsheet, and it is under this name that the table is saved to disk. If you don't specify a name when saving or you have just created a new table, then your table will be called NONAME by default.

The Command Menu

The top line of the screen presents a panel with a two-level menu called the **Command Menu**. You can activate these menus by pressing the *Alt* key, in which case you will enter **menu mode**, rather than the normal spreadsheet **editing mode**.

In menu mode, the arrow keys move you around the menu bar, highlighting the current menu item rather than around the cells in the spreadsheet. Pressing *Return* will select the highlighted menu item or display the contents of the second level menu, whilst pressing *Esc* will drop you back into editing mode. A full listing of the available tasks is given below:

Top Level Item	Second Level Item	Executed Task
File	New	Discard the current table and create a new blank one.
	Save	Save the current table to disk.
	Load	Load an old table from disk.

Table Continued on Following Page

Top Level Item	Second Level Item	Executed Task
	Exit	Close down EasyCalc
Calculation	Manual	Force the user to indicate which cells to recalculate
	Auto	EasyCalc organizes the recalculates

Choosing the Mode of Recalculation

When formulae are present in a table, we must at some point perform recalculations, so that the values in the cells featuring formulae can incorporate recent changes to other cells.

There are two modes of recalculation in EasyCalc - Manual and Auto. In manual mode, when you enter data into the current cell, the calculations are performed only for that cell. The values in the rest of the cells remain untouched. For recalculation of values in all cells, the user should press the function key *F5*.

In auto mode, when the new cell has finished receiving its instructions (i.e. you press *Return*), EasyCalc immediately performs the recalculation of all formulae throughout the spreadsheet.

Shortcut Key Menu

While in edit mode, you will be able to see a list of available shortcut keys at the bottom of the screen. These keys allow you to immediately perform the appropriate task without the need for the Command Menu. However, if you do activate the Command Menu, these shortcut keys no longer apply, and to represent this fact, the listing is removed and replaced by either a new list of options or by a description of the currently highlighted menu item.

The Entry Panel

The penultimate line of the screen is taken up by the data entry panel, which displays the physical contents of the current cell and allows the user to change those contents. All the information given here is only passed to the cell's current contents when the user hits the *Return* key, and not before. The user can abort any changes to the cell's contents at any time before this point by hitting the *Esc* key.

> **The maximum length of data that can be entered into the entry panel is 66 characters, but you should remember that only 13 characters are available for display in each cell. This should never affect your formula results, but it will have an effect on any text that you enter here. If the text entered into a current cell exceeds the 13 character limit, then the text on screen is truncated from the right. This doesn't mean that text data is lost - if you make that cell current then the entry panel will display the whole line - it just won't all appear in the cell.**

The Makeup of a Cell

As we have just been talking about the exact moment when cells are updated, it would be a good idea to look at what exactly makes up a cell. Hopefully, this discussion should prepare you for some of the reasons for why the spreadsheet is coded the way that it is.

The cell is the main object of data storage and is characterized by a number of parameters:

▲ Its address (A1 for example)

▲ Its contents. The cell can be empty or it can contain some data, usually a formula or some text.

▲ Its value, which is either the contents of the cell or the resolution of the formula stored in the cell's contents

It is important to understand the distinction between these final two parameters. In all cases, with the exception of a formula, a cell's contents and value will be identical. It is the special case that makes the spreadsheet so powerful, allowing the cell to provide both the means for working out the value and the value itself.

Formula Functionality

Usually, spreadsheets have a lot of functions enabling the users to execute complicated calculations on their data simply by using some shorthand notation in the formula, and EasyCalc is certainly not the odd one out. As well as the usual array of mathematical operators, EasyCalc features a host of additional functions:

▲ The functions **SIN (X)** and **COS (X)** calculate the sine and cosine of **X**, giving the answer in radians.

▲ The function **LOG (X)** calculates the natural logarithm of **X**. The argument of the function should always be positive.

▲ The function **SQR (X)** calculates the square root of **X**. The argument of the function should always be non-negative.

▲ The function **EXP (X)** calculates the exponential of **X**.

▲ The function **SUM (X:Y)** calculates the sum of the numerical values contained in all the cells within the range **X:Y**.

The arguments of the first four of these functions can be the addresses of other cells, numeric constants or even expressions, while SUM's argument must be a range of cells. Each function returns a result and places it into the cell's value (and so on screen), when the user presses *Return*.

Getting Help

Most commercial applications offer on-line help systems these days to guide the new user around the package. EasyCalc help system is purely context-sensitive, which means that a help screen will pop-up when you press *F1*, but the content of the help window will depend upon where you are when you press *F1*.

> *As a consequence of being purely context-sensitive, EasyCalc's help system doesn't support the kind of keyword search facility found in other spreadsheet packages.*

If you press *F1* while in edit mode, the help window will display information about moving table cursor on the screen:

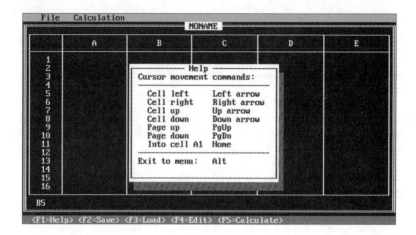

If you press the *F1* key in entry mode (you are halfway through entering a cell's contents), information about relevant keys and functions for input and editing will be displayed. The help information is not just limited to this though, because there are individual pages for several other key functions, primarily where input from the user is required.

Well, that concludes the tour of the EasyCalc system environment, and should hopefully have given you some ideas for future projects of your own. This program is an excellent example of how to build a large, practical application and, like the paint project of the subsequent chapter, should set a high standard for you to follow.

Let's now take a closer look at the code behind the program, so that you can learn the techniques behind developing such a large and involved application.

Developing EasyCalc

The EasyCalc program is probably one of the largest programs you will have come across, and in an effort to retain readability it is split into 28 procedures. Throughout this section of the chapter, we will be discussing the actual code for the spreadsheet package, so you might find it useful to have the program loaded. This will give you the opportunity to view the code as a whole, while it allows us to concentrate on some of the more interesting sections here in the book.

You should be able to find the spreadsheet on the accompanying disk called **\CHAP14\CH14_1.BAS**. If you haven't already tried it then this would be a good time to do so.

Data Storage

Just as we learned in Chapter 7, Program Design, a program's data structure is the most important thing to clarify as soon as possible. In this section, we will try to explain how and why we have decided to store the data in the way we have.

The following table presents the definition of all the global variables:

Variable	Description
`Column`, `Row`	Coordinates of table cursor
`LastColumn`, `LastRow`	Last column and last row of active part of table
`FirstRow`, `FirstColumn`	Coordinates of first cell on screen
`Name$`	Name of data file
`EditField$`	Contents of current cell
`CalcMode`	Indicator of mode of recalculation (0 - Manual, 1 - Auto)
`Table$()`	Array for storing data of table
`CellType`	Type of cell ('F' - formula; 'S' - string; "" - empty cell)
`Value()`	Array of numeric values of table's cells
`SyntaxError`	Error number (analyzed in procedure Errors)
`AnyChange`	Indicator of changes in table (0 - no changes in table since loading; 1 - otherwise)
`LastButton`	ASCII code of last pressed key
`MenuItem`	Current menu item
`ActiveMenu`	Indicator of menu activity (0 - menu is displayed on the screen, but not activated; 1 - menu is activated)
`MenuNumber`	Number of option in menu
`InputLineLen`	Maximal length of contents of a cell in characters (used while entering in procedure `InputLine`)
`WindowLevel`	Number of windows on screen (for correct erasing the windows)
`HelpContext`	Indicator of help context (1 - while navigating the table; 2 - while entering the contents of a cell; 3 - while entering file name)
`C(1)`, `C(2)`	Color of text and background of main screen
`C(3)`, `C(4)`	Color of text and background of menu
`C(5)`, `C(6)`	Color of text and background of a current menu item
`C(7)`	Color of background of warning message
`C(8)`	Color of shadow of a pull-down menu
`C(9)`, `C(10)`	Color of text and background of information message
`C(11)`, `C(12)`	Color of text and background of a current cell
`C(13)`	Color of framework of electronic table
`C(14)`	Color of index of cell
`C(15)`	Color of border
`C(16)`, `C(17)`	Color of text and background of information window
`C(18)`, `C(19)`	Color of text and background of error window
`C(20)`, `C(21)`	Color of text and background of help window

Let's examine some of the more important global variables in a little more detail.

Table$()

Without a doubt, the most significant block of data that we must store for our spreadsheet, is the representation of the cells in memory. First of all, we have to store the physical values, i.e. the exact data that the user types in. We'll call this variable **Table$()**.

CellType()

We also need a variable to store what type of cell it is; whether it's a formula, plain text or if it's empty. We shall call this variable **CellType()** and the content of this variable will be one of the following entries:

Value	Description
F	Formula
S	Character or text string
" "	Empty cell

Value()

The last variable for storing the cell data must hold the actual value of the specified cell, and we shall call this one **Value()**. If the cell is of the type 'S' or it is empty, then the value will be 0, otherwise the value of the cell is calculated from a formula, the text of which is stored in the given cell's **Table$()** variable. The calculation of the elements of the value array proceeds simultaneously with a syntax analysis of the formula, both occuring when the input of a given cell is completed or when a recalculation occurs.

Accessing These Variables

All three variables will need to be accessed from some sort of key, and logically this would be via their X and Y co-ordinates in the grid. Therefore they will become accessed in this form:

```
Table$(X,  Y)

CellType(X,  Y)

Value(X,  Y).
```

The following figure shows the entry panel, the memory status and the view of cell B1 after the user has entered the string of characters, "Spreadsheet EasyCalc into cell B1:

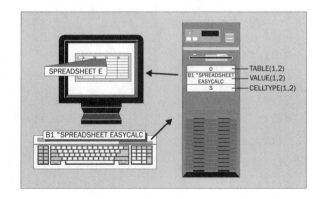

If you take a look at our spreadsheet's main module, you'll see that the first thing we do (apart from comments and subroutine declarations) is define and initialize all of our variables. After we have defined our data structures, we need to design our main module.

Designing the Main Module

The overall controller of **\CHAP14\CH14_1.BAS** can also be found in the main module and takes this form:

```
ON ERROR GOTO RunTimeError
CALL Title
CALL InitEnvironment
CALL New
CALL RunSpreadsheet
END
'===============================================================
RunTimeError:
   SyntaxError = 11
RESUME NEXT
'===============================================================
DataBox:
' *** Data for Box procedure ***
DATA Ú, Ä, ¿, ³, À, Ù
DATA É, Í, », º, È, ¼
DATA Õ, Í, ¸, ³, Ô, ¾
DATA ±, ±, ±, ±, ±, ±
'===============================================================
Colors:
' *** Set of Colors ***
DATA  15,1,0,7,15,0,4,8,15,3,10,13,3,11,6,0,7,14,4,0,2
'===============================================================
```

The first thing that the program does is to executes the **ON ERROR GOTO** operator setting up the error handling procedure, **RunTimeError**. It then continues by calling the **Title** procedure which outputs a simple, but effective title page onto the screen, which remains until a key is pressed.

The InitEnvironment Procedure

The procedure **InitEnvironment** is then called to initialize all the environment variables that EasyCalc will use. Specifically it initializes the global variables **C(1):C(21)**, **MenuNumber()**, **MenuItem()**, **ActiveMenu()**, **InputLineLen()**, **WindowLevel()** and **HelpContext()**.

We also take this opportunity to display a non-active Command Menu on the screen by calling the **Menu** procedure. This is so that the next procedure **New** can concentrate on producing a new table, and not worry about the rest of the environment.

The New Procedure

This procedure initializes a new table in memory by resetting all the table storage variables to zero or null depending on the existing variable type. It then call the **InitSpreadsheet** procedure to draw a table on the screen, border it with a rectangular framework through a call to the **Box** procedure, and then output the name of the table in the upper part of the framework thanks to a call to the **PrintName** procedure.

We then initialize our global variables, **AnyChange()**, **Row()**, **Column()**, **FirstRow()**, and **FirstColumn()** and then the cells of the new table are filled with our default data values (zeros) using the procedure **PrintSpreadsheet**.

The PrintSpreadsheet Procedure

The procedure **PrintSpreadsheet** first of all reproduces the cap and the side of electronic table on the screen, and then outputs the contents of the cells with a call to the **PrintCell** procedure, before displaying a table cursor with the **CursorOn** procedure. The **PrintInputLine** procedure is then called to update the data entry panel with the name of the current cell and its contents.

Let's take a closer at the procedure **PrintCell**:

```
SUB PrintCell
  ' Output the current cell of electronic table on the screen
  X = (Row - FirstRow) + 6
  Y = (Column - FirstColumn) * (CellSize + 1) + 10
  LOCATE X, Y                       ' Locate the cell position
  SELECT CASE CellType(Row, Column)
     CASE "F"                       ' If the cell contains a formula
        S$ = STR$(Value(Row, Column))   ' then take the value string
     CASE "S"                       ' If the cell contains a string
        S$ = Table$(Row, Column)    ' then take the text string
  END SELECT
  IF LEN(S$) > CellSize THEN
     PRINT LEFT$(S$, CellSize);
  ELSE
     PRINT S$ + SPACE$(CellSize - LEN(S$))
  END IF
END SUB
```

If the data in the current cell is a formula, a numeric value corresponding to the cell is extracted from the array **Value**, converted into a string and output onto the screen, complemented by a necessary number of blanks. If the data in the cell is a string, the first 13 characters of the corresponding string from the array **Table$** are displayed.

As you can see, the data displayed is taken from different sources depending upon the content of the variable, **CellType**, which is essentially a demonstration of an effective and unusual style of data structure.

The RunSpreadsheet Procedure

After setting up the data and the screen, control is passed to the last procedure in the main module, **RunSpreadsheet**:

```
SUB RunSpreadsheet
  ' Control of spreadsheet
  DO
     HelpContext = 1
     Key$ = ""
     ScanCode = 0
     WHILE Key$ = "" AND ScanCode <> &H38
        Key$ = INKEY$
        IF (INP(&H61) AND 128) = 0 THEN
           ScanCode = INP(&H60)
        END IF
```

```
        WEND
        IF ScanCode = &H38 THEN              ' Alt
          CALL Menu
        ELSE
          SELECT CASE Key$
          CASE CHR$(32) TO CHR$(255)         ' Symbol
            LastButton = ASC(Key$)
            CALL EditCell
          CASE CHR$(0) + CHR$(71)            ' Cursor Home
                  ...                        ' Code removed from here
          CASE CHR$(0) + CHR$(72)            ' Cursor Up
                  ...                        ' Code removed from here
          CASE CHR$(0) + CHR$(73)            ' Cursor PageUp
                  ...                        ' Code removed from here
          CASE CHR$(0) + CHR$(75)            ' Cursor Left
                  ...                        ' Code removed from here
          CASE CHR$(0) + CHR$(77)            ' Cursor Right
                  ...                        ' Code removed from here
          CASE CHR$(0) + CHR$(80)            ' Cursor Down
                  ...                        ' Code removed from here
          CASE CHR$(0) + CHR$(81)            ' Cursor PageDown
                  ...                        ' Code removed from here
          CASE CHR$(0) + CHR$(59)            ' F1
            CALL HelpWindow
          CASE CHR$(0) + CHR$(60)            ' F2
            CALL Save
          CASE CHR$(0) + CHR$(61)            ' F3
            CALL Load
          CASE CHR$(0) + CHR$(62), CHR$(13)  ' F4 or Enter
            LastButton = 13
            CALL EditCell
          CASE CHR$(0) + CHR$(63)            ' F5
            CALL Recalculate
            CALL PrintSpreadsheet
          END SELECT
        END IF
      LOOP
    END SUB
```

The procedure begins with the assignment of the value 1 to the indicator of the contextual help variable, **HelpContext**, which will define which information page the Help window displays if *F1* is pressed.

The Input Routine

The following block of code which effectively controls the whole program, implements the acceptance and recognition of a keypress. As **INKEY$** doesn't recognise the *Alt* key, we need to utilize the **INP** function to cover this possibility.

Reading the scan-code of an arbitrary pressed key is carried out by reading the byte from port **&H61** with the built-in function **INP(&H61)**. And then the curent 7th bit of this byte is set by **AND**ing the 7th bit (128) with this command using **INP(&H61) AND 128**. If the 7th bit is equal to zero then this indicates that the 7th was set and that the byte from port **&H60** contains the scan-code of the keyboard.

The loop cycle, **WHILE**, polls the keyboard until a recognisable entry from the standard keyboard is found (i.e. different to an empty string), or the *Alt* key is pressed, whose hexadecimal scan-code is 38. When a key has been recognised as having been pressed, the procedure then goes on to analyze the codes returned and undetake the appropriate actions.

Processing the Alt Key

Of all the keys that effect an action in the spreadsheet, the *Alt* key is processed first. And in doing so, the control is passed to the aforementioned procedure, **Menu**, activating the command menu. The subsequent selection of each option in the Command Menu is completed by a call of the subroutine **Action**:

```
Action:
  SELECT CASE MenuItem
    CASE 1                          'The File Menu
      SELECT CASE SubMenuItem
        CASE 1                      'New option
          CALL New
        CASE 2                      'Save option
          CALL Save
        CASE 3                      'Load option
          CALL Load
        CASE 4                      'Exit option
          CALL ProgramExit
      END SELECT
    CASE 2                          'The Calculation Menu
      SELECT CASE SubMenuItem
        CASE 1                      'Auto option
          CalcMode = 1
          Recalculate
          PrintSpreadsheet
        CASE 2                      'Manual option
          CalcMode = 0
      END SELECT
  END SELECT
RETURN
```

The two arguments of the **Action** subroutine are the two selections from the menu system : which menu the selection is on, **MenuItem**, and the individual option on that menu, **SubMenuItem**. Depending on these two values the relevant procedure is called to execute the selected option.

The EditCell Procedure

Pressing any of the alphanumeric keys results in the assignment of an appropriate character to a global variable **LastButton** and a call to the procedure **EditCell**:

```
SUB EditCell
  HelpContext = 2
  IF LastButton = 13 THEN                     'F4 or Enter
    'No operation
  ELSE
    EditField$ = CHR$(LastButton)
  END IF
  DO
    CALL EditString(EditField$, 23, 8, C(1), C(2), InputLineLen)
    IF LastButton = 27 THEN                   'Esc
      CALL PrintInputLine
      EXIT SUB
    ELSE                                      'Enter
      CALL SyntaxAnalysis((EditField$), CellType$, CellValue!)
      IF SyntaxError THEN
        CALL Errors(Row, Column)
```

```
         ELSE
            AnyChange = 1
            IF Row > LastRow THEN LastRow = Row
            IF Column > LastColumn THEN LastColumn = Column
            EXIT DO
         END IF
      END IF
   LOOP
   CellType(Row, Column) = CellType$
   IF CellType$ = "S" THEN
      Table$(Row, Column) = MID$(EditField$, 2)
   ELSE
      Table$(Row, Column) = UCASE$(DelSpaces$(EditField$))
   END IF
   Value(Row, Column) = CellValue!
   CALL CursorOn
   IF CalcMode = 1 THEN                    'Auto recalculation
      Recalculate
      PrintSpreadsheet
   END IF
END SUB
```

The **EditCell** procedure begins with the assignment of the appropriate help context and is immediately followed by a check of the **LastButton** global variable. If the check reveals a value of 13 i.e. *F4* or *Enter* was pressed, **EditField$** remains unchanged, otherwise we perform the following assignment:

```
EditField$ = CHR$ (LastButton)
```

This assignment causes the variable **EditField$** to be assigned to the character corresponding to the last pressed key.

The procedure **EditCell** then organizes a loop whose body begins by calling the procedure **EditString**, which carries on editing the variable **EditField$**. The exit from the procedure **EditCell** is only possible after pressing *Esc* or *Return*.

At an exit via the *Esc* key the contents of the current cell are displayed in the entry panel and the execution of the **EditCell** procedure is completed. No changes in the current cell are made in the process.

When exiting from the **EditString** procedure using *Return*, the variable **EditField$** is transmitted to the **SyntaxAnalysis** procedure for examination and for the calculation of the cell's numeric value. If a syntactic error is detected or a formula can't be resolved, a warning message is displayed and the cycle is repeated anew. If the procedure **SyntaxAnalysis** doesn't find any errors, an assignment is performed:

```
AnyChange = 1
```

testifying to the change of data in the spreadsheet. When necessary, the values **LastRow** and **LastColumn** defining the bounds of the active part of the table, are changed and we exit from the loop.

After quitting the cycle, an element of the array **CellType(Row,Column)** is assigned with the type of cell calculated in the **SyntaxAnalysis** procedure. The element **Table$(Row,Column)** is assigned some string value defined by the values of variables **CellType$** and **EditField$**. If **CellType$** is equal to 'S' then this value is obtained from the value of the **EditField$** by removing the leading inverted commas. Otherwise the new value results from the removal of leading blanks from the variable **EditField$** and the conversion of all lower case letters to capitals.

The removal of leading blanks from the variable **EditField$** is achieved using a procedure-function called **DelSpaces$**. The procedure **EditCell** then assigns to the element of the array **Value(Row,Column)** a value **CellValue** calculated previously by **SyntaxAnalysis**.

Upon completion of these assignments a table cursor is displayed on the screen and if **CalcMode = 1**, the recalculation of the spreadsheet's cell values takes place and the procedure ends.

Implementing Disk Interaction

Any serious software application must offer the user some method of storing data disk and the ability to retrieve this data at a later date. EasyCalc features two procedures, **Save** and **Load**, that allow you to to interact with disk files in this manner. The following code taken from the **Save** procedure demonstrates the complexity of file interaction:

```
' Write table on disk
HelpContext = 3
CALL OpenWindow(" Save ", 7, 25, 13, 54, C(16), C(17))
LOCATE 10, 28
COLOR C(16), C(17)
PRINT "File Name :"
OldName$ = Name$
DO
  TrueName = 0
  CALL EditString(Name$, 10, 41, C(16), C(17), 8)
  IF LastButton = 27 THEN                    'Esc
    Name$ = OldName$
    CALL CloseWindow
    EXIT SUB
  END IF
  GOSUB FileName
LOOP UNTIL TrueName
```

After defining the context of the help system, the procedure calls the filename entry panel - a window that is used to accept a filename to be input from the keyboard.

Using Window Dialog Boxes

In order to present this dialog, we must pass several important parameters to the **OpenWindow** function:

```
OpenWindow(WindowName$, Row1, Col1, Row2, Col2, Color1, Color2)
```

The parameters for this function are as follows:

▲	**WindowName$**	The header to be printed at the top of the window.
▲	**Row1, Col1**	Coordinates of the left upper corner of the window.
▲	**Row2, Col2**	Coordinates of the right lower corner of the window.
▲	**Color1, Color2**	Color of the framework and background of the window.

The **OpenWindow** function looks like this:

```
SUB OpenWindow (WindowName$, Row1, Col1, Row2, Col2, Color1, Color2)
  ' Open a window with shadow
  WindowLevel = WindowLevel + 1
  PCOPY 0, WindowLevel
  CALL Box(Row1 + 1, Col1 + 1, Row2 + 1, Col2 + 1, 4, C(8), C(8))
  CALL Box(Row1, Col1, Row2, Col2, 1, Color1, Color2)
  LOCATE Row1, (Col1 + Col2 - LEN(WindowName$)) / 2
  COLOR Color1, Color2
  PRINT WindowName$
END SUB
```

This procedure increments the value of the global variable **WindowLevel** and stores the current screen in video memory on the page number according to this variable. Then two frameworks are drawn by twice calling a procedure called **Box** and displays the title in the top of the window. Once the Save dialog window has been completed it should look like this:

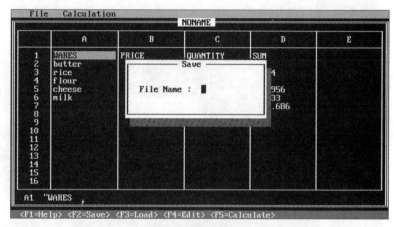

The **Save** procedure then opens a **Do...Loop** cycle to implement the input of the user's filename for their spreadsheet. The main load in the routine is born by a procedure called **EditString**, that ensures that the entering and editing of a string of characters goes as smoothly as possible. All the traditionally available text editing functions are implemented by **EditString**, including *Backspace*, *Delete*, *Home*, *End*, *Enter* and *Esc*. The **EditString** procedure is very similar to the input procedures we considered in the previous chapter on 'Programming the User Interface', so we shall refer you back there for further explanation.

If the user aborted the save using *Esc*, the procedure **CloseWindow** restores the screen previously stored in video memory on page number **WindowLevel**, and decrements the value of the global variable **WindowLevel**.

Filename Analysis

If the entry of a filename was completed by pressing *Return*, then the **FileName** subroutine is called to analyze the filename entered for validity:

```
FileName:
  FOR I = 1 TO LEN(Name$)
    C = ASC(MID$(Name$, I, 1))
    SELECT CASE C
      CASE 48 TO 57, 65 TO 90, 95, 97 TO 122   'Letters or digits
        ' No operation if entry is a number, letter or _
      CASE ELSE
        SyntaxError = 20
        CALL Errors(Row, Column)
        TrueName = 0
        RETURN
```

```
      END SELECT
    NEXT I
     TrueName = 1
    RETURN
```

This procedure steps through the entry made by the user one character at a time, checking for invalid characters.

Displaying Error Messages

If this subroutine detects an illegal character, it generates an error message by calling the **Errors** procedure after setting **SyntaxError** to 20:

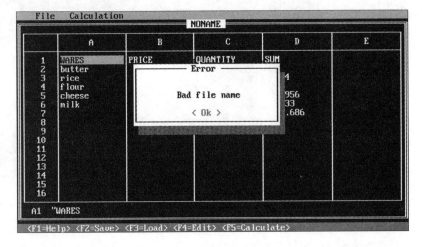

The simplicity of this procedure doesn't require for us to expand on it further here, but for your reference here is a list of all the error messages that can be generated in **\CHAP14\CH14_1.BAS**:

Error code	Error message
0	Overflow in XY
1	Operation expected
2	Error in expression
3	')' expected
4	'(' expected
5	Bad number or cell index
6	':' expected
7	Number too large
11	Division by zero in XY
20	Bad file name

After the output of a filename error message, the user can either correct their mistake or abort the save altogether.

The Save Procedure

If the user has entered a syntactically correct filename, the **Save** procedure appends the **.TAB** extension to it and creates that file in the same directory as your **QBASIC.EXE** file. A symbol 'ü' and two numbers, **LastRow** and **LastColumn**, describing the size of the active part of the spreadsheet are entered into the open file:

```
' Save file
OPEN Name$ + ".tab" FOR OUTPUT AS #1
  PRINT #1, "ü"
  PRINT #1, LastRow
  PRINT #1, LastColumn
  FOR I = 1 TO LastRow
    FOR j = 1 TO LastColumn
      IF CellType(I, j) = "S" THEN
        PRINT #1, "ü" + Table$(I, j)
      ELSE
        PRINT #1, Table$(I, j)
      END IF
    NEXT j
  NEXT I
  CLOSE #1
```

Then the contents **Table$(i,j)** of each cell (i,j) of the active part of the current table are recorded into the file. In doing so, the cells storing string data are prefixed with the 'ü' character.

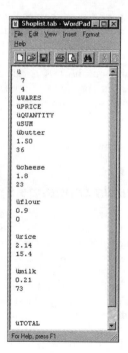

After recording the active part of electronic table in a file, the window with the entry panel closes (the procedure **CloseWindow** again) and the specified filename is used as the new heading of the current table - this is standard practise. At this point, the procedure **Save** has been completed.

To read the electronic table back in from disk, the **Load** procedure is used. Basically this procedure follows a similar vein to **Save**, except that it reads the data instead of writing it.

Recalculating the Electronic Table

When you select the Auto menu item, the **Action** subroutine assigns the value of 1 to **CalcMode** and calls the **Recalculate** procedure:

```
SUB Recalculate
' Recalculate the values of all cells
  FOR I = 1 TO LastRow
    FOR j = 1 TO LastColumn
      IF CellType(I, j) = "F" THEN              'Formula
        CALL SAFormula((Table$(I, j)), Value(I, j), 1)
        IF SyntaxError THEN
          CALL Errors(I, j)
        END IF
      END IF
    NEXT j
  NEXT I
END SUB
```

This procedure determines the type of a given cell and, if it finds a formula, it calls the **SAFormula** procedure to ascertain its value. If the formula cannot be calculated for some reason, an appropriate message with an indication of the cell's name is displayed, and the value isn't defined.

Syntax Analysis of Formulas

So far, we have quickly passed over the need for a procedure to check the syntactic correctness of a given formula. In this section, we'll be considering whether a string, **Cell$**, contains a valid formula and if so, what that value is.

The program used to carry out this task is called an interpreter, while its process is called the interpretation. During the interpretation of a possible formula, the interpreter reads the formula, checks the syntax against a predefined set of rules, and calls the appropriate routines to perform the necessary calculations. In EasyCalc, all of this functionality is encapsulated in the **SyntaxAnalysis** procedure.

Before we take a look at how this procedure is coded, let's see how the basic set of syntactic rules is detailed.

Depiction of Formula Language Syntax

When you are going to code a large set of rules into a program, it is sometimes necessary to breakdown those rules into smaller and smaller chunks, thus mapping out all of the options that you should cover. In the realms of mathematics (this is really just a type of set notation and description), there are a variety of ways to perform this task, but we shall be concentrating on Backus-Naur Form (BNF).

To begin with, let's start at the other end of the problem and define some basic terms. BNF provides us with a set of basic rules for illustrating what elements could replace the term when the given formula is resolved. For example, the set called 'Digits' looks like this:

<Digit> ::= 0|1|2|3|4|5|6|7|8|9

You can read this as 'You can replace the term Digit with 0 or 1 or .... or 8 or 9'. In a similar way, you can also define the set called 'Letter':

<Letter> ::= A³B³C³D³E³F³G³H³I³J³K³L³M³N³O³P³Q³R³S³T³U³V³W³X³Y³Z

Using these two basic sets, you can now create more complex versions. Consider the following definition:

<Cell> ::= <Letter><Digit>

By following the ideas we have looked at so far, you can explain the term Cell as 'You can replace the term Cell with any two character combination as long as the first comes from the set called Letter and the second comes from Digit'. Some examples of Cell values include A1, H5 and Z9.

Unfortunately, the name of this new set is misleading. With this set, you can't refer to all the cells on our spreadsheet - you can't refer to H11. To overcome this problem we need to define a new set called 'Digits':

<Digits> ::= <Digit>³<Digit><Digits>

In this definition, we are introducing a new use of the | symbol - using it to add different options to the sets contents as opposed to new elements - and a new idea - that of recursion. BNF allows you to build a definition based upon itself. To understand this idea, let's take a closer look at what this new definition actual means.

> You should note that it doesn't matter what order the options appear on the right hand side of the defintion. In other words, <Digit>³<Digit><Digits> is the same as <Digit><Digits>|<Digit>. However, you cannot rearrange the order of the terms inside an option - <Letter><Digit> is not the same as <Digit><Letter>.

Concentrating on the right hand sign of the definition, the left option indicates that the term 'Digits' can be replaced by any of the elements in the Digit set, but the right option is more interesting. It indicates that if you have an element of Digits, you can easily create another element of the set by prefixing it with an element from the Digit set.

This means that all the following elements can replace the term Digits:

    1
    31
    631
    8631

Let's also introduce one more convention. For simplicity, BNF allows you to write <Digit>³<Digit><Digits> as <Digit> {<Digit>} - you can read the curly brackets as 'repeat zero or more times'. This avoids the use of a new set (we know that we can do it, so why show it all the time!), is simply to understand than the recursive version and takes less time to write down!

Using this new definition, we can now make a much better attempt at describing the term Cell:

<Cell> ::= <Letter><Digits>

Using these same basic ideas, it is now possible to create a whole variety of exact defintions:

<Number> ::= <Digits> ³ <Digits>.<Digits> ³ .<Digits>

defines a term 'Number', that can be replaced by any of the following: 023, 79.54 and .61.

Let's stop messing around the realm of mathematics and get back to real life. Using these rules and this notation we can now define the syntax rules for our formulae:

```
<Digit> ::= 0|1|2|3|4|5|6|7|8|9
<Letter> ::= A|B|C|D|E|F|G|H|I|J|K|L|M|N|O|P|Q|R|S|T|U|V|W|X|Y|Z
<Multiplicative operation> ::= *|/
<Additive operation> ::= +|-
<Digits> ::= <Digit>|<Digit><Digits>
<CellIndex> ::= <Letter><Digits>
<Function> ::= SIN(<Formula>)|COS(<Formula>)|EXP(<Formula>)|LOG(<Formula>)|
SQR(<Formula>)|SUM(<CellIndex>:<CellIndex>)
<Term> ::= <Number>|<CellIndex>|(<Formula>)|<Function>|+<Term>|-<Term>
<Item> ::= <Term> {<Multiplicative operation><Term>}
<Formula> ::= <Item> {<Additive operation><Item>}
```

Unfortunately, there is one problem with these definitions, not due to the mathematics, but based on the real-life modelling of our spreadsheet. As you already know the maximum number of rows in our table is 100 - our definitions pay no attention to this restriction. This restriction can be included in the model, but it would make the definitions unnecessarily cumbersome for this example and would restrict the flexibility of the spreadsheet if we ever wish to increase the size of the table.

From Metaformulas to Programs

Now we have defined our rules, we can now attempt to put them into practice. In EasyCalc, we use a procedure called **SyntaxAnalysis** to coordinate the checking and evaluation of the formula:

```
SUB SyntaxAnalysis (Cell$, CellType$, CellValue!)
' Syntax analysis of table's cell
  SyntaxError = 0
  IF Cell$ = "" THEN                        'Empty cell
    CellType$ = ""
    CellValue! = 0
  ELSEIF LEFT$(Cell$, 1) = CHR$(34) THEN    'String
    CellType$ = "S"
    CellValue! = 0
  ELSE                                      'Formula
    CellType$ = "F"
    Formula$ = UCASE$(DelSpaces$(Cell$))
    CALL SAFormula((Formula$), CellValue!, 1)
  END IF
END SUB
```

This procedure performs a quick sweep of **Cell$** variable and if it can identify the contents as a string or the cell as being empty, it performs the appropriate assignments to **CellType$** and **CellValue!** and ends the procedure. However, if the sweep detects a possible formula, the entry is sanitised and passed to the **SAFormula** procedure for the actual syntax checking.

To perform the syntax checking of a given formula, we use a trio of procedures to break the formula down into small testable chunks. The main controlling function of the group is **SAFormula**:

```
SUB SAFormula (F$, FormulaValue!, Sign)
' Syntax analysis of formula F$
```

```
      CALL SAItem(F$, ItemValue!, Sign)
      IF SyntaxError THEN EXIT SUB
      FormulaValue! = ItemValue!
      DO WHILE F$ <> "" AND SyntaxError = 0
        C$ = LEFT$(F$, 1)
        IF C$ = ")" THEN
          SyntaxError = 4
          EXIT DO
        END IF
        IF C$ = "+" OR C$ = "-" THEN
          F$ = MID$(F$, 2)
          CALL SAItem(F$, ItemValue!, 0)
          IF SyntaxError THEN EXIT DO
          SELECT CASE C$
            CASE "+"
              FormulaValue! = FormulaValue! + ItemValue!
            CASE "-"
              FormulaValue! = FormulaValue! - ItemValue!
          END SELECT
        ELSE
          SyntaxError = 1
        END IF
      LOOP
    END SUB
```

As you can see, the calls to **SAItem** are used to break the current formula down at key points, i.e. when the character reader detects an opening bracket or an additive operator outside of a bracket. If the character reader detects an opening bracket, you obviously need to calculate the contents of the bracket before you can add the result to the running total. A similar rule applies to the additive operators outside of a bracket.

The rest of this procedure either deals with the calculation of the final value, taken from the results of call to **SAItem** or some error handling. Simply by setting **SyntaxError** to an appropriate value for the problem, this procedure will detect the fault, scrub the procedure and fall back to **EditCell** where the error is immediately handled by a call to **Errors**.

SAItem is used for exactly the same purposes as **SAFormula** except that it deals with the multiplicative operators. You should also note that this procedure doesn't have to worry about the bracket problem as **SAFormula** handles this. As you can see, this is quite a simple procedure:

```
  SUB SAItem (F$, ItemValue!, Sign)
  ' Syntax analysis of summand F$
    CALL SATerm(F$, TermValue!, Sign)
    IF SyntaxError THEN EXIT SUB
    ItemValue! = TermValue!
    DO WHILE F$ <> "" AND SyntaxError = 0
      C$ = LEFT$(F$, 1)
      IF C$ = "*" OR C$ = "/" THEN
        F$ = MID$(F$, 2)
        CALL SATerm(F$, TermValue!, 0)
        IF SyntaxError THEN EXIT DO
        SELECT CASE C$
          CASE "*"
            ItemValue! = ItemValue! * TermValue!
          CASE "/"
```

```
                ItemValue! = ItemValue! / TermValue!
        END SELECT
      ELSE
         EXIT DO
      END IF
    LOOP
  END SUB
```

The previous two procedures are really just to organise the use of the real meat of the analysis tool, **SATerm**. It is this procedure that actually identifies each individual term in the formula and applies the appropriate mathematical operator to the current value. It is here that the BNF of the formula really comes into its own. By following the structure of the term, you can logically sort out all the different options that are available, dealing with them in the appropriate manner.

```
SUB SATerm (F$, TermValue!, Sign)
' Syntax analysis of term F$
  IF F$ = "" THEN
    SyntaxError = 2
    EXIT SUB
  END IF
  C$ = LEFT$(F$, 1)
  IF Sign AND (C$ = "+" OR C$ = "-") THEN         'Signed term
    F$ = MID$(F$, 2)
    CALL SATerm(F$, TermValue!, 0)
    IF SyntaxError THEN EXIT SUB
    IF C$ = "-" THEN TermValue! = -TermValue!
  ELSE                                            'Unsigned term
    IF C$ = "(" THEN                              'Formula
      GOSUB FormulaSub
    ELSEIF "0" <= C$ AND C$ <= "9" OR C$ = "." THEN 'Number
      GOSUB NumberSub
    ELSE                                'Function or cell index
      CCC$ = LEFT$(F$, 3)
      SELECT CASE CCC$
        CASE "SIN"
          F$ = MID$(F$, 4)
          GOSUB FormulaSub
          TermValue! = SIN(TermValue!)
        CASE "COS"
          F$ = MID$(F$, 4)
          GOSUB FormulaSub
          TermValue! = COS(TermValue!)
        CASE "EXP"
          F$ = MID$(F$, 4)
          GOSUB FormulaSub
          TermValue! = EXP(TermValue!)
        CASE "LOG"
          F$ = MID$(F$, 4)
          GOSUB FormulaSub
          TermValue! = LOG(TermValue!)
        CASE "SQR"
          F$ = MID$(F$, 4)
          GOSUB FormulaSub
          TermValue! = SQR(TermValue!)
        CASE "SUM"
          F$ = MID$(F$, 4)
```

```
            GOSUB SumSub
        CASE ELSE                              'Cell index
            GOSUB CellIndexSub
            TermValue! = Value(Index, ASC(Letter$) - 64)
      END SELECT
    END IF
  END IF
EXIT SUB
'==============================================================
FormulaSub:
        . . .
RETURN
NumberSub:
        . . .
RETURN
CellIndexSub:
        . . .
RETURN
DigitsSub:
        . . .
RETURN
SumSub:
        . . .
RETURN
'==============================================================
END SUB
```

The only interesting sections of this code are the recursive call to **SATerm** if the current term is signed and the use of five further subroutines to handle some of the more repetitively run tasks.

The five further routines include:

- ▲ **FormulaSub**
- ▲ **NumberSub**
- ▲ **CellIndexSub**
- ▲ **DigitsSub**
- ▲ **SumSub**

FormulaSub

This procedure simply work outs whether or not you have an equivalent number of opening and closing brackets in a given formula.

```
FormulaSub:
  F$ = MID$(F$, 2)
  Brackets = 0
  I = 0
  DO WHILE I < LEN(F$) AND Brackets >= 0
    I = I + 1
    C1$ = MID$(F$, I, 1)
    SELECT CASE C1$
    CASE "("
```

```
          Brackets = Brackets + 1
      CASE ")"
          Brackets = Brackets - 1
      END SELECT
    LOOP
    IF Brackets >= 0 THEN
      SyntaxError = 3
      EXIT SUB
    END IF
    F1$ = LEFT$(F$, I - 1)
    F$ = MID$(F$, I + 1)
    CALL SAFormula(F1$, TermValue!, 1)
    IF SyntaxError THEN EXIT SUB
  RETURN
```

If the brackets balance in the formula, this procedure performs a recursive call to **SAFormula** in order to deal with the contents of the first set of brackets, otherwise the **SyntaxError** variable is set to the appropriate value for the error and the procedure is ended.

NumberSub

This procedure translates the string version of a number to its numerical value. It uses recursive calls to **DigitsSub** to identify the decimal point, translating first the integer part, handling the decimal point and finally translating the decimal places:

```
NumberSub:
  IF LEFT$(F$, 1) = "." THEN
    F$ = MID$(F$, 2)
    GOSUB DigitsSub
    TermValue! = VAL("." + Digits$)
    IF ERR THEN
      SyntaxError = 7
      EXIT SUB
    END IF
    RETURN
  END IF
  GOSUB DigitsSub
  IF LEFT$(F$, 1) <> "." THEN
    TermValue! = VAL(Digits$)
    IF ERR THEN
      SyntaxError = 7
      EXIT SUB
    END IF
    RETURN
  END IF
  Digits1$ = Digits$
  F$ = MID$(F$, 2)
  GOSUB DigitsSub
  TermValue! = VAL(Digits1$ + "." + Digits$)
  IF ERR THEN
    SyntaxError = 7
    EXIT SUB
  END IF
RETURN
```

In essence, it is this procedure, along with its partner, `DigitsSub`, that makes the spreadsheet work on a numerical level. It also illustrates that a device that users consider to be a numerical number-cruncher has more to do with letters than they would care to imagine.

DigitsSub

As we have already outlined, this procedure simply identifies where the decimal point comes in a given string:

```
DigitsSub:
  Digit$ = LEFT$(F$, 1)
  IF F$ = "" OR "0" > Digit$ OR Digit$ > "9" THEN
    SyntaxError = 5
    EXIT SUB
  ELSE
    I = 2
    DO
      Digit$ = MID$(F$, I, 1)
      IF "0" > Digit$ OR Digit$ > "9" THEN EXIT DO
      I = I + 1
    LOOP
    Digits$ = LEFT$(F$, I - 1)
    F$ = MID$(F$, I)
  END IF
RETURN
```

Notice that this procedure alters the content of `F$` each time that it runs. This is a requirement if the check on the first character in `F$` during the `NumberSub` is to function correctly.

CellIndexSub

This simple procedure is used to strip away the number and the letter from a cell reference. It also checks the validity of the letter component before attempting to strip and validate the numerical component:

```
CellIndexSub:
  Letter$ = LEFT$(F$, 1)
  IF "A" > Letter$ OR Letter$ > "Z" THEN
    SyntaxError = 2
    EXIT SUB
  END IF
  F$ = MID$(F$, 2)
  GOSUB DigitsSub
  Index = VAL(Digits$)
  IF Index <= 0 OR Index > RowNumber THEN
    SyntaxError = 5
    EXIT SUB
  END IF
RETURN
```

Note the use of the variable `RowNumber` in the numerical validation. The use of this variable allows the size of the spreadsheet to be increased and the error checking to still work.

SumSub

This final procedure uses the **CellIndexSub** to breakdown the two cell references into their component parts, checks to see if they appear in the correct order (A1:B1, not B1:A1), fixing them as appropriate and finally calculates the sum using two for loops to sweep over the required part of the table:

```
SumSub:
  IF LEFT$(F$, 1) <> "(" THEN
    SyntaxError = 4
    EXIT SUB
  END IF
  F$ = MID$(F$, 2)
  GOSUB CellIndexSub
  Letter1$ = Letter$
  Index1 = Index
  IF LEFT$(F$, 1) <> ":" THEN
    SyntaxError = 6
    EXIT SUB
  END IF
  F$ = MID$(F$, 2)
  GOSUB CellIndexSub
  IF LEFT$(F$, 1) <> ")" THEN
    SyntaxError = 3
    EXIT SUB
  END IF
  F$ = MID$(F$, 2)
  IF Letter1$ > Letter$ THEN SWAP Letter1$, Letter$
  IF Index1$ > Index$ THEN SWAP Index1$, Index$
  TermValue! = 0
  FOR I = Index1 TO Index
    FOR j = ASC(Letter1$) TO ASC(Letter$)
        TermValue! = TermValue! + Value(I, j - 64)
    NEXT j
  NEXT I
RETURN
```

By using these additional functions, we have translated the information into the appropriate format so that the recursive calls can unravel, the procedure call stack can be cleared and either a solution or an appropriate error message code can be returned to **EditCell**.

Context-Sensitive Help

As we have already noted, the help system in EasyCalc is context-sensitive, i.e. the help page displayed depends on mode that the spreadsheet is in when the user hits *F1*. Fortunately, the concept of a context-sensitive help system is an easy one to code.

A global variable is introduced, which changes as the spreadsheet moves between operating modes. When the user calls for help, the help system kicks in and selects the help page to display based on the current value of this variable.

The function called when the *F1* key is pressed is as follows:

```
SUB HelpWindow
' Global help
```

```
SELECT CASE HelpContext
  CASE 1                             'navigation about the table
    ...                              'Code removed from here
  CASE 2                             'editing a cell of table
    ...                              'Code removed from here
  CASE 3                             'Entering filename
    ...                              'Code removed from here
  END SELECT
  DO
    Key$ = ""
    WHILE Key$ = ""
    Key$ = INKEY$
  WEND
  LOOP UNTIL Key$ = CHR$(13) OR Key$ = CHR$(27)   'Enter or Esc
  CloseWindow
END SUB
```

The global variable **HelpContext**, is changed upon program entry to the following procedures:

Procedure	Value
InitEnvironment	1
EditCell	2
Load	3
Save	3
RunSpreadsheet	1

Let's now look at how we can tie in our data to a user-friendly way of presenting our data - graphs.

Using Graphics to Represent Data

There is a limit to the usefulness of text, when you need to represent results, summaries or conclusions to tables of numerical data. When such a time arises, representing the essential aspects of a horde of data using graphical means is the best route to take. There are many different methods of statistical representation available to us, so lets have a look at some of the more effective types of graphics to represent data.

Standard 2D Bar Charts

Bar charts are often constructed using pseudo-graphic symbols, such as the solid rectangles in this program:

```
REM Creating a bar chart using pseudo-graphics
REM \CHAP14\CH14_2.BAS

CLS

'Define double DATA
DATA Jan,15,  Feb,17,  Mar,24,  Apr,26,  May,29,  Jun,31
```

```
DATA Jul,27,  Aug,30,  Sep,32,  Oct,36,  Nov,40,  Dec,45
PRINT "Bar-chart showing production for 1994"
PRINT

'Reading and printing DATA
FOR I = 1 TO 12
    READ M$                          'Read the data statements
    READ Y                           'in on-the-fly
    PRINT M$; " ";
    FOR J = 1 TO Y                   'Draw a line of square boxes
        PRINT CHR$(&HFE);            'corresponding to production
    NEXT J                           'amount of that month
    PRINT
NEXT I

'Printing horizontal axis
PRINT "   |_____|_____|_____|_____|_____|"
PRINT "   0        10       20       30       40       50"

END
```

The advantage of this method is that it allows you to create a histogram in text mode. When you run this program you'll get this image:

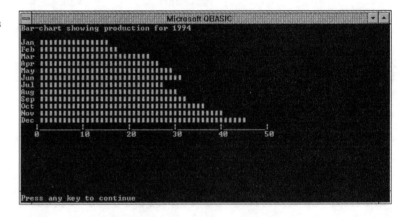

Unfortunately, this method of presentation also has a disadvantage - resolution. This program doesn't provide the tools for scaling the sizes of the horizontal columns of the linear bar chart, so the length of the columns must be calculated manually. These type of charts are typically used when time is a factor, so that you can quickly try out several ideas and get a feel for what's actually going on almost instantaneously.

Graphics-based 2D Bar Charts

Bar charts created in graphics mode are free from the aforementioned shortcoming. In the next program, we take advantage of this by producing a histogram contains a set of columns in the form of rectangles. To improve the presentation, the columns are painted or hatched to make them look a little more interesting.

You should note that our program only allows you to construct a maximum of 12 columns:

```
REM Constructing a Planar Bar Chart
REM \CHAP14\CH14_3.BAS

CLS : SCREEN 0: 'Clear screen and set text mode
```

534

```
Get.Number:
INPUT "Input number of bars between 1 and 12 "; N
IF N > 12 OR N < 1 THEN GOTO Get.Number

DIM X(N)
XMAX = 0

'Input DATA
FOR I = 1 TO N
    PRINT "Input X"; I; "="; : INPUT X(I)
    IF X(I) > XMAX THEN XMAX = X(I)
NEXT I

'Clear screen, set graphic's mode and draw axis
CLS : SCREEN 1
LINE (20, 0)-(20, 170)
LINE (20, 170)-(300, 170)
LOCATE 22, 1: PRINT "0"
LOCATE 1, 1: PRINT XMAX

'Drawing bars (columns)
DX = 142 / N
FOR I = 1 TO N
    X = 30 + (I - 1) * 2 * DX            ' Calculate X co-ordinate
    Y = 170 - X(I) * 160 / XMAX          ' Calculate Y co-ordinate
    LINE (X, 170)-(X + DX, Y), , B       ' Drawing Bars
    PAINT (X + 1, Y + 1), CHR$(97 - I)   ' Paint Bars
    LOCATE 23, INT(100 * X / 800) - (I < 10)
    PRINT I;
NEXT I

M$ = INPUT$(1):                         ' Pause

END
```

When creating a histogram, you can't rely on the data automatically fitting the maximum size of your graph. For example, the columns may all be to large or too small, so reducing the effectiveness of the histogram. To avoid this problem, we need to normalize the data before creating the graph.

> By normalizing the data, we mean that all of the values are re-scaled relative to the largest in the group, while the largest is re-scaled to fit the graph paper.

To include this feature in your program, you must determine the maximum value of the entered data, a task that is best performed as the data is entered. Every new number is compared to the value **XMAX**, which is set to zero to begin with. If the entered value is higher than **XMAX**, then **XMAX** is set to this value. By using this technique, **XMAX** will be equal to the largest value of the entered data set when the entry is complete.

Each of the values is stored in the array **X** as it is entered, while the number of columns, limited to the range 1 to 12, is stored in the variable **N**. When it comes to the actual painting of the histogram, the values are read from the array, normalized and passed to a temporary variable ready for the **Paint** command to actually draw the histogram.

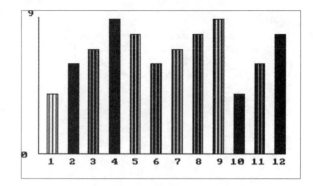

The last program illustrates the dialog approach to developing programs - asking the user for the number of columns, and then prompting the user for the quantitative data for each column. The chart is finally drawn after all the data is input and processed, and should resemble this:

To make the bar chart more illustrative, the columns are painted in different colors, and hatched in a variety of distinct styles. Column hatching is performed with the statement:

```
PAINT (X + 1, Y + 1), CHR$(97 - I)
```

By changing the arithmetic expression **(97 - I)**, you can change the hatching style. Colored diagrams are rarely used - only when data is output onto the screen of a colored display, or when a colored printer or plotter is available. In books, newspapers, and articles, bar charts are often presented in black and white, so in these cases it's better to distinguish the columns using patterns.

> A good program for creating your own patterns, together with an explanation of how it works, was given back in Chapter 8, and maybe worth a recap if you want to add that personal touch to your columns.

Standard 3D Bar Charts

The appearance of a standard 2D bar chart can be further improved by adding another dimension to it. The following program illustrates the construction of a 3D histogram:

```
REM Demonstration of a 3D Bar Chart
REM \CHAP14\CH14_4.BAS

DATA 6,20,40,80,100,90,120

SCREEN 1: CLS

'Read DATA and draw bars
READ N: DIM A(N): W = 150 / N: W1 = W * .25
FOR I = 1 TO N
    READ Y(I): GOSUB Column3D
NEXT I

'Draw global box and print the axes
LINE (0, 170)-(300, 170)
LINE (0, 170)-(0, 0)
LINE (0, 85)-(3, 85)
LINE (0, 0)-(3, 0)
```

```
LOCATE 23: PRINT "1990    1991  1992  1993    1994  1995"
LOCATE 1, 2: PRINT "100%"
LOCATE 11, 2: PRINT "50%"
A$ = INPUT$(1)

END

Column3D:                           'Subroutine for constructing a 3D-column

X = 5 + 2 * W * (I - 1)             'Calculate X co-ordinate
PSET (X, 170)                       'Set the basic point
YI = Y(I)                           'Read height of current column

'Drawing columns
D$ = "U=" + VARPTR$(YI) + "R=" + VARPTR$(W)
D$ = D$ + "D=" + VARPTR$(YI) + "E=" + VARPTR$(W1)
D$ = D$ + "U=" + VARPTR$(YI) + "L=" + VARPTR$(W)
D$ = D$ + "G=" + VARPTR$(W1) + "R=" + VARPTR$(W)
D$ = D$ + "E=" + VARPTR$(W1)
DRAW D$

RETURN
```

This program doesn't require data entry by the user. Instead the necessary data is supplied in the first line of the program in the **DATA** statement. The first data element specifies the number of columns, while the rest of the data specifies the height of each column in pixels. The subroutine `Column3D` actually creates each column:

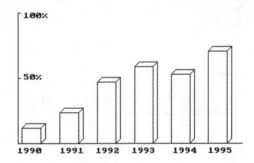

You may have noticed that we haven't normalized the height of the columns this time, as we know what the data will be. However, this is the perfect opportunity to see the problems that can occur when you don't normalize the data before it is displayed. Try altering the values of the data statement (remember that the first value represents the number of entries to follow) and seeing what effect that has on the display.

Special Bar Charts

Standard bar charts, although widely used, are sometimes simply too boring, or don't illustrate the information in the best manner. You can spend a lot of time selecting the correct patterns or positioning the columns to improve the presentation when a completely different type of graph would provide the required results with much less time and effort.

Double 3D Bar Chart

There may be times when you need to compare several sets of data, for instance, you may want to look at the monthly production output for the last couple of years all at once. You could use separate bar charts on subsequent screens but this isn't the most illustrative method for comparisons. Instead you may want to construct a combined bar chart. The following program constructs two histograms in one graph.

```
REM Constructing Two Bar Charts
REM \CHAP14\CH14_5.BAs

DIM M$(12), S(12), T(12)
FOR I = 1 TO 12: READ M$(I): NEXT I
DATA Jan,Feb,Mar,Apr,May,Jun,Jul,Aug,Sep,Oct,Nov,Dec

'Initializing the Data to be used
MINS = 1: MAXS = 1: MINT = 1: MAXT = 1
FOR I = 1 TO 12
    PRINT "For the month of "; M$(I); " Input Number1, Number2 ";
    INPUT S(I), T(I)
    IF T(I) < T(MINT) THEN MINT = I
    IF S(I) < S(MINS) THEN MINS = I
    IF S(I) > S(MAXS) THEN MAXS = I
    IF T(I) > T(MAXT) THEN MAXT = I
NEXT I

'Setup the screen
CLS : SCREEN 1: COLOR 16
LINE (20, 0)-(20, 170): LINE (20, 170)-(319, 170)
FOR I = 1 TO 12
    FOR J = 1 TO 3
        LOCATE 22 + J, 2 + 3 * I
        PRINT MID$(M$(I), J, 1);
    NEXT J
NEXT I

'Drawing columns
LOCATE 1, 1
DS = S(MAXS) - S(MINS): DT = T(MAXT) - T(MINT)
FAKS = 160 / DS: FAKT = 160 / DT
FOR I = 1 TO 12
    XTEMP = 5 + I * 24
    YT = 165 - (T(I) - T(MINT)) * FAKT
    YS = 165 - (S(I) - S(MINS)) * FAKS
    X = XTEMP + 6: Y = YT: COL.FLAG = 1  'Do the first column
    GOSUB Column3d2
    X = XTEMP - 1: Y = YS: COL.FLAG = 2  'Do the second column
    GOSUB Column3d2
NEXT I
W$ = INPUT$(1)

END

'Subroutine for drawing two columns
Column3d2:

'Check colors
 FOR K = 0 TO 3
    LINE (X + K, Y - K)-(X + 10 + K, 170), 0, BF
    IF COL.FLAG = 1 THEN COL = 2 ELSE COL = 1
NEXT K

'Draw lines
LINE (X, Y)-(X + 10, 170), COL, BF
LINE (X, Y)-(X + 10, 170), 3, B
```

```
LINE (X + 3, Y - 3)-(X + 13, Y - 3), 3
LINE (X, Y)-(X + 3, Y - 3), 3
LINE (X + 10, Y)-(X + 13, Y - 3), 3
PAINT (X + 2, Y - 1), 3, 3
LINE (X + 13, Y - 3)-(X + 13, 169), 3
LINE (X, 170)-(X + 13, 170), 3
PAINT (X + 12, 168), 0, 3
RETURN
```

Notice that all the data is entered via a friendly dialog, with the maximum and minimum values for each chart being calculated on the fly using the following code:

```
IF T(I) < T(MINT) THEN MINT = I
IF S(I) < S(MINS) THEN MINS = I
IF S(I) > S(MAXS) THEN MAXS = I
IF T(I) > T(MAXT) THEN MAXT = I
```

Once all the data has been painstakingly entered, the resulting bar charts are displayed, like thus:

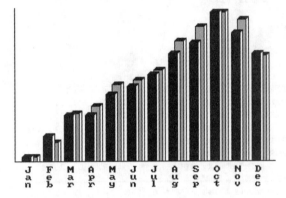

As you can guess from this screenshot the program uses different colors for the respective columns of the two bar charts. Differentiating the two obviously separate charts by color is just used to emphasize their offset screen location and to increase the aesthetic effect.

3D Bar Chart Shaped Like a Pile of Coins

If you choose a bar chart to represent financial data, you could choose to construct its columns as piles of coins. At a glance, it is clear that the bar chart deals with money and not the distribution of butterflies throughout Africa. Here's our version of the coin bar chart, a chart which provides information about the wages of a family for 1992-1995, together with a forecast for 1996:

```
REM Demonstration of a Bar Chart with the Rouleaux of Coins Scenario
REM \CHAP14\CH14_6.BAS

DECLARE SUB Title (T$, X0!, Y0!)
DECLARE SUB ColCir (R!, X!, N!, CC!, CL!)

SCREEN 9
Title "Family's Wages", 200, 20
LOCATE 25, 1: PRINT "                         ";

R = 25                          'Set the coin radius
FOR I = 1 TO 5                  'Get Bar Info
```

```
        READ N
        ColCir R, I * 100, N, 14, 12
    NEXT I


    LINE (10, 0)-(10, 300)


    'Y axis tick marks
    FOR I = 0 TO 5
        LINE (10, 300 - I * 60)-(14, 300 - I * 60)
    NEXT I


    'Rest of y axis detail
    LOCATE 1, 3: PRINT "50000 $ (USA)"
    LOCATE 22, 3: PRINT "0"
    LOCATE 24, 11
    PRINT "1992          1993          1994";
    PRINT "        1995          1996";
    F$ = INPUT$(1)


    END


    DATA 20,30, 42,40,45


    SUB ColCir (R, X, N, CC, CL)
        CIRCLE (X, 300), R, CC, 3.141, 0, .2
        CIRCLE (X, 300 - N * 6), R, CC, , , .2
        LINE (X - R, 300)-(X - R, 300 - N * 6), CC
        LINE (X + R, 300)-(X + R, 300 - N * 6), CC
        PAINT (X, 299), CC
        FOR I = 0 TO N - 1
            CIRCLE (X, 300 - I * 6), R, CL, 3.141, 0, .2
        NEXT I
        CIRCLE (X, 300 - N * 6), R, CL, , , .2
        LINE (X - R, 300)-(X - R, 300 - N * 6), CL
        LINE (X + R, 300)-(X + R, 300 - N * 6), CL
    END SUB


    SUB Title (T$, X0, Y0)
        LOCATE 25, 1
        PRINT T$;
        FOR Y% = 0 TO 11
            DX = .6 * Y% + X0: DY = 2 * Y%
            FOR X% = 0 TO 319
                Z = POINT(X%, 349 - Y%)
                IF Z <> 0 THEN
                XI = DX + 2 * X%
                LINE (XI, Y0 - DY)-(XI - 1, Y0 + 2 - DY), 15
                END IF
            NEXT X%
        NEXT Y%
    END SUB
```

The external procedure **ColCir** draws a 3D-column with the following parameters:

▲ The radius, **R**, of the coins in the column

▲ The coordinates of the center of the column

▲ The number of coins,   **N**, (up to 50) in the column

▲ The color **CC** of the column

▲ The color of the lines, **CL**

The columns are constructed in two stages. First, the general contour of a column is drawn and painted with the specified color **CC**, before all the other details are added - the semi-ellipses to separate the coins, the ellipse at the top of the column and the vertical lines which bound the column. These additional details are all drawn using lines with the color code **CL**.

You should note that the maximum number of coins that can appear in any one column is restricted to 50 - this is simply due to space constraints, i.e. we can't phsysically fit any more on screen Whereas, this is quite sufficient for drawing illustrative diagrams, they aren't meant for accurate quantitative evaluations.

Here is what your chart should look like:

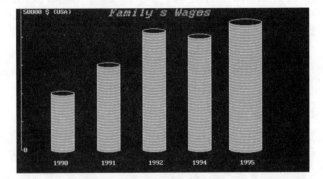

Notice the effective use of the large heading that we covered in Chapter 8 - Bit-mapped Graphics. If used sparingly and in the right places then it can make a presentation look so much better.

Multi-directional Bar Chart for Heterogeneous Data

Occasionally, you may wish to graph two related ranges of data, one of which illustrates a positive effect while the other measures a negative. As an example of this kind of situation, consider the paper industry. An environmentalist might consider the trees used as a negative while the paper mill owner would consider the reams of paper produced as a positive. Here's how the resulting graph may look, paper produced on top, trees cut down below:

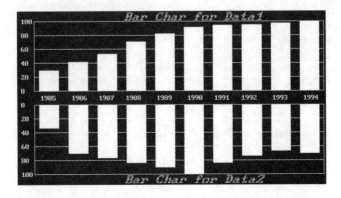

541

The program **DOUBLE.BAS** draws two bar charts in one diagram with an automatic normalization of the height of each column in relation to the highest one:

The program specifies the number of columns, **N**, to be drawn and three associated sets of data; the upper chart, the lower chart, the years to which the data relates. The external procedure **Axis** creates the scale grids for both bar charts, while the **Title** procedure displays the respective chart titles at the top and bottom of the diagram

You can easily add color to the chart by including a **PAINT** command into the statements which draw the columns. Try modifying this program yourself to get columns of different colors, and perhaps you might even be able to squeeze in a few more columns.

Pie Charts

Pie charts offer another interesting way of representing data for the purposes of comparison. When creating a pie chart, the data is usually normalized using 360 degrees to equate to the sum of the individual data values. This creates several 'pie slices', each representing a given data value, the size of which is reflected in the size of the slice.

All circular diagrams are best constructed using a polar coordinate system. This involves calculating the angles of the arc ends of each sector and using them to construct the sectors.

Here is the main control block of the program:

```
REM Pie Chart Creator
REM \CHAP14\CH14_7.BAS

CONST PI = 3.1416                'Value of pie

'Define Table
NoOfQtrs = 4                     'Number of quarters
DIM QtrTbl(NoOfQtrs)             'Table of quarterly sales

DATA   120,132,140
DATA   154,160,159
DATA   186,190,197
DATA   195,198,220

ControlModule:
   GOSUB LoadTable
   GOSUB SetUpGraphicsArea
   GOSUB DrawGraph
   GOSUB ReturnTextScreen
END
```

This fine exponent of modular programming effectively manages the whole program. The following variables are used within this program:

Variable	Description
Angle	Angle of the sector

Table Continued on Following Page

542

Variable	Description
P$	Screen pause
Percent	Ratio of quarterly sales to total sales
Pend	Angle for end of sector
Pstart	Angle for start of sector
Q	Table subscript
Sales	Variable for monthly sales
TotSales	Total sales
X, Y	Coordinates of label

And here are the five modules that form the bones of the program:

```
LoadTable:
  TotSales = 0
  FOR Q = 1 TO NoOfQtrs
      FOR Month = 1 TO 3
          READ Sales
          QtrTbl(Q) = QtrTbl(Q) + Sales
      NEXT Month
      TotSales = TotSales + QtrTbl(Q)
  NEXT Q
RETURN

SetUpGraphicsArea:
  SCREEN 1
  PALETTE 1, 0
  COLOR 1, 3
  CLS 0
  LOCATE 1, 10
  PRINT "Quarterly Sales 1994"
RETURN

DrawGraph:
  PStart = 0
  FOR Q = 1 TO NoOfQtrs
      Percent = QtrTbl(Q) / TotSales
      Percent = Percent * 360 / 57.3
      PEnd = Percent + PStart
      CIRCLE (160, 100), 75, , PStart, -PEnd
      GOSUB LabelQuarter
      PStart = PEnd
  NEXT Q
  P$ = INPUT$(1)
RETURN

ReturnTextScreen:
  SCREEN 0
  WIDTH 80
RETURN
```

```
LabelQuarter:
  Angle = (PStart + PEnd) / 2
  X = 160 + 40 * COS(Angle)
  Y = 100 - 40 * SIN(Angle)
  LOCATE INT(Y / 8), INT(X / 8)
  PRINT Q
RETURN
```

Here's the pie chart created by this program:

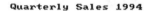

Quarterly Sales 1994

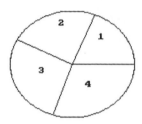

Circular diagrams tend to lose their illustrative quality when there are too few (less than 3) or too many (over 10) sectors. By changing the scales along the X and Y axes, you can obtain elliptic diagrams which sometimes look more attractive.

To create a pie chart, essentially what you do is sum up all the values and work out each as a percentage of the total. You then multiply this percentage by **2 * PI** (since there are 2Pi radians in a circle) to get the angle for each value's segment.

The **LabelQuarter** subroutine automatically arranges the labels inside the pie chart. The co-ordinates **x** and **y** are calculated from the parametric equation of a circle. The values **(x/8)** and **(y/8)**, rounded off to integers, are then used as the parameters of the positioning statement **LOCATE**. This is performed for each sector of the pie chart. Unfortunately, these algorithms only work well for small labels and a small number of sectors.

A Pie Chart with Various Fill Patterns

Some types of monitor (such as monochrome or CGA) offer just a small number of colors, in which case, you may want to use various patterns instead. You can use the **PAINT** statement to create various paint patterns, which is simpler than applying specialized hatching algorithms based on drawing each individual line. Here is the main block of code:

```
REM Pie Chart with various hatching patterns
REM \CHAP14\CH14_8.BAs

DECLARE SUB AssignTilingPatterns (tile$())
DECLARE SUB CountAndTotalData (count!, total!)
DECLARE SUB DrawChart (count!, total!, tile$(), scale!)
DECLARE SUB DisplayLegend (count!, tile$(), scale!)
scale = 1
DIM tile$(1 TO 10)
CALL AssignTilingPatterns(tile$())
CALL CountAndTotalData(itemCount, sumOfData)
CALL DrawChart(itemCount, sumOfData, tile$(), scale)
CALL DisplayLegend(itemCount, tile$(), scale)
WHILE INKEY$="":WEND
```

```
'Data: number of people (in millions) that speak language (approx)
DATA 182, 176, 979, 425, 119, 305, 169, 290, 301, 2005, -1
'Data: the major languages
DATA Arabic, Bengali, Chinese, English, French
DATA Hindi, Portuguese, Russian, Spanish, other
'Data: title for pie chart
DATA Principal Languages of the World

END
```

You should be fairly familiar with the different methods of creating patterns in QBasic after Chapter 8 - Bit-mapped Graphics. Here we create ten different patterns, one for each country, which we will use to fill in their segment in the pie chart:

```
SUB AssignTilingPatterns (tile$())
   tile$(1) = CHR$(136) + CHR$(136) + CHR$(170)
   tile$(2) = CHR$(85) + CHR$(0)
   tile$(3) = CHR$(128) + CHR$(32) + CHR$(8) + CHR$(2)
   tile$(4) = CHR$(3) + CHR$(12) + CHR$(48) + CHR$(192)
   tile$(5) = CHR$(170) + CHR$(170) + CHR$(0) + CHR$(0)
   tile$(6) = CHR$(17)
   tile$(7) = CHR$(168) + CHR$(168) + CHR$(0)
   tile$(8) = CHR$(1) + CHR$(16)
   tile$(9) = CHR$(255)
   tile$(10) = CHR$(5)
END SUB
```

This is the next subroutine to be called from the main block of code, and basically all it does is count and total the number of entries for the pie chart. Notice that it uses yet another method to read the data into memory - this time we are using a **DO...LOOP**, escaping when we read in the end-of-data delimiter, -1:

```
SUB CountAndTotalData (count, total)
   count = 0
   total = 0
   READ itemValue
   DO UNTIL itemValue < 0
       total = total + itemValue
       count = count + 1
       READ itemValue
   LOOP
END SUB
```

The following subroutine displays the comprehensive key for the chart, drawing a small box with the appropriate pattern inside and the country name alongside:

```
SUB DisplayLegend (count, tile$(), scale)
   heightInRows = 25: widthInColumns = 40
   WINDOW SCREEN (0, 0)-(widthInColumns, heightInRows)
   boxWidth = 2: boxHt = 1
   legendTop = (heightInRows - (boxHt + 1) * count) \ 2
   leftEdge = widthInColumns * (scale / 2) + 2
   FOR i = 1 TO count
       READ itemName$
       boxBottom = legendTop + (boxHt + 1) * i
       boxTop = boxBottom - boxHt
```

```
              rtEdge = leftEdge + boxWidth
              LINE (leftEdge, boxTop)-(rtEdge, boxBottom), , B
              PAINT (leftEdge + boxWidth / 2, boxBottom - boxHt / 2), tile$(i)
              LOCATE boxBottom, leftEdge + boxWidth + 2: PRINT itemName$
          NEXT i
          READ title$
          LOCATE heightInRows - 1, (widthInColumns - LEN(title$)) / 2
          PRINT title$;
      END SUB
```

The last subroutine finally draws the pie chart according to the data entered earlier:

```
      SUB DrawChart (count, total, tile$(), scale)
          windowWidth = 4: windowHeight = 3
          SCREEN 1, 0: COLOR , 0
          WINDOW (0, 0)-(windowWidth, windowHeight)
          twoPi = 8 * ATN(1)                          '2*pi
          radius = scale * windowWidth / 4
          xcenter = radius: ycenter = windowHeight / 2
          startSector = .00001
          RESTORE                                     'use first data statement again
          FOR index% = 1 TO count
              READ itemValue
              endSector = startSector + twoPi * (itemValue / total)
              IF endSector > 6.283 THEN endSector = 6.283
              CIRCLE (xcenter, ycenter), radius, , -startSector, -endSector
              theta = (startSector + endSector) / 2
              x = xcenter + radius * COS(theta) / 2
              y = ycenter + radius * SIN(theta) / 2
              PAINT (x, y), tile$(index%)
              startSector = endSector
          NEXT index%
          READ itemValue                              'read the sentinel value
      END SUB
```

Here's the pie chart drawn by this more substantial piece of programming:

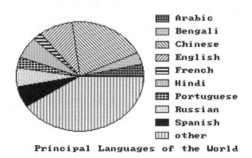

Principal Languages of the World

It certainly looks more impressive than our previous effort.

A Colored Pie Chart with a Cut-out Segment

One of the more exciting tasks that you can perform with a pie chart is to pull one slice out of the pie. To do this, you must simply radially shift the center of the given segment away from the centre of the pie. This slice is usually used to illustrate the important value in a given list and can be coded as follows:

```
REM Demonstration of a Separated segment in a pie chart
REM \CHAP14\CH14_9.BAS

SCREEN 7: CLS : COLOR 15, 0:
DIM M(20), T$(20), X(20), Y(20)
PI = 3.141592: PI2 = 2 * PI
DEF FNWIN (X) = .02 * PI * X
A = 0: F = 1.745329E-02
MX = 160: MY = 100: RADIUS = 90: ASPECT = 5 / 6

'Input the number of sectors and accept data from the user
INPUT "INPUT Nsectors="; N
FOR I = 1 TO N
    PRINT "INPUT M"; I; "  Text"; I; : INPUT M(I), T$(I)
NEXT I

'Input text labels
INPUT "INPUT Nlabel="; WB
FOR I = 1 TO N
    T = T + M(I)
NEXT I
CLS

'DATA conversion
FOR I = 1 TO N
    M(I) = M(I) * 100 / T
NEXT I: A = 0

'Drawing N sectors
FOR I = 1 TO N
    V = FNWIN(M(I))
    IF A + V > PI2 THEN A = PI2 - V
    WIN = (A + A + V) / 2: X(I) = RADIUS * .2 * COS(WIN)
    Y(I) = -(RADIUS * .2 * SIN(WIN) * ASPECT): A = A + V
NEXT I
A = .000001
FOR I = 1 TO N
    IF I = WB THEN
        XT = X(I): YT = Y(I)
    ELSE XT = 0: YT = 0
    END IF
    V = FNWIN(M(I)): COL = I
    IF A + V > PI2 THEN A = PI2 - V
    CIRCLE (MX + XT, MY + YT), RADIUS, COL, -A, -(A + V)
    WIN = (A + A + V) / 2: X = MX + RADIUS * .5 * COS(WIN)
    Y = MY + RADIUS * .5 * SIN(WIN) * ASPECT
    PAINT (X + XT, 200 - (Y - YT)), COL, COL
    A = A + V
NEXT I

'Printing character labels with automatic positioning
A = 0
FOR I = 1 TO N
    IF I = WB THEN XT = X(I): YT = Y(I) ELSE XT = 0: YT = 0
    V = FNWIN(M(I)): IF A + V > PI2 THEN A = PI2 - V
    WIN = (A + A + V) / 2: X = MX + RADIUS * .8 * COS(WIN)
    Y = MY + RADIUS * .8 * SIN(WIN) * ASPECT
```

```
        LOCATE 1 + (200 - (Y - YT)) / 8, 1 + (X + XT) / 8
        IF (X + XT) < MX THEN PRINT STRING$(LEN(T$(I)), 29);
        PRINT T$(I); : A = A + V
    NEXT I: T = 0
    LINE (10, 0)-(309, 199), 3, B
    M$ = INPUT$(1)
```

One feature of this program that is worth mentioning is the principle by which the segments are painted. A segment is constructed by the **CIRCLE** statement with negative values for the start and end angles. As well as the arc, the radial line segments are also drawn in the process - in other words, the whole segment is drawn at once.

However, a problem arises with the first segment whereby the initial angle is 0 and the radial line isn't constructed. To get around this, the value **A** is defined follows:

```
    A = .000001
```

The method by which we make one of the segments stand out is handled in the following section of code. The user is asked which segment they wish to shift from the centre of the pie chart, and the number of this segment is stored in the variable **WB**. The offset co-ordinates of the chosen segment are thus stored in **XT** and **YT**:

```
    IF I = WB THEN
        XT = X(I): YT = Y(I)
    ELSE XT = 0: YT = 0
```

What you see here is the black and white equivalent of the resulting circular histogram:

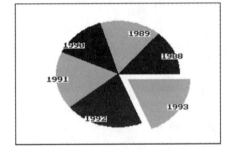

Combined Graphs

Sometimes combined graphs are a better option for presenting information; for example, the monthly production yield is illustrated by a column histogram or a linear graph, and the quarterly yield by a pie chart. Putting them both onto one chart can produce some impressive effects, as can be demonstrated by the **COMBINED.BAS** program on the accompanying disk.

This program combines the code of two earlier examples, with a supplementary sub-routine **LineGraph** which draws a linear graph on the background of a column bar chart. This is sort of combinatorial effect that can prove invaluable when presenting data:

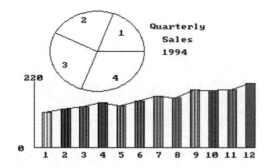

As you have seen, QBasic allows you to create a wide variety of graphs to represent your data. The only constraint that you as a programmer face is that of imagining a new way of presenting your data. What we have attempted to do here is present you with some algorithms and working examples as a starting point for your own projects.

Summary

In this chapter, we have examined how you can implement a basic spreadsheet program and we have given you some algorithms and worked examples for painting your own graphs on the screen. We have examined the ideas behind of Backus-Naur Form and a real world use of recursive procedure calls. In fact, we have covered all the important aspects of a commercial spreadsheet package.

What we haven't done is provide you with a complete package - one of the major omissions is the connection between EasyCalc and the graphing routines. You will have to modify the program to read the values from the spreadsheet into the graph procedures yourself.

In fact, if you are interested there are several other features that you can add to EasyCalc including:

- ▲ Sorting the rows of a spreadsheet based on the contents of one column.
- ▲ Copying a formula from a definite cell into a specified range of cells.
- ▲ Add extra mathematical functions to the predefined list such as Tan(x).
- ▲ Copy and Paste from cell to cell.
- ▲ Import from or save as an Excel spreadsheet.

When you have integrated the graphics procedure into EasyCalc, you might want to add the following features:

- ▲ Automatic redraw when the source data changes.
- ▲ Re-color the graphs on the fly.
- ▲ Allow the user to define the text for labels and legends at run-time.

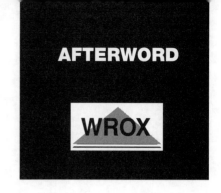

Where Do We Go from Here?

There really aren't very many important topics left to cover now, I'm afraid. You've gone from being a QBasic beginner to a fully qualified QBasic expert, albeit in theory. There are several paths that you can take to ensure that your newfound knowledge doesn't go to waste - and they are all called *practise*! If you haven't looked at many of the programs on the accompanying disk, now would be a very good time to do so. A full list of programs not specifically used in this book is given in Appendix B. There are so many different topics covered by every program that one or two are bound to strike a chord with you, wherever your interests in QBasic lie.

Take what you have learned and what you have seen and try to write your own programs, enhancements and versions. Sometimes, it can be very worthwhile to take a look at an existing program that you think you would like to write and try to write it from scratch. This way, if you ever get stuck, you can cheat and take a look at how someone else solved a particular problem. This method of learning is second only to having your own tutor so, hopefully, you can find some program that you like, or that you think needs improving.

If you would like to learn more about QBasic, or just hang out with the rest of us, take a look at Appendix A which details other relevant resources in the form of web sites, mailing lists, `ftp` sites, books, etc. In particular, if you have access to the World Wide Web, check out the BASIC resource page at the Wrox Web Site, http://www.wrox.com, which features regular updates of popular QBasic programs, news, information and the best new quality programs.

Are you interested in writing or reviewing any of our future books? We warmly welcome any willing contributors that can help Wrox publish even better books. If you're interested, contact us right away - see the details at the back of this book.

You can also contact Wrox via the reply card at the back of this book, or you can correspond with us by any of the following means:

Snail mail   **Wrox Press Ltd, Unit 16, 20 James Road, Birmingham, B11 2BA, United Kingdom.**

Electronic mail (e-mail)   **johnf@wrox.com**

World Wide Web   **http://www.wrox.com**

Compuserve   **100063,2152**

Telephone   **(44121) 706 6826**

Facsimile   **(44121) 706 2967**

QBasic
Resource Guide

The popularity of BASIC has enabled a phenomenal growth in the number of programs, archives, source code libraries, users, Internet sites and all manner of other enthusiast-related documents. This book and disk only represent a small snapshot of all the QBasic programs ever written, so where do you go for more? Well, this is the function of this appendix, where we will inform you of where all the best places to find like-minded BASIC individuals and oodles of source code. Let's now dip into this treasure trove of goodies, and don't forget to mention that Wrox sent you!

Books

For further reading of the subjects covered in this book, we recommend the following texts:

 **Graphik auf den IBM PC's Programmierhandbuch**, by Gabriel Cueller (Carl Hanser Verlag Munchen Wien, 1985).

 **QBasic Programming**, by D.I.Schneider, Brady Publishing, 1991.

If you want to recommend a guide for programming novices then look no further than our:

 **Beginner's Guide to QBasic**, written by Olga Melnikova, Anna Bonushkina and Victor Krylov.

It comes with an interactive tutorial on the accompanying disk and features everything a new computer user could ever want to get into our programming world. Its ISBN is 1-874416-16-8.

Newsgroups

There are basically (no pun intended) only two newsgroups relevant to QBasic programmers:

 alt.lang.basic

 comp.lang.basic.misc

Both should be checked out for the latest QBasic news, code, tips and information, but the best reason for browsing these newsgroups is for the contacts. If you require help on a particular QBasic-related subject then here you will find enough willing individuals to help you out.

There are hundreds of other computer-related newsgroups that may also be of interest to QBasic programmers who would like to learn more about a particular topic, but it is beyond the scope of this book to list them all here.

Don't forget to be careful when posting on the newsgroups because there are rules of etiquette and if you don't follow them you may upset other users. Please make sure that you read up about how to use the newsgroups first so that you can avoid a nasty flaming.

User Group

The QBasic Users Club is a UK-based society devoted to furthering the cause of QBasic. Run by Louis O'Brien, this user group distributes monthly newsletters to all its members, featuring articles, code, advice, adverts, reviews and competitions. For further details write to:

The QBasic Users Club
54b Massie Street
Cheadle
Cheshire
SK8 1DU
United Kingdom
Tel : +44 161 491 3282

Fanzines

There are several BASIC programming fanzines which regularly provide help, tips, code and information. The best of these is The Internet BASIC fanzine, edited by Peter Cooper, which is distributed monthly on the BASIC newsgroups. For more information, e-mail peter@trenham.demon.co.uk.

ftp Sites

File transfer protocol is a method of downloading files from computer systems at other sites across the Internet. Unlike the World Wide Web this method isn't graphics based, and so a grasp of UNIX commands wouldn't go amiss when using this system. The following `ftp` sites are of particular value:

Site	Directory
`ftp.coast.net`	`simtel/msdos/basic` (or any Simtel mirror site)
`users.aol.com`	`blood225`

Check out the introductory pages of these sites for details of mirror sites closer to your geographic location.

Forums

Across the Internet there are places where you can discuss QBasic-related issues until the cows come home. Similar in concept to newsgroups, these forums are a fantastic source of QBasic information, source code and help. Probably the best is Compuserve's MS-BASIC forum. Although this forum is split into over twenty different subjects, mostly devoted to Visual Basic, there is one folder, DOS/MacBasic, which features a host of QBasic-related threads. Compuserve also features a library of source code, under the same folder name, which contains hundreds of programs uploaded by users of Compuserve.

Web Sites

The World Wide Web is a vast network of information, that unsurprisingly features a huge amount of excellent BASIC and QBasic information and source code. All the following sites come highly recommended:

- http://www.jumbo.com/prog/dos/qbasic/
- http://www.fys.ruu.nl/~bergmann/basic.html
- http://www.coast.net:80/Simtel/msdos/qbasic.html

Then there's the Wrox web site which you can find by aiming your browser at the following URL:

- http://www.wrox.com

It features great support not only for all our books, but also for all our readers who are members of the QBasic community. This resource is constantly updated with the latest and best developments.

Disk Reference

Here are all the extra programs that are not featured within the chapters but are included on the accompanying disk. If you don't have access to a 3.5" disk drive then send away for the 5.25" equivalent floppy disk, details of which can be found at the back of the book.

AMUSE\AVG.BAS	A fine implementation of the brilliantly simple animal, vegetable or mineral game.
AMUSE\DARTS.BAS	A program to control scoring in darts.
AMUSE\GOSSIP.BAS	A simple pattern-recognition version of Eliza.
AMUSE\MAGIC.BAS	A classic game in which the computer attempts to guess the number you are thinking of.
APPS\BINGO.BAS	A bingo caller's dream program.
APPS\BOOKS	An on-line catalogue of books published by Wrox Press, featuring all the details of each book you require in database form for **DSTORE.BAS**.
APPS\CALENDAR.BAS	Print or display your own calendars.
APPS\DSTORE.BAS	A generic database creator and manipulator, allowing you to develop your own stores of data and then manipulate them to suit your own needs. It is written in pure QBasic and allows you to add, sort, search, save and load different databases.
APPS\FET.BAS	Switch on powerful FET transient analysis with spline VAC approximation.
APPS\FIXTURES.BAS	Computes each week's fixtures for a fully definable league of your choice.
APPS\LECAWIT.BAS	Linear electronic circuits analysis with topological input.
APPS\LOTTERY.BAS	Random number generator to take the pressure off producing winning numbers.
APPS\LTRACKER.BAS	A program to set up and store results in a league, whilst maintaining the current positions.
APPS\MANUAL.BAS	An on-line manual for **DSTORE.BAS**.
APPS\PLANETS	A small sample database for use with **DSTORE.BAS**. Provides a host of information about each of the seven planets in our solar system.

`APPS\SPECTRAL.BAS`	Parallel spectral analysis and trigonometric interpolation with graphics output for piecewise linear functions.
`APPS\TALLC.BAS`	Transient analysis for linear ladder circuits.
`GAMES\ADVENTUR.BAS`	A modern version of the traditional text adventure game.
`GAMES\ANAGRAM.BAS`	Test your anagram-solving skills.
`GAMES\BATTLE.BAS`	A hugely entertaining and nervewracking two-player war game where each player takes it in turn to fire a missile at their opponent. The first one to hit the other wins.
`GAMES\BLOCKM\BLOCKM.BAS`	BlockMaster, a faithful and well presented version of the ever-addictive Tetris.
`GAMES\CAVERNS.BAS`	An action game where you must guide your character through the caverns using just one key.
`GAMES\DODGE2.BAS`	The standard two-player version of the classic Tron game.
`GAMES\DODGE3.BAS`	A unique version of Tron for *three* players.
`GAMES\DODGEPRO.BAS`	The best version of Tron, for two players, featuring extra graphics and fifty preset screen layouts.
`GAMES\EV\EV.TXT`	A description of the author, information and how to register for version 2.
`GAMES\EV\EV11.BAS`	Extreme Velocity, a top quality shareware racing game with a selection of difficult tracks.
`GAMES\LAGON.BAS`	A fast action game.
`GAMES\MAGAZINE.BAS`	A difficult strategy game where you, editor of a magazine, have to make it a financial success.
`GAMES\MAZEGAME.BAS`	Get through the randomly created maze as quickly as you can.
`GAMES\MINES.BAS`	Classic version of minesweeper which features multiple hi-score tables.
`GAMES\MOLES\MOLE.BAS`	A simple yet very addictive mouse-based game. You must hit as many moles on the head within sixty seconds. Hitting moles on the head very lightly does them no harm at all - and besides they seem to come back for more.
`GAMES\NOCTURNAL\INV\` `QBINVADE.EXE`	QBasic invaders games.
`GAMES\NOCTURNAL\MATRIX\` `QMATRIX.BAS`	A top-quality Tetris shareware variant.
`GAMES\NOCTURNAL\SPRITE\` `SPRITE.EXE`	Excellent sprite creator.
`GAMES\QUIZ\CAPITALS.QIZ`	A set of questions based on the capital cities of the world for `QUIZ.BAS`.

`GAMES\QUIZ\GENERAL.QIZ`	A huge set of general-knowledge questions for **QUIZ.BAS**.
`GAMES\QUIZ\MONEY.QIZ`	A set of quiz questions based around the currencies of different countries for **QUIZ.BAS**.
`GAMES\QUIZ\PROVERBS.QIZ`	A large set of questions based on old-fashioned proverbs for **QUIZ.BAS**.
`GAMES\QUIZ\QUIZ.BAS`	A quiz program that can ask up to three people different sets of questions. Well-designed and good fun.
`GAMES\QUIZ\QUIZGEN.BAS`	A friendly designer that lets you create your own sets of questions for **QUIZ.BAS**.
`GAMES\RALLY.BAS`	A car racing game - just stay on the track!
`GRAPHICS\BALL.BAS`	A fast bouncing-ball routine.
`GRAPHICS\CYCLING.BAS`	Comparison between the two color cycling methods.
`GRAPHICS\DUPLIC.BAS`	Random plotter with three mirror images.
`GRAPHICS\ETCH.BAS`	Etch-a-sketch.
`GRAPHICS\GLOBE.BAS`	3D globe drawing program.
`GRAPHICS\JULIA.BAS`	Fractal depiction of the Julia set.
`GRAPHICS\LANDSCAP.BAS`	Draws a rolling landscape.
`GRAPHICS\LASERC.BAS`	Draws a bouncing pixel trail which, when a key is pressed, cycles impressively through the colors.
`GRAPHICS\LASERT.BAS`	Bounces a text block around the screen.
`GRAPHICS\MAZEGEN.BAS`	Draws a random maze of programmable size.
`GRAPHICS\PROJECT.BAS`	A user-definable projectile tester.
`GRAPHICS\SNOWFALL.BAS`	Demonstrates the effect of falling snow on a screen.
`ROUTINES\BORDERS.BAS`	A selection of interesting screen borders.
`ROUTINES\CHARBYCH.BAS`	An alternative text-string printing routine.
`ROUTINES\CLEARS.BAS`	A selection of useful screen wipes.
`ROUTINES\RADAR1.BAS`	A simple radar system.
`ROUTINES\USEFUL2\` `USEFUL.BAS`	A vast library of useful functions and procedures that will be useful in any program.
`TOOLS\ASCIFIND.BAS`	Searches a specified text file for a specific text string.
`TOOLS\ASCII.BAS`	A program to automatically produce your system's ASCII table on the screen.
`TOOLS\ATOB.BAS`	Converts an ASCII file into a BASIC program using either **DATA** or **PRINT** statements.
`TOOLS\COLORS.BAS`	A program to display the colors and their information.

`TOOLS\DIRMAN.BAS`	A directory manager.
`TOOLS\PRIMES.BAS`	Prime number generator.
`TOOLS\PRINTER\FONTS.BAS`	A program to display a variety of fonts to your printer.
`TOOLS\PRINTER\FRACTION.BAS`	A routine to print the normally unprintable user-definable fractions to your printer.
`TOOLS\PRINTER\MUSIC.BAS`	Print music staves on your printer.
`TOOLS\TANALYST.BAS`	A program that summarizes grammatical details of your text files.

Each program featured on this disk has been selected for the quality of the code and, although each has been thoroughly tested, we can't guarantee that all programs are bug-free. If you find an error, please send in your solution so that we can all share the enhancements.

Don't forget that the disk also features *every* piece of source code listed or referenced in the book.

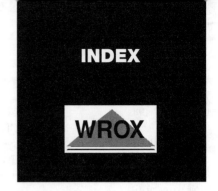

INDEX

Special 5.25" Disk Offer

Don't worry if you don't have access to a 3.5" drive. For a small fee ($5 US), we will send you a 5.25" floppy featuring all the files on the 3.5" disk. Just call us at (312) 465-3559 or toll-free on 800-USE-WROX. Alternatively, send a check for $5 to Wrox Press Inc, 2710 W. Touhy Avenue, Chicago, Illinois 60645.

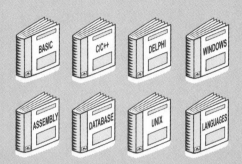

The Beginner's Guide to Visual Basic 4.0

The sequel to the best selling 'Beginner's Guide to Visual Basic 3.0' this is a practical guide to 32-bit programming with Visual Basic 4.0 Standard Edition. After a walk through the VB4.0 environment, it will take you straight into the Common Controls and writing real code for Win95. The book contains practical lessons in object-oriented programming, utilizing graphics and interacting with the Win95 API. You will also learn how to write powerful database applications with the Jet database engine. By the end of this book you will understand dialogs, handling data and list controls, OLE and DLLs and how to manipulate them in useful Windows applications.

Every topic is illustrated with 'Try It Outs' - real code examples that augment each concept as you progress. Comes with a disk containing all the source code from the text.

Author: Peter Wright   ISBN: 1874416559
Price: $34.95 C$48.95 £32.99

Beginning Visual C++

The book starts by teaching the reader the basics of C++ programming, covering such things as using variables and the different variable types available, how to perform loops and branches in the code, using pointers and how to write structured programs with functions. It then goes on to describe how to use C++ to write object-oriented programs. This is used as an introduction to Windows programming using Visual C++ and, in particular, how to use the Microsoft Foundation Classes (MFC). The main parts of the MFC are divided into logical sections, detailing such things as how to create and react to menus, drawing to the window, displaying text, using dialog boxes, using files, how to write your own DLL and finally how to write your own OCX.

Author: Ivor Horton   ISBN: 1874416591
Price: $36.95 C$51.95 £34.49

The Revolutionary Guide to Assembly Language

The teaching of Assembly in this book is taken step-by-step: from DOS, to hands-on usage of ASM for Intel chips. Now a recognized companion book for ASM courses, this title is a perfect tutorial and reference to low level, 16-bit, PC programming with MASM. Contains practical examples on writing and linking with the Macro Assembler/Linker and debugging with CodeView. You will learn how to control basic hardware: keyboard, video, disks, printers and mouse. This is not a reference to protected mode or XMS, but will give easy to follow methods for BIOS and DOS services, creating TSRs and interfacing your Assembly code modules with high level languages. The book has an extensive reference section to DOS and BIOS services, machine instructions, ASCII and keyboard scan codes. Comes with a tutorial disk that contains source code and extra ASM routines.

Authors: Maljugin et al   ISBN: 1874416125
Price: $39.95 C$55.95 £34.95

The Revolutionary Guide to MS Office 95 Development

The book initially has primers for WordBasic and Visual Basic for Applications (VBA), and gives details of DDE and OLE technology which is the 'glue' which holds the Office 95 applications together. Stand-alone applications in Word, Excel and Access are developed to complete the readers understanding of these applications. The book then goes into detail of Client/Server design, before developing applications hosted in, again, Word, Excel and Access, that show how it is possible to combine functionality of the host application with the other applications in Office 95. Information on mail-enabling applications is also provided, using Exchange as well as the built-in mail capabilities. A detailed explanation of the workflow paradigm is given, before showing a complete office system built from the components so far discussed. The book finishes off with how to extend Word's capabilities by writing a WLL (using C), and finally considers what is required to make an application ready for distribution.

Author: Steve Wynkoop   ISBN: 1874416699
Price: $49.95 C$69.95 £46.99

Wrox Press Presents
Their New *Bestselling* Author

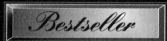

Could This Be You?

Have you ever thought to yourself "I could do better than that"?

Well here's your chance to prove it! Wrox Press are continually looking for

new authors and contributors. It doesn't matter if you've never been published before.

If you are a professional programmer, or simply a great developer,

we'd be very interested to hear from you.

Contact John Franklin at:

Wrox Press, Unit 16, 20 James Road, Birmingham, B11 2BA, UK

from US call: **800 814 3461**

or

e-mail: **johnf@wrox.com**

compuserve: **100063,2152**

WIN FREE BOOKS

TELL US WHAT YOU THINK!

Complete and return the bounce back card and you will:

- Help us create the books you want.
- Receive an update on all Wrox titles.
- Enter the draw for 5 Wrox titles of your choice.

FILL THIS OUT to enter the draw for free Wrox titles

Name _____

Address _____

_____

_____

_____ Postcode/Zip _____

Occupation _____

How did you hear about this book?

☐ Book review (name) _____

☐ Advertisement (name) _____

☐ Recommendation

☐ Catalogue

☐ Other _____

Where did you buy this book?

☐ Bookstore (name) _____

☐ Computer Store (name) _____

☐ Mail Order

☐ Other _____

I would be interested in receiving information about Wrox Press titles by email in future. My email/Internet address is:

_____

What influenced you in the purchase of this book?

☐ Cover Design

☐ Contents

☐ Other (please specify) _____

How did you rate the overall contents of this book?

☐ Excellent   ☐ Good

☐ Average   ☐ Poor

What did you find most useful about this book? _____

What did you find least useful about this book? _____

Please add any additional comments. _____

What other subjects will you buy a computer book on soon? _____

What is the best computer book you have used this year?

Note: This information will only be used to keep you updated about new Wrox Press titles and will not be used for any other purpose or passed to any other third party.

WROX PRESS INC.

Wrox writes books for you. Any suggestions, or
ideas about how you want information given in
your ideal book will be studied by our team.
Your comments are always valued at WROX.

Free phone in USA 800 USE WROX
Fax (312) 465 4063

Compuserve 100063,2152.
UK Tel. (44121) 706 6826 Fax (44121) 706 2967

———— *Computer Book Publishers* ————

NB. If you post the bounce back card below in the UK, please send it to:
Wrox Press Ltd. Unit 16, Sapcote Industrial Estate, 20 James Road, Birmingham, B11 2BA